CRYSTAL REPORTS®
2008
OFFICIAL GUIDE

"In this guide, you'll find everything from the basics to get you started on your first report, to using even the most advanced features. Listen to these experts – they will show you how to create any type of report you may need."

—James Thomas, Vice President, Product Management,
Volume Products, Business Objects,
an SAP company

NEIL FITZGERALD
BOB COATES
RYAN GOODMAN
MICHAEL VOLOSHKO

PREVIOUS CONTRIBUTORS:
KELLY BYRNE
JAMES EDKINS
ANNETTE JONKER
RYAN MARPLES

Sams Publishing
800 East 96th Street
Indianapolis, IN 46240 USA

CONTENTS AT A GLANCE

CRYSTAL REPORTS® 2008 OFFICIAL GUIDE

ISBN-13: 978-0-672-32989-0
ISBN-10: 0-672-32989-1

Library of Congress Cataloging-in-Publication Data is on file

Printed in the United States of America

First Printing September 2008

Trademarks

All terms mentioned in this book that are known to be trademarks or service marks have been appropriately capitalized. Sams Publishing cannot attest to the accuracy of this information. Use of a term in this book should not be regarded as affecting the validity of any trademark or service mark.

Warning and Disclaimer

Every effort has been made to make this book as complete and as accurate as possible, but no warranty or fitness is implied. The information provided is on an "as is" basis. The authors and the publisher shall have neither liability nor responsibility to any person or entity with respect to any loss or damages arising from the information contained in this book or from programs accompanying it.

Bulk Sales

Sams Publishing offers excellent discounts on this book when ordered in quantity for bulk purchases or special sales. For more information, please contact

U.S. Corporate and Government Sales
1-800-382-3419
corpsales@pearsontechgroup.com

For sales outside of the U.S., please contact

International Sales
international@pearson.com

SAMS Publishing

Associate Publisher
Greg Wiegand

Acquisitions Editor
Michelle Newcomb

Development Editor
Kevin Howard

Managing Editor
Patrick Kanouse

Project Editor
Jennifer Gallant

Copy Editor
Mike Henry

Technical Editors
James H. Brogden, Jr.
Tim Rodine
Brian Yaremych

Indexer
Ken Johnson

Proofreader
Gill Editorial Services

Publishing Coordinator
Cindy Teeters

Book Designer
Anne Jones

Compositor
Bronkella Publishing LLC

Business Objects

Business Objects Press
Editorial Board
Paul Clark
John McNaughton

CONTENTS

III Advanced Crystal Report Design

About the Lead Author

Neil FitzGerald is an entrepreneur who has successfully started or contributed to multiple consulting companies in the IT consulting domain. Neil combined his bachelor's degree in computer science from Queen's University in Kingston, Canada and his MBA from the Ivey School of Business at the University of Western Ontario with his more than 8 years of experience at Business Objects in a variety of senior roles to help provide information solutions to Fortune 500 companies across North America. He has spent more than 13 years in the information delivery domain and is available for onsite or remote consulting to companies large and small. Neil can be contacted at neil_fitzgerald@hotmail.com.

About the Contributing Authors

Bob Coates has worked for Business Objects, an SAP company (through the Crystal Decisions and Business Objects acquisitions), for more than 11 years. While there he worked in technical support, global services, and sales consulting. Presently Bob is a principal sales consultant working on the SAP Synergy Team—a branch of the Strategic Technology Group focused on the top 100 SAP customers. Bob would like to thank his wife Amanda for her infinite patience and support.

Ryan Goodman is the founder of Centigon Solutions Inc. As a previous technical evangelist and sales consultant at Infommersion and then Business Objects, Ryan has implemented hundreds of Xcelsius projects spanning more than 4 years. His interactive data visualization and design background coupled with his business insight and technical aptitude have made him one of the top Xcelsius experts in the world. Ryan continues to push the envelope and evangelize Xcelsius on his blog: www.ryangoodman.net/blog.

Michael Voloshko is a principal solutions architect for the financial services vertical at Business Objects, an SAP company.

DEDICATION

To my growing family, including my daughter Maya and her expecting mom, Arlene.

—Neil FitzGerald

Dedicated to my wife Amanda for all of her love and support.

—Bob Coates

To my mentors and counterparts who have contributed to my growth, both as a professional and as a person.

—Ryan Goodman

To all the people throughout the years who have inspired me to continue achieving and advancing in life.

—Michael Voloshko

ACKNOWLEDGMENTS

Neil FitzGerald—Thanks to all the authors for delivering on our joint goals of making this book a reality and for truly applying yourselves against tight deadlines. You are all world-class, and it was a treat to work with each of you.

Special recognition also goes to the Crystal Product and R&D teams for delivering this world-standard suite of products and the truly great leaders at Business Objects—you know who you are.

Bob Coates—I want to acknowledge my wife, Amanda Cousins, who helps me every day with both the technical and nontechnical aspects of my job; Patrick Sims for being a great boss and friend; and Andy Hillaker for supporting my success.

Ryan Goodman—I would like to thank Neil for the opportunity to contribute to this book. I would also like to commend the Xcelsius engineering team for the passion and innovation that it pours into Xcelsius.

Michael Voloshko—I would like to thank Neil for giving me the opportunity to contribute to this book and the rest of the team at Business Objects for all the hard work that goes into creating great products.

We Want to Hear from You!

As the reader of this book, *you* are our most important critic and commentator. We value your opinion and want to know what we're doing right, what we could do better, what areas you'd like to see us publish in, and any other words of wisdom you're willing to pass our way.

You can email or write me directly to let me know what you did or didn't like about this book—as well as what we can do to make our books stronger.

Please note that I cannot help you with technical problems related to the topic of this book, and that due to the high volume of mail I receive, I might not be able to reply to every message.

When you write, please be sure to include this book's title and author as well as your name and phone or email address. I will carefully review your comments and share them with the author and editors who worked on the book.

Email: feedback@samspublishing.com

Mail: Greg Wiegand
Associate Publisher
Sams Publishing
800 East 96th Street
Indianapolis, IN 46240 USA

Reader Services

Visit our website and register this book at informit.com/register for convenient access to any updates, downloads, or errata that might be available for this book.

INTRODUCTION

In this chapter

INTRODUCTION TO INFORMATION DELIVERY

Organizations of all sizes today find themselves increasingly awash in data, yet hungering for information to help them meet their business objectives. These corporations, from Main Street and Wall Street alike, have spent large amounts of time and money over the past 10 or so years implementing systems to help collect data on and streamline their operations. From monolithic Enterprise Resource Planning (ERP) systems (SAP, PeopleSoft, Oracle Financials, and so on) through Customer Relationship Management (CRM) systems (Siebel, Rightnow.com, Salesforce.com, and so on) to Custom Data Warehousing projects, these firms are now looking for ways to extract value from the collective body of data to help them run their businesses more productively and competitively. These firms are looking for a strategic information delivery or business intelligence solution to help them become more productive and ultimately compete more effectively. The products covered in this book are geared toward meeting that challenge.

The information delivery products and solutions presented in this book are often categorized under the *Business Intelligence (BI)* banner. BI is the industry of value-added information delivery based on structured data sources—essentially providing meaningful, business-driven value and information to business end users by connecting them to data with appropriate tools and products. Figure I.1 highlights the conceptual divide of information delivery solutions into the structured and unstructured world. Although evidence suggests an eventual blurring of the boundaries between these discrete industries over time, the Business Objects products covered in this book most aptly fit under the BI banner.

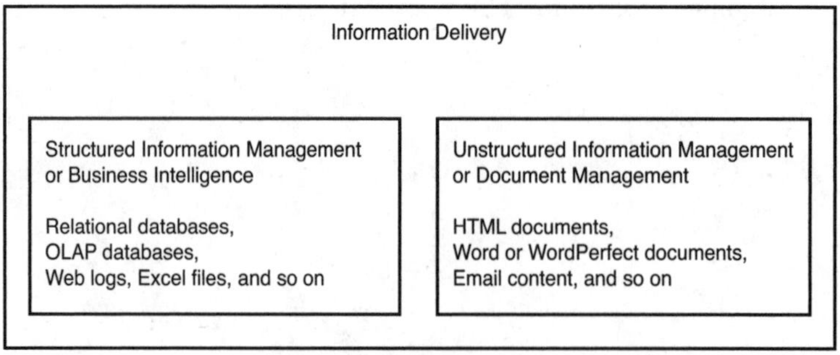

Figure I.1
The information delivery industry divides broadly into structured and unstructured information management.

Information Delivery	
Structured Information Management or Business Intelligence	Unstructured Information Management or Document Management
Relational databases, OLAP databases, Web logs, Excel files, and so on	HTML documents, Word or WordPerfect documents, Email content, and so on

Industry analysts in the information delivery area regularly highlight the impressive adoption rates of BI products in the past few years as testimony to their value. The dynamic double-digit percentage growth rates for industry leaders such as Business Objects are especially impressive when the difficult macroeconomic operating environment of recent years is taken into account. Ironically, many suggest, this same poor economic environment has largely driven the increased worldwide demand for BI functionality as firms work to increase their productivity and competitiveness by leveraging existing investments—and doing more with less. The next section covers the BI industry driver along with a few others.

SPECTRUM OF BUSINESS OBJECTS PRODUCT USAGE

BI products such as those distributed by Business Objects (Crystal Reports, Crystal Reports Server, BusinessObjects Enterprise, Crystal Xcelsius, and Web Intelligence) are deployed and used in about as many different ways as there are product implementations—and there are millions. However, as you examine a broad swath of BI clients and their implementations, you can find definite themes to their deployments. Taking a step back, distinctive drivers to worldwide BI product adoption become evident. The following sections discuss a few of the most common.

CUSTOM INFORMATION DELIVERY APPLICATIONS

Despite the increasing functionality of turnkey software and web applications available today, corporations of all sizes still regularly look to custom-developed applications to provide them with unique competitive advantage and to meet their proprietary business requirements. These applications run the gamut in size from small business applications through large departmental applications to enterprise intranet and extranet applications. The key component of these custom projects is the integration of BI functionality, such as formatted reporting, ad hoc query, dashboarding, self-service web reporting, and/or analytic capabilities, within an internally developed application. Table I.1 highlights some typical examples of custom applications using the Business Objects suite of products to help deliver custom applications.

TABLE I.1 SAMPLE CUSTOM INFORMATION DELIVERY APPLICATIONS

Application	Application Audience	Product Usage
Small retail chain's internal Java-based sales metrics application	Approximately 20 sales employees and managers	Using Crystal Reports Java Engine, the developer provides the sales team with Web access to on-demand metrics reports built into the intranet application.
Large portfolio	10,000+ high value customers of firm	Using Crystal Xcelsius and Crystal Reports Server, the management firm's developer provides access to the scalable client extranet application reporting infrastructure and facilitates those customers getting online web access to their portfolio reports.
Asset management firm's report batch of institution scheduling application	50,000+ clients	Using the Business Objects reporting server and scheduling engine, the developer's application dynamically creates tens of thousands of customized reports daily and automatically emails them to the appropriate clients in PDF and XLS formats.

A key strength of the Business Objects suite of products is that it lends itself readily to integration into custom applications. From the inclusion of basic formatted reports within Java/J2EE or .NET applications through the inclusion of rich ad hoc query and self-service reporting functionality in proprietary information product applications to provision of large-scale enterprise BI analytics, scheduling, and security functionality in a globally deployed application, the Business Objects suite of products can meet your requirements. Table I.2 provides a jump-point for those looking for each type of application integration covered in this book.

TABLE I.2 CUSTOM APPLICATION CHAPTERS OVERVIEW

Development Environment	Required Functionality	Part or Chapters
Java/J2EE	Prebuilt reports included in custom Java application	Part IV, Chapter 18
.NET	Prebuilt reports included in custom .NET application	Part IV, Chapter 19

ENTERPRISE BI INITIATIVES

With the proliferation of BI tools and the acceleration of product adoption around the globe, there has been concurrent pressure for the involved companies to standardize on a single set of products and tools—effectively a BI infrastructure or platform. The main arguments for such standardization include the following:

- Reduced total cost of product ownership
- Creation of enterprise centers of excellence
- Reduced vendor relationships
- Movement toward a BI infrastructure/platform

As BI products have matured from different areas of historical strength and their marketplace acceptance has grown, end user organizations have found themselves with disparate and incompatible BI tools and products across or even within the same departments in their organization. To eliminate the costliness of managing such a broad set of tools, many firms are now moving to adopt a single BI platform such as BusinessObjects Enterprise (or Crystal Reports Server for smaller businesses).

The infrastructure of BusinessObjects Enterprise provides a single architecture to manage all the content and tools required to serve an organization's structured information delivery requirements. Figure I.2 shows an end user map of a typical organization. To be productive, each type of end user in a company requires different types of tools. There are clear organizational benefits to a common infrastructure or centrally managed center of excellence, such as BusinessObjects Enterprise, which can meet the various end user and IT requirements.

Figure I.2
Organizational end user requirements map from Business Objects.

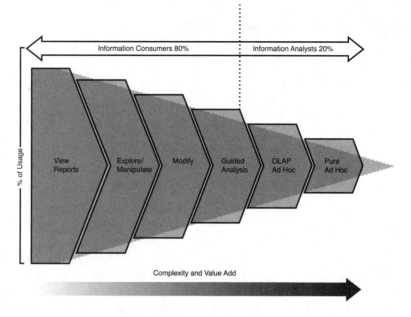

Details of the breakdown of this book are included later in this Introduction, but to jump-start your learning on this type of BI application, Table I.3 can point you to the sections and chapters of particular relevance.

TABLE I.3 ENTERPRISE BUSINESS INTELLIGENCE CHAPTER OVERVIEW	
Enterprise Business Intelligence Focus	**Chapter**
Out-of-the-box product using Crystal Reports Server for small- and medium-sized businesses	Part IV, Chapter 17
Using crystalreports.com to distribute reporting content	Part IV, Chapter 17

SPECTRUM OF BI TOOL USERS

Across the usage profiles of the thousands of BI scenarios/implementations, there generally exists a consistency in the types of people who become involved. Figure I.3 provides a relatively high level yet accurate graphic that shows a typical distribution of the people involved in BI implementations.

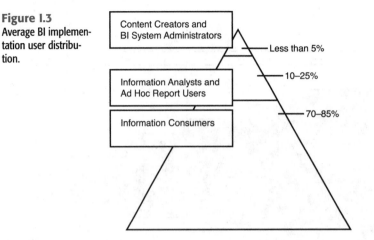

Figure I.3
Average BI implementation user distribution.

Content Creators and BI System Administrators — Less than 5%

Information Analysts and Ad Hoc Report Users — 10–25%

Information Consumers — 70–85%

Each of the three communities outlined in the pyramid plays a key role in the ongoing success and operation of any BI implementation. The content creators and system administrators play perhaps the most important role in ensuring the short- and long-term success of any deployment because their work sets up the system content and tools from which the other users derive benefit. The information analysts generally come from across an organization's typical functions and are highly demanding users who require rich and highly functional interactive tools to facilitate their jobs as analysts. The last group is by far the largest group and includes employees, partners, customers, and suppliers who rely on the BI implementation to provide timely, secure, and reliable information or corporate truths. This group tends to span the entire corporate ladder from foot soldiers right up to the executive suite—all of whom have the same requirement of simple information provision to enable them to complete their regular day-to-day assignments successfully.

Figure I.4 provides a schematic highlighting the distinction between the different content creation tools and the content delivery tools—BusinessObjects Enterprise, Crystal Reports Server, or Java/.NET reporting engines. This book breaks down into two sections covering these two themes: content creation (Chapters 1–16) and content delivery in all of its possible forms (Chapters 17–21) using some of the Business Objects suite of products.

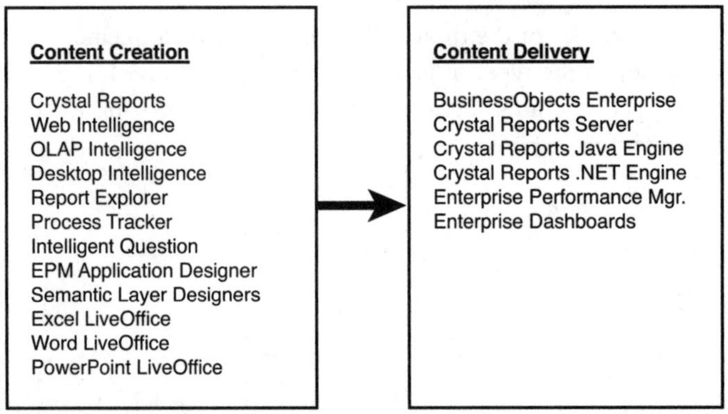

Figure I.4
Content creation and content delivery schematic.

Content Creation

Crystal Reports
Web Intelligence
OLAP Intelligence
Desktop Intelligence
Report Explorer
Process Tracker
Intelligent Question
EPM Application Designer
Semantic Layer Designers
Excel LiveOffice
Word LiveOffice
PowerPoint LiveOffice

Content Delivery

BusinessObjects Enterprise
Crystal Reports Server
Crystal Reports Java Engine
Crystal Reports .NET Engine
Enterprise Performance Mgr.
Enterprise Dashboards

CONTENT CREATORS (INFORMATION DESIGNERS)

Content creators provide the foundation to any BI implementation. This group uses content creation tools such as Crystal Reports, Crystal Xcelsius, Web Intelligence, Desktop Intelligence (formerly BusinessObjects), Excel, and so on. These users—primarily composed of IT folks but sometimes complemented with technically savvy business users—create the report content, dashboards, OLAP cubes, and reporting metadata that facilitates system usage and benefits derived from the other system users. Because these tasks are of paramount importance in an enterprise suite deployment, the entire first half of the book is dedicated to providing these folks with a comprehensive tutorial and reference on content creation using Crystal Reports and Crystal Xcelsius.

After content exists, it is ready for distribution through an infrastructure such as BusinessObjects Enterprise, the new Crystal Reports Server product, or a custom application. Finally, the content requires management. Another small but critical group of BI system users—the BI administrators—need to ensure that the system is deployed and tuned correctly to ensure optimal performance for the business end users.

INFORMATION ANALYSTS

Although not the primary group in number, the information analysts in a BI deployment are those who are primarily responsible for the extraction of new business insights and actionable recommendations derived from the BI implementation. Using such analytic tools as Web Intelligence, Crystal Xcelsius, and Excel, these users spend their time interrogating, massaging, and slicing and dicing the data provided in the various back-end systems until they glean nuggets of business relevance. These users tend to come from a wide variety of functional areas in a company, including operations, finance, sales, HR, and marketing and all work with the provided BI tools to extract new information out of the existing corporate data set. Chapters 20 and 21 provide detailed information on using Crystal Xcelsius, and www.usingcrystal.com provides information on Web Intelligence and Microsoft Live Office plug-ins.

INFORMATION CONSUMERS

This group of users composes the clear majority of those involved with a BI implementation. They are also the most diverse group and come from every rung on the corporate ladder. Executives who view corporate performance dashboards fit into this category, as would truck drivers who receive their daily mileage and shipping reports online through a wireless device. The common characteristic of members of this group is that their interactions with the BI system are not indicative of their primary jobs. Unlike the content creators and information analysts, information consumers have jobs outside of the BI implementation, and the key measure of success for them is that the BI system helps facilitate their variety of assignments. Chapter 17 provides an introduction to the out-of-the-box Crystal Reports Server interfaces.

THE PRODUCT FAMILY FROM BUSINESS OBJECTS

As Figure I.4 showed, the product family distributed by Business Objects is broken into two major segments: content creation and content delivery. This book is roughly split in two, with each section covering one of the topics in great detail. The primary products in the family covered in these sections are Crystal Reports (first section) and Crystal Reports Server, the Crystal Reports SDKs, and Crystal Xcelsius (second section). The content creation section of the book introduces Crystal Reports version 2008—the world standard for professional formatted reporting across the largest spectrum of data sources. The Crystal Reports Application Designer benefits from more than 15 years of development and provides an unparalleled combination of powerful functionality and report-design flexibility.

The content delivery half of the book covers the following Crystal Products and SDKs:

- **Crystal Reports Server**—New since version XI, Crystal Reports Server provides all the functionality of BusinessObjects Enterprise but is limited to a single multi-CPU server and is aggressively priced for small- and medium-sized businesses. This solution is a very attractive option for deploying BI and reporting solutions.

- **Crystal Xcelsius**—Xcelsius 2008 is a dynamic and customizable data visualization tool that enables users of different skill levels to create insightful and engaging dashboards from any data source with point-and-click ease. Xcelsius 2008 offers a comprehensive set of new features and integrations with Crystal Reports 2008, making it easy to put the power of dashboards into the hands of business users.

- **Crystal Vision**—New to version XI release 2, Crystal Vision provides a combination of the functionality of Crystal Reports Server with the newly acquired Crystal Xcelsius dashboarding functionality.

- **Crystal Reports Engine for .NET Applications**—The only third-party tool distributed with Visual Studio .NET, this reporting component enables .NET developers to quickly embed limited but powerful reporting functionality into their .NET applications.

- **Crystal Reports Engine for Java Applications**—Embedded in Borland's JBuilder and other Java IDEs, this reporting component enables Java developers to quickly embed limited but powerful reporting functionality into their Java applications.

WHAT IS IN THIS BOOK

This book is broken down into several sections to address the varied and evolving requirements of the different users in a BI deployment.

The entire first half of the book (Parts I through III) focuses exclusively on content creation with Crystal Reports. Through hands-on step-by-step examples and detailed descriptions of key product functionality, you learn to leverage the powerful report creation capabilities of Crystal Reports v2008. Some profiles of people who find these sections of particular relevance:

- New and mature Crystal Reports designers
- Professional Crystal Reports designers upgrading to 2008
- Existing and new OLAP Intelligence, Web Intelligence, and Desktop Intelligence (formerly Business Objects) designers and analysts
- Existing and new BusinessObjects Enterprise (formerly Crystal Enterprise) administrators
- New Crystal Reports Server administrators

The second section of the book (Part IV) focuses on the distribution or delivery of the valuable content created in the first half and additional insights into advanced content creation with Crystal Xcelsius. An introduction to Crystal Reports Server, crystalreports.com, and the offline Crystal Reports Viewer complements a comprehensive introduction to Crystal Xcelsius. This extends with an introduction to the .NET and Java SDKs around Crystal Reports. Some profiles of people who find these sections of high value:

- New Crystal Reports Server administrators
- New or existing Crystal Reports Server users
- .NET-based application developers
- Java/J2EE-based application developers
- Application developers looking to integrate report design or modification into their applications

PART I: CRYSTAL REPORTS DESIGN

Part I should familiarize you with the foundations of Crystal Reports and get you up and running as quickly as possible. It is critical for someone who is new to Crystal Reports and includes the fundamental report design concepts that even experienced users can use for the rest of their Crystal Reports–writing career. This section also provides powerful exercises and real-world usage tips and tricks with which even seasoned reporting experts can become more productive.

PART II: FORMATTING CRYSTAL REPORTS

Part II focuses on some of the more subtle nuances of Crystal Report design: effective report formatting and data visualization through charting and mapping. Improper formatting and incorrect use of visualization techniques can make reports confusing and not user friendly. This section also provides powerful exercises and real-world usage tips and tricks, enabling mature reporting experts to become more productive.

PART III: ADVANCED CRYSTAL REPORTS DESIGN

Part III presents a host of advanced Crystal Reports design concepts that involve features such as subreports, cross-tabs, report templates, and alerts. This part also touches on advanced data access methods such as JavaBeans, XML objects, SAP, and PeopleSoft systems. The section also provides powerful exercises and real-world usage tips and tricks, enabling mature reporting experts to become more effective in their report design work.

PART IV: REPORT DISTRIBUTION AND ADVANCED REPORT DESIGN WITH CRYSTAL XCELSIUS

Part IV focuses on the different methods of distribution of the Crystal Reports content created in the first three sections. These methods include Crystal Reports Server, crystalreports.com, the .NET and Java SDKs, and the offline Crystal Reports Viewer. This section provides a comprehensive introduction to advanced visualizations and dashboard creation with Crystal Xcelsius.

EQUIPMENT USED FOR THIS BOOK

You can find various supporting material that will assist you in the completion of the exercises in this book, as well as supplemental documentation on related topics. You should have access to a computer that has at least a 450MHz Pentium II or equivalent processor, 128MB of RAM, and Windows 2000, Windows 2003, or Windows XP Professional.

WEB RESOURCES

You can find all the source code and report samples for the examples in the book, as well as links to great external content, at www.usingcrystal.com. You'll find report samples to download and code for you to leverage in your report design and sharing efforts. Also, a great deal of additional product-related information on the Business Objects suite of products including Crystal Reports, Web Intelligence, OLAP Intelligence, Desktop Intelligence, Crystal Reports Server, and BusinessObjects Enterprise can be found at www.businessobjects.com.

INTENDED AUDIENCE

This book was written to appeal to the full range of Crystal Reports, Crystal Reports Server, and Crystal Xcelsius users. You'll find this book useful if you've never used the Business Objects suite of products before, if you are a mature Crystal Reports user looking for some new productivity tips, or if you want to explore some of the new features found in version 2008 and their related SDKs.

You don't have to be an expert, but you should have a basic understanding of the following concepts:

- Database systems such as Microsoft SQL Server, Oracle, Sybase, and Informix
- Operating system functions in Windows 2003/XP/Vista
- General Internet/intranet-based concepts such as HTML, DHTML, ActiveX, and Java

Parts I through III build on each other, so skipping around those parts isn't the best approach unless you have some familiarity with Crystal Reports 2008. Even if you are familiar with Crystal Reports, many new features have been introduced in recent versions, so you are encouraged to read the entire first three sections of the book so that you don't miss anything. Part IV focuses on the different methods of content delivery, so you can approach each part independently without loss of context.

REQUIREMENTS FOR THIS BOOK

All reports are based on sample data available from the businessobjects.com website, so you have access to the same data used in this book. You'll need to install Crystal Reports to get the most out of the examples included in each chapter in the first half of the book.

CONVENTIONS USED IN THIS BOOK

Several conventions are used within this book to help you get more out of the text. Look for special fonts or text styles and icons that emphasize special information.

- Objects such as fields or formulas normally appear on separate lines from the rest of the text. However, there are special situations in which some formulas or fields appear directly in the paragraph for explanation purposes. These types of objects appear in a special font like this: Some Special Code. Formula examples appear on the Sams Publishing website as well.
- In some cases, I might refer to your computer as a *machine* or *server*. This is always in reference to the physical computer on which you have installed Crystal Reports.
- You'll always be able to recognize menu selections and command sequences because they're implemented like this:
  Use the File, Open command.
- New terms appear in *italic* when they are defined.
- Text that you are asked to type appears in **boldface**.
- URLs for websites are presented like this: http://www.businessobjects.com.

NOTE

Notes help you understand principles or provide amplifying information. In many cases, a Note emphasizes some piece of critical information that you need. All of us like to know special bits of information that make our job easier, more fun, or faster to perform.

TIP

> Tips help you get the job done faster and more safely. In many cases, the information found in a Tip comes from experience rather than through experimentation or documentation.

Sidebar

Sidebars spend more time on a particular subject that could be considered a tangent but will help you be a better Business Objects product user as a result.

Real World sections provide some practical and productivity-enhancing usage insights derived from the author's real-world experience designing and deploying hundreds of Crystal Reports.

Troubleshooting sections provide some quick chapter summary notes and examples that are useful reminders on the product operations.

CRYSTAL REPORT DESIGN

CHAPTER 1

CREATING AND DESIGNING BASIC REPORTS

In this chapter

INTRODUCING THE CRYSTAL REPORTS DESIGNER

This chapter takes you through the required steps to create your own basic reports in the Crystal Reports Designer. After you install the Crystal Reports 2008 Designer, you are ready to open it and familiarize yourself with the environment. This section briefly introduces the following components of the application interface:

- Report sections
- Application toolbars
- Application menus

If you have already registered your installation, you should be presented with the Start page shown in Figure 1.1. This page provides quick access to existing Crystal Reports files and enables you to begin designing new reports via the Report Expert Wizards or from a blank report template. This page also enables you to quickly access the five most recently viewed reports with a single click.

Figure 1.1
The Start page provides quick access to existing Crystal Reports files and the Report Expert Wizards.

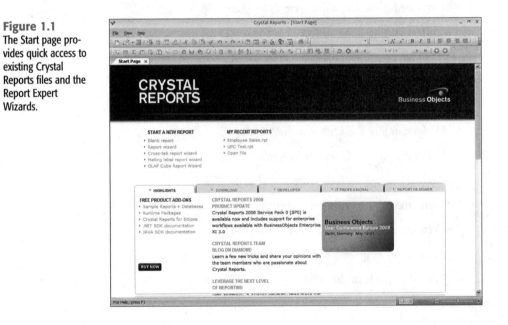

CRYSTAL REPORT SECTIONS

From the Start page, select the Blank Report link (listed below the Start a New Report heading). You'll see a window labeled Database Expert; click Cancel. If the Field Explorer window now displays on the right side of the New Report screen, click the Close button (an X). A new Report1 tab appears beside the original Start Page tab.

The Report1 tab presents a blank report template divided into five report sections. As Figure 1.2 illustrates, names on the left side of the design area identify the report sections.

These sections segment the Crystal Reports design environment into logical areas to facilitate more intuitive report creation—these include the Report Header, Page Header, Details, Report Footer, and Page Footer sections. (If your install displays initials instead of these report section names, go to the File menu, choose Options, and uncheck Short Section Names under the Layout tab). Each section has unique properties and printing characteristics that you can modify. When creating reports, you place objects (such as data fields) into the various sections according to report requirements. If a report object such as an image is placed in the Report Header section, the image displays and prints only once per report, on the first page. If the same image is placed in the Page Header section, the image displays and prints once per page. The same holds true for custom sections, such as Group Headers and Group Footers. The Details section specifies that whatever is placed in this section displays and prints once for each row retrieved from the data source.

Figure 1.2
Report sections provide an intuitive way to create and organize your data when designing reports.

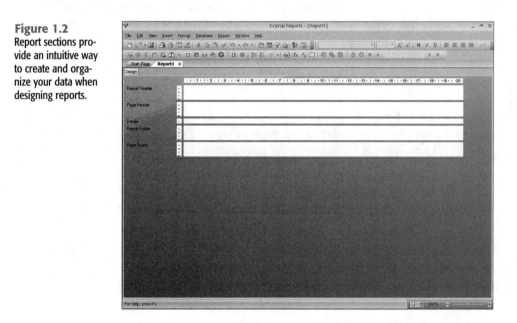

NOTE

Although a commonly used web-reporting initiative, the Crystal Reports design environment is built on a paper metaphor that uses *pages* to facilitate the presentation of information.

Report sections can contain a variety of object types, including database fields, text, pictures, charts, and map objects. You can position additional objects, such as formula and subreport objects, within report sections—later chapters in the book cover this topic in detail.

The Section Expert is for viewing and modifying the properties of the report sections. To access the Section Expert, perform one of the following actions:

■ Right-click on the section's label (or name, located on the left sidebar) you want to work with, and then select Section Expert from the pop-up menu.

■ Click on the Section Expert button.

■ Select the Section Expert option from the Report menu.

NOTE

When designing reports, you should consider the following items when working with report sections:

• Print a validating test page of each report you design.

• Consider keeping all font sizes the same within each section for maximum eye appeal.

• Print preprinted forms on the same machine to avoid discrepancies in the interpretation of the report layout by different print drivers and printers.

Crystal Reports also provides some more advanced section formatting options, reviewed later in the book, such as underlaying and suppressing sections based on certain criteria (formulas). These features are accessible from the Section Expert dialog.

USING TOOLBARS AND MENUS

Toolbars are the graphical icon bars at the top of the Crystal Reports application environment. They contain various buttons that you can click to activate the most frequently used application commands. Toolbars act as shortcuts to access commonly used functions of the design application; you can enable and disable them to appear and disappear at the top of the application area by selecting Toolbars from the View menu, which is located in the uppermost area of the application. As Figure 1.3 shows, there are six main toolbars for use within the Crystal Reports design environment:

■ **Standard**—The most commonly used application functions, including New, Open, Save, Print, Preview, Export, Copy, Cut, Paste, and Help.

■ **Formatting**—Functions that pertain specifically to modifying object properties with regard to Font, Font Size, Bold, Italic, Underline, Alignment, Currency, and Percentage formats.

■ **Insert Tools**—Quick access to the building blocks of all reports, including Text Objects, Summary Fields, Groups, Online Analytical Processing and Cross-Tab Grids, Charts, Maps, and Drawing items such as lines and boxes.

■ **Expert Tools**—Functions that enable you to access the main application experts quickly, such as the Database, Group, Select, Section, Formula Workshop, and Highlighting Experts.

- **Navigation Tools**—Functions that enable refreshing of the report data and navigation through the pages of the involved reports.

- **External Commands**—New to v2008, this toolbar provides access to third-party applications. After you add an application to Crystal Reports, you can access it through an icon on this toolbar.

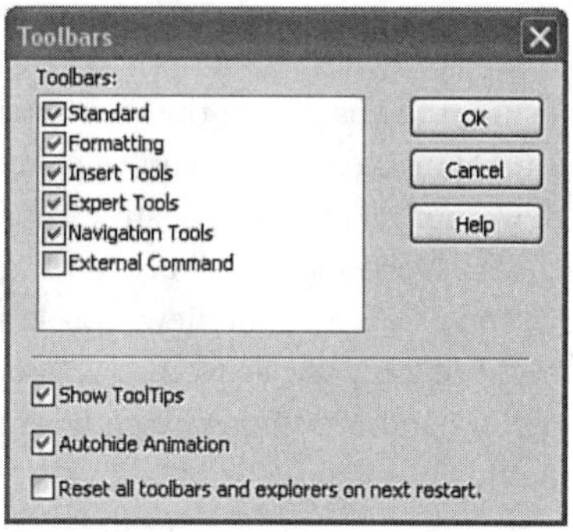

Figure 1.3
The six Crystal Reports Design toolbars provide quick and easy access to commonly used application commands during report design.

N O T E

ToolTips are pop-up descriptions that appear when your cursor rests over any of the toolbar buttons. Crystal Reports enables ToolTips by default. To disable ToolTips on your toolbars, deselect the Show ToolTips check box from within the Toolbars dialog.

In much the same way that the toolbars offer quick and easy access to commonly used commands, the menu items at the top of the application environment provide listings to virtually all the application functions available in Crystal Reports. The menu items act as shortcuts to all the commands within the design application, and they include the following items:

- The File menu includes file-specific commands to create a new report file, open an existing report, close a current report, save a report, save a report with an alternative filename, export to a different file format, and save the current data set with a report. In addition, the File menu contains commands that enable you to send a report to a printer, select a specific printer, modify the page setup and margins, add summary information to a report, and set a variety of report options.

- The Edit menu includes commands used to modify various aspects of a report, including commands to undo and redo actions, as well as to cut, copy, and paste report and OLE (Object Linking and Embedding) objects. Additionally, you can edit fields, formulas, summaries, and subreport links.

NOTE

OLE enables you to insert objects (OLE objects) into a report from other applications and then use those applications from within Crystal Reports to edit the objects if necessary. If Crystal Reports did not make use of OLE, you would have to exit Crystal Reports, open the original application, change the object, return to Crystal Reports, delete the object originally inserted, and then insert the newly revised object.

- The View menu includes commands used to customize the user interface of the Crystal Reports application. The View menu commands enable you to navigate between the application's Design and Preview views, access the three main explorers (Field, Report, and Repository Explorers), access the XI Dependency Checker window, and access the XI Workbench window. In addition, you can access the new Locale settings, access the Toolbars dialog, zoom in and zoom out of a report, as well as turn on and off the application rulers, guidelines, grids, ToolTips, and group tree from both the Design and Preview views of the report.

- The Insert menu includes commands used to insert text objects, summaries (counts, sums, medians, and so on), field headings, groups, subreports, lines, boxes, pictures, charts, maps, report template objects, and the new Flash objects into your report. This menu also provides access to the new v2008 Sort control.

- The Format menu provides easy access to a variety of commands useful in formatting your reports for presentation purposes. This menu includes commands used to change the characteristics of the objects in a report. The Format menu provides quick access to commands for modifying font properties (color, size, borders, background color, and drop shadows for example), chart, line height, and hyperlink properties, and formatting for entire sections of the report. The Format menu also provides commands to arrange report objects (move, align, and size) and to specify desired highlighting characteristics via the Highlighting Expert.

- The Database menu includes commands used to access the Database Expert, from which you can add and remove data source tables for use within reports, specify links between data source tables, and modify table and field alias names. This menu also provides easy access to the set database location and enables you to log on and off SQL and ODBC servers, browse field data, and display and edit the report SQL syntax. In general, the Database menu enables you to maintain the necessary specifications for the report with regard to the data source(s) with which the report interacts.

- The Report menu includes commands used to access the main application experts (also referred to as *wizards*), identify the desired records or groups to be included in a report via the Select Expert and Selection Formulas (often referred to as applying report *filters*), construct and edit formulas, and create and view alerts. You can specify report-bursting indexes, modify grouping and sorting specifications, refresh report data by executing the query to run against the database, and view report performance information.

- The Chart menu is visible only after you select a chart or map object and includes specific commands used to customize your charts and maps. Depending on the type of chart you select, the Chart menu includes commands to zoom in and out of charts; apply changes to all instances of a chart; discard custom changes made to the chart; save the chart template to a file; apply and modify template specifications for the chart; change the titles, numeric axis grids, and scales of the chart; and auto-arrange the appearance of the chart. After you select a map object, the Chart menu includes additional commands for configuring the overall style of the map, reorganizing the layers of report elements, changing the geographic map, and hiding or showing the Map Navigator.

- The Window menu includes commands used to rearrange the application icons and windows, as well as provide a list of currently open report windows and a command that enables you to close all report windows at once.

- The Help menu includes commands used to quickly access the Crystal Reports online help references, commands to register Crystal Reports and locate the Getting Start page, and quick access to the About Crystal Reports dialog and several key Business Objects websites for technical support and product information. Last, and available since Crystal Reports XI, the Help menu provides online access to Crystal Reports updates, downloaded and installed automatically from the Web. These updates can be set to occur automatically or manually.

REPORT DESIGN EXPLORERS

Several report design explorers, meant to streamline the report design process, compose another key component to Crystal Reports 2008. The design explorers are application tools that greatly enhance a report designer's efficiency while working with reports. They are design tools you will use in building reports throughout the remainder of the book.

The report design explorers are dialog windows that display various objects relevant to the report in a hierarchical tree view, facilitating quick access to and formatting of each respective object and its properties. The explorers enable you to easily locate and navigate to specific report objects, such as the report header or a corporate logo image, to customize the object for design purposes. All the objects included in a report (report sections, groups, database fields, formulas, parameters, images, charts, and so on) are organized and displayed within one of the design explorers. There are three distinct explorers:

- **Report Explorer**—Provides a tree view of each report section in the report and each of the report objects contained within each section. You can work with each report object directly from the explorer rather than navigating to each object separately in either the Design or Preview tab of the report.

- **Field Explorer**—Displays a tree view of database fields, formulas, SQL expressions, parameters, running totals, groups, and special fields. You can add any of these field types directly to a report from the Explorer dialog. Fields that have already been added to the report or fields that are used by other fields (such as formula fields, groups, summaries, and so on) have a green check mark icon in front of them.

- **Repository Explorer**—Provides a tree view of each object contained in the Crystal Enterprise report repository. You can work with each report repository object directly from the Repository Explorer rather than locating each object separately for inclusion in the report during the report design process.

NOTE

> It is important to emphasize that since Version 10, the centralized Repository is available for use only with BusinessObjects Enterprise and/or Crystal Reports Server.

Locating and Using the Report Design Explorers

You can dock in place each Explorer dialog or use it in a free-floating state. By default, the report and field explorers appear docked on the right side of the report design environment. However, you can manually dock each of them in other locations if you prefer. You can also use the explorers in free-floating mode, in which case you can drag each the explorer dialog window to any location within the report design environment and let it float in place until you either close or reposition it. To view each report design explorer, click the View menu and select each desired explorer individually, as shown in Figure 1.4.

Figure 1.4
By default, the design explorers, workbench, and dependency checker are docked on the right side of the Report Designer application but can be moved about and toggled on and off to facilitate report design.

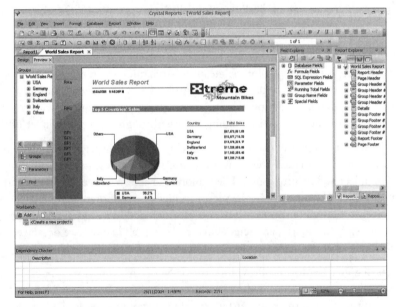

TIP

> To save space in the design environment, the individual explorers can be dragged on top of each other and provide their functionality through respective tabs in a single dialog. This is the default position for the Field and Report Explorer in a fresh install, but note in Figure 1.4 how the Report Explorer has been dragged into its own dialog with the Repository Explorer exposing itself through a tab in that same dialog. Also new since XI is the ability to autohide the explorer windows by clicking on the thumbnail toggle button at the top of each explorer. The explorers then autohide on the sides of your report until you are ready to use them again.

The report design explorers create an intuitive way for report designers to add and format report objects quickly while constructing reports. As you progress through the remainder of the book, you will use these explorers on a regular basis, so it's important that you understand the basics of these application features.

THE WORKBENCH AND DEPENDENCY CHECKER

Two new features presented since XI are the Workbench and the Dependency Checker. The Workbench provides a tool within the Crystal Reports Designer that enables the logical grouping and management of reports into projects. The Dependency Checker is another new tool that checks a specified report, or all reports in an existing Workbench report project for several types of errors, including formula compilation problems, database errors, repository object errors (if you're using BusinessObjects Enterprise), and hyperlink errors. You can check for these types of errors and invoke the Dependency Checker from under the main Report menu or from within the Workbench window. You can access both the Dependency Checker and the Workbench from the main View menu, and locate and lock them in the same way as the report explorers.

UNDERSTANDING DATA AND DATA SOURCES

The first step in creating a report is always to identify a data source. Today, Crystal Reports supports more than 100 different types of data sources. These data sources range from traditional databases such as Microsoft SQL Server, Oracle, IBM DB2, and Microsoft Access to other more abstract forms of structured data such as log files, email, XML, COM/.NET/EJB objects, and multidimensional (OLAP) data. Chapters 15, "Advanced Data Sources in Crystal Reports, and 16, "Formatting Multidimensional Reporting Against OLAP Data," cover many of the advanced data sources and their specific nuances in detail.

To determine which database driver to use to connect to a certain data source, it's best to understand the different types of database drivers. The following sections discuss direct and indirect access database drivers.

UNDERSTANDING DIRECT ACCESS DRIVERS

Direct access database drivers are built solely for reporting from a specific type of database, such as Oracle. If a direct access driver (sometimes called a *native* driver) exists for the database that you intend to report from, it is generally the best choice. Although they follow the standard model of a database driver, direct access drivers are tailored for that specific database. For example, if you choose the Microsoft Access direct access driver during the creation of a report, you receive a prompt for the filename of the Access MDB file. If you are using the Oracle direct access driver, you receive a prompt for a server name. Not only is the user experience more specific to that database, a direct access driver often results in better performance than other methods of connecting to the same data. Table 1.1 lists some of the most common direct access database drivers.

TABLE 1.1 COMMON DIRECT ACCESS DATABASE DRIVERS	
Direct Access Driver	**Description**
Microsoft Access	Used to access Microsoft Access databases and Microsoft Excel spreadsheets
Oracle	Used to access Oracle database servers
DB2	Used to access IBM DB2 database servers

UNDERSTANDING INDIRECT ACCESS DRIVERS

As you might guess from its name, an *indirect access driver* is one that connects indirectly to an actual data source. Indirect access drivers are not built for any one type of database, but rather are built to read data from a variety of data sources via a standard data access mechanism. The purpose of these drivers is to enable Crystal Reports to use data sources for which direct access drivers do not exist. The two major indirect access drivers provided are ODBC and OLE DB.

ODBC, which stands for *Open Database Connectivity*, is a long-standing technology built to connect various applications to various data sources via a common mechanism called an *ODBC driver*. Just as Crystal Reports has database drivers that enable data access to report developers, ODBC has ODBC drivers that enable data access to any application. The Crystal Reports ODBC database driver communicates with an ODBC driver, which in turn communicates with the actual database. The database vendors generally develop the ODBC drivers, which often come bundled with the database software.

OLE DB, pronounced *OH-lay-dee-bee*, is the evolution of ODBC. Like ODBC, OLE DB has a concept of database drivers, but it calls them *OLE DB providers*. Crystal Reports can read most OLE DB providers. Figure 1.5 illustrates the various ways to connect to your data.

Figure 1.5
The Crystal Reports data access architecture provides unparalleled data access.

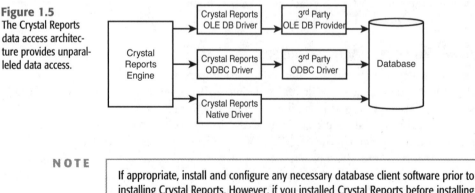

NOTE

If appropriate, install and configure any necessary database client software prior to installing Crystal Reports. However, if you installed Crystal Reports before installing the database vendor's client software, follow the directions located in the Crystal Reports Help files to ensure correct configuration of the Crystal Reports system data source names (DSNs).

INTRODUCING THE DATABASE EXPERT

Now that you have a basic understanding of what database drivers are and an idea of which one you might use to access a particular data source, let's look at the user interface for selecting the data source for a report. Because this is the first step in the creation of a report, it is only natural that this is the first step in the Report Wizard, as Figure 1.6 shows. Hosted inside the Report Wizard, the Database Expert is a tree control that enables you to identify the following:

- Which Crystal Reports database driver you want to use
- Which data source you want you use
- Which database objects you want to use

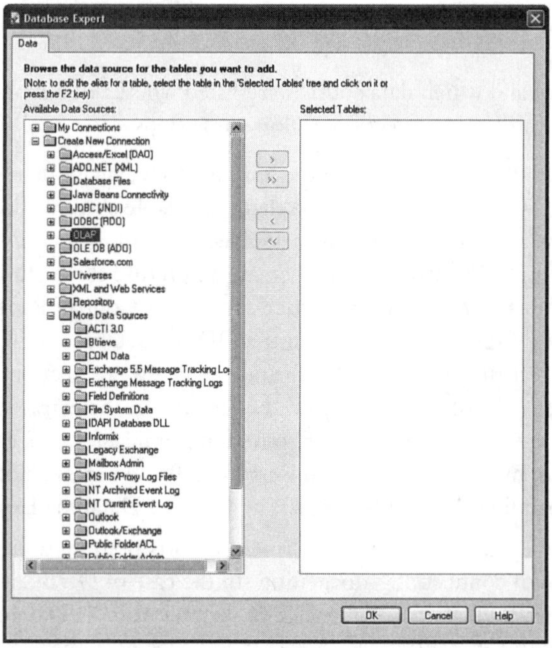

Figure 1.6
The Database Expert provides access to the multitude of supported Crystal Reports data sources.

To open the Database Expert, select File, New and select the type of report you want to create. Selecting Blank Report opens the Database Expert on its own, whereas selecting any other report type opens the Database Expert as part one to a multipart wizard dialog. The Database Expert represents data source connections organized into a number of categories. The following sections describe each of these categories, whereas Chapter 18, "Crystal Reports Java Components," discusses the Enterprise Repository.

CREATING A NEW CONNECTION

To specify a new connection, expand the Create New Connection node in the Database Expert. As Figure 1.6 shows, you can select from a multitude of data sources in this interface. There is a node in this section for each driver selected during the installation process.

> **NOTE**
>
> One node to take special note of is the More Data Sources node. When expanded, this node lists all database drivers that are available but not installed. Crystal Reports supports *install on-demand*, meaning that various features always appear as available, even if not installed. When you expand one of the database driver's node selections under the More Data Sources node, Crystal Reports installs that driver on demand. The next time you load the Database Expert, it lists that driver directly under the Create New Connection node.

Now that you understand which data sources are listed where, look at the process of creating a connection. To create a connection, follow these steps:

1. Expand the node that corresponds to the appropriate database driver. An easy one to play with is the Xtreme sample database that is available as a free download from Business Objects at http://support.businessobjects.com/downloads/samples.asp#07 . After downloading, extract the files and create an ODBC connection. To accomplish this, select Administrative Tools from your computer's Control Panel and then select the Data Sources (ODBC) option. From the ODBC Database Administrator window that displays, select the System DSN tab and add a new connection specifying Microsoft Access (MDB) as the type and the location of the extracted file. You should call this database Xtreme Sample 12 or something similar for ease of future reference. After these steps, move back to Crystal Reports 2008 and create a connection to this database by expanding the ODBC (RDO) node in the Database Expert.

2. Notice that when you expand a node, Crystal Reports presents a dialog that allows for the specification of connection information. In the case of ODBC, the DSN is the only thing required. In the list of available DSNs, Xtreme Sample Database 12 is visible—it is preinstalled with Crystal Reports. Select it and click on Finish.

3. Focus returns to the Database Expert, and there should be a node called Xtreme Sample Database 12. Below that node is the list of available tables, views, and stored procedures, as well as the Add Command option for adding a SQL command (discussed shortly).

You could also use the Xtreme Sample Database via the OLE DB or direct Access driver. Note that when prompting the report developer for connection information when using one of these drivers, Crystal Reports asks for different information. ODBC requires the selection of a DSN, whereas OLE DB needs the specification of a provider.

Using My Connections

The My Connections node lists all currently open database connections. In other words, if a report is or was recently open, the My Connections node lists that connection. The first time you open the Crystal Reports Designer, the My Connections node is empty because no connections have been initiated. This is indicated by the …no items found… item shown when the My Connections node is expanded. This is a quick way to select the same connection as another report currently open. Figure 1.7 illustrates the presentation of multiple open connections to the user.

Figure 1.7
Quickly add open connections to a report using the My Connections node.

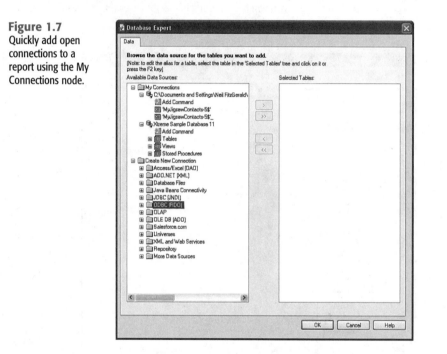

Adding Database Objects to Your Report

The term *database objects* describes the various forms of data that you can add to a report. Specifically, Crystal Reports can use the following types of database objects as data sources for a report:

- Tables or system tables
- Views
- Synonyms
- Stored procedures
- SQL commands

Crystal Reports lists database objects underneath connections in the Database Expert, and it groups them by object type. Figure 1.8 shows the various database objects for the Xtreme Sample Database. In this case, there are tables, views, system tables, and stored procedures. The Add Command node gives you the ability to add SQL commands to this report.

TIP

> You can control the objects displayed in the Database Expert by setting selection, description, and filtering options from either the Database tab of the Options dialog under the File menu or the Options menu option of the database's right-click context menu. This can be particularly useful when you are reporting off databases with hundreds of tables.

Figure 1.8
The Database Expert presents database objects in their logical categories.

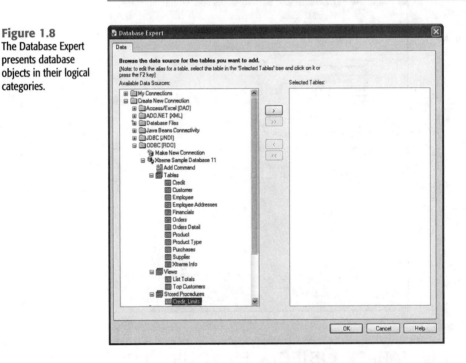

The following sections describe the most common database object types in further detail.

REPORTING ON TABLES

Tables are the most basic form of a data structure. Simply put, a *table* is a set of fields bound together to represent something in the real world. A Customer table might contain fields that describe all the customers of a given business. An Employee table might store information about a corporation's employees, such as name, title, or salary.

To add a table to a report, select the table in the Database Expert and click the arrow (>) button. Crystal Reports adds the table to the Selected Tables list on the right side of the dialog, below its corresponding connection. Most database administrators give the tables meaningful names; however, sometimes tables can have arcane names, such as RM564_321. That name isn't very descriptive, so renaming the table to something more meaningful is useful. To rename a table, select it in the Selected Tables list and press the F2 button (F2 is a standard convention for renaming things in Windows). Crystal Reports refers to renaming a table as *aliasing* a table.

REPORTING ON VIEWS

A *view* is a query stored by the database that returns a set of records that resemble a table. Views often perform complex query logic, and good database administrators create them to simplify the job of people (such as report developers) extracting data out of the database. For example, the Top Customers view in the Xtreme Sample Database returns all customers who have sales of more than $50,000. From a report developer's perspective, views act just like tables, and a designer can add them to the report in the same way.

REPORTING ON STORED PROCEDURES

Stored procedures, in the context of Crystal Reports, are similar to views in that they are pre-defined queries in the database that return a set of records. The major difference is that a stored procedure can be parameterized. This means that rather than having a preset query that returns the same data every time it runs, a stored procedure returns different data based on the values of parameters passed in.

Adding a stored procedure to a report works much the same way as tables and views. However, if the stored procedure has a parameter, a dialog appears when you attempt to add the stored procedure to the report, as shown in Figure 1.9. The dialog asks you to provide values for each stored procedure's parameters. After you complete this and click the OK button, focus returns to the Database Expert, and the stored procedure appears in the list of selected tables. At this time, a parameter is created in the report that corresponds to the stored procedure parameter, and any values that parameter is given are passed to the underlying stored procedure.

Figure 1.9
Adding a stored procedure with a parameter invokes the Enter Values dialog.

REPORTING ON SQL COMMANDS

When reporting from tables, views, and stored procedures, Crystal Reports generates a query behind the scenes using the *Structured Query Language (SQL)*. This is beneficial because the report developer does not need to understand the complexity of the SQL language, but rather can just drop fields onto the report and get data back that matches those fields. However, sometimes report developers are quite experienced with databases and, specifically, the SQL language. Because of this, they sometimes prefer to write their own SQL query rather than have Crystal Reports generate it for them. For an introduction to the SQL language, refer to the XI Downloads section at www.usingcrystal.com and download Appendix A: "Using SQL Queries in Crystal Reports."

SQL commands enable you to use your own prebuilt SQL query and have the Crystal Reports engine treat that query like a *black box*. This means any query, whether simple or very complex, that returns a set of records can be a data source for a Crystal Report. To create a SQL command, select the Add Command item under the database connection, and then click the arrow (>) button. This initiates a dialog that enables the user to type in a SQL query. Figure 1.10 illustrates a typical query.

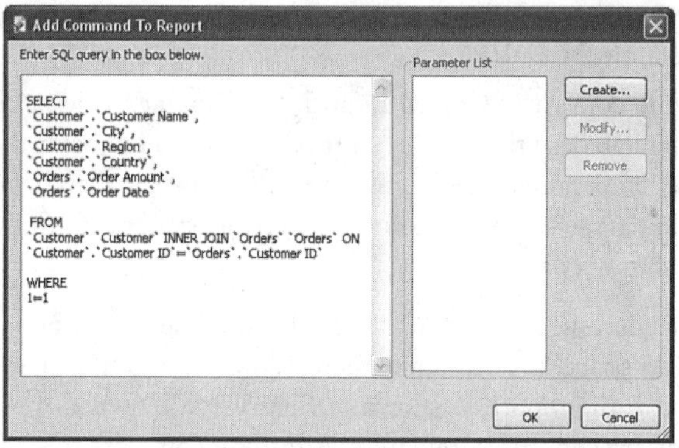

Figure 1.10
Adding a typical SQL command to a report.

After the user types in the query and clicks on the OK button, focus returns to the Database Expert, which represents the newly created command as `'Command'` underneath its corresponding connection in the Selected Tables area. As with all database objects, selecting the command and pressing the F2 button enables the user to rename the object.

One key feature of SQL commands is parameterization. If you had to create a static SQL query, much of the power of SQL commands would be lost. Fortunately, SQL commands in Crystal Reports support parameters. Although you can use parameters in any part of the SQL command, the most common scenario is to use a parameter in the WHERE clause of the SQL statement to restrict the records returned from the query. To create a parameter, click the Create button in the Modify Command dialog. This initiates a dialog that enables you to specify a name for the parameter, the text to use when prompting for the parameter value, a data type, and a default value. After you click the OK button, the parameter appears in the Parameter list. To use this parameter, place the cursor where the SQL query should use the parameter, and double-click the parameter name.

When the report developer creates a SQL command with a parameter, Crystal Reports prompts for a parameter value. This works much the same way as parameterized stored procedures in that Crystal Reports automatically creates the report that maps to the SQL command parameter.

CAUTION

> Unlike previous versions (9 and before), SQL commands can no longer be centrally stored and accessed in a centralized Crystal Repository without the BusinessObjects Enterprise or Crystal Reports Server products. In fact, the Repository and all its reusable objects are now available only through BusinessObjects Enterprise or Crystal Reports Server. A Repository Migration Wizard is distributed with the Enterprise product to facilitate quick migration from the V.9 Crystal Reports–based Repository.

JOINING DATABASE OBJECTS

Until this point the discussion has covered reports based on only a single table, view, stored procedure, or SQL command. However, it is quite common to have several disparate database objects in the same report. Crystal Reports treats all types of database objects as peers, which means that a single report can contain multiple tables, views, stored procedures, and SQL commands. Because all database objects are peers, from now on, the term *table* describes any of those database objects.

Because of the inherent basis on relational data in Crystal Reports, anytime it uses multiple tables, they must link together so that the sum of all database objects is a single set of relational records. The good news is that, most of the time, Crystal Reports handles this automatically and the report developer need not worry about linking.

To see this in action, create a connection to the Xtreme Sample Database and add both the Customer and Orders tables to the report. When you click the Next button, the Report Wizard displays the linking between the tables, as shown in Figure 1.11. A window represents each table. In addition to the name, the window lists each field in the table, and those fields defined as indexed fields in the database are marked with colored arrows. Arrows connecting the key fields from two tables represent any links defined between tables. Based on general database theory, linking to an indexed field generally results in a better-performing query, and in this dialog the color-coded icons displayed beside the field names highlight indexing.

By default, Crystal Reports creates links based on name. In this case, both tables have fields with a name of Customer ID, so it already created a link. To accept this link, simply click on Next to move to the next step in the Report Wizard. If there was no common field name, selecting the By Key option and clicking Auto-Link would cause Crystal Reports to attempt to create a link based on the fields defined in the database as keys. If neither method of automatic linking works, you must manually create the link. This is simple to do: Simply drag the field to link from one table and drop it onto the field from a second table.

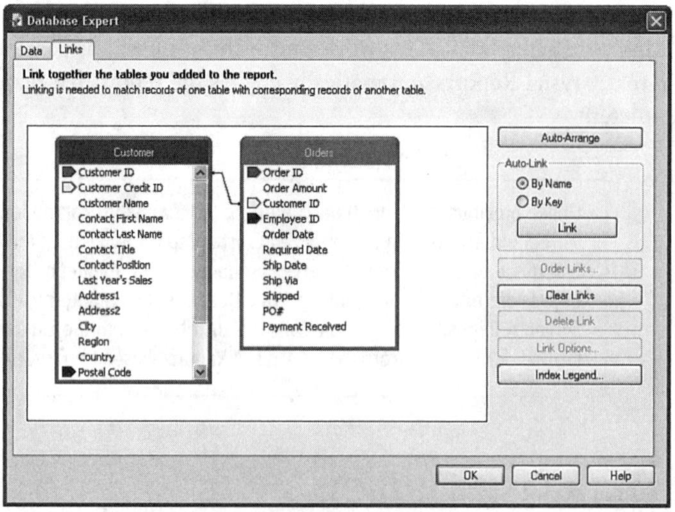

Figure 1.11
You can link multiple tables in the Report Wizard.

After creating links, you can configure them by clicking on the link arrow connecting two tables (it turns blue when selected) and then clicking the Link Options button. Links have two options: join type and link operator. These settings determine how Crystal Reports matches records from both tables. The default join type is an inner join, which means that only records with a matching key in both tables are included. The default link type is equal. For most cases, these two settings do not need to be modified.

UNDERSTANDING THE DIFFERENT JOIN TYPES

In Crystal Reports, the Link tab of the Report Wizard (and Database Expert) provides a visual representation of the relationship between multiple database objects. Defining the appropriate join strategy for any given report is reflective of the data within the database objects and of how the report needs to read and display that data. Join type settings enable you to control more precisely the query results based on your unique requirements. The following is a list of the most common types of joins and their associated descriptions:

- **Inner**—The resultset includes all the records in which the linked field value in both tables is an exact match. The Inner join is the standard type of join for most reports, and it is also commonly known as the *Equal join*.

- **Left Outer**—The resultset includes all the records in which the linked field value in both tables is an exact match. It also includes a row for every record in the primary (left) table for which the linked field value has no match in the secondary (lookup) table. For example, if you would like your report to display all customers and the orders they have each placed—including the customers who have not placed any orders—you can use a Left Outer join between the Customer and Orders tables. As a result, you would see a row for every customer who has not placed any orders.

- **Not Equal**—The resultset includes all records in which the linked field value in the primary table is not equal to the linked field value in the secondary (lookup) table. For example, if you needed to report on all orders not shipped on the same date they were ordered, you could use the Not Equal join type to join the OrderDate field in the Orders table with the ShipDate field in the OrderDetails table.

- **Full Outer**—The resultset includes all records in both of the linked tables. That is, all records in which the linked field value in both tables is an exact match, in addition to a row for every record in the primary (left) table for which the linked field value has no match in the secondary (lookup) table, and a row for every record in the secondary (lookup, or *right*) table for which the linked field value has no match in the primary table. The Full Outer join is a bidirectional outer join, which essentially combines the characteristics of both the Left Outer and Right Outer joins into a single join type.

NOTE

> Version 10 introduced the capability to enforce links created in a report. Enforcing a link between two tables ensures that the report's respective SQL uses this link, regardless of whether fields are required from either or both of the involved tables. The default setting is Unenforced Links, meaning that Crystal Reports uses the link only if the report's respective SELECT statement requires it. You access the different enforcement options by right-clicking on a link and selecting the Link Options menu item.

After you create a report, select Database Expert from the Database menu to return to the Database Expert. Here you can add, remove, and rename tables and SQL commands just as you could from the Database Expert in the report creation process.

USING THE REPORT CREATION WIZARDS

After that quick introduction to the Crystal Reports development environment and data access review, a good place to begin creating reports is with the default report wizards. The report wizards are provided to expedite the report design process for report designers of all skill levels, but they are especially useful for new users of Crystal Reports.

The report wizards, also commonly referred to as *report experts*, provide a simplified interface and a guided path to constructing the fundamental elements found within most reports. As a result, you can design interactive, professional-looking reports in a matter of minutes.

This section reviews the various wizards available for different report styles you might require. This chapter also provides a tutorial that walks you through the report design process using the Standard Report Creation Wizard to create a useful, professionally styled report.

TIP

> Using the default report wizards as a starting point for beginners on most reports is a good idea. The report wizards offer a shortcut to establishing the core elements required for most reports.

GETTING STARTED WITH THE REPORT WIZARDS

You can access the report wizards from either the Start page previously highlighted in Figure 1.1 or by selecting File, New from the New menu. The four report wizards facilitate the guided visual creation of four types of reports.

As Figure 1.12 illustrates, the New menu option of the File menu serves as the gateway to accessing and using the various report creation wizards. From this menu, you can select from one of the four provided report wizards:

- **Standard**—Used to create traditional columnar-styled reports
- **Cross-Tab**—Used to create summary styled cross-tab reports
- **Mailing Label**—Used to create reports with multiple columns, such as address labels
- **OLAP Cube**—Used to create summary styled cross-tab reports based on an OLAP data source

Figure 1.12
The Crystal Reports
New File menu pro-
vides quick access to
the various report
creation wizards.

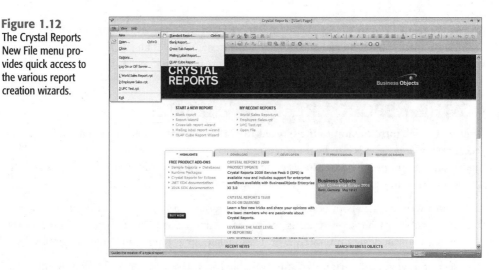

The remainder of this section focuses on exploring and using the Standard Report Creation Wizard. It is the most commonly used report wizard, and it provides a good introduction to the components of the report design process. If your interests lie in OLAP cube and cross-tab reports, rest assured that later chapters will cover them.

USING THE STANDARD REPORT CREATION WIZARD

The Standard Report Creation Wizard is the most frequently used design assistant in Crystal Reports. It provides multiple dialogs common to creating reports based on conventional corporate data sources. The Standard Report Creation Wizard guides you through selecting a data source, linking data source tables, adding data source fields to the report, specifying field groupings, identifying summary (total) fields, and setting the desired sort criteria for your report.

Additionally, the Standard Report Creation Wizard walks you through creating chart objects, applying record selection criteria (data filters), and applying predefined templates (layouts) to your report.

> **NOTE**
>
> Commonly, the term *filter* describes the data selection criteria that narrow the scope of the data extracted by the report from the underlying data source. For example, by using a filter such as Country = USA, you can easily limit your report to include only the information you are interested in extracting.

The Standard Report Creation Wizard consists of nine dialog screens that enable you to specify the criteria mentioned previously to quickly create a professional-looking report. The sequence of the wizard's dialog screens is dynamic and directly associated with the items selected in each of the progressive screens. For example, if you do not choose to identify any summary items for your report, you do not receive a Chart dialog screen. In general, charts apply best to summarized data, so if you have not identified any summary fields, the wizard assumes that you do not want to include a chart object in your report.

> **NOTE**
>
> You can create charts from base-level data, although to do this you must appropriately specify the On Change Of option and use the advanced settings in the Chart Expert. Generally, it makes more sense to base chart objects on summary-level data, such as regional sales by quarter—where you are charting the total sales for each quarter rather than each sales transaction in each quarter.

The following exercise steps through the wizard and builds a sales report to display last year's sales by country. By making use of the Standard Report Creation Wizard, you include the country, city, customer name, and last year sales database fields, graphically display a summary of last year sales by country, and apply professionally styled formatting to the report. To create the sales report, follow these steps:

1. From the main File menu, select the New option, and then select the Standard Report Wizard from the wizard list.

2. As shown in Figure 1.13, the Standard Report Creation Wizard presents the first dialog: Data. From the Data dialog screen, expand the Create New Connection node and then expand the ODBC listing as well. This should present the ODBC Data Source Selection dialog.

Figure 1.13
The Standard Report Creation Wizard begins by requesting a data source for your report.

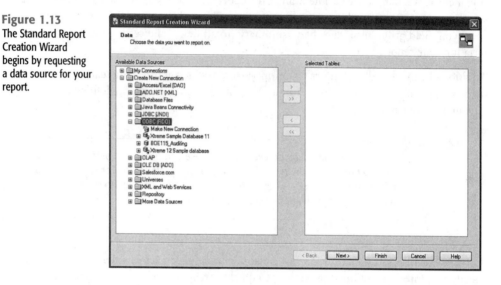

3. Select the Make New Connection option, and from the ODBC Data Source Selection dialog, scroll to the end of the Data Source Name list, and select Xtreme 12 Sample Database or the name that you applied to it, as shown in Figure 1.14. Click on Next to continue.

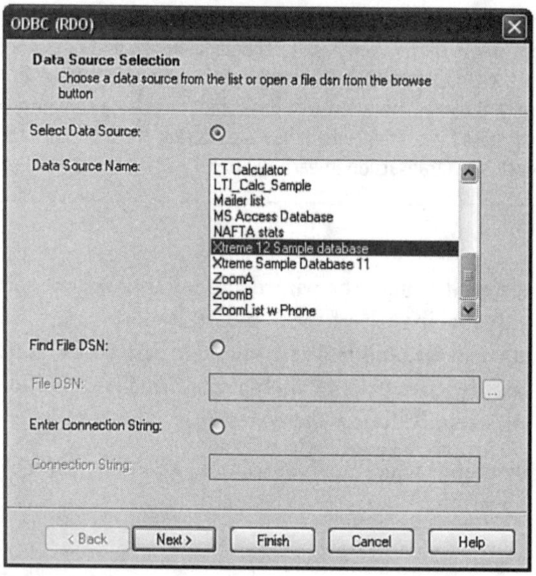

Figure 1.14
The ODBC Data Source Selection dialog enables you to select a valid connection to access your ODBC data sources.

4. Verify that the Data Source Name is correct and click on Finish from the ODBC Connection Information dialog. No password is necessary to access this database.

5. After you successfully identify and connect to Xtreme 12 Sample Database, you see the item listed under the ODBC node in the Available Data Sources area of the Data dialog, as shown in Figure 1.15.

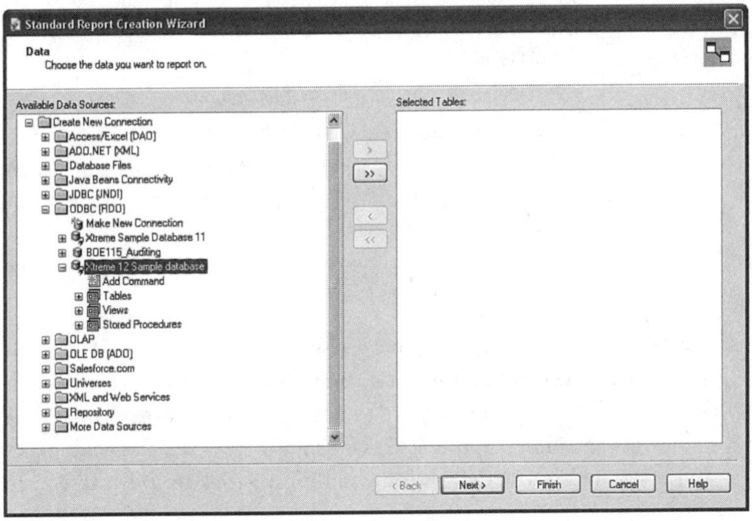

Figure 1.15
The Xtreme 12 Sample Database is under the Available Data Sources area of the Data dialog.

On expanding the Xtreme 12 Sample Database item, you see three or four distinct data source items listed: Tables, Views, and Stored Procedures—and possibly System Tables, depending on your options settings (shown in Figure 1.16).

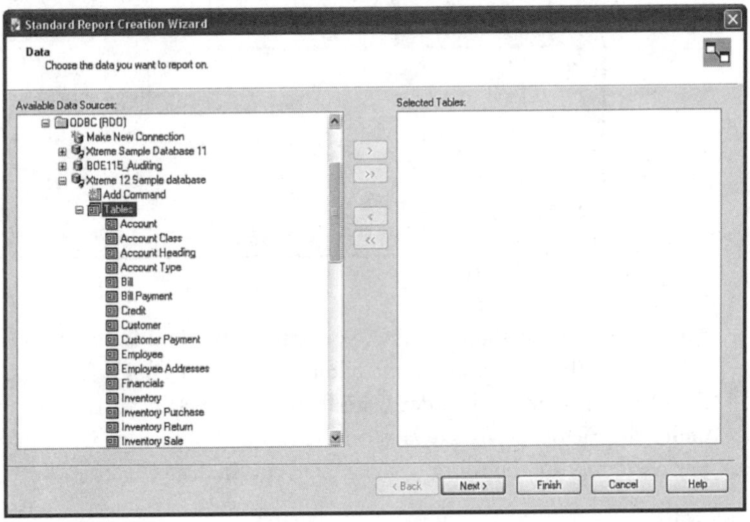

Figure 1.16
When you expand the Xtreme 12 Sample Database item, you see a list of multiple database items.

6. Within the Data dialog screen, select the Customer and Orders tables so that the Selected Tables area on the right lists them. After selecting those two tables, click on the Next button to continue to the Linking dialog.

TIP

> There are multiple ways to include tables in your report from within the Data dialog screen. From the list of available tables on the left side of the dialog, you can perform any one of the following actions to populate the Selected Tables list on the right side of the dialog area:
>
> • Double-click on each desired table item.
>
> • Drag-and-drop each desired table item.
>
> • Highlight the table item on the left (or multiple tables by using Ctrl-click) and click on the respective arrow icon (> or >>) between the two listing areas to populate the listing on the right.

7. The Link dialog screen presents a visual representation of the relationship between these two tables and permits you to modify the defined relationship by specifying the exact join links that you require to accurately report on the data within the selected tables. As shown in Figure 1.17, you should now see the Link dialog screen. For our purposes, accept the default join condition. Click on Next to continue.

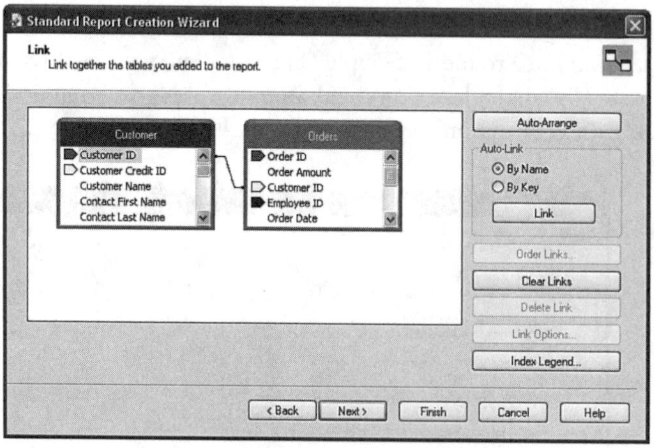

Figure 1.17
The Customer and Orders tables link via the Customer ID field.

8. After specifying the table linking, you will see the Fields dialog screen, shown in Figure 1.18. Select the Customer Name, Country, and City fields from the Customer table and the Order Amount and Order Date fields from the Order table so that they appear under the Fields to Display area on the right. If necessary, you can use the up and down arrows to modify the order of these fields in the list. Click on Next to continue.

Figure 1.18
The Customer Name, Country, City, Order Amount, and Order Date fields should appear under the Fields to Display area.

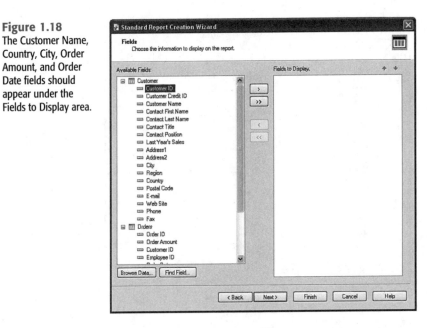

NOTE

If you're not sure of the data contained in any of the respective field items on the left, you can highlight a field name and click the Browse Data button to view a list of values from this field, as shown in Figure 1.19. This can be particularly useful if you are unfamiliar with the database and need to locate a field based on the values it contains, such as account numbers, policy codes, or employee names.

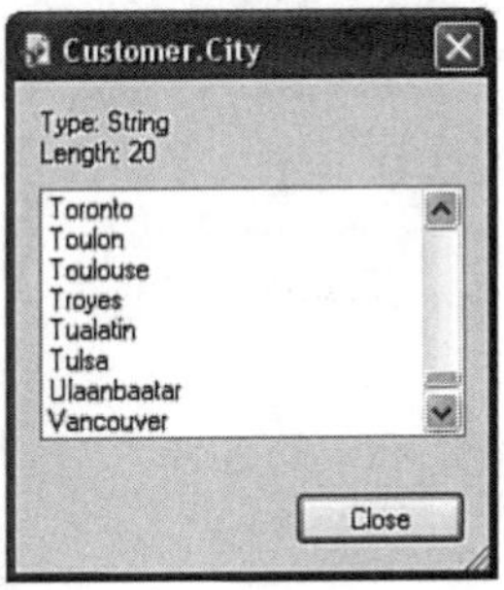

Figure 1.19
The Browse Data button enables you to view a list of values from any of the available database field items.

9. You now see the Grouping dialog screen. This dialog enables you to specify logical groups of information within your reports and whether they will be sorted in ascending or descending order. For this example, select to group by the Country field only and leave the default sorting order, as shown in Figure 1.20. Click on Next to continue.

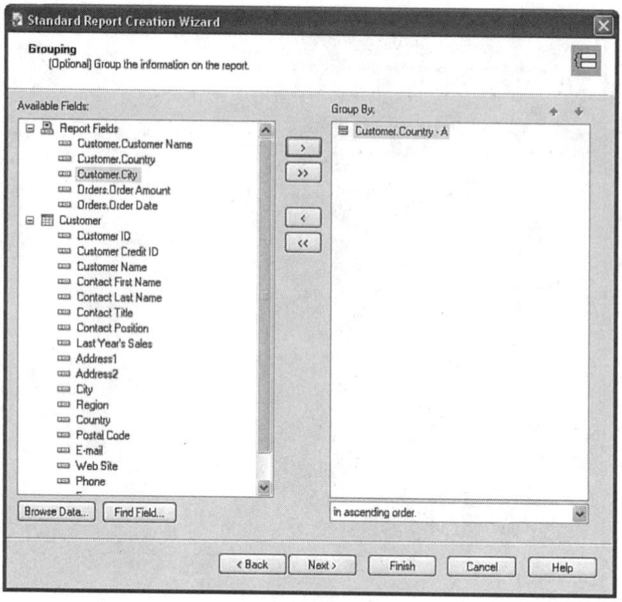

Figure 1.20
The Grouping dialog enables you to create structured groupings of information within your report.

10. You now see the Summaries dialog screen. The Summaries dialog screen enables you to identify summary values (such as sums, counts, and so on) for your reports. If you have not identified grouped items in a report, the Summaries dialog does not appear because summaries are applicable only to grouped data. To apply a summary object to the report, select the Order Amount field so that it appears under the Summarized Fields list on the right, as shown in Figure 1.21. Click Next to continue.

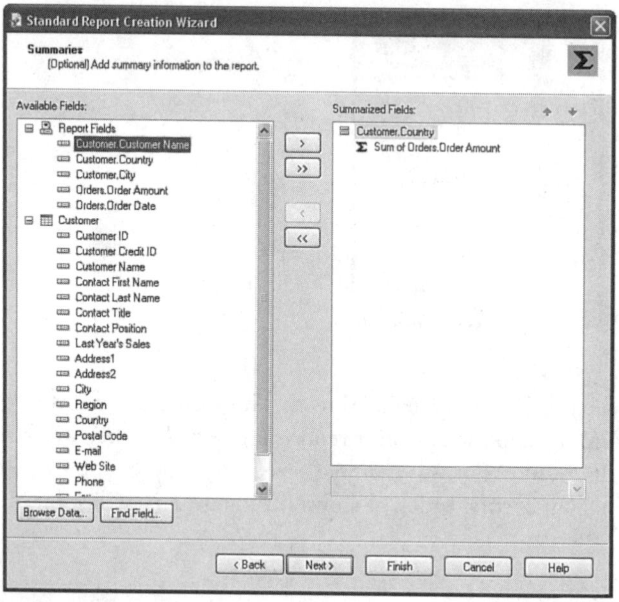

Figure 1.21
The Summaries dialog screen enables you to create summarized values that are frequently used in coordination with the grouping structure within reports.

NOTE

> As you might notice, Crystal Reports automatically chooses a summary for you if you choose to group your report data. It examines the detail information you specified for the report and builds a summary on the first available numeric field. However, you can easily modify the default summary criteria in the wizard.

NOTE

> By default, the Order Amount field that appears under the Summarized Fields area on the right is aggregated as a sum of the actual field value. As shown greyed out in Figure 1.21, the drop-down list located in the lower-right area of the Summaries dialog screen enables you to select from a variety of summaries, including sum, average, maximum, minimum, count, correlation, covariance, and standard deviation.

11. Now sort the report based on the total order amounts of the top five countries. The Group Sorting dialog screen enables you to sort the grouped fields based on the summarized totals. From the Group that Will Be Sorted drop-down list, select the Country field (the only option in the example here) and select the Top 5 Groups option from the Group Ordering choices. Also, select the Sum of Order Amount item (the only option in the example here) from the Comparing Summary Values drop-down list, as shown in Figure 1.22. Click Next to continue.

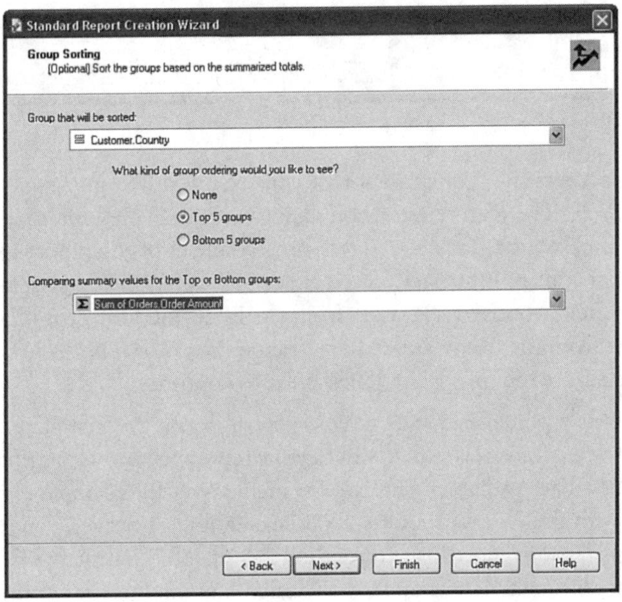

Figure 1.22
The Group Sorting dialog enables you to sort your report based solely on the Group values you want to include in the report results.

12. Charting can be added through the wizard to display the data already selected. From the Chart dialog screen, you can select a chart object to be included in the report based on the group and summary items you identify here. For this example, add a bar chart and select the Country field from the On Change Of drop-down list and the Sum of Order Amounts item from the Show Summary drop-down list. Change the chart title to `Total Order Amounts by Country`—see Figure 1.23 for additional guidance. Click Next to continue.

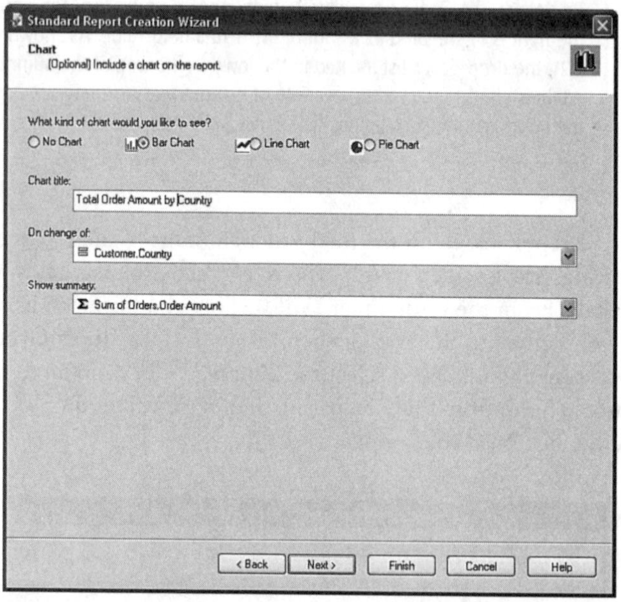

Figure 1.23
The Chart dialog enables you to select a chart object for a report based on the previously identified group and summary criteria.

13. Now you address the requirement that you are interested in customer orders from only the year 2003. The Record Selection dialog screen enables you to identify selection criteria, often called *data filtering*, to focus the resultset of the report to include only the information you are interested in returning. To accomplish this, select Order Date as the Filter Field, choose Is Between from the filter operator drop-down list, and select a data range from the newly created date-range drop-down boxes to incorporate all the dates in 2003 (see Figure 1.24). Click Next to continue.

14. Finally, apply a predefined style to your report. From the Template dialog screen, you can select predefined styles to apply to your report for formatting purposes, as shown in Figure 1.25. The Available Template list includes various sample templates that are included with the Crystal Reports 2008 installation. However, you can also create your own templates for report formatting. For this example, select the Corporate (Blue) template. For additional details on how to design and implement your own templates, see Chapter 14, "Designing Effective Report Templates."

Figure 1.24
The Record Selection dialog permits you to narrow your resultset based on the selection criteria identified here.

Figure 1.25
The Template dialog permits you to select predefined styles to apply to your report.

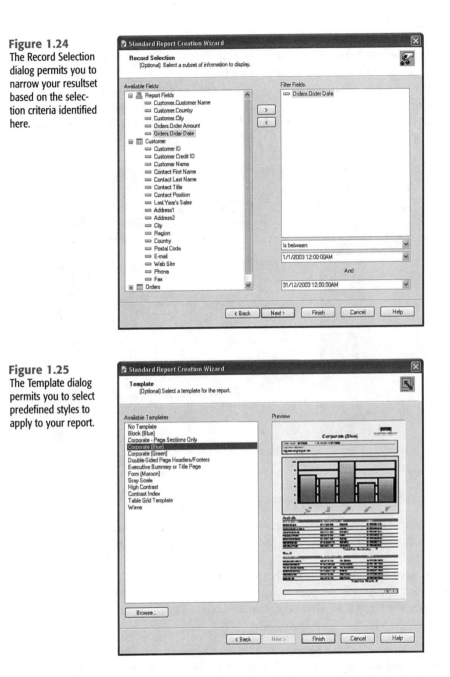

This concludes the Standard Report Creation Wizard example. When you click Finish, you execute the report that you just created and receive a preview of the corresponding resultset. At this point, you can click Finish if you are satisfied with the report design criteria. When you are presented with the preview of your report, save your new report by selecting Save As from the File menu. Name this report Chap1Wizard.rpt or anything you like.

As Figure 1.26 shows, creating a useful and professional-looking report is extremely simple when using the Standard Report Creation Wizard. In the preceding exercises, you connected to a database, identified the tables and fields you wanted to include in your report, linked the tables, grouped and summarized the data, sorted the data, applied filtering criteria, included a chart object for enhanced visualization of the report results, and applied a report template for quick and easy formatting—all in just a few clicks of your mouse! This process speaks to both the ease of use and the power of the Crystal Reports design application.

Figure 1.26
The executed resultset and preview of the report you have just created using the Standard Report Creation Wizard.

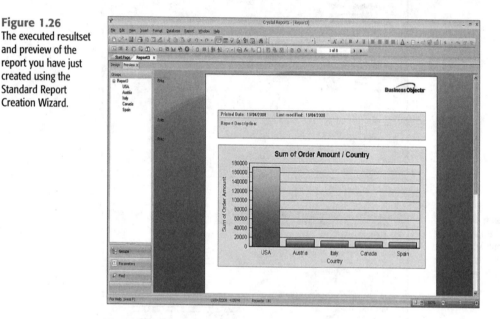

CREATING A REPORT WITHOUT WIZARDS

As with many software tools, educational tools and facilitators such as the Report wizards are often the best way to begin a learning process. They are by their nature, however, limited in functionality, and it generally does not take long before maturing students want to roll up their sleeves and discover the raw power and incredible flexibility that lies beneath. This section reintroduces the report just created in the Report wizard through a manual design process in the Crystal Reports Designer. Create the beginning of that same Sales Report from scratch with the following steps:

1. Select a blank report. After opening Crystal Reports, select the New option from the File menu. From the submenu that appears, select the Blank Report option.

2. Select an appropriate data source. From the Database Expert dialog that comes up, in the Available Data Sources list, browse to Create New Connection, ODBC. As soon as you choose ODBC, the ODBC (RDO) dialog pops up. Scroll until you find Xtreme 12 Sample Database. Select it and click on Finish. (There are no other settings to get this database working, so you can ignore the Next button.)

3. Select the appropriate tables. After choosing the appropriate database to connect to, you need to select the tables for this report. Move down in the left list box and expand the Tables item. Choose the Customer and Orders tables by using the right-arrow (>) button, shown in Figure 1.27.

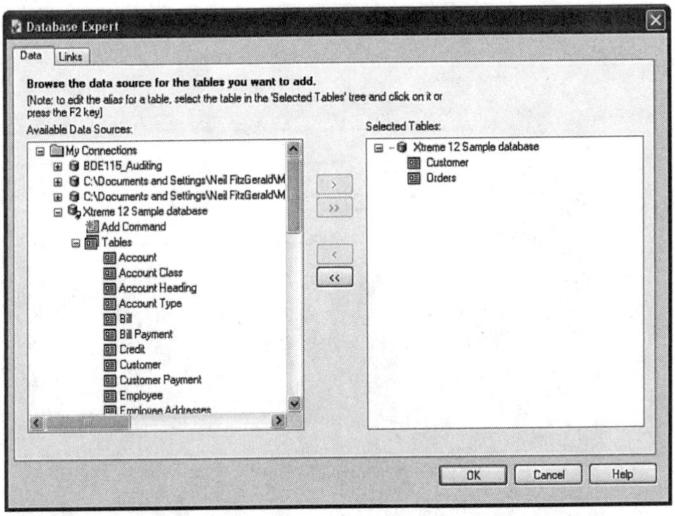

Figure 1.27
The Data tab from the Database Expert dialog shows the two tables you just added to the report.

TIP

Remember that you can choose each table separately and click the arrow button or hold down the Ctrl key to select all tables that you want and then press the arrow button only once. Also, if you want to select several tables in a row, the Shift key helps you with that.

4. Link tables from the database. Move to the next tab in the Database Expert dialog by either clicking on the OK button or selecting the Links tab. Notice that all the tables are already linked. Crystal Reports attempts to link tables using similar field names and sizes whenever possible. You can optionally turn off this automatic smart linking in the Database tab (accessed from File, Options). You don't need to make any changes at this point, so just click on the OK button.

TIP

You can enlarge this dialog by using the stretch markers so that you can increase the display area and see more tables at once. The next time you enter this dialog, Crystal Reports remembers the adjusted size.

5. Add detail records to the report. First confirm that the Field Explorer is displaying so that you can use it to add the fields to the report. If it is not, choose View, Field Explorer. In the Field Explorer that becomes available, open the Database Fields item

and then the Orders and Customer tables to expose the fields to add. Select each field separately and drag it to the Design tab. Place them side by side in the Details Section: Customer Name and Customer City from the Customer table, and Order Date and Order Amount from the Orders table. Figure 1.28 highlights the desired result.

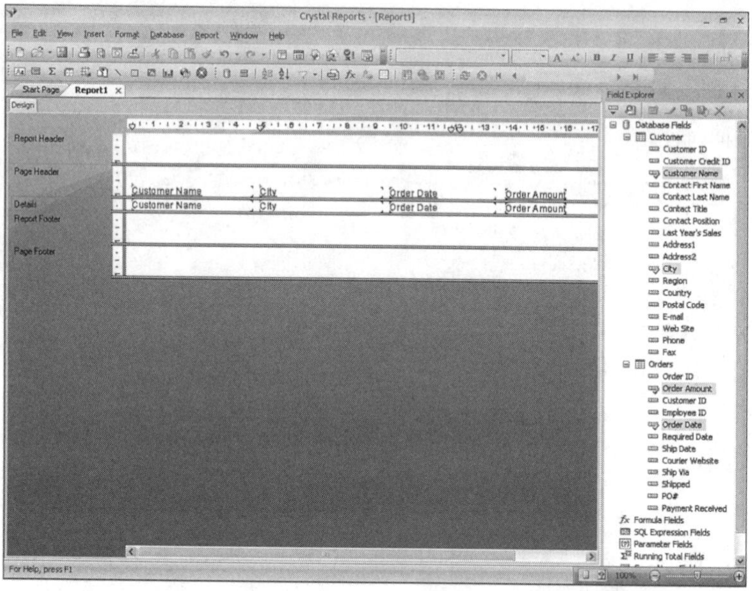

Figure 1.28
This is the Design window after you add all the fields.

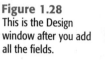

6. Create a logical grouping of data by Country. To accomplish this, choose Insert, Group. When the Insert Group dialog appears, scroll down the first list box until Country under the Customer table is available. Select it, as shown in Figure 1.29, and then click on OK.

   Notice that in the Design view of the report, two new sections become available: Group Header #1 and Group Footer #1. Within Group Header #1, the Group Name #1 field is also automatically added.

7. Add a summary value of total Historical Order Amount by Country to the report. Choose Insert, Summary to get the Insert Summary dialog to appear. In this dialog, select the Order Amount field in the Field to Summarize drop-down box. Next, because you plan on finding out how much has been ordered in each country, you need to set the summary operation in the second list box to Sum. Last, because the desired summary is per country, set the location of the summary to show Group #1, as shown in Figure 1.30. Click on OK.

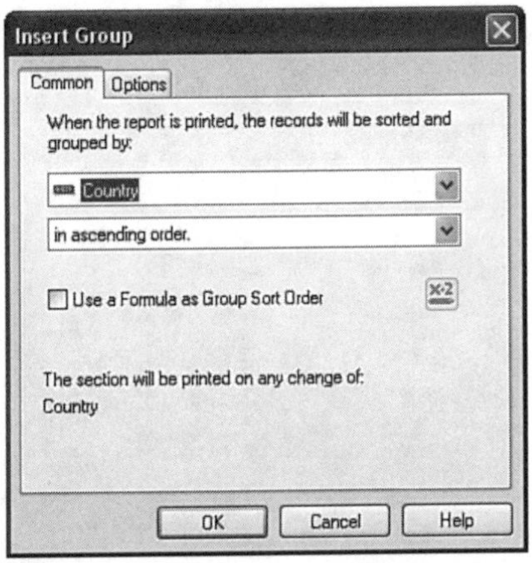

Figure 1.29
The Common tab of the Insert Group dialog with the Country field selected.

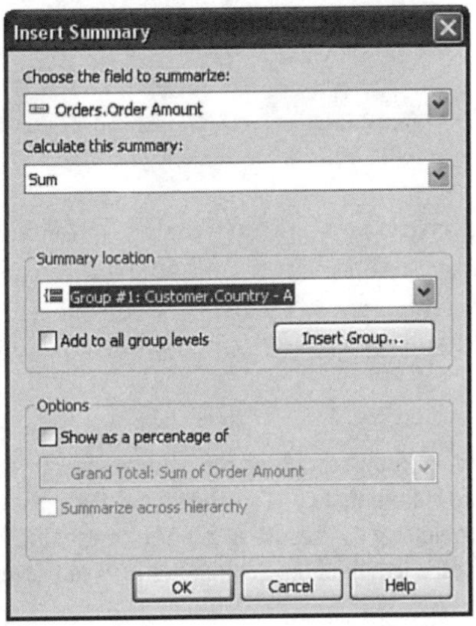

Figure 1.30
The Insert Summary dialog with Order Amount summed by Customer Country selected.

> **TIP**
>
> A shortcut to the Insert Summary command (and running total command described later) is accessible for each field on the report by right-clicking the involved field in the Report Designer.

Notice that in the Design view, in Group Footer #1, Crystal Reports has added the Sum of Order Amount field.

8. View the report. Look at the report by choosing Report, Refresh Report Data or by either pressing the F5 key or clicking the Refresh button in your Crystal Reports Designer. The Preview tab displays a report with all the data represented in the last wizard-driven report you created, as shown in Figure 1.31.

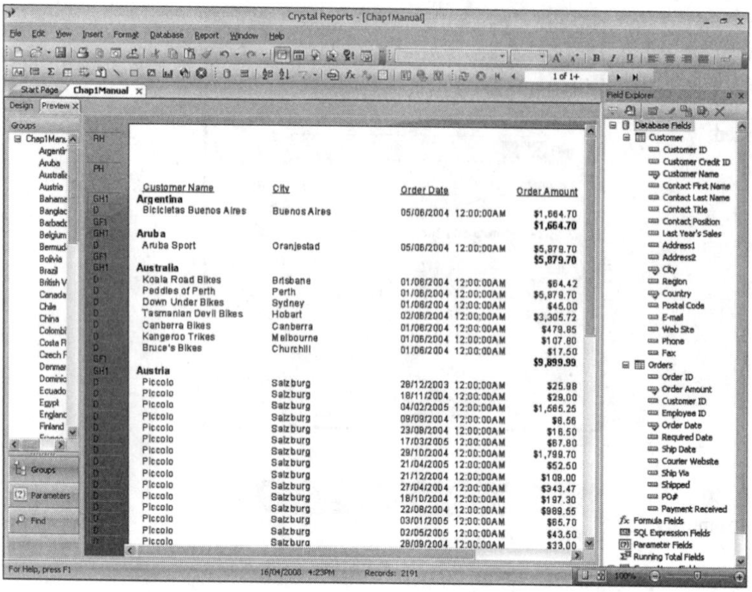

Figure 1.31
The resulting report based on steps 1 through 8 in the Preview tab.

9. Save the report. Choosing File, Save opens the Save dialog. Provide a suitable name for the report, such as Chap1Manual.rpt. You are welcome to explore the charting and report template features now to replicate the Chap1Wizard report, but Chapter 8, "Visualizing Your Data with Charts and Maps," and Chapter 14 cover them in detail.

TIP

> If you are concerned about losing work between manual saves of a report, Crystal Reports has an autosave feature that you can enable. Set this option by navigating to File, Options, and then selecting the Reporting tab. You can set the Autosave Reports After option and specify the length of time in minutes between saves in the Edit box for this option.

TROUBLESHOOTING

I am having difficulty accessing the Database Expert.

To access the Database Expert for a new report, select File, New and select the Blank Report option or any of the Report wizards. For an existing and open report, select the Database Expert from the main Database menu.

I want to update my Crystal Reports Installation with new patches.

To check for new updates in an on-demand mode, select the Check for Updates option under the Help menu. To have this handled for you proactively, select the Check for Updates on Start Up option under the same menu.

CRYSTAL REPORTS IN THE REAL WORLD—HTML PREVIEW

Mature report designers know that to ensure end user happiness and to deploy reports with absolute confidence in the expected results, it is critical to preview the report in the desired distribution format. Because many reports are distributed through the Web and a DHTML viewer, Business Objects added a productivity feature called HTML Preview.

To see an HTML rendering of a Crystal Report design as it will appear when published to the Web, click the HTML Preview button on the Standard toolbar or select HTML Preview from the View menu. Unlike the standard Crystal Reports Preview tab, the HTML Preview tab shows a converted format. By calling up both the Preview and the HTML Preview tabs, you can quickly preview your web-distributed copy of the involved report and make rapid adjustments to yield ideal web results.

The Preview HTML feature is available when you publish reports to Crystal Reports Server or BusinessObjects Enterprise. In the case of reports published to either of these web distribution environments, no configuration is required, and the HTML Preview feature works automatically.

The feature is also available for standalone reports if you use the Report Application Sever (RAS) to generate the preview. To enable the feature in this situation, configure the HTML Preview feature under the Smart Tag & HTML Preview tab of the Options dialog box in Crystal Reports. In this tab, you need to specify the involved web server, platform, virtual server URL, and RAS server.

CRYSTAL REPORTS IN THE REAL WORLD—SQL COMMANDS

Experienced report developers will have noticed that the sample database is simple (only a dozen tables) and that all the fields in the tables have useful names. In practice, it's very common for a database to have many more tables with very complex relationships and field names that are not descriptive. This is where SQL commands can help. This section explores the advantages of using SQL Commands to create reports. To take SQL commands for a test drive, follow these steps:

1. Open Notepad and type the following lines of SQL exactly as they appear here:

```
SELECT
`Customer`.`Customer Name` AS 'Name',
`Customer`.`City` AS 'City',
`Orders`.`Order Amount` AS 'Amount',
`Orders`.`Order Date` AS 'Date'
 FROM
`Customer` `Customer` INNER JOIN `Orders` `Orders` ON ➡ `Customer`.`Customer
ID`=`Orders`.`Customer ID`
```

This is the SQL statement to use in the report.

2. Select a blank report. After opening Crystal Reports, select File, New and select Blank Report.

3. Select an appropriate data source. From the Database Expert dialog that opens, in the Available Data Sources list, browse to Create New Connection, ODBC. As soon as you choose ODBC, the ODBC (RDO) dialog pops up. Scroll until you find the Xtreme 11 Sample Database. Select it and click Finish. (There are no other settings to get this database working, so you can ignore the Next button.

4. Rather than selecting tables, double-click the Add Command option. The Add Command to Report window pops up. Copy the SQL command from Notepad into the box as shown in Figure 1.32.

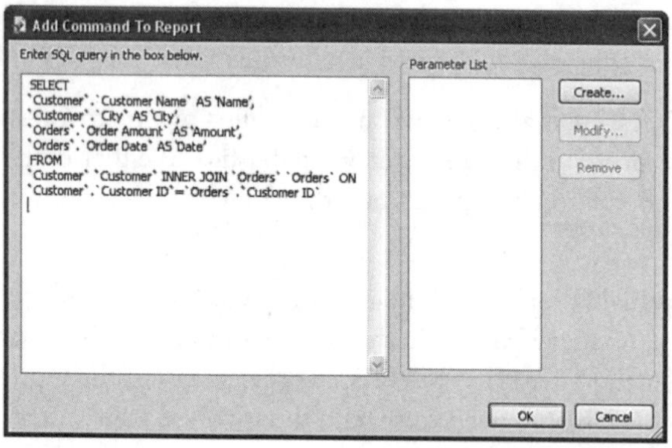

Figure 1.32
The Add Command to Report window with the SQL command pasted into the text box.

Click on OK; notice that there is no need to link the tables because the SQL command already defines the relationship between the tables. Notice also that there are only four fields to choose from and that their names changed.

The SQL command does four things:

- **Hides database complexity**—Converts many tables into one view with the table relationships defined.

- **Hides unnecessary fields**—Many database fields are ID fields that simply aren't intended to be seen by users. You can construct the SQL command so that these fields don't pass through.

- **Renames database fields**—Database field names are often unreadable and give no hint about what they contain. The SQL command can rename these obscure names into something more meaningful.

- **Empowers SQL Experts**—If you are a SQL expert or have them in your organization, you can leverage their expertise in creating optimally performing SQL through use of SQL commands.

Currently you cannot create SQL commands against native connections on Sybase, DB2, and Informix. To leverage the power of this functionality, you can create an ODBC connection against these data sources and then create a SQL command against that ODBC source.

CHAPTER 2

SELECTING AND GROUPING DATA

In this chapter

INTRODUCTION

The Field Explorer, introduced in Chapter 1, "Creating and Designing Basic Reports," provides a quick and easy way to select and display fields on your report and then easily drag and drop them onto the Report Design area. In addition to choosing existing fields from your selected data sources, the Field Explorer enables you to create calculated (formula) fields, parameter fields, running total fields, and group summary fields, as well as choose from a predefined set of default special fields. These additional objects enable a great deal of flexibility and power in the information you can deliver through the reports you create.

In addition to selecting the fields that make up the raw content for a report, it is often beneficial to group base-level data by country, region, or product line. Grouping the data facilitates relevant business user analysis and enables meaningful summarizations in your reports. Crystal Reports provides easy-to-use grouping functionality that enables nested groups, hierarchical grouping, and drill-down analysis into the different levels of grouping selected.

This chapter covers the following information:

- Understanding the different types of field objects
- Adding grouping to your reports
- Adding multiple groups to your report and reordering them
- Hierarchical grouping
- Creating and using drill-down in your reports
- Hiding and suppressing detail records in your reports

UNDERSTANDING FIELD OBJECTS

As described in Chapter 1, the Field Explorer displays a tree view of data fields in your report. It shows database fields, formula fields, SQL expression fields, parameter fields, running total fields, group name fields, and special system fields that you have defined for use in your report. This chapter introduces you to all the standard field types available in Crystal Reports.

To activate the Field Explorer, either select it from the View menu or click on the Field Explorer button in the Crystal Reports Standard toolbar. Figure 2.1 shows the sample Crystal Report created in the last chapter with the Field Explorer activated and docked on the right side of the screen. As previously mentioned, you can dock the Field Explorer on either side of the designer or at the bottom of the screen. Alternatively, the Field Explorer can freely float over any part of the design window by simply dragging and dropping it.

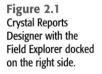

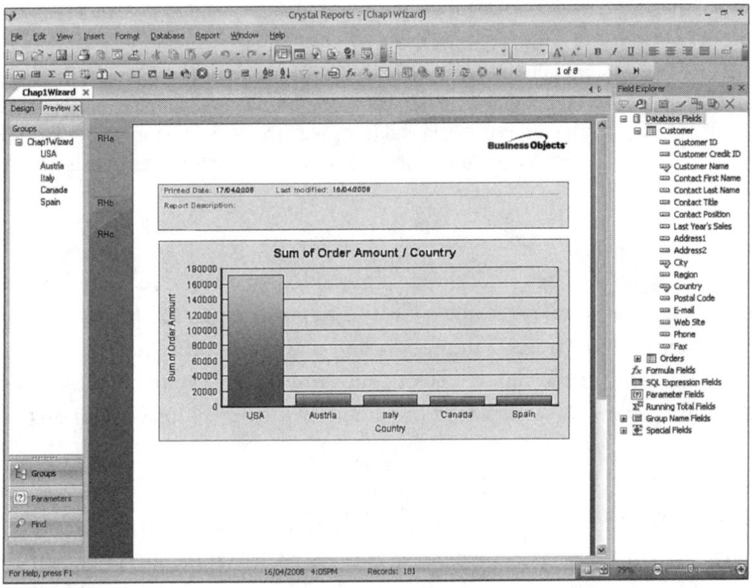

Figure 2.1
Crystal Reports
Designer with the
Field Explorer docked
on the right side.

The next seven sections introduce the different types of fields accessible from the Field Explorer and provide ideas on where you might use them in a report. Later chapters in the book cover some advanced uses of these types of fields. Before moving on to explore these different types of fields, here are some common traits shared by all field types:

- Fields used in the report and fields that have been used by other fields (for example, formulas) in the report are highlighted with a green check mark in front of them.

- The buttons along the top of the Field Explorer (Insert, Browse, New, Edit, Rename, and Delete) are enabled or disabled based on the availability of the selected Field type.

Detailed report field formatting, positioning, and resizing are covered in Chapter 6, "Fundamentals of Report Formatting."

ACCESSING DATABASE FIELDS

The Database Fields branch of the Field Explorer tree adds database fields to your report. The fields that you can add to your report are those from standard database tables, views, stored procedures, synonyms, and system tables. To add additional tables or other data sources to your report, use the Database Expert under the Database menu.

To insert the database fields available from the Field Explorer into your report, either click and drag them into the desired location on the report or select them, click the Insert to Report button (or Insert to Report action from the right-click menu), and then select the desired location on the report for the highlighted fields.

TIP

> If you are uncertain of which fields to add to your report because of ambiguous (for example, WERKS, MENGE, LEAFS) or similar (for example, District, Region, Locale, Division) field names, you might be able to determine the appropriate field by selecting the respective field and using the Browse button (or the Browse action from the right-click menu) to view the data type and sample values of data from the table.

Multiple fields can be highlighted simultaneously in the Field Explorer and placed in the report designer window at once. Crystal Reports drops the first of the multiple chosen fields in the selected location on the report and places the subsequent fields in order to the right of the initial field. If the report's layout runs out of real estate on the right side of the report, the subsequent fields are placed one line down, and the placement algorithm continues.

ACCESSING FORMULA FIELDS

Formula fields provide a means to add derived fields (that is, those not directly available in your database) such as a calculation into your Crystal Reports. Crystal Reports treats derived formula fields in the same manner as it does original database fields. Some examples of where formulas might be used on the sample report from Chapter 1 would include the following:

- **Days Until Shipped**—A date formula determining the difference between the two database fields: Order Date and Ship Date

- **Next Year's Sales Projection**—A numeric formula that multiplies the database field Last Year's Sales by 110%

- **Custom Name Field**—To include the first letter of a customer contact's First Name (a database field) concatenated with a space and the contact's last name (another database field)

The Formula Fields branch of the Field Explorer tree is used to add existing or new formula fields to a report. A listing of previously created formulas appears in this part of the Field Explorer tree. Once created, existing formulas are added to the report by either clicking and dragging and dropping or by selecting the formula and using the Insert functionality—available through the right-click menu or Field Explorer action button—and then selecting the location.

TIP

> Both simple and complex formulas can be created on any type of field, including numeric, date, string, Boolean, or memo fields. This is explored in Chapters 11, "Using Record Selections, Sort Controls, and Alerts for Interactive Reporting," and 13, "Using Formulas and Custom Functions."

If a new formula is required, it can be created directly from the Field Explorer by using the New toolbar button. You are prompted to name the new formula and then select the method of creation. Figure 2.2 displays the Formula Name dialog.

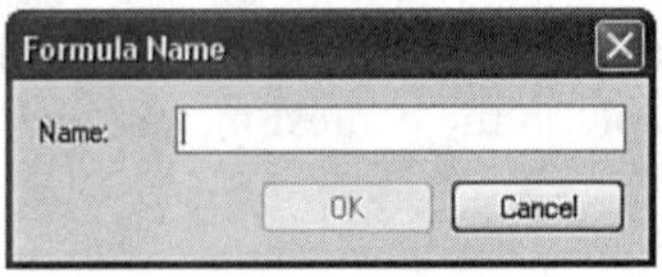

Figure 2.2
The Formula Name dialog requires specification of a formula name.

Using the Xtreme Sample Database and the sample report created in Chapter 1 (chap1Wizard.rpt), one simple formula you might want to add is a Full Name field that comprises both the first and last name of the customer's contact person (Contact First Name and Contact Last Name in the Customer sample table).

To perform this task, perform the following steps:

1. After opening the Chap1Wizard report, highlight the Formula Fields branch of the Field Explorer tree.

2. Select New either by using the New button or right-clicking and selecting New from the fly-out menu over the Formula heading.

3. Enter the Formula Name **Full Name** in the Formula Creation dialog and select OK to enter the Formula Editor.

4. Scroll down in the Report Fields window (the leftmost window of the three at the top in the main frame) to locate and open the Customer table. Select the Contact First Name field by double-clicking on it. The field displays in the main Formula Editing window.

5. Add a space after the Contact First Name field and then type in + " " +. This concatenates the two fields and adds a space between the first name and the last name.

6. Scroll down in the Report Fields window (the upper-left window in the main frame) to locate and open the Customer table. Select the Contact Last Name field by double-clicking on it. The field displays in the main formula editing window.

7. When you have confirmed that the main formula window looks exactly like that shown in Figure 2.3, save the Full Name formula by clicking the Save button and then closing the main Formula Editor window or by simply clicking the Save and Close button.

By selecting Save in the Formula Editor, when you return to the Field Explorer, the new formula, Full Name, is now available to be placed on the report. Finish this section by placing the Full Name Formula field onto the report beside or underneath the Customer Name.

ACCESSING SQL EXPRESSION FIELDS

The SQL Expression Fields branch of the Field Explorer tree is used to add existing or new SQL expression fields to a report. A listing of previously created SQL expressions appears in this part of the Field Explorer tree. Once created, existing SQL expressions are added to the report by either clicking and dragging and dropping or by selecting the SQL expression—using the Insert into Report button or action on the context menu—and selecting the location.

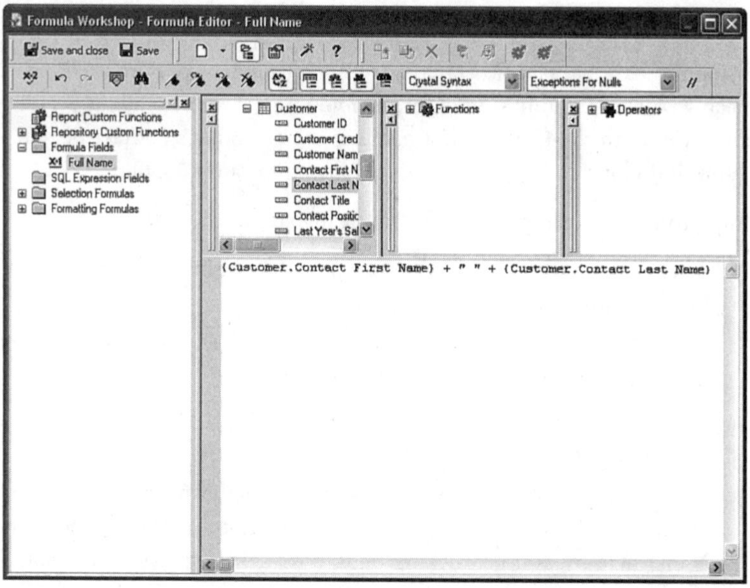

Figure 2.3
This is the Formula Editor after you created a string concatenation formula.

SQL expressions are created in the same Formula Editor as formulas but use Structured Query Language (SQL) statements (rather than the formula syntax). SQL expressions are used in cases where report-processing efficiency is critical. Using SQL expressions can give report designers greater report-processing performance by pushing data processing to the database server instead of the Crystal Reports engine because it is generally more efficient.

> **NOTE**
>
> The SQL syntax created in SQL expressions must be appropriate to the source database. Different databases support various syntactical versions of SQL and even diverse degrees of functionality. This is explored in a document named "Using SQL Queries in Crystal Reports," which is available from the Downloads section of www.usingcrystal.com.

ACCESSING PARAMETER FIELDS

Parameter fields provide a means to create dynamic reports and provide your business users with an interactive method of driving the report content or layout they view. When a

Crystal Report contains parameters, it requests certain pieces of information from the business user before processing. The involved Crystal Report can then use those inputted parameters to filter the data presented or even suppress entire report sections. Some examples of where parameters might be used include

- A region parameter on a sales report
- A profit center on a financial report
- Beginning and ending dates on a transactional report
- A department on an HR salary listing report
- A salesperson name on a customer order listing report

The Parameter Fields branch of the Field Explorer tree is used to add existing or new parameter fields to your report. A listing of previously created parameters appears in this part of the Field Explorer tree. Once created, Parameter fields are added to the report by either clicking and dragging and dropping or by selecting the Parameter field—using the Insert into Report button or action on the context menu—and selecting the location.

If a new parameter is required, it can also be created directly from the Field Explorer by using the New toolbar button. You are prompted to name the new parameter and enter some supporting information. This dialog is displayed in Figure 2.4.

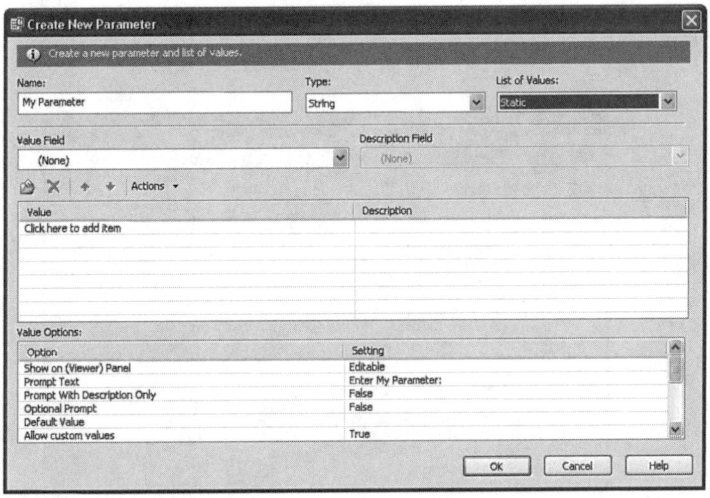

Figure 2.4
The Create New Parameter dialog enables you to specify a parameter name and supporting parameter type information.

→ For detailed information on parameter creation and use as a means to filter report information, **see** "Creating and Implementing Parameters Fields," **p. 134**.

At this point, it is important only to note the location of this field type.

IMPLEMENTING RUNNING TOTAL FIELDS

Running total fields provide a means to incrementally calculate a total on a report as the records are processed. In contrast to the summary fields you will learn about later in the book, running total fields enable you to control how a total is calculated, when it is reset, and when it is displayed. Some examples in which running total fields might be used include

- Running total of website hits over multiple days/weeks/months and so on
- Running total of sales expenses over weeks in a quarter or fiscal year
- Running total of average order amount over time
- Running total of employee count over time

The Running Total Fields branch of the Field Explorer tree is used to add existing or new running total fields to your report. A listing of previously created running totals appears in this part of the Field Explorer tree. Once created, existing running total fields are added to the report by either clicking and dragging and dropping or by selecting the Running Total Field—using the Insert into Report button or action on the context menu—and selecting the location.

If a new running total is required, it can be created directly from the Field Explorer by using the New toolbar button. You are prompted to name the new running total. Select the field to calculate the running total on, the type of running total (for example, sum, average, variance, and so on), and some other supporting information about when the running total is to be evaluated, and reset as shown in Figure 2.5.

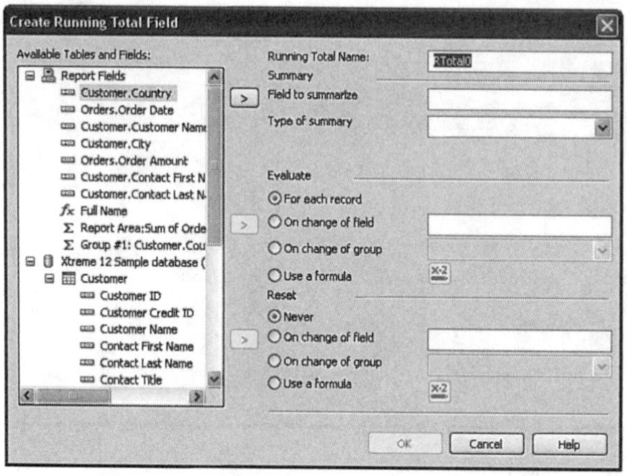

Figure 2.5
The Create Running Total Field dialog enables you to specify a running total name and its supporting information.

In the sample Customer Order Listing report from Chapter 1, an interesting running total to add would be one on the average order amount over time within each country. This running total tells senior sales management whether the average order size for each country is increasing or decreasing over time. To create this running total, follow these steps:

1. Open the sample report from Chapter 1 (Chap1Manual.rpt). Sort the data by ascending date by accessing the Record Sort Expert from either the Report menu or the Record Sort icon on the Expert Tools toolbar. Then select Order Date as a secondary sort order after Country.

2. Highlight the Running Total Fields branch of the Field Explorer tree.

3. Select New using either the New toolbar button or by right-clicking and selecting New from the pop-up menu. This opens the dialog shown in Figure 2.5.

4. Enter the name **Avg Order Size** for the running total name.

5. Select the Order Amount field from the Order table as the field to summarize by highlighting it in the field selection window and clicking on the Select button (>).

6. Because you want an average summary instead of the default Sum summary, select this from the Type of Summary drop-down box.

7. You want to calculate the average order amount after each order, so select the For Each Record option in the Evaluate section.

8. Because you want to calculate this independently for each country, select the Reset On Change of Group option and select the Country group in the Reset. Then and click on OK to finish.

Figure 2.6 shows the completed Create Running Total Field dialog.

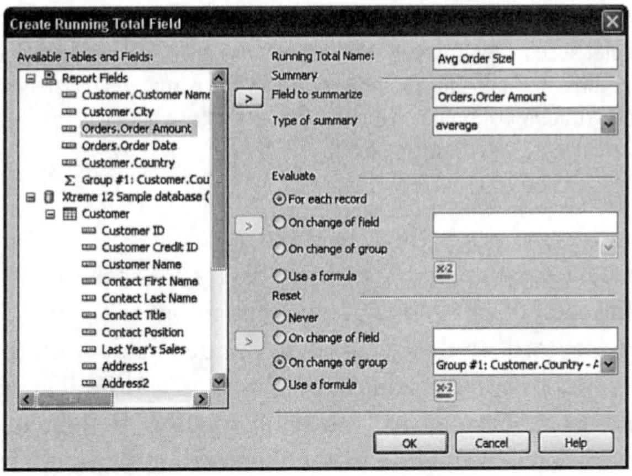

Figure 2.6
The Create Running Total Field dialog with average order size running total information entered.

After the running total has been created, it needs only to be dragged onto the report in the appropriate section. In this example, the appropriate section is the Detail section to show a changing average order size for every order. The updated sample Customer Order report is shown in Figure 2.7. Notice the changing average order size calculated for each record. This type of report can now provide increasing value to senior sales management.

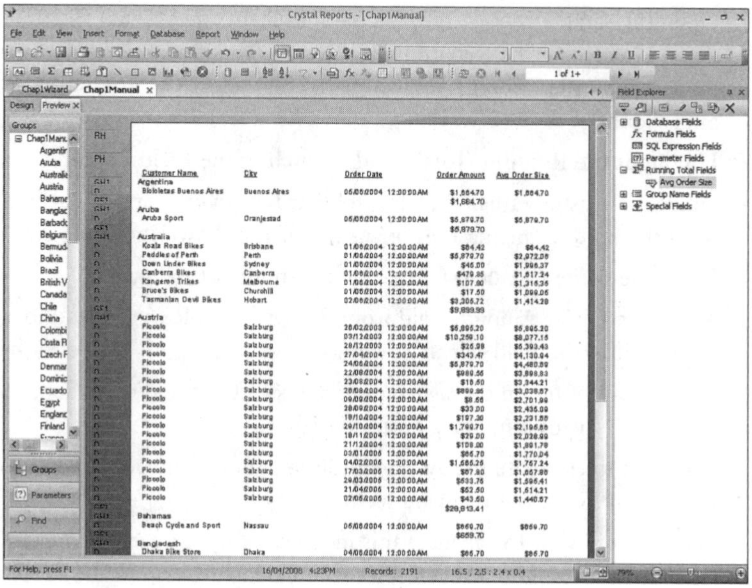

Figure 2.7
A sample Customer Order report with running average total on order size for each sales rep.

TIP

It's not necessary to place running total fields exclusively in the Detail section of your reports. By placing running total fields in different sections of your report, you can receive very interesting results. For example, if you place a running total in a Group Footer section, the running total displays the selected running total up to and including the current group. This can be very useful when analyzing average order size over time and grouping by month or quarter (for example, where you are interested only in some form of aggregated running total).

As highlighted in the Create Running Total Field dialog, it is possible to both evaluate and reset the running total fields based on four different options. The first three are self-explanatory—for each record, on the change of a specified field, or on the change of a specified group. The last option, using a formula, is a powerful and flexible option that you more fully explore after reviewing Chapter 13 on formula creation. In its simplest description, this option enables the creation of a conditional running total or the reset of that running total based on the results of a formula you have created.

TIP

A good use of this conditional summing is the creation of a running total that calculates the sum of all orders but evaluates (or sums in this case) the running total only when the total order amount on a given record is greater than a certain amount (for example, 1,000). This running total, in effect, provides a running total of only large orders so that business analysts can determine the percentage of revenue derived from large orders. Another common usage of this functionality is for financial statements (such as income

> statements) where a number of general ledger transactions compose the rows retrieved from the database and different running totals are used to conditionally add the associated transaction value to their total if and only if certain conditions are met (for example, a certain account code is associated with the transaction value). The resulting running totals are then placed in a report to present financial statement–oriented information such as total revenue, operating costs, investment income, taxes, and so on.

USING GROUP NAME FIELDS

Group Name fields exist in a report only after you specify one or more groups to add to your report. You will read about that functionality later in this chapter. Group Name fields are created at the same time you add a grouping to a report. Once created, existing Group Name fields are added to the report by either clicking and dragging and dropping or by selecting the group name—using the Insert into Report button or action on the right-click menu—and selecting the location.

SPECIAL FIELDS

The special fields in the Field Explorer are a number of system fields that Crystal Reports provides. Table 2.1 presents those system fields and a brief description of each. The fields that were new to version 10 are suffixed with a *10, the fields new to version XI are suffixed with *XI, and the field new to version 2008 is suffixed with *2008.

TABLE 2.1   SPECIAL FIELDS AVAILABLE IN CRYSTAL REPORTS

Field	Description	Valid Locations on Report
Content Locale*XI	The locale setting of the current user—found in the Control Panel under regional settings.	Anywhere
Current CE User ID*10 BusinessObjects Enterprise (BOE)	The ID number of the current user (if one exists).	Anywhere
Current CE User Name*10	The username of the current BusinessObjects Enterprise user (if one exists).	Anywhere
Current CE User Time BusinessObjects Enterprise	The time zone of the current user (if one exists).	AnywhereZone*XI
Data Date	The date the data in your report was last retrieved.	Anywhere
Data Time	The time the data in your report was last retrieved.	Anywhere

continues

TABLE 2.1 CONTINUED

Field	Description	Valid Locations on Report
Data Time Zone*XI	The time zone of the data last retrieved in your report.	Anywhere
File Author	The author of the report. This is set in Document Properties (File, Summary Info in the menu).	Anywhere
File Creation Date	The date the report was created.	Anywhere
File Path and Name	The file path and name for the report.	Anywhere
Group Number	An automatically created group numbering field.	Group Header or Group Footer sections only
Group Selection Formula	The current report's group selection formula. This is created by using the Select Expert covered in Chapter 6.	Anywhere
Horizontal Page Number*10	The current horizontal page number of a report using either a cross-tab or an OLAP grid.	Anywhere
Modification Date	Date that the report was last modified (in any way).	Anywhere
Modification Time	Time that the report was last modified (in any way).	Anywhere
Page N of M	Indicates current page on report relative to total number of pages.	Anywhere
Page Number	The current page number.	Anywhere
Print Date	Either the current date or a date specified in the Set Print Date and Time dialog under the Reports, Set Print and Date Time option.	Anywhere
Print Time	Either the current time or a time specified in the Set Print Date and Time dialog under the Reports, Set Print and Date Time option.	Anywhere
Print Time Zone*XI	The time zone of the machine where the report printed.	Anywhere

TABLE 2.1   CONTINUED

Field	Description	Valid Locations on Report
Record Number	An automatically created number that counts the records in the detail section of your report.	Details Section
Record Selection	The current report's record selection formula. This is created by using the Select Expert covered in Chapter 7, "Working with Report Sections."	Anywhere
Report Comments	Comments summarizing the report. This is set in the Document Properties dialog. (Choose File, Summary Info in the menu.)	Anywhere—but only the first 256 characters are printed
Report Title	The title of the report set in the Document Properties dialog (File, Summary Info in the menu).	Anywhere
Selection Locale*2008	The locale setting of the machine that your report is running on. (The machine's locale is usually found in the Control Panel's Regional Settings.) This updates each time you refresh your report's data.	Anywhere
Total Page Count	The total number of pages for this report.	Anywhere

These special fields are added to the report by either clicking and dragging and dropping or by selecting the Special Field—using the Insert into Report button or action on the context menu—and selecting the location.

WORKING WITH GROUPS

Grouping data in a report facilitates business user analysis and enables meaningful summarizations. Examples of common and useful groupings in reports include

- Sales reports that group by sales rep, product line, sales district, or quarter
- HR reports that group by department, management level, or tenure with the company
- Financial reports that group by company division, product line, or quarter
- Inventory reports that group by part number, supplier, or manufacturing plant

Crystal Reports provides easy-to-use grouping functionality that enables multiple types of powerful and flexible data grouping.

INSERTING GROUPS

Taking the sample report from this or the previous chapter, you can realize the flexibility and power of grouping in a few short steps. Assume that senior sales management in a hypothetical company is interested in viewing customer order information by employee/sales representative, in addition to the existing grouping by country. The following steps guide you through an example of how grouping can help this company accomplish this task:

1. Select the Group option from the Insert menu or click on the Insert Group button located on the Insert toolbar. This opens the Insert Group dialog shown in Figure 2.8.

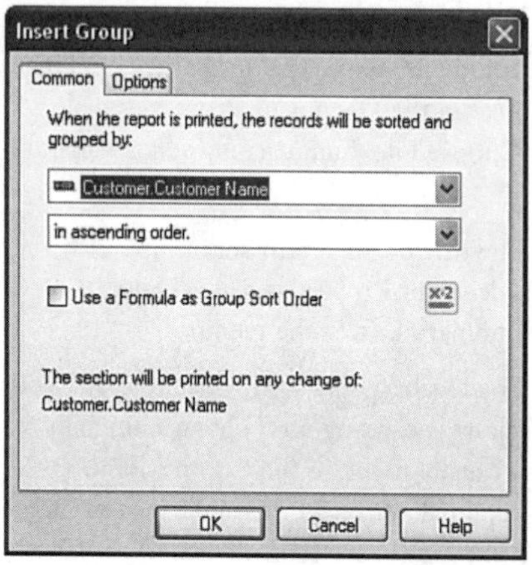

Figure 2.8
The Insert Group dialog requires selecting the field to group on and enables specification of some custom grouping options.

2. The Insert Group dialog prompts for the data field on which the group is based. The field you select can be an existing database field already on the report, a database field included in your data sources (perhaps not yet on the report), a formula field, or a SQL expression. For this exercise, select the Employee ID field from the Orders table for the grouping field.

3. Select In Ascending Order for the sort order.

4. Click OK, and the report changes to reflect a new grouping on Employee ID.

The results of this new grouping are shown in Figure 2.9. Note that the Employee ID grouping is automatically selected to be the lowest-level grouping. This is the standard and expected behavior when inserting new groups, but based on the sales management's hypothetical request, you will need to edit the grouping order so that Employee ID becomes the highest level and you can view an employee's sales across countries. You will do that in the next section.

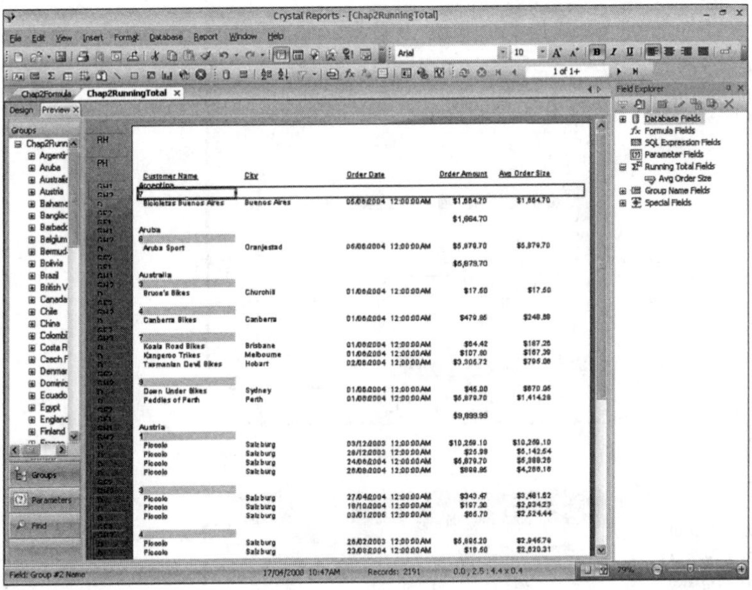

Figure 2.9
Here is a sample
report grouped by
Country and
Employee ID.

NOTE

The specified order selection (as opposed to ascending or descending order) of the Insert Group dialog is particularly interesting because of the flexibility it provides. With this option, you can dynamically create both groups and a custom order of appearance on the report. A related geographic example would be the creation of a Continent grouping based on the country field in the database with the groupings and order of appearance specified in the Insert Group dialog. Notice that when you select the specified order and name the group, two more tabs appear in the Change Group Options dialog (see Figure 2.10). These tabs enable you to specify or create dynamic groupings and to select a method of handling the other elements that do not fit into your dynamically created groups.

Another custom ordering option new to XI is the ability to conditionally sort a group based on a formula. This option is enabled through the Group Dialog box and the Use Formula as Sort Order check box. A formula can then be entered by clicking on the X+2 box.

A last note on the Change Group Options dialog is that options around group naming are available for customization. These options are accessed through the Options tab and facilitate the process of making your reports most presentable. For example, in another situation you might want to group on a country code instead of a country name for report processing efficiency (that is, numeric fields are sorted faster than string fields), but you still want to present the actual country name in the report. You could perform this customization through the Options tab in the Change Group Options dialog as shown in Figure 2.11.

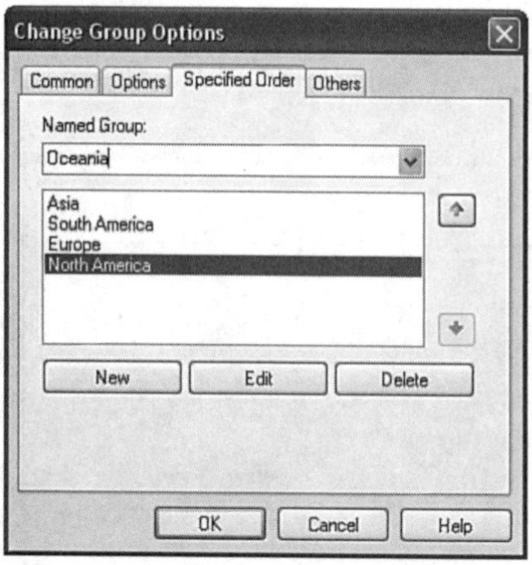

Figure 2.10
The Change Group Options dialog displaying the Specified Order tab.

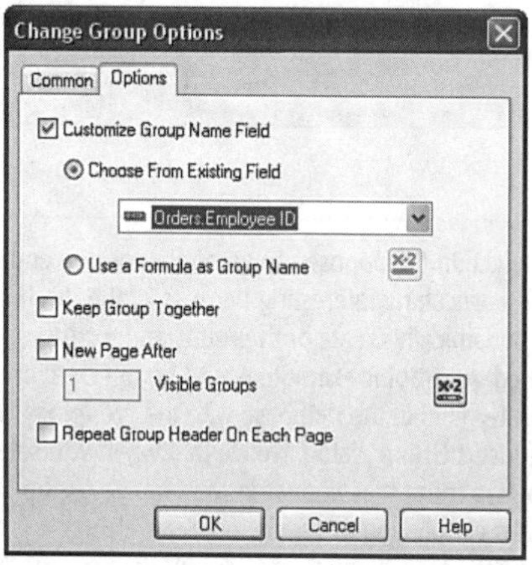

Figure 2.11
The Options tab of the Change Group Options dialog enables you to set some custom grouping options, such as the displayed group name.

REORDERING GROUPS

As you can imagine, it is quite common to want to group data by different fields within a single report. It is also quite common to receive multiple reporting requests for different views of data by various levels of grouping. Some examples might be

- View sales numbers grouped by product, region, and sales rep
- View sales numbers grouped by region, product, and sales rep
- View sales numbers grouped by sales rep, product, and region

During report design, one of these different grouping orders could be created initially, as you did in the last section with the groups Country and Employee ID. If other grouping orders were required, these could be quickly realized through either the Crystal Reports Design window or the Group Expert. Working in the leftmost report section area of the Design tab of Crystal Reports (not the Preview tab), the different groups (sections) can be dragged and dropped before or after each other, quickly rearranging the grouping order. To complete the sales management's reporting request from the last section (to group by Employee ID at the highest level and Country below that), follow these steps:

1. Click on the Design tab of the Crystal Reports Designer if you are not already on that tab.

2. After double-clicking and holding the last click on either the Employee ID Group Header or Footer, drag that group to the outside of the Country grouping to dynamically re-sort the grouping order. A hand replaces the normal cursor image when you grab a group, and blue lines highlight the intended drop location before you release your click and re-sort the grouping order.

TIP

To facilitate identification of groups while in the Design tab, hover over a group header or footer section, and a descriptive rollover tip temporarily appears.

3. Click on the Preview tab, and you will see the benefits of your work—the same report with the groupings instantly rearranged. Figure 2.12 highlights your intended results.

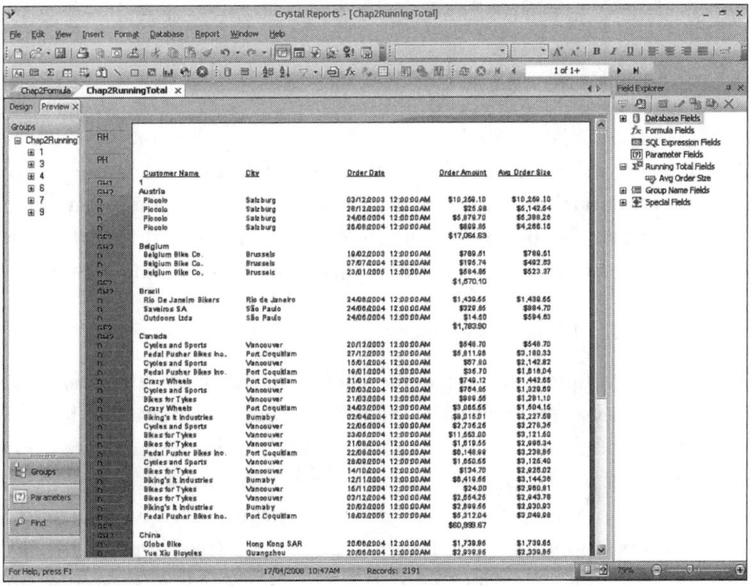

Figure 2.12
A sample customer orders report regrouped by sales rep (employee ID) and then country.

NOTE

Note the change in the group tree as you move back to the edited Crystal Report. The group tree provides an easy-to-use navigation system for end users of this report because they can drill into the group tree and then link to the exact location and group they desire.

An alternative and powerful method for reordering groups is provided with the Group Expert. It is accessed from the Report menu, and the different groups can be reordered through the up and down buttons within the Grouping dialog. This quick reordering can present your data in completely different ways, serving multiple analysis requirements with very little report development effort. The next section explores the power of the Group Expert.

USING THE GROUP EXPERT

Crystal Reports provides an easy method to add multiple groups simultaneously and a central location for accessing all your current groups—the Group Expert dialog. Accessed from the Report menu, the Group Expert dialog, shown in Figure 2.13, enables you to add multiple groups at one time and quickly reorder any specified groups.

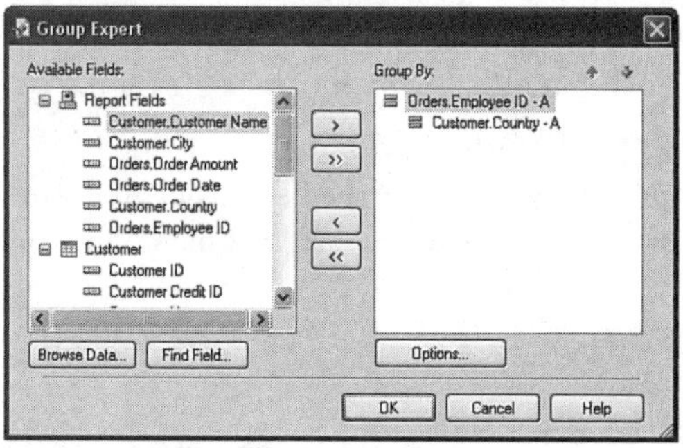

Figure 2.13
The Group Expert dialog accessed from the Report menu enables macro-level report group reordering and option setting.

This dialog enables the selection of multiple groups in one location and provides access to the same functionality as the Change Group Options dialog through the Options button. The groups can also be easily reordered from within this dialog through use of the up and down arrow buttons, located on the upper right of the dialog area.

GROUPING ON DATE/TIME FIELDS

One type of grouping that is common across most organizations is date- and time-related grouping. Analysts from all industries want to see how numbers (for example, sales revenue, units shipped, units produced, employees hired, and so on) change over various periods. To facilitate this type of analysis, Crystal Reports provides some built-in flexibility around date-and-time grouping. When you are creating a group based on a Date or Time field, an extra drop-down box appears in the Insert Group dialog (see Figure 2.14). This extra Print by Section box enables the user to group the detail records in the report automatically by any number of time-related criteria. Examples include By Day, By Hour, By Quarter, or even By Second. These automatic grouping options enable quick time-oriented analysis.

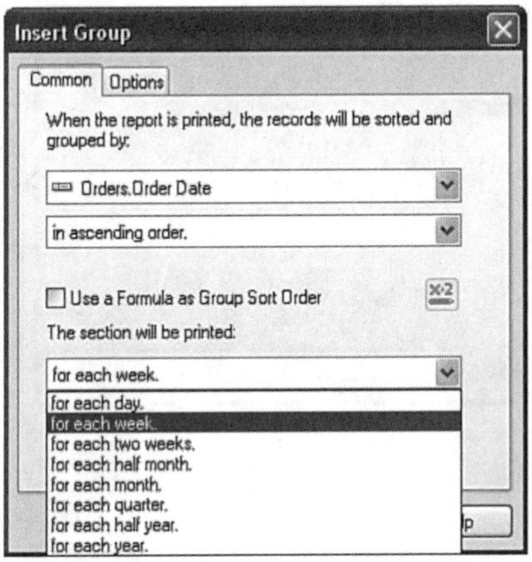

Figure 2.14
The Insert Group dialog with the date/time grouping drop-down box expanded.

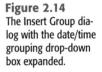

HIERARCHICAL GROUPING

Another type of special grouping that is available in Crystal Reports is hierarchical grouping. This special type of grouping enables your report data to be dynamically grouped on a hierarchy kept within a single table of your database. To enable hierarchical grouping, a group of the base-level data should be created through the standard group creation dialogs described previously. The Hierarchical Group option dialog can then be selected from the Report menu. To walk through a quick example, follow these steps:

1. Create a new blank Crystal Report and connect to the Xtreme 12 Sample Database.

2. Select the Employee table for the report and click on the OK button in the Database Expert.

3. Open the Field Explorer; select the First Name, Last Name, Extension, and Position fields from the Employee table; and drop them into the detail section of the report.

4. Insert a group on Employee ID using the Insert Group dialog (accessed from the Insert menu) and select ascending sort order. Move to the Options tab of the Insert Group dialog before finishing, click on the Customize Group Name Field check box, and select the Employee Last Name field as the field to display. Now click OK in the Insert Group dialog.

5. Select Hierarchical Grouping Options from the Report menu. You are presented with the dialog displayed in Figure 2.15. Click on the Sort Data Hierarchically option and select either Employee Supervisor ID or Employee Reports To as the parent field with an indent of 0.5 centimeters.

6. Click on OK and view your new report by pressing the F5 key. Figure 2.16 displays a report that should be similar and highlights the power of hierarchical grouping.

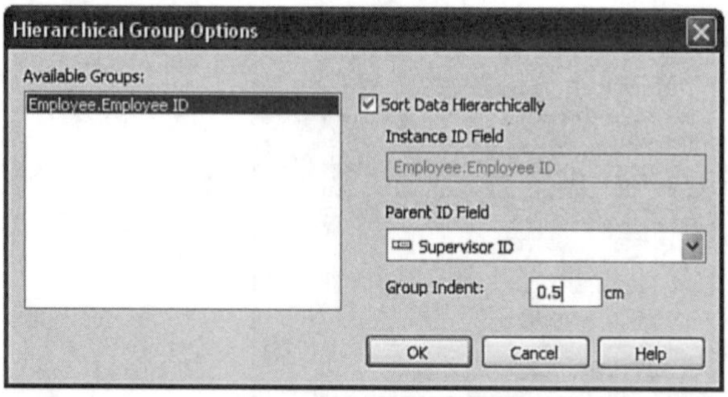

Figure 2.15
The Hierarchical Group Options dialog accessed from the Report menu enables specification of hierarchical grouping options such as parent field and indentation.

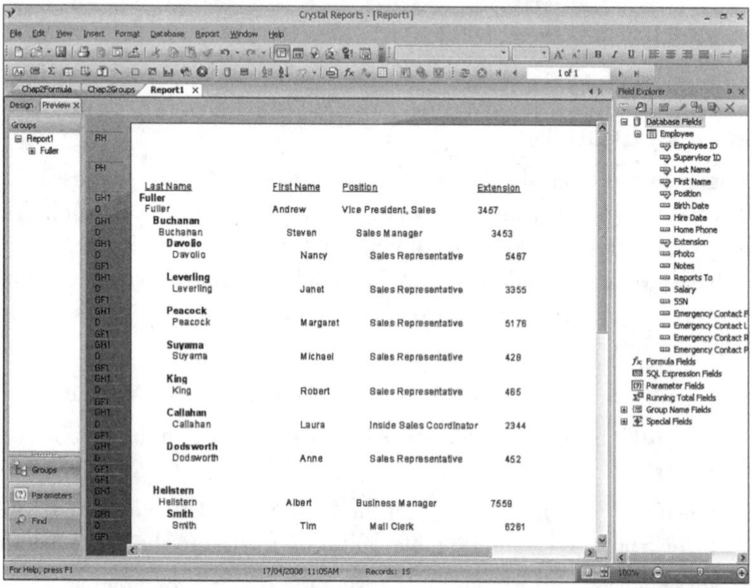

Figure 2.16
A sample report that highlights the hierarchical grouping and indentation functionality.

CAUTION

When creating a hierarchical group, the only eligible parent fields are those fields in the selected data source that have the same field type (for example, number, string, date) as the Grouped On field.

As shown in Figure 2.16, the value you enter in the Group Indent field affects all other objects in the same report section as your hierarchical group fields. For example, the Position and Extension fields also indent when you add the Employee field as a hierarchical group with supervisor. Starting with version XI, a new function was added to enable indentation of only the hierarchy records and not the other objects. This is accomplished by leaving this value as 0 (zero) and using the new conditional-X-position feature with the new `HeirarchyLevel()` function. A sample formula is provided in the Crystal Reports help file and a working sample report is available for download from usingcrystal.com.

UNDERSTANDING DRILL-DOWN REPORTS

As you have learned, grouping data facilitates data analysis for business users and enables meaningful summarizations in your reports. Having both the group level and the detail level data available in a view of a report enables the simultaneous analysis of both group-level summaries and the supporting detail records (for example, database fields, formulas, and so on). There are situations, however, in which a report consumer or analyst wants to view only aggregated group-level information initially and then selectively drill down into detail records where relevant (that is, drill down only where the aggregated group level information is interesting, appealing, or stands out). This is easily and quickly accomplished in Crystal Reports through the use of the built-in drill-down capabilities in the product.

NOTE

When the term *drill-down* is used, it implies that a business user has the capability to move from an aggregated or grouped view of the data (for example, sales revenue for each sales district) to a more detailed level of the data (for example, sales revenue for each salesperson in a selected sales district). In Crystal Reports, this is as easy as double-clicking on the involved group data or aggregated graphic.

CREATING A DRILL-DOWN REPORT

By default, whenever a group is created within Crystal Reports, an automatic drill-down path is created from the respective group headers into the child groups and detail records. The drill-down icon, a magnifying glass, appears in your Crystal Reports Preview tab as you hover over a group header with drill-down enabled. A sample report with Grouping and associated drill-down on Employee ID and Country is shown in Figure 2.17.

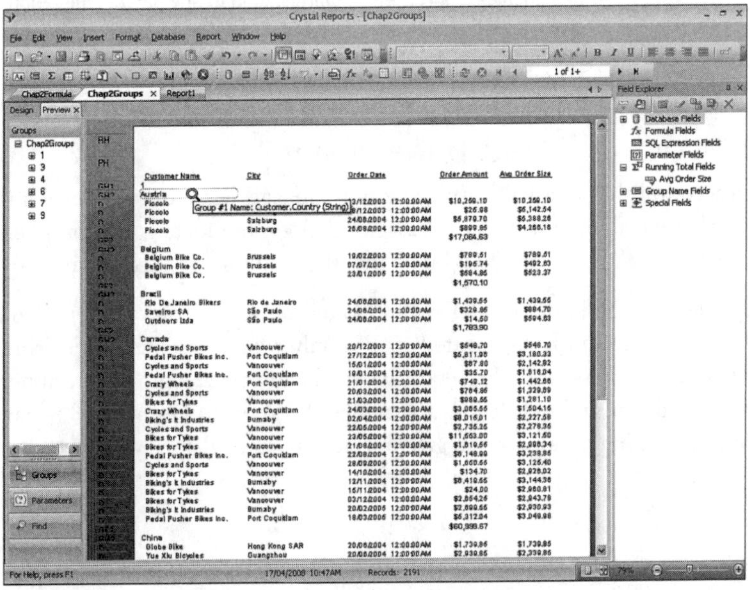

Figure 2.17
A sample report with drill-down groups available for end user navigation/drilling.

By double-clicking on the involved group header (such as Austria in Figure 2.17), a new viewing tab is opened with only the relevant group header's supporting information. Figure 2.18 highlights one of these views.

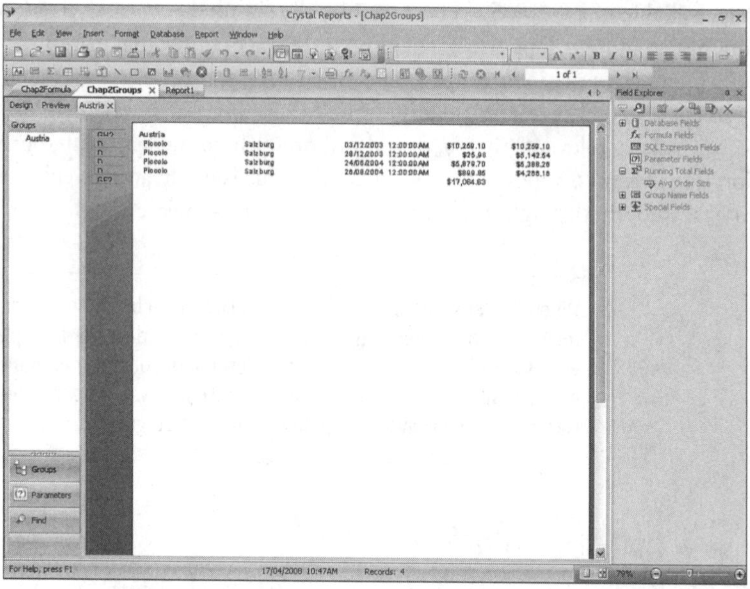

Figure 2.18
The drill-down view-
ing tab in Crystal
Reports Preview
mode highlights the
drill-down results.

NOTE

An alternative method of navigating through report data is to use the Group Navigation tree that is exposed through all Crystal Report Viewers. The advantage of this is that it does not initiate new viewing tabs like those shown in Figure 2.18. The Group Navigation tree enables report users to quickly jump to any point in the report by highlighting the group level that they are interested in viewing.

HIDING DETAILS ON A DRILL-DOWN REPORT

To accomplish the task of displaying only the aggregated group-level information in the sample report and not the details, right-click on the Details section in either the Design or Preview window. Figure 2.19 highlights the resulting context menu.

By selecting the Hide (Drill-Down OK) option in the context menu, your report now shows the details within the aggregated groups only when a business user drills down into them. Figure 2.20 shows what the report looks like in Preview mode. From here, the business user can drill down to the drill-down viewing tabs (refer to Figure 2.18 for an example) by double-clicking on any of the group header rows or data.

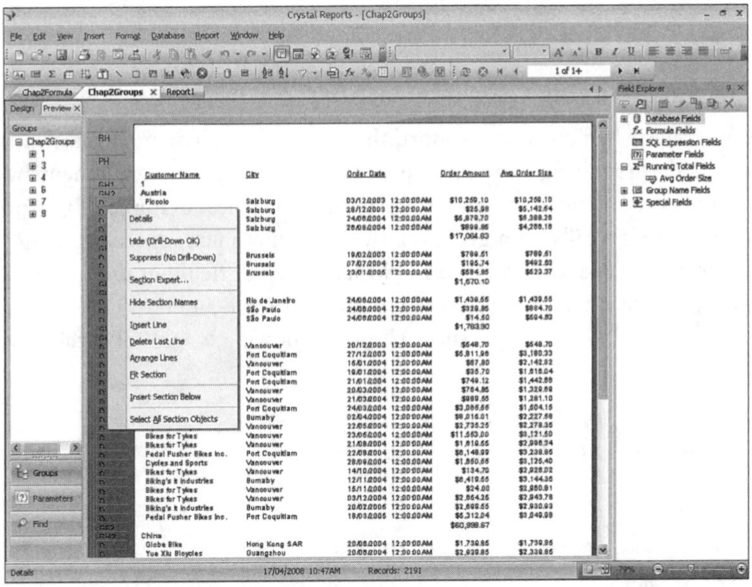

Figure 2.19
The Details section context menu enables hiding (or even suppression) of the detailed section.

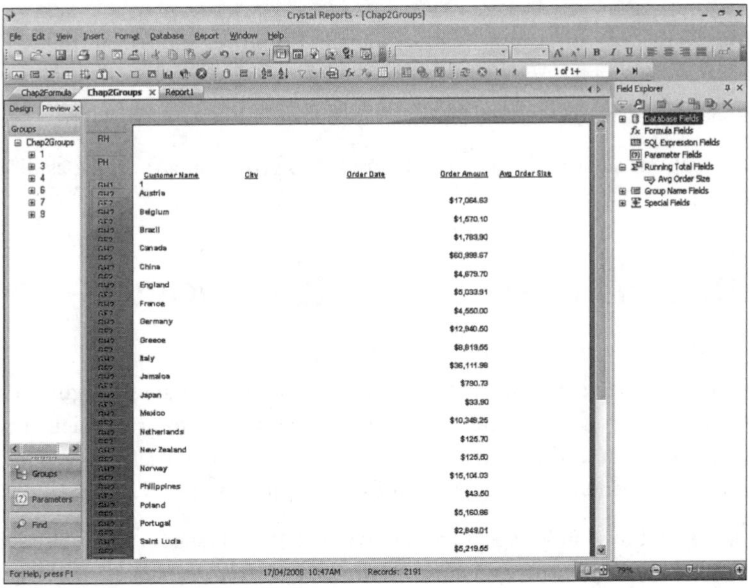

Figure 2.20
A sample report with Details section hidden but available in drill-down.

NOTE

The Suppress (No Drill-Down) option from the context menu shown in Figure 2.19 can provide another viewing option to report designers and essentially turn off drill-down in your report. If the aggregated group level section data is to be viewed by business users but they are not allowed to view detailed section data, this can be accomplished by suppressing the Details section.

TROUBLESHOOTING

GROUP ON A FORMULA

Sometimes when creating a report, the involved database might not natively contain the data specified as requiring a group; that is, the required grouping elements will need to be based on some criteria unavailable in the database. A typical example of this problem occurs when a report design calls for a grouping by a demographic range, such as age or income bracket. In the case of age, the database might have an Age field but the business case calls for some form of market analysis by the age ranges 0–19, 20–34, 35–49, 50–64, and 65 and above. A formula called Date Range, similar to the following, could solve the reporting problem:

```
Select {@Age}
    Case Is < 19 :
        "0-19"
    Case Is > 19, Is < 34 :
        "20-34"
    Case Is > 34, Is < 49 :
        "35-49"
    Case Is > 50, Is < 64 :
        "50-64"
    Case Is > 64:
        "65+"
```

For the record, this sample is based on the Employee table from the Xtreme Sample Database and uses another formula called @Age that resolves to

```
(Today - {Employee.Birth Date}) / 365
```

In situations such as these, it can be useful to group on a formula, as discussed in the next section.

CRYSTAL REPORTS IN THE REAL WORLD—GROUP ON A FORMULA

Sometimes when creating a report, the development database might not be complete or might be in production; there might be a requirement to group elements based on some criteria that is not in the database. In these cases, it can be useful to group on a formula. To explore the benefits of grouping on formulas, follow theses steps:

1. Open the sample report from Chapter 1 (Chap1Manual.rpt). Create a new formula, name it Continent, and click on the OK button.

2. Type the following text into the code window so it appears like Figure 2.21:

```
WhileReadingRecords;
WhileReadingRecords;
Select {Customer.Country}
    Case "Canada","Mexico","USA":
        "North America"
    Case "Australia", "New Zealand":
        "Oceania"
    Default:
        "Outside North America and Oceania";
```

Figure 2.21
A sample formula to group information on a formula.

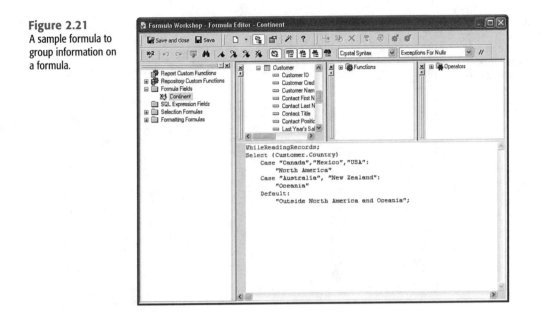

3. With the text entered, click the Save and Close button.

4. From the Report menu, select Group Expert. Find the Group1 formula from the Available Fields list and add it to the Group By fields list. Finally, because the Group1 field is a higher level than the For Country field, select it and move it up using the arrow button. Figure 2.22 displays the results.

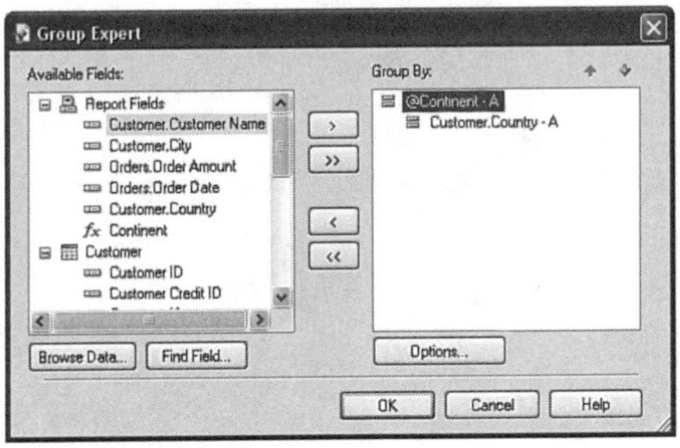

Figure 2.22
The report correctly grouped, highlighting the capability to group on formulas and create increasingly flexible reports.

5. Click on OK to see the completed report that looks like that presented in Figure 2.23.

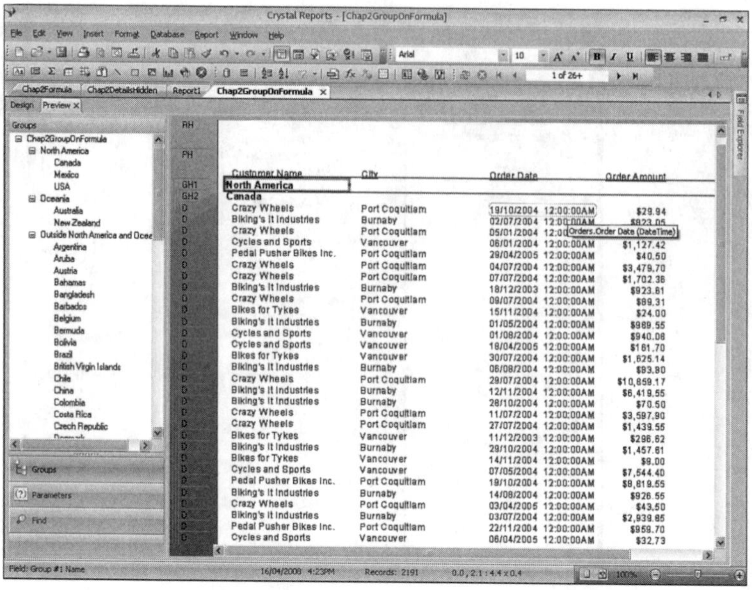

Figure 2.23
A report with a group based on a formula highlights the powerful capabilities of custom grouping.

CHAPTER 3

FILTERING, SORTING, AND SUMMARIZING DATA

In this chapter

INTRODUCTION

In the first two chapters, you created reports that display the rows of data in your database onto the report surface with minimal manipulation of that data. The value of Crystal Reports is its inherent capacity to convert those rows of raw data into valuable information. The information reveals something about the data that cannot be found by simply poring over pages and pages of records. In the previous chapter, you began to take advantage of the power of Crystal Reports by applying grouping to a report to organize the data into categorical groups. In this chapter, you build on that by learning how to create reports that perform the following actions:

- Filter data based on a given criteria
- Sort data based on field values
- Summarize and subtotal data

→ For more detailed information on grouping data, **see** "Working with Groups," **p. 63**.

FILTERING THE DATA IN YOUR REPORT

So far, the reports you have created have returned all the records from your database. Sometimes this is appropriate, but often reports need to filter the data based on specified criteria. This is most relevant when you're working with large databases in which there can easily be hundreds of thousands of records returned from a query, especially when table joins are applied.

As with many features in Crystal Reports, there are multiple ways to filter data:

- **Using the Select Expert for Records**—This simple method provides a visual way to specify filtering.
- **Using the Record Selection Formula**—This more granular, yet powerful, method involves creating a custom formula language expression to determine the filter criteria.

Regardless of the method you use to filter your report, you should always make best efforts to filter on indexed database fields. By filtering on indexed fields, you realize the greatest performance on the database server. You can determine the indexed fields in a table by using the Crystal Reports Links tab on the Database Expert accessible from the Database menu. Use the Index Legend button and dialog provided to understand the different index markers in your database tables.

WORKING WITH THE SELECT EXPERT

The Select Expert is a design tool that enables you, the report designer, to specify basic yet powerful filters for the current report using a graphical design dialog. Figure 3.1 shows the Select Expert dialog.

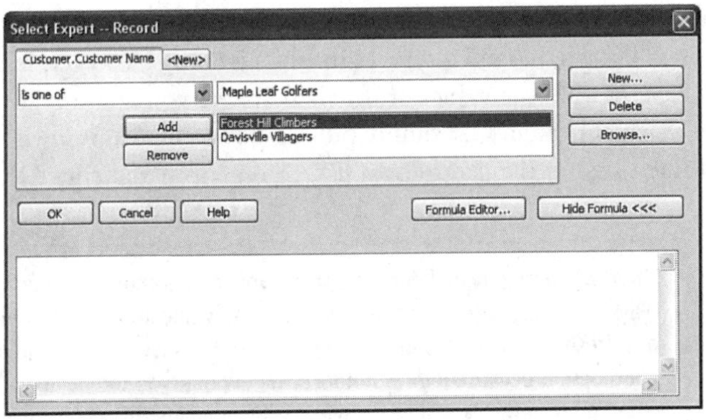

Figure 3.1
The Select Expert for Records provides access to easy-to-use filtering functionality from a graphical interface.

Let's work through an illustrative example of filtering using the Select Expert. Taking what you have learned so far about creating simple columnar reports, create a new report from the Xtreme 12 Sample Database, adding the Customer Name and Last Year's Sales fields from the Customer table to the Details section of the report. Follow these steps to add a filter to this report:

1. To invoke the Select Expert for records, click its button (funnel) found on the Experts toolbar and select Records or, alternatively, select the Select Expert option from the Report menu and select Records from the fly-out menu.

2. The first step in creating a filter is to choose which field the filter should be created on. Accordingly, the Choose Field dialog is displayed. Both fields that are present in the report and fields from the database are listed. A field does not need to be on the report to create a filter using it. At this point, if you forget which values are stored in any of the fields listed, click the Browse button to see a sample list of values. For this example, choose Last Year's Sales field and click on OK. The Select Expert dialog appears, as shown in Figure 3.1.

> **TIP**
>
> Another quick and direct method of accessing the Select Expert for records is through the context menu available on any data field. This method opens the Select Expert for records directly with the specified field already selected as the filtered field and bypassing the Choose Field dialog.

3. The Select Expert for records has a group of tabs—one for each filter defined inside that report. In the case of your sample report, there is only one tab for the Last Year's Sales field and another called <New>, which is used to define additional filters. By default, the filter setting on the Last Year's Sales tab is set to Is Any Value. This means that regardless of the value of the Last Year's Sales field, all records are included in the report. To change the filter in a report, change the value of the drop-down list. For this example, change it to Is Equal To.

4. When this option is selected, another drop-down list appears. If the exact value to filter the field on is known, it can be typed into this list box. However, in this case, you might not know exactly what the values of the field are, so you are provided with the capability to browse that field's values by simply pulling down the drop-down list. Choose the $300.00 value listed in the drop-down list, or type it in and click OK.

TIP

> Often when modifying filters and selections in the report designer, Crystal Reports displays a message asking the user whether she wants to use the saved data in the report or refresh the data from the database. Using the saved data in the report is usually a good option because it does not incur a new query to the database. However, especially when modifying filters, it can cause some confusing results because the set of saved data in the report might or might not consist of all the records in the database; that is, a filter might have already been applied. So, when modifying filters, it's best to refresh the data whenever Crystal Reports asks you.

5. When returning to the report, you should notice that the report now only displays a single record: the Has Been Bikes company that had sales of $300. A more useful filter would be to show all records that were above or below a threshold. To accomplish this, reopen the Select Expert. This time, change the Is Equal To criteria to Is Greater Than and type **100,000** into the list box. When closing the Select Expert and returning to the report, a small collection of records should be returned (approximately 17). In just a few seconds, you've created a report showing your top customers.

A few more filter types can be applied to a report. Apply these various types of filters with the following steps:

1. Open the Select Expert again and change the criteria from Is Greater Than to Is Between.

2. This time, two list boxes are presented, each corresponding to an upper and lower bound. Type in the values **2000** and **3000** respectively (as shown in Figure 3.2), and click on OK. The report displays all customers with sales between $2,000 and $3,000.

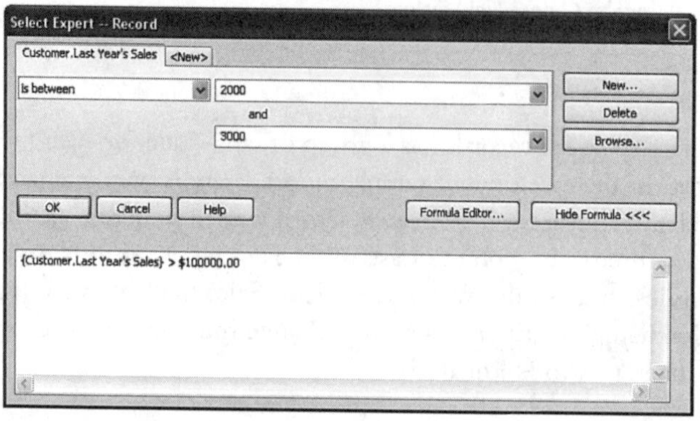

Figure 3.2
Modify the report to display customers with sales between $2,000 and $3,000.

3. So far, only the Last Year's Sales field has been used as a filter. However, any field can be used as a filter, although there are slightly different options for various field types. Go back into the Select Expert and, on the Last Year's Sales tab, click the Delete button to remove that filter.

4. Add a new filter on the Customer Name field by clicking the New button and selecting the Customer Name field from the subsequent dialog.

5. To have the report show only a single customer's record, leave the criteria as Is Equal To and choose Alley Cat Cycles from the drop-down list. Applying this filter results in the report only showing a single record.

6. Return to the Select Expert and change the criteria to Is One Of. This option enables you to choose multiple values. Each time a value is selected from the drop-down list, it is added to the bottom of the list box. Select Alley Cat Cycles, Bikes R Us, and Hikers and Bikers and notice how the report now reflects those three records.

7. Next remove the three values previously selected by highlighting them and clicking the Remove button. Now change the criteria to Is Like and type Wheel* into the drop-down list. Click Add or press Enter to add this item to the list. Applying this filter results in the report showing all customers whose names begin with the word *Wheel*.

NOTE

When using the Is Like option, an * acts as a wildcard for any number of characters, whereas a ? acts as a wildcard for only a single character. This can be quite useful when you're searching through textual fields for a specific text pattern.

The last thing this chapter covers with respect to the Select Expert is applying multiple filters. To do so, perform the following steps:

1. Start from scratch and delete any filters you have applied by clicking the Delete button on each tab.

2. Click the New button and add a new filter using the Last Year's Sales field.

3. Change the criteria to Is Less Than and the value to 5,000. This filter results in showing all customers with sales of less than $5,000, but let's apply another condition.

4. Click the New button and add a new filter based on the Country field. Note that this is slightly different from the previous filters that have been created—not only because more than one filter is being applied at the same time, but also because the filter being created is based on a field that is not present on the report.

5. Change the criteria for the Country filter to Is Equal To and choose Canada from the drop-down list. Clicking OK applies this filter, resulting in a report with multiple conditions: customers from Canada with sales below $5,000. See Figure 3.3 for the filtered output of this report.

Figure 3.3
A filter is applied to show all Canadian customers with sales less than $5,000.

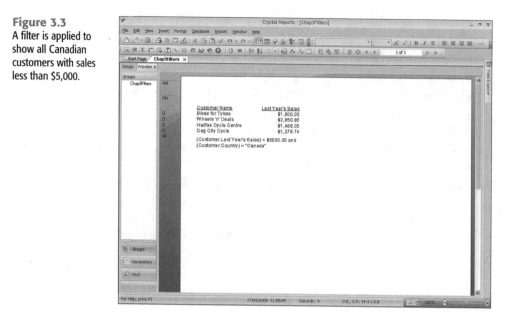

NOTE

The two filters that were just added to the report are concatenated together by default with a logical AND statement, that is, All Customers with Last Year's Sales of less than $5,000 AND from Canada. This can be edited in the Formula Editor accessible from the Show Formula button on the Select Expert. This is discussed in the next section.

THE RECORD SELECTION FORMULA

Although the Select Expert is quite powerful, there are certain situations where you need to define a filter that is more complex than the Select Expert allows. Fortunately, Crystal Reports has a built-in formula language that enables you to define custom expressions as a filter. In fact, this is one of the strengths of the Crystal Reports product: using the formula language to attain a high level of control in various aspects of report creation.

Although you might not have realized it, even when you were using the Select Expert, a formula was being generated in the background that defined the filter. To see this in action, open the Select Expert and click the Show Formula button. This expands the Select Expert dialog to reveal the formula being generated. This formula is called the *record selection formula*. Notice that the formula's value is as follows:

```
{Customer.Last Year's Sales} < $5000.00 and
{Customer.Country} = "Canada"
```

The formula language is covered in more detail in Chapter 11, "Using Record Selections, Sort Controls, and Alerts for Interactive Reporting," but the following are the key points to learn right now. In formulas, braces denote a field. For database fields, the table and field names are included and are separated by a period. The rest of the formula is a statement that tests whether the sales value is less than $5,000.

Think of a record selection formula as an expression that evaluates to a true or false result. For each record in the database, Crystal Reports applies the record selection formula, plugging in the current field values in place of the fields in braces. If the result of the statement is True, the record is included in the report. If the result of the statement is False, the record is excluded from the report. Let's look at an example. The first record in the Customers table is that of City Cyclists who had sales of $20,045.27.

For this record, Crystal Reports evaluates the preceding formula, substituting $20,045.27 in place of {Customer.Last Year's Sales}. Because this value is not less than $5,000, this statement is False, and the record is not included in the report. To see what other formulas look like, change the filter using the Select Expert to a few different settings and observe how the formula changes.

TIP

> When working with filters, it is almost always helpful for your report viewers to know at a glance what those filters were when viewing a report. This can be quickly accomplished by adding the Special Field called Report Selection Formula to your report—perhaps in the header or footer. A sample of the preceding report with this extra feature is available for download at www.usingcrystal.com and is displayed in Figure 3.3.

WORKING WITH THE FORMULA EDITOR

The formula shown at the bottom of the Select Expert is not just for informational purposes: It can be edited in-place. However, a much better editor exists for formulas. It's called the Formula Editor (shown in Figure 3.4), and it can be invoked by clicking the Formula Editor button in the Select Expert or by selecting the Report menu and choosing Selection Formulas, Record. Although the formula language doesn't change, the process of creating formulas becomes much simpler because of a focused user interface.

Learn to use the Formula Editor by creating a simple record selection formula. This formula attempts to filter out any customers who owe more than $5,000 in tax. Tax liability is defined as 2% of the customer's sales figure. To implement this, work through the following steps:

1. To begin, launch the Formula Editor as described previously and delete the existing selection formula.

2. Next, create an expression that calculates the tax liability. To do this, enter the following expression:
   ```
   {Customer.Last Year's Sales} * 0.02
   ```

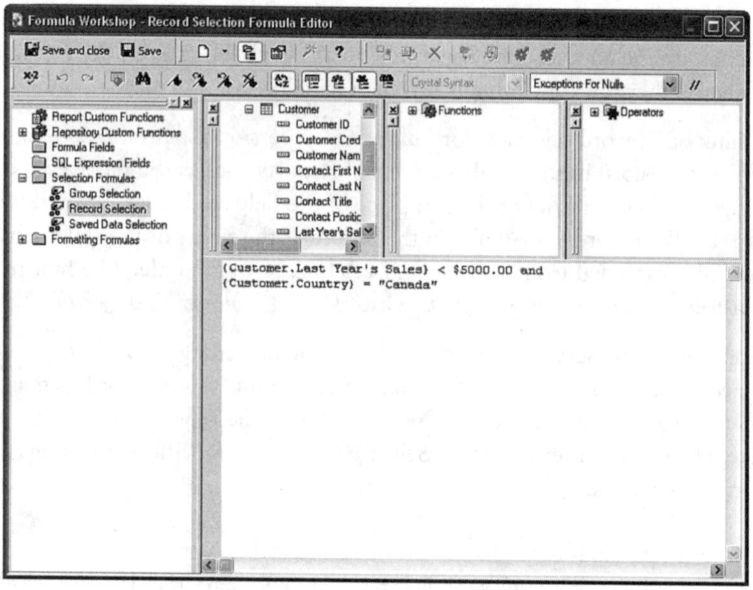

Figure 3.4
The Formula Editor provides quick access to powerful formula creation capabilities.

3. The previous expression now represents the customer's tax obligation. To complete the expression to filter out all customers who owe less than $5,000 in tax, modify the formula to look like this:

```
({Customer.Last Year's Sales} * 0.02) > 5000
```

4. To complete the formula and apply the filter, click the Close button at the upper-left corner of the Formula Editor window, and then click OK to close the Select Expert. Focus returns to the report, and when data is refreshed, only a handful of customers should be listed on the report.

Both the formula language and the Formula Editor are topics unto themselves and will be discussed in more detail in Chapter 4, "Understanding and Implementing Fomulas" and Chapter 11.

LEARNING TO SORT RECORDS

Although filtering is one of the key components of an effective report, it alone is not enough. Often, to properly highlight key pieces of data, a report needs to be sorted. Crystal Reports is quite flexible when it comes to sorting, allowing any field type to be sorted, as well as multiple ascending or descending sorts. Sorting is applied using the Sort Expert.

WORKING WITH THE SORT EXPERT

The Sort Expert is launched from a button on the Experts toolbar and via the Record Sort Expert item on the Report menu. Figure 3.5 shows the Sort Expert.

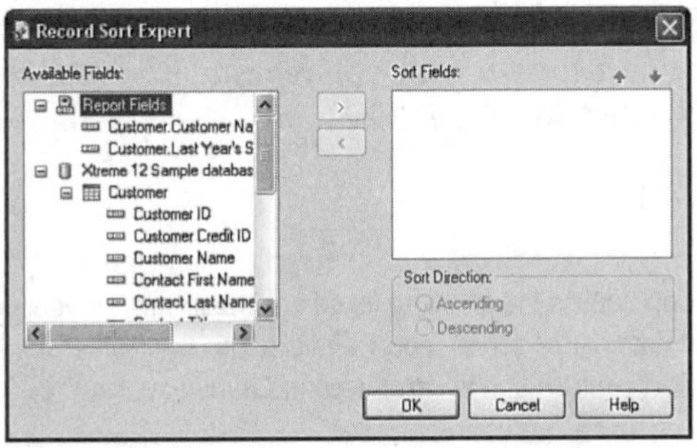

Figure 3.5
The Record Sort
Expert dialog
accessed from the
Report menu.

To apply sorting to the report, select a field from the list of available fields on the left side of the dialog area, and click on the arrow (>) button to add that field to the Sort Fields list. Note that like filters, sorts can use fields both on the report and fields not otherwise used in the report.

> **TIP**
>
> In addition to sorting on report and database fields, you can sort on formula fields. Creating a formula field enables you to sort a report based on a custom expression.

To see this in action, follow these steps:

1. Create a new report using the Employee table of the Xtreme Sample Database and add the First Name, Last Name, and Salary fields to the report.

2. Initially, this report doesn't tell you a lot because the data is in seemingly random order. However, if the report were sorted by last name, it would be more useful. To accomplish this, first launch the Sort Expert.

3. Select the Last Name field from the available fields list and click on the arrow (>) button to apply a sort on it. Click OK to return to the report. Notice how the report's records are now sorted in alphabetical order by last name.

The Sort Expert enables you to sort on both alphabetic and numeric fields. To modify this report to sort by salary instead of last name, follow these steps:

1. Return to the Sort Expert and remove the current sort by selecting the Last Name field from the Sort Fields list and clicking on the < button.

2. Now select the Salary field and add it to the Sort Fields list.

3. Alphabetic fields are usually sorted in ascending order (from A to Z), but numeric fields are often sorted both ways. In this case, select the Salary field in the Sort Fields list and click on Descending for the sort direction. This lists the employees with the top salary first. Click on OK to apply the sort and return to the report.

Notice that some employees have the same salary level. If you want to perform a secondary sort within duplicates of the primary sort field, you can simply add another sort field. The sort fields can be arranged up and down using the buttons near the upper-right corner of the Sort Expert.

NOTE

New to version 2008 is the ability to enable direct sorting on your reports and their associated saved data by the actual report viewers. This is accomplished through a new concept called Sort controls and is introduced in Chapter 11.

CREATING EFFECTIVE SUMMARIES

The third key aspect of a good report after filtering and sorting is summarizing. Summarizing creates totals and subtotals that help the viewer of the report understand the data better. The following sections discuss various types of summarizing.

CREATING GRAND TOTALS

The simplest kind of summary is a grand total. This takes a single field and creates a total at the end of the report. To try this out, create a new report from the Orders table and add both the Order ID and the Order Amount fields onto the report.

Initially, this report is more than 30 pages long. A report of this length would make it very difficult to estimate the total amount of all orders, but a summary does that quite easily. Right-click the Order Amount field and select Insert, Summary from the context menu. This opens the Insert Summary dialog shown in Figure 3.6.

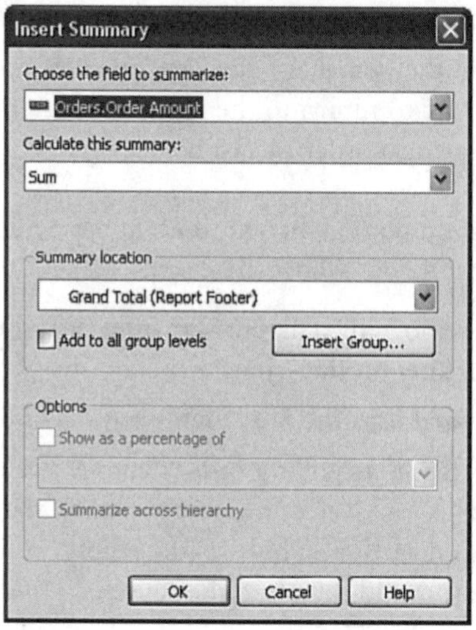

Figure 3.6
Inserting a summary based on the Order Amount field.

To insert a summary, the first thing you need to specify is the field to summarize. Because you right-clicked the Order Amount field, this is already filled in for you. The next piece of information to fill in is the summary operation. The default is Sum, which is what you want in this example, so leave it as is. Finally, Crystal Reports needs to know for which group the summary should be performed. Because there is no grouping in this report, the only option is Grand Total, which is already filled in for you. Click on OK to close this dialog.

NOTE

New to version 2008, an option to add a summary to all group levels has been added to the Insert Summary dialog. This small feature will prove to be a good time-saver for you when building reports with multiple groups and multiple levels of summary.

When looking at the end of the report, you see that a grand total of the order amount is now visible in bold text. To edit the summary, right-click on it and select Edit Summary from the context menu. This opens the Edit Summary dialog. Try changing the calculation from Sum to Average. This now updates the summary to show the average order amount. There are various calculations to choose from, including minimum, maximum, variance, count, deviation and median.

Besides the order amount total, it might be helpful to know how many orders there are. To do this, right-click the Order ID field and select Insert, Summary. Change the calculation from Sum to Count and click OK. Now besides the order amount summary, there is a count of all orders.

CREATING GROUP SUMMARIES

Although grand totals are useful, summarizing starts to become really powerful when it is applied at the group level. This enables totaling for each level of a group and tells more about the data than a simple grand total does because it measures the relationships between the various groups. To apply a group summary, a group must first exist in the report.

Using the same report from the last example with the Order ID and Order Amount fields, insert a group on the Ship Via field. This produces a report showing all the orders grouped by shipping method, for example, FedEx, Loomis, and so on. To compare the different methods of shipment, right-click the Order Amount field and select Insert, Summary. Previously, when you created a grand total, you accepted all the defaults in this dialog. But this time, the summary location needs to be changed. Change Grand Total (Report Footer) to Group #1: Orders.Ship Via in the Summary Location drop-down box, make sure the summary type is set to Average, and click on OK.

Now a summary field is inserted into the report, which acts much like the grand total except that the average is repeated for each group. By examining these summaries, you can determine that the largest average order amount was shipped via UPS. You could also add a group-level summary to the Order ID field to determine the count of orders for each shipping method. Doing this reveals that the most orders were shipped via Loomis. These conclusions would have been difficult to reach without effective summaries.

NOTE

> When groups have many records inside of them, it sometimes becomes difficult to compare summaries because they aren't all visible on the page at the same time. A good tip for comparing these values is to hide the Details section, which contains all the records, and display only the group header and footer that normally contains the group name and its summary. To hide the Details section, move to the Design tab, right-click on the Details bar on the left side of the screen, and select Hide.

USING GROUP SELECTION AND SORTING

Following closely on the topic of group summaries are group selection and sorting. These bring together both filtering and summarizing concepts. Group selection and sorting are to groups what record selection and record sorting are to records. In other words, defining a group selection or sorting defines which groups are included in the report and in which order, respectively. A key point to understand is that whereas record selection and sorting work from values of individual fields, group selection and sorting work from summary fields.

In the example from the previous "Creating Group Summaries" section, you created a report that displayed all orders grouped by the shipment method, but to determine which shipment method shipped the highest dollar value of orders, you had to manually browse through the report comparing the numbers. Applying a group sort would provide an easy way to see the rankings. And what if you wanted to show only the top three shipment methods? Group selection provides a way to filter out groups in such a manner.

As you might expect, there is an expert for applying group selection and sorting. It's called the Group Sort Expert, and it can be found on the Experts toolbar, as well as from the Group Sort Expert item on the Report menu. When the Group Sort Expert is launched, it displays one tab for each group in the report. In the previous example, there was only a single group on the Ship Via field, so that's what you should see. Inside that tab, there is initially only a single list box with a value of No Sort. Changing this list box to All displays a set of options very similar to that of the Record Sort Expert—except instead of having a list of all report fields to choose to sort on, only summaries are listed.

Assuming that you continue to use the latest report created, the Group Sort Expert should have initially selected the Average of Orders.Order Amount summary field and selected Ascending Order. In this case, because it's more useful to see the highest dollar value first rather than last, change the sort order to Descending. Clicking on OK closes the Group Sort Expert and returns focus to the report, which should have reordered the groups from largest to smallest. It's easy to see now that UPS was the method that shipped the highest dollar amount because it is the first group to appear.

There are only six shipment methods, but you can imagine reports that contain many more groups than six. Even if the groups are sorted, sometimes it's just too much data for the consumer of the report to absorb. To solve this problem, you can apply a group selection. To do this, launch the Group Sort Expert and change the All option on the left to Top N. Notice that the options are different from sorting. Applying a Top N selection implies that the groups will be sorted but enables you to only display a specified number of the top groups in order. The default value is 5; change this value to 3.

NOTE

New since version XI is the ability to set the N value of a Top or Bottom N sort to a formula. These formulas are created in the Formula Workshop accessed by the X+2 button beside the N value. This new functionality combined with parameters, covered in Chapter 5, "Implementing Parameters for Dynamic Reporting," enables improved report flexibility and allows report viewers to dynamically determine the N value of the Top/Bottom N at report-viewing time.

Another important option is relating to the set of groups excluded by the group selection. By default, all these groups are combined under a new group called Others. You might or might not want to include this Others group in your report. If you choose not to, uncheck the option labeled Include Others. Clicking on OK returns focus to the report that now should display only the top three shipment methods based on the total order amount.

NOTE

Like the record selection, the group selection has a formula that can be defined to use a custom expression to determine which groups to include in the report. The group selection formula can be found on the Report menu, under Selection Formulas, Group.

Some other options available in the group sort expert include Bottom N, which is the opposite of Top N, and Top and Bottom Percentage, which allow a filtering of the top x percent of groups.

CAUTION

It is instructive to note that group selection formulas execute on the second pass of the Crystal Reports Engine. The second pass takes place after grand totals, group subtotals, and the group navigation tree have been created. To understand the nuances of multipass reporting, review the last topic in Chapter 4.

CREATING RUNNING TOTALS

The last kind of summary discussed in this chapter is a running total. In some older versions of Crystal Reports, to create a running total, you had to create a collection of formula fields, so a feature was added in version 9 just to handle running totals. To create a running total, follow these steps:

1. Create a new report using the Orders table. Add the Order ID, Order Date, and Order Amount fields to the Details section of the report. You can reformat the order date to a more user-friendly format if you prefer by right-clicking the field and selecting Format.

2. Add a sort based on the Order Date field in ascending order. This report now shows all orders in the order they were placed. This is a perfect scenario for a running total that would show a cumulative total of orders so that the viewer of the report could see what the current total order amount was at any given time.

3. To add a running total, right-click the Order Amount field and select Insert, Running Total from the Context menu. The Create Running Total Field dialog is shown in Figure 3.7.

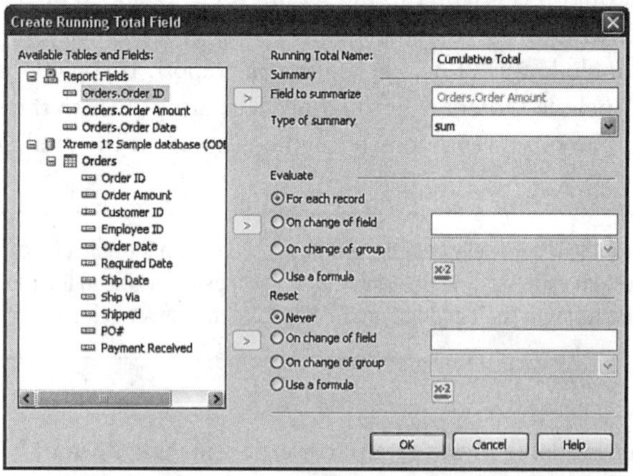

Figure 3.7
Creating a Running Total field is quickly accomplished through the Create Running Total Field dialog.

Four pieces of information need to be provided in this dialog, including

- **Name of the running total field**—The default is somewhat cryptic; it's best to give this a more meaningful name.

- **The summary to perform**—The Field to Summarize should be prepopulated for you, but you can change the summary type from the default of sum to other standard summary types. Some of the more useful types for a running total are Count and Average.

- **When to evaluate the running total**—The default and most common setting here is For Each Record, but this can be modified to be evaluated only when the value of another field is changed or a group value is changed, or you can define a custom formula that defines the evaluation criteria.

- **When to reset the running total**—This setting determines whether the running total should reset itself. If no groups are present in the report, you'll likely want to keep the default of Never. But if you have groups, you might want to reset the running total for each group or define more complex criteria with a formula.

4. For this example, give the running total a name of `Cumulative Orders` and leave all other settings at their defaults. Completing this running total adds the new field to the report next to the Order Amount field and provides a cumulative total of orders. The output of this report is shown in Figure 3.8.

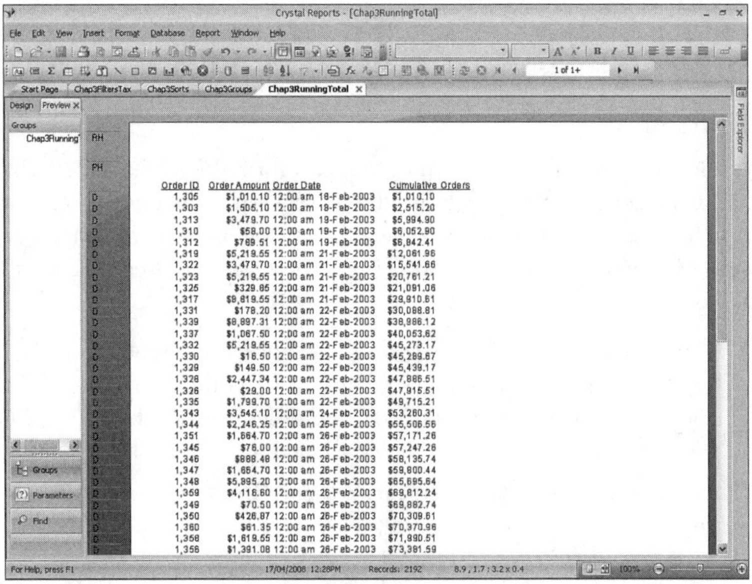

Figure 3.8
A cumulative orders report using a Running Total field.

NOTE

Running totals can also be created from the Field Explorer by selecting the Running Total Field item and clicking on the New button or right-clicking and selecting New from the context menu. Creating a field in this way does not automatically add it to the report; you need to place it on the report in a desired location yourself.

TROUBLESHOOTING

GROUP SELECTION FORMULA

Where can I find the group selection formula?

The group selection formula can be found on the Report menu, under Selection Formulas, Group.

COMPLEX RECORD AND SELECTION FILTERS

The Record and Group Selection dialogs do not allow me to create the complexity of filter that I would like to use. Is there a way to free-form edit the record and group selection filters?

From the Record and Group Selection dialogs, a Show Formula button is available that enables you to see the current filter and to manually modify it with Crystal formula syntax.

CRYSTAL REPORTS IN THE REAL WORLD—NESTING FORMULAS

It's common to combine some more complex formulas to provide specific insight into report data. For example, a user might need to have a report that lists all customers with their total sales, but also show the average value of sales over a given amount. As described previously, there are many ways that a report design expert can approach this; what follows is one method.

1. Open the report Chap3RunningTotal.rpt, or use the report you just created in the last section. Insert a group on Customer ID. Select the running total field, right-click it, and choose Edit Running Total. Under the Reset section, choose On Change of Group. Now the report is ready for the new functionality and should look like Figure 3.9.

2. Create a new formula named Large Orders from the Field Explorer with the following code:

```
WhileReadingRecords;
If {Orders.Order Amount} > 3000 Then
    {Orders.Order Amount}
Else
    0;
```

3. Add this formula to the report. Right-click on the new formula field and select Insert, Summary and for the section Summary Location, change this value to your Group 1 field. This creates the numerator for your average.

4. Next, to determine the value for the denominator, right-click the Large Orders formula and choose Insert, Running Total. Name the running total Large Order Count; for Type of Summary, select Count; for Evaluate, select Formula and enter the following code:

```
{@Large Orders}>0
```

Under Reset, select Group 1. Check your settings against Figure 3.10.

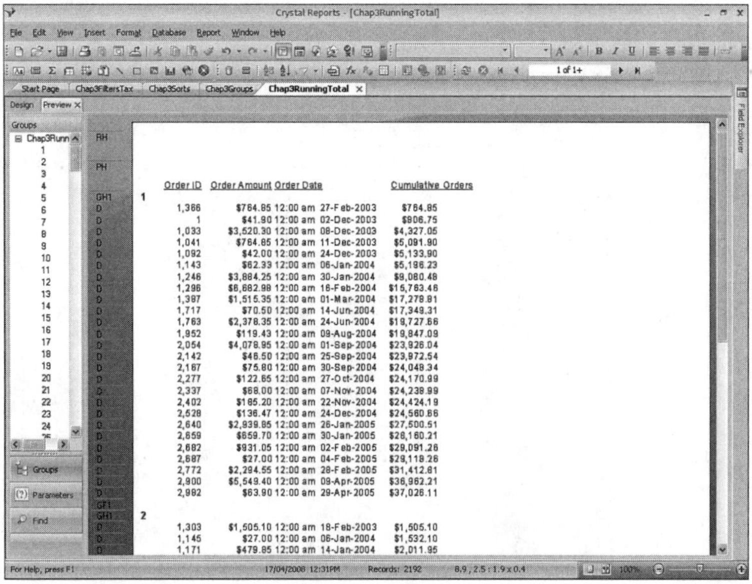

Figure 3.9
This is the starting point for the new functionality.

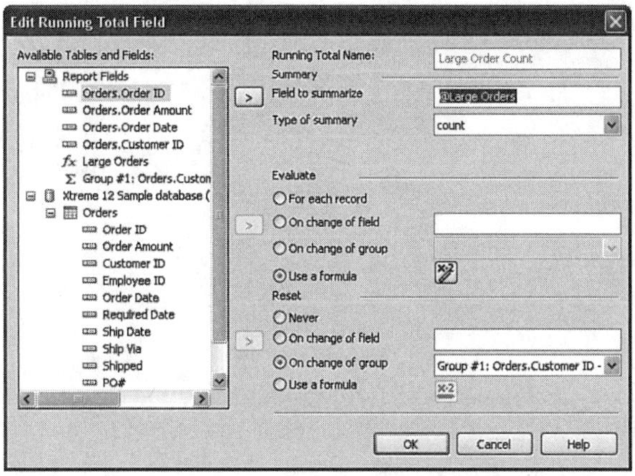

Figure 3.10
Create running totals easily using the Running Total Expert.

5. Now with the numerator and denominator values defined, simply create a new formula called Avg Large Deal Size with the following code:

```
Sum ({@Large Orders}, {Orders.Customer ID})/{#Large Order Count}
```

6. Insert this new formula onto the Group Footer. The report now has a summary value showing the average of all orders greater than $3,000 for each customer (see Figure 3.11).

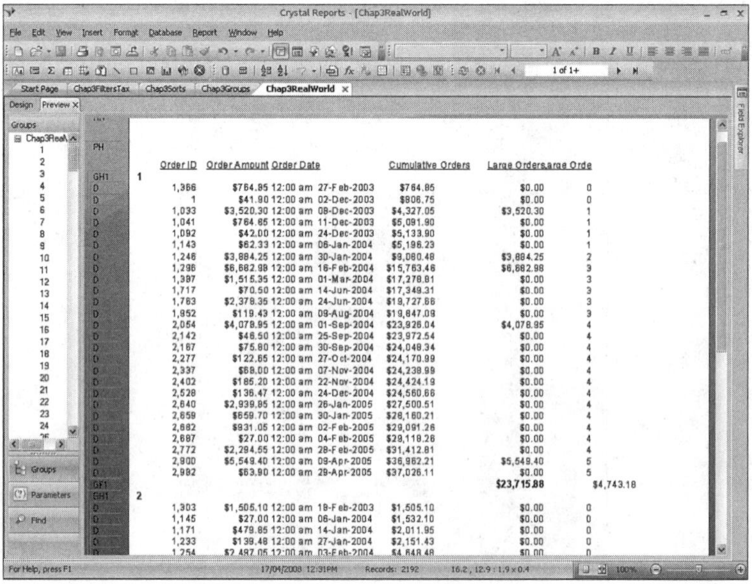

Figure 3.11
A report complete with complex formulas.

Order ID	Order Amount	Order Date	Cumulative Orders	Large Orders	Large Order
1,366	$764.95 12:00 am	27-Feb-2003	$764.95	$0.00	0
1	$41.90 12:00 am	02-Dec-2003	$806.75	$0.00	0
1,033	$3,520.30 12:00 am	08-Dec-2003	$4,327.05	$3,520.30	1
1,041	$764.85 12:00 am	11-Dec-2003	$5,091.90	$0.00	1
1,092	$42.00 12:00 am	24-Dec-2003	$5,133.90	$0.00	1
1,143	$62.33 12:00 am	06-Jan-2004	$5,196.23	$0.00	1
1,246	$3,884.25 12:00 am	30-Jan-2004	$9,080.48	$3,884.25	2
1,396	$6,682.98 12:00 am	16-Feb-2004	$15,763.46	$6,682.98	3
1,397	$1,516.35 12:00 am	01-Mar-2004	$17,278.81	$0.00	3
1,717	$70.50 12:00 am	14-Jun-2004	$17,349.31	$0.00	3
1,763	$2,378.35 12:00 am	24-Jun-2004	$19,727.66	$0.00	3
1,952	$119.43 12:00 am	09-Aug-2004	$19,847.09	$0.00	3
2,054	$4,078.95 12:00 am	01-Sep-2004	$23,926.04	$4,078.95	4
2,142	$46.50 12:00 am	25-Sep-2004	$23,972.54	$0.00	4
2,167	$75.80 12:00 am	30-Sep-2004	$24,048.34	$0.00	4
2,277	$122.65 12:00 am	27-Oct-2004	$24,170.99	$0.00	4
2,337	$68.00 12:00 am	07-Nov-2004	$24,238.99	$0.00	4
2,402	$185.20 12:00 am	22-Nov-2004	$24,424.19	$0.00	4
2,528	$136.47 12:00 am	24-Dec-2004	$24,560.66	$0.00	4
2,640	$2,939.85 12:00 am	26-Jan-2005	$27,500.51	$0.00	4
2,659	$659.70 12:00 am	30-Jan-2005	$28,160.21	$0.00	4
2,682	$931.05 12:00 am	02-Feb-2005	$29,091.26	$0.00	4
2,687	$27.00 12:00 am	04-Feb-2005	$29,118.26	$0.00	4
2,772	$2,294.55 12:00 am	28-Feb-2005	$31,412.81	$0.00	4
2,900	$5,549.40 12:00 am	09-Apr-2005	$36,962.21	$5,549.40	5
2,982	$63.90 12:00 am	29-Apr-2005	$37,026.11	$0.00	5
				$23,715.88	$4,743.18
1,303	$1,505.10 12:00 am	19-Feb-2003	$1,505.10	$0.00	0
1,145	$27.00 12:00 am	08-Jan-2004	$1,532.10	$0.00	0
1,171	$479.85 12:00 am	14-Jan-2004	$2,011.95	$0.00	0
1,233	$139.48 12:00 am	27-Jan-2004	$2,151.43	$0.00	0
1,254	$2,497.05 12:00 am	03-Feb-2004	$4,648.48	$0.00	0

CHAPTER 4

UNDERSTANDING AND IMPLEMENTING FORMULAS

In this chapter

INTRODUCTION

Chapter 2, "Selecting and Grouping Data," introduced the concept of formulas and showed you how to create them and subsequently drop them into a report from the Field Explorer. This chapter explores the Formula Editor in more detail.

Formulas provide great flexibility and power when creating Crystal Reports by enabling you to create *derived* fields not directly stored in available data sources. Formulas also enable you to create advanced conditional object formatting and use flexible selection formulas in a report.

Crystal Reports has a number of built-in tools that facilitate the formula creation and formula reuse processes, the Formula Editor being a good example. The Formula Workshop provides a single convenient access point to almost all your formula fields within a given report. You can access SQL expression fields, record and group selection formulas, formatting formulas, and custom report- and Repository-based functions from the new Formula Workshop.

This chapter covers the following topics:

- An introduction to the Formula Workshop
- A review of the Formula Workshop tree elements
- Formula Editor
- Arithmetic, date, and string formulas
- Type conversion
- Variables in formulas
- Formula Expert
- Formula Extractor
- Multipass reporting

USING THE FORMULA WORKSHOP

You have already been introduced to the record selection and group selection functionality of Crystal Reports that each independently leverages the formula capabilities of the product for enhanced flexibility. As you create more advanced reports, you will come across more functional areas that exploit the formula capabilities of Crystal Reports. Figure 4.1 displays the familiar Formula Editor within the new Formula Workshop interface.

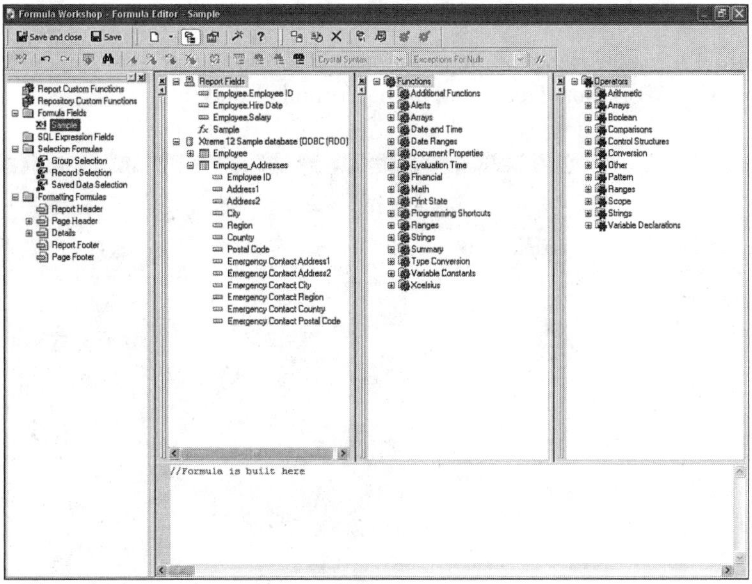

Figure 4.1
The Formula Editor within the new Formula Workshop.

You can use the Formula Editor in the following functional areas of Crystal Report creation:

- Creation of derived fields (formulas, SQL expressions)
- Report section formatting
- Report object formatting
- Record selection formulas
- Group selection formulas
- Running total conditions
- Formula-based hyperlinks (covered in Chapter 9, "Custom Formatting Techniques")
- Alert conditions (covered in Chapter 11, "Using Record Selections, Sort Controls, and Alerts for Interactive Reporting")
- Use of report variables (covered later in this chapter and in Chapter 12, "Using Subreports for Advanced Reports")

Although the independently accessed Formula Editors for each reporting area provide powerful capabilities, a great productivity feature introduced in Crystal Reports version 9 is the capability to access almost all the formulas held in a report in a single interface called the Formula Workshop—essentially a one-stop shop for all formulas. At the time of writing, the only exceptions to the rule were the Running Total and Alert Condition formulas.

The Formula Workshop consists of a toolbar, a tree that lists the types of formulas you can create or modify, and an area for defining the formula itself either through the Formula Editor or a Formula Expert.

NAVIGATING THE FORMULA WORKSHOP WITH THE WORKSHOP TREE

Figure 4.2 shows some of the new Formula Workshop features you see by expanding the Formula Workshop Tree found in the Formula Editor.

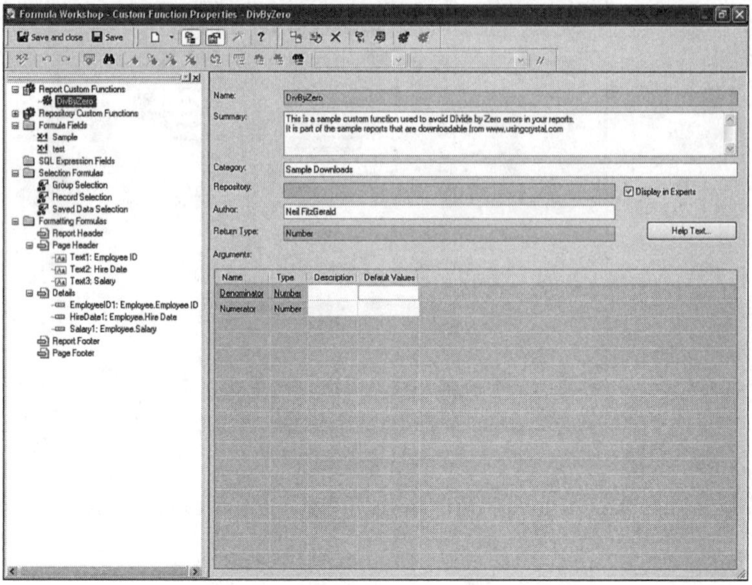

Figure 4.2
The Formula Workshop with expanded Formula Workshop Tree and the properties for a custom function displayed.

The Workshop Tree is a container for report and Repository functions, formula fields, SQL expression fields, selection formulas, and formatting formulas—all of which the following sections explain in more detail.

REPORT CUSTOM FUNCTIONS

Report custom functions are ones created by Crystal Reports designers and stored within the current report file. It is important to note that custom functions are accessed from the Formula Workshop along with other types of formulas and functions. New custom report functions are created through the Formula Editor by accessing the right-click menu on any part of the Report Custom Function section of the Formula Workshop or by selecting Custom Function from the New menu drop-down list.

→ For more information on custom functions, **see** "Crystal Reports in the Real World—Custom Functions," at the end of this chapter and Chapter 13, "Using Formulas and Custom Functions."

REPOSITORY CUSTOM FUNCTIONS

Repository custom functions are ones created by Crystal Reports designers and then stored centrally within the BusinessObjects Enterprise (or Crystal Reports Server) Repository. The repository acts as a central library for these custom functions among multiple other reusable objects. Note that Repository functions are accessed from the Formula Workshop along with the other types of formulas and functions. You upload new Repository functions by creating a report function and subsequently adding it to the Repository through the Add Repository option accessed by right-clicking any specific custom report function.

> **TIP**
>
> Although the Crystal Repository was introduced and made available in Crystal Reports version 9, it is now available only to Crystal Report designers licensed for BusinessObjects Enterprise (or Crystal Reports Server). When requesting any Repository-related function or activity, a logon prompt for BusinessObjects Enterprise (or Crystal Reports Server) is presented to the designer and must be successfully completed before the functionality is made available.
>
> Remember that when you add a custom function to the Central Repository for other report developers to use, you must first create it locally as a report custom function and only then can it be added to the central Repository. Custom functions cannot be directly added to the central Repository.

FORMULA FIELDS

As you learned in previous chapters, formula fields provide a means to add derived fields (that is, those not directly available in your database), such as a calculation into your Crystal Reports, as well as provide your business users (report consumers) with additional views of data. After you create derived formula fields, Crystal Reports treats them in the same manner as it does original database fields. The majority of this chapter is dedicated to introducing the different methods of creating formulas through two interfaces: the Formula Editor and the Formula Expert. Both are discussed next, and Chapter 13 explores some advanced features of formula creation and use.

SQL EXPRESSION FIELDS

SQL expressions provide a means to add derived fields (that is, those not directly available in your database), such as a calculation into your Crystal Reports, that are based exclusively on *Structured Query Language (SQL)* statements rather than standard Crystal formula syntax. As a reminder, SQL expressions are used in cases where report-processing efficiency is critical.

Using SQL expressions facilitates pushing data processing to the database server instead of the Crystal Reports Server, and this is usually most efficient. Like formulas, SQL expressions are created in the Formula Editor but provide only a subset of the functionality because of the dependency on the SQL supported by the report's attached data source. A downloadable chapter called "Using SQL Queries in Crystal Reports" provides a good introduction to SQL and is available from www.usingcrystal.com.

SELECTION FORMULAS

As discussed in Chapter 3, "Filtering, Sorting, and Summarizing Data," selection formulas come in two varieties in Crystal Reports: group and record. A record selection formula provides a filtering mechanism on records to be included in the final report. Similarly, a group selection formula provides a filtering mechanism on the groups to be included in the final report. Each selection formula can be accessed and edited through the Formula Workshop by using the familiar Formula Editor component. The Formula Editor will be described in detail in the next major section and in extended detail with respect to selection formulas in Chapter 11.

FORMATTING FORMULAS

Formatting formulas provide flexibility in the presentation of Crystal Report's report sections and all the report objects contained within report sections. Examples of object- and section-formatting options include Background Color, Suppression, ToolTip, Border Color/Style, Section Underlay, and so on. All the formatting capabilities available in the Format Editor dialog (see Figure 4.3) and the Report Section Expert (see Figure 4.4) that provide access to an X+2 icon can be set—and be set conditionally—through these formatting formulas.

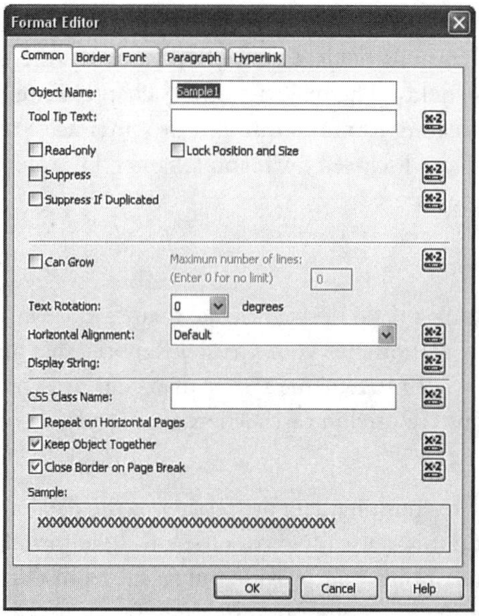

Figure 4.3
The Format Editor dialog provides access to numerous formatting settings and additional access to the Formula Editor for conditional formatting.

Coverage of the formatting functionality provided through these dialogs continues in Chapter 6, "Fundamentals of Report Formatting," but you should note that it is accessed and set through the Formula Workshop's Formula Editor. When you select the New Formatting Formula option by either clicking the New button or right-clicking on a Section or Field element under the Formatting Functions tree, you can access all formatting functions that can be modified through a formula.

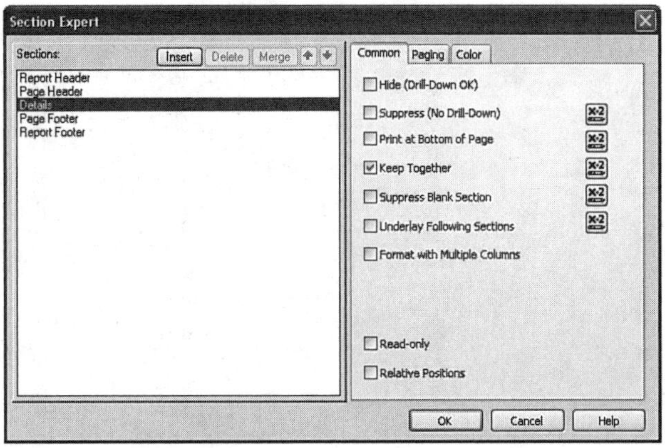

Figure 4.4
The Section Expert provides access to numerous section formatting settings and additional access to the Formula Editor for conditional settings.

USING THE WORKSHOP FORMULA EDITOR

The Formula Editor, shown in Figure 4.5, is a common tool used across all the different types of formulas accessible through the Formula Workshop. The Formula Editor is composed of five distinct areas:

- The Fields area (at the upper-left frame of the Formula Editor) includes all the available report, formula, summarization, and database fields that you can add to the current formula.

- The Functions area (at the upper-center frame of the Formula Editor) includes the prebuilt Crystal Reports functions and custom functions that you can add to the currently edited formula.

- The Operators area (at the upper-right frame of the Formula Editor) includes a number of operators that you can use in the currently edited formula. Examples of operators include +, *, IF/THEN/ELSE, SELECT CASE, AND/OR, and so on.

- The Editing area (the large bottom frame of the Formula Editor) is the free-form text-editing area where you create formulas through either direct typing or double-clicking selections from the other three Formula Editor frames.

- The toolbar area contains a number of Formula Editor options, including toggles on the different frames, a new toggle on the Formula Editor or Expert, some bookmarking options, a formula syntax checking button (x+2), and, importantly, the Crystal versus Basic Syntax drop-down box.

NOTE

Crystal Reports provides two different formula languages for use in creating formulas. Basic syntax is very similar to the Visual Basic programming structure and provides a natural fit for report designers with a Visual Basic programming background. The other more commonly used syntax—Crystal syntax—has no programming language affiliation but is highly evolved and easy to use for nonprogrammers. For the rest of this chapter, the examples are created using the more common Crystal syntax.

Figure 4.5
The Formula Editor provides a one-stop shop for formula development.

The available elements in each of the top three areas of the Formula Editor vary depending on what type of formula you are creating. For example, when you create a formatting formula, the Functions frame presents a Formatting section not available while editing or creating other types of formulas. Another familiar example is the limited set of fields, functions, and operators presented when creating SQL expressions. This is, of course, dependent on the supported SQL for the current report's data source.

To facilitate your understanding of the Formula Editor, the following hypothetical business problem provides a hands-on experience with creating formulas within reports. The CEO of Maple Leaf Bikes is planning an initial public offering (IPO) of his stock to the marketplace. Having recently acquired another company called Xtreme Cycles, he wants to fairly share the success of the overall company with these new employees. As such, he wants to allocate stock options to them based on tenure with Xtreme Cycles (a metric of loyalty) and their current salary (a metric of expected contribution). Therefore, the CEO has determined that a fair allocation would be 100 shares for each year of tenure and 100 shares for each $10,000 in salary, and he wants a report outlining these allocations so that he can present this proposal at the next board of directors meeting. The following steps demonstrate a solution for this problem:

1. Create a new report based on the Xtreme Sample Database ODBC Connection using either the Standard Report Wizard or through the main Report Design menus.

2. Select the Employees and Employee_Addresses tables to use in the report. They should be automatically smart-linked on their indexed (noted by the red icon in the linking dialog) Employee ID fields.

3. Add the Employee ID, Salary, and Hire Date fields into the detail section of the report.

At this point, the design window (from the Design tab) for the report should resemble Figure 4.6.

Figure 4.6
The Crystal Reports Design window with a sample report.

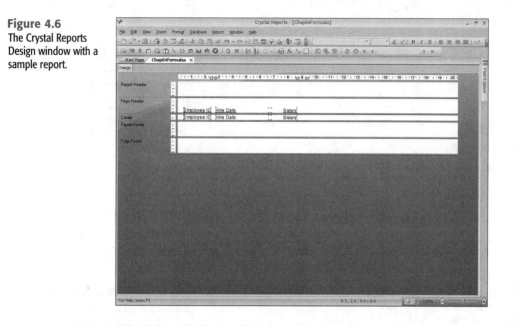

The basic building blocks to the requested report have now been added to the sample report, but there is clearly work to be done to capture the CEO's intent. This report is flushed out through the next few sections as different formula functions are systematically introduced.

ARITHMETIC FORMULAS

Arithmetic formulas are those derived from existing numeric fields (or fields converted into numbers—type conversion information is discussed later in this chapter). These formulas can be simple multiplication or addition operations, or they can be as complex as standard deviations, sums, or correlations. Arithmetic formulas are created within the Formula Editor by selecting any combination of numeric fields, numeric operators, or numeric-oriented functions. Figure 4.7 displays the Formula Editor resized to highlight some common arithmetic functions and operators.

With hundreds of formula functions and operators built into Crystal Reports and the new capability to expand that set with custom functions, it's easy to be overwhelmed by all the available formula possibilities. One very helpful source of information on the many built-in formulas in Crystal Reports is the provided help files accessed through the F1 key. By clicking on the Index tab of the Crystal Reports help screen and searching on functions or operators, you can access a detailed description of each of the hundreds of different Crystal Reports functions and operators. Figure 4.8 displays the Crystal Reports Help dialog with an Aging function highlighted.

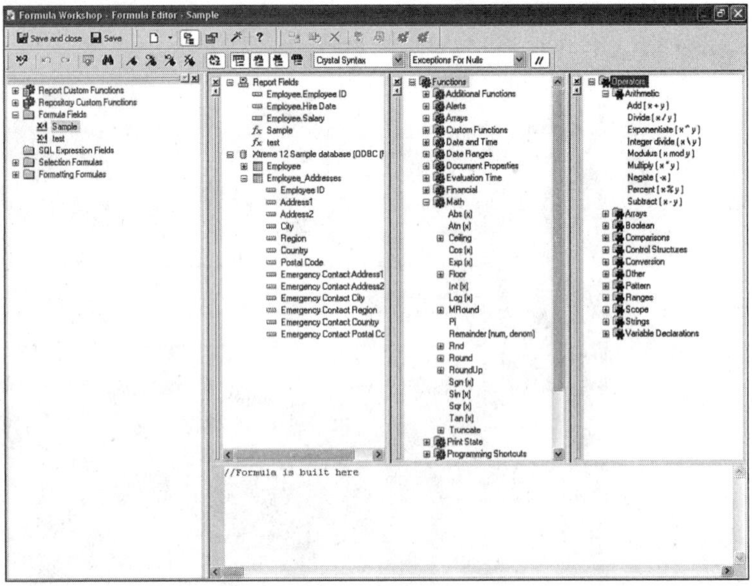

Figure 4.7
The Formula Editor highlighting some arithmetic functions and operators.

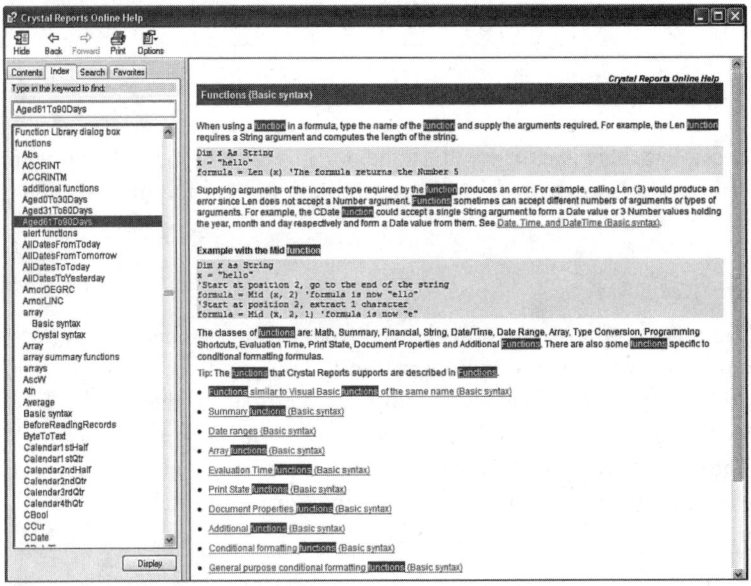

Figure 4.8
Crystal Reports functions help—a great reference for understanding the syntax of formula functions.

To create an arithmetic formula (as any other kind of formula) within the Formula Editor, either double-click on the appropriate elements from each of the Fields, Functions, and Operators frames or select them by single-clicking and dragging and dropping them into the formula editing frame. Using either method, you begin to construct a formula in the formula editing area/frame. Alternatively, experienced users can create formulas by typing the formula directly into the formula editing area and periodically checking the formula's syntax with the X+2 toolbar button, which provides error-checking functionality.

TIP

For users who prefer to work in the Formula Editor and type in their formulas by hand, Crystal Reports provides an auto complete capability, accessed by using the Ctrl+spacebar key combination. A list of formula functions that could complete the most recently typed characters is made available for instant selection.

Revisiting the Maple Leaf Bikes reporting scenario, the CEO has designated two criteria for stock option allocation to the Xtreme Sports employees: tenure and salary. The salary component is based on a derivation from a numeric field (salary) and lends itself to the creation of an arithmetic formula based on the requirements that each $10,000 of salary contributes to 100 stock options. The following steps, continued from the last section, move toward a reporting solution for the CEO and provide exposure to the formula creation process in the Formula Editor:

1. If the Field Explorer is not already open in your Crystal Reports Design window, open it now either by clicking on the Field Explorer icon or by toggling to the Field Explorer option under the View menu. Figure 4.9 displays the Crystal Reports Design window with the Field Explorer displayed.

Figure 4.9
Maple Leaf Bikes CEO report with Field Explorer displayed.

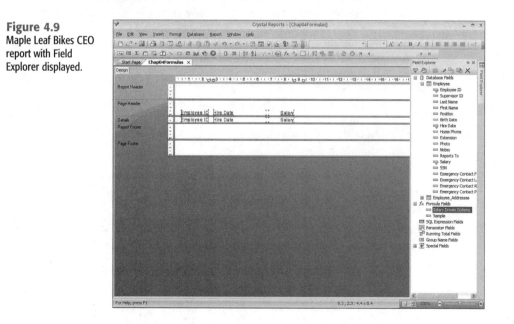

> TIP
>
> To maximize report design real estate in the Design tab, you can shorten the Report Section names by accessing the Show Short Section Names option from the right-click menu accessed from any report section heading. Similarly, to maximize the preview real estate in the Preview tab, a capability exists through the Hide Section Names menu option.

2. Create a new formula by clicking on the Formula Fields field and either accessing the New option on the right-click menu or clicking the New button in the Field Explorer toolbar. You will be prompted for a formula name—call this formula Salary Driven Options and select the Use Editor button to create the formula. If you accidentally click the Use Expert button, have no fear; simply click the Formula Editor/Expert toggle button in the Formula Workshop toolbar. The Formula Expert is explored later in this chapter, but for now, the Formula Editor is your primary focus. The familiar Formula Workshop (as you saw in Figures 4.2 and 4.5) appears.

3. Logically stepping through the CEO's request, the first database field you need to access to determine the salary-driven component of stock option allocation is Salary, so find the Salary field in the Fields frame and double-click on it.

> TIP
>
> More than just providing access to those fields already selected for viewing in the report, the Formula Editor Fields frame provides access to all available database fields for those tables selected as report data sources. Additionally, existing formulas, sums, running totals, and so on can be accessed here, which can be included in other formulas.

Because the CEO wants to provide 100 stock options for each $10,000 in existing salary, you logically need to divide each employee's current salary by $10,000 and then multiply by 100. To do so, you could either access the arithmetic operators (/ for division and * for multiplication) in the Operators frame and double-click on those or simply type them in.

4. To accomplish this task, you need to type in the numeric constants regardless, so type the following into the Formula Editor so that it resembles Figure 4.10:
   `{Employee.Salary} / 10000 * 100`.

5. Perform error-checking on your report by clicking on the X+2 icon. After you confirm that no errors are found and your formula is identical to that in Figure 4.10, save the formula with the Save button and exit the Formula Workshop by clicking on Close.

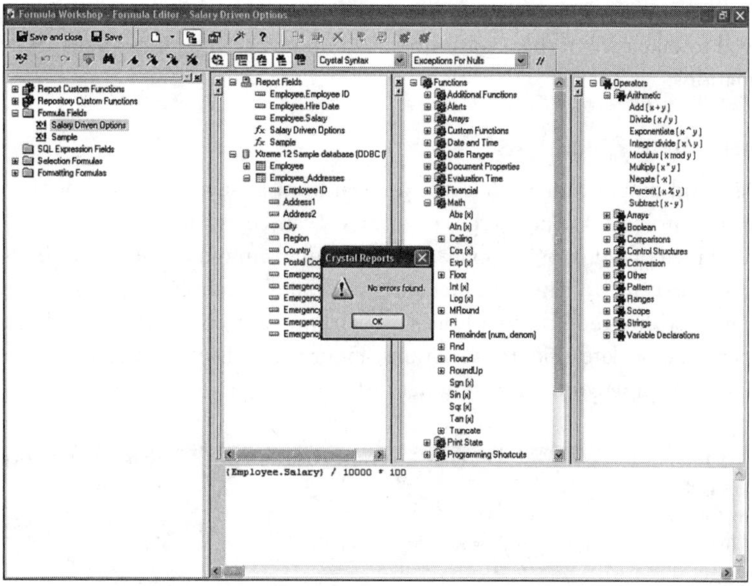

Figure 4.10
Salary-driven options formula creation example.

6. Add the new formula into the report beside Employee ID and try to format it to display zero decimals and no currency symbol (hint—right-click on the object and select the Format option or use the shortcut buttons from the Formatting toolbar). At this point, also remove the original Salary and Hire Date fields from the report by deleting them. Note that the Salary Driven Options field can exist without its underlying support fields (Salary) existing on the report. The Preview tab of the CEO's report should now resemble that shown in Figure 4.11.

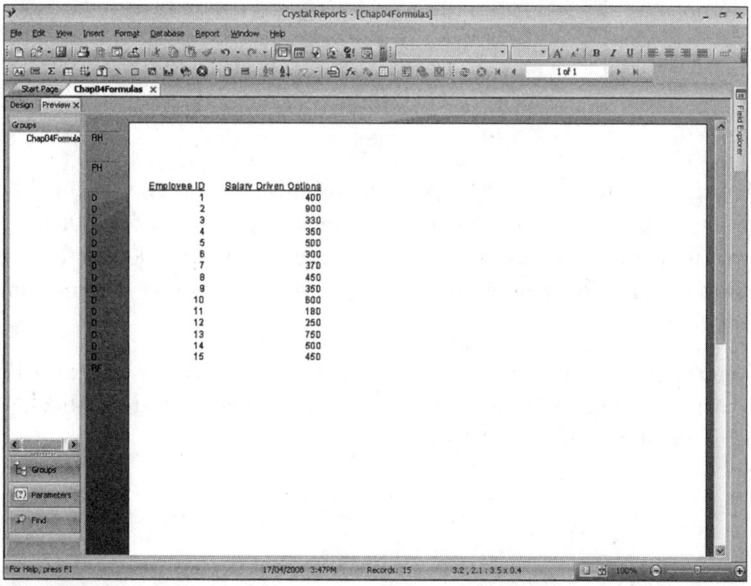

Figure 4.11
The interim version of the Maple Leaf Bikes CEO sample report.

The current version of the report takes the content of the report to about half complete. You need to take care of the tenure-driven component of the CEO's request with some date calculations.

DATE AND TIME FORMULAS

Date and time formulas are those derived from existing date or time fields (or fields converted into dates). These types of formulas can be as simple as extracting a month name from a date field or as complex as determining shipping times in business days (the difference between two dates not including weekends and holidays). Date and time formulas are created within the Formula Editor by selecting any combination of date and time fields, date operators, or date-oriented functions. Figure 4.12 displays the Formula Editor resized to highlight some common date functions.

Figure 4.12
The Formula Editor highlighting some date and time functions.

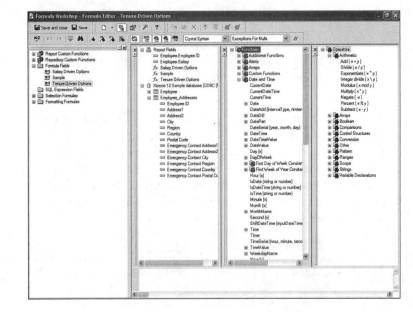

To create a date/time formula (as with arithmetic formulas) within the Formula Editor, either double-click on the appropriate elements from each of the fields, functions, and operators frames or select them with a single-click and drag and drop them into the formula editing frame. Using either method, you begin to construct a formula in the formula editing area/frame.

Some operators commonly used with dates include + and -. Those are displayed in Table 4.1 with some quick examples and their effect. These operators work equally well on time fields and date fields.

TABLE 4.1   COMMON DATE OPERATORS, THEIR FUNCTIONS, AND EXAMPLES

Common Date Operator or Function	Formula Usage Example	Effect
+ operator	`{Employee.Hire Date}` `+ 365`	Returns the one year anniversary date of the given employee in a date format.
- operator	`{Orders.Ship Date}-` `{Orders.Order Date}`	Returns a numeric field representing the days taken to ship after receiving an order.
- operator	`{Orders.Warranty` `Expiration Date} - 365`	Returns a date representing the purchase date of the given item.

Functions commonly used with dates include the prebuilt date ranges and date type conversion formulas in Crystal Reports.

- Conversion functions are found under the Date and Time section in the Functions frame of the Formula Editor.

- Range functions are found in the Date Ranges section of the same Functions frame and provide a number of built-in date ranges that can be automatically created in Crystal Reports and used in comparisons. Range examples include Aged61To90Days, Next30Days, or AllDatesFromTomorrow. These ranges can be used with the control structures introduced later in this chapter (for example, IF statements) to determine whether dates fall within certain predefined ranges.

Revisiting the Maple Leaf Bikes reporting scenario, the tenure component of option allocation still needs to be created in the report. It is based on a derivation from two date fields (Hire Date and the current date) and lends itself to the creation of a date formula based on the requirements that every 365 days of tenure contributes to 100 stock options.

The following steps move toward a final reporting solution for the CEO and provide exposure to date-focused formula creation in the Formula Editor:

1. Create a new formula called Tenure Driven Options in the Field Explorer.

   Because the CEO wants to provide 100 stock options for each year (365 days) of tenure, you logically need to determine each employee's tenure in days by finding the difference (with the - operator) between the current date (with a built-in Crystal Reports function) and the hire date (with a provided database field). This employee tenure measured in days must then be divided by 365 to find the tenure in years before being multiplied by 100 to determine the number of tenure-driven options.

2. To accomplish this, add the Current Date function (CurrentDate) to the formula by accessing it under the Date and Time section of the Functions frame in the Formula Editor. You could alternatively add this by typing **Cu** in the editor box, pressing

Ctrl+Spacebar, and selecting the CurrentDate function from the list. Add the - operator (found under the Arithmetic section in the Operators frame) after that, and then add the database field Hire Date to the formula by double-clicking on it. Finally, add the / 365 and * 100 formula pieces by typing them in and, more importantly, wrap two round brackets around the CurrentDate-{Employee.Hire Date} section of the formula to ensure the proper order of calculation.

NOTE

> The Crystal Reports Formula Editor respects the standard mathematical order of operations. In order, this is brackets, exponents, division and multiplication, and, finally, addition and subtraction.

3. Ensure that your formula resembles what Figure 4.13 shows, and save it before closing the Formula Workshop.

Figure 4.13
A Tenure Driven Options sample formula highlighting some date formulas.

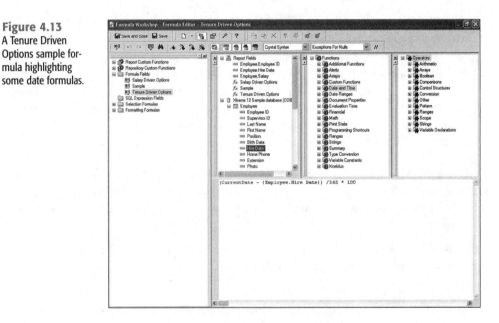

4. Place the new formula on the report beside the Salary Driven Options field and format it to have no decimal places and no currency symbol.

It has likely struck you that most CEOs would not appreciate having to take the two options numbers you have created and add them themselves. It seems like a good opportunity for another formula to sum up those two numbers.

5. Create a new formula called Total Options and make that formula be the sum of the two previously created formulas. (Hint: The previously created formulas appear in the Fields frame under the Report Fields Tree node, and you can use the addition operator.)

6. Add this new field to the report, remove the Hire Date and Salary fields, and reformat it to make your sample resemble that displayed in Figure 4.14.

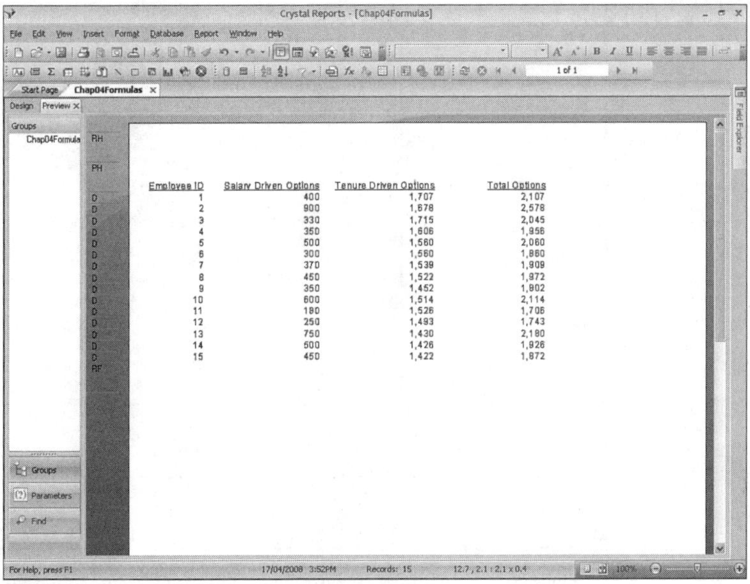

Figure 4.14
Maple Leaf Bikes CEO report with options formulas.

The CEO of Maple Leaf Bikes should be quite happy with the turnaround time on this report. Having created the results so quickly, it might be a good move in career management to spend a little time on the presentation and readability of this report. The next sections and chapters introduce some additional capabilities provided in Crystal Reports and the Formula Editor that increase the presentation quality of this report.

STRING FORMULAS

String formulas are created from existing string fields (or fields converted into strings—type conversion is covered later in the chapter in the section "Using Type Conversion in Formulas"). These formulas can be as simple as concatenating two string fields or as complex as extracting some specific piece of information from a string field. String formulas are created within the Formula Editor by selecting any combination of string fields, string operators, or string-oriented functions. Figure 4.15 displays the Formula Editor resized to highlight some common string functions.

The most commonly created string-based formulas involve the concatenation of multiple existing fields from a data source. This is accomplished through the Formula Editor with either the formal Concatenate function from within the Strings section of the Operators frame or by using the much simpler + and & concatenate operators. These last two operators enable the dynamic linking of one or more string fields into one large string field.

Figure 4.15
The Formula Editor with string-oriented functions expanded.

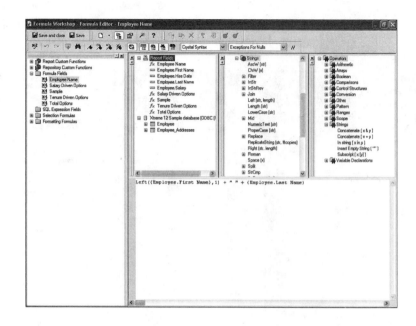

4

TIP

Although the + operator requires all its arguments to be of the same string type when concatenating, the & operator performs dynamic conversion to text on any nonstring fields included in the operation—a nice time-saving feature.

Revisiting the Maple Leaf Bikes reporting scenario and focusing on increasing the readability of the report, Employee ID can be replaced with Employee First Initial and Last Name.

NOTE

When creating a string formula that is meant to join two existing strings (for example, First Name and Last Name, or Address 1 and Address 2), the concatenation features of Crystal Reports dynamically resize the resultant formula to exclude any redundant spaces between the end of the first joined field and the beginning of the next. This is an important presentation feature that prevents the requirement to trim all fields before joining them.

To use the string capabilities of the Formula Editor and enhance the report, follow these steps:

1. Create a new formula called `Employee Name` in the sample report.

2. Because you want to present only the first letter of the employee's first name, you need to use the `Left` function under the Strings section of the Functions frame. Add this to your formula, and note that the cursor is automatically placed in the expected location for the first parameter to this function—a string.

3. Without moving the cursor in the Editing area, find the First Name field of the Employee table and double-click on it. (You will likely need to expand the Xtreme Sample Database section because this field is not currently added to the report.) This adds it as the first argument to the Left function.

4. Move the cursor in the editing area to the location of the second expected parameter for the Left function—after the comma—and type 1 (the number of characters to extract). This creates the entry Left ({Employee.First Name}, 1) in the Formula Editor and instructs the Formula Engine to take the leftmost single character from the First Name field.

5. To concatenate this with the Last Name in a nice-looking manner, type + ". " + into the editing area and then double-click on the Last Name field of the Employee table. Your new formula should resemble Figure 4.16.

Figure 4.16
String formula sample in the Formula Editor.

6. Replace the Employee ID field in the CEO's sample report with the new Employee Name formula you just created, and rearrange your report to resemble Figure 4.17.

TIP

If you wanted to continue to provide the CEO with the capability of determining an actual Employee ID but didn't want to squeeze the report real estate anymore, you could use a clever Crystal Reports feature called ToolTips. This enables a pop-up window to show up with additional information (such as Employee ID) when the end user (in this case, the CEO) scrolls over any employee name. This is implemented from the Format Field window (under the Common tab) and the ToolTips Text X+2 button. You can accomplish this by using the following formula: "Employee ID: " + CSTR({Employee.Employee ID},0).

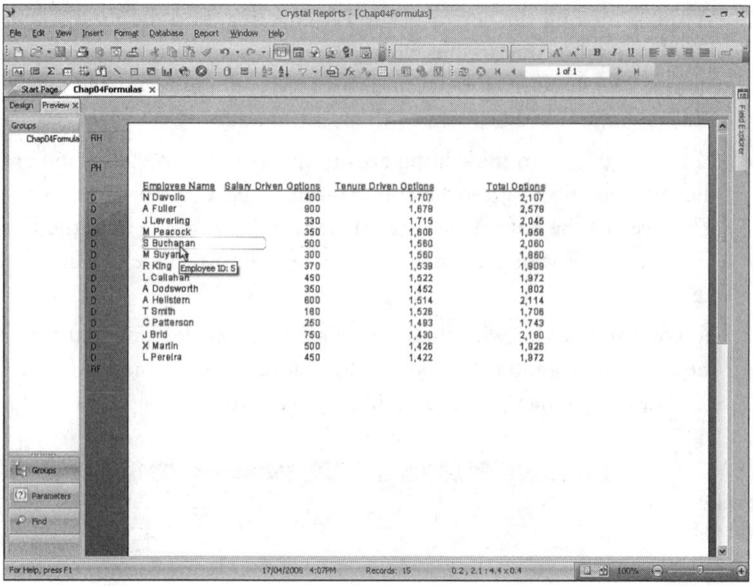

Figure 4.17
Maple Leaf Bikes CEO report with string formula and ToolTip with Employee ID displayed.

Having covered the primary data types used in strings, it is useful for operating in the real world to know how to move between those data types. The next section discusses data type conversion.

TIP

> Comments can be added to formula statements to better document the formula. To insert comments, use the double forward slash (/ /) at the beginning of a line of code to comment out the entire line. Thus, any text on this commented line is not processed as part of the formula. There is also a toolbar command within the Formula Editor that enables you to add this syntax into formulas quickly, as indicated with the double slash (//) icon. If you're using the Basic syntax, the apostrophe (or rem) commands can be used for commenting.

USING TYPE CONVERSION IN FORMULAS

Often, data is not accessible in the format that is required for a particular operation. A common example is when numeric fields are stored in a database as string fields and are required in an arithmetic formula. For any number of additional reasons, it often happens that data needs to be converted to and from different data types. The Formula Editor provides numerous built-in functions that facilitate this conversion process. These functions are accessible from the Type Conversion section under the Functions frame of the Formula Editor. Figure 4.18 displays the Formula Editor with the Type Conversion section expanded.

Figure 4.18
The Formula Editor provides you with many different type conversion functions.

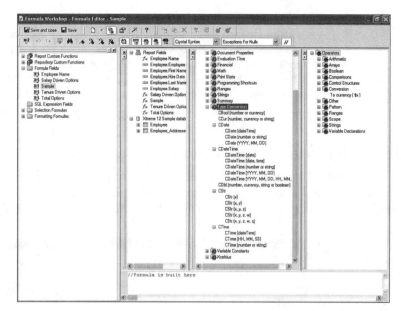

A great deal of flexibility is provided with the numerous type conversion functions built into Crystal Reports and these should enable all required conversions. Additionally, Crystal Reports provides some automatic conversions in the following cases: Number to Currency, Date to DateTime, and basic type to a range value of the same underlying basic type. Some of the most commonly used Type Conversion functions are

- **CStr() or ToText()**—These identical functions convert Number, Currency, Date, Time, and DateTime values to text strings.

- **CDbl() or ToNumber()**—These identical functions convert Currency, text string, or Boolean values to a number. Often used in combination with IsNumeric() or NumericText() to validate input arguments.

- **CDate(), CDateTime(), or CTime()**—These functions convert their given arguments (numeric, string, and specific fixed formats) to a respective Date, DateTime, or Time value.

A couple of more interesting type conversion options include the following:

- **Roman()**—This function converts a number ranging from 0 to 3999 into its Roman numeral equivalent (for example, Roman(2004) = MMIV).

- **ToWords()**—This function converts a number or currency value to a string representation of that number (for example, ToWords($134.15, 2) = one hundred thirty four and 15/100). This is a nice function for facilitating the delivery of checks.

> **NOTE**
>
> Barcode conversion functions are also available through a third party, Azalea, at www.azalea.com/CrystalReports/index.html. These enable you to convert numbers to standard barcodes that can be embedded on your Crystal Reports. New to version 2008 is the ability to convert existing strings or numbers to barcodes directly from the context menu on your report objects.

Control Structures—Conditional and Looping Structures

The Formula Editor provides additional power in formula creation through a set of control structures made available in the Operators and Functions frames. Figure 4.19 displays the involved sections of those respective frames that include the provided control structures.

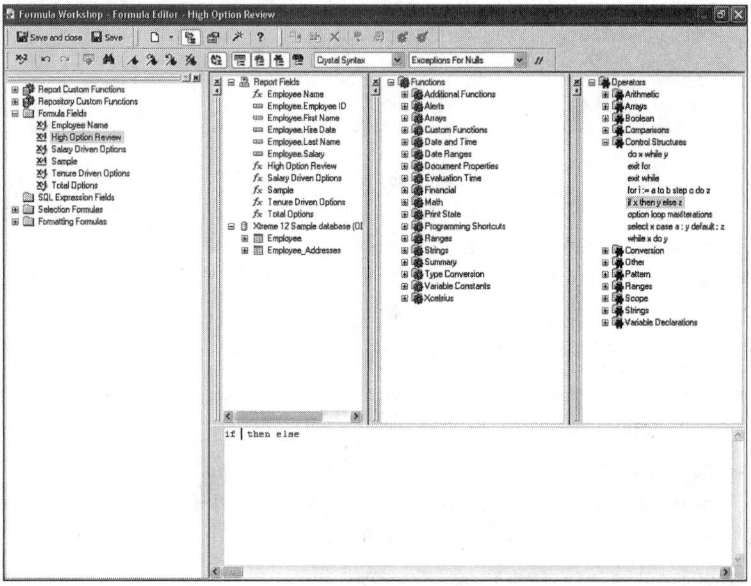

Figure 4.19
The Formula Editor provides several control structure functions and operators.

One of the most useful control structures is the `If/Then/Else` construct. This structure enables the inclusion of conditional logic in Crystal Reports formulas. The `If/Then/Else` works particularly well when a condition leads to either one of two settings. Although this construct can handle multiple potential settings through nested `If` statements, creating this type of complicated formula can be avoided with the `Select Case` operator that allows for multiple settings and multiple potential results.

Revisiting the Maple Leaf Bikes example, assume that the CEO has provided a new requirement specifying that employees with a recommended stock allocation of greater than 2000 stock options need to be highlighted for his personal review. Of course, with Crystal

Reports, there are multiple methods of providing this highlighting; to use the `If/Then/Else` control structure, follow these steps:

1. Create a new formula called `High Option Review`.

2. Add the `If/Then/Else` control structure to the formula.

3. Add the condition that the `Total Options` formula (@Total Options field) is greater than 2000 between 'If' and 'Then' so that the beginning of the formula text is `IF {@Total Options} > 2000 THEN`.

4. Now when any employee meets this condition, you need to highlight that record for the CEO's special review. To do this, add text similar to `"** Review **"` (with the double quotes surrounding the text) to the area after the `Then` part of the `If` statement construct.

5. When that condition is not met, you can simply print a space or dash. Do this by adding `"-"` (including the double quotes) after the `Else` part of the `If` statement so that your new formula resembles that shown in Figure 4.20.

Figure 4.20
A sample formula with an `If` control structure.

NOTE

Carriage returns (via the Enter key) can be inserted into the construction area of the formula, such as between lines and logical breaking points, to make formulas more readable. If you're using the Basic syntax, you can extend single code lines over multiple lines for readability by using the underscore character (_) preceded by a space.

6. Add the new formula to the CEO's report so that it resembles the sample report shown in Figure 4.21.

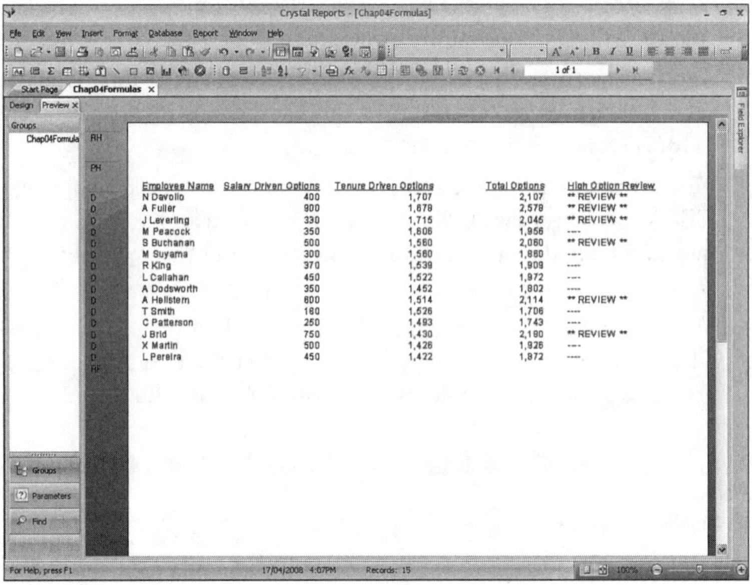

Figure 4.21
The revised sample report includes a High Option Review indicator.

The conditional logic inherent in the If/Then/Else and Select/Case statements provides clear flexibility in formula creation. Another valuable formula capability that programmers appreciate immediately is the looping functionality. The Formula Editor provides three different looping constructs (For/Step/Do, Do/While, and While/Do), and each enables the evaluation of formula logic multiple times for each evaluation of the formula. Table 4.3 describes the most common types of control structures and their usage.

TABLE 4.3 COMMONLY USED CONTROL STRUCTURES

Control Structure		Description Usage
If/Then/Else and IIF()	Conditional structures that select an execution path based on the evaluated conditions.	This construct is best used when evaluating conditions with a minimal set of potential execution options.
Select Case	Conditional structure that selects an execution path based on the evaluation conditions.	This construct is best used in place of the if/then/else construct when evaluating conditions with multiple potential execution paths.

TABLE 4.3   CONTINUED

Control Structure	Description	Usage
Switch	Another conditional structure that selects a value from a set of expression/value pairs where the expression evaluates to `true`.	This is especially effective when creating report selection filters because it allows for the pushing of the results down to the database or faster report execution—this is not possible with the other conditional constructs. It is also useful for compact conditional formula creation.
For/Step/ Loops	For loops enable you to evaluate a sequence of statements a fixed numbers of times. An `Exit` statement can end this looping prematurely.	This construct is best used when you `Do` know the number of times that the expressions need to be evaluated in advance or the loops are dependent on a variable in the report. `For I = X to Y Step Z Do (statements)`
Do/While Loops	`Do/While` loops execute until the `While` condition is no longer met. They always execute at least once. The `Exit While` statement can end this looping prematurely.	`While` loops can be used to execute a fixed block of statements an indefinite number of times. `Do statements` `While condition`
While/Do Loops	`While/Do` loops execute until the `While` condition is no longer met. It is possible that not a single iteration takes place if the condition is immediately false. `While condition Do (statements)`	`While` loop can be used to execute a fixed block of statements an indefinite amount of time. The `Exit While` statement can end this looping prematurely.

CAUTION

The Crystal Reports engine has a built-in safety mechanism that displays an error message and stops processing any formula if it includes more than 100,000 loop iterations. This is important to consider when including any of the loop constructs in a formula. It is also important to note that this built-in governor works on a per-formula basis and not per loop. This means that if any one formula contains any number of loops that tally more than 100,000 looping iterations, the formula stops processing with an error. Another control structure function called `Option Loop` can be used for limiting iterations to a number different from 100,000.

VARIABLES

Crystal Reports has included yet another programming construct, variables, in the Formula Editor to provide even further flexibility in formula creation. Variables give you a powerful means to store and retrieve information throughout the processing life of any report—essentially providing a temporary storage space for valuable information. Examples of information that might be useful to store and retrieve later are previous detail section information, previous group section information, or a one-time calculation that needs to be incorporated into many subsequent report formulas.

Several different types of variables can be declared (for example, String, Number, Date, Time, Boolean, and so on) and three different scopes for each of these variables are as follows:

- **Local**—Accessible only in the same formula within which they are declared
- **Global**—Accessible from all formulas in the main report, but not accessible from subreports.
- **Shared**—Accessible from all formulas in both the main report and all subreports

Both the variable declaration and scope operator listings are accessible from the Operators frame in the Formula Editor. To use variables in your report formulas, they must be declared first. This applies to every formula that accesses any given variable—not just the first processed formula.

TIP

> Another important function to remember when using multiple variables in multiple formulas with calculation dependencies is the EvaluateAfter() function. This formula function can force certain formulas (and their variable logic) to be processed after another formula (and its variable logic). This can be very useful when the order of formula calculation is important because of variable and formula dependencies. A good discussion of when things are evaluated in Crystal Report's multipass engine is provided at the end of this chapter.

It is worth noting that variables can provide significant power in report creation in their capability to maintain persistent information outside the regular processing path of the report. A practical hands-on use of variables is explored in Chapter 12.

CREATING FORMULAS WITH THE FORMULA EXPERT

The Formula Expert creates formulas based on existing custom functions, either from the current report or the Crystal Repository. It appears when you click on the Formula Expert/Editor toggle button (the magic wand) in the Formula Workshop. The Formula Expert leverages the power of the custom functions and repository functionality introduced first in version 9. Figure 4.22 displays the Formula Expert dialog.

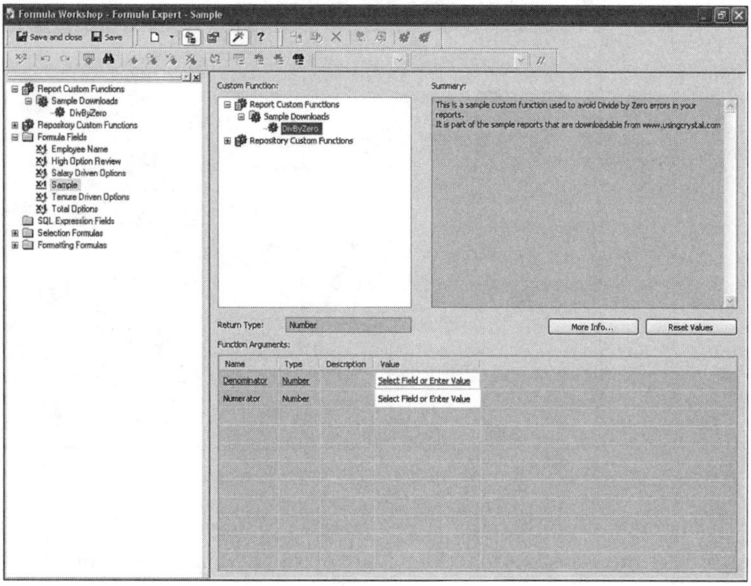

Figure 4.22
The Formula Expert
dialog enables rapid
creation of formulas
through a wizard-type
interface.

To use the Formula Expert, follow this simple three-step process:

1. Find the custom function that meets your formula requirements by searching through the Report and Repository Custom Function libraries. The supporting Help description and More Info button can aid in this search.

2. For each parameter of the selected function, select a field from your report data source or enter a constant.

3. Save the new formula using the Save button.

The created formula is now accessible through the Formula Editor and can be enhanced or edited with that tool.

USING THE FORMULA EXTRACTOR TO CREATE CUSTOM FUNCTIONS

The Formula Expert enables you to create formulas from existing custom functions. The Formula Extractor does the opposite: It enables you to create custom functions from previously created formulas. This functionality is accessible by creating a new custom report function and selecting the Use Extractor button. Figure 4.23 displays the Extract Custom Function from Formula dialog accessed when creating custom report functions.

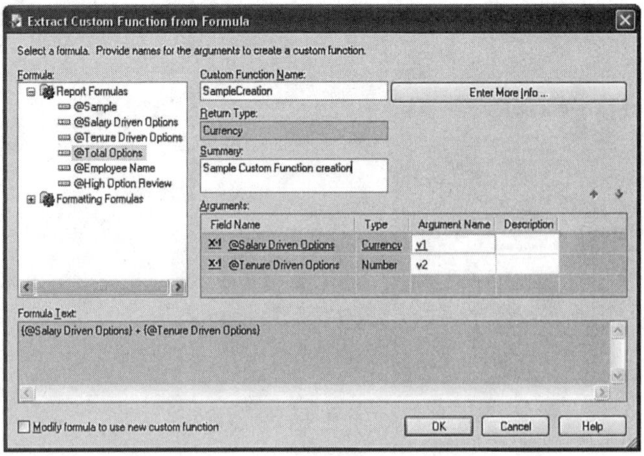

Figure 4.23
The Extract Custom Function from Formula dialog enables the creation of a custom function from an existing formula.

By using the Formula Extractor, it is possible to migrate existing formula logic from a formula field into a custom function. The appropriate part of the migrated formulas can subsequently be replaced with the new custom function and eventually be added to the Crystal Repository. To create a custom function from an existing formula using the Formula Extractor dialog, follow these steps:

1. In the Formula Workshop, create a new custom report function. Select the Formula Extractor by clicking on the Use Extractor button after you have ensured that the custom function name you select follows your personal or organization's standard naming convention.

2. Edit the default argument names (v1, v2, and so on) and descriptions that represent the required parameters for the new function. These argument names and descriptions should communicate the expected information to future users of the custom function. The importance of meaningful information here cannot be underestimated with respect to the future usefulness of the newly created custom function.

3. Add an appropriate summary description to the Summary window so that future report designers using this custom function will understand its proper use.

4. Click on the Modify Formula to Use New Function check box (in the lower-left area of the Extract Custom Function dialog) to place the new custom function into the formula on which you are basing it. This is not a mandatory step, but it is a nice feature that enables you to quickly take advantage of the reusability of your new custom function.

5. Click the Enter More Info button to add additional support information for the custom function. Figure 4.24 displays the More Info dialog.

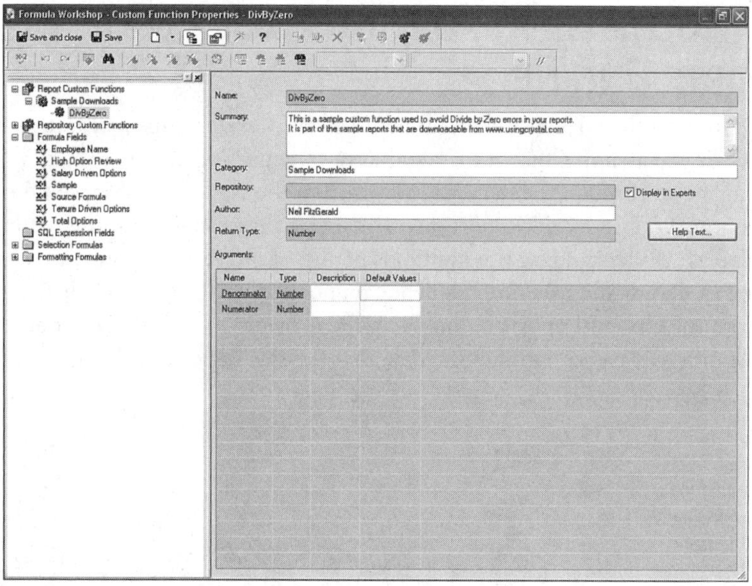

Figure 4.24
The Custom Function Enter More Info dialog enables the specification of supporting information for the newly created custom function.

6. Enter the custom function author (likely yourself) and custom function category information in their respective text boxes.

NOTE

> When entering a custom function category, it is possible to create it at more than one level of subfolder depth by using forward slashes in the Category text box. For example, by entering `MapleLeafBikes/HR`, the newly created formula will be added to the Custom Function library under the Maple Leaf Bikes category and the HR subfolder. By adding and maintaining your custom functions in a logical hierarchy, future users will find accessing them much easier.

7. Optionally, set default values for your custom functions arguments by clicking on the default value cells and filling in the Default Values dialog.

8. Add Help text describing the custom function by clicking on the Help Text button. Again, it is important to consider future report designers using this custom function when deciding on the detail that you should include in this description.

THE MULTIPASS REPORTING PROCESS OF THE CRYSTAL REPORTS ENGINE

Despite all the Crystal Reports functionality covered to this point, it would be understandable if you assumed that the Crystal Reports reporting engine provides all this power with a single pass through the data it retrieves from the database. That would be a faulty assumption, however: Crystal Reports actually uses a three-pass reporting methodology to generate reports. Understanding the multipass nature of the reporting engine can facilitate effective report design and expedite the debugging of potential reporting challenges. Figure 4.25 from the Crystal Reports online Help file provides a good starting point for understanding the different passes through the data that Crystal Reports makes and what is calculated on each pass.

Figure 4.25
Understanding the Crystal Reports multi-pass report engine flow can help in creating and debugging Crystal Reports.

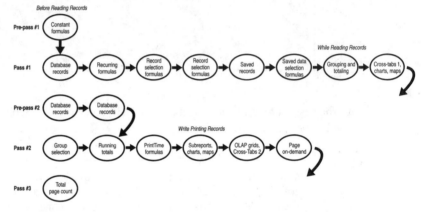

CRYSTAL REPORTS PROCESSING ENGINE—PRE-PASS #1

In the Pre-Pass phase of report creation, only constant formulas are processed. A constant formula example might be 1967*10. These formulas are evaluated at the beginning of the print generation process and are never evaluated again. This process is known as BeforeReadingRecords.

CRYSTAL REPORTS PROCESSING ENGINE—PASS #1

After the constant formulas have been processed, Crystal Reports begins reading the database records. During the record reading process, known as WhileReadingRecords, the following occurs:

- **Database connection and record retrieval**—If possible, record selection and sorting are pushed down to the database in this step.
- **Evaluates recurring formulas**—These formulas are those that contain database fields but do not contain references to subtotals or summary information. This evaluation time is referenced as WhileReadingRecords and can be specified within a formula.

Formulas that contain references to subtotals or summary information are processed in the second pass.

- **Local record selection applied**—If the record selection is too complex to be pushed down to the database, it is applied by Crystal Reports in this step. This is common where the record selection could not be specified in a proper SQL expression.

- **Sorting, grouping, and summarizing**—The data is sorted and, separated into groups, and then subtotals and summaries are calculated for each group.

- **Cross-tab, chart, and map generation**—Only cross-tabs, charts, and maps that are based entirely on database fields and recurring formulas are generated in pass #1.

- **Storage of saved data**—After the totaling process is complete, all the records and totals are stored in memory and to temporary files. Crystal Reports does not read the database again, but instead uses this saved data during all subsequent processing.

CRYSTAL REPORTS PROCESSING ENGINE—PRE-PASS #2

During Pre-Pass #2, groups are ordered in the report for top/bottom N or hierarchical grouping. The reporting engine looks at group instances from Pass 1 and takes the top N as appropriate, or it orders the groups based on the specified hierarchical group settings.

CRYSTAL REPORTS PROCESSING ENGINE—PASS #2

Crystal Reports moves through the saved data, if required, to complete any remaining operations and initiates printing of the records in this phase known as `WhilePrintingRecords`. During this phase, the following takes place:

- **Application of group selection formula**—If applicable.

- **Evaluates print-time formulas**—These formulas are those that contain any print-time formula functions such as `Previous()` or `Next()` or explicitly use the `WhilePrintingRecords` function within the formula.

- **Running totals calculations**—If applicable.

- **Charts, maps, cross-tabs, and OLAP grids**—Cross-tabs, charts, and maps that include running totals or print-time formulas, and charts that are based on cross-tabs or OLAP grids are generated.

- **Subreports**—All in-place subreports are calculated during pass #2. When you're using variables within subreports and expecting certain behavior in the main report based on these shared variables, keep in mind when they are processed relative to everything else in the main report.

CAUTION

Subtotals, grand totals, and summaries might appear incorrectly if the report has a group selection formula. This occurs because the grand totals and summaries are calculated during pass #1, but the group selection formula filters the data again in pass #2. Running total fields or formula fields with variables can be used instead of summaries to total data successfully with group selection formulas.

CRYSTAL REPORTS PROCESSING ENGINE—PASS #3

In the third and final pass, the total page count is determined. This applies to reports that use the total page count, or Page N of M special fields.

Understanding the multipass reporting paths of the Crystal Reports engine helps in the general development and debugging of your production reports. Additional leveraging of the built-in formula functions discussed previously (`BeforeReadingRecords`, `WhileReadingRecords`, and `WhilePrintingRecords`) in combination with the `EvaluateAfter()` function enable you to design more flexible reports and formulas. These functions also enable you to leverage advanced variable usage and successful sharing among subreports.

TROUBLESHOOTING

ADDING A CUSTOM FUNCTION

I cannot add a custom function directly into the central Repository.

Custom functions cannot be directly added into the central Repository. When you add a custom function to the central Repository for other report developers to use, you must first create it locally as a report custom function and only then can it be added to the central Repository. With version XI (and 10) of the Enterprise suite of products, you must also be licensed for either BusinessObjects Enterprise or Crystal Reports Server to leverage a central Repository.

CONVERTING A NUMBER TO A STRING WITH NO DECIMAL PLACES

When trying to convert an existing database numeric field to a string, my result strings are always suffixed with two zeros.

When converting an integer to a string field using the `CStr()` function, the default result will be automatically set to have two decimal places (for instance, 555.00). This can be eliminated through the addition of a second argument in the function that explicitly specifies the number of decimal places to be set to zero. For example, `CStr({Purchases.Units in Stock},0)` would work.

CRYSTAL REPORTS IN THE REAL WORLD—CUSTOM FUNCTIONS

Some examples of custom functions include handling divide-by-zero errors and handling multilanguage text. Both of these examples are described in this section. A common reason for divide-by-zero errors is simply that a field might not be populated. If a given field has not been populated but it is used in the report, Crystal Reports converts it to a default value. Unless modified, the default value for a numeric field that returns NULL is 0. This means that if there is a formula calculating percent of capacity (Current_Amount/Max_Amount) but the item is new and therefore no max amount has been set, then the Max_Amount field in the database is likely blank. When the preceding formula is applied to the database fields, then the result will be a divide by zero error and the report will fail. `Current_Amount/Max_Amount` would resolve to some real value divided by `NULL`, the `NULL` would be converted to the default value of `0`, and the result would be some number divided by zero—and a divide-by-zero error be the result. To avoid this, create a custom function to handle all division. The custom function simply checks for a denominator of 0 and handles it appropriately.

To create the custom function, follow these steps:

1. Open the sample report Chap4Formulas.rpt or the report you have created through this chapter. From the Field Explorer, select Formula Fields and click New. Type in a name for the formula such as **Source Formula** and click Use Editor.

2. When the Formula Workshop window opens, enter the following formula:
```
If {Employee.Supervisor ID} = 0 Then
    0
Else
    {Employee.Employee ID}/{Employee.Supervisor ID};
```

> **NOTE**
>
> Although it seems (and is) odd to build a formula using ID fields in a calculation, what is important is the field types. The fields are used to build the custom function based on their data types rather than actual content. The previous fields are abstracted to simply numeric fields named v1 and v2.

3. With the Formula Workshop still open, mouse over the New button near the top of the window and click the down arrow. From the list, choose Custom Function, enter the name **DivBy0**, and click on the User Extractor button.

4. When the Extract Custom Function from Formula window opens, select the @Source Formula item from the list of formulas. Rename the arguments from v1 and v2 to Denominator and Numerator, respectively (see Figure 4.26).

5. Click on OK to close the window, and the function is now part of the report. If you are using BusinessObjects Enterprise (or Crystal Reports Server), you could now right-click on the function name and choose Add to Repository. When prompted, enter the logon information for your BusinessObjects Enterprise system, and the custom function will be added to the Enterprise Repository making it available to all the users who have access to the repository and enabling all report writers to avoid fatal divide-by-zero errors in their reports.

6. Click on Save and Close (see Figure 4.27) .

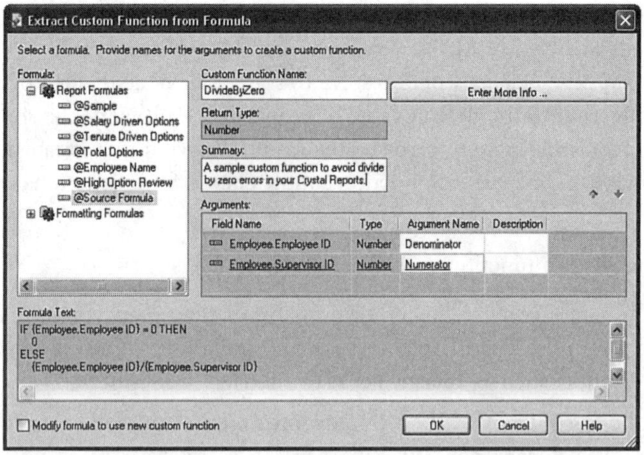

Figure 4.26
Using the Custom Function Extractor to create a custom function from a formula.

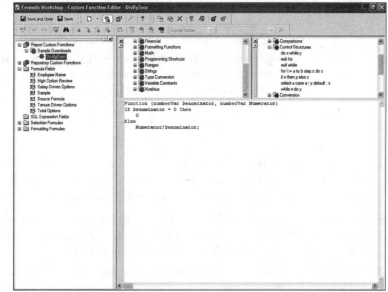

Figure 4.27
The custom function is now part of the repository, making it available to users who have appropriate rights.

Another example of a custom function might be how to handle some standard text options. For example, it might be useful to have a parameter drive the column header for a field.

1. Keep the report open. From the Field Explorer, create a new parameter named Language with the potential input values of English, French, or Italian (described in Chapter 5, "Implementing Parameters for Dynamic Reporting"). Also add a new formula named `Country Source` (described previously). Add the following formula code:

```
If {?Language} = "English" Then
    "Country"
```

```
Else If {?Language} = "French" Then
    "Pays"
Else If {?Language} = "Italian" Then
    "Paese";
```

2. Repeat steps 3, 4, 5, and 6 from the preceding example to create a new custom function called Country extracted from the Country Source formula.

3. To use the new custom function, create a new formula named Country. From the list of functions, expand the custom functions and double-click the Country formula. The function takes one argument; pass in the Language parameter (see Figure 4.28).

Figure 4.28
The custom function accepting the Language parameter. This parameter determines what the function does.

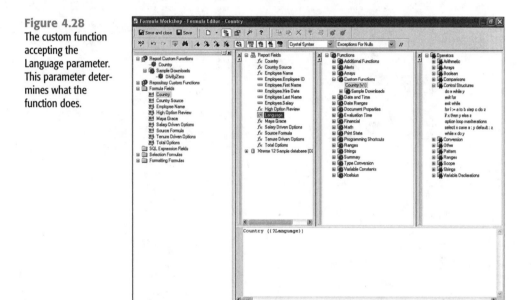

4. Click on Save and Close. If prompted, enter the text **English**. Place the new formula in the group header alongside the other column headers and add the Country field from the Employee Addresses table below it on the detail line. You will also need to delete the default Country header that will be added when you add the field.

5. Save the report as Chap4FormulaswithCustom.rpt. Refresh the report, passing in "English," "French," and "Italian" to see the effect (see Figure 4.29).

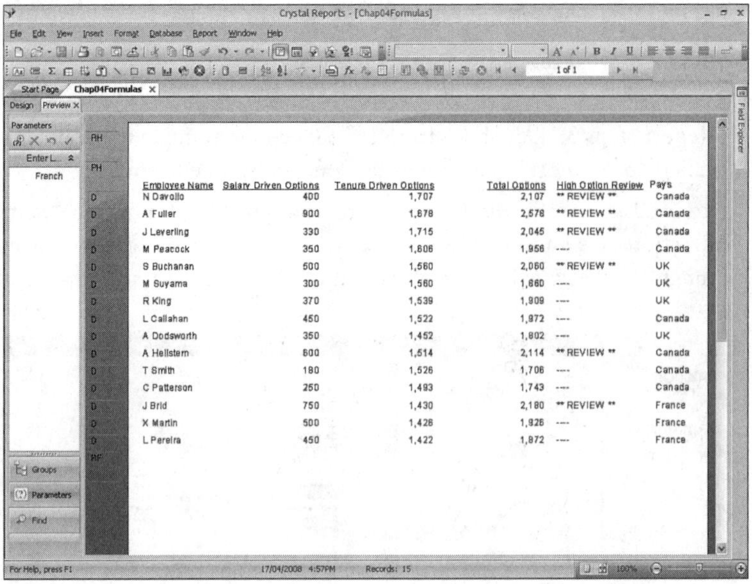

Figure 4.29
The field header changes to display the Country heading in appropriate languages.

CHAPTER **5**

IMPLEMENTING PARAMETERS FOR DYNAMIC REPORTING

In this chapter

INTRODUCTION

A common goal of report design is providing a single report that can service very specific reporting requirements and accommodate a large audience of business users. Parameter fields enable you to satisfy this requirement and provide three primary benefits:

- **Additional level of interactivity for business users when viewing reports**—A marketing report can prompt a business user for a specific brand or product line she wants to analyze.

- **Ability to segment reports in many different ways to reduce the number of reports necessary to service the demands of the business users**—A sales report can be segmented by district to service the needs of all district-level business users with one report.

- **Greater control over the report query for administrators by filtering the report results to include only the selected parameter value(s)**—A sales report can be filtered to include only data for the appropriate district. This also includes the capability to constrain the report query to avoid including excess or sensitive data.

In this chapter, you take a closer look at using parameters in your reports as well as how to create and implement parameter fields. Like many Crystal Reports application features, working with report parameters is very logical, but understanding the underlying mechanics facilitates the creation of effective reports.

This chapter covers the following topics:

- Understanding the value of parameters
- Creating and implementing parameter fields
- Creating and implementing dynamic and cascading parameter fields
- Using parameters with record selections

UNDERSTANDING THE VALUE OF PARAMETERS

By using parameter fields that enable business users to select from a list of one or more parameter field values (such as district, country, or account type), you can make reports more valuable for business users while limiting the volume of data that the report retrieves. For example, a sales report is likely to be more valuable for a sales professional if it allows him to select his specific territory or district, and the report runs more efficiently because it retrieves only the desired data and not an unnecessarily large data set. Parameter fields can prompt users for a variety of information that you can use in a number of flexible ways within reports. Good examples include controlling the sort order, grouping order, record selection (filter), report title and descriptions, report language, alert thresholds, formula inputs, N value for a Top/Bottom N sorting/grouping, and so on.

Parameter fields prompt report users to enter information by presenting a question that the user must answer before executing the report. The information that the user enters determines what appears in the resulting report and that report's formatting and presentation.

One of the greatest benefits of parameter fields for report designers is the opportunity to have a single report service a large audience while also empowering the users to personalize the information they are viewing within the report. Designers can use parameter fields in coordination with record selections to segment a single report in many different ways. Parameter values that business users enter can also be used within record selection formulas to determine what data is retrieved from the database.

TIP

> New since version XI is the ability to set the N value of a Top/Bottom N grouping or sorting through a formula. Combining this new functionality with a user-driven parameter enables end users to drive the value of N in a given report. You do so by creating the parameter and then selecting it as the value of the formula for the selected Top/Bottom N formula.

For example, consider a World Sales Report for a large organization. This report could potentially include a tremendous amount of data. Not only is the report itself large, but also many of the business users are not concerned with the entire worldwide scope of the sales data. Rather than allow each salesperson to generate the report to include worldwide data, you can include a parameter dialog that asks the salesperson to select from a list of available countries, as shown in Figure 5.1. The report would return the results for only the specified countries. By using a parameter field to enable the salespeople to select from a list of countries, the report becomes more valuable for the business users and limits the scope of the query by using the selected parameter value(s) to filter the report and reduce the volume of data retrieved.

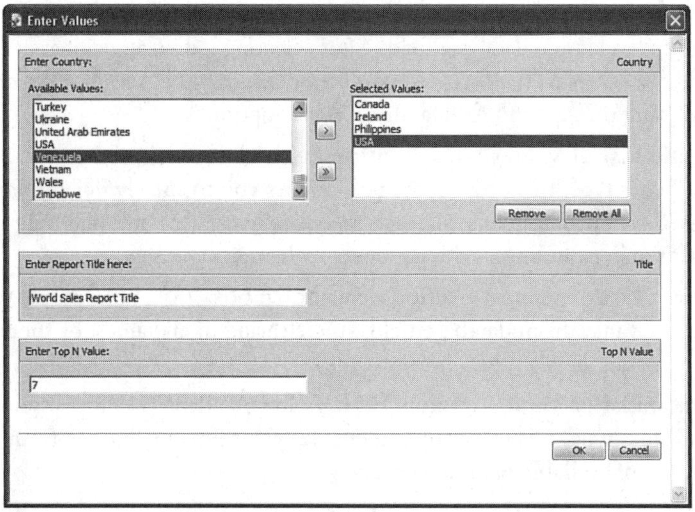

Figure 5.1
Prompts enable business users to select values to populate the parameter field.

CREATING AND IMPLEMENTING PARAMETERS FIELDS

The process of using parameter fields in reports includes two distinct steps:

1. Creation of the parameter field
2. Implementation of the parameter field into the report

The remainder of this chapter uses the example mentioned earlier, the World Sales Report, to create and implement parameter fields into a report. The World Sales Report is one of the many sample reports provided by Business Objects online at http://businessobjects.com/product/catalog/crystalreports/samplereports.asp.

REVIEWING PARAMETER FIELD PROPERTIES

Before you learn how to create and implement parameter fields, it is useful to understand a few common input options and properties associated with creating parameter fields. The Create New Parameter dialog presents each of the following input properties, shown in Figure 5.2:

- **Name**—A logical name for the parameter field.
- **Value Type**—A list of available field types that correspond to how you want to use the parameter field within the report, including String (the default option), Boolean, Currency, Date, Date Time, Number, and Time.
- **List of Values Type**—New since XI, you have the option of sourcing a list of values for the involved parameter from either a static list that does not change over time or a dynamic list that is live or updates regularly. The dynamic list of values can cascade and include multiple levels of selection with increasing granularity and filtering as you move through the levels. For instance, selecting a Country leads to a filtered list of states/provinces for end user selection at the next level and so on.
- **Static List of Values—Value field**—Available when you select Static as the List of Values type, this drop-down box enables you to specify the list of available parameter values based on a database field. After selecting a desired database field here, you can add the values to the involved parameter through the Action drop-down list and by selecting the Append All Database Values option.
- **Static List of Values—Description field**—Available when you select Static as the List of Values type, this drop-down box enables you to specify default parameter descriptions based on a database field. Designers typically use this optional field to facilitate the end user's understanding of the parameter selection.
- **Static List of Values—Action drop-down box**—A list of options that enable the insertion of values from database fields, the clearing of all values, or the import and export of the existing list of values into text files.
- **Static List of Values—Value Table field**—Available when you select Static as the List of Values type, this table column enables you to manually specify an entry for a value in the list of available parameter values.

- **Static List of Values—Description Table field**—Available when you select Static as the List of Values type, this table column enables you to manually specify an entry for a description in the list of available parameter descriptions.

- **Dynamic List of Values—Prompt Group Text**—An optional title that displays to end users when they are prompted for the list of dynamic and potentially cascading report parameters. Designers typically use this only when utilizing cascading parameters—it's redundant otherwise.

- **Dynamic List of Values—Choose a Data Source**—A user selection enabling either creation of a new set of dynamic parameters or use of an existing list of values. The existing option displays only if existing lists of values are present in the report or the report attaches to a BusinessObjects Enterprise repository that has them.

- **Dynamic List of Values—Value Table field**—Available when you select Dynamic as the List of Values type, this table column enables you to specify the list of available parameter values based on a database field.

- **Dynamic List of Values—Description Table field**—Available when you select Dynamic as the List of Values type, this table column enables you to specify the list of available parameter descriptions based on a database field.

- **Dynamic List of Values—Parameter Table field**—Available when you select Dynamic as the List of Values type, this table column enables you to create a parameter in the underlying report that is automatically used in the creation of the involved cascading parameter.

- **Show on (Viewer) Panel**—New in version 2008, this option allows the report designer to display (or not) the involved parameter on the end user's report viewer panel. There are three options: Do Not Show, Editable, and Read-Only. The Editable option enables the end user to change this parameter in the actual report viewer, whereas the Read-Only option provides another display mechanism.

- **Prompt Text**—A statement or question presented to the business user within the report prompt dialog for the parameter field.

- **Prompt with Description Only**—A Boolean option that allows the report designer to prompt end users with only a parameter value description (if set to `True`) or both the parameter value and description (if set to `False`).

- **Optional Prompt**—New in version 2008, this Boolean option allows report designers to make specific parameters optional for report viewers. When designing reports with optional parameters, it is important to be careful that the report can operate successfully whether or not the involved parameter is entered.

- **Sort Order**—Enables specification of the sort order and the sort field that the parameter values sort on.

- **Default Value**—An option that allows the report designer to set a default value for the static list of values.

5

- **Allow Custom Values**—If the designer sets this option to True, the business user can enter a custom parameter value. If the designer sets this option to False, end users can only select predetermined parameter values.

- **Allow Multiple Values**—Enables the business user to enter more than a single value for the parameter field.

- **Allow Discrete Values**—Enables the business user to enter only a single value for the parameter field.

- **Allow Range Values**—Enables the business user to specify a range, using start and end values, for the parameter field.

- **Length Limit**—The minimum and maximum length limits for the parameter field.

- **Edit Mask**—Used to enter an edit mask for String data types rather than specifying a range of values. The edit mask can be any of a set of masking characters used to restrict the values you can enter as parameter values. (The edit mask also limits the values you can enter as default prompting values.) Table 5.1 provides a listing of the masking characters and instructions on how to use them.

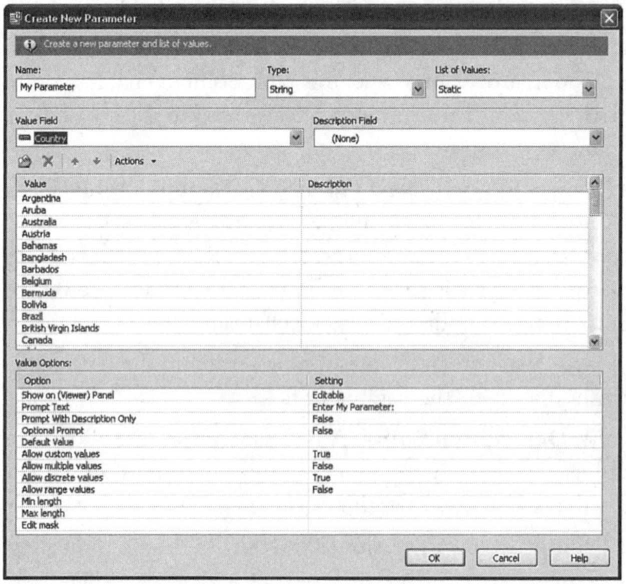

Figure 5.2
The parameter field options and properties presented within the Create New Parameter dialog.

5

TABLE 5.1   EDIT MASK CHARACTERS

Mask Character	Mask Description
A	Requires entry of an alphanumeric character for its place in the parameter value.
a	Enables an alphanumeric character but does not require the entry of a character for its place in the parameter value.

Mask Character	Mask Description
TABLE 5.1	CONTINUED
0	Requires a digit (0 to 9) for its place in the parameter value.
9	Enables a digit or a space but does not require such an entry for its place in the parameter value.
#	Enables a digit, space, or plus/minus sign but does not require such an entry for its place in the parameter value.
L	Requires a letter (A to Z) for its place in the parameter value.
?	Enables a letter but does not require such an entry for its place in the parameter value.
&	Requires a character or space for its place in the parameter value.
C	Enables any character or space but does not require such an entry for its place in the parameter value.
. , : ; - /	Inserting separator characters into an edit mask is akin to hard-coding the (separator characters) formatting for the parameter field. When you place the field on the report, the separator character appears in the field object frame, like this: L0L-0L0. This example depicts an edit mask for a Canadian Postal Code (such as M2M-2L5) with a forced display dash.
< or >	Forces subsequent characters in the parameter to be converted to lowercase (<) or uppercase (>).
\	Forces the subsequent character to display as a literal.
Password	Enables the setting of the edit mask to "Password" so that subsequent conditional formulas can specify certain sections of the report to become visible only after the entry of certain user passwords.

When using optional parameters, it is important to provide the end user with some guidance that a parameter is optional. You can add that information to the parameter prompting text or within the report's description information, if you're using Crystal Reports Server (or BusinessObjects Enterprise or Edge). Another important item to keep in mind when using optional parameters is that, although the Select Expert automatically prefixes the optional parameter with the HasValue() function, this does not happen by default in the Formula Workshop. Therefore, it is critical to manually insert the HasValue() function whenever you reference an optional parameter directly within the Formula Workshop. If you do not do this, the report engine generates an error when it comes across an optional parameter with no value.

Now that you understand the primary parameter field properties, you can use them while creating parameters for a World Sales Report, as mentioned earlier in the chapter.

5

CREATING PARAMETER FIELDS

The first step in using a parameter within a report is to create the actual parameter field and define the primary properties associated with it. In the following exercises, you use the Field Explorer dialog to create three new parameter fields for the World Sales Report:

- A manual text entry field to use as the report's title
- A database field that prompts the business user to select one or more countries and uses this selection to filter the data returned for the report
- A Top N parameter field that specifies how many countries display in the edited World Sales report

To begin your exercise, open the World Sales sample report within the Crystal Reports designer. You can quickly access all the sample reports from the 'Sample Reports + Databases' link on the Crystal Reports start page. Alternatively, you can download the sample reports from Business Objects at http://businessobjects.com/product/catalog/crystalreports/samplereports.asp. The World Sales report will be located within the Demonstration Reports category at this link. After you open the World Sales report, you can begin the steps necessary to create the parameter field objects in the following way:

1. Remove the existing report title text object. After you open the World Sales Report, navigate to the Design tab view. Highlight and delete the text object currently used as the report's title, *World Sales Report*, located in the Report Header A section. Your parameter field, which you create later, will populate the report title.

2. Open the Field Explorer dialog by either clicking the appropriate toolbar button or using the View menu.

3. Open the Create Parameter Field dialog. To do this, right-click on Parameter Fields within the Field Explorer and either select New from the pop-up menu or click on the New button at the top of the Field Explorer.

> **NOTE**
>
> In addition to using the right-click menu to create a new parameter field, you can use the Field Explorer's toolbar commands to create, edit, rename, and delete parameter fields. The operations available on this toolbar depend on what you selected in the Field Explorer dialog. New since XI is the ability to use the Parameter Order dialog in Figure 5.3 to sort the parameter display order. You access this option from the right-click menu on the Parameter sections of the Field Explorer.

4. You first create a manual text-entry parameter field to enable the business user to define a title to display on the report. Within the Create Parameter Field dialog, enter `Title` in the Name property, ensure that String is the selected Value Type, and provide a meaningful prompting text so that the business user understands the use of the entered value, such as `Enter a title to be used for this report`.

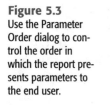

Figure 5.3
Use the Parameter Order dialog to control the order in which the report presents parameters to the end user.

5. Ensure that both the Allow Discrete Values and the Allow Custom Values properties under the Options area are set to `True`, and click on OK to return to the Field Explorer.

6. You should now see the `Title` parameter field listed under Parameter Fields in the Field Explorer. Insert this `Title` field into the report's Report Heading either by using the right-click menu option or by dragging and dropping the field onto the report. Figure 5.4 shows the results.

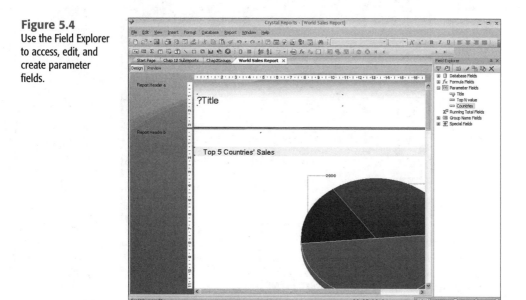

Figure 5.4
Use the Field Explorer to access, edit, and create parameter fields.

7. You now create two more parameter fields to use later in the chapter when discussing how to use parameter fields in coordination with record and Top N selections. After you learn this technique, you can enable your end users to select filters on the involved report data according to their selected parameter values.

8. Open the Create Parameter Field dialog. To do this, highlight the Parameter Fields item and click the New toolbar button inside the Field Explorer dialog.

9. Define the key properties for the second parameter object. Within the Create Parameter Field dialog, enter `Top N Value` in the Name property, select Number as the parameter Type, and provide a meaningful prompting text, such as `Please select the top N selling countries to display on this report`, so that the business user understands the use of the entered value.

10. Ensure that both the Allow Custom Values and Allow Discrete Values properties in the Value Options area are set to `True`. The Allow Multiple Values property should be set to `False`. Click OK to save the parameter and return to the Field Explorer.

11. Create another parameter called Countries (or Country). Within the Create Parameter Field dialog, enter `Countries (or Country)` in the Name property and provide a meaningful prompting text, such as `Please select one or more countries for this report`, so that the business user understands the use of the entered value.

12. Ensure that both the Allow Multiple Values and Allow Discrete Values properties under the Value Options area are set to `True`, as shown in Figure 5.5.

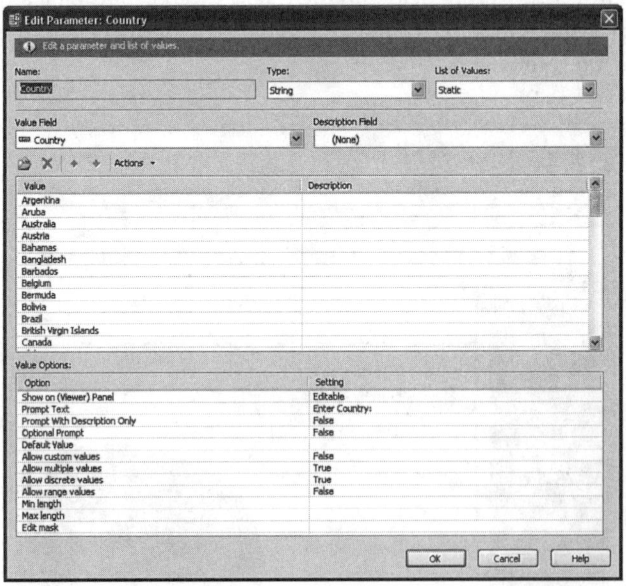

Figure 5.5
Use the Edit Parameter dialog to create and edit parameter fields.

SETTING DEFAULT VALUES FOR PARAMETER FIELDS

You now want to define the Countries parameter field to include all database values within the Country field of the Customer table. You can accomplish this by mapping the parameter field to this database field and quickly importing the values. This enables the business user of the report to select one or more country values from the available list.

When setting default parameter values for a static parameter, Crystal Reports can read a list of default values from the database, or the designer can enter them manually to provide the business user with a list of available values from which to choose. With static parameters,

Crystal Reports enables you to define the default values list when you are designing reports. No direct database connection exists to populate the prompting parameter field list when the business users run the report. New since XI, Crystal Reports enables the creation of dynamic parameters that access an underlying database in real-time when a business user is running the report. You learn more about these later in this chapter. For now, populate the static Country parameter by following these steps:

1. Access the Edit Parameter dialog if you closed it by highlighting the Countries parameter and clicking on the Edit toolbar button. In the Value Field drop-down list, select the Country field from the Customer table and then select the Append All Database Values action from the Actions drop-down list. Crystal Reports adds all countries listed in the Customer table as parameter options for this parameter, as shown in Figure 5.6.

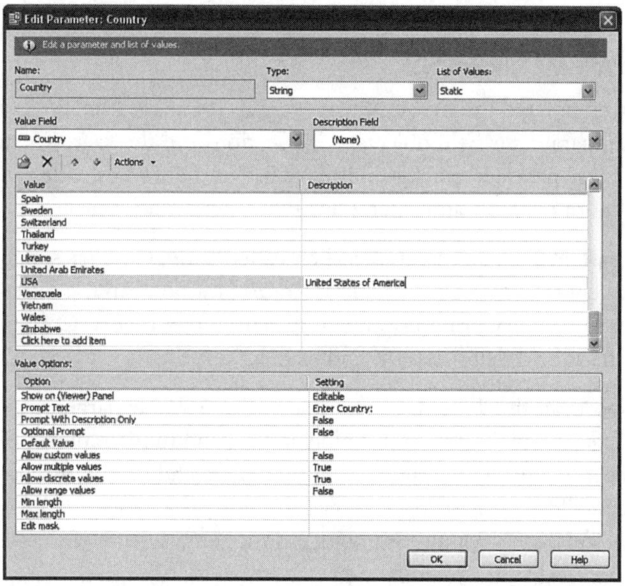

Figure 5.6
The Edit Parameter dialog enables you to define the default selection values for parameter fields.

Continuing the process, you now add a sample description to the default values that you added to the parameter field.

2. Locate and highlight the USA value in the Value list. Click in the Description field located just beside the Value field displaying USA.

3. Add **United States of America** as the description for USA, and click on OK to close the Edit Parameter dialog. If you want, repeat this step for any additional default values.

4. Click on OK to return to the Field Explorer. You should now see the Countries and Top N Values parameter fields listed under Parameter Fields in the Field Explorer. These parameters are now part of your Crystal Report, but they do not become functional filters until you attach them to record selection criteria, as described in the next section.

TIP

There are a few considerations to keep in mind when working with parameter fields, such as

- Any parameter field prompting text more than one line in length automatically word wraps.

- The creation of a manual pick list enables the business user to select parameter field values from drop-down boxes instead of needing to enter them manually. You can export, and subsequently import, manually created lists into other reports as a means of list reuse.

- You do not have to place a parameter field in a report to use it in a record or group selection formula. You can create the parameter field and then enter it in your formula as you would any other field.

IMPLEMENTING PARAMETER FIELDS

You have now completed the first task necessary to use parameter fields within a report: creating the actual parameter field objects. This section, and the exercises included here, discuss how to apply these parameter fields and make use of them to provide the business user of the report with a more dynamic and interactive reporting experience.

First add the parameter fields created earlier, called Title, Countries, and Top N Value, for display on the report. This example demonstrates how you can use different parameter fields to add useful commentary or descriptive information to a report. Continue working with the same report, the World Sales Report, and follow these steps:

1. Add and position the Title, Countries, and Top N Value parameter objects onto the report. Open the Field Explorer dialog and expand the Parameter Fields list. Click on the Title parameter field, drag it onto the report, and drop it into the upper-left corner of the Report Header A section, shown in Figure 5.7 in a size 20 Arial font. Place the Countries and Top N Value parameters in the same section with size 10 Arial font.

2. Preview the report. To see the use of this parameter within the generation of the report, run the report by clicking on the Refresh toolbar button (represented by the two blue arrows indicating a counter clockwise rotation) or pressing F5 or via the Refresh Report Data option on the Report Menu. As shown in Figure 5.8, the report prompts the business user to enter a value to use as the report's title.

NOTE

If you have already run the report at least once and then select to refresh the report, Crystal Reports presents the Refresh Report Data dialog that asks you to select one of the two following options:

- Use Current Parameter Values

- Prompt for New Parameter Values

To enter or select new values for any existing parameter fields, select the Prompt for New Parameter Values option.

Figure 5.7
Drag and drop the parameter fields into the left side of the Report Header A section.

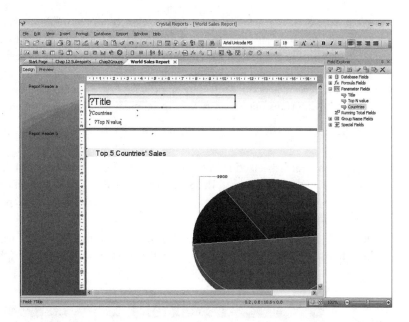

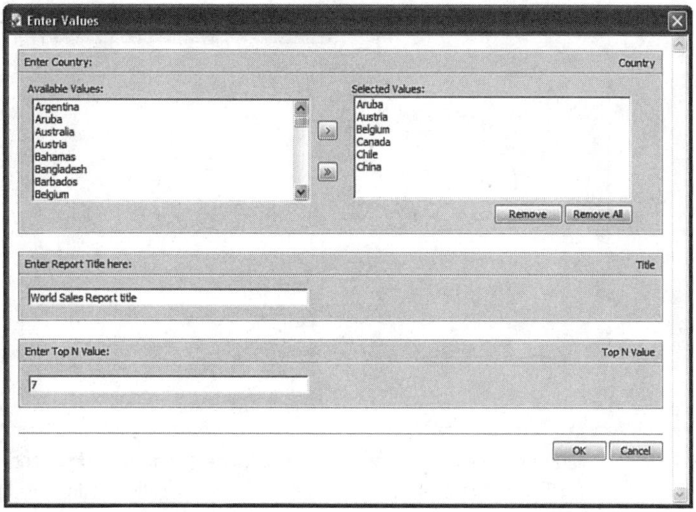

Figure 5.8
Parameter fields offer a means to add additional interactivity for the business users within the report.

USING PARAMETERS WITH RECORD SELECTIONS

Now that you have completed the task of adding a parameter field onto a report, you learn how to use a parameter field to filter the data retrieved by a report. You can use parameter values that business users enter within record selection formulas to determine the data retrieved from the database.

In the following exercises, use the same World Sales Report to implement the Countries parameter field (created earlier in the chapter) to filter the report results by including the parameter field within a record selection definition (using the Select Expert dialog). In this case, you enable the business user of the report to select one or more country values to be included in the record selection, thus filtering the report results to include only the desired data. The following steps demonstrate how to segment a single report many different ways:

1. Open the Select Expert dialog by clicking the Report menu and choosing Select Expert, Record.

2. Create a new record selection definition. To create a new record selection definition, click on the <New> tab within the Select Expert dialog. This opens the Choose Field dialog. Choose Customer.Country from the Report Fields list and then click on OK to return to the Select Expert dialog.

3. Define the selection formula Select Is Equal To from the drop-down list on the left, and then choose the {?Countries} option from the drop-down list on the right, as shown in Figure 5.9.

Figure 5.9
You can quickly add parameter fields to record selection formulas via the Select Expert dialog.

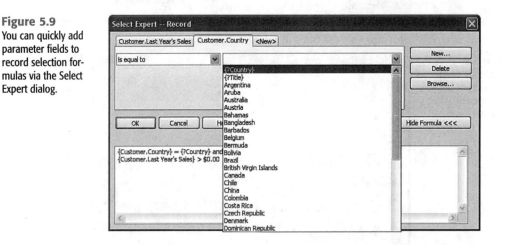

5

4. Preview the report. To view the use of the parameter within the generation of the report, run the report by clicking on the Refresh toolbar button (or pressing F5). As shown in Figures 5.10 and 5.11, the report prompts the business user to select from a list of country values that filter the data retrieved by the report and present only the requested values in the report.

Figure 5.10
Business users can select one or more countries to include in the report results.

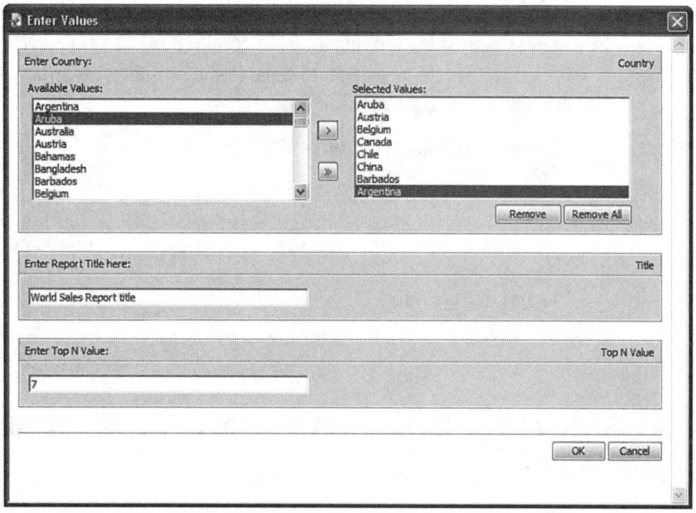

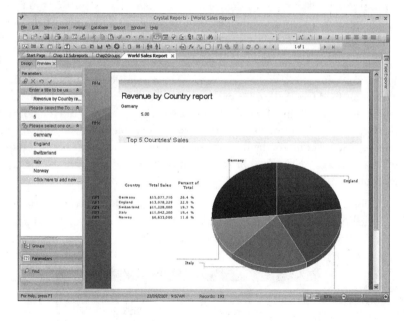

Figure 5.11
Based on the selected parameter field values, the report results display only the desired data.

NOTE

As Figure 5.11 highlights, when you add a multivalue parameter (Countries in this case) to a report, only the first value displays. This is because the multiple values of the parameter are stored in an array, and by default the parameter field shows only the first element of the array. To show different values, you can either create a formula and use the Join() function or use the parameter and an index (for instance, {?Countries}[2] to show the second country in the list). Using the Join() function, you could simply specify in your string formula a `Join({Countries},",")` command, and the individual countries would be listed and separated by commas. To show all the values, you could also create a formula like this:

```
Local StringVar CountryString := "";
Local NumberVar i;
For i := 1 To Ubound({?Countries}) Do
(
    CountryString := CountryString + ", " + {?Countries}[i]
);
CountryString
```

USING PARAMETERS WITH TOP/BOTTOM N GROUP SELECTIONS

New since version XI, you can use a parameter to dynamically affect the value of a top or bottom group selection (for instance, top five countries for sales or top five selling products). You have already completed the task of implementing a parameter field called Top N Value within this chapter's sample report. Now you learn how you can use this parameter field to filter the data retrieved by a report.

In the following steps, you use the same World Sales Report to implement the Top N Values parameter field (created earlier in the chapter) to filter the report results by including the parameter field within a formula definition that specifies the Top (or Bottom) N value (using the Group Sort Expert dialog). In this case, you enable the business user of the report to select a value that filters the report results to include only the specified number of top-selling countries' data. The following steps demonstrate how this single report can display multiple Top/Bottom N views:

1. Open the Group Sort Expert dialog displayed in Figure 5.12 by clicking on the Report menu and choosing Group Sort Expert or using the Group Sort Expert toolbar button. Ensure that you are on the Country Group tab.

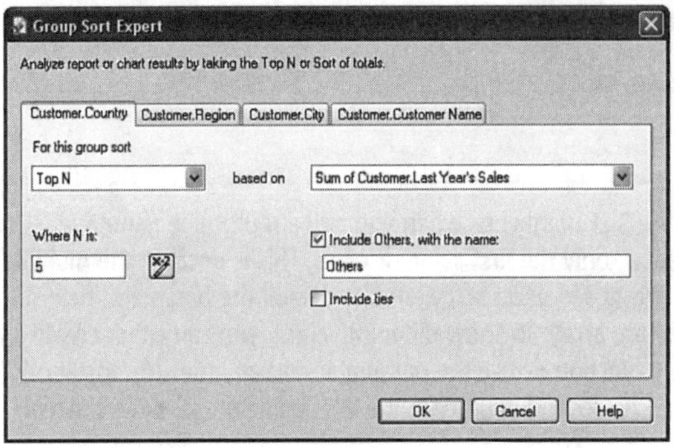

Figure 5.12
The Group Sort Expert enables specification of a dynamic Top/Bottom N value through the X+2 button.

2. Ensure that the Top N sorting order is selected in the first drop-down box and it is based on the Sum of Last Year's Sales. Click on the X+2 button beside the Top N value box. This brings up the Formula Workshop where you add the {?Top N Value} parameter field to the formula. You have now connected the selected number of top-selling countries to display in the report to the N value specified by the end user through the Top N Value parameter.

3. Change the value of the various parameters and refresh the report a few times to see the impact of an end user changing just these three parameters.

NOTE

After creating the parameters and implementing them into a report, no extra effort is required for parameters to work within Crystal Reports Server and the BusinessObjects Enterprise solution also. See www.usingcrystal.com for some additional chapters from previous books on BusinessObjects Enterprise, or view updated information at www.businessobjects.com.

CREATING AND IMPLEMENTING DYNAMIC AND CASCADING PARAMETERS

New since version XI, Crystal Reports now provides the ability to base report parameters on dynamic values derived directly from a database or from the BusinessObjects Enterprise repository (if using BusinessObjects Enterprise, Edge, Crystal Decisions, or Crystal Reports Server). This new functionality enables end users to select from the most recent list of elements dynamically retrieved from the database at runtime.

An additional new powerful feature provided since version XI is the ability to link dynamic parameters in a cascading manner. Cascading parameters enable end users to select parameter values by entering information at multiple levels, with all levels leading to the application of dynamic filters to all subsequent level parameters. The most common example of this is filtering a City parameter based on the linked Country parameter, as described earlier in the chapter. Specifically, if Canada is the only country selected, only cities in Canada are available for selection in the linked City parameter. Dynamic, cascading parameters are set through the same Create Parameter dialog used for static parameters.

The following steps take you through a practical example of the creation and implementation of a dynamic, cascading set of prompts:

1. Open the sample report that you previously created in this chapter. Remove the Country record selection and the Top N Value formula, delete the existing Countries parameter, and save this as a new report with a name of your liking.

2. Create a new parameter called Cities, of type String, and select the Dynamic List of Values type.

3. Ensure that the New radio button is active, and click on the Value field of the parameters table. Ensuring the New radio button is selected, click on the Value field of the parameters table and you are prompted with a drop-down list box where the Country field from the Customer table is selected.

4. Ensure that the Allows Multiple Values property is set to True. You have now created Country as the highest level parameter of this group.

5. Now click on the Value field in the next row of the parameters table and you are prompted with a drop-down list from which you select the City field from the Customer table. Ensure that the Allows Multiple Values property is set to True. You have now created City as the second and currently lowest level parameter of this group.

6. To complete the parameter creation process, click on the parameter fields for each of the Country and City rows in the parameter table. The prompting text of `Click to Create a Parameter` changes to the specific parameter name consisting of the top-level parameter name suffixed by the involved field name. Figure 5.13 highlights what this should look like. Click on OK.

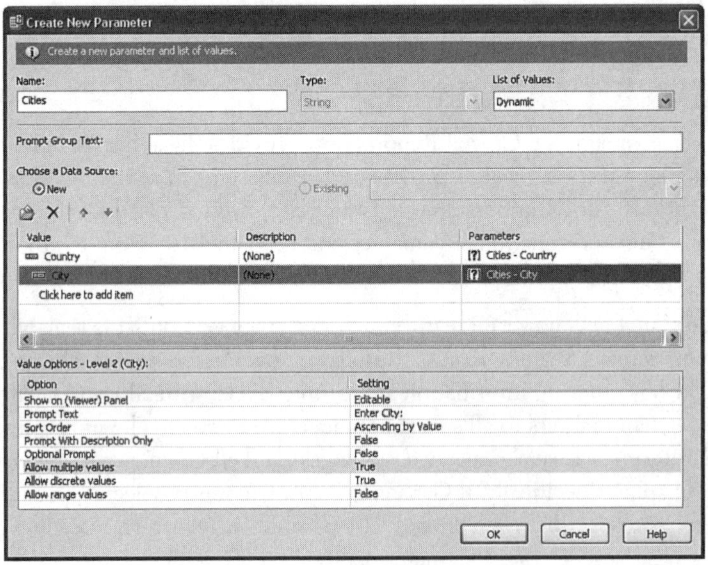

Figure 5.13
The Create New Parameter dialog enables rapid creation of dynamic and cascading parameters.

7. Now add a new record selection through the Record Select Expert that filters the report where the City field from the Customer table is equal to the newly created parameter {?Cities – City}.

8. Finally, refresh the report, and you receive the parameter selection screen shown in Figure 5.14. As you add countries to the list of countries selected in the Cities parameter group, the list of available cities in the City parameter dynamically filters. After testing the filtering process, select USA, Canada, and Ireland as countries with only Las Vegas, Philadelphia, Vancouver, Toronto, and Dublin as selected cities. Click on OK, and your report resembles the one in Figure 5.15.

Figure 5.14
The dynamic and cascading parameter feature enables increased productivity in report design and a better end user experience.

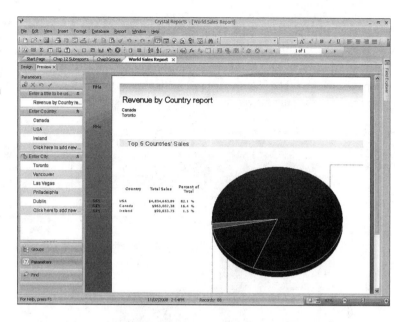

Figure 5.15
The results of a dynamic and cascading parameter–driven World Sales Report.

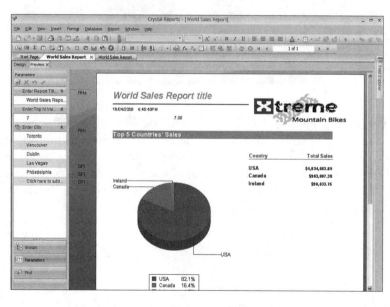

This new powerful cascading parameter feature enables increased end user productivity through reduced and focused selection sets. When you design reports, give careful consideration to use of these dynamic and cascading parameters versus the static parameters. Dynamic parameters are ideal for data sets that change frequently. Static parameters are best when the involved list of values does not change often because no additional database hits are required.

USING THE PARAMETER PANEL IN THE PREVIEW TAB

New to version 2008, a Parameters panel resides in the Preview tab of the Crystal Reports Designer. Figure 5.16 highlights the Parameters panel located in the same frame as the Groups tree viewer. The Parameters panel allows you to quickly examine the current parameter values of the current version of the report you are viewing.

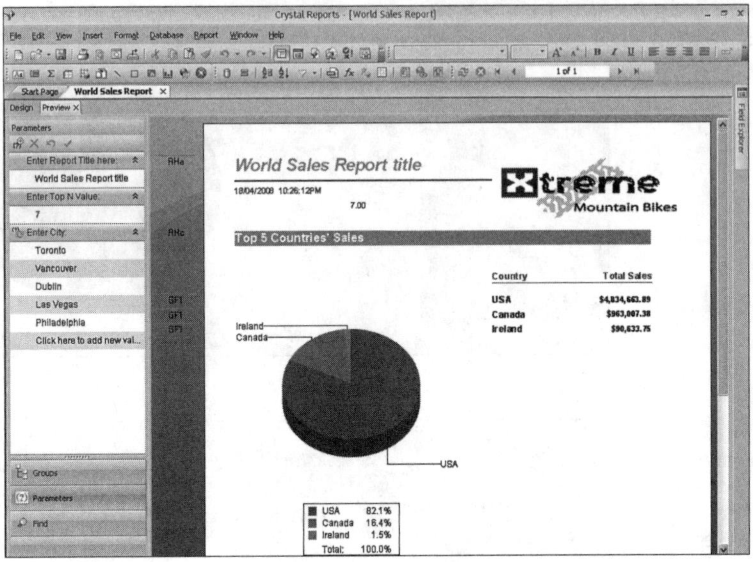

Figure 5.16
A report highlighting the Parameters panel in the Preview tab.

The Show on (Viewer) Panel property that you set in the Edit Parameter dialog determines whether parameters show in the Parameters panel. Setting the property to Editable enables viewing and editing the parameter from the Parameters panel, whereas setting it to Read-Only allows viewing the values but not editing them. For parameters set to Editable, you can add, delete, and modify the report values directly from the Parameters panel by making the appropriate changes and then clicking on the Apply button.

TROUBLESHOOTING

PARAMETER REUSE ACROSS REPORTS

Is there a way to store parameters so that I can reuse them across multiple reports?

You can store dynamic and cascading parameters' lists of values, and even their associated update schedules, in the repository. However, this is available for use only with the Crystal Reports Server or the BusinessObjects Enterprise, Edge, or Crystal Decision product.

CRYSTAL REPORTS IN THE REAL WORLD—CUSTOM FILTERING

Sometimes a report needs to return all records for a parameterized field where the designer created a record selection filter on this parameter. Although it would certainly be possible to create a parameter and select all valid values for it, there certainly must be a better way—and there is. This example adds a filter to a report so that if a user enters a specific value or a list of values, the report returns only those values. Alternatively, if the user enters an asterisk (*, or another predefined symbol, such as All Values), the report returns all values. The following steps highlight this capability:

1. Open the sample report created in the first half of this chapter. Within the Countries parameter Edit dialog, set the Allows Custom Values property to `True` and change the Top N sort condition to All in the Group Sorting Expert.

2. From the Report menu, choose Selection Formulas, Record. Remove the following line of text:

   ```
   {Customer.Country} = {Countries}
   ```

3. Replace the text with the following (as shown in Figure 5.17):

   ```
   (If {?Countries} = "*" Then
        True
   Else
        {Customer.Country} = {?Countries};)
   ```

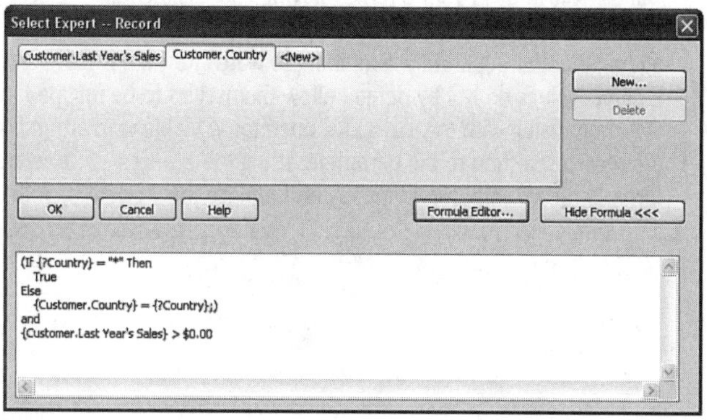

Figure 5.17
The updated Record Selection Formula Editor enables the end user to select All Values with one easy selection.

4. Click Save and Close.

When prompted for a new parameter value, remove any existing values, enter the * symbol as a manual custom entry, click on the Add (>) button to add the symbol to the list of values, and click on OK. You should see something like Figure 5.18.

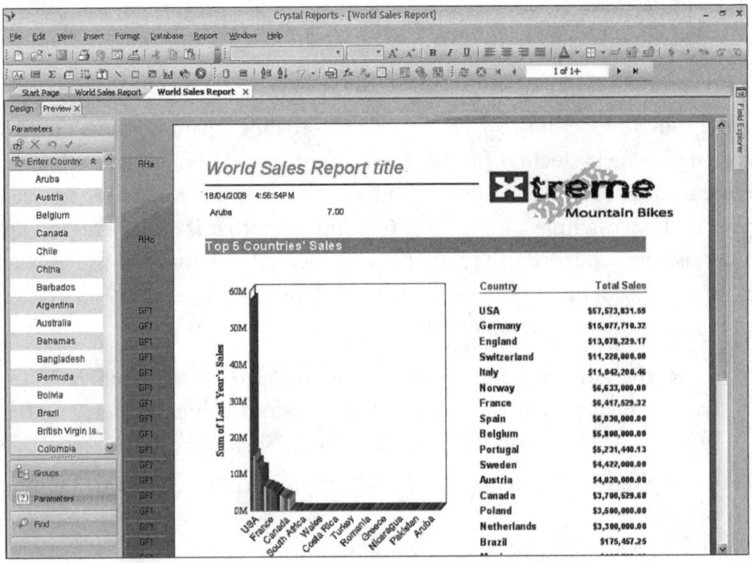

Figure 5.18
The report returns all values when * is passed in as a parameter. In this figure, the chart has been edited slightly (changed to bar chart with labels removed) from the original report, but you can clearly see that all countries were returned.

NOTE

Another way to implement an All Values parameter option for the report consumer is to create a record selection through the Record Selection dialog that uses the `is like` operator instead of the `equals to` operator. Using this operator enables you to use the * and ? wildcards in your filter. By having end users enter '*' or providing that as one of the default parameter selection options, the users can specify All Values without adding them all separately. One thing to watch for here is that parameters that allow multiple values do not by default allow themselves to be mapped to in the Record Selection dialog with the `is like` operator. A viable workaround, however, is to map the record selection to the parameter using the `equals to` operator and then edit the formula record selection manually and replace the = operator with the `like` operator.

PART II

FORMATTING CRYSTAL REPORTS

CHAPTER **6**

FUNDAMENTALS OF REPORT FORMATTING

In this chapter

INTRODUCTION

To this point, the majority of material you've seen in this book has focused on the various functions of the Crystal Reports design application. Equally important, however, is the form (or format) of the report—especially when a report is used as a corporate or industry standard document that projects a company's image externally (such as an income statement or balance sheet). This chapter focuses on form over function and discusses a myriad of formatting techniques.

You have already reviewed the Crystal Reports 2008 development environment and learned about creating a report from a blank canvas, as well as how to select, group, filter, sort, and summarize your report data. Now you move on to the cosmetic aspects of report design. Working with report formatting and object properties to create professionally designed reports is very straightforward, but it does require familiarity with various features of the design application environment. This chapter reviews the most commonly used object-formatting techniques—fonts, borders, page and margin properties, and object layering—and provides a tutorial to apply these techniques to one of the sample reports created earlier in the book.

This chapter covers the following topics:

- Positioning and sizing report objects
- Modifying object properties for formatting purposes
- Combining and layering report objects
- Configuring report page and margin properties

POSITIONING AND SIZING REPORT OBJECTS

After you have completed your functional report design tasks—connecting to the data source, adding report objects, and structuring the report—the next step in the report design process is to format the various objects on a report. As demonstrated in Chapter 1, "Creating and Designing Basic Reports," objects can be added to a report via a variety of methods—dragging and dropping objects from the design explorers, or selecting objects from toolbar and menu commands and placing them in the desired locations—for quick and intuitive report creation. After you successfully add objects to your report, each object can be positioned, sized, and formatted for display purposes, as demonstrated in the following exercise.

As a visual example of the difference that report formatting efforts can make, compare the presentation value of the report samples shown in Figures 6.1 and 6.2. These two reports accomplish the same functional tasks, but the report in Figure 6.2 is much more visually appealing.

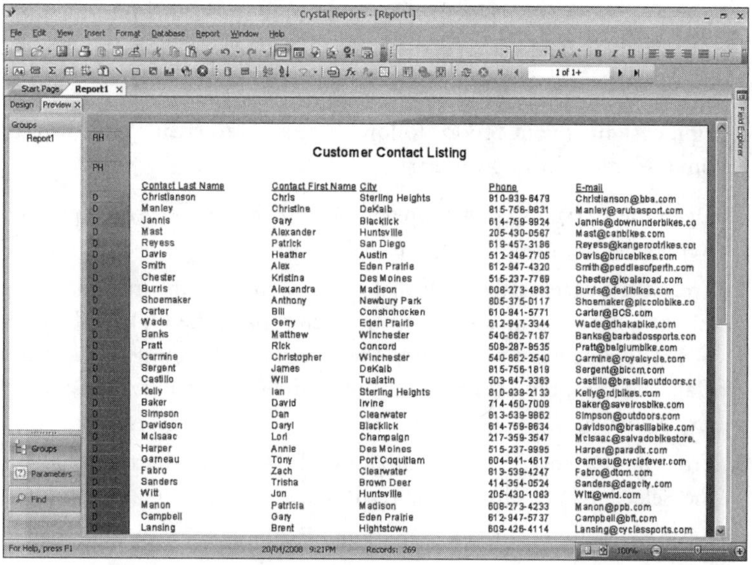

Figure 6.1
A customer contact listing report with little to no formatting applied.

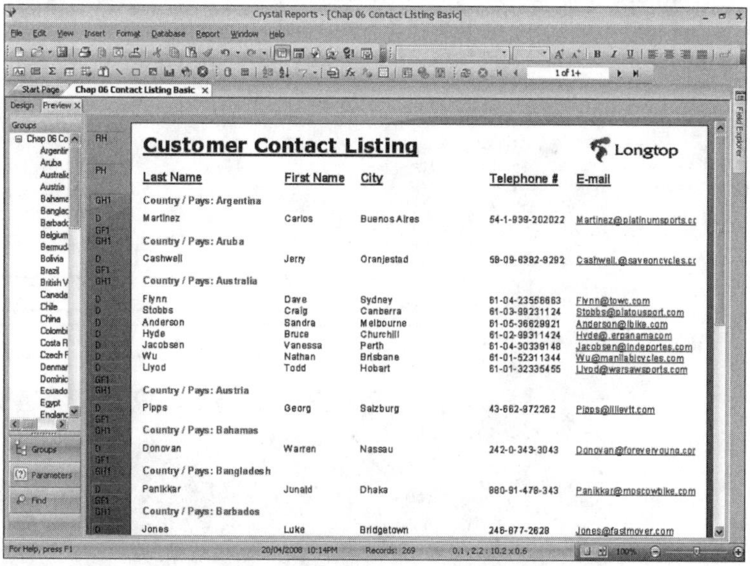

Figure 6.2
A customer contact listing report with a moderate amount of formatting applied.

You will spend the remainder of this chapter reproducing many of the visual transformations from Figure 6.1 to Figure 6.2. By completing the following exercises, you create a Customer Contact Listing report using a variety of applied formatting techniques, such as adding a group definition to logically structure customers into their respective countries, and formatting the font styles of the report title, column titles, country description, and email address fields to make for a more precise presentation of the report information. By combining the Country database field with a text field, you also provide for a bilingual display of the country description.

To begin designing your report, follow these steps to create your own nicely formatted Customer Contact Listing report:

1. Open the Crystal Reports application and choose Create a New Report Using the Blank Report Layout from the start page.

2. From the Database Explorer dialog accessed from the main database menu, expand the Create a New Connection list, and then expand the ODBC (RDO) node to present the ODBC dialog window that lists the available data sources. Select the Xtreme 11 Sample Database from the list of data sources, and click on Finish to continue to the Database Expert dialog.

3. From the Database Expert dialog, use the arrow (>) button to add the Customer table to the Selected Tables list on the right. Click on OK to continue.

4. From the View menu, select the Field Explorer command to open the Field Explorer dialog.

5. From the Field Explorer, expand the Customer table by clicking the plus symbol. Then click and drag the Contact Last Name field onto the report's design view and place it to the far left of the Details section area, as shown in Figure 6.3.

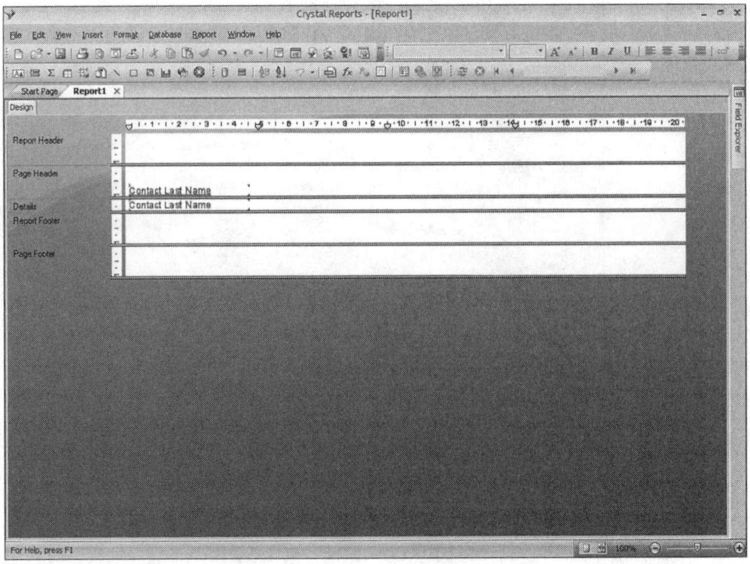

Figure 6.3
Add the Contact Last Name field to the Details section of the report.

6. Follow the previous step to add the Contact First Name, City, and E-Mail fields to the Details section of the report, as shown in Figure 6.4.

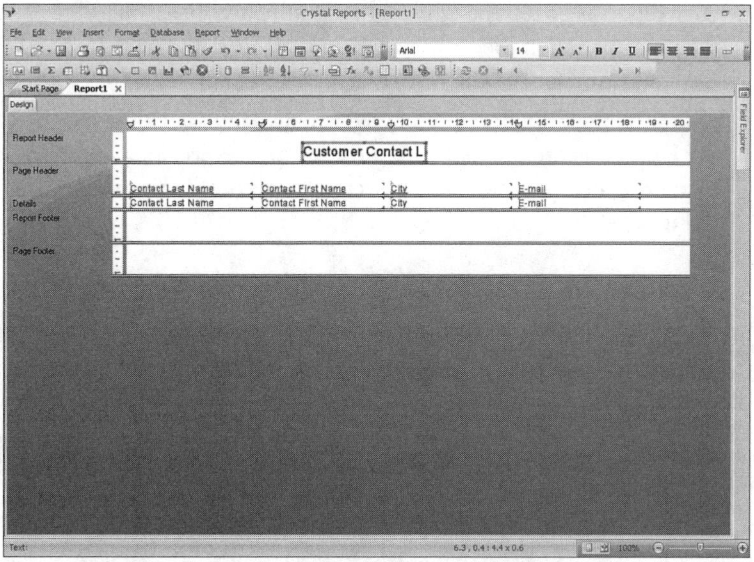

Figure 6.4
The selected fields displayed within the respective sections of the report and a hidden Field Explorer dialog.

7. From the Insert menu, select Text Object, drop the object into the middle of the Report Header section, and type **Customer Contact Listing** in the text field. Click anywhere outside the text object to remove the cursor focus from the text object, and increase the size of this field to 14 by reselecting the object, and then changing the font size through the Formatting toolbar.

   Now that the report includes the field and text objects identified previously, focus on positioning and resizing these fields for display purposes.

8. As Figure 6.4 shows, now you might not be able to see the entire text entered into the report title text object because it is not wide enough to display the text entry by default. To resolve this, click once on the report title text object located in the Report Header section so that it highlights. Using the dark blue handles that encompass the object's perimeter, float over the handle located on the right side of the text object with the mouse pointer; then click and hold the mouse button while dragging the handle farther to the right to widen the text object's display area. Refer to Figure 6.5 to see the result of this action.

   NOTE

   > Notice that when you float over the perimeter handles of an object with your mouse cursor (or pointer), the cursor icon turns into an alternative shape, such as horizontal or vertical arrows, to illustrate that you can modify the object if you click on the handle.

9. Now that you have widened the display area of your report title object using the object handles, repeat this same step to modify the width of the field objects within the Details report section so that you can insert one additional object into the Details section of

your report between the City and E-Mail fields. To facilitate this resizing, you can view the report through the Preview tab and dynamically see the effect of your resizing on the resultant data and the report's appearance.

10. Using the Field Explorer, insert the Phone database field from the Customer table into the Details section of your report. Based on the previous steps, practice positioning and sizing the objects in the Details section to accommodate all the database fields, as shown in Figure 6.5.

Figure 6.5
The sample report Design tab displays five database field objects in the Details section, five database field column header text fields in the Page Header, and one text object in the Report Header section.

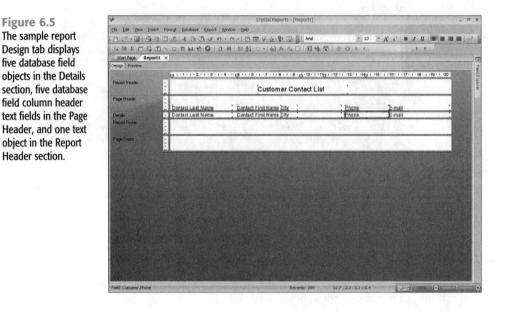

TIP

Although many formatting activities can be exercised on field objects in both the Design and Preview tabs, some formatting facilities are available only within the Design tab. One useful feature to take note of is the capability to move a highlighted field (or even a set of fields) and its associated column title with the arrow keys on your keypad. This technique is a great help when you're moving around report fields, as you did in step 9.

NOTE

As you might have noticed, the field sizes are often large enough to show the entire field name in the Design view of the report. But from the Preview tab view of the report, you see that fields (such as the E-mail or Phone fields here) are cut off from the display area. This is not unusual, and it might require you to resize the field objects to ensure that they are appropriate for the report display area. It is often useful to use the report's Preview tab as the active window when finalizing the formatting and layout of your reports.

11. Now click on the Preview tab to see a preview display of what the report actually looks like, as shown in Figure 6.6.

NOTE

If the Preview tab is not displayed in the application, you have not yet run the report against the database. To run the report, press the F5 key or click on the Refresh toolbar icon to execute the report to run. The Refresh toolbar icon is represented by the two blue arrows indicating a counterclockwise rotation.

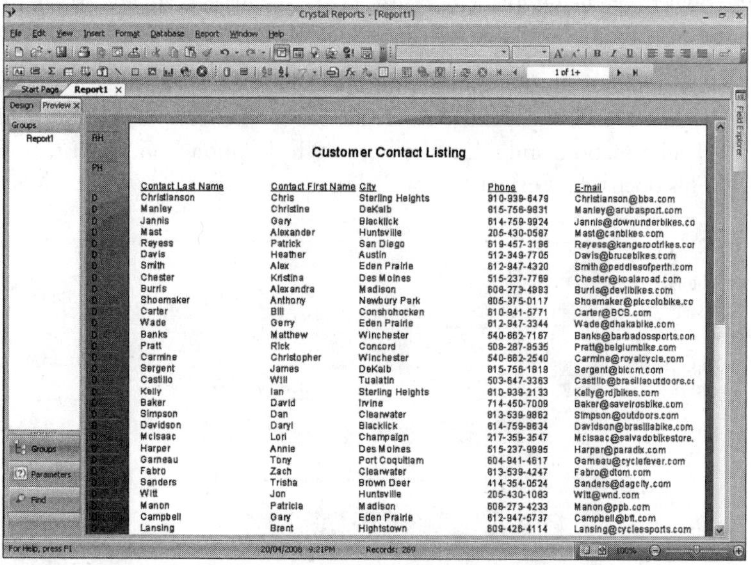

Figure 6.6
To preview your report, press F5, select the Preview tab, or click on the Refresh button.

NOTE

Although it's important to understand the basics of report formatting, you will not necessarily have to go through the often arduous process of formatting reports every time. Report templates can be used to apply predefined and meaningful formatting characteristics in a very quick manner. Additionally, object formatting can be copied from existing objects to other unformatted objects through use of the Format Painter introduced in version 10. The Format Painter is accessed through the right-click menu of any object whose format you want to copy.

→ For more details on designing and using report templates, **see** "Creating Useful Report Templates," **p. 336**.

MODIFYING OBJECT PROPERTIES FOR FORMATTING PURPOSES

Now that the foundation of our report is complete, it is time to focus on how to improve the form and aesthetic appearance of the report.

By modifying various object properties, you can greatly improve the presentation value of the report. In doing so, you will be using the Format Editor to access a variety of specific properties, such as fonts, borders, colors, and alignment. The Format Editor is commonly used to quickly and easily modify all report objects, and its contents are reflective of the specific object type being formatted (text, chart, database field, and so on). To explore these formatting capabilities, follow these steps:

1. Continuing with the report from the chapter's earlier exercise, return to the Design tab of your report and right-click on the report title text object (located in the Report Header section) and select the Format Text option from the list, as shown in Figure 6.7. This opens the Format Editor dialog.

Figure 6.7
The Format Editor dialog is accessed from the context menu on most Crystal Reports objects.

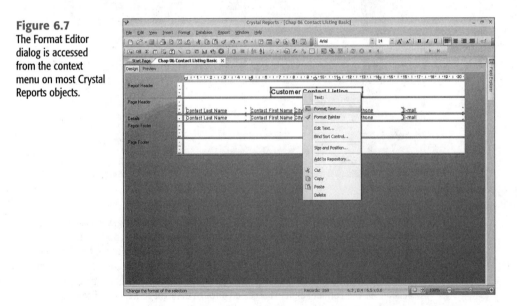

2. The Format Editor dialog (displayed in Figure 6.8) enables you to set and adjust a variety of properties of the object. For this exercise, navigate to the Font tab of the Format Editor and select the bold font style, a font size of 14, and a font color of red. Also, select the Paragraph tab of the Format Editor and choose Centered from the Horizontal Alignment drop-down list.

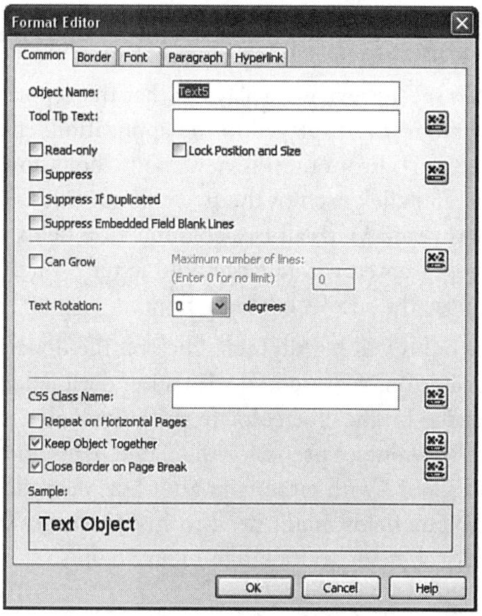

Figure 6.8
The Format Editor dialog provides quick and easy access to a variety of report object properties.

3. Now select the Border tab from within the Format Editor and then select Single from each of the four border Line Style drop-down lists (left, right, top, and bottom). Under Color, click the Background check box and select Yellow from the drop-down list as the background color. Based on all your selected properties in the Format Editor, you should now see a representative example of the text object in the Sample area at the bottom of the dialog box. Click OK to save these settings and return to the Design tab on your report.

4. To improve the effectiveness of your report, you can modify the database field column titles to provide more meaningful descriptions for the business users of your report. Working within the Design tab of your report, double-click on the Phone title object in the Page Header section of the report. When the cursor's focus is on this object, you can delete, append, or update the text as you choose. Modify this text to read `Telephone #` and then click anywhere outside the object to remove the cursor's focus from the object. Make similar adjustments to the Contact First Name and Contact Last Name fields by removing the Contact prefix.

TIP

As an alternative to the Format Editor, you can also use the toolbars and menu commands to quickly apply common formatting techniques, such as font and alignment characteristics.

5. From the View menu, select Toolbars to present the Toolbar dialog. Make sure all the Standard, Formatting, and Insert toolbar items are selected, and click on OK.

6. Click on the Preview tab to see a preview display of what the report will actually look like. Again, if the Preview tab is not displayed in the application, click the Refresh toolbar button to execute the report. From the Preview mode, hold down either the Shift or Ctrl key on your keyboard and click each of the five column titles so that they are all highlighted with a blue perimeter. With all five columns title fields highlighted, click the Bold toolbar button, represented with a large bold letter B on the Formatting toolbar. Refer to Figure 6.9 to see the results of this action.

7. With the five column title fields still highlighted, click on the downward arrow located on the Font Color toolbar button, represented with an underlined letter A on the Formatting toolbar. Select the bright blue color from the available list, as shown in Figure 6.9. Lastly, remove the contact prefix for the name fields and increase the size of these column titles to font size 12 with either the Font Size drop-down box or the A+ Increase Font Size button. The fields might need to stretch vertically to fit the new font size, but they can eventually be made to look like Figure 6.9.

NOTE

If certain formatting buttons do not appear on your Formatting toolbar, it might be because of limited display real estate. They are, however, still available for use by clicking on the double arrows at the right extreme of the involved toolbar.

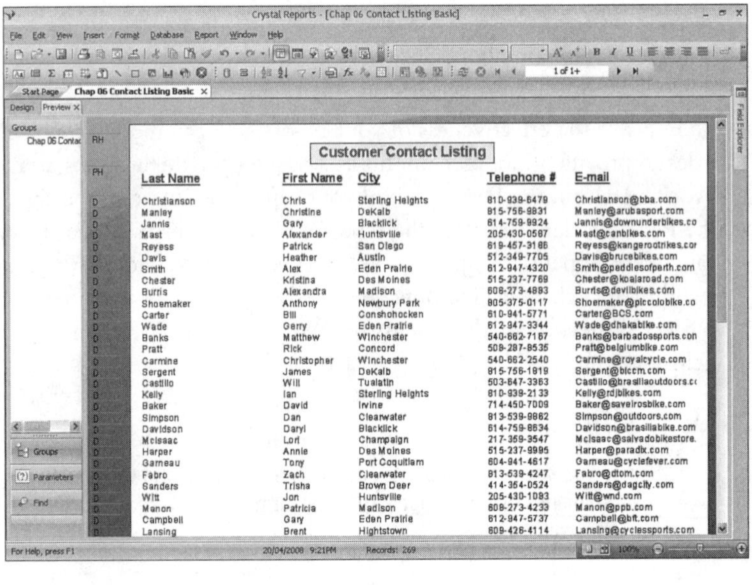

Figure 6.9
Common formatting properties can be quickly specified via the Formatting toolbar commands (such as font styles, font size, colors, borders, and so on).

To make the E-Mail field appear more meaningful to the business users of the report, let's format the E-Mail database field values to resemble and behave like standard hyperlink text.

8. To remove the cursor focus from the five column titles fields, click anywhere outside these field areas or press the Esc (Escape) key on your keyboard.

9. In the Preview tab, click any of the actual E-Mail field values to highlight the E-Mail database field objects, and right-click on the same object to present the context menu. From the context menu, shown in Figure 6.10, select the Format Field item.

Figure 6.10
Right-clicking on any field object presents you with a list of commands for that particular object.

10. Select the Hyperlink tab after you have opened the Format Editor. From the available Hyperlink Types, select Current E-Mail Field Value—this option automatically creates a hyperlink based on the values stored within this field in the data source assuming that these values are formatted as proper email addresses in the data source, such as abc@domain.com.

NOTE

You can use the Hyperlink tab within the Format Editor to create hyperlinks to a website, email address, file, or another Crystal Report. A hyperlink is saved with your report and is available to other users as a way of linking to additional external information from your report. Hyperlink definitions can also be defined by formulas to enable context-sensitive, data-driven hyperlinks—a very powerful feature of Crystal Reports.

6

11. Now let's make the E-Mail field appear as a standard hyperlink value, commonly known to have a blue underlined font style. Select the Font tab within the Format Editor dialog to apply the blue font color, and select the Underline check box. Click on OK to return to the report preview, and then press Esc to remove the cursor focus from all report objects.

12. Based on the completion of the previous step, your mouse pointer should now change into a hand icon as it floats over any of the E-Mail field values on the report. This indicates that upon clicking on any of the E-Mail values, you initiate an email message to be sent to that address, as shown in Figure 6.11.

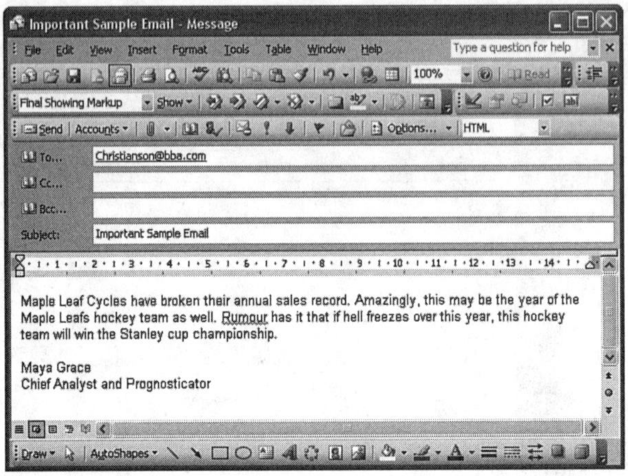

Figure 6.11
By applying an email hyperlink, report end users can initiate a context-sensitive email to any of the respective customer contacts.

By using the Format Editor as well as the toolbar commands to modify report object properties, you have very quickly and easily enhanced your report's presentation quality. Not only did you enhance this report example visually, but you also easily incorporated hyperlink functionality to add an additional level of interactivity to your report. For more information on using hyperlink functionality in reports, see Chapter 9, "Custom Formatting Techniques."

EXPLORING THE FORMAT EDITOR DIALOG COMMON OPTIONS

The previous exercises introduced the Format Editor—the dialog where the appearance of report fields and other report objects can be manipulated. Different Crystal Reports objects present different tabs within the Format Editor, and each provides specific editing functionality for the underlying object types (such as Date and Time, Boolean, Hyperlink, and so on). The next few sections introduce the most commonly used tabs and underlying formatting options.

THE COMMON TAB OF THE FORMAT EDITOR

The Common tab of the Format Editor provides basic functionality for the majority of Crystal Reports' objects. The most commonly used formatting features accessed through this tab include the following:

- **Object Name**—Assigned by default, this name is referenced primarily for use with report part viewing (that is, when specifying which report parts to view in a report parts viewer).

- **ToolTip Text**—Enables a text bubble to be displayed as the end user hovers over report fields. A common and powerful use of ToolTips is to provide the end users with a database-driven description of the involved field from an associated metadata table. To see this functionality in Design and Preview tabs, you must turn on the ToolTips option under the Layout tab of the Options dialog, accessed from the File menu.

- **Read Only**—This option makes the selected report object read-only so that it can't be formatted. When this option is selected, all other choices in the Format Editor except Repeat on Horizontal Pages and Lock Position and Size become inactive.

- **Lock Position and Size**—This option locks the position of the selected report object so that it can't be moved or resized.

- **Suppress**—Enables the suppression of the selected object in the Preview tab and on any report printing. This option is often used with intermediary formula components that the end user is not intended to view or on fields that the user is meant to view only conditionally. The X+2 button is used to suppress (or display) the selected field based on certain data conditions being met (for example, show "ALERT" text object only if shipping date is five or more days after order date for a specified field).

- **Suppress If Duplicated**—This option enables the suppression of repeated field names in a report.

- **Can Grow**—Enables variable-length fields to grow vertically in the report and word wrap automatically. A maximum number of lines can be set with this option to control rogue or large data elements.

- **Text Rotation**—Enables the rotated display of the involved object by 90° or 270°. This feature is highlighted in Chapter 9.

- **Horizontal Alignment**—Provides the capability to align the data within an object justified left, center, right, or both.

- **Display String**—This custom string functionality enables the conditional formatting and display of field types (for example, number, currency, date, time, date and time, Boolean, string, running total, formulas, parameters, and so on) as a custom string (for example, displaying the number 1,500,000 as the custom string 1.5M). The following sample formula snippet highlights how this would work:

```
Switch (
CurrentFieldValue > 1000000000, ToText(CurrentFieldValue/1000000000, 2) + "B",
CurrentFieldValue > 1000000, ToText(CurrentFieldValue/1000000, 2) + "M",
CurrentFieldValue > 1000, ToText(CurrentFieldValue/1000, 2) + "K",
True, ToText(CurrentFieldValue, 2))
```

6

- **CSS Class Name**—Provides the capability for Crystal Reports to leverage existing CSS (Cascading Style Sheets) style sheet classes when deployed in a web application or with BusinessObjects Enterprise.

- **Repeat on Horizontal Pages**—Introduced in version 10, this option enables the repetition of a report object that does not expand horizontally (such as text objects, field objects, OLE [Object Linking and Embedding] objects, charts, maps, lines, boxes, and so on) for each additional horizontal page that a cross-tab or OLAP grid might create as it expands horizontally.

- **Keep Object Together**—This option keeps an object on a single page. If there is enough room, the program prints the object on the current page. If there is not enough room, the program prints the object on the next page. This is clearly not possible with objects that span more than a single page.

- **Close Border on Page Break**—This functionality ensures that borders created on the object close at the bottom of any page and begin again as the object is continued on the next page. This provides for a much slicker-looking border format for your reports.

THE BORDER TAB OF THE FORMAT EDITOR

The Border tab of the Format Editor provides border, background, and drop-shadow formatting functionality for Crystal Report objects. The most commonly used formatting features accessed through this tab include the following:

- **Line Style drop-down boxes**—The Left, Right, Top, and Bottom drop-down boxes enable specification of the different types of supported borders (Single, Double, Dashed, or Dotted). For basic borders, this functionality is more easily accessed through the Borders button on the Formatting toolbar.

- **Tight Horizontal**—This option specifies that a border tightly wraps around the involved object's contents and not the entire field as placed on the report (that is, no spaces are included within the border).

- **Drop Shadow**—This format prints a drop shadow to the right and below the specified object.

- **Border Color**—The color of the border and drop shadow is specified here through the drop-down box.

- **Background Color**—The background check box enables you to specify that a background be displayed for the given field. An additional drop-down box enables you to select the color for the background after the check box has been selected.

THE FONT TAB OF THE FORMAT EDITOR

The Font tab of the Format Editor provides the capability to change the fonts, font size, and font style for text and data fields in your Crystal Reports. The most commonly used formatting features accessed through this tab include the following:

- **Font, Style, Size, and Color**—Enable the designer to specify a variety of available formatting fonts (such as Arial, Courier, Verdana, Times Roman, and so on), styles (such as Bold and Italic), sizes (including manually entered 1/2 sizes), and colors.

- **Strikeout and Underline**—Enable you to specify the selected formatting on the current report object.

- **Character Spacing Exactly**—Use this option to specify the space that each character in the selected font occupies. The value is defined as the distance in number of points measured from the start of one character to the start of the next. When the character spacing is edited, only the spacing between adjacent characters changes—not the actual font size of the characters. Using 0 enables the default font character spacing.

THE HYPERLINK TAB OF THE FORMAT EDITOR

The Hyperlink tab is used to create hyperlinks to external websites, email addresses, files, or other reports and report objects from report objects within the current report. These hyperlinks can be data-driven (that is, change on the data coming back from the database) and provide a rather intuitive method for integrating Crystal Reports into a business workflow. The helpful hint section of this tab provides in-place coaching for each type of hyperlink used. The most commonly used formatting features accessed through this tab include the following:

- **Website on the Internet**—Enables the specification of an external website with or without dynamic context-sensitive components of the URL (uniform resource locator) driven from the database. An example of a context-sensitive web address would be www.google.com/search?q= + {Customer.Customer Name}, where the link would take the end user to a Google search page full of results based on the current value of the customer name.

- **E-mail address**—Enables you to add a link to an email address that would need to be typed into the E-Mail address text box or through the associated formula editor X+2 button.

- **File**—Enables the linked object to call a specified file and launch its associated application upon end user activation of this link. Report designers can specify EXE files with command-line parameters through the Formula Editor accessed by the X+2 button.

- **Current Website or E-mail Field Value**—Creates a website or email link to the underlying object on which the hyperlink is being created. The formatting of the data for the involved field must be correct (that is, a proper email address or website URL).

- **Report Part Drilldown**—The Report Part Drilldown option lets you define a hyperlink so that the Report Part Viewer can emulate the drill-down functionality of Crystal Reports. The Report Part Viewer displays only destination objects; therefore, to make drill-down work, you need to define a navigation path from a home object to one or more destination objects, all residing in the same report section. Initial report part specification for a given Crystal Report is set within the Report Options dialog accessed from the main File menu. The drill-down path is then set for each report part in the

6

navigation path through this option. Not all Crystal Reports objects have this option available based on their report section location and their type of object.

- **Another Report Object**—This option enables the definition of a hyperlink to objects in the same or different reports. When defining a hyperlink path to a different report, that report must be managed in a BusinessObjects Enterprise environment. To specify report objects, you must copy them using the right-click Copy command from their source report and then paste them into the current object's Hyperlink tab using the Paste Link button.

OTHER FORMAT EDITOR TABS

The remaining tabs found in the Format Editor depend on the type of object selected in the involved Crystal Report. The other tabs that you find and some of the most common formatting options provided in each are as follows:

- **Paragraph tab**—Enables you to specify formatting for string/text fields, including spacing, reading order, and horizontal alignment.

- **Numbers tab**—Enables detailed formatting on numbers and currency objects, including the handling of zeros, decimal point specification, negative number formatting, rounding, and thousands separator specification. The Customize button enables access to the majority of these formatting features.

- **Date and Time tab**—Provides detailed formatting on dates, times, and datetime objects. Many default display options are available, with a great deal of granularity provided through the Customize button.

- **Boolean tab**—Enables the selection of the format for the return values of Boolean field objects.

- **Box, Line, Rounding, Subreport, and Picture tabs**—Provide for granular-level formatting of each involved Crystal Reports object.

COMBINING AND LAYERING REPORT OBJECTS

The concept of combining and layering report objects becomes relevant when you need to precisely control the relationship between two or more objects occupying a common space on the report. For example, assume that rather than having your Country field read USA, you would like to combine the Country database field with a text object so that it reads Country/Pays: USA—displaying the textual description for country in both English and French. To accomplish this, you can easily combine a text and a database field into one common report object.

The previous exercises can be enhanced by adding a more descriptive text object to your report as that described earlier. To complete this, start by adding a group to your report. The group enables you to logically present each customer within his country. To add this grouping, perform the following steps:

1. From the Insert menu, select Group to present the Insert Group dialog. Select the Country field (located under the Customer table) from the uppermost drop-down list. Leave the sort order as Ascending, and click on OK to return to the report.

2. Verify that you are working in the Design view of the report—click on the Design tab if necessary. You should now see two new sections listed in the left column area of the design environment: Group Header #1 and Group Footer #1. From the Insert menu, select Text Object and drop the object to the right of the Group #1 Name field in the Group Header section. Type **Country/Pays:** for the textual content of this new object (including a space after the colon), as shown in Figure 6.12.

Figure 6.12
The Insert menu enables you to quickly add a group and text object into your report. The resultant group and text object are shown here in the Report Designer.

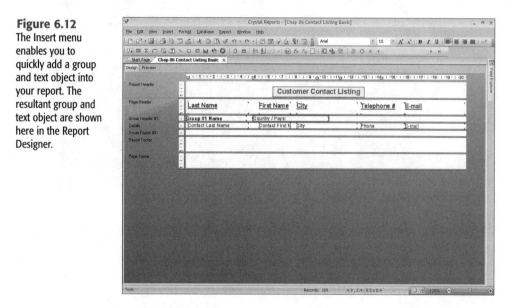

3. Highlight the Group #1 Name field object. Click and drag it over the new text object field (you can drag the entire object after the mouse pointer has turned into a four-way cross icon), and drop it onto the text object when the flashing vertical cursor indicates that it falls precisely to the right of the textual description you entered.

> **NOTE**
>
> Dragging and dropping objects to combine them is a very precise maneuver and might require some practice. If you dropped the Group Name field in the wrong place, click the Undo button (curved arrow pointing backward) and try again until you are comfortable and successful with this technique.

4. After you have successfully combined these objects, the design application still references the newly combined object as a text object. You now need to widen the object's

display area. Click this object to highlight it, and drag the left-side perimeter handle farther to the left until you reach the left margin of the design area, as shown in Figure 6.13.

Figure 6.13
You have now combined a database field object with a text object to form one common report object.

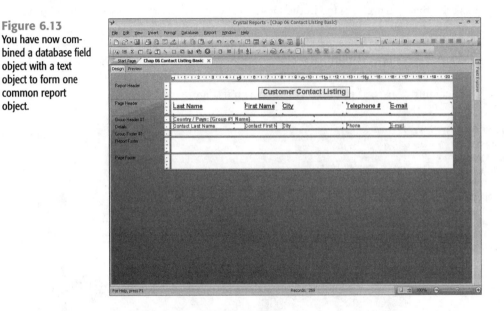

5. With the combined text object highlighted, use the steps identified earlier in this chapter to modify the object's properties to present the field values in a bold red font style, as shown in Figure 6.14. Click the Preview tab to see how the report results are displayed. (Use the Refresh toolbar button if the Preview tab is not visible.)

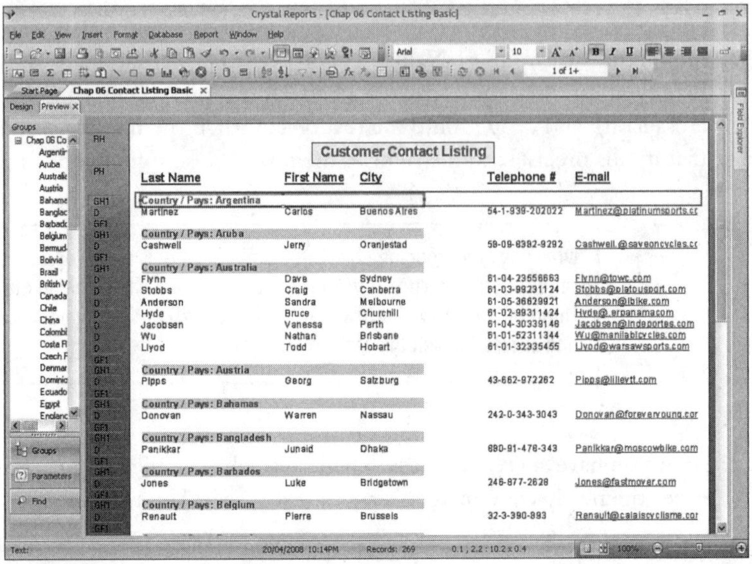

Figure 6.14
After combining two or more objects, you can specify formatting properties for the newly combined report object.

6

6. Now let's add a corporate logo to your report and use it to display object layering. You need to have a picture file saved in bitmap, TIFF, JPEG, or PNG format available for use. You can use the Business Objects logo (downloaded from the www.usingcrystal.com website for this example) or any other image that you prefer. Select the Picture menu option from the Insert menu. Navigate to and select the Business Objects logo image and drag it into the Report Header section. Drop the image into the Report Header section so that its left perimeter is aligned directly above the left perimeter of the Telephone Number column, as shown in Figure 6.15.

Figure 6.15
Drag and drop the Business Objects logo image object into place in the Report Header section.

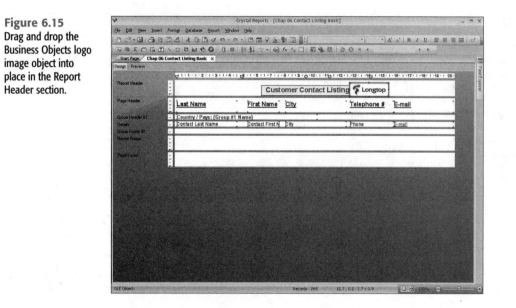

Notice, as illustrated in Figure 6.15, that you have partially covered the report title object with the new logo image. This could have certainly been avoided by placing the image object farther to the right, but for demonstration purposes, use the Move property of the report title field to once again make it visible.

7. Right-click on the report title text object, select Move, and then select To Front from the additional pop-up options. This positions the report title object on top of the logo image, as you can see in the report preview.

8. To resolve the issue of overlapping objects in the Report Header section, adjust the two objects so that the report title displays farther to the left of the logo image, as shown in Figure 6.16. Also, at this time, add a hyperlink to the Business Objects logo to the Business Objects website at www.businessobjects.com. As a reminder, you can do this by right-clicking the photo and going into the Format Editor by selecting Format Graphic. Select the Hyperlink tab and choose A Website on the Internet. Add the site after http:// in the website address.

6

9. As a final step to re-create the report in Figure 6.2, use the Format Expert dialog to modify the report title text so that it appears in a bold, navy blue, underlined, size 20 Verdana font with no displayed borders.

Because of these exercises, you now have a very useful report that displays each customer contact record distinctively grouped within the country in which they are located. The formatting applied introduces the capabilities that make Crystal Reports the undisputed champion of professionally formatted reports.

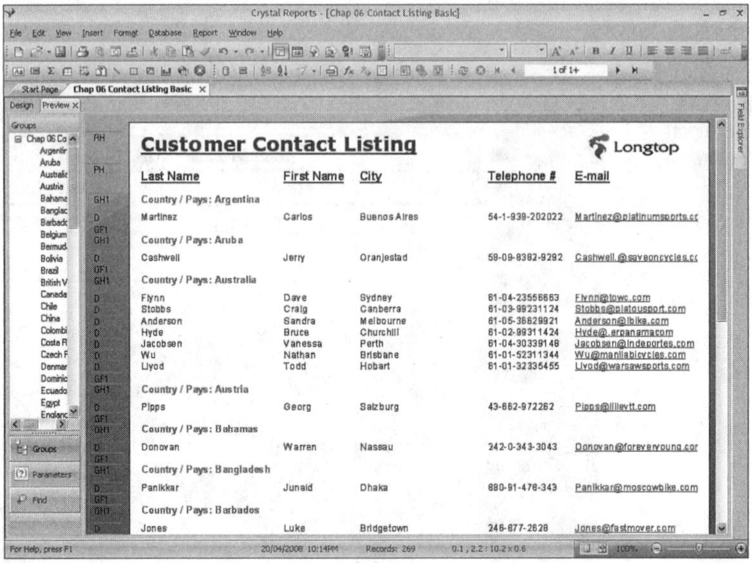

Figure 6.16
By adjusting the objects located in the Report Header, you have resolved the need to layer these objects; however, layering does provide flexible display options for future reports.

CONFIGURING REPORT PAGE AND MARGIN PROPERTIES

With Crystal Reports, page margins can either be set to use specific manually set margin definitions or selected to automatically adjust to the report margins. To set your report margins to meet exact specifications, follow these steps:

1. From the File menu, click Page Setup, and the Page Setup dialog appears as shown in Figure 6.17.
2. Modify the default page margins for your exact requirements.
3. Click OK to save your changes.

NOTE

Each margin setting is calculated from the paper edge. Consequently, a left margin of .25 inches causes the printing of the report page to start exactly one-quarter of an inch in from the left edge of the paper.

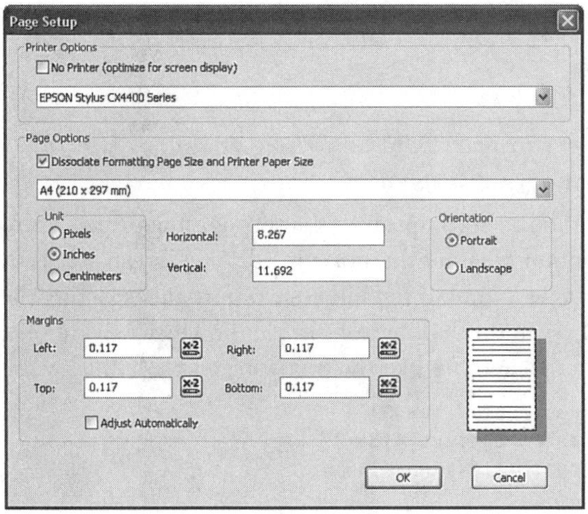

Figure 6.17
Use the Page Setup dialog to specify report margin settings.

As an alternative to specifying exact report margins, you can select the Adjust Automatically check box if you want Crystal Reports to automatically adjust the report's margins when the paper size changes. This option maintains the ratio of the margins to the printable area of the report by enlarging or reducing the left/right and top/bottom margins by the same factor. For example, this setting could ensure that a report designed for a printer that can only print within .5 inches of the paper's edge would maintain the same overall margin ratio when printed on a printer that could print to within .25 inches of the paper's edge.

The Page Setup dialog also enables you to select a printer for your report or specify no printer at all for optimized web viewing. Based on the printer selection, you are able to set different page sizes and either portrait or landscape orientation. New to XI, a preview of the selected paper size is shown at the top of the Page Setup dialog.

TIP

If you decide to select the Adjust Automatically check box margins options for your reports, there are two common issues to be aware of when printing reports (also described in the Crystal Reports Help files):

- When printing a report in another environment in which the printer's default margins are *greater* than the report's setting, the report objects on the right side of the report print off the page.
- When printing a report in another environment in which the printer's default margins are *smaller* (enabling a larger printing area), the entire report moves to the left side of the page.

As a result, it is recommended that you specify your own report margins. You are encouraged *not* to select the Adjust Automatically check box margins option in the Page Setup dialog to avoid these common problems. It is advisable to set your report margins manually using the Page Setup dialog, even if the margins you want to specify are the same as the default margin settings. This issue becomes especially important when you distribute your reports over the Web and have no idea what type of printer the business user will be using.

6

TROUBLESHOOTING

FORMATTING PHONE NUMBERS

I need phone numbers that are stored in the underlying database as 5554161010 to display as (555)416-1010. Is this easily accomplished?

Yes. The simplest method to accomplish this is through the display string functionality accessed under the Common tab of the Format Editor. You can access this dialog by right-clicking on the Telephone_Number field in your report and selecting the Format Field option. Once here, click on the X+2 button beside the Display String title (near the bottom of the dialog) and enter something like the following to accomplish your goal:

```
"(" + Left (CurrentFieldValue,3) +
") " + Mid(CurrentFieldValue,4,3) +
"-" + Right(CurrentFieldValue,4)
```

Or use

```
Picture (CurrentFieldValue, "(XXX) XXX-XXXX")
```

CRYSTAL REPORTS IN THE REAL WORLD—EXPORTING OPTIONS

To eliminate the need to set and reset commonly used exporting options, the XI and 2008 versions of Crystal Reports now enable the saving of report export configuration information with the report itself. You can preset your preferred export options (examples include exporting Page Headers and Footers only once per report in Excel, or creating page breaks in Excel for each page in the report) and have end users automatically use those options when exporting through their report viewers. This new feature results in rapid report deployment and fewer end user requirements in the setting of export options.

NOTE

> A new RTF Export format is available since version XI. This format is optimized to facilitate easy editing of the generated files. This new feature complements the existing RTF export that is optimized for accuracy and forms processing. The result is that you can now choose from two different RTF export formats, depending on your need for either accuracy or the ability to edit.

CRYSTAL REPORTS IN THE REAL WORLD—REFERENCING EXTERNAL RESOURCES

A very powerful use of hyperlinks is to be able to take advantage of the many resources on the Internet. Many Internet sites make use of what is called a *query string*. By knowing the URL and query string that drive a particular site, you can customize a report hyperlink to open a website and perform some functionality. In the next example, supporting encyclopedic information of the customer countries can be opened in wikipedia.org by using a hyperlink:

1. Start by opening the report Chap 06 Contact Listing Formatted.rpt or the report you have created in these last exercises. From the Insert menu, choose Text Object. Add the text Wikipedia to the report beside the country title, as shown in Figure 6.18.

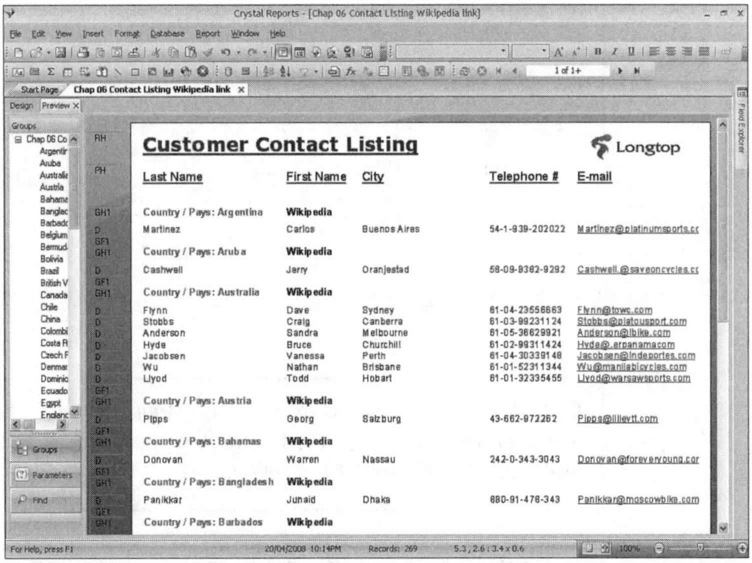

Figure 6.18
A new Wikipedia field added to the report provides a dynamic hyperlink directly to Wikipedia information of the client's country.

2. Right-click on the newly added text object and choose Format Text. Click the Hyperlink tab, select Website on the Internet Hyperlink option, and click the X+2 button beside the Website Address input box. Figure 6.19 highlights the formula you enter to provide a dynamic data-driven link to Wikipedia showing supporting information on the client country locales. Enter the following code into the Formula Editor:

```
StringVar URL;

// The prefix of the URL that will not change;
URL := "http://en.wikipedia.org/wiki/";

// Add the country suffix
URL := URL & {Customer.Country};

// Output the result
URL
```

3. Click on Save and Close to close the code window. Click on OK to close the Format Editor window. Format the hyperlink using the same method used to format the email address to show the user it is an actionable hyperlink.

6

Figure 6.19
Code that builds a dynamic data-driven URL to enable hyperlinks to the Wikipedia website from a Crystal Report.

TIP

Other websites that you might consider linking your reports to include Google for supporting Internet searches on report information and MapQuest for supporting map information for addresses featured on your reports.

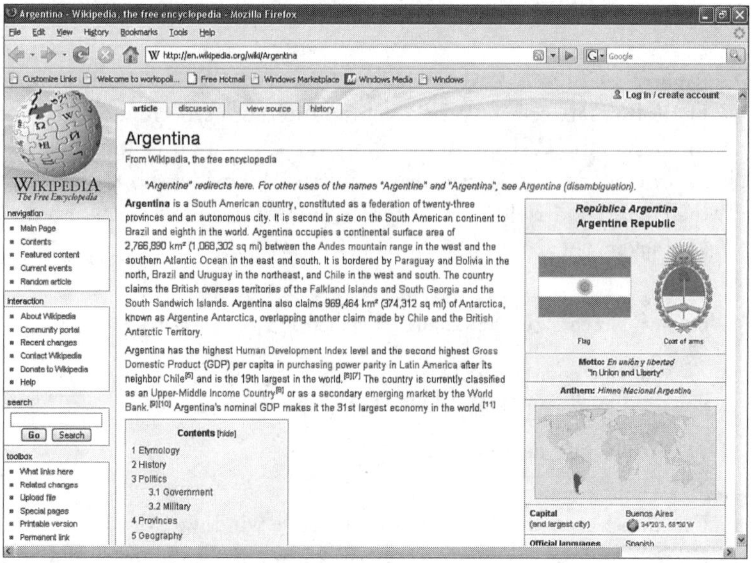

Figure 6.20
A Wikipedia website that has received a dynamic data-driven request directly from your Crystal Report.

CHAPTER 7

WORKING WITH REPORT SECTIONS

In this chapter

INTRODUCTION

You should now be familiar with some of the most common formatting features within the Crystal Reports 2008 designer. Building on the concepts and techniques covered in Chapter 6, "Fundamentals of Report Formatting," for report object formatting, this chapter explains how you can format entire sections within your reports. Just as any report object has specific modifiable properties available for formatting, report sections also have unique properties. This chapter examines those properties and explores their use in creating effective professionally styled reports.

→ For more information on report formatting, **see** "Exploring the Format Editor Dialog Common Options," **p. 166**

This chapter covers the following topics:

- Formatting report sections
- Modifying report section properties
- Using multiple report sections

FORMATTING REPORT SECTIONS

Earlier chapters introduced the concept of report sections such as the Details section and the Group Header and Footer sections. *Report sections* segment reports into logical areas that facilitate logical report design. A name on the left side of the design (or preview) environment identifies each report section. By default, each report includes a Report Header and Footer, Page Header and Footer, and Details section. If you have inserted any groups into your report, you also have a Group Header and Footer for each defined group item. As you created reports in the previous chapters, you placed objects such as database fields, text fields, and corporate logo images into the various report sections and organized them based on the report design requirements.

Each section has unique display properties and printing characteristics that you can modify. For example, if you place a report object, such as an image, in the Report Header section, the image displays and prints only once per report, on the first page. If you place the same image in the Page Header section, the image displays and prints once for every page of the report. The same principles hold true for other custom sections, such as Group Header and Footer, where items display for each specified group. The name of the Details section implies that whatever you place in it displays and prints once for each row retrieved from the data source.

NOTE

A paper metaphor forms the basis of the Crystal Reports design environment, with pages the driving concept in structuring the presentation of report information. The page metaphor applies when referencing report printing and with respect to various presentation characteristics of report formatting.

You can use the report you created in Chapter 6 to take a closer look at how to format report sections. The following exercises demonstrate how to format sections such as the Group Header and Group Footer to improve the overall presentation of a Crystal Report. In addition to modifying display properties, conditional logic is applied that modifies the behavior of the Page Header section based on the result of the defined condition (format formula). The Section Expert is the central location for viewing and modifying the properties of each report section throughout the following exercises.

NOTE

As you might have noticed, the long name (descriptive name) of each section displays to the left of the design environment within the Design tab, whereas only the short name (abbreviated name) of each section displays while you view reports from the Preview tab. This maximizes the report viewing space while working in the Preview tab. You can access the long names, however, either by hovering the mouse cursor over the section or by right-clicking on the section name or label.

There are three distinct ways to access the Section Expert; these include

- Right-clicking anywhere on the report canvas in Design or Preview mode, or on the name of the section you want to work with and selecting Section Expert from the pop-up menu

- Clicking on the Section Expert toolbar button located on the Expert Tools toolbar

- Selecting the Format menu and choosing Report, Section Expert

To start the hands-on learning, follow these steps:

1. Open the report you created in Chapter 6. Alternatively, open the report entitled Ch07start.rpt (available for download at www.usingcrystal.com or by searching for the book's ISBN—0-7897-3417-6—at Que Publishing's website, www.quepublishing.com).

2. Open the Section Expert. From either the Design or Preview mode, right-click on the report canvas, select the Section Expert from the pop-up menu and select the Group Header #1. This presents the Section Expert dialog displayed in Figure 7.4.

3. Now apply a background color to your Group Header #1 report section so that the report consumers can quickly distinguish between country sections and determine which customer contacts belong to each country. In the Section Expert, select the Group Header #1 item from the Sections list on the left, and then click on the Color tab on the right. Click on the Background Color check box so that it activates, and select Navy from the drop-down list of color options. Click OK to continue.

NOTE

From within the Section Expert, you can easily navigate from modifying the properties of one report section to another without closing this dialog window. Regardless of how you open the Section Expert dialog window, you can quickly toggle to other report sections, providing a central location to access and modify the properties of all report sections.

7

4. Select the Preview tab to view your report display.

5. The red font used for the object in the Group Header #1 does not look good against the navy background color. To resolve this, highlight the text object, actually a combined object consisting of a text object and a database field object, and change its font color to white, as shown in Figure 7.1.

Figure 7.1
Formatting a report section can make reports more readable and friendly to end users.

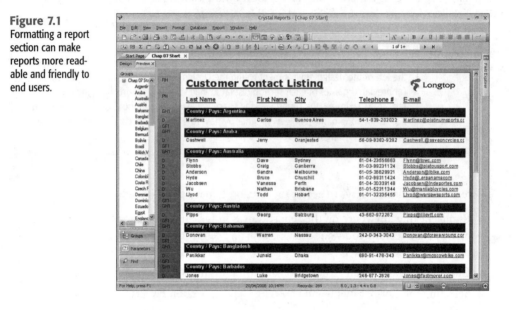

6. To complement the current report grouping on the Country field, add a summary count of the contacts for each country in the Group Footer #1 section. To do this, select Summary from the Insert menu to open the Insert Summary dialog and select the following items:

- Customer.Contact Last Name field from the Choose the Field to Summarize drop-down list
- Count from the Calculate This Summary drop-down list
- Group #1: Customer.Country from the Summary Location drop-down list

NOTE

To access the Insert Summary dialog so that you can add a summary field to your report, you can use the Summary command from the main Insert menu. Alternatively, you can use the Insert Summary button located on the Insert toolbar, or simply right-click on any report field already in the report and access the Insert Summary menu option from the right-click menu. This last option prepopulates the Choose the Field to Summarize drop-down box and saves you one unnecessary step.

7. After you make these selections from the Insert Summary dialog, click OK to continue.

8. You should now see the Count Summary field listed in the Group Footer #1 section of your report. To align the field values to the left and make them noticeable, use the Align Left and Font buttons located on the Formatting toolbar to apply the desired alignment and a red font color.

9. Now add additional report section formatting to the Group Footer #1 section. From the Report menu, select the Section Expert command to present the Section Expert dialog. From the Sections list on the left, select Group Footer #1 and then select the Color tab on the right. Check the Background Color check box, specify a silver background color for this section, and click on OK to return to the report preview, shown in Figure 7.2.

Figure 7.2
Apply section formatting to specific sections of your report for a more meaningful report presentation.

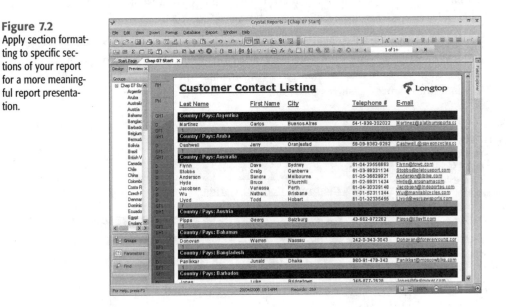

10. As a final step, change the font color of the database field column titles. From either the Design or Preview view, right-click on the Page Header section title and choose Select All Section Objects from the pop-up menu. After highlighting all the column title objects, select Teal from the formatting toolbar Font Color button.

Formatting the various sections of your report is very straightforward. Each section has unique and specific properties that you can modify and use collectively to enhance the presentation quality of the entire report.

TIP

> To quickly remove blank space within report sections and tighten up the alignment of the objects positioned within the sections, you can use the Fit Section command. The Fit Section command is available from the right-click menu of each report section. This raises the bottom boundary line and reduces unnecessary space within the section.

7

MODIFYING REPORT SECTION PROPERTIES

In addition to formatting properties, each section has a variety of general properties that manipulate the behavior of that section within the overall report. For example, you can use the Section Expert to suppress a particular section from the report display, or hide a detail-oriented section from the initial display but enable business users to navigate to the underlying details.

Using the report you created in the previous exercise, relocate the Count summary field into the Group Header and hide the Details section to enable viewers of the report to access this section only if they double-click on the Group Header summary values—commonly known as *drilling down* on report data. The following steps guide you through formatting several fields and sections, creating a drill-down report:

1. Highlight the Summary field currently located in the Group Footer #1 section (Count of Contact Last Name) and drag it up in the Group Header #1 section so that it is positioned to the right of the Country/Pays field, approximately under the Telephone # column title. Figure 7.3 shows the results.

Figure 7.3
Report objects can be repositioned into the various report sections to change the presentation of the report.

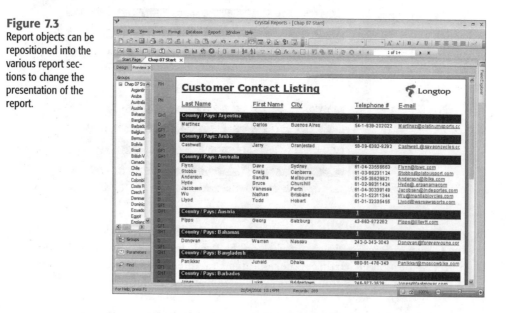

2. While the Summary count field is still highlighted, modify its font properties so that it is underlined and in a bold yellow color.

3. Using what you learned in the previous exercises, remove the background color of the Group Footer #1 section—the background color property can be located on the Color tab of the Section Expert. Figure 7.3 shows what your report should now look like.

4. To display the listing of customer contacts for each country on a separate and unique page, open the Section Expert and select Group Footer #1 from the section list on the

left. As Figure 7.4 shows, the Common tab within the Section Expert provides access to a variety of properties unique to the section that you selected. In this case, check the box next to the New Page After item on the Paging Tab and click on OK to continue.

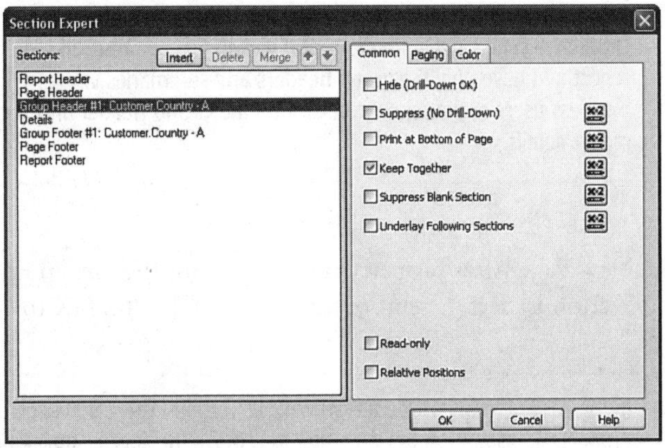

Figure 7.4
The Section Expert provides access to a variety of section formatting properties and enables the specification of what happens before and after each section prints.

TIP

Common report section commands, such as Hide, Suppress, Delete, Hide Section Names, and Select All Section Objects, are accessible via the pop-up menu when you right-click on the applicable section's name. Some of these commands are also available within the Section Expert dialog, although unlike the Section Expert, the right-click pop-up menu pertains only to the specific section you have selected.

---

5. Looking at the preview of your report, you should now see each country's list of contacts on a separate page. Although this might be desirable for those countries with a considerable number of contacts in this report, such as Canada, France, and the United States, it is not necessarily the most visually pleasing presentation for countries that have only one or two customer contacts. A potential solution is to conditionally create a New Page After the Group Footer section only when a country has a significant number of contacts. You accomplish this using a formula that you enter by clicking on the X+2 button adjacent to the New Page After check box. A simple solution might include adding the following formula:

```
Count ({Customer.Contact Last Name}, {Customer.Country}) > 5
```

The formula is evaluated for every Group Footer section (for every country) and causes a new page after the involved Group Footer only when the current country has more than five contact names.

It is likely that the majority of the business users for this hypothetical report are primarily interested in the total number of contacts for each country rather than the actual

7

list. However, a few of the business users also want to be able to access the complete contact list. To accommodate both groups, you can manipulate the properties of the Details section.

NOTE

Drill-down functionality makes report viewing easier. You can hide the details of your report and have only the group headers and summaries visible. When necessary, the business users of the report can click on the Group Header or Summary field to view the report details.

Disable the New Page After property that was set for the Group Footer #1 section. You can use the Section Expert to remove this setting. Click on OK to continue.

NOTE

In the case of many properties within the Section Expert, including the New Page After property, it is important to note that to remove the specific functionality, you must *both* deselect the associated check box *and* remove any existing formula that was previously created and accessed under the X+2 formula button.

7. From either the Design or Preview view of your report, right-click on the Details section title to the far left of the application area and select Hide (Drill-Down OK) from the pop-up menu.

NOTE

To indicate to the business user of the report that more detailed information is available behind the Summary group level, the mouse pointer turns into a magnifying glass icon when it floats over a drillable section (for example, the yellow count field of customer contacts, located in the Group Header #1 section).

As shown in Figure 7.5, you created a list of each country with the total number of contacts displayed. Additionally, by double-clicking on the count of contacts (displayed with the underlined, yellow number), a business user of the report can quickly drill down into the Details section to see the actual customer contact specifications.

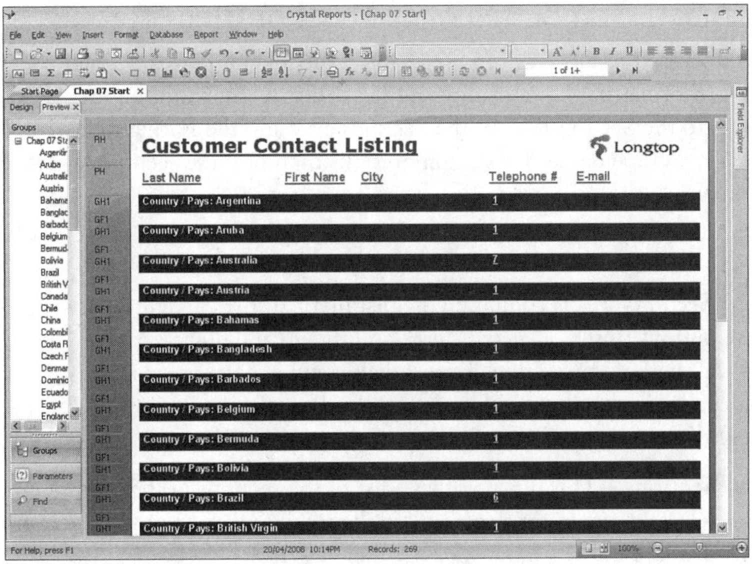

Figure 7.5
A manager receives a summary list of customer contacts by country and can access the customer contact details by drilling down.

As you can see in Figure 7.6, after the business user drills down into a particular group's detail listing (France in this example), that group's detailed contact list is displayed in the Crystal Reports application in a separate tab and is cached so that it can be easily accessed for future reference. When a business user of the report selects a refresh on the report, Crystal Reports removes all cached tabs because there is no guarantee that the data it retrieves from the database is the same as the previously cached page. The end user would have to drill back down into France to view the detailed contact listing again. It is also instructive to note that the Section Expert is unavailable to access when viewing a drill-down view of the report.

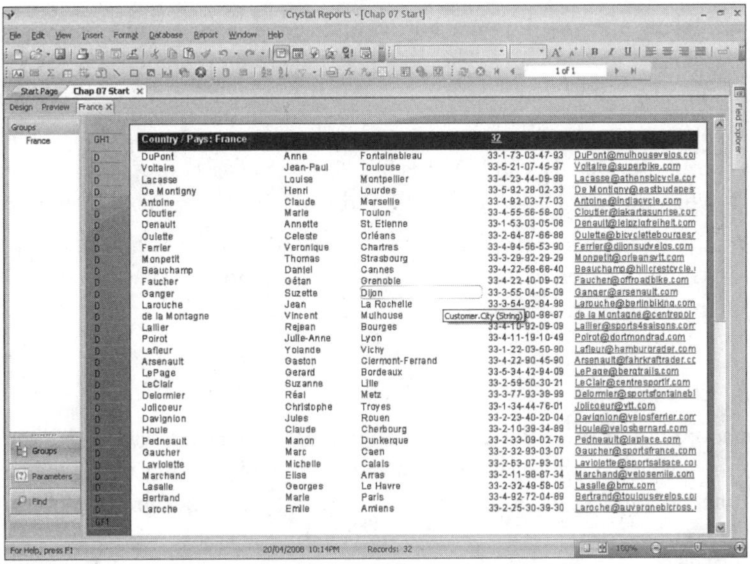

Figure 7.6
The detailed list of customer contacts for France.

THE SECTION EXPERT SETTINGS AND FUNCTIONALITY

As discussed to this point in the chapter, the Section Expert provides a great deal of powerful report formatting functionality and flexibility. As shown in Figure 7.4, there are two major areas to the Section Expert: the Sections area and the Formatting tabs (Common, Paging, Color, and Layout). This section presents each of these sections and their associated functionality.

THE SECTIONS AREA

The Sections area is composed of a listing of all the current report's sections and five separate buttons: Insert, Delete, Merge and the up and down arrows. The Sections area takes up the left half of the Sections Expert dialog and enables you to create, delete, merge, and reorder entire sections within the involved report. The following list describes each component of the Section Expert Sections area:

- **Sections**—This box provides a list of the sections in the current report. When you select a section, the program highlights the other Section Expert properties and buttons that you can set, modify, or use for the selected section.

- **Insert button**—This button enables you to add sections below the currently highlighted section. The newly added section is of the same type as the currently selected section. For example, inserting a section while on the Details section creates another Details section called Details b, the original Details section is called Details a, and both exist under a parent node called Details.

  In addition to the parent section, each child section has different available formatting and display properties. Creating multiple Details (or other) sections dramatically increases the flexibility with which you can display information because each independent child section can have unique formatting and display properties applied (for example, Only Show Column Titles in Details a Section Every 10th Row).

- **Delete button**—Use this button to delete existing highlighted sections from the current report. You can delete only inserted children sections (as described previously)— not original primary sections.

- **Merge button**—This button enables you to merge two related children sections (for example, Details a and Details b) into one new section. This button is only available when the user clicks on the top of the involved sections to be merged.

- **Up and Down Arrow buttons**—These buttons enable you to reorder children sections within the currently selected report. You cannot reorder the original parent sections from the Section Expert.

THE COMMON TAB

In addition to the Section Expert options that you have already used, the following segment of the chapter provides an overview of the available settings presented on the Common tab of the Section Expert. A subset of or all these options become available when you select a section in the Sections area, as described earlier. The following options are available in the Common tab:

- **Hide (Drill-Down OK)**—This option hides the respective section from the report's initial visual display but still enables report users to access the section's content with end-user drill down.

- **Suppress (No Drill-Down)**—Hides the respective section from the report's visual display and disables any drill-down capabilities such that the section's content is *not* available to report users. This is very useful for eliminating the display of sections that contain no data (such as redundant or empty Group Footer sections).

- **Print at Bottom of Page**—Causes the current section to print at the bottom of the page. This setting is most useful for printing invoices and other reports where you want summary values to appear toward the bottom of the page in a fixed position.

- **Keep Together**—Keeps a particular section together on one page without splitting the section between multiple pages. For example, in a customer list, data on a single customer might extend over several lines. If the standard page break falls within the data for a customer, the data splits—part on one page and the remainder on the next. You can use the Keep Together setting to insert the page break before the record begins so that all the data prints together on the following page.

- **Suppress Blank Section**—Hides the report section if it is blank and prints it only if it is not blank. This is a powerful display control for eliminating unnecessary blank space in reports.

- **Underlay Following Sections**—Permits the selected section to underlay the following section(s) when it prints, making the current section transparent. This feature is often used for the printing of watermarks (such as "Internal Use Only," "Draft," or a company logo) on a report. It is also often used to display data in different sections beside each other (for example, an underlying summary pie chart from the Report Header to show beside the actual details of a pie chart in the Group and Details sections).

- **Format with Multiple Columns**—Only available on the Details section, this option presents the Layout tab (otherwise hidden from view) within the Section Expert and enables you to use multiple columns in a given report. This powerful feature enables the presentation of row data in the Details section as columns in a report. It is particularly useful when presenting summarized information for comparison or a lengthy list—a topic discussed later in this chapter.

- **Clamp Page Footer**—When this check box is selected, the program removes any extra white space at the bottom of a report. This functionality can minimize unnecessary scrolling for reports when viewed online and is only available to be applied to the Page Footer section.

- **Reserve Minimum Page Footer (Page Footer section only)**—Reserves space at the bottom of each page for your Page Footer sections (a default setting). This enables you to minimize the space reserved for your Page Footer sections, thus maximizing the

7

space available for other report information on each page. This option affects only a Page Footer area with multiple sections.

- **Read-Only**—Locks the formatting and position of all report objects within the section so that they can't be formatted or repositioned.

- **Relative Positions**—Locks the relative position of a report object next to a grid object within a section. For example, if you place a text object one inch to the right of a cross-tab or OLAP (Online Analytical Processing) grid object, the program pushes the text object to the right during report generation to maintain the one inch of space regardless of the width of the cross-tab or OLAP grid object.

The presence of an X+2 button to the right of the majority of the options indicates that those options can be set via a formula in addition to setting them via the dialog. Setting an option via formula is referred to as *conditional formatting* because the formula typically evaluates a condition.

To implement a conditional option, click on the X+2 button associated with the option; the Formula Editor opens. Within the Formula Editor, create a formula that the program evaluates for every iteration of the section. If the formula evaluates to a value of True, the involved option is applied; otherwise, it is not. A simple but practical example of conditional section formatting could be a marketing campaign list where the marketing department wants to contact customers in the USA by phone and everywhere else by mail. You could create two Details sections: one that includes Contact Name and Phone Number, the other with Contact Name and Mailing Address. The first Details section can be conditionally suppressed with the formula {Customer.Country} <> "USA" to show that section only for USA-based customers. The second Details section could be conditionally suppressed with {Customer.Country} = "USA" to show only non–USA-based customers.

THE PAGING TAB

The following segment provides an overview of the available settings presented on the Paging tab of the Section Expert. A subset or all of these options are available when you select a section in the Sections area, as described previously. The following options are available in the Paging tab:

- **New Page Before**—Inserts a page break before it prints the section. This option is applicable only to the Group Header, Group Footer, Report Footer, and Details sections.

- **Reset Page Number After**—Resets the page number to one (1) for the following page after it prints a group total. When this option is used in conjunction with Print at Bottom of Page, a single group prints on a page, the group value is printed at the bottom of the page, and the page number is reset to 1 for the next page. This option is useful whenever you are printing multiple reports from a single file (such as customer invoices), and you want each report to be numbered beginning with page 1.

- **New Page After**—Inserts a page break after it displays and prints a section. For example, you can use this setting in the Group Footer section to print each group on a separate page. This option is not available for the Page Header, Page Footer, or Report Footer sections. Of additional note, two additional options become available for the report designer when this option is selected for a Details section: After End of Section and After a Specified Number of Visible Records.

- **Orientation**—Allows you to set page orientation for each section in the report except for the Page Header and Page Footer sections. The default setting is the same as the report page orientation in the Page Setup dialog box.

THE COLOR TAB

Use the Color tab to set the background color for the entire highlighted section, either absolutely or conditionally. A good example of a conditionally colored background is when presenting a lengthy list of detailed items. To enable easier reading of the report, every second row can be conditionally colored silver with the formula in Listing 7.1.

LISTING 7.1   ALTERNATE ROW COLORING FORMULA

```
IF RecordNumber Mod 2 = 1 THEN
    Silver
Else
White
```

THE LAYOUT TAB

As mentioned, the Layout tab appears only when you have the Details section selected and the Format Groups with Multiple Column check box has been selected on the Common tab. This tab enables multicolumn formatting. As described earlier, this kind of report enables you to present multiple columns of standard row data and have the data flow from column to column. This tab, shown in Figure 7.7, has four distinct settings:

- **Detail Size**—This box enables the specification of the dimensions (height and width) of each detail column.

- **Gap Between Details**—This box enables the specification of the empty area between detail columns and rows. The horizontal gap is the distance between the details going across the page, and the vertical gap is the distance between rows going down the page.

- **Printing Direction**—This option enables the specification of the flow path to be followed when printing the detail column and rows on a report page. The Across Then Down option prints details across the columns in one row first before moving onto the next row of data. The Down Then Across option prints details down an entire column before moving onto the next column.

- **Format Groups with Multiple Column**—This option formats groups with multiple columns using the Width, Gap Between Details, and Printing Direction options specified for the selected Details section.

7

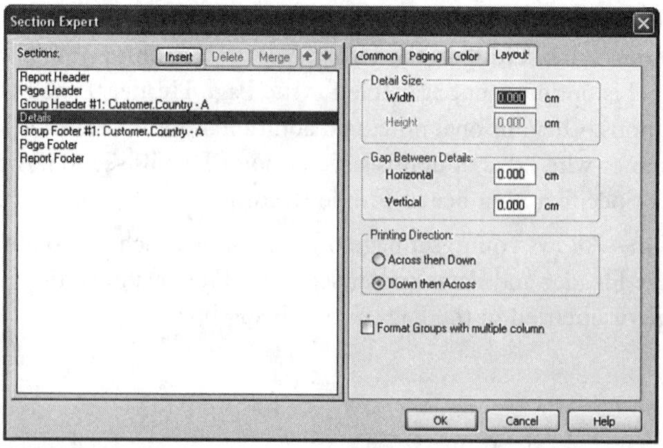

Figure 7.7
The Layout tab is available only for advanced multicolumn reports.

TIP

When you format a report to show multiple columns, the Crystal Reports engine reviews the fields in the Details section and sizes the columns in the rest of the report based on the width of the Details fields. If you place data labels (text fields) in the Details section for row identification, you increase the width of the report's columns and reduce the number of columns that fit on each page. To place such fields, consider putting them in a Page Header or Group Header section and underlying them on the Details section.

To begin to truly understand the powerful formatting capabilities of multicolumn reporting, it is instructive to edit your current contact list report using this functionality. Figure 7.8 highlights some appropriate layout settings you can set after you check the Format with Multi-Columns check box. (Remember that it's available only for the Details section.) At this time, do not check the Format Groups with Multiple Column option; set the Width and Gap options instead. Increase the height of the Details section and stack the current Details columns on top of one another for the best display. After completing vertical rearrangement of report fields, you can check the Format Groups with Multiple Column option to view the benefits of this functionality.

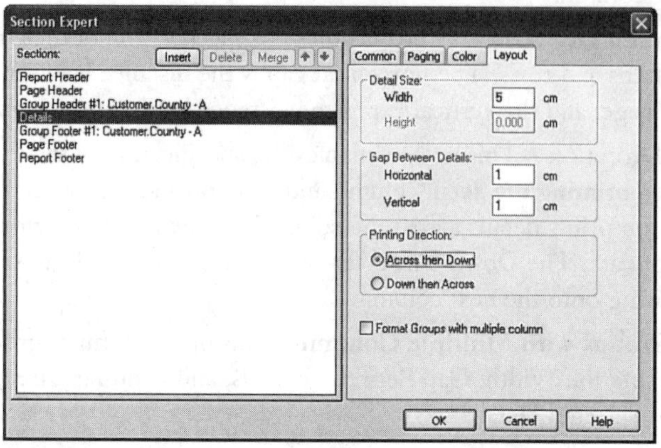

Figure 7.8
The Layout tab is available for the Details section only when the Format Group with Multiple Column option is set.

Figure 7.9 shows the results of this small report modification. The report now shows the pertinent customer contact information in multiple columns across the page. Designers often use this flexibility effectively in the creation of financial statements and other reports where a columnar display paradigm is natural or expected.

Figure 7.9
A multicolumn version of your customer contact report.

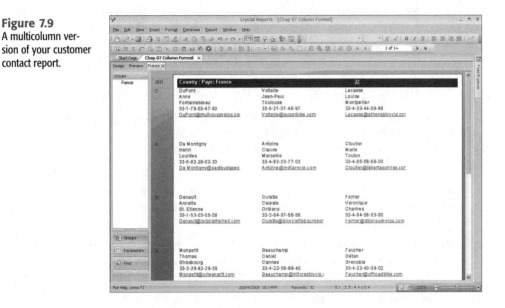

USING MULTIPLE REPORT SECTIONS

Including multiple sections within each section area of your report provides for an extremely flexible presentation of your report data. Chances are good that you do not need to create more than one occurrence of any of the existing report sections for basic reporting needs. However, Crystal Reports enables you to define multiple report sections within any given section area and to identify section-specific properties for challenging formatting requirements within more complex reports. The most efficient way to perform certain reporting tasks is by creating multiple sections within an area.

For example, multiple report sections are very useful when you want to create a form letter for your customers and you need it to display only one of two possible return addresses: an American address for customers based in the United States and a Canadian address for the Canadian customers. To accomplish this, you need to insert two Report Header sections into your report and use conditional formatting to dynamically apply the appropriate return address based on the customer's location.

To demonstrate how to implement and use multiple report sections, you first need to review the basic operations of resizing, inserting, removing, and merging report sections.

7

RESIZING REPORT SECTIONS

Report sections might require resizing to accommodate for various-sized report objects, such as large database fields, lengthy text objects, or corporate logo images, but they cannot exceed the size of the report page itself. From the Design tab of the report environment, you can drag the bottom boundary of the various sections up and down with the mouse to resize each section. Using the mouse, float the pointer over the horizontal boundary lines of the different sections. When the mouse pointer changes into a double-headed arrow icon, click and hold the left mouse button while dragging the boundary line to the desired position.

INSERTING NEW REPORT SECTIONS

To display only one of two possible return addresses on a form letter based on the country of the customer, you need to insert a second Page Header section into the report. The following steps walk you through constructing the following report using the Customer table from the Xtreme Sample database:

1. Create a new Crystal Report using the standard Report Wizard, connecting to the Xtreme Sample database and selecting the Customer table. Do not add database fields to the report. Click on the Finish button in the Fields Selection dialog.

2. Create a group (by choosing Insert, Group) based on the Customer Name field, but remove the Customer Name field from the Group Header section. The Group field should automatically appear in the Group Header section when you create the group.

3. Select the New Page After property for the Group Footer #1 section.

4. Ensure that the Report Header section is suppressed.

5. Create and insert text objects in the appropriate report sections, as shown in Figure 7.10.

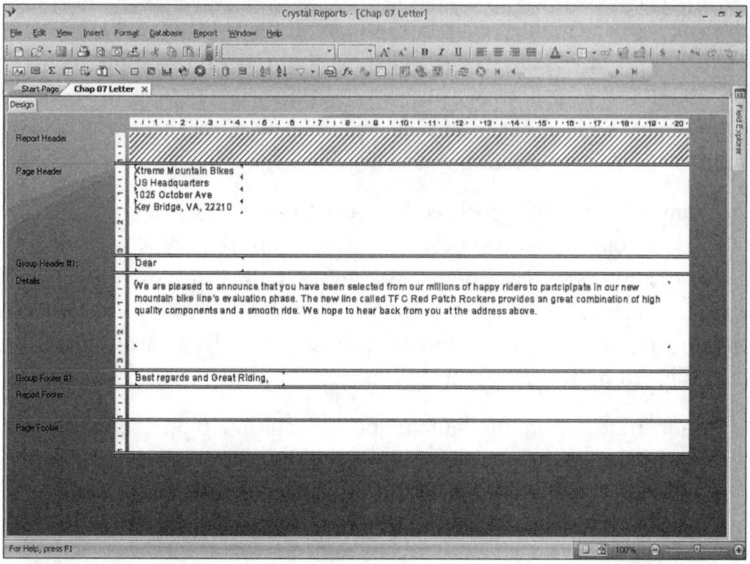

Figure 7.10
This simple form letter report shows the correct return address, chosen conditionally.

> Notice that in this sample form letter report, each report object displayed on the report is just a text object inserted into the appropriate section. The report includes no database fields yet.

Next you insert a new Page Header section to display an alternative return address for Canadian customers. The following steps take you through the process:

1. To insert a new Page Header section, locate the existing Page Header section, right-click on the section name (on the left of the design environment), and select Insert Section Below from the pop-up menu.

   The new section's name is Page Header b, and the original section's name changes to Page Header a so that there are now two Report Header sections within your report. The application follows this naming convention whenever you add multiple report sections.

2. After you insert a new Page Header section (labeled Page Header b), insert text objects to display a Canadian return address for the non–U.S.-based recipients of the form letter, as shown in Figure 7.11.

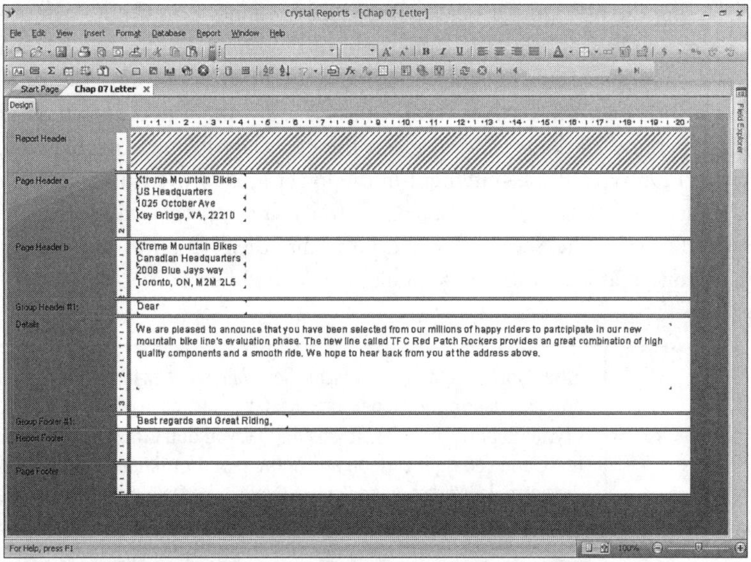

Figure 7.11
The form letter report now shows two Page Header sections.

Now that the report has two different return addresses and report sections, you must create the logic within the report to implement the appropriate Page Header section based on each customer's location—whether they are based in the United States or Canada. Evaluate each customer's mailing address on the Country field from the

Customer table. For this example, you're concerned with only North American customers, so if the Country field is equal to USA, use Page Header a to display the return address. If the Country field is equal to Canada, use Page Header b.

3. To isolate your report for only North American (excepting Mexico) customers, choose the Select Expert, Records option from the Report menu. From the list of available fields, select the Country field from the Customer table listing and click on OK to continue.

4. You should now see the Select Expert dialog. From the drop-down list on the left, select Is One Of and include Canada and USA in the list box. Click on OK to close the Select Expert dialog and accept your changes.

5. To add additional personalization to the form letter, use the Field Explorer to insert the Customer Name field into the Text object (located in the Group Header #1 that reads "Dear Customer") so that it appears as Dear {Customer Name} in the Design tab of your report. To do this, you'll need to modify the text portion of this combined object to read "Dear " (the word *Dear* followed by a space), and then followed by the database field object.

Finally, you need to apply the logic to display the appropriate return address on the form letter. To do this, you apply a conditional formatting statement (format formula) to each of the two Page Header sections.

6. Using the Section Expert for Page Header a, click on the X+2 button (with the pencil symbol) located directly to the right of the Suppress (No Drill-Down) option on the Common tab. After clicking this icon, the Format Formula Editor dialog (see Figure 7.12) opens. You can use the Field, Function, and Operator windows (located in the upper area of the dialog) to insert the necessary format formula within this dialog, or you can type in the statement in the lower area of the Editor dialog so that it reads {Customer.Country} = "Canada". After you insert this statement, click Save and Close to return to the Section Expert. Note that the X+2 button has changed color (to red) to signify that a conditional formula was created here.

> **TIP**
>
> When you are entering a specific field value (for example, Canada or USA) into a suppression filter or any other formula, take advantage of the direct paste option that Crystal Reports provides. To ensure that you don't mistype and that exact field values are used, you can right-click on any of the report or database fields in the top left frame of the Formula Workshop and select the Browse Data option. From the dialog that pops up, you can paste database values directly into your formulas and filters.

7. You now need to implement a very similar formatting condition for the Page Header b section. Following the same procedure used for the first section, use the Section Expert to insert a statement that reads {Customer.Country} = "USA".

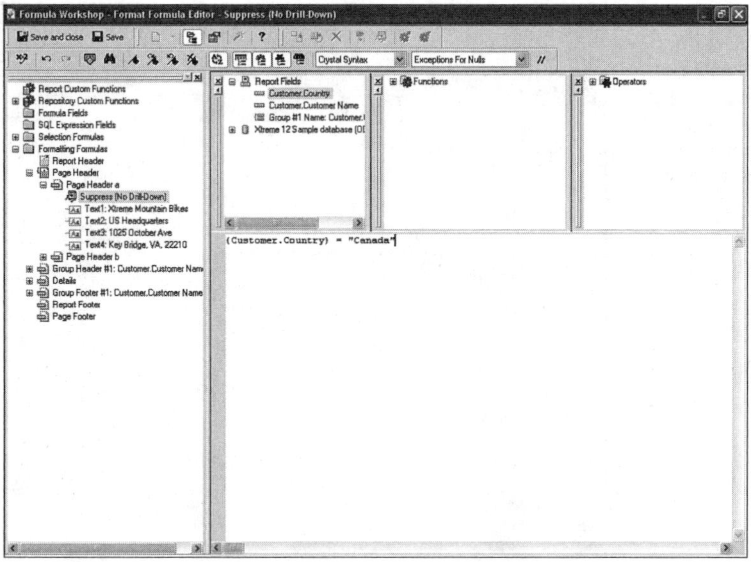

Figure 7.12
The report section is suppressed only if the conditional statement defined in the Format Formula Editor is `True`.

NOTE

You do not need to check the Suppress (No Drill-Down) check box in the Section Expert dialog for either report Page Header section. By inserting a format formula, you effectively apply conditional formatting that suppresses the section if the format formula evaluates to `True`. In this case, one of the two format formulas should always be `True` because the customers are located in either the United States or Canada.

8. Close the Section Expert dialog by clicking on OK. After refreshing the report by pressing F5 or by selecting the View, Preview menu option, your report should now display only one of the two possible return addresses on the form letter. To verify that the appropriate return address is populating on the form letter report for each customer, you can browse through the multiple pages of the report and verify that the return address changes. Figure 7.13 highlights the report output with only one return address displayed per customer.

DELETING REPORT SECTIONS

In much the same manner you inserted sections, you can quickly remove unused report sections from reports by right-clicking on the section name and selecting Delete Section from the pop-up menu. Be aware, however, that deleting a section from a report also deletes any report objects positioned within it. If any objects within a section you want to delete are required, you must relocate them to alternative report sections before deletion.

7

Figure 7.13
A simple form letter report, dynamically formatted with the appropriate return address based on the customer's location.

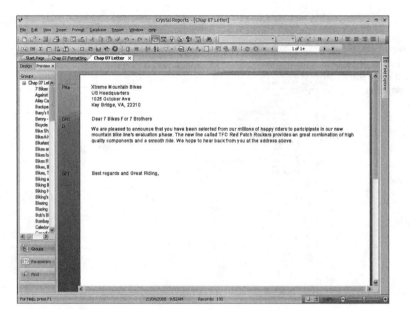

NOTE

Crystal Reports requires at least one section to be present for certain section types in every report—the Report Header and Footer, Page Header and Footer, and Details sections. When you create a new report, these report sections generate by default. Also, if Group objects exist within a report, you cannot remove the Group Header and Footer sections unless you first remove the Group object from the report.

MERGING REPORT SECTIONS

When designing reports, you might want to merge two report sections to simplify the layout of a report. To merge the two Page Header sections from the earlier example, right-click on the Page Header a section title and select Merge Section Below from the pop-up menu. The Merge Section Below command is available from the right-click menu of any report section that meets two criteria:

- There are more than one of the given section type (Page Header) within the section area.

- The section is not last in a series of sections (Page Header) consisting of the same section types within a common area.

For example, if three Page Header sections are present on a report (as shown in Figure 7.14), the Merge Section Below command would be accessible from the right-click menus of Page Header a and Page Header b, but not from Page Header c.

7

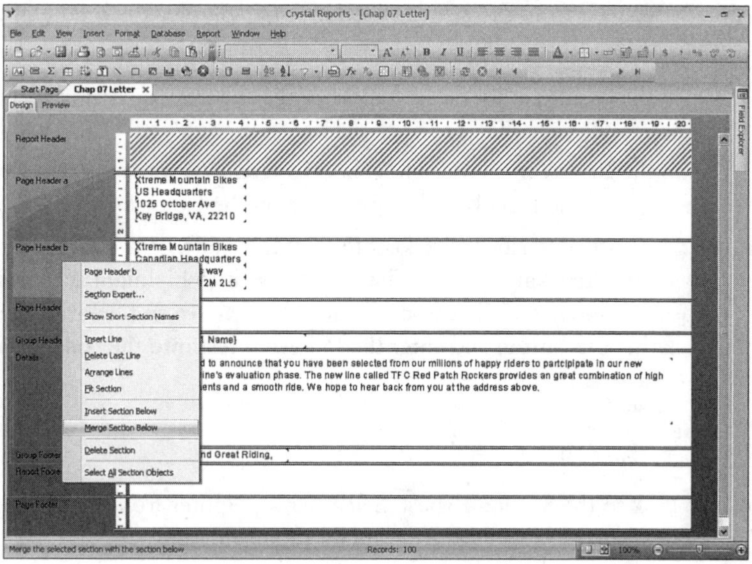

Figure 7.14
The Merge Section Below command is available from the right-click menu of certain report sections.

TROUBLESHOOTING

REPORT SECTION FORMATTING

I keep getting blank spaces above and/or below my data fields in my report sections, and I need a quick way of removing them.

To quickly remove blank spaces within report sections and tighten up the alignment of the objects positioned within the sections, use the Fit Section command available from the right-click menu of each report section.

SHOWING GROUP SECTION HEADERS ON DRILL-DOWN

I want the Group Header sections of each Group section to display as I drill down into the report's grouping hierarchy. By default, this does not happen, and creating conditional suppress functions on each section can be time-consuming.

To change the default behavior to always show Group Header sections on drilling down, access the Report Options dialog from the File menu and check the Show All Headers on Drill-Down option box.

CRYSTAL REPORTS IN THE REAL WORLD—ADVANCED FORMATTING

A report section often needs to be more than simply one color or another. A report with many rows might need some color to help guide the reader's eye and make each line distinctly separate from the next. In the following sample, you modify the report you created earlier to improve readability:

1. Open the Chap7RealWorld.rpt report or the report you created at the beginning of this chapter.

2. From the Report menu, select Section Expert. When the Section Expert dialog box opens, select the Details section and click on the Color tab.

3. As previously described, checking the Background Color box enables you to set all the Detail lines to a single color. The intent here is to highlight the detail lines so that they appear distinctly different from the detail line above and below to improve readability. Click the X+2 button and enter the following text into the code window:

```
If Remainder(RecordNumber,2)=1 Then
    crAqua
Else
    DefaultAttribute;
```

4. Go back to the Section Expert. Select Group Footer from the list of sections, and check the box labeled New Page After under the Paging tab.

5. Each group now starts on a new page, and long groups have detail lines defined by color. You can see the color improvement on page 3 of the report, as shown in Figure 7.15.

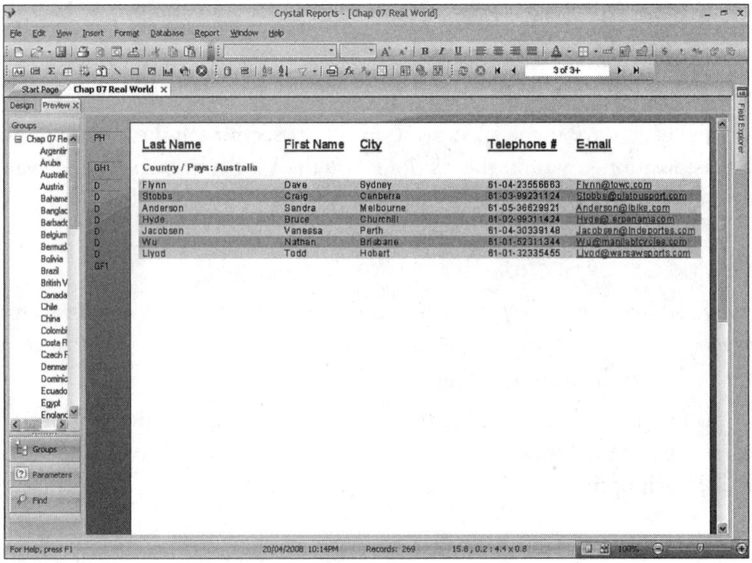

Figure 7.15
Records delimited by color for improved readability.

6. Save the report.

CRYSTAL REPORTS IN THE REAL WORLD—ADVANCED FORMATTING ON DRILL-DOWN REPORTS

Many reports deployed across the Crystal Reporting world include one or more levels of grouping that ideally require varied column headers at each of the different levels of grouping and drill-down. A powerful function in the Crystal Reports function library allows report designers to conditionally show or hide different report elements such as column headers based on the level of user drill-down. This function is called `drilldowngrouplevel` and, used in combination with the conditional suppression capabilities of Crystal Reports, enables reports to show different column elements based on the user's current level of drill-down. This function returns 0 when the current user view is the original report view, returns 1 when the current user view is the first level of drill-down, and returns n on the nth level of user drill-down.

In the following sample, you will take the report just created in the previous Real World section and conditionally show the column headings only when the user is viewing the drill-down details below the country group level.

1. Open the `Chap7RealWorldDrilldown.rpt` report or the report you created in the last Real World section.

2. Prepare the report by hiding the Details section to make it available on drill-down but not apparent in the original report view. You can accomplish this by right-clicking on the Details section header and selecting the Hide (Drill-Down OK) menu option. Additionally, insert a summary in the Group Header that counts the number of Details rows for a given country group. As a final preparation step, remove the the New Page After option from the Group Footer section.

3. Insert a new Group Header section underneath the current section, and move all of the column headers from the original Page Header section into this new section. This is the section of column headers that we only want to show up if the user has drilled down into the report details.

4. Go to the Section Expert and create a suppression formula by clicking on the X+2 formula button beside the Suppression option. Enter the following suppression formula.

   ```
   DrillDownGroupLevel = 0
   ```

   This will enforce suppression of the newly inserted Group Header section (and the column headers) in the original report view as shown in Figure 7.16. This is meaningful since we have hidden the report details in this original view, so showing their column headings would be redundant.

5. Preview the report and note that the column headings are not shown until you actually drill down into the report details by double-clicking on the count summary group field. Figure 7.17 highlights the appearance of the column headings after the user has drilled down on the Australia country group summary.

7

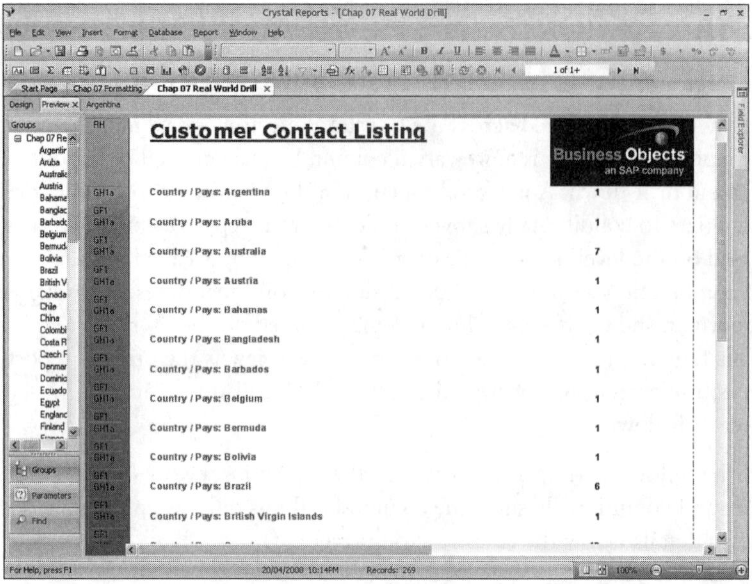

Figure 7.16
Detail record column headings hidden in original report view.

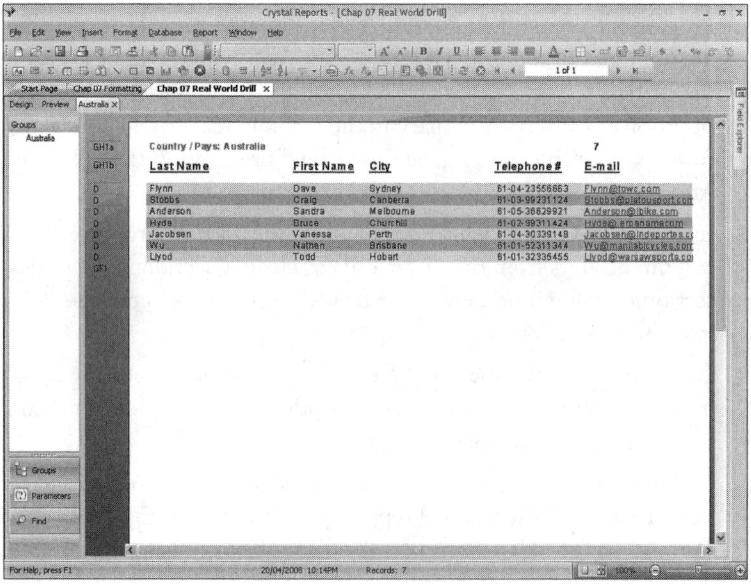

Figure 7.17
Detail record column headings displayed in drill-down report view.

7

CHAPTER 8

VISUALIZING YOUR DATA WITH CHARTS AND MAPS

In this chapter

INTRODUCTION

Chapter 2, "Selecting and Grouping Data," and Chapter 3, "Filtering, Sorting, and Summarizing Data," introduced the importance of grouping and summarizing in report generation. When doing so for business users, it is often effective to present these groups and summarizations using various visualization techniques. The charting and mapping features in Crystal Reports provide a very effective way to communicate relevant information using powerful visualization techniques.

Charts and maps with Crystal Reports provide an extensive array of data visualization options to report designers. In addition to familiar chart types, including bar charts, pie charts, scatter charts, line charts, and bubble charts, new chart types in recent versions include the following:

- Histogram charts (v.XI)
- Funnel charts (v.10)
- Gantt charts (v.9)
- Gauges (v.9)
- Numeric axis charts (v.9)

Geographic mapping with color-coding and integrated charting options provides another effective method of conveying macro-level information to report consumers.

This chapter introduces various charting and mapping techniques, including

- Enhancing the sample reports from previous chapters with charts and maps
- A review of the Crystal Reports charting expert
- An introduction to the newer chart types: Gantt, gauge, numeric axis, funnel, and histogram charts
- A review of the Crystal Reports Map Expert
- Manual chart and map formatting

The Chart Expert is a good place to begin adding visualizations to your reports.

USING THE CHART EXPERT

Reflecting back on the sample reports used in Chapters 2 and 3, you might find that there are opportunities for enhancement through the addition of meaningful charts. As you learned with groupings in Chapter 2, it is quite easy to summarize the data you collect for a report into meaningful categories or groups. Chapter 2 reviews some examples of grouping based on fields such as country and employee ID. By hiding or suppressing the detail sections of reports, you learned how to bring the meaningful summarizations around these types of groups to the forefront. To further bring this aggregated data to the business user's attention, you can create a chart on this grouped data using the Chart Expert.

To open the Chart Expert, either click on the Chart icon located on the Insert toolbar, or select the Insert Chart option under the main Insert menu and then, after placing the chart placeholder on your report in the desired section, access the Chart Expert menu option from the chart's context menu. Figure 8.1 displays the Chart Expert.

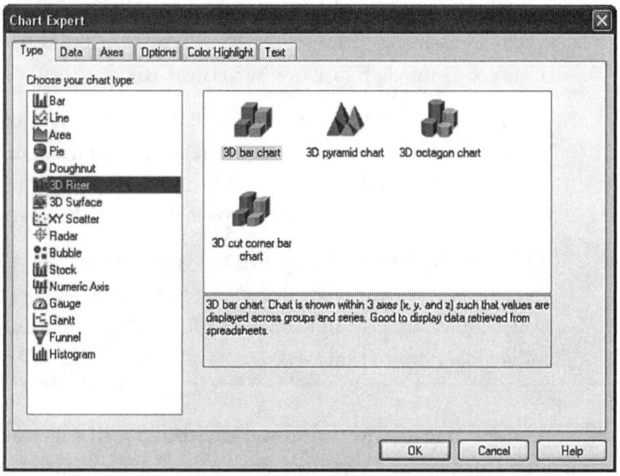

Figure 8.1
The Chart Expert dialog enables the rapid addition of valuable charts to reports.

After you access the Chart Expert, several steps are required to actually complete the chart. These are reviewed in the next six sections.

USING THE CHART EXPERT TYPE TAB

The Chart Expert consists of six different tabs. The initial display tab on the Chart Expert is the Type tab, as shown in Figure 8.1. On that tab, the type of graphic or chart is selected. In Crystal Reports version 2008, there are more than 40 different basic chart types from which to select.

In addition to the classic bar, line, pie, and area charts, new chart types in versions 9, 10, and XI are listed in Table 8.1.

TABLE 8.1 NEW CHART TYPES IN CRYSTAL REPORTS VERSIONS 9, 10, AND XI

New Chart Type	Chart Type Description
Numeric axis (v.9)	A numeric axis chart is a bar, line, or area chart that uses a numeric field or a date/time field as its On Change Of field. With numeric axis charts, you can create a true numeric x-axis or a true date/time x-axis.
Gauge(s) (v.9)	A gauge chart presents data using a speedometer visual and is often used to measure percentage completed against target type metrics.

continues

8

TABLE 8.1 CONTINUED	
New Chart Type	**Chart Type Description**
Gantt (v.9)	A Gantt chart is a project-focused horizontal bar chart used to provide a graphical illustration of a project schedule. The horizontal axis shows a time span, whereas the vertical axis lists project tasks or events. Horizontal bars on the chart represent event sequences and time spans for each task on the vertical axis.
Funnel (v.10)	Funnel charts are most often used to represent stages in a sales cycle and visually depict proportionality of the different phases in that sales process. A funnel chart is similar to a stacked bar chart in that it represents 100% of the summary values for the groups included in the chart.
Histogram (v.XI)	Histograms show the frequency of occurrence of data elements in a data set. The x-axis is divided into intervals that denote ranges of data values. Each histogram bar shows the number of data elements whose value falls into that interval.

These charts have been added to expand the visual capabilities of Crystal Reports and enrich your report presentations. Let's create a sample customer order listing report and add a chart to it that highlights the company's top 10 customers in the following steps:

1. Quickly create the basics of this sample report by selecting the Customer Name, Order ID, and Order Amount fields from the Xtreme 12 Sample Database (Customer and Orders tables). Then select Group by Customer Name and Summarize Order Amount by the Customer Name group.

2. To restrict the data to the top 10 customers, access the Group Sort Expert from the Report menu option. Select a top 10 sort based on the sum of order amount, and do *not* include others or ties.

3. Insert a Chart object onto the report using the Chart toolbar icon or the Chart option from the Insert menu. You will then decide where to place the chart on your report. Drop the Chart object identified by a colored outline in the Report Header section. The location of the report is important in determining the recurrence of the chart. By placing it in the Report Header, the chart appear only once. If you had placed it in the Group Header or Footer for Country, a new and separate chart would be created for every group.

4. Right-click on the newly created Chart object and select the Chart Expert option. Select a bar chart as the main chart type in the list box by clicking on it.

5. Select the two-dimensional side-by-side bar chart subchart type (top left option) by clicking on the associated graphical icon to the right of the Chart Type list box.

Figure 8.2 displays the result of these five steps. You will continue creating this chart in the next four sections.

Figure 8.2
The Type tab on the
Chart Expert dialog
for the Sample Top 10
Customers report.

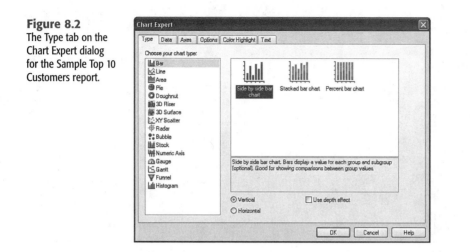

Table 8.2 highlights some common reports, their contained graphics, and the benefits of using them.

TABLE 8.2   COMMON REPORTS WITH CORRESPONDING CHART TYPES

Report	Chart Type	Report and Chart Benefit
Company Sales Report	Pie or Donut Chart	Highlights the regional breakdown of product sales across continents or countries, facilitating analysis of revenue contribution.
Product Profitability Report	Horizontal or Vertical Bar Chart	Highlights the profit margin per product that a company sells, facilitating comparative analysis of profitability.
Actual versus Target Report	Gauges	Highlights the progress being made against specified targets through the use of a speedometer visual. When used across projects or divisions, it is relatively easy to compare how they are performing against certain initiatives.

USING THE CHART EXPERT DATA TAB

After you select a chart type in the Type tab, click on the Data tab. The Data tab enables the selection of the specific data on which the chart is based and the chart's location on the report. Figure 8.3 displays one view of the second tab of the Chart Expert. This view might vary depending on the different Chart Type options you have selected. The Data tab is composed of two sections: Layout and Data. These sections and corresponding options are discussed next.

Figure 8.3
The Data tab of the
Chart Expert enables
specification of layout
and data options.

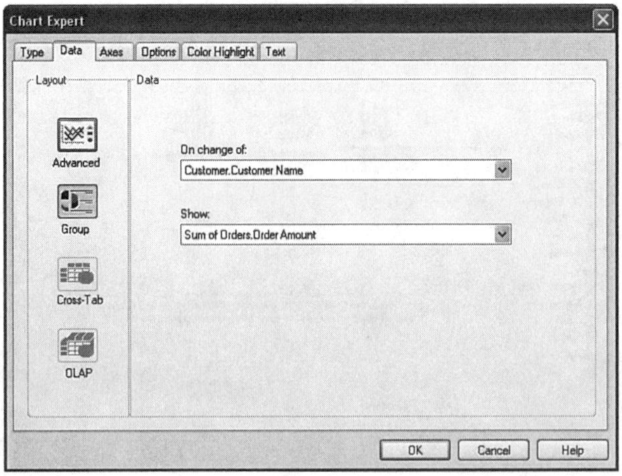

SPECIFYING CHART LAYOUT

The Chart Layout section specifies the data selection options that the selected chart provides to the report designer. The actual data is selected in the Chart Data section. Note that the options presented in that section depend on the specific Chart Layout button you selected. Table 8.3 lists the different layout buttons and their typical uses.

TABLE 8.3 LAYOUT BUTTONS AND TYPICAL USES

Layout Button	Description	Typical Uses
Advanced	This layout button provides complete flexibility in chart creation by providing you with control of all charting options.	Creation of charts based on summaries not already created in the report or charts to be created for every detail record.
Group	Although this button is presented second, it is the default layout. This layout limits the Chart Data Selection options (see the following "Specifying Chart Data" section) to two drop-down boxes specifying the On Change Of and Show Values and expedites the creation of a chart at the cost of some of the flexibility provided by the Advanced layout button.	Quick creation of charts based on summarized fields already in the report and to be displayed at the Report or existing Group level.
Cross-Tab	This layout button appears as an option only when your current report is a Cross-Tab report.	Creation of a chart based on an existing Cross-Tab in the report.
OLAP	This layout button appears as an option only when your current report is based on an OLAP data source.	Creation of a chart based on an existing OLAP grid in the report.

The Cross-Tab and OLAP layout buttons and their related options are explored in Chapters 10, "Using Cross-Tabs for Summarized Reporting," and 16, "Formatting Multidimensional Reporting Against OLAP Data," because they relate to very specific report types. The next section explores the detailed data options that the Advanced and Group layout buttons enable.

SPECIFYING CHART DATA

Figure 8.3 displays the Data tab with the Group layout button selected. As previously described, this layout option facilitates the quick creation of a chart with a minimal amount of effort. To accomplish this rapid chart creation, two pieces of information are requested through two drop-down boxes—On Change Of (grouping item) and Show (field to be shown in the chart) selections. The On Change Of field determines where the selected chart breaks the displayed report data. The Show field specifies the summary field to display for each break of the data.

To continue adding a bar chart to the sample report, follow these steps:

1. Ensure that the Group layout button from the Layout section is selected.

2. Select Customer Name in the On Change Of field. This indicates that the chart breaks for each different customer.

3. Select Sum of Orders.Order Amount for the Show field. This indicates that the chart reflects this sum for each customer. Figure 8.3 reflects the results of these steps in the Chart Data tab. You will continue creating this chart in the next section.

NOTE

> When leveraging the Rapid Chart Creation functionality of the group layout option, it's worth noting that you are limited to chart creation based on existing summary fields already created in your reports and inserted into existing group sections. For more flexible chart creation, you can use the Advanced layout option described later.

Figure 8.4 displays the Data tab with the Advanced layout button selected. The additional options presented here give you more flexibility in the charts that you can create.

The On Change Of and Show Values fields should be recognizable in this new window, although they are selected in a much more flexible manner (see the right side of the Data section beside the Available Fields listing) described next.

The On Change Of field is now only one selection option (among three) in its own drop-down box. If you need to create a chart based on changing a specific field (as you did with the standard group layout), select the On Change Of charting option and then specify the field or fields to break the chart sections on by selecting any of the fields in the available fields listing. Unlike the drop-down box under the Group layout, you can select any of the available report fields in this interface, dynamically order them with the Order button, or restrict their display on the report to a specified Top or Bottom N with the Top N button. You can also dynamically select multiple fields for the chart to break on. None of the selected fields need to be already on the report or have summary fields previously existing on the report for them.

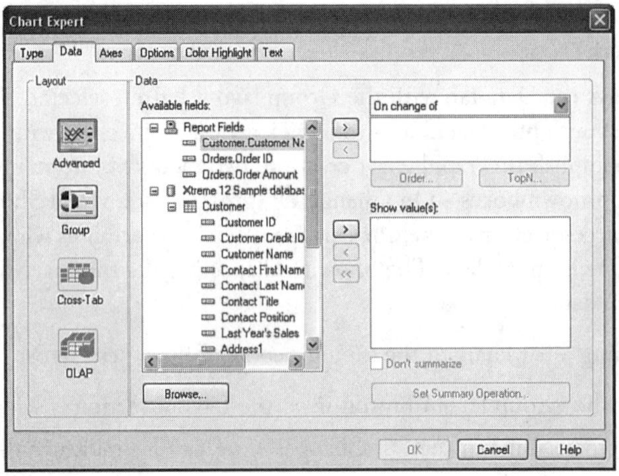

Figure 8.4
The Data tab with the Advanced layout button selected.

The remaining two options in the On Change Of drop-down box are For Each Record and For All Records. These two options enable you to create charts either against all data in a report or for each detailed record in a report.

TIP

> When using the For All Records charting option, you can select the field to display for each break by selecting a field from the Available Fields list in the list box beneath the For All Records drop-down box.

After selecting any of these options, you need to select a Show Value(s) field to enable the chart's creation. This selection specifies the summary field to display for each break of the data and can come from any field (database, report, formula, and so on) listed in the available field's list. To select the Show Value fields, highlight the intended field and use the selection arrow buttons adjacent to the Show Values list box.

NOTE

> You do not need to have an existing summary on your report to use it for a graph in the Advanced Charting layout options. You can add any field to the Show Values list and then dynamically create a summary by clicking on the Set Summary Operation button. These dynamically created summaries are created automatically and used by the chart. This is one of the unique features of Crystal Reports that provides you with more charting flexibility.

USING THE CHART EXPERT AXES TAB

The third tab in the Chart Expert dialog, the Axes tab enables you to customize chart gridlines, data value scales, data value ranges, and data value divisions. Figure 8.5 displays the Axes tab of the Chart Expert dialog for a bar chart.

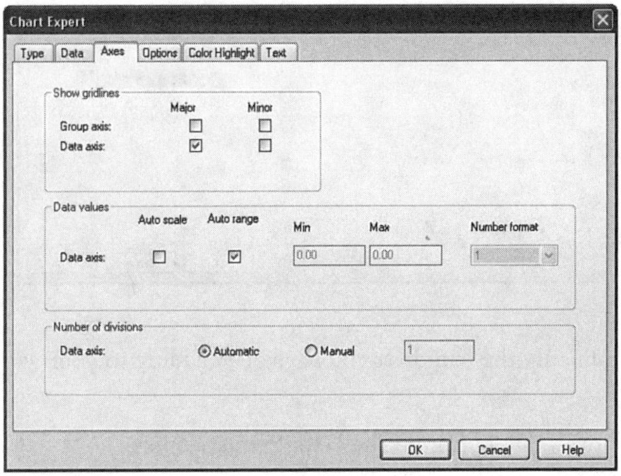

Figure 8.5
The Axes tab of the Chart Expert allows specification of gridline display, axis ranges, and divisions.

> **NOTE**
>
> This tab appears only when the selected chart type has axes within it (for example, a bar chart or line chart) and does not display for other chart types, such as pie charts.

To continue adding a bar chart to the sample report, try the following step: Select the Major Gridlines check box for the data axis. This facilitates the reading of the bar charts. You will finish creating this bar chart in the following section.

> **TIP**
>
> By manually setting both the Min/Max Data Ranges and the Number of Divisions options, you are able to customize your data axis gridline display labels.

USING THE CHART EXPERT OPTIONS TAB

The Options tab in the Chart Expert enables you to customize chart coloring, data point labeling, legend placement, legend format options, and several other chart type–specific formatting options. Figure 8.6 displays the Options tab of the Chart Expert dialog for a bar chart.

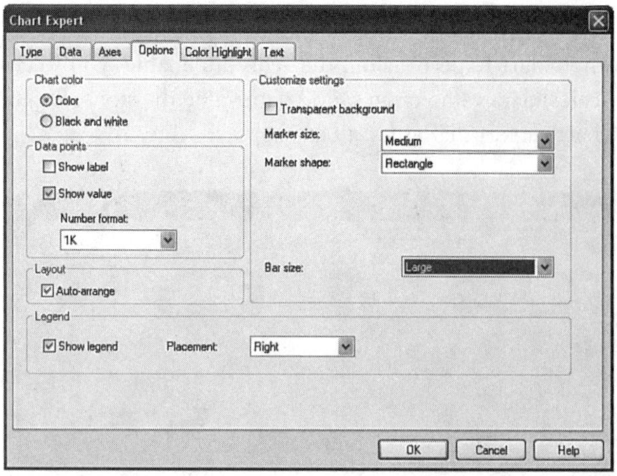

Figure 8.6
The Chart Expert
Options tab allows
specification of data
points and legends
for the involved chart.

To continue customizing the bar chart you have been adding to your working sample report, follow these steps:

1. Select the Show Value button in the Data Points section.

2. Select the 1K format from the Number Format drop-down box.

3. Click on the OK button.

USING THE CHART EXPERT COLOR HIGHLIGHT TAB

New since version XI, the Color Highlight tab provides you with an easy method of controlling the color of the different elements (such as bars, pie slices, and so forth) in your created charts. This functionality was hard to find in previous versions of Crystal Reports, but it was previously available through the Format button under the Chart Expert Options tab.

> **TIP**
>
> The color highlighting functionality enables you to create charts with consistent coloring both within and across your reports. In the sample report in this chapter, you could specify the color of any particular customer, or you could specify the color of multiple bars based on the sum of the Orders Amount field. An example might be that where the sum of Orders Amount is greater than 75,000, the involved bar should be colored black to highlight the positive impact on Xtreme's bottom line.

USING THE CHART EXPERT TEXT TAB

After specifying a chart type and data, select the Text tab. This tab on the Chart Expert dialog enables you to specify titles and title formatting that the chart displays when it is placed on the report. Figure 8.7 shows the Text tab of the Chart Expert.

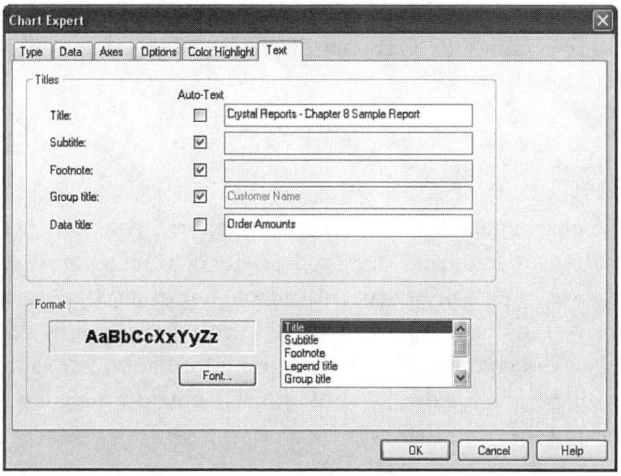

8

Figure 8.7
The Text tab of the Chart Expert allows specification of text labels for the associated chart.

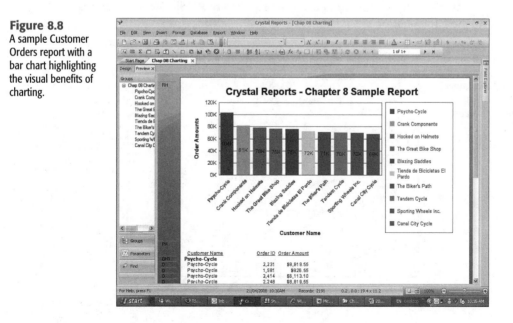

To finish adding the bar chart to the sample report, follow these steps:

1. Deselect the Auto-Text check box beside the Title entry. You should now be able to modify the text box for the title. Change the title to `Crystal Reports—Chapter 8 Sample Report`.

2. Deselect the Auto-Text check box beside the Data Title entry. Change the Data Title entry to `Order Amounts`. Click on OK, and you will find a bar chart similar to that in Figure 8.8, providing a snapshot of the top 10 customers for this report.

Figure 8.8
A sample Customer Orders report with a bar chart highlighting the visual benefits of charting.

If you find your chart is slightly different in appearance or imperfect, that is okay. You have plenty of powerful fine-tuning tools at your disposal, and you will explore them at the end of this chapter.

USING THE MAP EXPERT

As you explore the charting capabilities of Crystal Reports, you will discover numerous powerful data visualizations that enhance the productivity of your reports and business users. Another valuable form of data presentation available in Crystal Reports is geographic mapping. This enables you to create reports that are logically grouped by geographically related information and that can communicate meaningful information in a familiar mapping model. When working with geographic data, you can quickly create a map or a map/chart combination on this data using the Map Expert.

TIP

> The maps and mapping functionality provided within Crystal Reports are bundled from a third-party company: MapInfo. Additional map layers and types can be purchased directly from MapInfo and can be made accessible from Crystal Reports by adding them to the mapping folders under \Program Files\Map Info X. You can order additional mapping information from MapInfo at www.mapinfo.com.

To open the Map Expert, either click on the Map Globe icon located on the Insert toolbar or select Insert, Insert Map from the menu bar. Figure 8.9 displays the Map Expert dialog with the Group button selected.

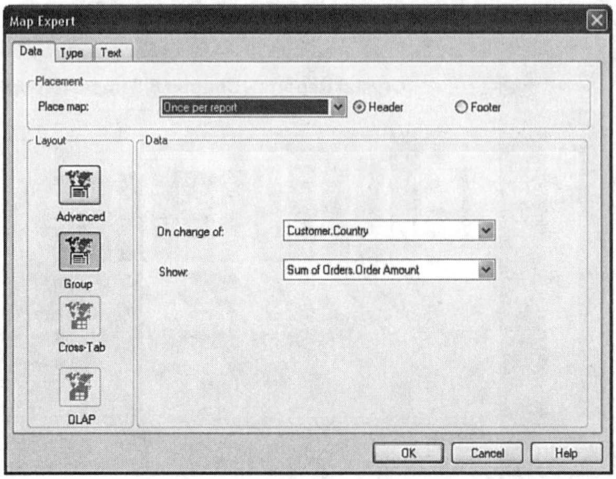

Figure 8.9
The Map Expert dialog enables the rapid addition of mapping visuals to a report.

The next three sections introduce you to the functionality of the Map Expert and escort you through a brief tutorial on the addition of a map to a sample Order Listing report slightly different from the one you just created.

USING THE MAP EXPERT DATA TAB

The Data tab on the Map Expert dialog enables you to select the specific data that the map is based on and where it is placed on the report. Figure 8.9 displays this tab of the Map Expert. The Data tab is composed of three different sections: Placement, Layout, and Data. These sections and their corresponding options are discussed next.

SPECIFYING MAP PLACEMENT

The Map Placement section enables the selection of the location of the map on the report and consequently the recurrence of the map throughout the report.

Using the Place Map drop-down box, select the section of the report where the map will be located (for example, Group 1, Group 2, and so on). The options available in this drop-down box are limited to the groups previously created in the report in addition to the option to create the graphic only once for the entire report. Using the radio buttons located beside the drop-down box, choose the header or footer of the selected report section. By making these selections, you also determine the map's recurrence in the report because the map repeatedly appears in every section you specify (for example, for each country in the group based on country).

To begin with a walkthrough of an example, perform the following steps:

1. Quickly create a new report similar to the report created earlier in this chapter based on the Xtreme 12 Sample Data database. Add a few columns of data in the detail section, including Order Amount, and group the report by Customer Country and by Customer Name. Finally, add summary fields on Order Amount for each of the Country and Customer Name groups.

2. Open the Map Expert via the Insert Map menu option or by clicking on the Map Global icon on the toolbar.

3. Select Once Per Report in the Placement drop-down box and select the header as the map's intended location. The following sections contain more steps for this example.

SPECIFYING MAP LAYOUT

The Layout section specifies the data that the map uses. The actual data is selected in the Map Data section (described next), but the options presented in that section depend on the Map Layout button you select. Table 8.4 lists the different layout buttons and their typical use.

8

TABLE 8.4 MAP EXPERT LAYOUT BUTTONS AND TYPICAL USE

Layout Button	Description	Typical Use
Advanced	This layout button provides complete flexibility in map creation by giving you control of all mapping options.	Creation of maps based on summaries not already created in the report or maps based on geographic fields not contained in predefined report groups.
Group	Although this button is presented second, it is often the default layout if the involved report has predefined groups and summary fields already created. This layout limits the Map Data Selection options (see next section) to two drop-down boxes specifying the On Change Of and Show Values and expedites the creation of a map at the cost of some of the flexibility provided by the Advanced layout button.	Quick creation of Maps based on summarized fields already in the report and to be displayed at the Report or existing Group level.
Cross-Tab	This layout button appears as an option only when your current report is a Cross-Tab report.	Creation of a map based on an existing Cross-Tab in the report.
OLAP	This layout button appears as an option only when your current report is based on an OLAP data source.	Creation of a map based on an existing OLAP grid in the report.

→ For information on the Cross-Tab and OLAP layout buttons and their related options, **see** Chapter 10, **p. 253**, and Chapter 16, **p. 369**.

The next section explores the detailed data options enabled by the Advanced and Group Layout buttons.

CAUTION

> If you attempt to create a geographic map based on a nongeographic field, the Map Expert accepts your request and then displays a blank map when it cannot resolve the selected field values to geographic entities. Make sure you select a valid geographic field in the Geographic Field item of the Advanced layout section or the On Change Of field in the Group layout section.

SPECIFYING MAP DATA

As you saw earlier, Figure 8.9 displays the Map Data section with the Group layout button selected. As described in Table 8.4, this layout option facilitates the quick creation of a map with a minimal amount of user interaction. To accomplish this rapid map creation, two pieces of information are requested through two drop-down boxes.

The first drop-down box requests you to select the On Change Of field and the second requests the Show field. The On Change Of field determines where the selected map breaks the report data to display (for example, Country, State, or Province). The Show field specifies the summary field to display for each break of the data.

NOTE

> When using the Rapid Map Creation function of the Group layout option, you are limited to map creation based on existing summary fields already created in your reports and inserted into existing group sections. For more flexible map creation, use the Advanced layout option described later.

Figure 8.10 displays the Map Data tab with the Advanced layout button selected. The additional options presented provide you with improved flexibility in the maps that you can create.

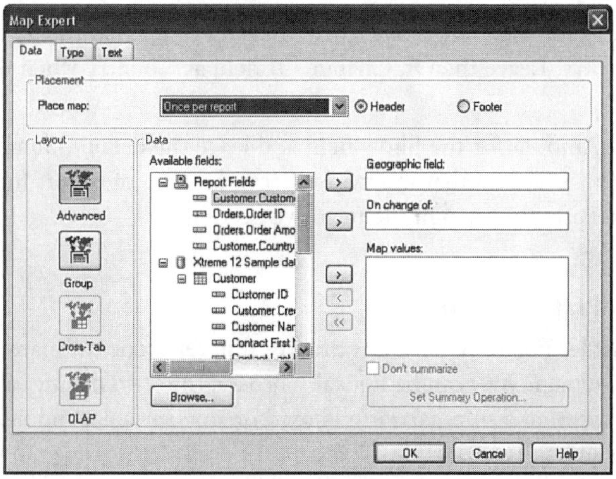

Figure 8.10
The Data tab with the Advanced layout button selected allows flexible selection of mapping data, layout, and placement.

The familiar On Change Of field should be recognizable in this new window, although it is selected in a more flexible manner using the selection buttons in the interface. It is selected in the same manner as the Geographic field selection in this interface by selecting any of the fields in the Available Fields listing and clicking on the selection button.

NOTE

> The Geographic and On Change Of fields are often the same but can be set to be different. They are set to different field values when you want to present pie or bar charts on top of the involved map and for each different value in the selected Geographic field. An example of this would be presenting a pie chart for each country that highlights the different order amounts by company—indicated in the On Change Of field.

After selecting your Geographic and On Change Of fields, you must select a Map Values field to enable the map's creation. This selection specifies the summary field to display for each break of the data and can come from any field (database, report, formula, and so on) listed in the available field's list. To select the Show Value fields, highlight the intended field and use the selection arrow buttons adjacent to the Map Values list box.

NOTE

As mentioned previously, you do not need to have had an existing summary on a report to summarize on it using the Advanced Mapping layout options. You can add any field to the Map Values list and then dynamically create a summary by clicking on the Set Summary Operation button. These dynamically created summaries are automatically created and used by the map.

To continue adding a map to your sample report, follow these steps:

1. Ensure that the Advanced layout button from the Layout section is selected.

2. Select Country for the Geographic field. This indicates that the map breaks for each different country. Leave the On Change Of field as Country when this populates automatically.

3. Select Order Amount for the Show field and leave the default, Sum, as the summary operation. This indicates that the map reflects this sum of orders for each country. You will finish creating this map in the next two sections.

USING THE MAP EXPERT TYPE TAB

The Type tab enables you to select from the five different types of maps available for presentation. The five map types can be logically broken into two distinct and separate categories: maps that present a summarization based on one variable, and maps that present a summarization based on two variables. Figure 8.11 depicts the Type tab with these five map types. All five map types are also described in Table 8.5.

The first three map types shown base their maps on the summary of the selected Show Value field and for each Geographic field—the single fluctuating variable. The last two map types base their maps not only on the changing Geographic field, but also on a second fluctuating variable selected in the On Change Of field. Based on this second variable changing, either bar or pie charts display on top of each involved Geographic field. Table 8.5 describes the different map types and includes a sample scenario for each.

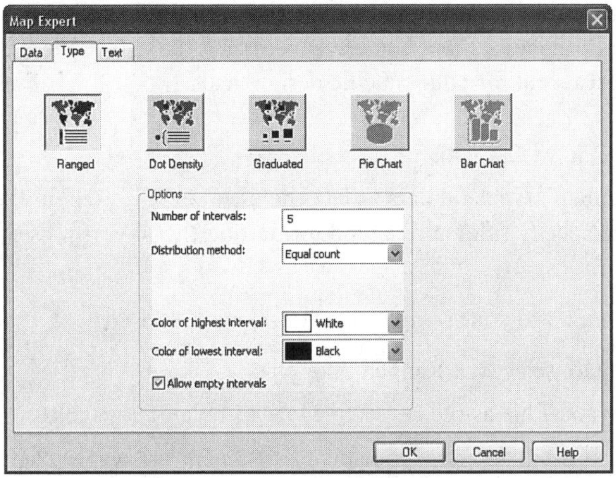

8

Figure 8.11
The Map Expert Type tab enables you to select from the different types of maps available for display in your report.

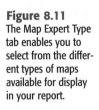

TABLE 8.5   MAP TYPES WITH CORRESPONDING SAMPLE REPORTING SCENARIO

Map Type	Description	Sample Scenario
Ranged	Breaks data into specified ranges and displays geographic areas on the map in different colors.	A U.S.-based firm looking for a Sales Map that highlights the states that fall into a specified number of sales/revenue ranges.
Dot Density	Displays a dot for each occurrence of a specified item.	A growing wireless company in Eastern Canada wants to view the density and point location of new customers and map that to ongoing marketing campaigns.
Graduated	Displays data that is linked to points rather than precise geographical areas.	An Irish beverage company wants a report on geographically dispersed distributors, proportionately highlighting the amount of product being distributed.
Pie Chart	Displays a pie chart over each geographic area. Each slice of the pie represents an individual summarization relative to the whole for the given geographic area.	An employee head-count report for the United States with a pie chart over each state that highlights the breakdown of the employees by status including salaried, hourly, or temporary.
Bar Chart	Displays a bar chart over each geographic area. Each bar represents an individual summarization relative to the other summarizations for the given geographic area.	A marketing media report for a U.S.-based company with a bar chart that highlights the amount of advertising and marketing dollars spent in different media in each region: TV, Internet, newspaper, magazine, and so on.

8

Each map type has a small number of associated options that can be set to customize the appearance of that particular map. You are encouraged to explore these options to help you find the maps most useful for your specific design goals.

USING THE MAP EXPERT TEXT TAB

After you select a map's type and data, select the Text tab. This tab on the Map Expert dialog enables you to specify titles and legend formatting that the map uses when it is placed on the report.

To finish adding a map to your sample report, follow these steps:

1. On the Type tab, select the Ranged map type.

2. Select Yellow and Blue as the respective low and high range colors.

3. Click on the Text tab and give your map a title such as `Crystal Reports 2008—Chapter 8 Map Sample`.

4. Click on OK, and you will find a geographic map added to your report that should look similar to Figure 8.12.

Figure 8.12
A sample Customer Orders report with a geographic map.

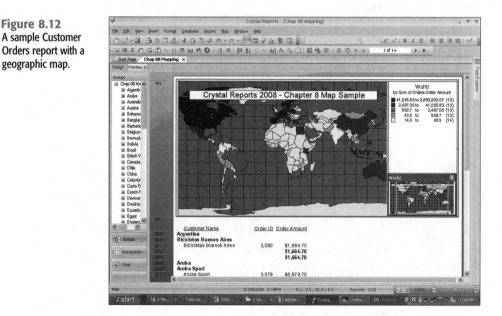

MODIFYING CHART AND MAP PROPERTIES

After you successfully create a chart or map and place it on your report, you have a number of post-creation editing options at your disposal within the Crystal Reports Designer. Both charts and maps provide a number of easy-to-use methods to revisit and edit your charts or maps. The following sections list several of the most common editing methods.

MODIFYING CHART PROPERTIES

After you create a chart and place it on your report, you can perform numerous post-creation edits by right-clicking on the chart object while in Preview mode. From the Chart menu that appears, you have both the ability to revisit the Chart Expert and use a number of more finely tuned post-creation editing tools, including the powerful and flexible Chart Option functions.

NOTE

> Version 2008 of Crystal Reports gives you the great ability to perform numerous in-place edits to chart objects. For example, you can grab a chart title (or other object) and move its location or change its font directly in place. Before version 9, this functionality was mostly accessible from a separate tab called the Chart Analyzer. That tab is no longer available.

FORMAT CHART OPTIONS

As introduced in Chapter 6, "Fundamentals of Report Formatting," the Format Chart dialog enables you to add common formatting options for the involved chart. Common options set here for charts include borders, ToolTips, and/or general hyperlinks. Review Chapter 6 for a detailed discussion of the different general formatting options you have for the chart.

USING AND CREATING CHART TEMPLATES

The Load Template selection provides direct access to a set of almost 100 custom charts in eight categories, including Basic, Big Data Sets, Corporate, Gradients, Letter Size B&W, Letter Size Color, Surveys, and User Defined. By selecting one of these predefined templates, all the formatting attributes of the selected template overwrite those on your existing chart. The Save Template option enables the saving of your own personal charting templates and enables future reuse of those across other reports. Chart templates can be particularly useful if you want to apply standard corporate chart formatting across your organization.

SPECIFYING CHART SIZE AND POSITION

This option enables you to identify very specific x and y coordinates in addition to height and width measurements for the involved chart. Charts can also be dynamically resized and repositioned by grabbing any of the sizing handles that appear on the frame of the chart after it is selected.

MODIFYING CHART OPTIONS

The Chart Options menu choice enables you to fine-tune the look of your charts at a granular level not available in the standard Chart Expert. The following sections explore the variety of chart customizations and formatting options exposed through the Chart Options menu. These are especially useful where the functionality of the standard chart creation expert does not meet your exact requirements. The chart options are accessible through a rich multitabbed interface with a chart preview window. Figure 8.13 highlights the interface, and the following paragraphs describe the details of the respective tabs.

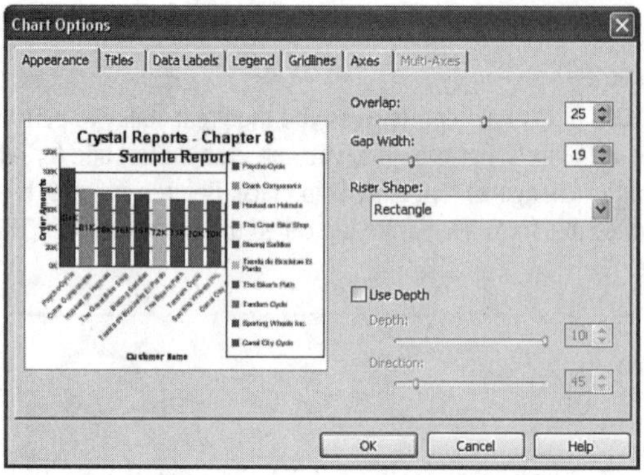

Figure 8.13
The Chart Options dialog provides advanced chart configuration functionality.

The Appearance tab provides general formatting options for each chart type. These settings give you a great deal of flexibility in controlling the details of the involved graphics (such as pie chart tilt, rotation, hole size, and exploding pie characteristics, or bar chart shape, overlap, width, depth, and so on).

Some common options for pie, bar, and other charts include the following:

- **Overlap**—Use this slider to change how much risers within each category overlap each other.

- **Gap Width**—Use this slider to change the gap between the group of bar risers in each category.

- **Riser Shape**—Use this list box to choose the shape of the chart's bars or risers.

- **Use Depth**—Use this check box to apply a depth effect or to make a completely flat chart.

- **Depth**—When Use Depth is selected, use this slider to specify the amount of depth to be applied to the chart risers and frame.

- **Pie Tilt**—Use this slider to tilt the involved pie charts.

- **Pie Rotation**—Use this slider to rotate the involved pie.

- **Explode Pie**—Exploding a pie or doughnut chart detaches all slices away from its center. Select the Series option from the context menu of a highlighted pie slice if you want to attach or detach an individual slice from a chart.

The Titles tab enables you to specify chart titles, subtitles, footnotes, and so on. Many charts also include axis title specifications (such as group axis title or data axis title) here.

The Data Labels tab provides formatting and display options for data labels. The different options enable you to select the presentation of data labels based on the underlying value representing the chart graphics, the associated label, or a combination of the two.

The Legend tab provides options for changing the appearance of the involved chart. The Color Mode drop-down box enables you to select a color scheme for the involved chart components. This is typically a decision between coloring by group or by series, although other options are provided for surface charts. The visual effects of these modes are truly seen only when you set more than one Change By field for the involved chart.

The remaining options surround the display of the legend (available on most charts) and its placement relative to the chart.

The Gridlines tab provides options for displaying or hiding gridlines for specified chart types. Typical options set here include gridline display for both the group and data axis.

The Axes tab provides display options for both the data and group axis. You can select to use dual y-axes for your chart if you previously selected two On Change Of fields in the Chart Expert. In addition, you can decide whether you want those dual axes split or shown in the same grid.

The Multi-Axes tab provides selection options for the display of your dual y-axes report. By default, when a dual y-axis report is selected, half of your series members will be assigned to each y-axis. You can change that default assignment in this tab. If a split axis has been selected, you can also select some display options about the proportion of the grid taken by each split of the y-axes.

SPECIFYING SERIES OPTIONS

This menu option applies formatting options to an individual series in a chart. The Series Option is available for selection only if a series was previously selected in the chart. This series selection is done in place in Crystal Reports (for example, highlighting a pie slice on a pie chart enables the Series Option functionality for that pie slice's series). Figure 8.14 highlights the Series Option dialog for the chart you created earlier in this chapter, and the following paragraphs describe the different tabs available on the Series Options dialog and some common usage scenarios.

The Appearance tab shows general formatting options for a selected series. Common display effects enacted here include altering the visual metaphor for a selected series so that it is different from the other series (for example, displaying the United States Sales results as an area visual on a bar chart). In certain charts, such as 3D charts, the selection of each series' riser shape is also available.

The Data Labels tab shows data label display options for the currently selected series. It enables you to specify series-specific data labels. This functionality is effective for highlighting a series of particular relevance. Unlike the General menu option's Data Labels tab, this series-specific functionality enables the setting of only numeric-based data labels.

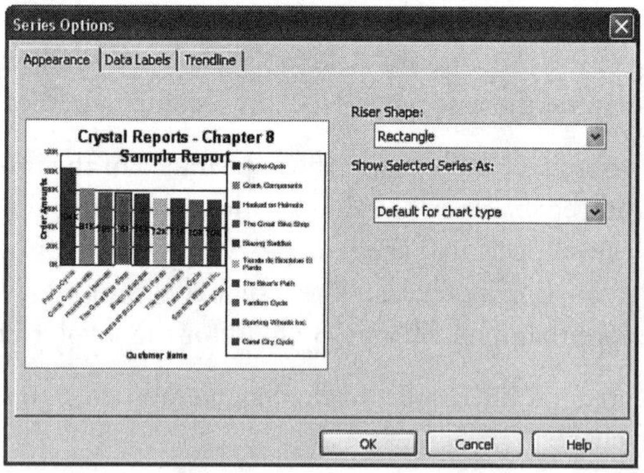

Figure 8.14
The Series Options dialog provides the capability to specify chart series options such as trendlines, data labels, and number formats.

The Trendline tab provides display and formatting options for a trendline selection. It enables you to represent trends in a data series graphically. You can add trendlines to data series in a number of unstacked charts (such as 2D area, bar, bubble, column, line, and scatter charts). Several different automatic trendline creations are possible, including linear, logarithmic, polynomial, or exponential trendlines, in addition to moving averages.

SPECIFYING X-AXIS AND Y-AXIS OPTIONS

These chart options format chart axes, axis numbers, gridlines, and scaling. Unlike versions before version XI, the axis options are accessed independently by selecting any axis object and its associated context menu and then choosing the involved Axis Options menu selection. When an axis dialog is selected, the tabs at the top of the dialog reflect the available formatting options for that axis. Figure 8.15 shows the Data (Y) Axis Settings dialog for this chapter's sample report, and the following paragraphs describe the different tabs available on the Axis Option dialogs and some common usage scenarios.

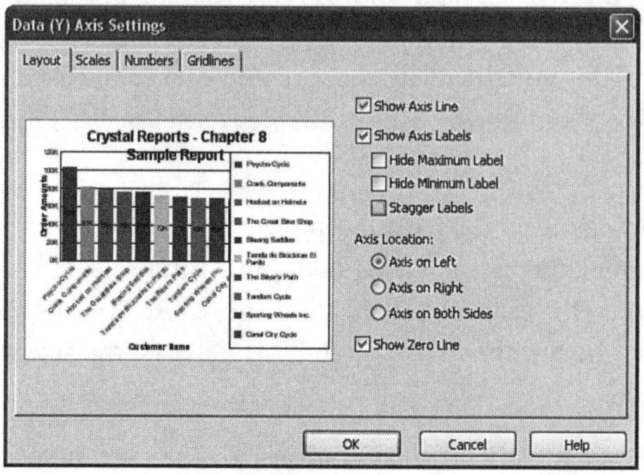

Figure 8.15
The Data (Y) Axis Settings dialog provides granular level control over chart axis display options. A similar dialog is available for the group (X) axis.

The Layout tab shows general formatting options for a selected axis. You can specify the location of the Axis labels (for example, top, bottom, left, right, both) through the Location of the Label radio buttons. Additional options of interest new since version XI are the abilities to stagger labels automatically and to skip a specified number of labels.

The Scales tab provides options around the scale for the involved axis. The most common options set in this tab are the manually set maximum and minimum scale options. These enable increased control over the range presented on the involved axis. Other options include settings around the logarithmic scale and forcing the inclusion of zero in the axis range. New since Version XI, settings for using a descending axis and for selecting a minor gridline interval can be made here.

The Numbers tab shows formatting options for data axis numbers. This tab enables you to specify data axis numeric data label formatting. The Category drop-down box enables you to select a general format for the numeric component of the data labels. After this is selected, more granular options are exposed for control over the display of each format. If you are looking to format the data label numbers displayed within the chart, you must select them and access the Format Data Label option from their right-click menu.

The Grid tab provides access to the Gridline formatting options for the involved data axis. This tab enables you to specify the involved axis' displayed gridlines, including Custom Gridlines specified at certain values and different grid formats.

SPECIFYING SELECTED ITEM FORMATTING OPTIONS

This Chart Options menu selection enables you to format line, area, and text objects in a chart. It is available only when a chart object is selected with the mouse or other pointer. Figure 8.16 highlights the Formatting dialog. Different tabs (Fill, Border) are highlighted and available based on the underlying selected chart item.

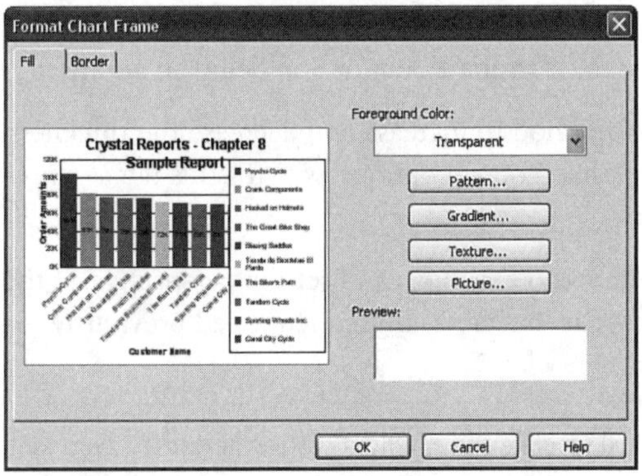

Figure 8.16
The Format Chart Frame dialog provides the capability to format user-selected objects within the involved chart.

SPECIFYING 3D VIEWING ANGLE OPTIONS

This menu option is only available for 3D charts. It enables you to edit the involved chart's viewing angles, position, wall thickness, and so on. The basic options enable you to select a predefined viewing angle template. The advanced options enable you to create new templates and refine the manipulation of the 3D chart. Figure 8.17 highlights the Choose a Viewing Angle dialog.

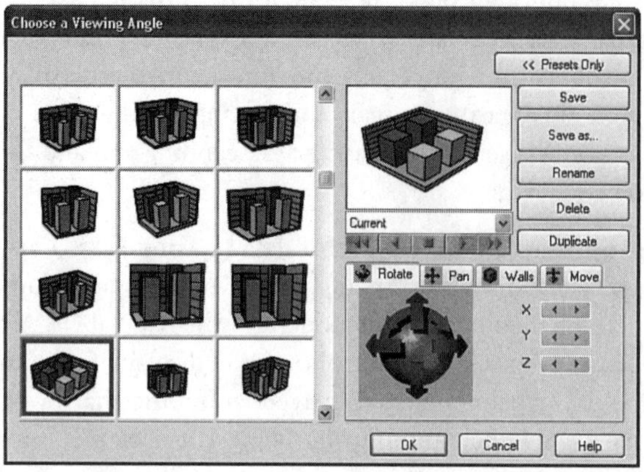

Figure 8.17
The Choose a Viewing Angle dialog provides the capability to specify precise viewing angles for 3D charts.

The Rotate tab and its X, Y, and Z dimension controls are used to rotate a 3D chart to any angle. There are three different methods or controls to change the rotation of the chart:

- Use the X, Y, and Z left and right control buttons to incrementally rotate the chart in the preview window.
- Use the directional arrows surrounding the globe to affect the rotation.
- Use the preview window itself to click and drag the previewed chart around the different axes.

The Pan tab is used to pan and zoom a 3D chart. The same control options exist here as described for the Rotate tab, with the Zoom option being an additional component.

The Walls tab provides a method to increase and decrease the thickness and length of the walls on a 3D chart. The same control options exist for this tab as those mentioned previously for the Rotate tab.

The Move tab provides a method to move and set the perspective of the 3D chart. The same control options exist for this tab as those mentioned previously for the Rotate tab.

NOTE

You will find separate and advanced charting help instructions for these granular options available through the Help button present on all the dialogs accessed from the Chart Options menu. This advanced Help is provided by 3D Graphics—the third party responsible for the charting in Crystal Reports.

MODIFYING MAP PROPERTIES

After you create a map and place it on your report, you can perform numerous post-creation edits by right-clicking on the map object while in the Preview mode. From the menu that appears when you right-click, you have the capability to either revisit the Map Expert or use a number of more finely tuned post-creation editing tools such as Zooming, Layer Control, Map Navigation, and Data Mismatch Resolution.

FORMAT MAP OPTIONS

As introduced in Chapter 6, the Format Map dialog enables you to add common formatting options for the involved chart. Common options set here for charts include borders, ToolTips, and/or general hyperlinks. Review Chapter 6 for a detailed discussion of the general formatting options available for the chart.

SIZE AND POSITION

This option enables you to specify very specific X and Y coordinates, in addition to height and width measurements for the involved map. Maps can also be dynamically resized and repositioned by grabbing any of the sizing handles that appear on the frame of the map after it is selected.

LAYER CONTROL

By clicking on the Layers menu option, you can specify the different layers that display on your map. Examples of this include World Capital Cities and the Mapping Grid. Crystal Reports 2008 is distributed with a number of built-in layers that are accessed through this Layer Control dialog. These layers and more detail-oriented layers can be added and removed from Crystal Reports using this dialog. Additional maps can be purchased separately from MapInfo (a third-party company) and integrated into Crystal Reports.

RESOLVE MISMATCH

The Resolve Mismatch dialog provides two very useful functions for maps. First, the Resolve Mismatch dialog enables you to select a specific map to use for your report. Several maps are provided out of the box with Crystal Reports, and others can be purchased separately. Additionally, you can match the field names stored in the Geographic field from which you are basing the map onto the names that the involved map is expecting. This powerful feature enables you to take raw, untransformed data and dynamically match it to a geographical map value that the mapping engine can understand. For example, on a map of Canada, you might have multiple inconsistent data entries in your database for the province of Ontario (for example, ON, Ont, Ontario, and so on). Using this dialog, you can match each of these to the expected value of Ontario, and the mapping engine successfully interprets them all.

ZOOMING AND PANNING

The Zoom In and Zoom Out options enable you to focus on a particularly relevant part of the involved map. The Panning option enables you to horizontally pan the view of the map to what is most interesting to you and your business users. When you select any of these options from the Map menu, you are placed in an interactive mode with the map and your mouse/touchpad. Clicking zooms you in and out, and double-clicking and dragging facilitates panning. When you are finished working in these special design modes, you can change back to the Select mode for standard map navigation.

TIP

When selecting from the Map menu, the Map Navigator provides a thumbnail of the entire map you are currently working with. As you saw earlier, Figure 8.12 highlights this Map Navigator in your report sample. The Map Navigator also provides a dotted outline of the area currently selected for display. You can fine-tune the area that displays by grabbing this dotted line, double-clicking on any of its corners, and subsequently dragging or expanding them out or collapsing them in while holding down your second click.

TROUBLESHOOTING

CHARTING ON A FIELD NOT ALREADY GROUPED IN THE REPORT

I want to create a chart based on changing a specific field but don't know how.

Select the On Change Of charting option under the Advanced layout option and then specify the field or fields to break the chart sections on by selecting any of the fields in the available fields listing. Unlike the drop-down box under the Group layout, you can select any of the available report fields in this interface, dynamically order them with the Order button, or restrict their display on the report to a specified Top or Bottom N with the Top N button.

DISPLAYING A CHART BESIDE RELATED REPORT DATA

I want to add a chart to a report that displays alongside or inline with other displayed report data.

You can do this by adding your charts into report sections (for instance, Group or Report Headers) above the data you want to display them beside. You can then use the Underlay Following Sections option accessed through the Section Expert dialog. With some design forethought, you can create nicely formatted reports that integrate both data and visuals very closely.

CRYSTAL REPORTS IN THE REAL WORLD—COMPLEX CHARTS

Charts can be particularly useful when they display data that is different but complementary. Although it is certainly possible to show data in multiple charts, showing complementary data in the same chart allows direct comparison of information and more efficient use of space. The following steps walk through a good example of this when an executive team wants to see how average order size varies over the largest customers:

1. Start by creating a new report using the Customer and Orders table from the Xtreme Sample Database. Add the Customer Name, Orders ID, and Orders Name field into the detail section of the report. Now, insert a group on Customer Name. In the chart that will be added, bars will eventually represent the total sales by customer, and a line will eventually show the average order amount for each of the involved customers.

2. From the Insert menu, select Chart and place it in the Report Header section. Open the new chart's Chart Expert, go to the Data tab and ensure that the Advanced button is selected. Select the Customer Name field and use the upper arrow (>) button to move the field to the On Change Of window. Finally, select the Order Amount two separate times and add it each time to the Show Values window using the lower arrow (>) button. Set the summary operation to Sum for the first entry and Average for the second addition. The results of this step should resemble Figure 8.18.

Figure 8.18
Creating an advanced chart with a two summary fields will enable some creative charting.

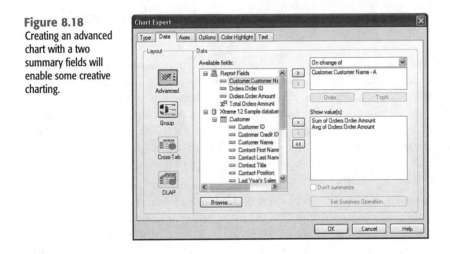

3. Now to focus the chart on the largest customers by total sales, select the Customer Name field in the On Change Of window and click the Top N button. When the Group Sort Expert window opens, select Top N from the drop-down box, enter **10** as the Top N value, uncheck the Include Others and Ties boxes, select Sum of Order Amounts as the field to sort on, and choose Descending as the sort order. Click OK to close the window.

4. Click the Text tab. Uncheck the Title Auto-Text boxes and type **Comparison Chart** into the Chart Title text box. Click on OK to close the window and return to the report.

5. Using the handles on the chart object, stretch the chart to fit the page width. Figure 8.19 provides a good benchmark for comparing your own report.

8

Figure 8.19
Bars representing both individual total client sales and average order size display on the same chart, effectively communicating multiple pieces of information in one chart.

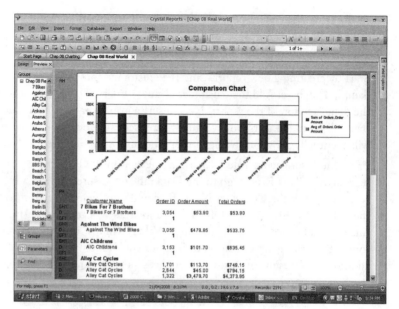

6. Notice that because the Total Customer Sales become such increasingly large values, the contrast between average order size values appears to be quite small using the automatically provided scale. To change this, the report can be changed to use a dual y-axis. This will enable you to show both sets of values on different and relevant scales while highlighting the contrast between individual elements within a set. To change the chart to a dual y-axis, right-click anywhere in the chart and choose Chart Options and then the Axes tab. Click on the Dual Axes box, ensure that the Split Dual Axis check box is not checked for this exercise, and then click on OK.

7. To enable this chart to better project both sets of information more clearly, you could either set a split dual axis back in the Chart Options dialog or you could change the display format of the involved series. To do the latter, click any of the individual average order size bars to select it, and then right-click the bar and select Chart Options, Series. Change the Chart Type list box from Default to Line and click on OK to close.

8. Save the report. It should ultimately resemble the report in Figure 8.20 and clearly shows both the largest clients by total sales on one y-axis while showing the average order size for each of these same important clients. The executive team is now able to analyze the data and take proactive action.

The preceding example provided a great example of displaying different data sets in the same chart. Another practical use of this functionality is displaying averages (or running total calculations) over time in the line chart to complement the other bar chart sums by some specified period (such as a month). Essentially, you could create a chart that represents a moving average laid on top of the monthly sums.

Figure 8.20
Bars represent individual client sales and a line represents total cumulative sales with two separate numeric scales displayed.

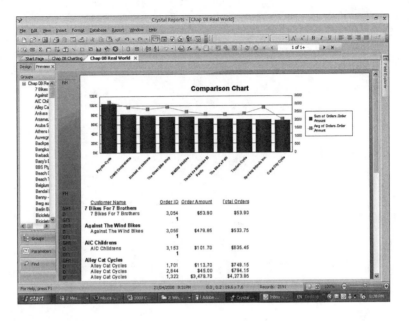

CHAPTER **9**

CUSTOM FORMATTING TECHNIQUES

In this chapter

INTRODUCTION

This chapter focuses on more complex formatting to make reports look like high-quality information portals rather than simply paper reports. Often a software suite is either powerful or easy to use, but Crystal Reports actually does a great job of being both and can be best described as having layers of complexity. For the beginner, a simple listing report can suffice, but the advanced user can extend this listing report with formatting, interactive reports, and powerful charts. The newest version of Crystal Reports offers some compelling and exciting new options explored in this chapter.

MAKING PRESENTATION-QUALITY REPORTS

Up to this point in the book, the focus of the chapters has been on making sure that the data appears as required. The next step, formatting, keeps users coming back to the reports time and time again. When we talk about formatting, users often assume that we're simply making a report "pretty" or "boardroom quality," and this simply isn't the case. With rich formatting, the data should be easier to read, understand, and navigate. Rich formatting should guide the reader's eye to those elements of the report that are most important and in the case of reports that mimic paper documents, your Crystal Report can be made to look identical to the original document. Adoption of your new report should be very impressive.

Formatting can take many different forms, from basic font coloring to hyperlinks to conditional formatting (formatting based on the data). This chapter examines a cross-section of all these types of formatting to give the report author a good basis for report formatting.

This chapter presents a series of tutorials to enable you to add formatting to a report started in an earlier chapter. Let's assume that you would like to improve the report named Contact Listing Formatted that was started in Chapter 6, "Fundamentals of Report Formatting."

COMMON FORMATTING FEATURES

The most common formatting feature is changing the font color or font face. This can be done by choosing the features directly on the Formatting toolbar, as shown in Figure 9.1.

Chapter 6 introduced the Highlighting Expert, so if more detail is necessary, you can find it there.

Figure 9.1
The Crystal Reports Formatting toolbar lets you change object formatting.

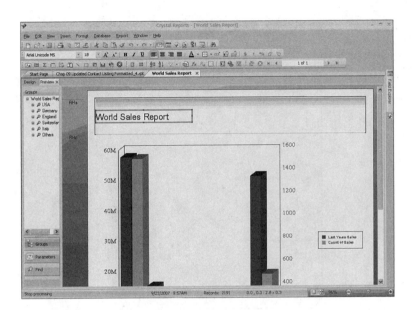

9

WORKING WITH TOOLTIPS

All report objects can have rollover text or ToolTips available when the report is viewed. For example, if you would like to use descriptive text to coach the users on what action they can take, you could do this with a ToolTip.

In the example created in Chapter 6, you now want to inform the end users that they can click on a field to email the contact person. The text should appear whenever a user mouses over the email field on the report. The following steps create a ToolTip:

1. Open `Chap 06 Contact Listing Formatted.rpt` or the report created earlier in Chapter 6. Select File, Open and browse to find `Chap 06 Contact Listing Formatted.rpt` and open it.

2. Format the email field at the far right. Right-click on it and choose Format Field.

3. Add the ToolTip text. In the Format Editor dialog, select the Common tab. To the right of the ToolTip Text box, click on the Formula Editor button (see Figure 9.2), and enter the following formula, which makes a custom message for each email address:

```
"Click here to compose an e-mail to " +
{Customer.Contact First Name} + " " +
{Customer.Contact Last Name} + "."
```

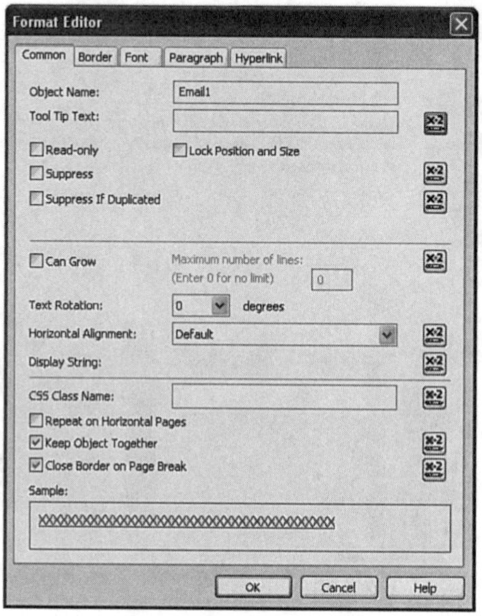

Figure 9.2
On the Common tab, click the ToolTip text formula button.

4. Test the ToolTip text. Click on OK to finish the formatting. In Preview, scroll the mouse over the email field and see that the rollover text now appears as a custom message, which is different when viewed by each email recipient. Before proceeding, save the report as Chap 09 Updated Contact Listing Formatted.rpt by choosing File, Save As.

LINES AND BOXES

Adding lines and boxes to a report can make it easier to read as well as visually grouping items for business users. To add lines under each Details section as well as a box around each group, follow these steps:

1. View Chap 09 Updated Contact Listing Formatted.rpt in Design mode. If the report is not already open, open it using Ctrl+O. Make sure that the report is in Design mode by choosing Ctrl+D.

2. Insert the line by choosing Insert, Line. The mouse changes to a pencil. Move the mouse to the lower left of the fields in the Details section. Hold down the left mouse button to begin drawing the line. Scroll the mouse to the right until you reach the end of the Details section. When you reach it, release the mouse button.

3. View the result in Preview mode. Select F5 to refresh the report to see the line with the data as shown in Figure 9.3.

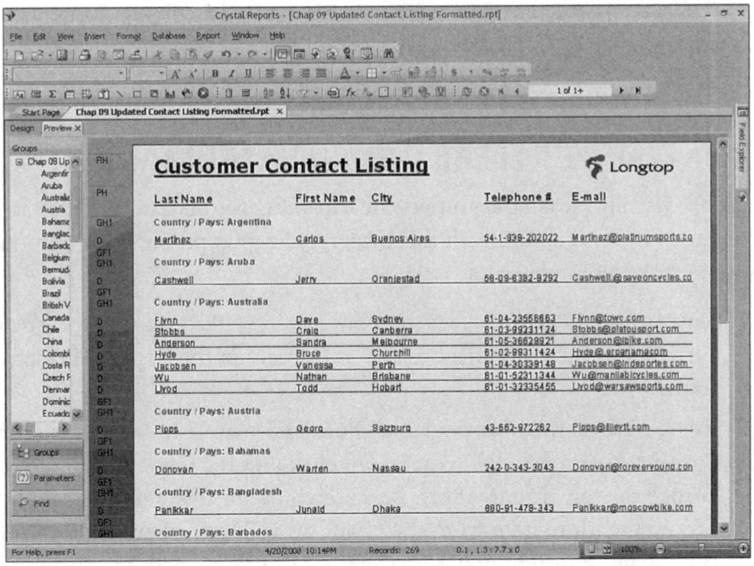

Figure 9.3
Use the Preview mode view of a report to show a line under each detail record.

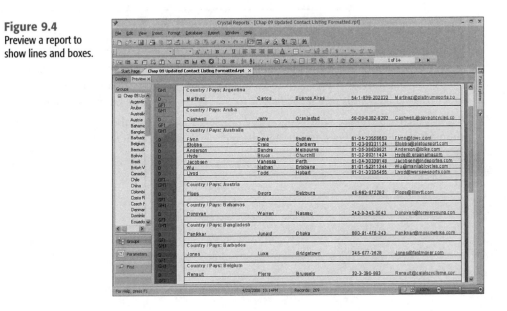

4. Add the box by choosing Insert, Box. The mouse changes to a pencil. Move the mouse to the upper left of the Country/Pays USA data in the Group Header. Hold down the left mouse button to begin drawing the box. Scroll the mouse down to the bottom left of the Summary amount in the Group Footer and then scroll to the right until the end of the Group Footer section. Once reached, release the mouse button. The resulting box should appear similar to Figure 9.4.

Figure 9.4
Preview a report to show lines and boxes.

5. Choose File, Save As and save the report as Chap 09 Updated Contact Listing Formatted_2.rpt.

CREATING A VERTICAL TEXT WATERMARK

Another visually pleasing feature is the capability to rotate text. This can be very effective when used in conjunction with the Underlay Section property for sections. Follow these steps to make a sample watermark:

1. Start by using Chap 09 Updated Contact Listing Formatted_2.rpt in Design mode. Choose Insert, Text Object to add a text field in the Report Header. Enter **DRAFT** for the text.

2. Right-click on the Text field and choose Format Text. Select the Common tab. Change the Text Rotation to 90 degrees and click on OK. Go to the Font tab, where you can change the font size to 48pts. Because you want this watermark to be semitransparent, choose the More item from the Color drop-down, where you can specify a custom color. Choose a light gray (or silver). Click OK to close the custom color dialog box. Increase the Character font spacing by specifying 70 pts in the dialog, and then exit the dialog by clicking on OK.

> **NOTE**
>
> This color section, common to all objects within Crystal Reports 2008, enables you to specify colors using RGB or hue, saturation, and luminance. By choosing corporate colors and adding them to the custom colors, you can extend corporate branding into report presentation.

3. Resize the field. Because the field needs to go down the page, it needs to be resized to be narrow and long. Select the field and choose the rightmost square on the field. Resize the object by holding down the left mouse button. Now choose the bottom square on the field and stretch the height to 5". Figure 9.6 shows how this should look.

4. Refresh the report to see your progress by pressing F5. It shows the text rotated, although it is not running down beside the records as shown in Figure 9.6.

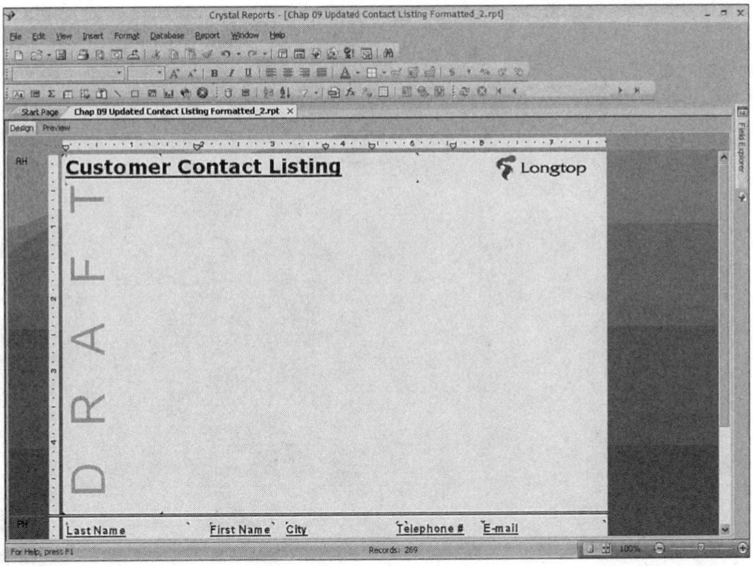

Figure 9.5
Design tab with text rotation applied to text field.

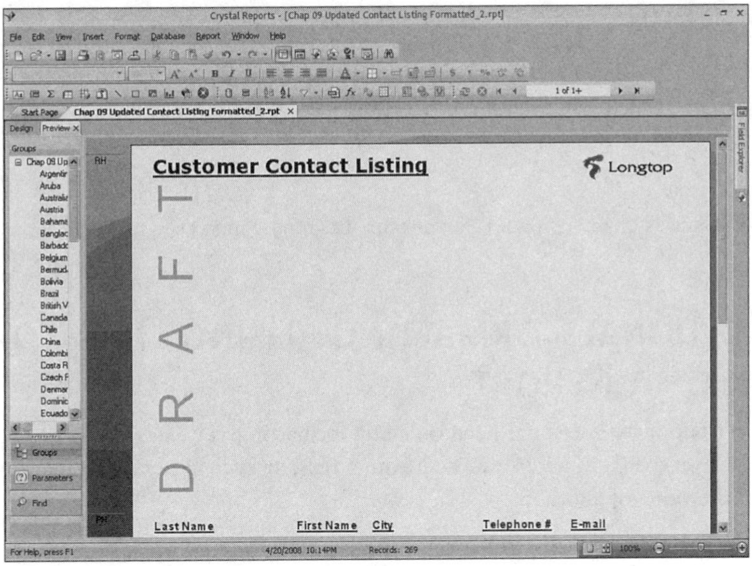

Figure 9.6
Preview of the report with text rotation.

5. Set the Report Header to Underlay. Because the text does not yet flow to the record level, it must be underlayed. This is a section property. Right-click in the Report Header section located on the left side of the report design area, choose Section Expert, and click on the Insert button near the upper left. Be sure to select Report Header B in the Sections window and put a check in the box to the left of Underlay Following Sections, and click on OK. Drag your text box into Report Header B. The desired results should appear similar to Figure 9.7.

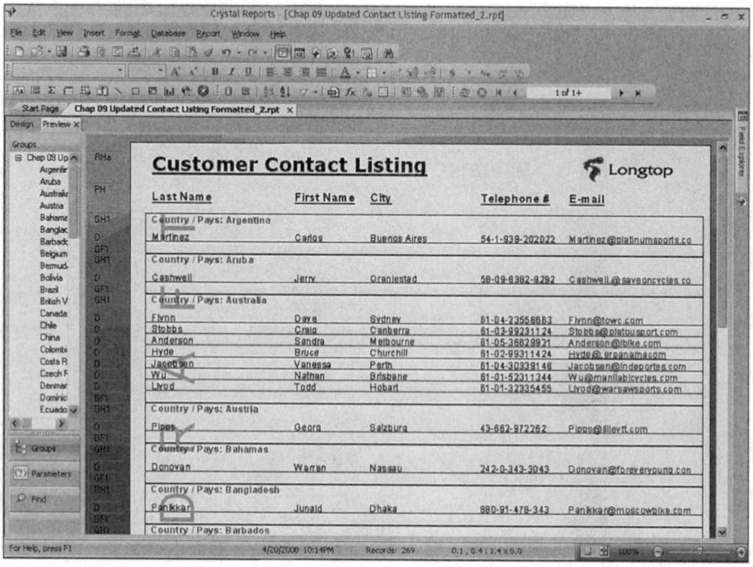

Figure 9.7
Preview of the report with rotated text flowing under the detail records.

CAUTION

Realize that when rotating text, the justification rules might be opposite of what would normally be expected. In the case of 90 degrees, the text must be right justified to have the company name appear to be top justified.

6. Save as Chap 09 Updated Contact Listing Formatted_3.rpt.

CONDITIONAL FORMATTING—USING DATA TO DRIVE THE LOOK OF A REPORT

Up to now, the focus has been on static formatting. The next step is to apply formatting based on the data being returned from a field or even applying formatting on one field based on the value of another.

Conditional formatting relies on formulas. Because the formula language is extensive, you can create complex statements. This chapter introduces fairly simple examples to illustrate.

The simplest way to add conditional formatting is to use the Highlighting Expert. This feature enables you to apply font face and font color changes to database fields based on their values.

9

> **TIP**
>
> Almost every formatting option can be conditional. To determine which ones are conditional, look at the X+2 button next to the option in the Formatting Editor dialogs.
>
> If a formatting option has already been set to a conditional format, the button appears with red text. Otherwise, it appears as blue text.

APPLYING FORMATTING FROM ANOTHER FIELD

1. In Design view, right-click on the Contact Last Name field, choose Format Field, and then navigate to the Font tab and click the formula button to the right of the Color drop-down. This opens the formula editor, driving your font color choice.

2. Enter the following formula:

```
SELECT {Customer.Last Year's Sales}
CASE 0 TO 1000: crRed
CASE 1001 TO 100000: crYellow
CASE IS > 100001: crGreen;
```

> **NOTE**
>
> Here you specified a color as the result of the CASE expression because the formula controlled color. In cases where the formatting option is Boolean (that is, either you turn the feature on or off), there is an assumed IF statement, and all you have to do is enter the condition (for example, {table.field} > 100). A full IF statement in cases like this should be built with both TRUE and FALSE results defined, or you might get unexpected results.

3. Refresh the report by pressing F5 while you're in the Preview tab. Now you see red, yellow, and green last names depending on the amount of last year's sales for that person (see Figure 9.8).

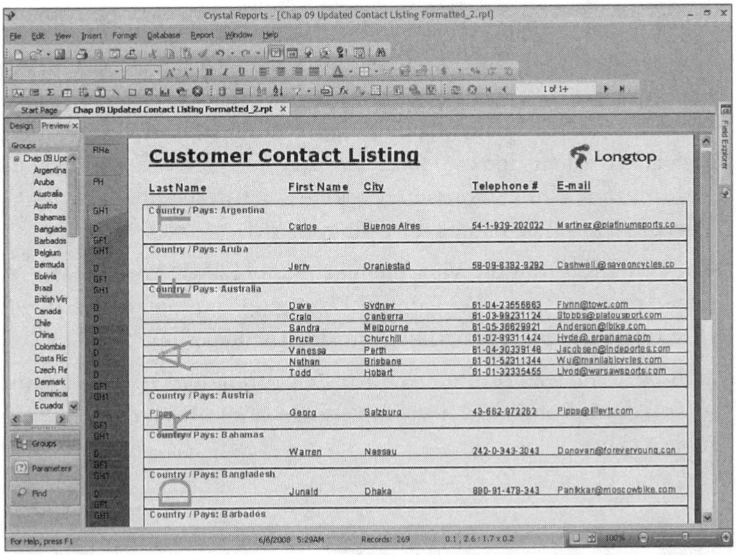

Figure 9.8
Conditional highlighting based on another field.

4. Save the report as `Chap 09 Updated Contact Listing Formatted_4.rpt`.

REPORT-TO-REPORT LINKING AND THE HYPERLINK WIZARD

No matter how well designed, no single report can address all the needs of a business. Even if it could be done, the report would be unhelpful to the users—overwhelming and hard to read. One way of making the information easy to manage is to break it out over several reports but make navigation easy by placing hyperlinks in the report to allow the user to move smoothly from report to report.

In the `Chap 09 Updated Contact Listing Formatted_4.rpt` report, you'll add a hyperlink that opens a report from BusinessObjects Enterprise.

REPORT-TO-REPORT LINKING

1. From the menu choose, File, Open. In the lower left of the Open dialog window is a button labeled Enterprise. Click the button, and if you aren't already connected to Enterprise, you are prompted to log on. If you don't know the appropriate information to log on, move to the next section. To leverage any BusinessObjects Enterprise integration, you must have installed the latest service pack of Crystal Reports 2008.

2. Browse to the `Report Samples` folder, and then the `General Business` folder, and finally to the World Sales Report and click open.

3. With the World Sales Report open, right-click on the chart and choose Copy. Using the Report tabs displayed right below the toolbars, go back to the `Chap 09 Updated Contact Listing Formatted_4.rpt` report.

4. Right-click on the Customer Contact Listing text, choose Format Text, and click the Hyperlink tab.

5. Select Another Report Object and click the Paste button. You will see much of the window get populated. If the Paste button is not enabled, go back to your World Sales Report, select the chart, right-click the chart, choose Copy, and try again. By copying the chart, you're actually trapping significant information about the chart that the designer interprets for you. Take a look at Figure 9.9. Even if you followed the steps perfectly, not all the information will be exactly the same. For instance, the value in Select From will be unique for your system.

6. Click on OK. From the View menu, choose HTML Preview. When the preview opens, mouse over the Customer Contact Listing text box and notice that the mouse cursor changes, indicating a hyperlink. Clicking the hyperlink opens the World Sales Report.

7. This powerful feature allows users to flow from one report to another with the potential to drill down from a high level to very low level of detail or to a completely different subject matter altogether.

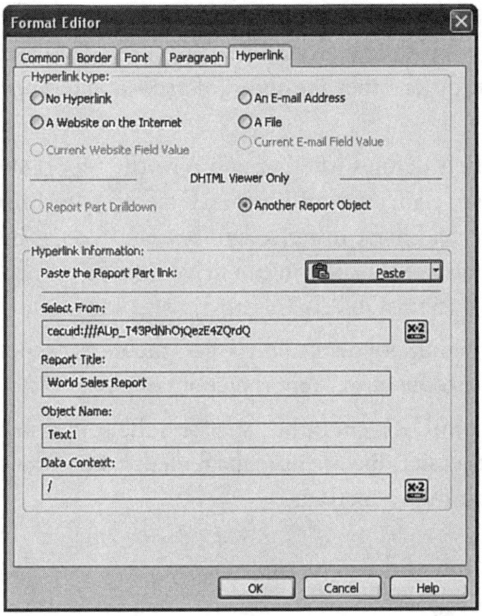

Figure 9.9
Creating a hyperlink
to another report.

HYPERLINK WIZARD

The Hyperlink Wizard offers a significant benefit over the Report-to-Report Linking above. In the preceding linking style, there are very few options available (but it is included for reference), but with the Hyperlink Wizard, you can specify some important criteria as detailed in the following steps:

1. Right-click on the Customer Contact Listing text, choose Format Text, and click the Hyperlink tab.

2. Select the option for A Website on the Internet, and the button named Create Enterprise Hyperlink will appear. Click the button. To leverage any BusinessObjects Enterprise integration, you must have installed service pack 0 of Crystal Reports 2008.

3. The dialog offers several options. First select the Document ID by clicking the Browse button, and select the target report using steps 1 and 2 from the earlier "Report-to-Report Linking" section.

4. Set the Target Window option. This defines whether the target report will open in the same or new browser window. Many users like to have reports open in the same window because it's easier to manage just a few open browsers.

5. Set the Output format option. This defines what document type will be used for presenting the report to the user. Options include HTML, PDF, Excel, and Word. The default is HTML, and unless there is a clear requirement to choose otherwise, the default should probably be retained because it offers valuable scalability and performance benefits that are too numerous to name here.

6. Set the Refresh on Open option. This defines whether the report instance will use data already in the report or get up-to-the-second data from the database. Sometimes current data is important, but other times the speed of accessing a report with saved data is more important.

7. Set the Instance option. This defines whether and how the report should fetch a report instance. Report instances are a feature of BusinessObjects Enterprise. Options include Do Not Use, Latest Instance, Latest Instance by User, and Latest Instance by Parameter Values. Proper use of this option can drive significant performance gains, but the details are specific to BusinessObjects Enterprise and so will not be detailed here.

8. The Parameter Settings section populates only when the target report has parameters. This allows passing values to the target reports parameters.

9. The Include Server Name in URL check box specifies the server name to be used. Checking this box permits easier document management when promoting documents from development through to production.

See Figure 9.10 for an illustration of the Hyperlink Wizard.

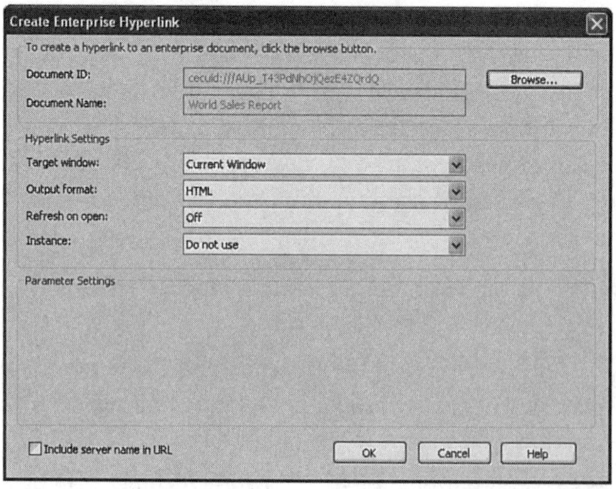

Figure 9.10
Create Enterprise
Hyperlink options.

FIND IN FIELD EXPLORER

Often a report will have many records in it. Finding the right record can be a significant challenge. New in Crystal Reports 2008 is the ability to search in all fields to find a value, show information about the found item, and drill to that value conveniently.

1. With `Chap 09 Updated Contact Listing Formatted_4.rpt` open, go to the Edit Find menu. Type **Martinez** into the Find text box and click on the spyglass key or press the Enter key.

2. The Find feature will display four found items (two fields on two different records) with additional information including page number and where in the group tree it was found (in this case, the country). Double-clicking a found item will navigate to that page and select the found item.

BARCODE SUPPORT

Although barcodes in Crystal Reports have been useable for many versions, new to Crystal Reports 2008 is a feature that makes these fonts easier to use than ever. With just a few clicks, a field can be converted to a barcode, formatted, and even changed back to the original font. This important feature simplifies making weigh bills, shipping labels, and more. Crystal Reports 2008 ships with Code39 barcodes (a very popular barcode font), but others can be added. See your barcode vendor for specific barcode fonts.

CONVERT TO BARCODE

1. Using the skills covered in Chapter 6, create a new report using the Inventory table from the sample database. Select all three fields from the table. See Figure 9.11 for an example of our start point.

Figure 9.11
Simple report list.

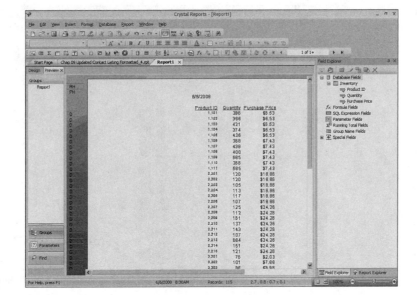

2. Right-click on the Product ID field, and choose Change to Barcode. Selecting a barcode font from the list causes details for that barcode to be displayed, including a sample input, sample output, and a button to go to the barcode vendor's website. Figure 9.12 illustrates the barcode window.

Figure 9.12
Barcode options window.

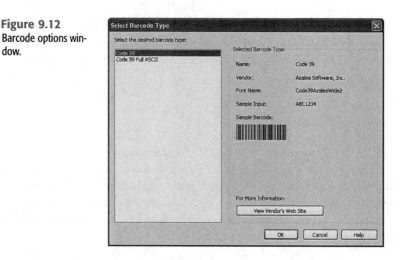

3. Click on OK. You might have to adjust the location of the field. The field now displays a barcode instead of the field value. Only number and string fields can be converted to barcode. Figure 9.13 shows our field value converted to a barcode.

Figure 9.13
Report with barcodes.

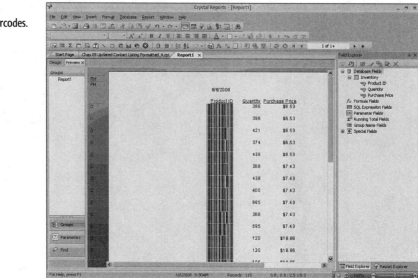

CONVERT FROM BARCODE

1. The Convert to Barcode option actually does three things in one step: It converts the font from the original to the specified barcode, changes the font size, and adds a formula to the display string. To undo these steps, you could use the Undo button. But if

that's not practical, right-click the barcode and choose Format Field, make sure to go to the Common tab, click the formula button to the right of Display String, and remove the text. Next go to the Font tab and change the Font Name field to the desired font and reduce the font size from 24 to be consistent with the rest of the report. Click OK.

2. Using the handles on the field, reduce its size so the height matches other fields on the detail line. Right-click on the label Detail or D at the left border of the report and choose Fit Section to reduce the additional whitespace on the report.

CRYSTAL REPORTS IN THE REAL WORLD—ADVANCED CHARTING

Nothing enables users to visualize data better than a chart. With a glance, charts enable users to see relative distribution, peaks, and valleys of values. This section describes how to use charting in creative ways. The following creates a report that charts the sum of sales and distribution of customers by country:

1. Download the demo sample reports from http://support.businessobjects.com/ communitycs/FilesAndUpdates/demonstration_samples.zip.asp.

    Open the World Sales Report. Stretch the chart so that it takes the full width of the page. In the left margin, right-click on the text Group Footer 1 (the text might simply say GF1 if you are using short section names), and choose Hide (Drill-Down OK) from the menu. Delete the headers from under the chart.

2. Right-click on the chart and choose Chart Expert. For Chart Type choose Bar, and from the options that refine which type of bar chart, choose the left option listed as Side by Side Bar Chart (see Figure 9.14).

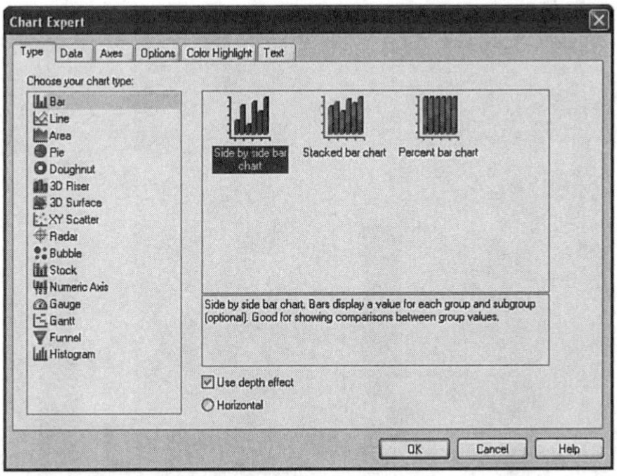

Figure 9.14
Choosing a chart type.

3. Click on the Data tab and the Advanced button. From the list of available fields, select Customer.Country and add it to the window below On Change Of. Again, from the list of available fields, choose Customer.Last Year's Sales and Customer.Customer Name and add them to the Show Values. Select Customer.Country in the On Change Of window and the Top N button enables. Click the Top N button and choose Top N from the list box. Leave the remaining defaults and click on OK (see Figure 9.15).

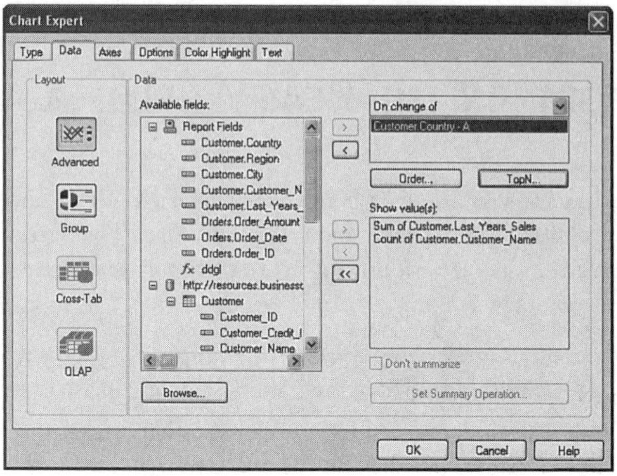

Figure 9.15
Selecting data for the chart.

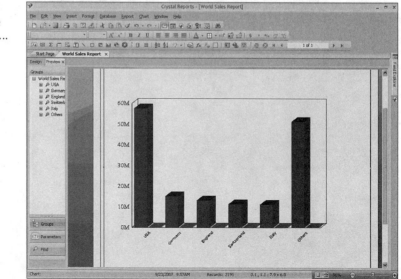

4. Click on the Options tab and uncheck the Show Label option. Click on OK to close the window.

5. The bar chart is almost complete. It contains the correct data, so it is technically accurate, but because the scale of the values is so different, it is unreadable for the user. See Figure 9.16.

Figure 9.16
Technically accurate but not helpful yet....

6. Because the scale of the data is significantly different, the chart needs to be broken into two axes. Right-click on the chart and choose Chart Options, Axes tab. Click the Dual Axis check box. Navigate to the Legend tab and click Show Legend and click OK. Right-click on a label in the legend and choose Edit Axis Label. Replace Sum of Customer.Last_Years_Sales with Last Years Sales and replace Count of Customer.Customer_Name with Count of Sales. The resulting chart should look like Figure 9.17.

Figure 9.17
Chart showing two scales of information.

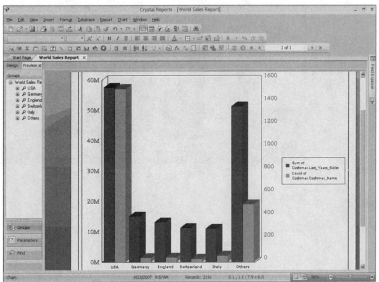

7. Finally, a trendline can be added to the chart to show a trend in the data. Right-click on the Customer Name bar and choose Series Options. Click the Trendline tab and add a check to the Show Trendlines check box and click on OK. The resulting chart should resemble Figure 9.18. Save the report as Chap 09 World Sales Report with Charts.rpt.

Figure 9.18
Chart showing two scales of information and a trendline.

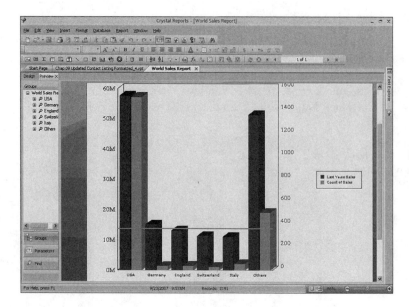

ADVANCED CRYSTAL REPORT DESIGN

CHAPTER **10**

USING CROSS-TABS FOR SUMMARIZED REPORTING

In this chapter

INTRODUCTION TO CROSS-TABS

Cross-tabs are highly formatted and densely populated reports that look a lot like a spreadsheet. This chapter gives you an understanding of how and when to use cross-tabs for your reporting needs.

A *cross-tab* is a fully summarized set of cells in a grid format. It summarizes values both across as well as down. It is a compact representation of information grouped on two different axes. There can be more than one level of grouping on either axis (row or column).

A *row* goes across the page with the header on the left or right, whereas a *column* runs down the page with the header at the top or bottom. The intersections between the rows and columns are called *cells*. Cells are places where a value to be summarized displays. Totals in the cells are summarized for each row and column as well as the break points for the different levels of groupings.

BENEFITS OF CROSS-TABS

Cross-tabs deliver data in a familiar spreadsheet format. They also summarize both vertically and horizontally, have a grid format, and can change size depending on the data.

Several of the most compelling reasons for using cross-tabs are

- Making better use of space
- Leveraging experience with the spreadsheet format
- Horizontal expansion
- Custom formatting

Because cross-tabs are grouped and summarized both vertically *and* horizontally, they are incredibly efficient at saving space as compared to a typical grouping report. They are very good at showing key information if the information required has at least two levels of grouping.

Here's an example: quarterly sales figures for the customers in a sales report. These need to be grouped by customer and quarter. If the report were shown in a standard grouping layout like you've worked with previously, it could be several pages long. Figure 10.1 shows a typical Crystal Report in which nine pages display only the USA customers grouped by customer and quarter.

Cross-tabs replicate the information contained in a sales report while resembling a spreadsheet. Managers get a one-stop view of all customers and their quarterly sales. Figure 10.2 shows how the information is more efficiently presented when a cross-tab is used to display the same information. Now the manager can view all the sales information at a glance.

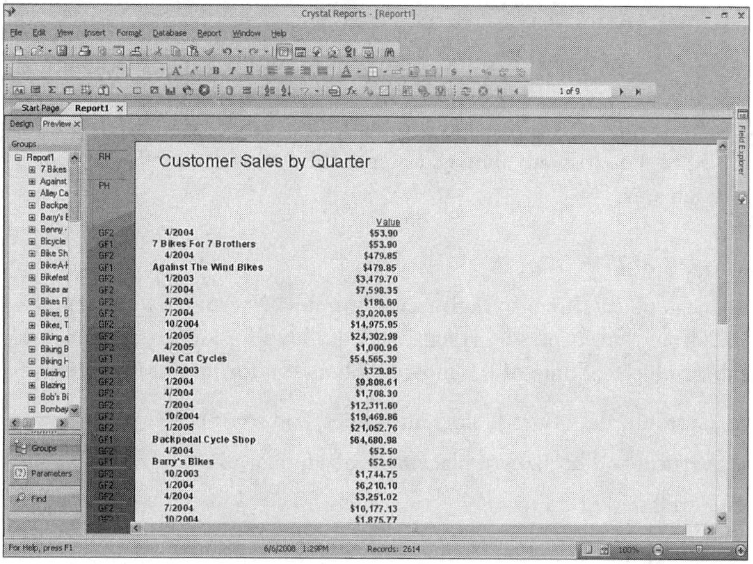

Figure 10.1
Standard grouping style used on a typical sales report.

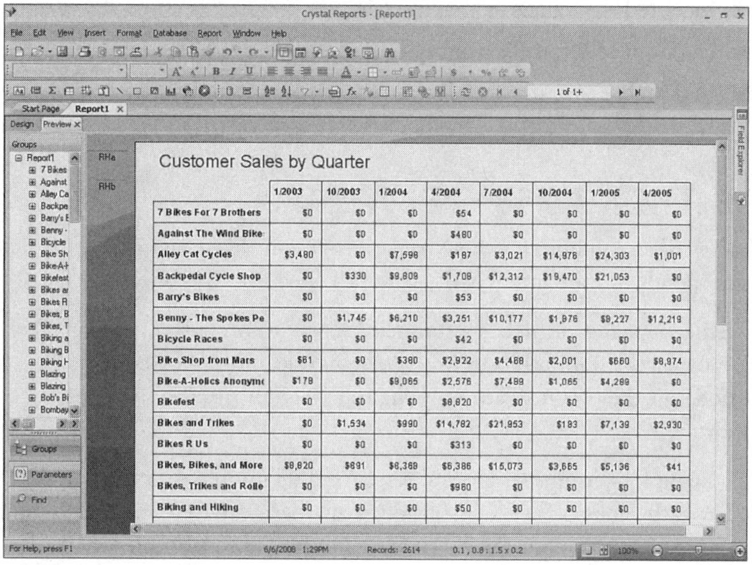

Figure 10.2
Sales shown in a cross-tab.

LEVERAGING EXPERIENCE WITH THE SPREADSHEET FORMAT

Another benefit of the cross-tab format is its familiarity to many users of spreadsheet applications. Many people use spreadsheets in their daily routines and are accustomed to their look and feel. Because cross-tabs appear very much like spreadsheets, Crystal Reports offers a familiar format and reporting style for many users. Again, providing the information in the format most comfortable to the user improves his productivity and your success.

HORIZONTAL EXPANSION

Cross-tabs, like spreadsheets, expand both vertically and horizontally. In Crystal Reports, cross-tabs are one of only two object types that expand across horizontal pages. Crystal Reports handles this expansion automatically. If there is more data to display than the original size of the cross-tab allows for, Crystal Reports doesn't cut off any critical data from the cross-tab area.

CUSTOM FORMATTING

Cross-tab objects are also highly customizable in terms of formatting. Everyone has different needs from their data, so Crystal Reports allows for a great deal of changes to the formatting of these objects. Some of the most highly useful formatting features used in cross-tabs are

- Customizable styles (colors, grid lines, and so on)
- Vertical and horizontal placement of summaries
- Formatted grid lines
- Toggle for summary totals (rows/columns)
- Cell margins
- Indented row labels
- Location of totals (beginning or end for both rows/columns)
- Repeatable row labels

USING THE CROSS-TAB WIZARD

Start with an example for the Xtreme Mountain Bike Company—the fictitious company that corresponds to the sample XML data provided for Crystal Reports.

Xtreme management needs a summary report to provide a quick glance at its shipped orders. The managers want to know how much has been spent by country for every six-month period, but they want to see only the top 10 countries. Follow these steps to create this report:

1. Begin by getting the Crystal Reports 2008 sample data from http:// www.businessobjects.com/product/catalog/crystalreports/samplereports.asp. Sample data is made available using XML files. Download the sample XML files and unzip to a folder.

2. Create a new report by choosing File, New and when the Report Gallery appears, choose As a Blank Report and then click on OK.

3. The Database Expert appears. In the Available Data Sources list, expand the following two nodes: Create New Connection, and XML and Web Services. When prompted use the button with three dots to browse for the local XML file named Customer.XML, and click on Next. Again using the three dots button, browse for the file named Customer.XSD, and then click on Finish. Expand the data root and add the Customer_Query source to the report. Double-click the Make New Connection link

under XML and Web Services, repeat the previous steps for the files orders.xml and orders.xsd, and add the orders_query connection to the report.

4. The Database Expert dialog appears again. Remove the link on Internal_ID and click OK again to accept the default linking and click Finish to go to the report.

5. Insert a cross-tab by choosing Cross-Tab from the Insert menu, or click on the Insert Cross-Tab button on the Insert toolbar (the fourth item from the left). This presents you with a shadowed box attached to your cursor. Place the box in any header or footer of your report (not on a page header or footer) and in this case put it in the upper-left corner of the Report Header. The box will become an empty cross-tab.

6. Set up the initial cross-tab. Right-click on the empty cross-tab and choose Cross-Tab Expert. The rows of the report are the countries, so select Country from the Available Fields and then click on the arrow button (>) under Rows. The column grouping is going to be by Order Date, so choose Order Date from Available Fields and then click on the arrow button (>) under Columns. Because the Order Date is supposed to be by quarter, click on the Group Options drop-down under Columns and change the third list box from Each Day to For Each Quarter. Finally, choose Order Amount from Available Fields and click the arrow button (>) under Summarized Fields so that the cell's summary is also selected. The final result looks like Figure 10.3.

Figure 10.3
Cross-Tab Expert–
Cross-Tab tab.

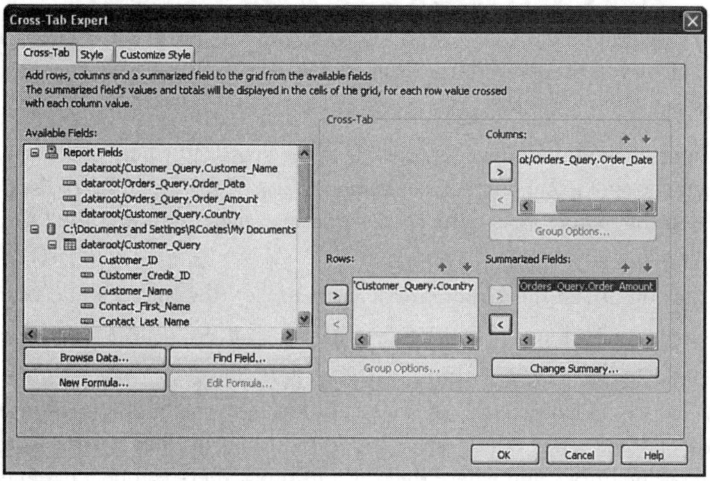

7. Click on the OK button to close the Cross-Tab Expert and see the result in the report Preview, as shown in Figure 10.4.

8. Before continuing, save your work. Choose File, Save As. Call this Chap 10 Cross-tab1.rpt and then click on OK.

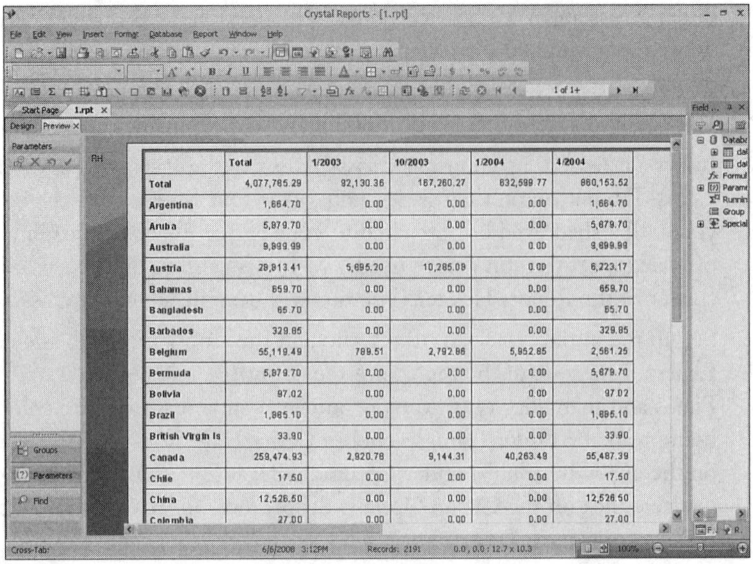

	Total	1/2003	10/2003	1/2004	4/2004
Total	4,077,785.29	92,130.36	167,260.27	632,599.77	860,153.52
Argentina	1,664.70	0.00	0.00	0.00	1,664.70
Aruba	5,879.70	0.00	0.00	0.00	5,879.70
Australia	9,899.99	0.00	0.00	0.00	9,899.99
Austria	28,813.41	5,695.20	10,285.08	0.00	6,223.17
Bahamas	659.70	0.00	0.00	0.00	659.70
Bangladesh	65.70	0.00	0.00	0.00	65.70
Barbados	329.85	0.00	0.00	0.00	329.85
Belgium	55,119.49	789.51	2,792.86	5,952.85	2,561.25
Bermuda	5,879.70	0.00	0.00	0.00	5,879.70
Bolivia	97.02	0.00	0.00	0.00	97.02
Brazil	1,865.10	0.00	0.00	0.00	1,895.10
British Virgin Is	33.90	0.00	0.00	0.00	33.90
Canada	259,474.93	2,920.78	9,144.31	40,263.49	55,487.39
Chile	17.50	0.00	0.00	0.00	17.50
China	12,526.50	0.00	0.00	0.00	12,526.50
Colombia	27.00	0.00	0.00	0.00	27.00

Figure 10.4
Cross-tab in Preview.

USING TOP N WITH CROSS-TABS REPORTS

Group sorts can be done on a report level so that the records are sorted and removed as necessary. However, there are times when the records are needed in the overall report but not in a cross-tab.

1. Right-click in the upper-left corner of the cross-tab where there are no data or words and choose Group Sort Expert. Choose Top N for the primary list box and change 5 to 10 in the Where N Is field. In this example, make sure that the Others option is not selected.
2. Click on OK in the Group Sort Expert to view the final result, as shown in Figure 10.5.
3. Save your work by choosing File, Save As. Call this `Chap 10 Cross-tab2.rpt` and then click on OK.
4. What would happen if there was a need to have the option of showing the top 5, the top 10, or some other value for N? In Crystal Reports 2008, a formula may be used to set the value of N—and where there is a formula, there can be a parameter. Using the skills you learned in Chapter 5, "Implementing Parameters for Dynamic Reporting," create a parameter.
5. To create a new parameter, open the Field Explorer, select Parameter Fields, and click on the New button. For Name, call this `Top N`, and set the type to Number. Because you've already learned about parameters, simply click on OK to move on.
6. Right-click on your cross-tab in the top left where there are no numbers or text, and select Group-Sort Expert. To the right of the number 10, click on the Formula button. When the window opens, simply double-click the parameter in the list of fields. Figure 10.6 shows what the formula should look like.

Figure 10.5
Cross-tab with a Top 10 Group Sort applied.

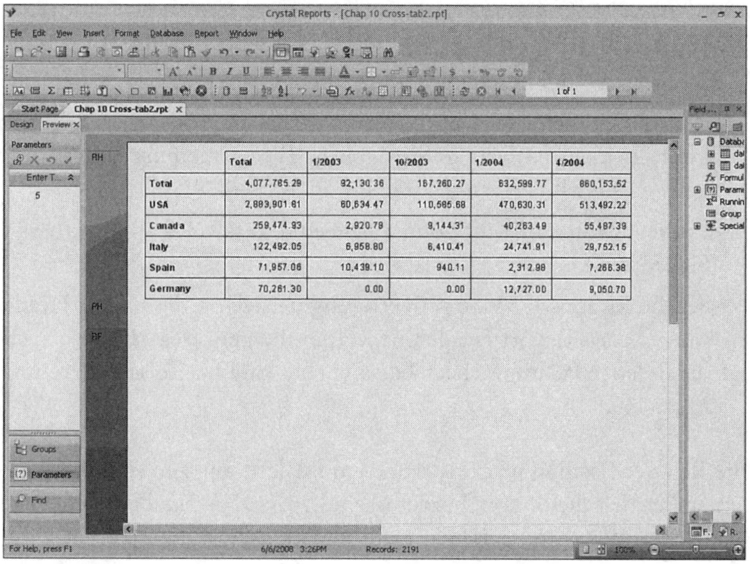

Figure 10.6
Setting the parameter to be the value for N makes this chart much more flexible.

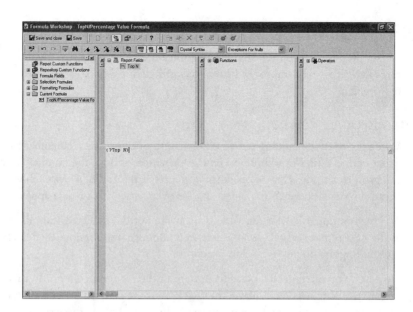

7. Refresh the report several times using different values for N. Save this report as Chap 10 Cross-tab dynamic N.rpt.

USING ADVANCED CROSS-TAB FEATURES

Crystal Reports version 9 introduced significant cross-tab improvements. The advanced features gave cross-tabs improved flexibility and functionality to satisfy even more reporting requirements.

SETTING RELATIVE POSITION

When it comes to planning the width or length of cross-tabs, remember that they expand dynamically. With the addition of new information or data, the number of rows or columns can grow or shrink. This makes putting objects at the end of a cross-tab very difficult because it's unclear when the object will be overwritten if new data appears.

An easy solution exists for the same issue at the bottom of a cross-tab. Place the new object in the next report section—even if it means adding a new section. By default, objects in Crystal Reports do not overwrite a section.

However, you often need to specify an item in the far-right column. In this report, you might want a logo to be displayed to the right of the cross-tab. But, in Design, the size of the cross-tab doesn't match what you see in Preview. Follow these steps to set the relative position:

1. Open `Chap 10 Cross-tab dynamic N.rpt`. Start with your last saved document by choosing it from the File list on the File, Open menu.

2. Ensure that the view is set to Design mode, and then insert a text object by opening the Insert menu and selecting Text Object. Type something into the text box and color the font red so that you can see it easily.

3. Preview the report. Click on F5 to see the result. It's not exactly as you intended (see Figure 10.7).

4. Set the Relative Position property. Right-click on the Report Header label (on the left where it says Report Header, or RH, in the gray area). Choose Section Expert. Toggle the Relative Positions check box and click on OK. To see the resulting report, refer to Figure 10.8.

The Relative Position property works on the left, top, and right borders of the cross-tab. Remember that the bottom border of the cross-tab is handled by the end of a section. Relative positions can be used in many situations. For example, showing a chart on the information in the cross-tab can be very useful.

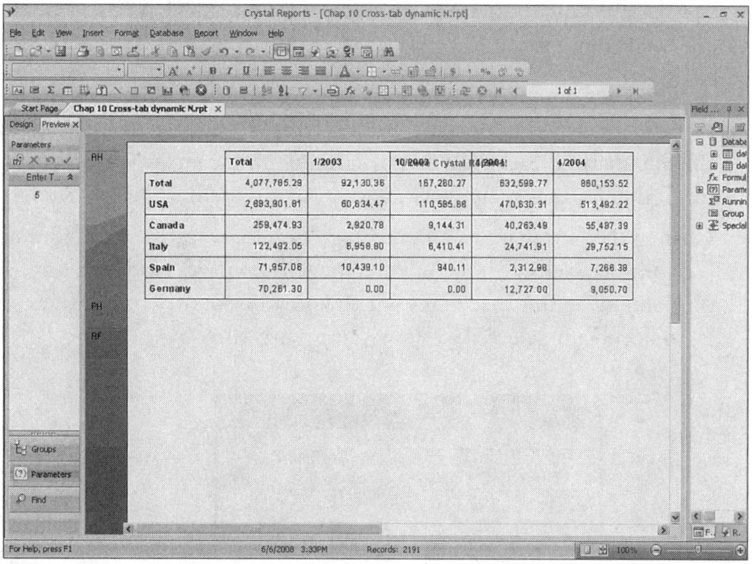

Figure 10.7
Design with cross-tab and text field in improper location.

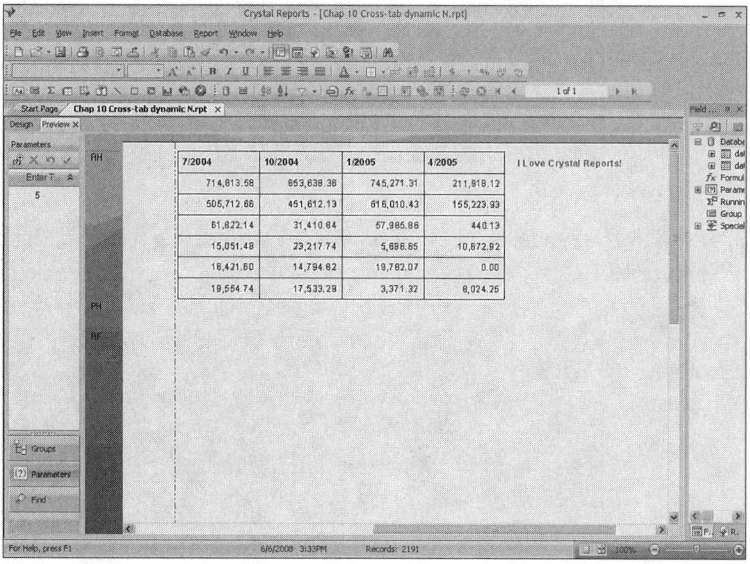

Figure 10.8
Preview of the cross-tab and text field as requested.

INSERTING A "PERCENTAGE OF" SUMMARY

Cross-tabs are great for compressing a lot of data into a small space, but it can be difficult to find the peaks or valleys in the data when just looking at the raw numbers. To highlight these peaks and valleys, summary values can be displayed as percentages of either the total rows or total columns:

1. Add another summary. Right-click in the upper left of the cross-tab where no data appears and choose Cross-Tab Expert. In the Cross-Tab tab, choose to add the Order Amount to the Summarized Fields list box by clicking on the arrow (>) button. Notice that it looks like it duplicates the summary above it, so choose the Change Summary button.

2. Change the Summary to a Percentage Summary. In the Edit Summary dialog in the Options box, select Show As Percentage Summary. Notice that it has an option for Row or Column. In this case you want to know by country (row) where the percentage split is, so keep Row selected as shown in Figure 10.9.

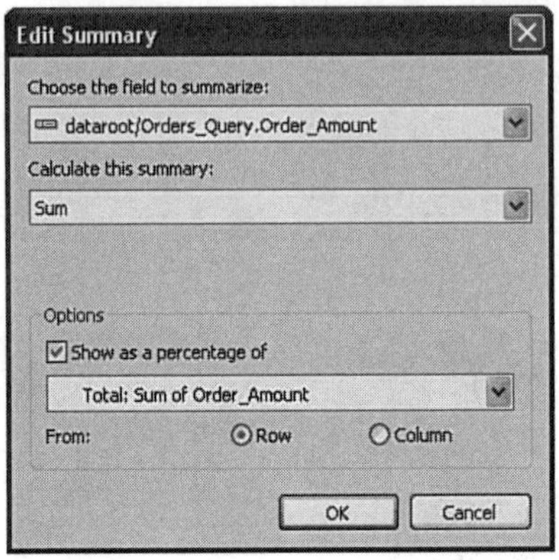

Figure 10.9
The Edit Summary dialog.

3. Preview the results by clicking on OK on both dialog windows. It should look like Figure 10.10.

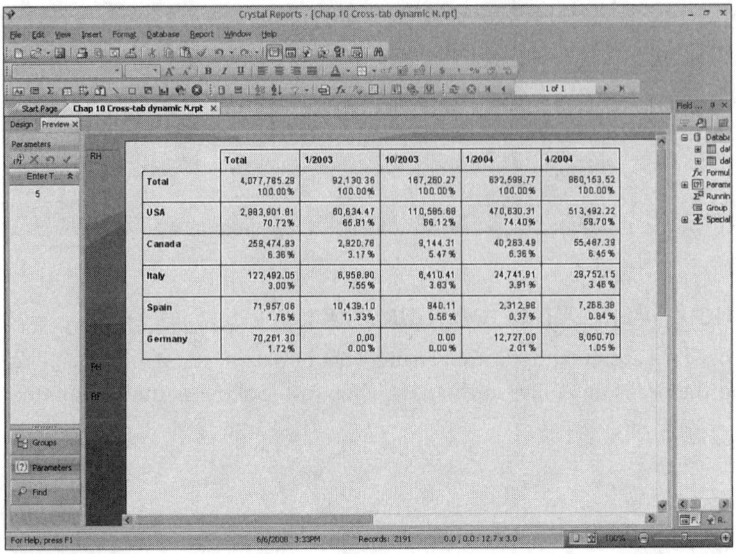

Figure 10.10
Monthly percentages by country.

Notice that the USA is consistently the largest percentage of Xtreme's orders. It's very easy to see this when percentages are added to the cross-tab.

HORIZONTAL AND VERTICAL PLACEMENT

Because the percentages add up to 100% down the page, it would be easier to understand if the summaries could be displayed side by side instead of one on top of the other. That way, the numbers down the page could be added up easily.

Crystal Reports allows the toggle between horizontal and vertical placement of summaries:

1. Launch the Cross-Tab Expert. Right-click in the upper left of the cross-tab again and choose Cross-Tab Expert. Select the Customize Style tab. Under Summarized Fields, choose Horizontal; select the Show Labels option.

2. View the report. Click on the OK button to see the changes made to the cross-tab (see Figure 10.11).

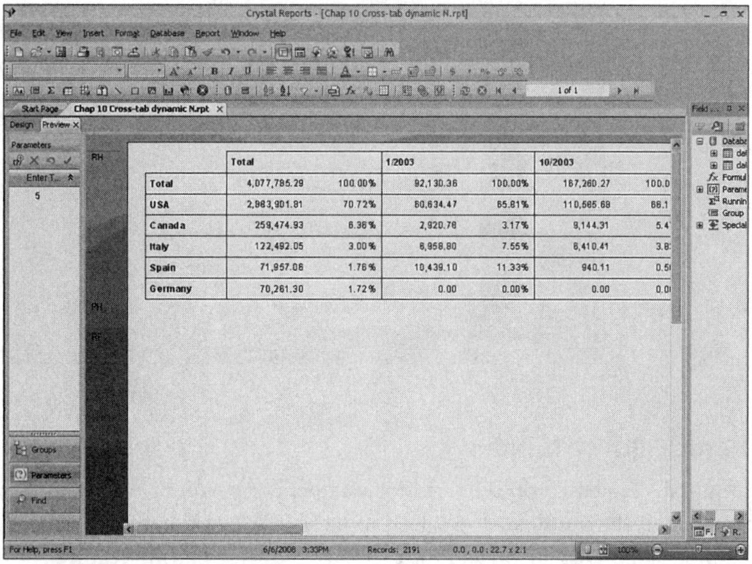

Figure 10.11
Horizontal placement of summaries.

INSERTING SUMMARY LABELS

Notice that on the report in Figure 10.11, the columns don't have a title to identify them. Right-click on the cross-tab as before and choose Cross-Tab Expert, go to the Customize Style tab, and make sure to select the Show Labels option. Both titles for the percentage and the summary are exactly the same (Order Amount). This is because Crystal Reports is showing the field that a summary is acting on. In this case, where the field is acted on twice, it's not a good choice. Crystal Reports enables you to edit these labels right on the cross-tab in both Design and Preview modes:

1. Edit the summary's title. Right-click on the first Order Amount title in the cross-tab and choose Edit Text. Delete the Order Amount text and add Sum instead. Then choose the Align Center button on the toolbar while the item is highlighted. Click off the object and see the result.

2. Edit the percentage title. Repeat the previous step for the second Order Amount field, but instead of changing the text to Sum, change it to %, as shown in Figure 10.12.

Figure 10.12
Cross-tab with both labels changed.

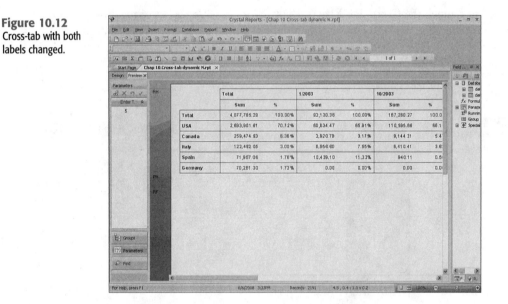

ADDING A DISPLAY STRING

Cross-tabs are based on the need for numbers or currency to be summarized, but there are times when the numbers don't need to be seen to get the point across. Crystal Reports has a feature, called Display String, for all fields. This formatting feature allows a different representation for a field than its underlying value. For example, a manager might want to see text beside a percentage mark, as shown in Figure 10.13.

As previously mentioned, cross-tab cells are always an intersection of rows and columns with a summary because the strings are the visual representation of the underlying summary being computed in the cross-tab. You can affect this string using the advanced Cross-Tab features of Crystal Reports.

Crystal Reports can now separate the data value from its display. This is a powerful feature and is *not* limited to cross-tabs, although it plays a major role in cross-tabs because of the requirement of summaries. To complete this report, ensure that all $0.00 amounts are shown as NONE on the report.

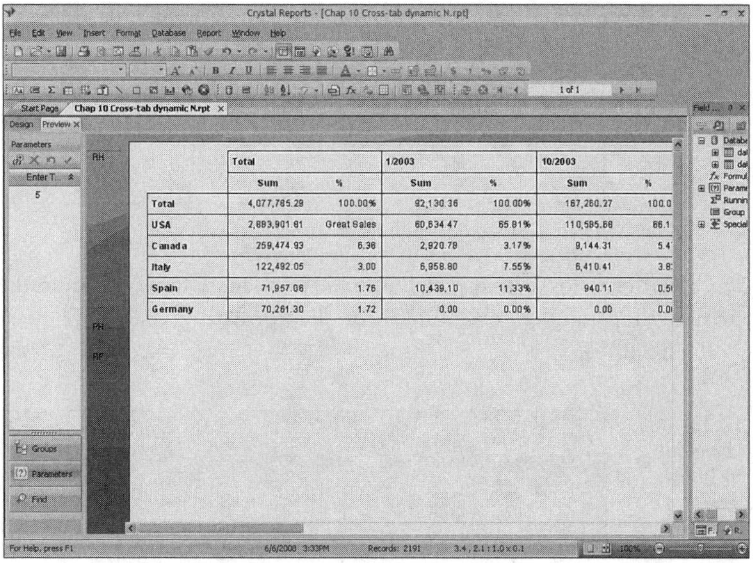

Figure 10.13
Sales report with text to identify great sales as display strings.

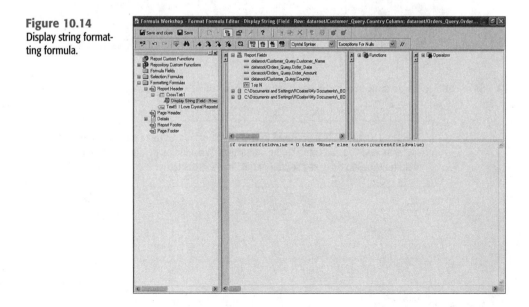

1. Format the Order Amount Summary. Right-click on one of the $0.00 amounts on the report and choose Format Field. Choose the Common tab and then choose the Conditional Formatting (X+2) button to the right of Display String. The Formula Workshop appears.

2. Format the formula for strings. Use an If/Then/Else formula structure to accomplish the task. The final result is If CurrentFieldValue = 0 Then "NONE" Else ToText(CurrentFieldvalue) (see Figure 10.14).

Figure 10.14
Display string formatting formula.

TIP

> Try to avoid using explicit field names in these formulas so that they can be reused in other places.
>
> Also, remember that these are string formulas. That's why ToText is needed around the CurrentFieldValue. Both Then and Else clauses must contain similar data types.

3. Close the dialog windows. Choose the Save and Close button on the Formula Workshop and then click on OK on the Formatting dialog. The result is shown in Figure 10.15.

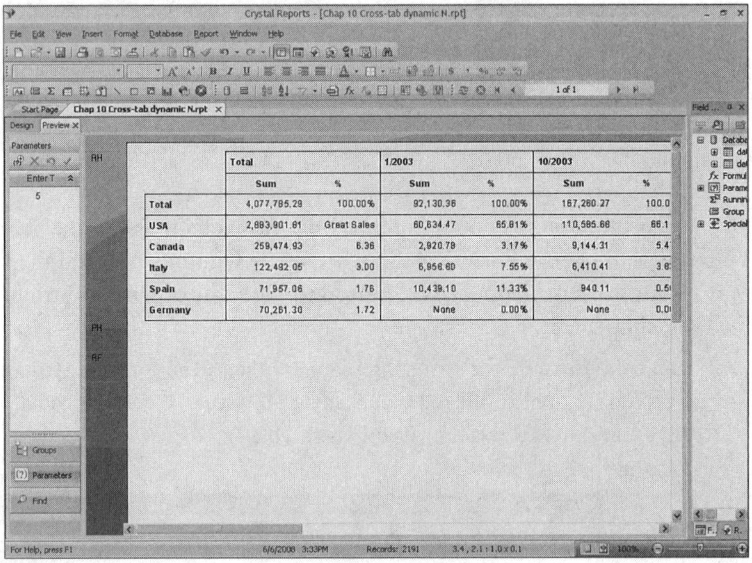

Figure 10.15
$0 changed to NONE by using the Display String feature.

4. Save the report as Chap 10 Crosstab3.rpt by choosing File, Save As.

TIP

> The same technique that you used to change the display value of the cell can be used on any area, and you can combine the interactivity provided by parameters and other formula functions to drive any section or field in the cross-tab.

WHAT'S NEW IN CROSS-TABS

Crystal Reports 2008 introduces some new and powerful capabilities. To illustrate how to leverage these new capabilities we'll start by defining some of the new functions and then we'll open one of the sample reports and re-create the custom cross-tab from scratch.

NEW CROSS-TAB FUNCTIONS DEFINED

There are some new functions that will be used commonly throughout cross-tab creation. Figure 10.16 is a sample cross-tab that will be referred to when explaining the functions that follow.

Figure 10.16
Sample cross-tab to help illustrate the formulas that follow.

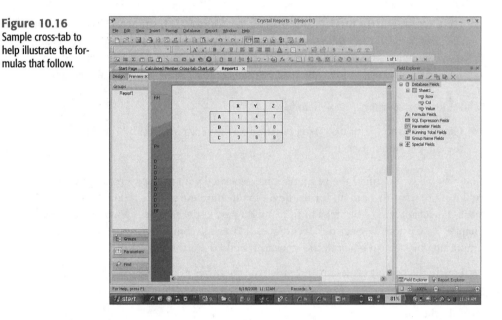

With an understanding of what these functions are meant to do, we can extend the cross-tab capabilities. These new functions are

- **GridValueAt(Row Index, Column Index, Summary Index)**—This returns the value of a given single cell within the cross-tab. It may be string or numeric depending on what that cell contains. `Row Index` and `Column Index` may refer to either the column in general or a specific cell within the row/column, but the value for `GridValueAt()` will be found at the intersection of that row and column. `Summary Index` refers to the summary value to be returned from the row and column intersection.

Valid values for Row Index include

- **CurrentRowIndex**—This function takes no arguments and returns the index of the current row.

- **GetRowPathIndexOf(Row Header Value)**—This function takes the value of the row header and returns the index identifying the row. For example, from Figure 10.16, GetRowPathIndexOf("B") returns the number 1 (this is a zero-based index) that identifies the row containing cell values 2, 5, and 8.

  Valid values for Column Index include

- **CurrentColumnIndex**—This function takes no arguments and returns the index of the current column.

- **GetColumnPathIndexOf(Column Header Value)**—This function takes the value of the header for the column and returns the index identifying the column. For example, from the figure 10.16 GetColumnPathIndexOf("X") returns the number 0 (this is also a zero-based index) that identifies the column containing cell values 1, 2, and 3.

Valid values for Summary Index include

- **CurrentSummaryIndex**—This function takes no arguments and returns the index of the current summary value.

Now that we've identified the key functions associated with the new cross-tab capabilities, we'll explore what this can do for us. Begin by opening the sample report Calculated Member Cross-tab Chart.rpt. The steps to find and download the sample reports can be found in Chapter 9, "Custom Formatting Techniques." We will rebuild the same cross-tab as in the sample step by step. In general, the steps to rebuild the cross-tab will be

- Create the default cross-tab and order the countries as needed.

- Add the blank rows and names for the continents.

- Edit the summaries.

1. Create the default cross-tab. From the Insert menu, choose Cross-Tab. This will attach a shadowed box to the mouse cursor. Move the shadowed box beside the upper-right corner of the cross-tab in the sample. Don't worry if the cross-tab doesn't look similar just yet. Figure 10.17 illustrates what the report should look like at this point. Right-click in the upper-left corner of our new cross-tab and from the context menu select Cross-Tab Expert. Move Customer.Country to the Rows and Customer.Last_Years_Sales to the Summarized Fields. With Customer.Country selected, the button Group Options will enable. Click Group Options. (If the button is still gray, see Figure 10.18 to ensure that Customer.Country is properly selected.) When the Group Options window opens, change the group order from In Ascending Order to In Specified Order. The window will change to allow picking the groups one at a time. Pick the groups in the following order Canada, USA, Mexico, Belgium, England, France, and Germany. Click on OK to close the Group Options window, and then click the Customize Style tab of the Cross-Tab Expert window. Uncheck Column Totals on

Top and click on OK. The cross-tab now looks very similar except for the new features. (Some subtle formatting differences remain, but the focus is on the structure of the cross-tab not formatting.)

Figure 10.17
A blank cross-tab.

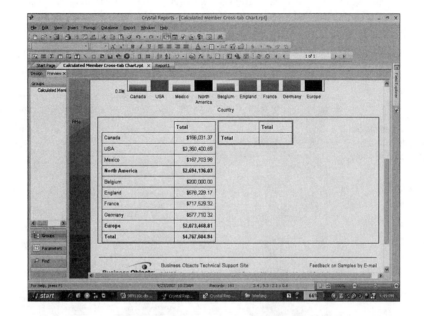

Figure 10.18
Cross-tab Expert settings.

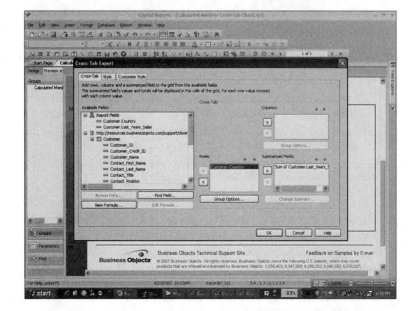

2. Add the blank rows and names for the continents. On our new cross-tab, right-click on the row header of Mexico, and from the context menu, choose Calculated Member, Insert Row. A blank row is inserted after Mexico. Right-click on the blank cell directly under Mexico, and from the context menu choose Calculated Member, Edit Header Formula. When the Formula Editor opens type **North America** and click on the Save and Close button. Do the same for Germany, but label the blank cell as **Europe**. Figure 10.19 illustrates the report to this point. The structure exists with only the continent summaries remaining.

Figure 10.19
Cross-tab with the structure defined but not quite complete. The continents show zero.

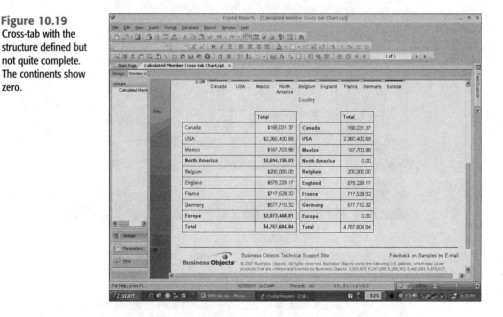

3. Edit the summaries. For both defined continents (North America and Europe), the totals show zero. Right-click the zero beside North America and from the context menu choose Calculated Member, Edit Calculation Formula. In the Formula Workshop window, enter the following formula:

```
GridValueAt(GetRowPathIndexOf("Canada"),
CurrentColumnIndex, CurrentSummaryIndex)
```

4. Click on the Save and Close button. Notice the North America value matches the Canada value. Edit the formula (right-click the formula and from the context menu choose Calculated Member, Edit Calculation Formula) and change Canada to USA. Click on the Save and Close button. Notice the formula now matches the value for USA. Edit the formula one more time but enter the following formula:

```
GridValueAt(GetRowPathIndexOf("Canada"),
CurrentColumnIndex, CurrentSummaryIndex)
+ GridValueAt(GetRowPathIndexOf("USA"),
CurrentColumnIndex, CurrentSummaryIndex)
+ GridValueAt(GetRowPathIndexOf("Mexico"),
CurrentColumnIndex, CurrentSummaryIndex)
```

5. Notice the formula now shows the sum for North America. Edit the formula for Europe, adding the following formula:

```
GridValueAt(GetRowPathIndexOf("Belgium"),
CurrentColumnIndex, CurrentSummaryIndex)
+ GridValueAt(GetRowPathIndexOf("England"),
CurrentColumnIndex, CurrentSummaryIndex)
+ GridValueAt(GetRowPathIndexOf("France"),
CurrentColumnIndex, CurrentSummaryIndex)
+ GridValueAt(GetRowPathIndexOf("Germany"),
CurrentColumnIndex, CurrentSummaryIndex)
```

The summary for Europe is now accurate, and the new cross-tab is complete. See Figure 10.20 to see the completed cross-tab.

Figure 10.20
Newly created complete cross-tab.

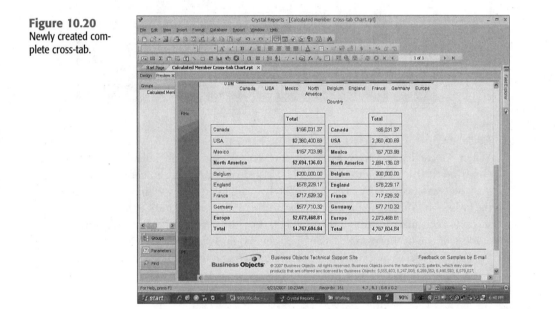

CRYSTAL REPORTS IN THE REAL WORLD—ADVANCED CROSS-TABS

Although a single cross-tab that covers all the data in a report can be quite useful, with some large data sets it can be quite unreadable. As an example, the Chap 10 Crosstab3.rpt report created earlier stretches across more than one page. A simple solution to this is to group the report and place the cross-tab in the group header or footer. Cross-tabs are context sensitive and if placed in a group header or footer will show only data for that group.

1. Open the Chap 10 Crosstab3.rpt report and, using skills learned in earlier chapters, create a group for Order Date and change it from For Each Day to For Each Year. See Figure 10.16 for the report's starting point.

Figure 10.21
Report framework.

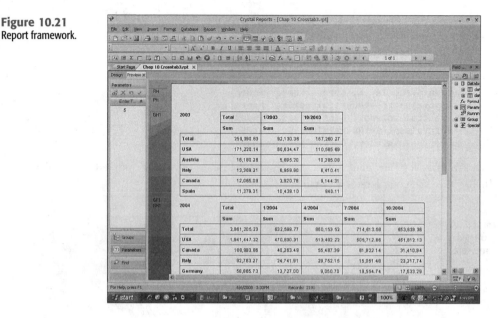

2. Edit the Cross-Tab Expert and remove the Percent field from the summarized fields. When done, click on OK. Next, right-click on the cross-tab in a blank area and choose Cut from the menu. Right-click on a blank area of the report and choose Paste. Notice that the cross-tab doesn't paste immediately. A silhouette shows a box that represents the cross-tab. Moving the box around with the mouse, you'll notice that the different sections get a shadow around them. When the silhouette for the cross-tab is inside the shadow of any of the group headers, left-click to deposit the cross-tab in the group header. If needed, you can click the Undo button and try again. Notice the cross-tab is aware of the context for the group. Only data for the correct year shows in the cross-tab for a given group.

3. Figure 10.17 shows the complete report.

4. Save the report as GroupedCrossTab.rpt.

Figure 10.17
Grouped cross-tabs can avoid confusion through improved readability.

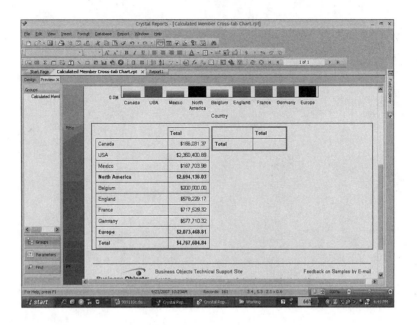

CHAPTER **11**

USING RECORD SELECTIONS, SORT CONTROLS, AND ALERTS FOR INTERACTIVE REPORTING

In this chapter

INTRODUCTION

Not all information is fit for all users, so this chapter discusses how record selection can limit the data in a report. Hand-in-hand with limiting the data (reducing the recordset also improves speed and performance) is a review of tuning the report. Even when a report is published to BusinessObjects Enterprise (discussed in later chapters) and much time is invested in correctly architecting and tuning the servers, the number one performance improvement is often in correct report authoring.

CREATING ADVANCED RECORD SELECTION FORMULAS

Although creating a simple report can be very useful for an end user, highlighting notable information can increase the utility of the report because it saves time spent looking for trends and crucial data. *Outliers*, data that fall above or below the average of a specified threshold, often contain key information. This chapter focuses on drawing attention to key data by using record selections and introducing SQL expressions, and it introduces report alerting.

Although many filters are simple enough to be defined using the Select Expert, most real-world reports require editing the record selection formula itself. Before covering the best practices for creating formulas, review the material on record selections introduced in Chapter 2, "Selecting and Grouping Data."

RECORD SELECTION REVIEW

Record selections, or filters, are defined by a record selection formula built using the Crystal syntax of the Crystal Reports formula language. You can build a record selection formula using the Formula Editor by opening the Report menu and choosing Selection Formulas, Record. A simpler way to build record selections is to use the Select Expert icon accessed via the Experts toolbar.

A record selection formula returns a Boolean value indicating whether a given record should be included in the report. It is evaluated for each record in the database. Any time a database field is used in the formula, it is replaced by the actual field value.

After this quick review, the following sections move on to some of the more important topics in creating record selection filters.

DISPLAYING RECORD SELECTIONS

Although the techniques discussed in this chapter allow powerful filtering, this should not be applied without the end user's knowledge in most cases. (Certainly there are cases where end users should not know of hidden data, but this more often is handled via filters to secure the data in a Business View or Business Objects Universe.) In these cases, you can simply display the current selection filter or other special fields by either dragging the fields onto the report from the Field Explorer, Special Fields area, or by using the same fields in a formula to change the way these fields display, as in the previous chapter.

DEALING WITH DATES

Use the Select Expert, which you access by choosing Report, Select Expert, to manipulate dates with the addition of four specific date-related comparators:

- **Is Between**—The selected items fall between these two dates.
- **Is Not Between**—The selected items do not fall between these two dates.
- **Is in the Period**—The selected items fall in the periods selected from the drop-down list.
- **Is Not in the Period**—The selected items do not fall in the periods selected from the drop-down list.

These date-specific operators appear when you have selected a field of type Date, and they prompt for the specific values. However, in more complicated situations, you are forced to create a formula in the Formula Editor rather than use the Select Expert to create the formula for you.

One of the most common record selection formulas is {field} = value, where {field} is a database field and value is a corresponding value of the same data type. An example of this would be

```
{Customer.Country} = "Canada"
```

This kind of formula is very easy to create but becomes more complicated when the data types of the values to be compared are not the same. Filtering data based on dates often causes this type of situation; for instance, this formula:

```
{Orders.Order Date} > "2/25/2000"
```

NOTE

> When you click the Check button to check the formula's syntax, Crystal Reports provides a message saying **A date-time is required here**. After you close the message box Crystal Reports highlights `"2/25/2000"`. Because the Order Date field has a data type of Datetime, the formula attempts to compare a Datetime to a String, which is not allowed. Comparisons must always be performed on objects of the same data type. To rectify this, instead of using a string literal to describe a date, the formula could use the `DateTime` function to return a Datetime value. Here is an example of the corrected formula:
>
> ```
> {Orders.Order Date} > DateTime(2000, 2, 25, 0, 0, 0)
> ```

Notice that when the DateTime function is used, it takes arguments for not only year, month, and day, but also for hour, minute, and second. This is because to compare this value to the Order Date field, it needs to be a Datetime value. In this case, you might not care about the time part of the Datetime value. The best way to solve this would be to first convert the Order Date field into a date from a Datetime, and then use the Date function instead of Datetime. The improved formula follows:

```
Date({Orders.Order Date}) > Date(2000, 2, 25)
```

To make this even simpler, the Crystal Reports formula language also supports dates specified in the following format:

```
#YYYY/MM/DD HH:MM AM/PM#
```

Using this syntax, the following formula is also valid:

```
{Orders.Order Date} > #2000/2/25 12:00 AM#
```

Another nice feature of this syntax is the capability to omit the time portion. When this is done, a default of 12:00 a.m. is used.

Various functions are available for converting between Strings, Dates, and Datetimes. These can be found in the Function Tree window of the Formula Editor, under the Date and Time folder.

Another issue that comes up often is filtering on a field in the database that contains dates but is defined as a string field. The following fictitious formula, although it does not return any errors when checking the syntax, does not accomplish what you might expect:

```
{Shipments.Ship Date} > "1/1/2001"
```

This will not perform a date comparison because both fields are of type String. To correct this formula, you could use the DTSToDate function provided by the DTS (datetime string) user function library.

11

> **NOTE**
>
> A *user function library* is a library of functions that can be used from the Crystal Reports formula language. Business Objects provides several of these with the product, and others are available from third-party vendors. If you are proficient with COM or Java programming, you could even create a user function library yourself. The user function library can be found under the `Additional Functions` folder in the Function Tree of the Formula Editor. Crystal Reports supports both COM and Java user function libraries but not at the same time—only one or the other. Similarly, BusinessObjects Enterprise supports only the COM versions of the user function libraries. Reports that embed the Java libraries will cause an error when viewed using BusinessObjects Enterprise. To take advantage of full support for the Enterprise product, it might be useful to build a custom function rather than a user function library.

The DTSToDate function takes a string in the proper date format and converts it to a Date value. The correct formula is shown here:

```
DTSToDate({Shipments.Ship Date}) > Date(2001, 1, 1)
```

where the Ship Date field contains a date in *DD/MM/YYYY* format.

WORKING WITH STRINGS

As with dates, simple string comparisons are easy to achieve using the record selection expert. Slightly more complex comparisons can easily become tedious unless you are armed with knowledge for effectively dealing with strings. A simple example is a listing of customer data for a set of countries. Creating a record selection formula like the following can become quite tedious:

```
{Customer.Country} = "England" or
{Customer.Country} = "France" or
{Customer.Country} = "Germany" or
{Customer.Country} = "Denmark"
```

Rather than using multiple comparisons, this can be accomplished with a single comparison using a string array.

NOTE

An array in the context of the Crystal Reports formula language is a collection of values that can be referenced as a single object.

The previous record selection formula can be rewritten to look like this:

```
{Customer.Country} in ["England", "France", "Germany", "Denmark"]
```

Notice that there are several differences. First, instead of using multiple comparisons, only a single comparison is used. This is both simpler to read and easier to maintain. The four country values combine into a string array. Square brackets with values separated by commas indicate arrays. Finally, instead of an = operator, the in operator is used. This operator, as its name implies, is used to determine whether the value on its left is present inside the array on its right.

NOTE

Although string arrays are described here, arrays can be made holding other data types, such as integers and currency values.

In this example, the countries are hard-coded into the selection formula. Although this makes it easy to read, the report would need to be modified if the country list were ever to change. A better way to handle this would be to create a multiple-value prompt and use it in place of the country list. If you did that, the formula would look like this:

```
{Customer.Country} in {?CountriesParam}
```

During the parameter prompting, the user is allowed to enter multiple values, and you can even provide a list of default values from which to choose.

PUSHING RECORD SELECTIONS TO THE DATABASE

When dealing with large sets of records, performance becomes important. The record selection used makes a significant difference in report performance. Crystal Reports does have the capability to perform database-like operations on the data, such as grouping, filtering, summarizing, and sorting. However, in general, asking the database to perform those

11

operations results in a faster overall transaction. Because of this principle, Crystal Reports attempts to ask the database to perform these operations if possible.

In the context of record selections, when Crystal Reports queries the database, it attempts to incorporate as much of the logic of the record selection formula as possible into the query. Ideally, all the logic can be incorporated into the query, which means that the database will perform all the filtering and return only the records that meet the criteria. However, because the SQL language doesn't support all the Crystal Reports formula language, there could be certain situations in which some or all the logic of the record selection formula cannot be converted to SQL. In this case, Crystal Reports needs to pull some or all the records from the database and perform filtering itself.

When working with a desktop database such as Access or FoxPro, the performance difference between the database engine and the Crystal Reports engine doing the filtering is minimal because it really comes down to which filtering algorithm is faster. Because databases are made for just this purpose and are customized for their own data structures, they generally perform this kind of operation faster. However, when dealing with client/server databases in which the database resides on a back-end server and Crystal Reports resides on your desktop machine, the difference becomes much more apparent. This is partly because of network traffic. There's a big difference between sending 50 records back over the network and sending 100,000. This performance hit becomes even worse when using a slow connection such as a dial-up modem.

To determine whether the logic you used in the record selection formula or Select Expert is incorporated into the query sent to the database, it's helpful to have a basic understanding of the SQL language. You need not be an expert at SQL, but being able to recognize whether the query is performing a filter on a certain field makes record selection formula tuning much more effective.

Although there are some guidelines for creating record selection formulas that will be fully passed down to the server, often the best approach is to simply check the SQL statement manually and determine whether the record selection logic is present. To view the SQL statement that Crystal Reports generated, select Show SQL Query from the Database menu. Figure 11.1 shows the resulting dialog.

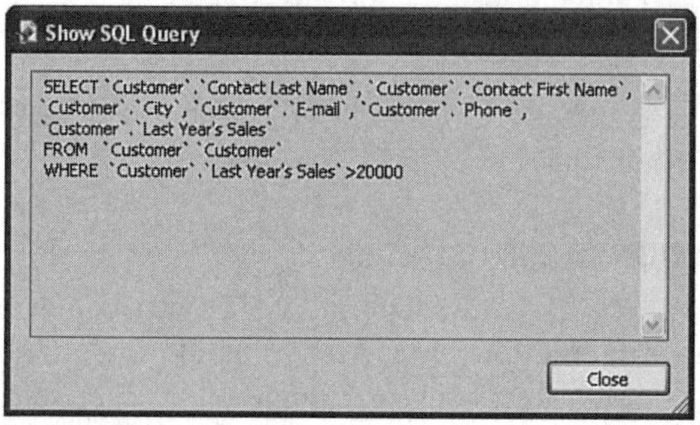

Figure 11.1
The Show SQL Query dialog displays the actual SQL code used to retrieve the results from the relational database.

```
Show SQL Query

SELECT `Customer`.`Contact Last Name`, `Customer`.`Contact First Name`,
`Customer`.`City`, `Customer`.`E-mail`, `Customer`.`Phone`,
`Customer`.`Last Year's Sales`
FROM `Customer` `Customer`
WHERE `Customer`.`Last Year's Sales` >20000
```

Close

You can infer from the preceding SQL query that this report is based on the Customer table, uses the Customer Name, email, and Last Year's Sales fields, and has a record selection of

```
{Customer.Last Year's Sales} > $20000
```

All the logic of the record selection formula has now been passed down to the database in the SQL query. However, if this report had a formula field that calculated the tax, that formula might consist of the following:

```
{Customer.Last Year's Sales} * 1.07
```

This formula field might be placed on the report to indicate the tax for each customer. A problem occurs when this formula is used in the record selection formula. Although the following formula seems logical, it is inefficient:

```
{@Tax} > $10000
```

If you were to look at the SQL query generated for this report, you would see that no WHERE clause is present. In other words, the report is asking the database for all the records and doing the filtering locally, which, depending on the size of the database, could result in poor performance. A better record selection to use—which would produce the same results, but perform the filtering on the database server—would be

```
{Customer.Last Year's Sales} > $142857
```

This works out because at a tax rate of 7%, $142,857 is the minimum a customer would need to sell to have tax of more than $10,000. Using the previous record selection would result in a SQL query with the following WHERE clause:

```
WHERE 'Customer'.'Last Year's Sales' > 142857
```

Although this approach returns the correct data, a slightly less cryptic approach would be to use a SQL expression.

AN INTRODUCTION TO SQL EXPRESSIONS

Crystal Reports formulas are useful because they enable you to use the full Crystal Reports formula language as well as a suite of built-in functions. However, as you learned in this chapter, they can be a factor in report processing performance. SQL expressions provide an alternative to this.

A *SQL expression*, as the name implies, is an expression written in the SQL language. Instead of consisting of a whole formula, a SQL expression consists of an expression that defines a single field just like a formula field does. The difference between a formula field and a SQL expression is based on where it is evaluated. Formula fields are evaluated locally by Crystal Reports, whereas SQL expressions are evaluated by the database server and therefore produce better performance when used in a record selection formula.

To better understand this, look at the example discussed in the previous section. The example had a report with a Crystal Reports formula that calculated tax based on the Last Year's

Sales field. Although there certainly are situations in which formula fields need to be used, this is not one of them because the logic being used in the formula is simple enough that the database server is able to perform it. Instead of creating a formula field, a SQL expression could have been created. SQL Expressions are created via the Field Explorer, which was introduced in Chapter 4, "Understanding and Implementing Formulas." Right-clicking on the SQL expressions item and selecting New begins the process of creating a SQL expression. When you're choosing to create a new SQL expression, the SQL Expression Editor is launched (see Figure 11.2).

Figure 11.2
The SQL Expression Editor.

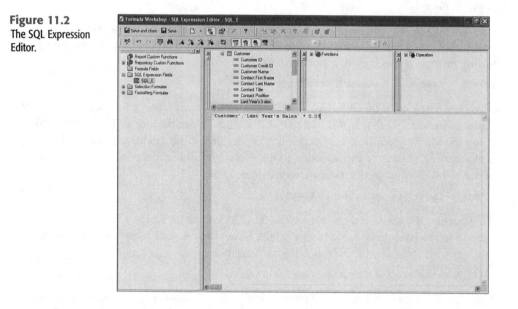

This editor is, in fact, the same editor used to create Crystal Reports formulas, but with a few small changes. First you'll notice that in the field tree, only database fields are present for use in the expression. Because SQL expressions are evaluated on the database servers, Crystal Reports constructs, such as prompt fields and formula fields, do not exist and thus cannot be used in the expression.

To create a SQL expression that calculates the tax, the following expression can be used:

```
'Customer'.'Last Year's Sales' * 0.07
```

Notice that instead of using the {Table.Field} syntax for fields, the 'Table'.'Field' syntax is used. This is because the quoted syntax is how you define fields in the SQL language.

When inserting this SQL expression into the report and checking the SQL query, you will find Crystal Reports has generated SQL similar to this:

```
SELECT 'Customer'.'Customer Name', ('Customer'.'Last Year's Sales' * 0.07)
FROM 'Customer' 'Customer'
```

The SQL expression defined in the report is inserted into the main SQL statement that Crystal Reports generates. This means that you can use any database-specific syntax or function inside a SQL expression.

Getting back to the topic of performance, you'll remember that using the tax calculation formula field in the record selection formula resulted in all the records being returned and Crystal Reports having to perform the filtering locally. Fortunately, any SQL expressions used in the record selection always pass down to the database server. Therefore, a better record selection for filtering out customers who pay less than $10,000 in tax would be the following:

```
{%Tax} > 10000
```

In this record selection formula, {%Tax} is the SQL expression discussed previously. This record selection formula would result in Crystal Reports generating the following SQL query:

```
SELECT 'Customer'.'Customer Name', ('Customer'.'Last Year's Sales' * 0.07)
FROM 'Customer' 'Customer'
WHERE ('Customer'.'Last Year's Sales' * 0.07)>10000
```

NOTE

> Remember that any formula evaluated after the first pass of the multipass system (for instance, grouping criteria or information to prompt a subreport) can cause slow report processing. Again, a SQL expression can retrieve the correct data in the first place, speeding report processing significantly. The next chapter of this book covers the multipass system in detail.

ADDING ALERTING TO YOUR REPORTS

Although you can call out outlying values by using conditional formatting, the alerting feature inside Crystal Reports allows for more interactive identification of key data as well as pushing of those alerts to end users via BusinessObjects Enterprise's alerting functionality.

A report *alert* is a custom notification created within Crystal Reports, triggered when a predetermined condition is met. An alert comprises three integral parts:

- Name
- Trigger (condition or threshold)
- Message

Alerts serve the dual functions of bringing end-user attention to a certain condition being met and focusing that attention on specifically relevant data in a report—thereby increasing user efficiency. Table 11.1 lists some examples of reports in which alerts could provide a benefit.

TABLE 11.1   REPORTS WITH POTENTIALLY USEFUL ALERTS

Report	Alert	Alert Trigger and Result
Product Sales Profitability Report	Product Profitability Warning	Trigger: Specific product profitability below 10% Result: A listing of the least successfully selling products
Customer Churn	Regional Customer Churn Warnings	Trigger: Specific regions where churn rate is higher than 3% in a quarter Result: A listing of regions to increase competitive analysis or to review regional management practice
Income Statement	Company Divisions with Net Losses	Trigger: Company division with net income < 0 Result: A listing of divisions where deeper business analysis is required

Report alerts trigger when the report is processed and the associated condition is met. When this condition is true, the alert message will be displayed. Figure 11.3 displays a triggered alert from within the Crystal Reports Designer.

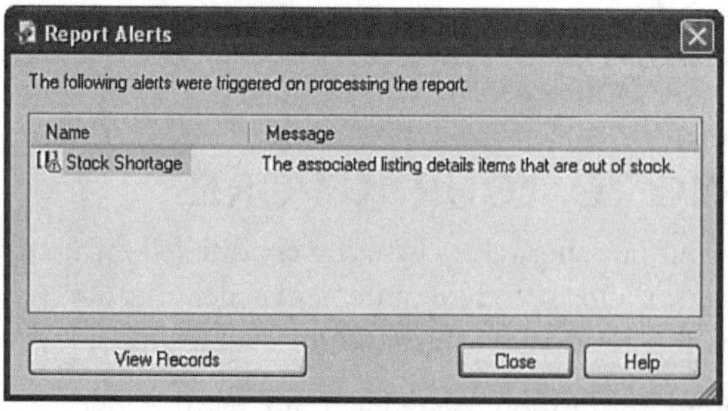

Figure 11.3
A report alert being triggered.

CREATING, EDITING, AND USING ALERTS

To create or edit alerts in Crystal Reports, select the Report, Alerts, Create or Modify Alerts menu items. The Create Alerts dialog (shown in Figure 11.4) enables you to create a new alert, edit existing alerts, and remove existing alerts.

To create the alert, follow these steps:

1. Give the alert a name. This name should be meaningful and will be displayed to the user when the alert is triggered.

Figure 11.4
Clicking Edit on the
Create Alerts dialog
opens the Edit Alert
dialog.

2. Specify a condition for which to trigger the alert. An example of this would be
   `{Customer.Last Year's Sales} < $10000`. The condition is simply a formula using
   either Crystal or Basic syntax that evaluates to a TRUE or FALSE result. TRUE means the
   alert should be triggered; false means that it should not.

   NOTE

   > You can use other formulas and prompts inside this condition. Using a prompt to deter-
   > mine the threshold on your alert is useful because the report could then be viewed by
   > different audiences with different thresholds, and they could still see the alert triggered
   > for their respective numbers.

3. Give the alert a message to display when it has been triggered. This can be a hard-
   coded string, or it can be a formula such as
   `"Sales are over $" + ToText({Customer.Last Year's Sales})`

To see your alert in action, refresh the report with data that meets your alert condition, and
triggered alerts will display.

Finally, not only are you notified that the alerts have been triggered, but you can click the
View Records button on the Report Alerts pop-up dialog to filter the report to show only
those records that triggered the alert. This is a good way to draw attention to the key outliers in the data.

USING ALERTS IN BUSINESSOBJECTS ENTERPRISE

The Report Alerts dialog displayed in Figure 11.3 is available only from within the Crystal
Reports Designer. If you are delivering your reports via another mechanism, such as the
Web, alerts are handled differently. To have your end users take advantage of Crystal

Reports alerting, you will need to either use BusinessObjects Enterprise for report distribution or exploit the built-in alert functions (`IsAlertEnabled()`, `IsAlertTriggered()`, and `AlertMessage()`) within formulas you create in your report.

→ For more information on BusinessObjects Enterprise, **see** online chapters from previous editions of this book downloadable at www.usingcrystal.com.

Typically, alerts can be shown to end users in a portal, which then links back to the report.

PERFORMANCE MONITORING AND TUNING

As reports grow in data size and complexity, ensuring optimal performance becomes increasingly important. This section serves as both a reminder of some performance tips already covered in the book to this point and as an introduction to some other tools and methods provided by Crystal Reports to optimize report performance in demanding environments.

GROUP BY ON SERVER

This Crystal Reports option enables you to push down the Grouping and Sorting activities to the database server. By performing these functions on the database instead of the Crystal server, less data is passed back to the Crystal Report and report-processing time is decreased. This option can be set locally under the Database main menu when the given report is being edited, or set globally on the Database tab of the Options menu accessed under the File main menu.

Some restrictions apply to the use of this option, including the following:

- The data source must be a standard SQL database.
- The report must have groups within it, and the groups must be based on database fields—not formula fields.
- The groups cannot contain specified order sorting.
- The Details section of the report must be hidden.
- Running totals must be based on summary fields. (That is, they do not rely on detail records for their calculations.)
- The report cannot contain average or distinct count summaries or use Top N values.

When this option is applicable and used, the involved reports perform faster. In addition, the detail level on these reports is still accessible through the standard drill-down functionality and makes dynamic connections to the database to bring back any user-requested detailed information.

SQL EXPRESSIONS IN RECORD SELECTIONS

As referenced and discussed previously in the book, SQL expressions are SQL statements that provide access to advanced database aggregations and functions. Using SQL expressions wherever possible in record selections and formula creation (versus using Crystal or Basic syntax) optimizes the amount of work that will be processed by the database server (versus the Crystal server)—and this increases your report's performance.

Some quick examples of SQL expressions that can be used in place of Crystal formula syntax:

Crystal Formula Syntax	SQL Expression (SQL Server Syntax)
IF/THEN/ELSE	CASE [Database Field]
Or	WHEN Condition THEN Value1
SELECT CASE	ELSE Value2 END
Concatenate	CONCAT([Database(x + y) Field1], [Database Field2])
MONTH(datefield)	MONTH([Database Field])

You should investigate the SQL capabilities of the report's database thoroughly when report performance and optimization becomes a critical business issue. Mature databases such as Oracle, DB2, SQL Server, and so on have mature SQL capabilities that you can often leverage in lieu of the Crystal formula language in field selection and record selection. Using SQL expressions can dramatically increase report performance in many instances.

USE INDEXES ON SERVER FOR SPEED

This is another performance option set under the Database tab of the Options dialog accessed from the main File menu. This option ensures that the involved Crystal Report uses any indexes that are present for the selected database and for the given report.

ON-DEMAND OR REDUCED NUMBER OF SUBREPORTS

As discussed in the chapter on subreports, these objects are reports unto themselves and maintain their own database connections and queries. As you can imagine, if too many subreports are added to a main report, this can lead to runaway report-processing times. A typical scenario where this might happen is when you want to include the data inside a subreport for every group within the main report. In a large report with hundreds or even thousands of groups, this can lead to that subreport running thousands of times—a palpable performance hit even when the subreport is small and/or optimized.

To minimize this challenge, it is a good idea to ensure that in-place subreports (as opposed to on-demand subreports) are used judiciously and that they are indeed required in performance-sensitive reports. Often times, only a very small subset of the subreports are ever viewed by a user, and an acceptable user experience can be provided with on-demand subreports instead.

PERFORMANCE MONITOR

After a report has been functionally designed, Crystal Reports provides the Performance Information tool to facilitate performance testing. This tool provides information that helps

11

in optimizing the current report for fastest performance. The Performance Information dialog shown in Figure 11.5 is accessed from the main Report menu by selecting Report | Performance Information.

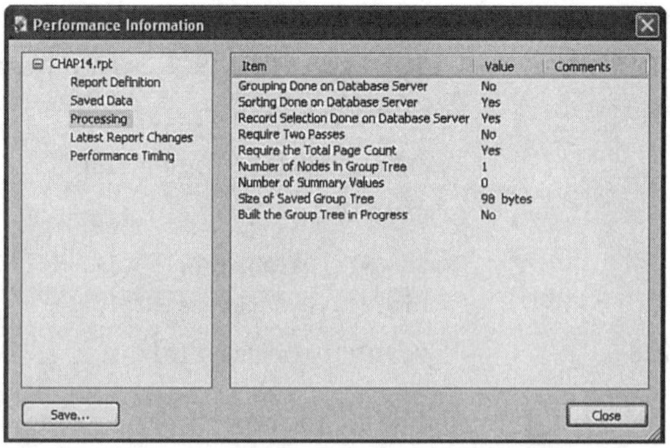

Figure 11.5
The Performance Information window provides detailed report performance metrics.

The left side of the Performance window provides a tree structure that facilitates navigation among the different report metrics areas maintained by this tool:

- **Report Definition**—This node provides information about the content of the report: the number of fields, the number of summaries, UFLs (user function libraries), Chart objects, and so on. Each of these objects will have some impact on the performance of the report dependent on its quantity and complexity. The Page N of M Used option is relevant because it specifies whether a third pass of the data is needed when processing this report. If not required, this can be eliminated by removing any Page N of M special fields on the report.

- **Saved Data**—This node provides information about the data captured in the involved report: the number of data sources used, the total number of records, recurring database record length, size of saved data, and so on. These metrics are of particular relevance when Group By On Server is properly used but can be generally used to monitor the effects of report changes.

- **Processing**—This node provides information about the processing of the selected report: Grouping on Server?, Sorting on Server? Total Page Count required? Number of Summary Values? and so on. The metrics provided here have a clear impact on performance and can be used to monitor the effective implementation of the optimization techniques described in this section.

- **Latest Report Changes**—This node provides information about recent changes to the report to facilitate performance monitoring.

- **Performance Timing**—This node provides the timing metrics based on opening the involved report and formatting its pages. These metrics provide the ultimate benchmark to determine the effectiveness of any implemented report optimization techniques.

Additional tree branches and nodes are displayed if the involved report contains subreports—each of these nodes appears under a new parent node for each subreport, facilitating performance analysis at a granular level.

One final note on performance monitoring: To facilitate record-keeping on the progress of any ongoing database or report optimizations, the Performance Information window provides the capability to save the involved report's performance information to a file for future reference and time comparison.

DYNAMIC CASCADING PROMPTS

Probably the most requested feature in years has been the desire to create dynamic *cascading prompts*—report prompts that adjusts scope as they're being used, such as selecting country, region, and city and having only relevant regions show for a selected country and so on. This is a powerful feature in Crystal Reports 2008. The following steps create a dynamic cascading prompt that allows the user to filter by country, region, and city.

1. Start by opening the sample World Sales Report. (See Chapter 9, "Custom Formatting Techniques," for steps on how to download the report samples.)

2. From the Field Explorer, select Parameter Fields, and click the New button. Figure 11.6 shows the new parameter window.

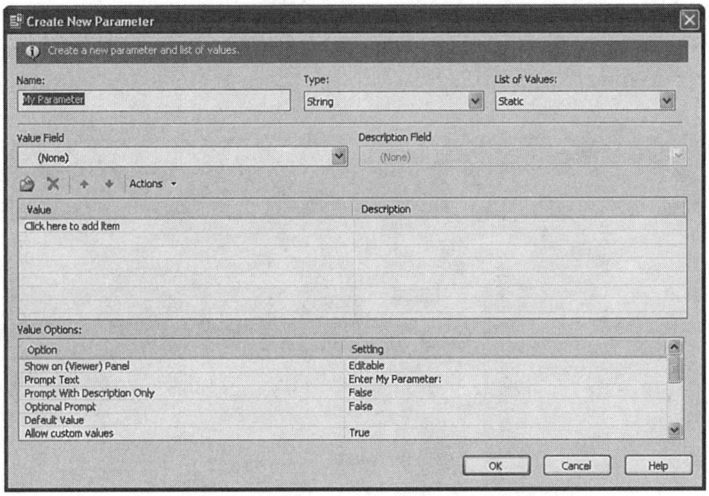

Figure 11.6
The new parameter window with default properties.

3. Start by giving the Prompt a name such as `Dynamic Territory`. From the List of Values list box, choose Dynamic, and for the Prompt Group Text, enter some helpful text for the report consumer (in this case type in **Select the territory from the list**).

4. When you click the box immediately below the Value header, you are able to select a report field. Choose Country. Click on the box below Country and select Region. Click

the box below Region and select City. In the three boxes below Parameter (where the text reads Click to Create Parameter), click on each box one time to generate the default parameter. When complete, the window should look like Figure 11.7.

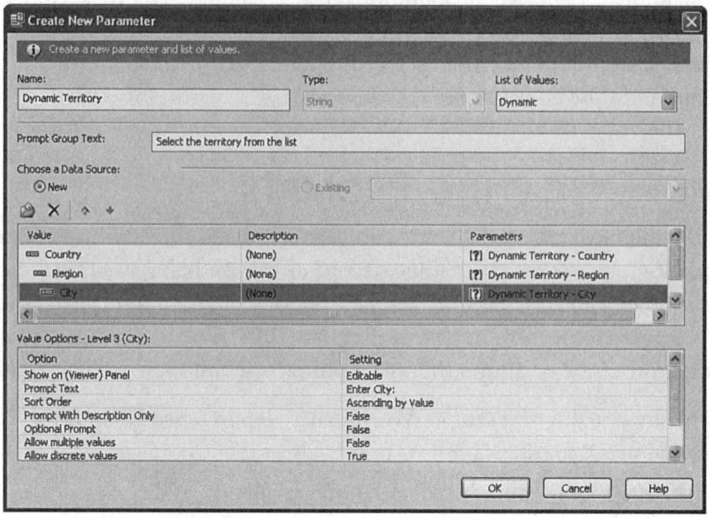

Figure 11.7
The new parameter window with the properties described in step 4.

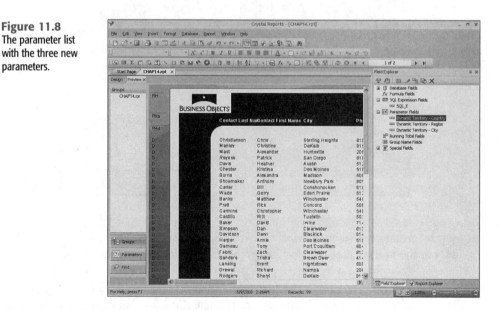

5. Now with the prompt created, click on OK to save it. Notice in Figure 11.8 that with this one step, three distinct prompts have been created. This will be used in the last step to filter the report.

Figure 11.8
The parameter list with the three new parameters.

6. To use these new parameters to filter this report, open the Record Selection Formula window (Report, Selection Formulas, Record). Enter the formula you see in Figure 11.9. To limit the risk of typing errors, you can simply double-click the fields and prompts from the list of report fields.

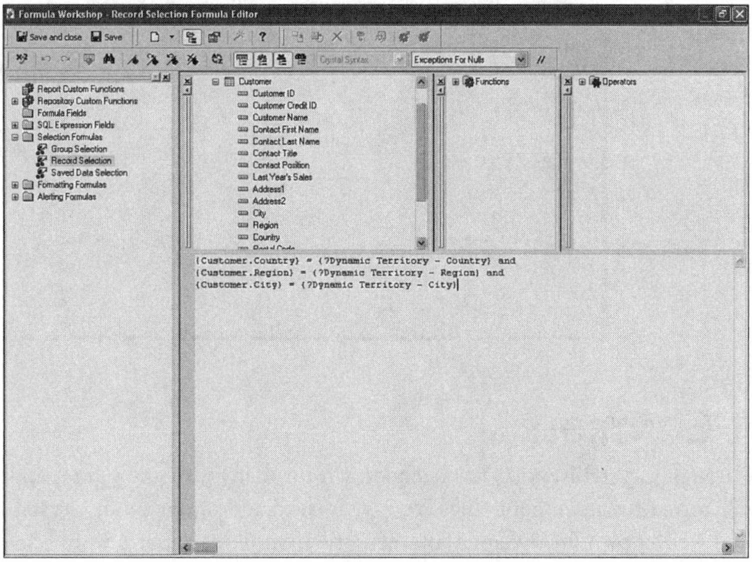

Figure 11.9
Using the new prompt to filter the report.

7. After clicking the Save and Close button, you should be prompted immediately to select a Country, Region, and City.

NOTE

Exploring the prompt window, you'll notice several useful features:

- Only the top-level item is enabled. Users cannot select a region or city until they select a country. The user is guided to the correct starting point.
- As the user selects a country (such as USA), only those regions appropriate to that country are listed (in this case, states). Also, only region becomes enabled; city does not become enabled until a region is selected.
- If the user selects a country, region, and city but has not yet clicked OK and then goes back and changes the country, both region and city will be blanked out and city will again become disabled until the user picks a valid region from the newly selected country.

At all points during the process, the users are guided to where they need to go next.

8. Select USA for country, CA for region, and San Diego for city. See Figure 11.10 to confirm your selection. Clicking OK runs the report, and the report is filtered according to your selection.

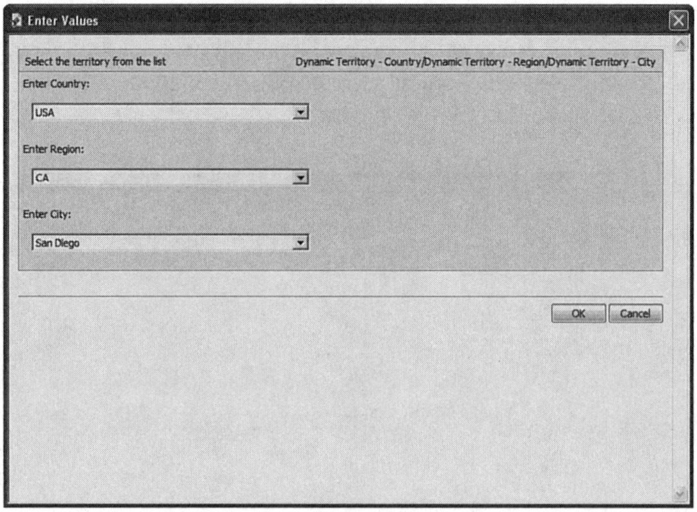

Figure 11.10
Set values for the dynamic cascading parameters.

SORT CONTROLS

Although Crystal Reports has been known for many years as a great application for building well-formatted documents that are easy to read and understand, Crystal Reports has not been well known for dynamic interactivity. Interactive reports were achievable, but it was not always easy and certainly not something that was considered out of the box. New in Crystal Reports 2008, Crystal Reports offers a Sort control that allows the user to sort a column with a click of the button.

1. Using the steps described in Chapter 10, create a new report off the Customer.xml sample data. Add the fields Country, Region, City, and Last Year's Sales to the report canvas and group the report by country, region, and city.

2. Right-click on the field header for Country and choose Bind Sort Control. In order to bind a field to the sort control, it must be added to the details section or be a group. This way, the users will be able to see the effects of their actions.

3. The dialog box prompts to select which sort to change. Select the Country field. Click the up and down arrows to see the sort order of the country group change. Repeat step 2 for both region and city.

Figure 11.11
Adding the Sort control to the field header.

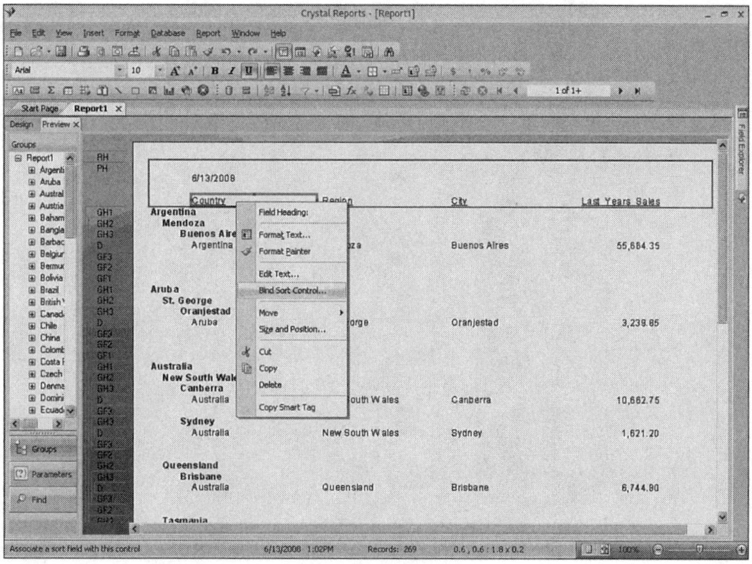

Figure 11.12
Binding the Sort control to a group.

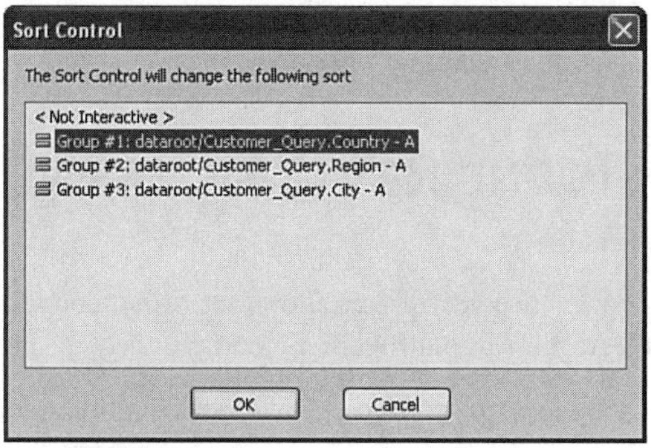

4. The Sort control can bind with a group because by default all groups have sorts associated with them. To bind a Sort control to the field Last Year's Sales, you must first manually add a sort to the field. From the Report menu, choose Record Sort Expert, find the field Last Year's Sales, and add it to the list of Sort Fields. Now repeat step 2 for the field Last Year's Sales.

Figure 11.13
Report with Sort controls.

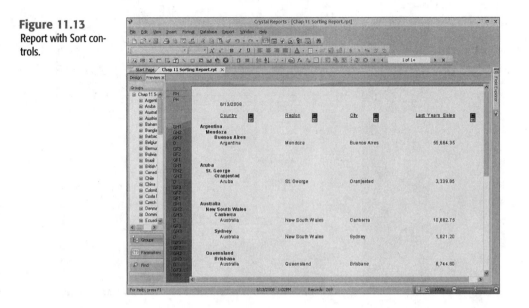

Explore the effects of the Sort controls by clicking them one at a time to see the report change. Save the report as `Chap 11 Sorting Report.rpt`.

CRYSTAL REPORTS IN THE REAL WORLD—WEB REPORT ALERT VIEWING

This Real World section covers two very practical options. First, you learn good uses of alerting and second, you learn how to put together a complex record selection formula.

There are many creative ways to employ alerting in Crystal Reports to direct the report consumer to information that requires attention. The following scenario helps you understand the use of alerting.

As part of her daily function, a sales executive views the World Sales Report multiple times. Although she is familiar with the report, it is easy to overlook an important piece of information if it is hidden in the pages to follow. Simply by looking at the first page of the report, it might not be clear if there is a problem that requires attention. The Sales report that is discussed here is grouped by country, region, city, and customer. The Details section shows the order date and order amount. For the purpose of the example, the problem in the business occurs when a sales order is booked for more than $5,000. An alert will be created that flags this circumstance (see Figure 11.14).

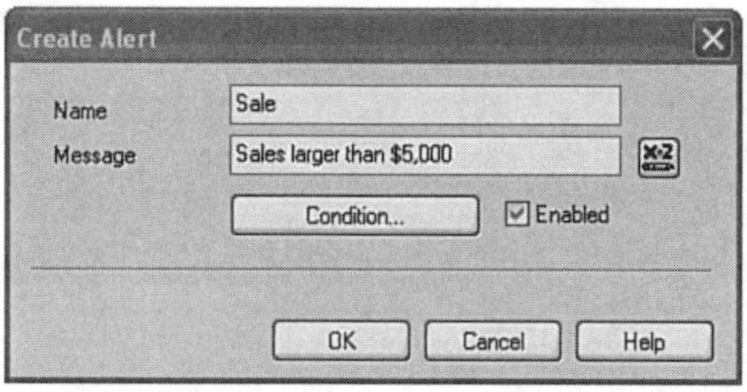

Figure 11.14
Create an alert and
set the properties.

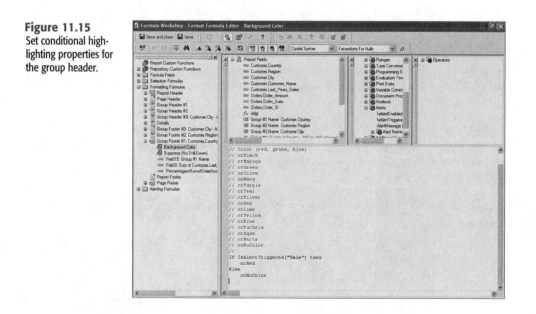

This sample report uses two techniques to draw the viewer's attention to the significant
records. The first step highlights the Group Header/Footer in red if any record in the group
sets the alert. To do this, the report evaluated the built-in function IsAlertTriggered
('Sale') and set the highlighting appropriately (see Figure 11.15). In the case of the World
Sales Report, apply this conditional formatting to each of Group Footer #1, Group Footer
#2, Group Footer #3, and Group Header #3. (If it isn't clear why all of these, try them one
at a time and explore the effects.)

Figure 11.15
Set conditional high-
lighting properties for
the group header.

Additionally, to help draw the executive to the order(s) triggering the alert, you will highlight the background of the detail record(s) that have triggered the alert. To do this, conditionally set the fill color of the Details section to yellow (see Figure 11.16).

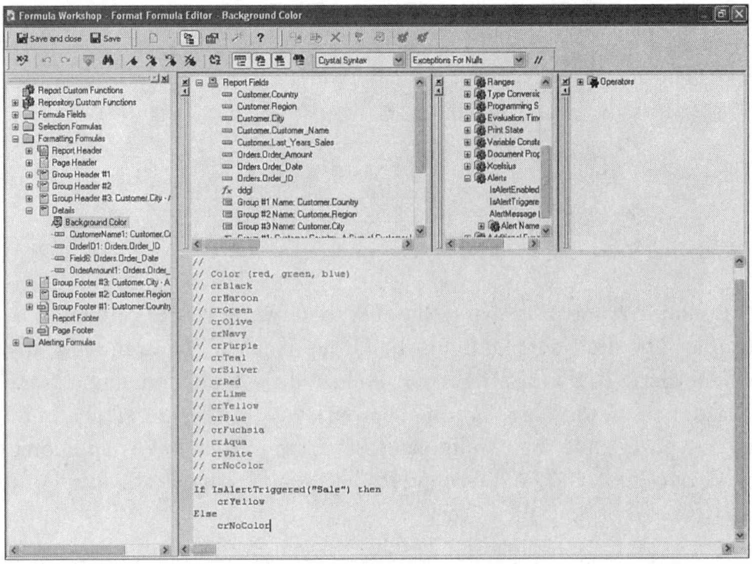

Figure 11.16
Set conditional highlighting properties for the detail line.

Now, when the executive views the sales report and drills to the detail data, the records highlighted in yellow indicate where the problem occurred. To effect this, when the report opens, an alert window pops up to inform the viewer that an alert has been triggered Click the View Records button on the Alert window.

Conditional formatting techniques described here can be applied to other attributes of report elements such as ToolTips. ToolTips can contain alert messages based on the triggered alerts. You can also conditionally hide or display report sections to highlight (see Figure 11.17).

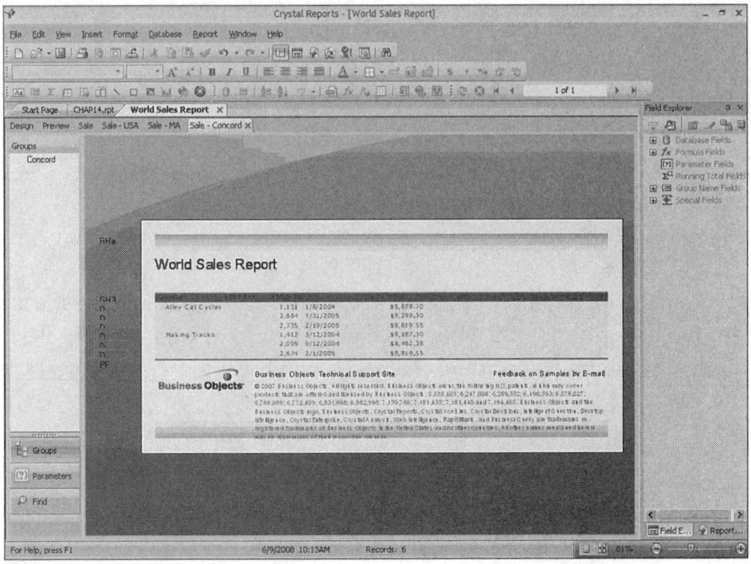

Figure 11.17
Report highlighting draws attention to critical records.

Now consider a complex record selection formula. The goal of a selection formula is to determine which records belong in a report. To do this, each record is evaluated against the given selection formula, and only those records that return TRUE are passed into the report. A number of very simple record selection formulas were listed earlier. These formulas, so far, have all compared one field to one value, but what happens if there is a need to evaluate several different criteria for the same record? Frequently when this occurs, report authors try to resolve this with a complex nested IF-THEN-ELSE statement. There is a very simple alternative, however.

Consider this situation. What if the World Sales Report (from the samples that ship with Crystal Reports) needed to be filtered on the following three items:

- Only orders from Canada/Mexico/USA
- Only orders greater than $5,000
- Only orders shipped within the last full month

The selection formula in Figure 11.18 explicitly shows how the different parts of the formula are evaluated and then combined to resolve to a single Boolean value. There are a number of ways to achieve this goal, and this formula could be written very differently—this example is just intended to show the method step by step.

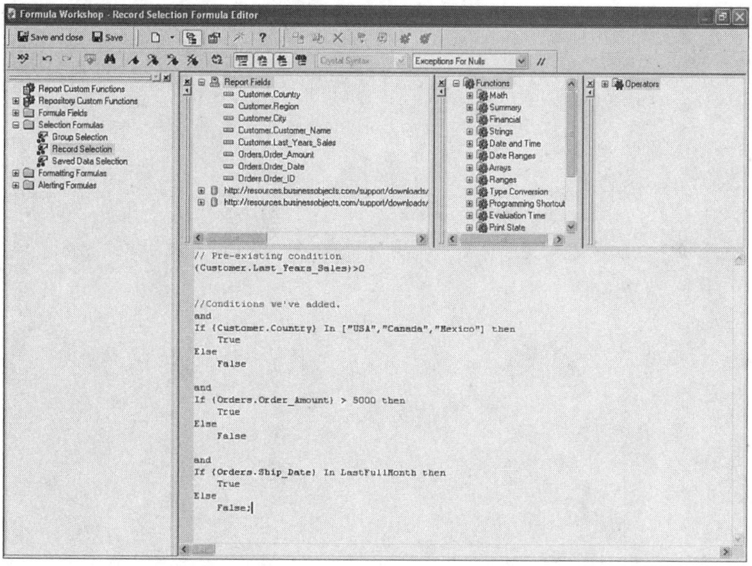

Figure 11.18
A sample record selection formula that explicitly evaluates each criteria and returns one final evaluation.

TROUBLESHOOTING

SELECTION FORMULAS

There should be data in the report, but no records are returned.

Start by breaking out the selection formula into the component parts. As an example, the selection formula from Figure 11.18 is made of three parts. Start by commenting out the existing formula and build it up one part at a time. Test to see when the expected result is different from what is returned. After the specific parts are identified, it should be easier to see what the problem is. Also, remember that the result of the selection formula is Boolean (TRUE or FALSE), and only those records that result in TRUE are accepted into the report.

CHAPTER 12

USING SUBREPORTS FOR ADVANCED REPORTS

In this chapter

INTRODUCTION TO SUBREPORTS

The previous 11 chapters of this book introduced you to the design of individual reports using single aggregated data sets. Crystal Reports provides further flexibility and reporting capabilities through the use of additional reports embedded directly within an original main report. These embedded reports, referred to as *subreports*, extend your reporting solutions into the expanded domain that this chapter explores.

The next two sections provide you with

- A further introduction to subreports
- An idea of when you might use them
- A lesson on how to use subreports

Crystal Reports provides the capability to embed multiple Crystal Reports within a single existing main report to allow for increased flexibility in report creation. Think of subreports as entire reports within reports, which can contain their own data sources, formatting, and record selections. You can create embedded subreports from existing Crystal Reports files or dynamically at report design time using the Insert Subreport functionality. When you're presenting a report that contains one or more subreports to business users, the subreports can be displayed either in-place, providing a seamless integration, or on-demand, minimizing the amount of required up-front report processing.

COMMON SUBREPORT USAGE

A few particular reporting problems are difficult to solve without the use of subreports. Here is a list of some of the most common problems and a specific example of each:

- **The presentation of data from two (or more) completely unrelated data sources on a single report**—Specific example: On a Manufacturing Plant Efficiency report sourced from your internal Oracle ERP system, you want to display industry average information sourced from a completely different and unrelated industry or trade database.

- **The combination of data from different tables with only derived (i.e. not direct) database field links**—Specific example: On a Customer Profile report, you want to combine Order Information from your ERP (for example, SAP, Oracle, Baan) system with call center information from your call center application (for example, Remedy) and your CRM system (for example, Siebel, PeopleSoft), but the employee ID field is stored slightly different in each system. Subreports enable linking of the different employee IDs by allowing linking on formulas or derived fields.

- **The presentation of the same data in two (or more) different ways in a single report**—Specific example: On a Sales Summary Report, senior management wants to present a high-level summary of sales by region but also wants to present a separate and personalized summary of sales by product for each salesperson viewing the report.

- **The inclusion of a summary field in the report that is unrelated to the established grouping in the main report**—Specific example: On an employee HR report, HR managers want to see employee salary information grouped by business unit, division, and department. Additionally, they want to view a count of the different departments that this employee worked for in the previous year. The main report groups employees by department (and by division and business unit), whereas the subreport groups departments by employee to determine a department count.

- **The inclusion of a reusable component (such as a standard reporting header or footer) that can be dynamically updated for all reports in a single location in numerous reports across an organization**—Specific example: A firm wants to deploy all reports in its organization with a standard header, including standard logos and titles. In addition to using the report templates and Repository, subreports can appear as a header within all the reports and provide a single location for updating the header.

Data presented in subreports often relates to data presented in the associated main report, but it does not have to be. Subreport data can be a twist on the main report's information or sourced from a completely different database.

ADDING SUBREPORTS TO YOUR REPORTS

Adding a subreport to your main report is as easy as adding any other Crystal Reports object. After clicking on the Insert subreport button on the Insert toolbar or selecting the Subreport option from the Insert menu, you are presented with the Insert Subreport dialog (see Figure 12.1).

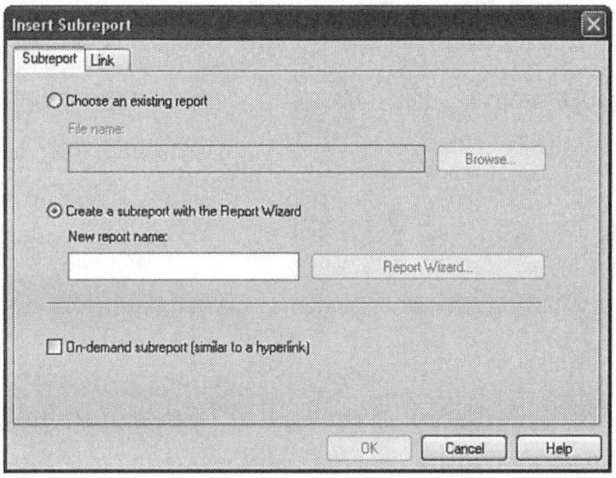

Figure 12.1
The Insert Subreport dialog enables you to add a subreport to your main report.

To explore one of the many challenges solved by using subreports, let's solve the hypothetical reporting problem faced by the Chief Operating Officer (COO) of Maple Leaf Bikes Corporation. This COO wants a single report that highlights the recently acquired company's (Xtreme) top-selling products in one bar chart and additionally highlights the company's top selling sales reps in a corresponding pie chart. The two charts are sourced from the same sales information but have no direct relation or links to each other. To resolve this request, complete the following steps:

1. Create a new report and point it at the Xtreme 12 Sample Database.

2. Select the Orders, Order Detail, and Product tables, accept the default table linking provided by Crystal Reports, and then select the Product Name and Order Amount fields to display on the report.

3. Group the report by product name and add a summary to the report that sums the order amount for each product name group. Also limit the report to display only the top five groups based on the Summarized field. (Reminder: You can use the Group Sort Expert under the Report menu option to accomplish this last task and ensure to not include an Others group by confirming that the associated check box is not checked.)

4. Add a bar chart in the Page Header to represent the top five selling products, and you should have a report similar to the one depicted in Figure 12.2.

Figure 12.2
Preliminary sample report to solve COO problem.

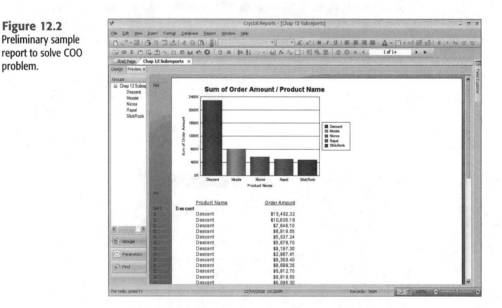

5. Make room for the COO's requested second visual by resizing the bar chart to take up only half of the page header's width.

6. Select the Insert Subreport option by either accessing that option from the Insert menu or clicking on the Insert Subreport icon. The Insert Subreport dialog in Figure 12.1 appears.

7. Select the Create a Subreport with the Report Wizard option by clicking on the associated radio button.

8. Enter a name similar to `Top Sales Reps` and click on the Report Wizard button.

9. As you step through the familiar Report Wizard to create this subreport, select the Xtreme 12 Sample Database and the Employee and Orders tables. Accept the default table linking provided by Crystal Reports, and from the list of available fields, select First Name and Order Amount.

10. Group the subreport on Employee First Name and create a summary on the sum of order amounts for each employee group. Limit the report to display the top five employees based on this sum, add a pie chart to this report, add a title `Top 5 Sales Reps` to the pie chart, and click the Finish button.

11. Ensure that the On-Demand Subreport check box is unchecked, and then click on OK on the Insert Subreport dialog. Drop the subreport on the right side of the main report so that it does not overlap the existing bar chart. The details of on-demand reports are described later in this chapter.

12. To clean up the final presentation of your main report and included subreport, edit the subreport by right-clicking on it and then hiding all the sections of the report except the report header a. You hide sections by right-clicking on the name of the involved sections in the Design or Preview tab and selecting the Hide option. Last, delete the Report Header b section in the subreport. Figure 12.3 shows the result of this quick report. If your result appears slightly different, review Chapter 8, "Visualizing Your Data with Charts and Maps," and revise the charts accordingly.

NOTE

As mentioned in previous sections, subreports *are* Crystal Reports in their own right, and as such they have their own Design tab in the Crystal Reports Designer. To format the details of a subreport, it is necessary to open the Design tab for that subreport from within the Designer of the main report by right-clicking on a subreport and selecting the Edit Subreport option. This can also be accomplished by double-clicking on the subreport within the main report. Figure 12.3 displays the tabs for both the sample's main report and the subreport.

12

With that introduction to subreports, you should begin to see some of the flexibility and power that they offer in solving difficult reporting (and even dashboard-related) problems. The next few sections explore this in more detail.

Figure 12.3
Sample report with subreport to solve COO problem.

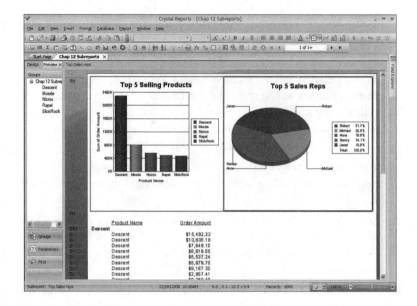

UNDERSTANDING LINKED VERSUS UNLINKED SUBREPORTS

The hypothetical COO scenario just explored highlights an example of an unlinked subreport. In Crystal Reports terminology, this means that the parent, or *main*, report did not have any specific data connections (or links) to its related child report (the subreport). Unlinked subreports are completely independent from their main reports and do not rely on the main report for any data. Many reporting problems in which multiple views of the same or different data sources are required in a single presentation can be resolved with unlinked subreports. If a requirement exists to share data between the parent/main report and its subreport, linked reports provide the answer.

In contrast to unlinked subreports, linked subreports are bound (or linked) to the data in their associated main report. You define the links in the Link tab of the Insert Subreport dialog shown in Figure 12.4.

The Link tab enables you to link report, database, or formula fields in the main report to fields in the subreport and enables you to filter the subreport based on the data passed in from the main report.

The Available Fields section of the Links dialog enables you to select the field from the main report to link. More than one field can be selected for linking. After you select at least one field, a separate Field Links section appears at the bottom of the Links tab. For each linked field, a parameter in the involved subreport must be selected to receive and hold that information. These parameters can be pre-existing parameters predefined in the subreport, or they can be parameters that are automatically created for each field you have selected to link. (These are automatically created in the subreport with the prefix ?Pm-.)

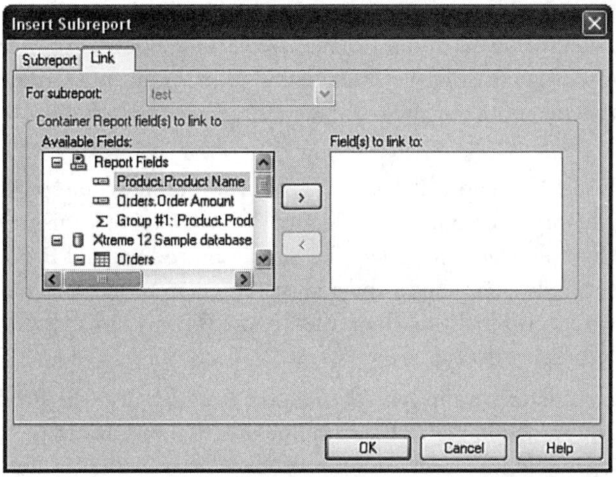

Figure 12.4
Link tab of the Insert Subreport dialog.

Finally, for each linked field from the main report, you can create a data filter in the subreport based on that parameter. You do so by checking the Select Data in Subreport Based on Field check box and selecting the report field, database field, or formula field in the subreport that you want to have filtered based on the linked parameter from the provided dropdown box. In effect, checking this box creates a selection filter in your subreport based on the selected filter field and the selected parameter field.

Linking Subreports and Reports with Formulas

The capability to link subreports and main reports with formulas gives you a flexible method of presenting data from different database tables that is not possible otherwise. The Crystal Reports Database Linking Expert enables joining only of fields from different tables and does not permit joining of formulas to fields. By using formulas and subreports, a derived formula can link to another database field in a subreport.

For example, this would be beneficial if a firm's order processing system (SAP, Oracle, Baan, and so on) stored a customer ID as a nine-digit number (999123888), but that same company's Customer Relationship Management (CRM) system (Siebel, Salesforce, Rightnow, and so on) stored the same customer ID as a nine-digit number prefixed with a regional code (ONT999123888). These fields could not be joined in the Crystal Reports Database Linking Expert, but they could be linked using a formula that extracts the nine-digit number from the CRM/Siebel customer ID and links to the SAP customer ID in a subreport.

To explore a reporting solution with linked subreports, solve the hypothetical reporting problem faced by the same COO of Maple Leaf Bikes Corporation. The COO now wants a single report that highlights the company's top-selling product *types* in one bar chart (similar to the previous example), enables drill-down into the actual products, and produces a list of suppliers for each product type to be available for review. Essentially, he wants a supplier's listing subreport linked to the main report based on the product type name. To accomplish this, follow these steps:

1. Open the previous sample report from this chapter and delete the previous subreport containing the Top 5 Sales Rep pie chart. Now add the Product_Type table to this

report through the Database Expert under the Database menu option. It is automatically and correctly linked to the Product table. Add another group for Product Type Name on top of the existing Product Name. (Hint: You can use the Group Expert under the Report menu and manually use the up arrow.) Then hide the Details section of this report.

2. Open the Insert Subreport dialog and create another new subreport called Supplier Info using the provided Subreport Report Wizard. Connect this new subreport to the Xtreme 12 Sample Database, select the Supplier, Product, and Product_Type tables (they will correctly smart-link), and add the Supplier Name, City, and Phone Number fields to the report. Finally, click on the Report Wizard Finish button, but do not exit the Insert Subreport dialog.

3. Click on the Link tab in the Insert Subreport dialog. Select the Product Type Name field from the Available Fields list as the field to link on. (It can be selected from the Product_Type table.) This initiates the Product Type Name ID Link section at the bottom of the dialog. Use the default (and automatically generated) parameter '?Pm-Product_Type.Product Type Name' for the link on the subreport.

4. Confirm that the Select Data in Subreport Based On Field check box is selected, and choose the Product Type Name field from the Product_Type table in the drop-down box. Essentially, you have just specified that this supplier's subreport filters on the product type name that passes in from the main report every time this subreport is called. Click on OK to add the subreport and place it in the Product Type Name Group Header on the right side of the report.

5. To ensure that the desired results are provided and provided in a clean way, edit the subreport to remove the default provided date, resize its Report Header Subreport section, and hide the report header a and the report footers in the subreport. You also need to specify that this subreport should return only a *distinct* list of suppliers because the COO is not interested in a repetitive list—this can be done through the Report Options selection under the File menu. Click on the Select Distinct Records check box.

6. Back in the main report, resize the bar chart graphic on the main report, and you have a new sample report resembling the report depicted in Figure 12.5 for the COO.

The COO can now make an informed analysis on whether his firm has too much reliance on a small number of suppliers, and you have learned some of the benefits of a linked subreport.

NOTE

Unlike the initial sample report presented in this chapter where you placed the Top Sales Rep Subreport in the Report Header and it ran once for the entire main report, the Product Suppliers Subreport is run multiple times—in fact, once for every product type. This is the case because you placed the subreport in the Group Header section of the main report, and it therefore executed for each different group in the main report. This is important to note with respect to performance, specifically when your databases and reports become large.

Figure 12.5
Sample report with linked suppliers sub-report.

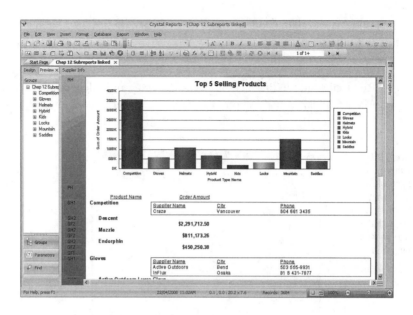

CONSIDERING SUBREPORT EXECUTION TIME AND PERFORMANCE

There are two types of subreports: In-Place and On-Demand. Both of the sample reports created previously in this chapter have been in-place subreports. An *in-place* subreport is virtually indistinguishable from the main report components when viewed because it is run at the same time as the main report. In-place subreports are displayed as components of the main report like any other report object and require no special business user interaction to view them. *On-demand* subreports, on the contrary, are not executed at the same time as the main report and require user interaction to be viewed.

All in-place subreports on a main report run at the execution time of the main report. In the two examples presented in this chapter, this has clearly not caused any performance problems, but it could on larger databases and reports. Imagine running the last sample report (with the Product Suppliers subreport in every group header) for a large conglomerate with thousands of products. The Product Suppliers subreport would need to run thousands of times to complete the presentation of the main report. Moreover, thousands of supplier subreports would be unlikely to be used by any given business user and would therefore have run extraneously. An elegant solution to that problem is the use of on-demand subreports.

Unlike in-place subreports, on-demand subreports execute only when a user requests them. They lie dormant until that time. The performance benefits of on-demand reports are clear; however, they come at the expense of a less seamless integration than in-place subreports and a small delay in viewing because the subreport executes dynamically after being requested.

12

Taking the last example, follow these steps to make the Product Suppliers subreport an on-demand subreport:

1. Open the most recent sample report if you have closed it.

2. Right-click on the Product Suppliers subreport and select the Format Subreport option. Many familiar formatting options are available here (see Figure 12.6), but click on the Subreport tab.

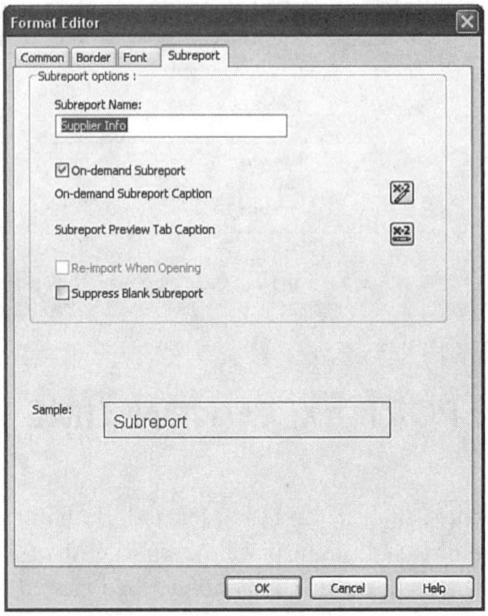

Figure 12.6
The Format Editor dialog enables specification of many standard formatting options, including whether a subreport is on-demand.

3. Click the On-Demand Subreport check box to turn on that option. Notice that the On-Demand Subreport Caption section is no longer grayed out.

4. Click on the On-Demand Subreport Caption button (X-2) and type `'Supplier List'` (include the apostrophes) in the Text Editing area. Click on the Save and Close button, and you should now have a main report that resembles Figure 12.7, where the Supplier List link dynamically runs the involved subreport if and only if a report consumer requests it.

TIP

Give careful consideration to report design when deciding between in-place and on-demand subreports. You must consider the trade-off between the seamless integration of in-place subreports and the performance benefits of on-demand subreports in addition to the specific requirements of the business users' overall experience.

Figure 12.7
Sample report with linked, on-demand Suppliers Subreport.

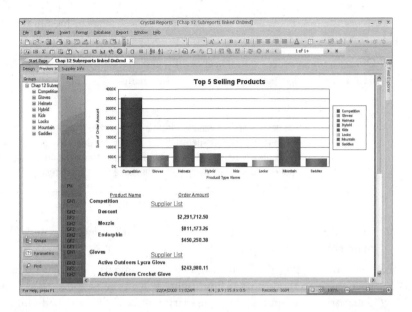

USING VARIABLES TO PASS DATA BETWEEN REPORTS

Up to this point in the chapter, the examples that involve passing data between a main report and a subreport have worked exclusively through the Subreport Linking tab or dialog. Although the functionality provided there is certainly powerful, circumstances might require more flexible passing of data between the main report and the subreport or the passing of data the other way—from a subreport to a main report.

With the use of variables, it becomes possible to pass data between the main report and any of the subreports or even among different subreports in the same main report. By declaring the same shared variable in formulas in both the main report and at least one subreport, data can be exchanged back and forth fluidly, and each report can leverage information from the other in a very flexible manner.

TIP

Using subreports and variables to pass data back to a main report from a subreport is an effective way to capture important summarizations or external information to your main report that is not possible otherwise because of the default groupings of the main report. A simple example in this chapter's last sample report would be the inclusion of a count on the number of suppliers for each product. Using only the default groupings provided in the main report (By Product), this count would be impossible to calculate. By using a subreport, however, that count can be calculated outside the main report (in a subreport), shared using variables, and eventually displayed on the main report.

12

To explore the power of shared variables, follow these steps to modify this chapter's last sample report:

1. Open the most recent sample report if you have closed it. Turn the Supplier subreport back to an in-place subreport (versus on-demand).

NOTE

> When passing shared variables from a subreport to a main report, the involved subreport cannot be set to on-demand. The reason, of course, is that subreports are not run until specifically requested by the business user. Therefore, their associated variables are not set until that time, making them unusable in the main report.

2. Edit the Supplier subreport by right-clicking on the subreport and selecting the Edit Subreport option.

3. Select the Supplier Name field and insert a summary field that counts the distinct supplier names in this report. (Hint: Right-click on the Supplier Name field and access the Summary menu option.) This summary will shortly be assigned to the shared variable that will be created and used to pass the information back to the main report.

4. Insert a formula into the Report Footer section of this subreport and call it `Assign Supplier Count`. In this formula, declare a shared numeric variable called `SupplierCount` and then assign this variable to equal the Supplier Summary created in the last step. (Reminder: You can access the summary created in step 3 for use in your formula by double-clicking on it.) The formula definition should resemble Figure 12.8. Click on Save and Close when finished.

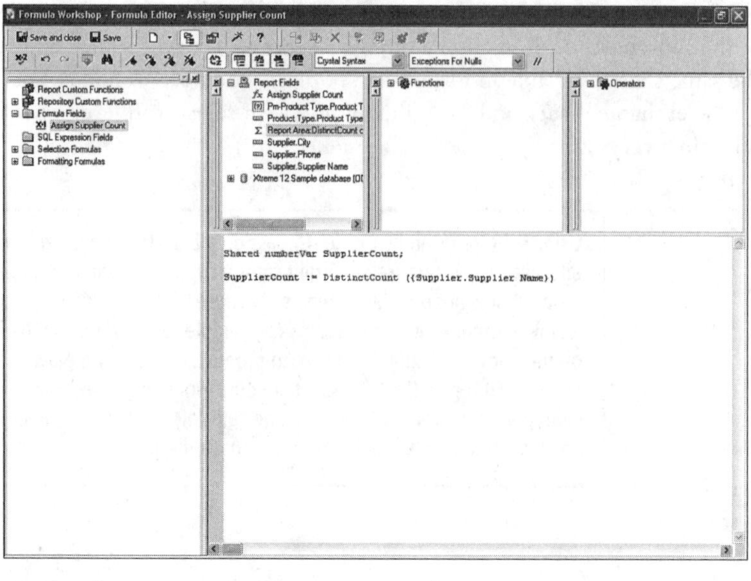

Figure 12.8
Formula with a shared variable declaration in the subreport.

5. Now click on the Preview or Design tab of the Crystal Reports Designer to take you back to the main report, insert a formula into the Product Type Group Footer section, and call it `Place Supplier Count`. In this formula, declare the same shared numeric variable, `SupplierCount`, and make this variable the output of this formula. Figure 12.9 shows what this formula should look like.

NOTE

> It is important to place this formula in the group footer of the Product Type Name group. This strategic placement ensures that the Supplier List subreport for the involved product type has already completed (as it is in the group header) and has set the shared SupplierCount variable appropriately. When using variables, give careful consideration to ensure that they evaluated at the time and order desired. In addition to the Top to Bottom and Left to Right default evaluation times of Crystal Reports, `EvaluateAfter()` and a few other functions discussed in the section "The Multipass Reporting Process of the Crystal Report Engine" in Chapter 4, "Understanding and Implementing Formulas," are useful in ensuring the desired reporting results.

Figure 12.9
Formula with a shared variable declaration and output in the main report.

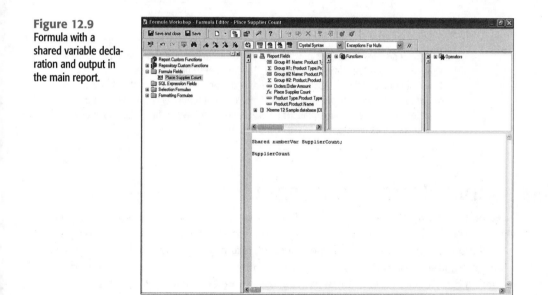

6. Add a text field to the report to complement the Supplier Count field called Supplier Count, hide the Details section on the main report, and with a little creative formatting and group sorting, the final result should resemble Figure 12.10.

Perhaps not the prettiest report ever designed, this quick example begins to convey the power and importance of shared variables in report design.

Figure 12.10
Sample report with
Supplier Count
sourced from a
shared variable in a
subreport.

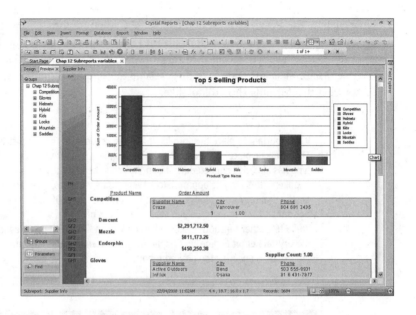

> **NOTE**
>
> As you discover the power of variables, you begin to leverage this programming feature in increasingly complex ways. The Supplier Count example just provided is a relatively simple example that scratches the surface of the power of variables. Another variable-based technique that can circumvent some common reporting challenges is to use variables to manage running totals. The flexibility provided within the Formula Editor and with variables enables you to create flexible condition-based running totals.

EMULATING NESTED SUBREPORTS

Based on the title of this section, you can deduce that it is not possible to nest subreports—why else would you need to emulate that behavior? Crystal Reports does not currently support subreports within subreports. Report hyperlinks and report parts do, however, provide a flexible method in advanced navigation between and within reports. This form of flexible navigation can emulate nested subreports and was covered in Chapter 9, "Custom Formatting Techniques."

TROUBLESHOOTING

FORMATTING THE DETAILS OF A SUBREPORT

I can't figure out how to format the details of a subreport.

Open the Design tab for that subreport from within the Designer of the main report by right-clicking on a subreport and selecting the Edit Subreport option or by double-clicking the subreport within the main report.

USING SUBREPORTS TO WRITE BACK TO A SOURCE DATABASE

I would like to enable report viewers (or end users) to be able to dynamically send updates back to a source database—can subreports help me accomplish this?

Using a clever combination of subreports and SQL commands, you can provide this capability to your end users. You can add on-demand subreports to your main report and have each of the on-demand subreports based on a SQL command that includes an INSERT SQL statement to write back to a data source. A sample SQL command could be

```
SELECT * FROM   "TestInsertfromCR"."dbo"."TableName";
INSERT INTO "TestInsertfromCR"."dbo"."TableName" VALUES _
    (9999,'test insert',9999,'test','test')
```

Each time a report-viewing end user requests that the on-demand subreport run, this SQL statement executes and updates the involved data source. To make this data updating process more dynamic, the preceding example could replace the inserted values fields with dynamic data fields from the report (for example, Customer ID or Employee ID).

CRYSTAL REPORTS IN THE REAL WORLD—MULTIPLE SUBREPORTS

As discussed earlier in the chapter, a single report often needs to show data from different and frequently unrelated pieces of information. In the next example, the main report shows both customer and supplier information with two separate subreports and each of them for a given geographic location using the main report's regional grouping hierarchy as a filter on the underlying subreports. You create a main report for the hierarchical geographic structure of country, region, and city hierarchy and then add one subreport to show customer information and another subreport for supplier information. Because there is no relationship between suppliers and customers, at least one of these pieces of information must come from a subreport. For this sample, both elements come from a subreport to highlight the capability to use multiple subreports in a single main report. Follow these steps to explore this capability:

1. Open the Report Designer and select Create New Report Using the Report Wizard. Click on OK and browse to the Xtreme Sample Database data source, expand the list of tables, and add the Customer table to the list of report tables by clicking on the > button. Click on Next.

2. In the Fields window, add the Country, Region, and City fields to the report in the listed order and click on Next. In the Grouping window, add the same fields to the Group By list and in the same order.

3. Click on Finish to complete the report. This builds the hierarchy used in the report.

4. Change to Design mode. Move the fields in the group header to the left, and indent them slightly at each lower level. Suppress all sections of the report other than the headers, and expand each of the header areas below the fields. See Figure 12.11 to view what the framework of the report should look like.

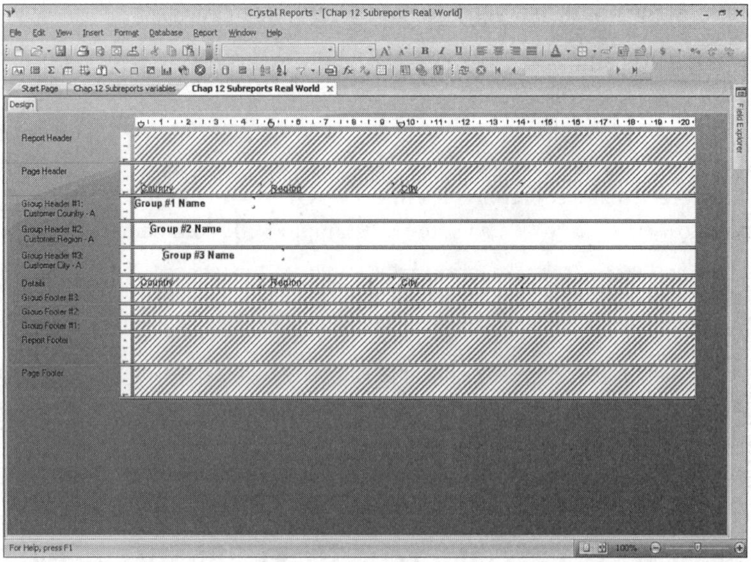

Figure 12.11
Report hierarchy to
act as the framework
for subreport content.

5. With the framework complete, the next step is to create the content. There are different ways to create subreports; in this instance, you create the subreports as separate files and later import them into the main report. Create the report for supplier information by navigating to the Start Page and selecting a new report with the Standard Report Wizard. Select the Xtreme 12 Sample Database connection, browse the list of tables for the Supplier table, and click on the > button to move it to the list of selected tables. Click on Next. From the Fields window, select Supplier Name and Phone and click on the > button to move them to the Fields to Display. Click on Finish to close the wizard. Minimize report content by changing to Design mode, deleting the Print Date field that was automatically added to the Page Header, moving the remaining fields to the left edge, suppressing sections with no fields, and minimizing whitespace. Figure 12.12 illustrates a sample Suppliers subreport. Save this report to your local machine.

6. Repeat step 5 for the Customer table, selecting the Customer Name and Phone number from the Customer table.

7. Add each subreport to the report three times, once each for country, region, and city. Use the Insert Subreport dialog accessed from the main Insert menu and, using the Choose an Existing Report option, browse to the location where you saved the recently created subreports. Now link the regional fields (Country, Region, and City) to each of the subreport's associated fields by accessing the Change Subreport Links option available on the right-click menu for each subreport. For the subreports based in the Country group header, you need to link the Country field from the main report to the Country field in the Suppliers table. You have to link both the Country and the Region fields for the subreports in the Region group header, and you have add City for those subreports in the City group header.

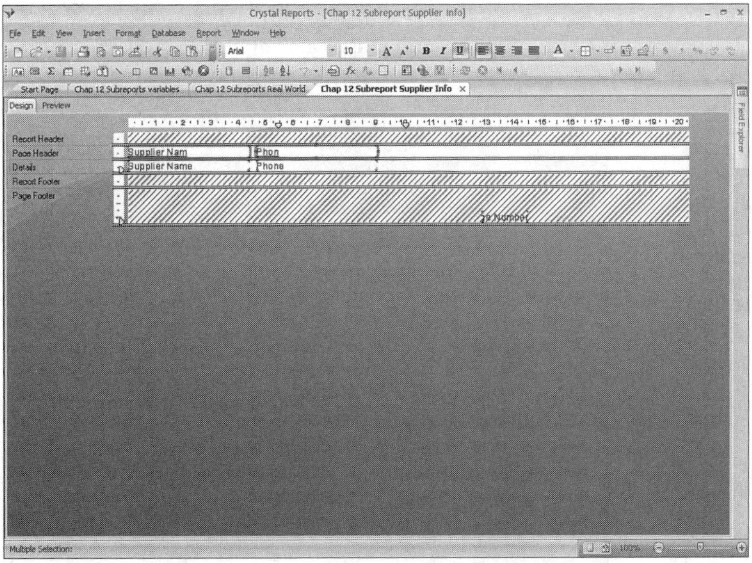

Figure 12.12
Supplier information subreport with extra whitespace reduced to a minimum.

8. For each subreport, ensure that the Keep Object Together formatting option is turned off. You access this option from the Format Subreport dialog on the Common tab. You can use the Format Painter to copy one subreport's format to the others to save you a few keystrokes.

9. From the Report menu, select Section Expert. In the list of sections, ensure the Keep Together option is not checked for each group header. Click on OK to close the window. Save the report. The design of the report should look like Figure 12.13, and the final result should resemble Figure 12.14.

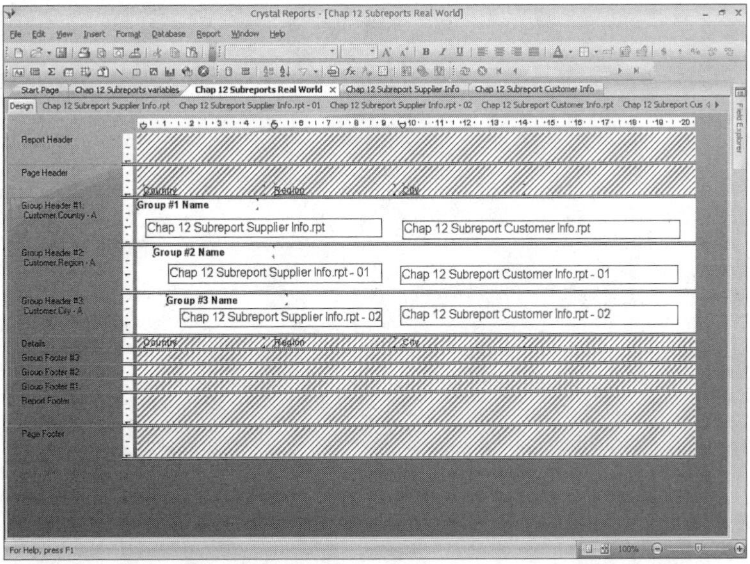

Figure 12.13
Report with hierarchy and subreports.

Preview the report. Notice that on the page displaying Canada, different and unrelated information for both Suppliers and Customers appears, and the information for both is specific to the location context.

Figure 12.14
Report preview showing a main report hierarchy on region. Multiple subreports filtering their customer and supplier lists by their placement in the main report.

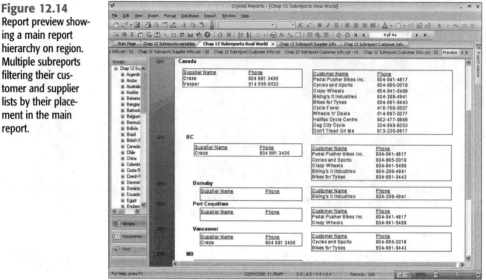

CHAPTER **13**

USING FORMULAS AND CUSTOM FUNCTIONS

In this chapter

INTRODUCTION

This chapter explores the use of advanced formulas and functions to accomplish many mundane and repetitive tasks. Also, you will look at how the formulas and functions can help alleviate redundancy in report design.

Whereas Chapter 4, "Understanding and Implementing Formulas," focused on the basics of formulas, this chapter focuses on some lesser-known facts and tricks to make formula work more productive as well as less repetitive.

CHOOSING A FORMULA LANGUAGE: CRYSTAL VERSUS BASIC SYNTAX

Previous chapters used the Crystal syntax for all formulas. However, formulas in Crystal Reports can be created, edited, and modified using one of two languages. The Crystal syntax is the most used language, but the Basic syntax is also available.

Both languages are equal in their functionality—meaning that if something was added to Crystal syntax, it was also added to Basic. The reason you're given a choice is for your comfort—you can use whichever language you are more comfortable with using.

UNDERSTANDING SYNTAX DIFFERENCES

The Crystal syntax is most similar to the Pascal or Delphi programming languages. It's not exactly like Pascal, but if you're a Delphi developer or a longtime Crystal Report developer, this syntax is probably your first choice.

The Basic syntax is most similar to Visual Basic as a programming language. If you're a Visual Basic developer, you'll likely find this syntax most beneficial. Some specific differences between the two languages are described in Table 13.1.

TABLE 13.1 DIFFERENCES BETWEEN CRYSTAL AND BASIC SYNTAX

Description	Crystal	Basic
Variable declarations	`StringVar <name>`	`Dim <name> As <type>`
Statement endings	`;`	None required
Comment characters	`//`	`'`
Variable assignment	`:=`	`=`
Formula statement	None required	Required
Formula returns	None required	`Return` statement
Multiline statement indicators	None required	_
If statement ending	`;`	`End If`

WHY BASIC SYNTAX WAS ADDED

Many functions and operators provided by the BASIC language increase the productivity of Crystal Reports users. By implementing the whole language, the existing Crystal syntax users could benefit from the new operators and functions and at the same time, newer users who are familiar with the BASIC language through other development endeavors could easily make the jump to creating formulas in Crystal Reports.

Some of the functions and operators that were added as a result of the addition of the Basic syntax are

- Date functions such as `DateAdd`, `DateDiff`, and `DateSerial`
- Financial functions such as Present Value (`PV`)
- Control structures such as `Do While`, `Do Until`, and `For Next` statements

SELECTING THE BEST SYNTAX FOR YOU

Whether you choose Basic or Crystal syntax, they are both equally capable of doing the job, and there is no performance implication in making this choice. The decision is entirely based on the comfort level and familiarity of each language for report designers.

TIP

> Whichever syntax you prefer to use most often, you can set it up as the default for all new formulas by going to File, Options, Formula Editor tab, and choosing the desired syntax in the Default Formula Language list box.

USING BRACKETS IN FORMULAS

Regardless of which syntax is chosen, some fundamental concepts to formula creation are important.

Several variations of brackets are used within the formula language, and it can be confusing to know which one to use at a particular time. To clear up some of the confusion, here is a way to remember them phonetically:

- {}French = Fields

  For example, `{Table.Field}` is used to refer to fields, formula fields, or parameter fields in the report definition.

- []Square = Selected

  For example, `{Table.Field}[1]` returns only the first character of a string field. Square brackets are used for indexes on array types (for example, strings or array data types).

13

- ( )Parenthesis = Parameters

  For example, Function (`{Table.Field}`) passes the field to the function. Parentheses are used to define which parts of a calculation or formula should be performed first (that is, defines order of precedence for mathematical and nonmathematical operations).

USING CHARACTERS IN FORMULAS

As with brackets, symbols in the formula language (or in the icons) have specific meaning. To shed some light on this, check out the listing of symbols that represent different field types in Crystal Reports:

@ = Formula	`{@Formula}` is a formula field
? = Parameter	`{?Param}` is a parameter field
# = Running Total	`{#RunTtl}` is a running total field
Σ = Summary	`ΣfieldName` is a summary field on the report
% = SQL Expression	`{%SQL}` is a SQL expression field

RECENT IMPROVEMENTS TO FORMULAS

Because Crystal Reports has been around for so many years and has released many versions over that time, it's not uncommon to come across users still using older versions. To bring those users up to speed, this section covers some of the recent additions and improvements to formulas over the past few versions.

MANIPULATING MEMO FIELDS IN FORMULAS

In the past, Crystal Reports developers were unable to access string fields that were longer than 255 characters within the formula language other than to find out whether they were null. This limitation was removed in Crystal Reports XI.

For the purposes here, assume that the Xtreme Mountain Bike Company management needs an HR report that shows only the female employees, but there is no gender field in the Xtreme database. In the Notes field in the Employee table, the word *she* is used for all female employees. However, Xtreme's management has indicated that it might need to search for other words as well, so they want to have a keyword search instead of hard-coding the search values. Follow these steps to create such a report to fulfill this reporting requirement:

1. Download the Employee Profile Report from the SAP website. You can find it (along with other prior version samples) and the Xtreme Sample Database here:

   ```
   https://websmp130.sap-ag.de/sap(bD1lbiZjPTAwMQ==)/bc/bsp/spn/bobj_download/
   main.htm
   ```

For the list box Software Product choose Crystal Reports. For the list box Product Version choose 2008. For the Software Type choose Sample. This will present you with a selection of zip files for reports and sample data.

Open the Employee Profile Report. Press Ctrl+O to open a report. Find the Crystal Reports XI sample report called Employee Profile.

2. Create a parameter field by selecting View, Field Explorer. Right-click on the Parameter Field item in the Field Explorer and choose New. In the Create Parameter Field dialog, call the parameter Search-A-Word. The prompting text should be What word would you like to search for?. The value type should be String.

3. Add "<none>", "she", and "he" to the list of default values. The final result should look like Figure 13.1.

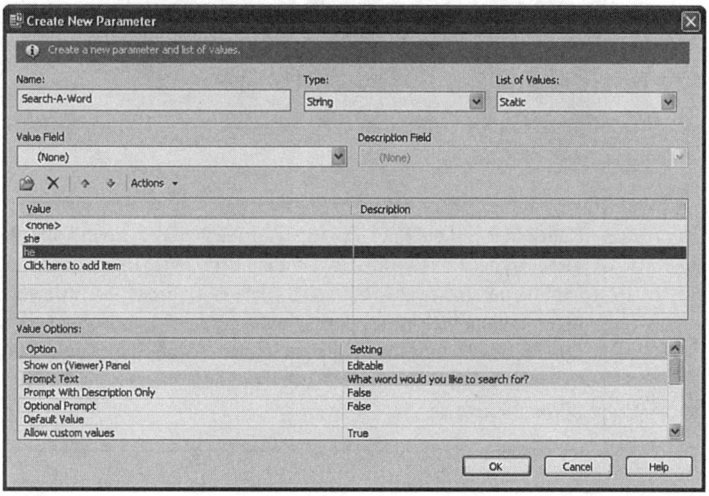

Figure 13.1
The default values and prompt settings for a Search-A-Word prompt.

4. Connect the prompt to the selection formula. Select the Formula Workshop via Report, Formula Workshop. Then choose Selection Formulas, Record Selection from the Workshop tree. Enter the following selection formula into the editor: **IF {?Search-A-Word} = "<none>" THEN TRUE ELSE ({?Search-a-Word}) IN LowerCase({Employee.Notes})** and click on the Save and Close button.

5. Run the report. When prompted, choose she from the Parameter Field prompt and choose to refresh the data. The result is that only the female employees appear on the report, as shown in Figure 13.2. Save the report as Chap13_1.rpt.

13

Figure 13.2
The employee profile showing female employees only.

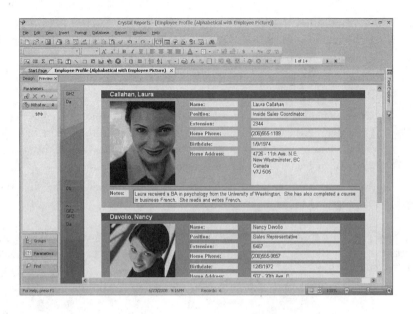

TIP

> Notice that you put the `LowerCase()` function call around only the `{Employee.Notes}` field and not the parameter. This is because you put the values into the parameter as lowercase by default. However, because you allow the business users to input their own values into the parameter, it might be a good idea to put the `LowerCase()` function on the parameter as well. This allows Crystal to compare apples to apples when evaluating these exact values. Alternatively, both could have been set to `UpperCase()`.

A keyword search is just one example of how to use a memo field in a formula. The 255-character limit for formulas that was removed in version 9 of Crystal Reports means that practically all database field types can now be accessed in formulas and manipulated. Remember that memo fields are really just long string fields, so they are treated as strings in the formula language. Wherever a string can be called, now a memo field can be called as well.

CAUTION

> Not all databases support the capability to search large string fields, so if this type of keyword search is required, more records than necessary might come across the network. For the preceding example, 15 records were returned from the data source, but only the 6 that were female were shown on the report. This is because the data source couldn't be passed this selection criteria to handle on the server side.
>
> It is a powerful new feature, but keep in mind that it might bring back more records than you expect.

WORKING WITH THE ADDITIONAL FINANCIAL FUNCTIONS

In older versions of Crystal Reports, the financial functions capability of the formula language was limited to 13 functions. However, Crystal Reports 2008 provides more than 50 financial functions. With overloads for parameters, these functions count up to about 200 variations.

These functions were implemented to give as much functionality as possible to a highly skilled group of report designers. In the past, they had to hand-code the financial functions. By including the standard financial functions that most users have seen in Microsoft Excel, these report developers can now develop their formulas much more quickly.

For more information on the financial functions available, refer to the Crystal Reports Help file. In the index, look up "Financial Functions" for a complete list of what is available.

CREATING CUSTOM FUNCTIONS IN YOUR REPORTS

Custom functions were introduced in Crystal Reports 9 and continue to be a powerful feature of Crystal Reports 2008. Although they were introduced in Chapter 4, this section focuses on some more detailed information on what they are and how they could be used in report development.

Custom functions are packets of business logic that are written in Basic or Crystal syntax. These functions do not have any reference to database fields. Because these functions contain logic that will change values and return a result, the values must be passed in, and the results of the logic must be passed out or returned.

Only 10% of a custom function is different from your average formula. As mentioned previously, parameters must be passed in to allow for data manipulation because a custom function is *stateless*. This means that it has no meaning outside the function it has called in. It acts just like all the other formula functions in the formula language. The only difference is that custom functions can be created, edited, and deleted, whereas Crystal formula functions are completely unchangeable.

Here is a custom function provided within the sample repository that comes with Crystal Reports:

```
Function cdExpandRegionAbbreviation (regionAbbreviation _
  As String, Optional country As String = "USA")
  Select Case UCase (country)
   Case "CANADA"
    cdExpandRegionAbbreviation _
      = cdExpandRegionAbbreviationCanada (regionAbbreviation)
   Case "USA", "U.S.A.", "US", "U.S.", "UNITED STATES", _
    "UNITED STATES OF AMERICA"
    cdExpandRegionAbbreviation _
      = cdExpandRegionAbbreviationUSA (regionAbbreviation)
    Case Else
        cdExpandRegionAbbreviation = regionAbbreviation
    End Select
End Function
```

13

Some of the things you will notice about the preceding code are as follows:

- It's in Basic syntax. This is not a requirement of custom functions. They can be in either Basic or Crystal syntax.
- It does not reference database fields directly. Any information needed from a database must be passed in via the parameters in the first statement (`regionAbbreviation`).
- It has an optional parameter (`Optional country As String = "USA"`). This means that this parameter does not necessarily need to be passed in for the function to work. If this parameter is not supplied by the developer in the formula, the value of `"USA"` is used by default.
- It calls other custom functions. `CdExpandRegionAbbreviationCanada` and `cdExpandRegionAbbreviationUSA` are also custom functions. In fact, they are Crystal syntax custom functions. (This shows that Basic and Crystal syntax can call one another.)
- It has a definite endpoint (`End Function`). This allows the result (the function's return) to be passed back out to the formula making the call.

> **TIP**
>
> The Enter More Info button takes you to another dialog where you can enter much more descriptive text around the custom function. It also contains fields for categorization and authors. From there, you can also add help text via another dialog. For more information on these dialogs, consult the online help.

SHARING CUSTOM FUNCTIONS WITH OTHERS

Two ways in which you can share custom functions are

- **By using them in multiple places at once**—Because custom functions are stateless, different parameters can be passed in to allow for instant function reuse.
- **By sharing them in the Crystal Repository**—Custom functions are one of four report object types that can be shared in the repository.

Custom functions can be used in many ways. Take your existing formulas, convert them, and share their logic with others.

UNDERSTANDING RUNTIME ERRORS

Crystal Reports 2008 provides the ability to get more information about variables within formulas when a runtime error occurs. In the past, when a runtime error (such as a divide by zero) occurred, Crystal would simply take you to the line of the formula giving the error. However, this was not altogether helpful, especially if the error was because the data being passed in from the database could have been at fault. So, since version 9 of Crystal Reports, there is a feature that shows all variables and data field values used in all related formulas when an error occurs. You can think of this as a variable stack.

13

The runtime error stack appears only when a runtime error occurs (when real-time data forces an error). It appears where the workshop group tree normally would in the Formula Workshop.

The runtime error stack shows all variables and all database field data related to the formula in question. If custom functions are called within the formula, their variables will appear above the formula as well. The last function to be called will appear at the top.

TIP

> The idea of a stack (reverse order) is useful in that the last function called most likely will be where the error is. But, of course, that might not always be the case.

This concept is best shown as an example. Assume that Xtreme Mountain Bike Company's management would like to take the World Sales Report and find out how much money is not accounted for by days when not shipped (`Calculation = Order Amount / Days until shipped`). To see how this works, follow these steps to simulate a formula error:

1. Use the samples download URL cited earlier to get the new World Sales Report.

2. Create a new formula called `Days Until Shipped` and use the following calculation: `{Orders.Required_Date}-{Orders.Ship_Date}`.

3. Use the Formula Workshop. Select Report, Formula Workshop. Right-click on the Formula Field branch in the workshop tree and choose New. Name the formula `Unaccounted Amount/Day`, and click on OK.

4. Add the required logic. In the Editor, enter the following: `"{Orders.Order_Amount}/{@Days Until Shipped}"`. Click on the Save and Close button in the upper-left corner. Choose Yes when prompted to save. If the report is not already in Preview mode, press F5 to refresh the report. If you don't see any data, choose Report, Section Expert and make sure that the Details section isn't suppressed. If it is, toggle the option and click on OK.

5. Drag the field onto the report. From the Field Explorer (View, Field Explorer), select the newly created formula and drag it onto the detail line of the report. Notice that the divide by zero error comes up right away. Click on OK.

6. View the Runtime Error Stack shown in Figure 13.3. In this case, the formula is quite straightforward. The problem is occurring because some of the orders are on time (zero day's wait). Xtreme's management would like to show 0 if the orders are on time, so change the formula to the following: `"If {@Days Until Shipped}=0 then 0 else {Orders.Order_Amount}/{@Days Until Shipped}"`. Click on the Save button.

7. Press F5 to refresh the report. See the values of the resulting formula as shown in Figure 13.4, and then save the report as `Chap13_2.rpt`. In the sample report created here, the new formula was colored red so it can be easily found. You will need to drill to the detail level to see this field.

Figure 13.3
Runtime error stack next to the newly updated formula.

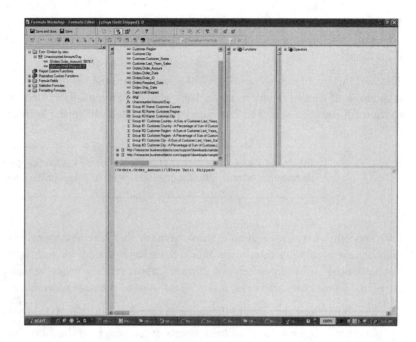

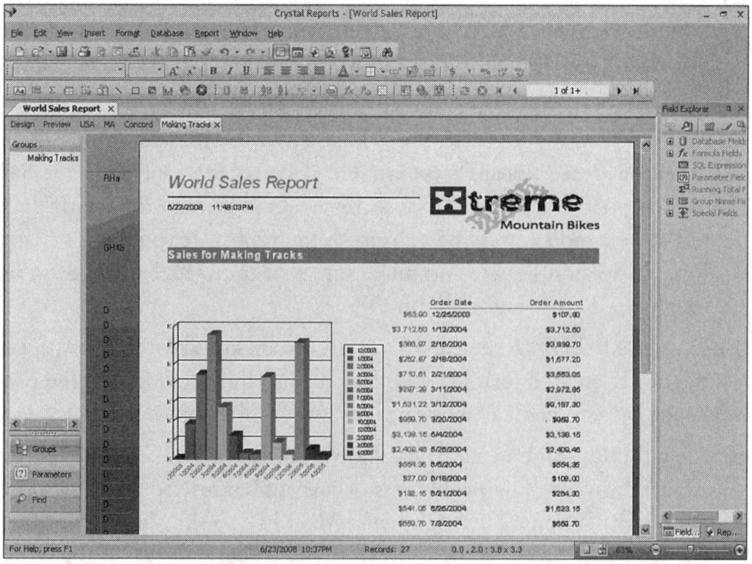

Figure 13.4
Resulting report with the latest Xtreme requirements added.

CRYSTAL REPORTS IN THE REAL WORLD—CUSTOM FUNCTIONS

As described in Chapter 4, custom functions can be prepared in advance and can be stateless so they can be used later in a variety of ways. In the next example, a name formula is created in such a way that it builds and formats names in a consistent and reusable manner.

1. Open the Employee Profile report. From the Field Explorer, select Formula Fields and click on New. Give the formula the name Title and click on OK. Enter the following text into the code window of the formula editor:

```
If InStr(LowerCase({Employee.Notes}), " he ")>0 Then
    "Mr."
Else If InStr(LowerCase({Employee.Notes}), " she ")>0 Then
    "Ms."
Else
    "";
```

2. Click on Save and Close. Next, create another new formula named Suffix and in the code window type only two double quotes (the string equivalent of NULL); this acts as a placeholder because the table doesn't have a suffix field. Finally, create a formula called Proper Name and add the following text into the code window:

```
Local StringVar strFullName;
strFullName := "";
If {@Title} <> "" Then
    strFullName := {@Title} & " ";
strFullName := strFullName & {Employee.Last Name}
        & ", " & {Employee.First Name};
If {@Suffix} <> "" Then
    strFullName := strFullName & " " & {@Suffix};
strFullName
```

3. Click on Save and Close. From the Report menu, choose Formula Workshop, right-click on Report Custom Functions in the upper-left corner of the window select New from the context menu, enter the name **ProperName**, and click on Use Extractor. In the list of formulas, select @Proper Name. Your screen should look like Figure 13.5. By default, the argument names are v1, v2, v3, and v4, but this won't help users of your formula, so change the names to Title, LastName, FirstName, and Suffix.

4. Click on OK to close the window. Crystal converts the formula from the way it's currently written into a generic custom function for later use. The new custom function is shown in Figure 13.6.

13

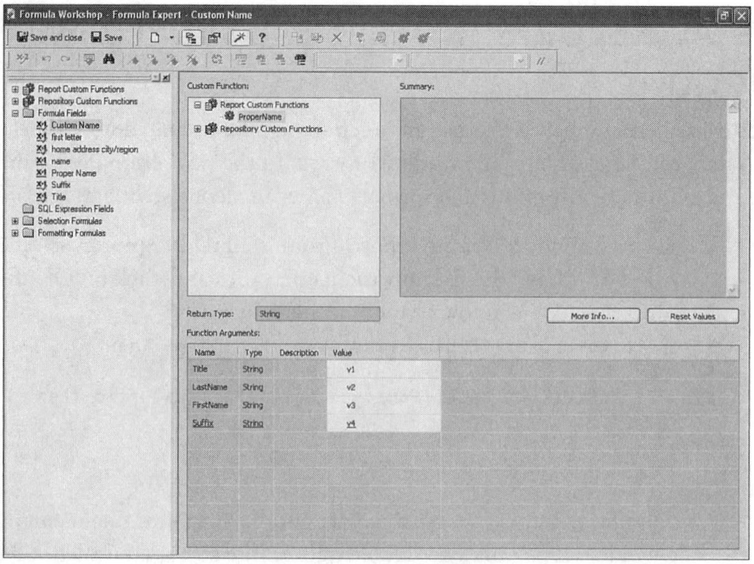

Figure 13.5
Custom function properties.

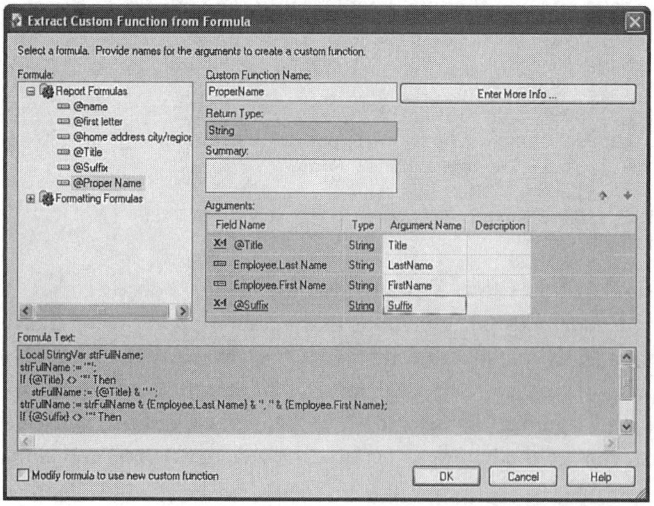

Figure 13.6
Custom function formula.

5. Click on Save and Close. The custom function is now available for use.

6. Finally, create the formula that will be used in the report. Create a new formula called Custom Name. From the list of functions, double-click on the ProperName function and pass in the following values:

```
Title: @Title
LastName: {Employee.Last Name}
FirstName: {Employee.First Name}
Suffix: @Suffix
```

Your completed formula should look like Figure 13.7.

Figure 13.7
Passing values to a
custom function.

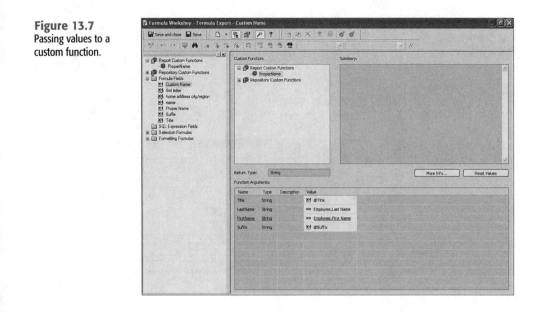

NOTE

In the sample database there is no Title field, but a formula can be used to generate the
title that will be passed to the custom function. The sample database also doesn't contain
a Suffix field, and because there's no way to determine whether the employee name has
a suffix, a null string will be passed to the custom function. The custom function can be
used later with tables that have both Title and Suffix fields.

7. Add the Custom Name formula to the report and replace the @name formula in the Group
   Header 2 section. Change the font to bold and white. Save the report as
   CustomName.rpt. Figure 13.8 shows the completed report.

Figure 13.8
Report using a name built using a custom function.

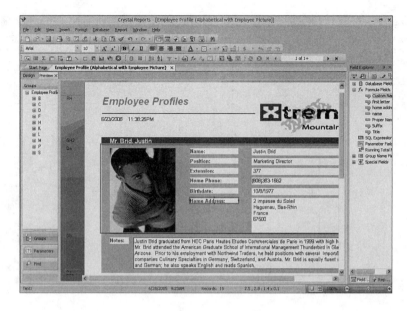

CHAPTER 14

DESIGNING EFFECTIVE REPORT TEMPLATES

In this chapter

Understanding the Importance of Reuse in Reporting

Up to now, you've been creating feature-rich reports that are very functional. Most likely, no two of the resulting reports from the previous chapters have a consistent look and feel.

One of the most demanding and time-consuming parts of report design is giving all of your reports a consistent look and feel. In many situations, report designers are asked to conform to a corporate standard like letterheads (all page numbers in the lower-right corner, and so on) or perhaps even something as demanding as Generally Accepted Accounting Principles (GAAP) or Securities Exchange Commission (SEC) standards.

In a perfect world that revolves around report designers, less work would be required if you were allowed to focus your efforts on one report and use it as a guide for all other reports that require visual, presentation-focused (yet time-consuming) features. After one report is complete with the appropriate formatting, why not apply its contents and format to other reports? Applying an existing report's layout to other reports is very straightforward with Crystal Reports 2008. This is made possible through enhancements to the report template's functionality.

Understanding Report Templates

A report template is nothing more than a regular report (.rpt) file. It can be any RPT file. Templates are applied to other reports so that their formatting and layout can be used as a basis for the other reports. What is useful about the application of templates to other reports is that formatting applies to the report as well as the layout. An example of this would be a report that has four fields in a Details section, where all sections are squished together before applying a presentation-quality template. After the template is applied, the location of the fields in the template force the fields in the existing report to span out and possibly even change some font information, depending on the specific template.

Using Report Templates

Think of a template as the form that everyone in a company must comply to. Templates can house many types of objects. These objects can be applied to a report after the data-intensive portion of the report design is completed. Applying an existing template to a report can save hours or potentially days of mundane formatting tasks.

Some types of tasks that can be accomplished by (but are not limited to) applying a template to a report are as follows:

- Corporate logos and other images
- Consistent page numbering formatting
- Font style/color/typeface for data fields

- Field border and background formatting
- Field sizing
- Group headers and footers formatting
- Summary field formatting
- Watermarks
- Tricky formatting
- Lines
- Boxes
- Repository objects
- Report titles
- Website links
- Formatting based on data field type

How Are Templates Better Than Styles in Older Versions?

Templates are better than the styles in older versions of Crystal Reports in so many ways that it's challenging to explain in a short section. However, because not all report designers have used Crystal Reports prior to version 10, they won't know how cumbersome styles used to be. For those of you new to Crystal Reports since version 10, feel free to skip this sidebar.

The main problem with the old Report Styles feature in older versions of Crystal Reports (such as 8.5) was that they were not customizable. The styles that one person created when the feature was introduced were the only options available. Even if you just didn't like the color red as the group name field and wanted to change it to blue, you were not able to, which was very limiting. This limitation alone made the Styles feature practically useless outside of learning how to create very simple reports.

These styles were also limited to data and group fields. No images or static text objects were included, and again because the styles could not be modified, they could not be updated in this way. The styles were hard-coded into the Crystal Reports Designer so that no external .rpt files were used, whereas templates enable the use of any .rpt file.

Using Existing Crystal Reports as Templates

Now that you've learned the major benefits of report templates, apply a template to one of the reports created in Chapter 6, "Fundamentals of Report Programming." The report Chap 06 Contact Listing Basic.rpt (shown in Figure 14.1) was pretty plain because the focus was on making sure that the data requirements were satisfied.

There wasn't a lot of time to play with formatting, so now you are going to apply a template that has some nice formatting and some rich elaborate corporate visuals applied. These steps walk you through that process:

1. Open the report. Choose File, Open to get the Open dialog box, and browse until the report is found. Choose it and click on Open to continue.

14

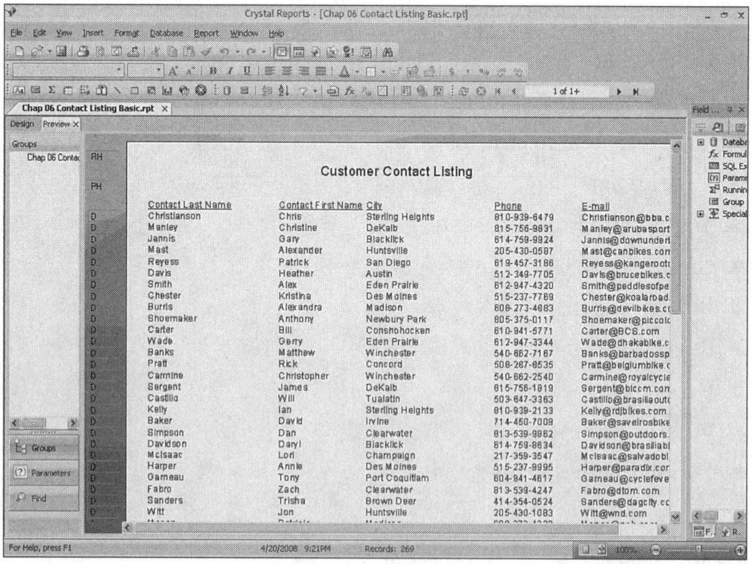

Figure 14.1
The original report before applying a template.

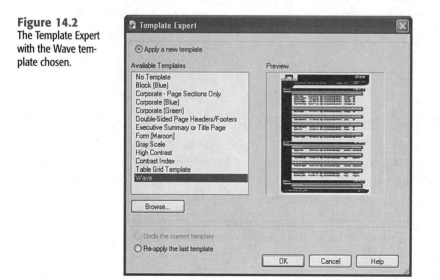

2. Look at the report prior to applying the template as shown in Figure 14.1. To get a good view of the application of the template, make sure that the Preview tab is selected. If the Preview tab is not selected or available, choose View, Preview.

3. Apply the template. To apply some formatting quickly, choose Report, Template Expert. In the Template Expert dialog, feel free to choose each file so that you can see the associated thumbnail. For this case, choose Wave, as shown in Figure 14.2, and then click on OK.

Figure 14.2
The Template Expert with the Wave template chosen.

TIP

> For more information on thumbnails, review the "Preview Pictures" sidebar at the end of this chapter.

4. Save the report. The report opens with the formatting from the applied template as shown in Figure 14.3. You can now save the report as CHAP14.rpt.

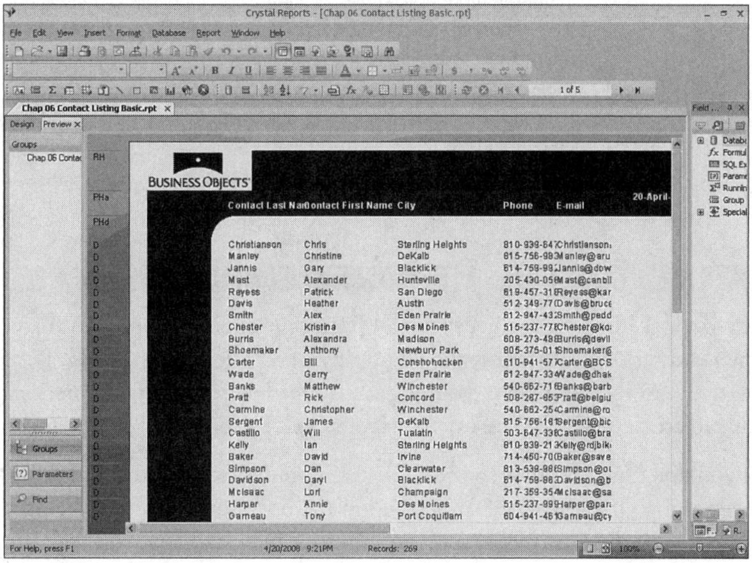

Figure 14.3
The target report with the Wave template applied.

NOTE

> You might have noticed that just about anything you do when designing a report can be undone if you don't like it. This is also true when applying templates. However, the mechanism of accomplishing this is slightly different from all other undo operations. It does not appear in the regular undo list on the Standard toolbar.
>
> If you don't like a template that you've just applied or it doesn't accomplish what you hoped for, you can undo this action by going back in to the Template Expert. At the bottom of the dialog box, you find a button that says Undo the Current Template. After selecting it and clicking on OK, the template is removed.

UNDERSTANDING HOW TEMPLATES WORK

A lot of report formatting tasks were accomplished in the two minutes it took to apply the template in the previous exercise, including

- Adding the Business Objects logo to the report (along with its ToolTip and hyperlink) from the Crystal Repository

- Adding an image that says "Confidential" as an underlay to each page of the report
- Modifying the fonts and positions of all the database fields
- Adding dashed lines between all items in the Details section
- Adding a rounded box at the top of the page
- Using a rounded box to show where groups start and end

> **TIP**
>
> One of the more advantageous features of templates is that even if more fields are in the target report's Details section than the template has, it duplicates the data field formatting for those extra fields. It puts them into a separate Details section (usually titled Details B) so that they will appear together but they won't overwrite each other. You can then move the fields around without having to worry about applying the same formatting by hand.

CREATING USEFUL REPORT TEMPLATES

If a Crystal Report already exists that has been regularly copied in the past or is viewed as the *perfect report*, consider it the beginning of an effective template. Because any report can be the basis for a template, you might just need to refine a few functional or formatting characteristics to make the existing report more robust for use as a formal template.

If you don't have reports to use for creating templates, you don't need to be concerned. Everything you've learned so far (and in the upcoming chapters) helps with effective template design. By creating a nice presentation-quality report, you have also created a likely candidate that you can use as a helpful report.

Keep in mind a few key things when using an existing report for a template. As previously mentioned, templates can be used to accomplish formatting tasks at lightning pace after data collection is done. Because any report can be used as a template, a Crystal Reports designer might already have a library full of ideas.

Applying one report layout as a template to another could cause some minor issues if the databases connected to each report are completely different in terms of schema, structure, or content. However, with some minor adjustments, the template report can be applied more effectively.

Formulas, for instance, can be problematic when applying a report as a template to another report. Because most formulas require database fields to function, they are closely tied to the actual database and structure of the data coming in to the report. Because formulas act on database fields, using them in templates is not very effective because errors might occur when applying a template report to another report that accesses a different database. However, some tools that can minimize this effect are available. Using custom functions instead of prewritten formulas can alleviate some of the data dependencies, as can using the CurrentFieldValue evaluator for formatting formulas.

Also, even relatively small things can make a significant difference. Sometimes just focusing on the page headers or footers can go a long way in effective report template design. By reducing the repetitive nature of general page formatting, you increase your report design productivity.

USING CUSTOM FUNCTIONS AS REPLACEMENTS FOR DATA-DEPENDENT BUSINESS LOGIC

Because custom functions were introduced in the previous chapter, the focus of this section is how to use custom functions to avoid formula errors when applying templates. For more information on custom functions, see Chapter 13, "Using Formulas and Custom Functions."

The reason custom functions are more useful in templates than straight formulas is that they are *stateless*, which means that they have no direct dependency on the database fields to get their data. Custom functions see the data only as parameters passed in to the report. Instead of searching through an entire formula to find all uses of a given field, by passing it in to a custom function once, Crystal Reports effectively repeatedly does the search-and-replace on the report designer's behalf.

Another advantage to using custom functions in a report template is that within the one report—the template report—it might be possible to use one custom function more than once because the logic might be used over and over with the only difference being the data that's used.

If a report that contains many formulas is applied as a template to a report that contains a different table name—for example, `template.field` and `target.field`—the formulas would not change over correctly. Therefore, all the formulas result in compiler errors on the first run of the report to the preview. Because the report designer would have to go through all the lines of business logic and replace every database field occurrence, it could be a very tedious process. If the search-and-replace time could be limited to one line per formula, you would be far more productive.

Of course, current formulas in a pre-existing report are already working, and you would not want to break them. Manually changing all relevant formulas to custom functions would be a big task. However, the Formula Extractor can automate this process for you.

By using the Formula Extractor, you can actually review the existing formula, break it down, find the data-specific pieces, convert them into parameters, and reformulate the formula to accept those parameters and save it as a custom function. It even rebuilds the initial formula that created the custom function to apply the new custom function so that the report designer doesn't have to go back and perform that step manually.

TIP

> In general, to make formulas even easier to work with, use the Formula Workshop as much as possible. This virtual all-in-one workspace for formulas means that navigation between formulas is quick and easy and you don't have to open each one separately or guess at their names.

14

Even after formulas are converted, you might need to make adjustments for data-specific fields that would need to be passed in as parameters to those functions. However, because most custom functions reduce the lines of code and pass in the data only once, the search-and-replace tasks are greatly reduced.

> **TIP**
>
> If you are concerned about losing old formula logic when converting the formula, just comment out the old formula code and put in the custom function. Of course, commenting each line by hand can be cumbersome. By using the Comment/Uncomment (//) button on the toolbar, you can highlight all the contiguous lines of code you want to comment out and then click this button. It comments out all the lines in one quick step.

USING THE `CurrentFieldValue` FUNCTION

When using formulas to create conditional formatting, they are usually designed to be data dependent—so much so that the database field name is used at every opportunity. However, to make formatting formulas more portable (and reusable), use the `CurrentFieldValue` formatting function instead of the actual field name that would always change depending on where the formula is located.

`CurrentFieldValue` is a special signifier in the formula language that tells the formatting formula to look at the value of the field it is associated with, without actually having to know the name of the field. This is advantageous in two ways:

- For general formatting, this allows for copying of formatting formulas and reusing the formatting formulas within a single report or within multiple reports without having to replace data-specific field names.
- For template formatting, this is especially useful because you can't be sure that the database field is going to be of the same name, let alone of the same data type.

By keeping the reuse factor in mind when creating and maintaining formulas from now on, creating effective templates will become much easier over time.

USING TEMPLATE FIELD OBJECTS

During the process of designing a report template, you might need to provide some specific formatting for a field not based on its position in the report, but instead based on the type of field it is. For example, a company might require that all date/time fields display in military time regardless of operating system defaults. For example, "6:02 p.m. on March 31, 2004" would have to look like "3/31/04 18:02". Another requirement could be a space as the thousands separator for all numbers (instead of the usual comma).

These requirements could easily be corporate or industry standard requirements, such as the ISO 9000 standard. At the time the template is created, it's unknown where these fields will be located in the report or how many of them there will be. You would have to find another way of handling special formatting requirements. Template Field objects help in this endeavor.

When designing a report specifically as a template, Template Field objects take the place of regular database fields in a report. They can be placed anywhere that a database field would normally be placed.

These fields are a special type of formula field that contains no data but allows formats to be applied to them as if they were of any data type. Template Field objects have a special dialog associated with them that exposes all the Formatting tabs of the Format Editor regardless of type. This provides a one-stop shop for all of your formatting needs regardless of the data type for a given position of a field in a report.

The best way to explain this is by actually performing it, so start by implementing the examples given previously in this section:

- **Military time**—"6:02 p.m. on March 31, 2004" to appear as "3/31/04 18:02"
- **Thousand separator as a space**—1,000 to appear as 1 000

Starting with a new report, follow these steps:

1. Create a new report. After opening Crystal Reports, click the New button. Then within the Crystal Reports Gallery dialog, choose As a Blank Report and click on OK.

2. Skip the data source step. Because this report is going to be a template, there is no need to associate a data source with it. Click on the Cancel button in the Database Expert to close this dialog.

3. Insert a Template Field object. To insert the first Template Field object, select Template Field Object from the Insert menu. Place the resulting field into the leftmost area of the Details section (see Figure 14.4).

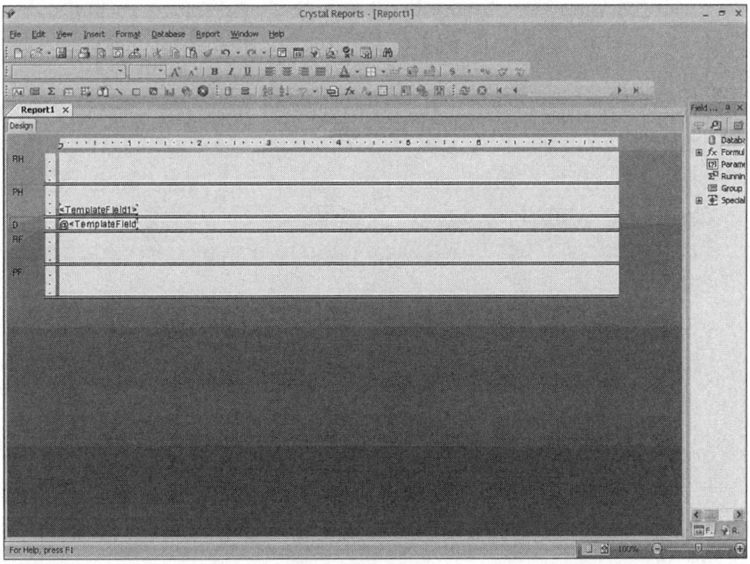

Figure 14.4
The Design tab with the first Template Field object added to the report.

14

4. Add five more Template Field objects. Repeat the previous step five more times and place each new field to the right of the last one. Once completed, the Design tab will look like Figure 14.5.

Figure 14.5
The Design tab with six template objects added to the report.

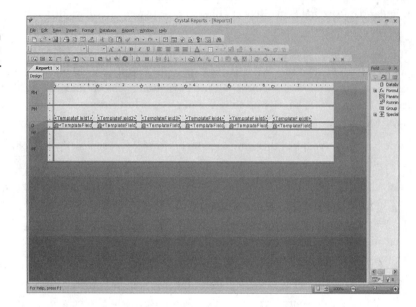

5. Select all template objects to format. To select all template objects, hold down the Ctrl key while single-clicking on each template object in the Details section. After all six objects are selected, right-click on the last object you chose and select Format Template Fields from the pop-up menu.

6. Format Date/Time to military time (3/31/04 18:02). After the Format Editor appears, select the Date and Time tab. Choose the third option in the Style list box that represents date/time as 3/1/99 13:23 because this is the option required, as shown in Figure 14.6.

7. Format Number with a space as the thousand separator (1 000), as shown in Figure 14.7. Now select the Number tab in the Format Editor dialog box. Because this style does not appear in the Style list box, select Customize. In the Custom Style dialog box, change the symbol from "," to " " (without the quotes). Click on OK to return to the Format Editor. Click on OK again to return to the Design tab with the changes applied.

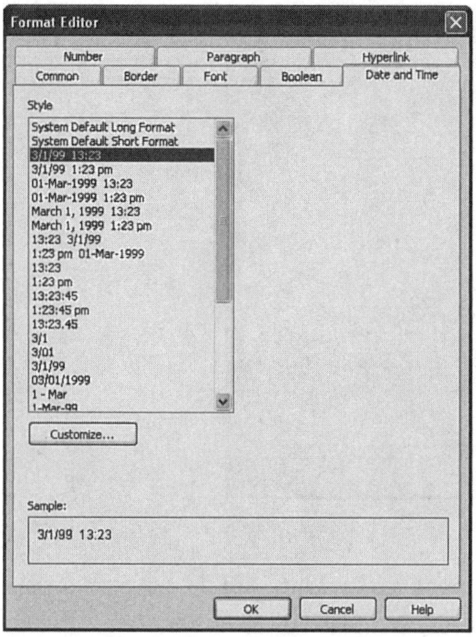

Figure 14.6
The Date and Time tab of the Format Editor with Military Date/Time selected.

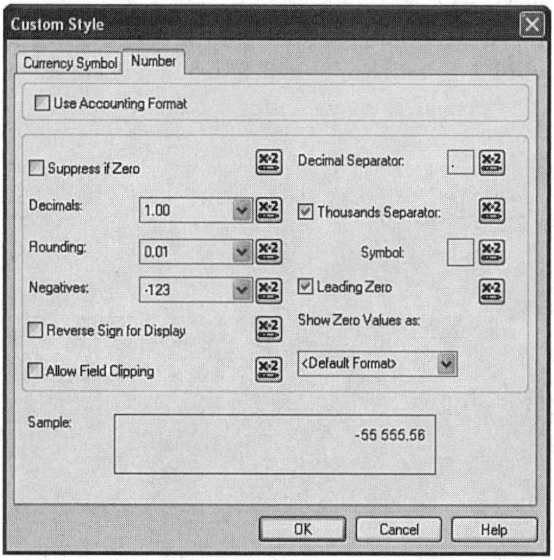

Figure 14.7
The Custom Style dialog box with the space set as the thousands separator symbol.

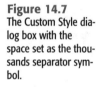

8. Give the template a name and a preview picture. When the report appears in the Template Expert, it will have a name associated with it. The name is saved as the Report Title. To change the Report Title, select File, Summary Info. Input the name **Military Time & Thousands** into the Title property field and select the Save Preview Picture check box as shown in Figure 14.8. Select OK to continue.

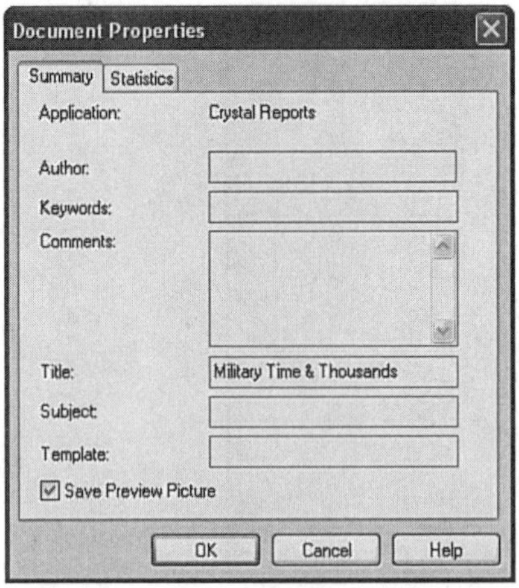

Figure 14.8
The Report Title set to describe the Template report.

9. Save the report to the Templates folder. Choose File, Save As to save the report. Call the report TemplateObjects.RPT and place it in the Templates folder. The Templates folder is usually found at C:\Program Files\Business Objects\Crystal Reports 12.0\Templates\en. When it is saved, close the report.

10. Open the report from the previous example (Chap14.rpt) and add the Last Year's Sales data field to the report. Notice that all the fields and numbers are in the standard format as is the Last Year's Sales field, as shown in Figure 14.9.

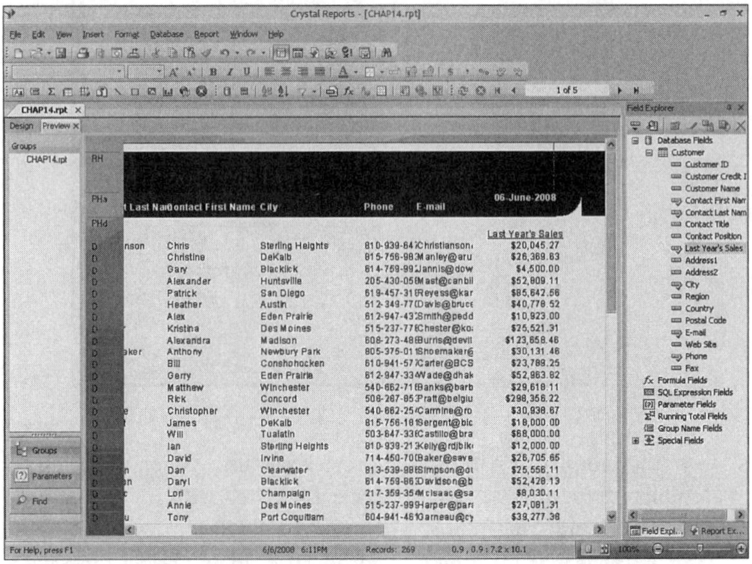

Figure 14.9
The Preview tab showing how the report looked when the original report was created.

11. Select the template. To select the template that was saved earlier, select Report, Template Expert. Select Military Time & Thousands from the Available Templates list, as shown in Figure 14.10.

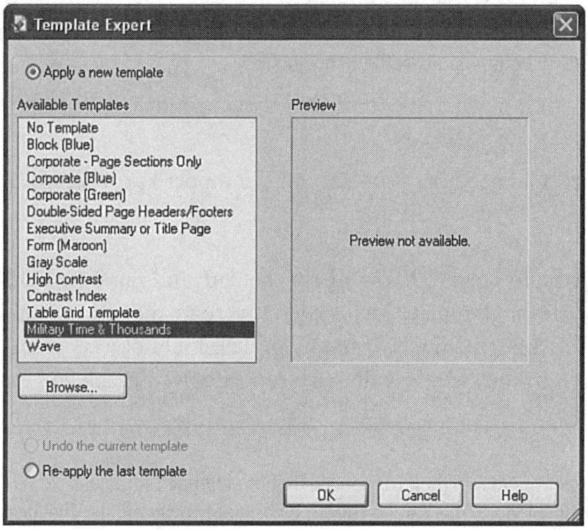

Figure 14.10
The Template Expert dialog box with a template selected.

12. To apply the template, simply click on the OK button. The report will appear as shown in Figure 14.11. You will notice that the report appears to close. Do not be alarmed because this is standard behavior. Crystal Reports saves a temporary file with the old look of the report and then applies the template during the new Open command.

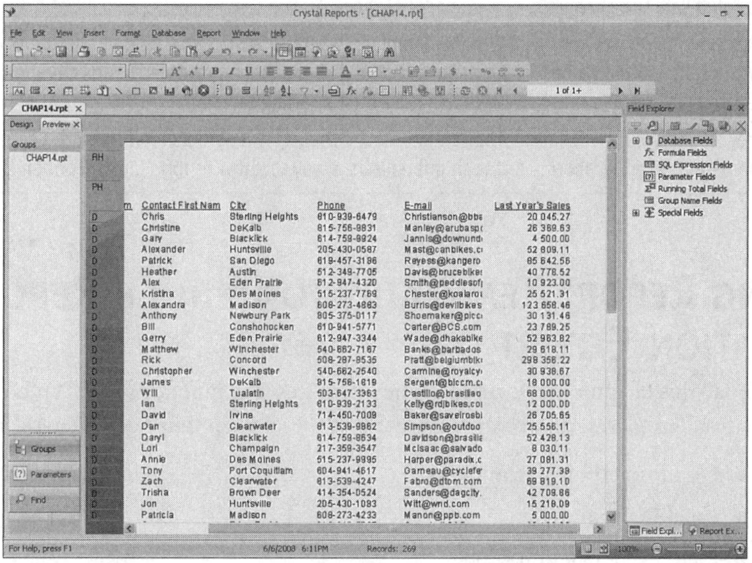

Figure 14.11
The Preview tab showing how the report looks after the template is applied.

TIP

> Undoing a template is always an option. If for some reason you do not like the look that the applied template gives your report, just return to the Template Expert and choose the Undo command at the bottom of the dialog box. Selecting this option and then clicking on OK lets Crystal Reports revert to the original report before the template was applied.
>
> Crystal Reports accomplishes this by opening up the temporary backup .rpt that it saved before applying the template file.

13. Save the report. Choose File, Save As, call the report templateapplied.rpt, and on click OK.

Notice that there was no need to know where the date and numeric fields were located in the report because all the Template Field objects were formatted to handle the different requirements for the different fields. Using Template Field objects along with the other template tips mentioned in the chapter will make report design quick and easy.

Preview Pictures

During the previous exercise, you might have noticed that the intended template did not show a preview picture on the right of the dialog window. This can be caused by one of two situations. The Save Preview Picture option in the Document Properties dialog box was not selected. If that option was checked and the thumbnail still did not appear, it was because the template report was not saved with a preview. In the example that you just completed, the template report was not previewed before the report was saved.

Preview pictures, or *thumbnails* as they are commonly called, are just that: pictures of the preview of the report. If a report has not been previewed, it will not have the thumbnail to save.

Another key point to notice on preview pictures is that if changes are made in the design of the template and then a save is done, the changes will not be reflected in the thumbnail because the Preview tab was not updated with the changes.

Preview pictures are very useful in the Template Expert because these images provide you with a visualization of what the template does to the existing report. To save them as a default with all reports, select the Save Preview Picture option in File, Options under the Reporting tab.

Preview pictures are also important to have if the reports will be delivered through Crystal Enterprise because the ePortfolio application uses the thumbnails as a way to show reports in the front end.

USING REPORT TEMPLATES TO REDUCE REPORT CREATION EFFORT

So far this chapter has focused on new features and functions that can be used to create templates. Templates can accomplish many of the more intense designer-related tasks, including

- Conditional formatting
- Field highlighting
- Page headers and footers

- Charting standards
- Lines, boxes, and borders
- Color standards
- Logos and images
- Websites, hyperlinks, and email addresses
- Standard custom functions
- Repository objects
- Locking size or position of any object
- Special fields

APPLYING MULTIPLE TEMPLATES

Because any report could be used as a template, it is also conceivable that many reports could be applied to any single report as a template.

This can prove quite useful if the templates do different things. For example, one template might be applying the standard page headers and footers to all reports within a company, whereas another template could apply department-based colors to the Details section. Because both templates are encapsulated separately, they can be applied separately and will not affect each other. The end result is one report with both the corporate style (headers and footers) as well as the specific department's colors (in the Details section) applied.

TIP

> Templates can be applied repeatedly, even if new fields are added to the report after the initial template was applied. Simply choose Reapply Template in the Template Expert to have the template address any new fields.

EXPORTING CAPABILITIES IN CRYSTAL REPORTS

The ability to take a snapshot of a report and convert it to another format (this is often referred to as exporting to another format) has existed for quite some time, going back to the earliest versions of Crystal Reports. This capability, however, has had some important updates in Crystal Reports 2008. We'll start by identifying the different output formats for exporting a Crystal Report.

Two important exporting properties are the output formats and available destinations.

Output formats:

- Crystal Reports (RPT)
- HTML 3.2
- HTML 4.0

14

- Microsoft Excel (97–2003)
- Microsoft Excel (97–2003) Data—only
- Microsoft Word (97–2003)
- Microsoft Word (97–2003)—Editable
- ODBC
- PDF
- Record Style—Columns with spaces
- Record Style—Columns without spaces
- Report Definition
- Rich Text Format (RTF)
- Separated Values (CSV)
- Tab Separated Text (TTX)
- Text
- XML

Available destinations (all destinations are supported by all above format types except the format type ODBC, where ODBC is a destination):

- Application
- Disk file
- Exchange folder
- Lotus Domino
- Lotus Domino Mail
- MAPI

The most common output formats have traditionally been PDF and Excel with XML garnering a lot of recent interest. Exporting to PDF is useful when a report exposes some interesting information and the report needs to be shared with others who don't normally have access to the report (don't have the report designer or access to the report on a web-deployed environment). The report consumer can use the exporting feature to convert the report from the native Crystal Reports format to PDF and send the PDF file to a user who then only needs the Adobe Acrobat Reader to view the report. This option also delivers the output format that most resembles the original report.

Exporting to Excel is useful when the report consumer would like to analyze the data. Once the data is in Excel, the consumer is then free to manipulate the data using all the features of Excel. If reports are frequently being exported to Excel, then the business should have a look at the LiveOffice capability of embedding report data into Excel while maintaining a connection to the report (and therefore the database). The data can then be refreshed over and over directly from within Excel without repeating the manual steps of exporting. This delivers the benefits of exporting but with less manual intervention.

Exporting to XML is gaining popularity where businesses want to take the data from a report and make it available to third-party products. In the past this capability could be challenging to manage as the XML structure was not flexible enough to adjust to different customer needs. The result was that the report data was exported to XML but customers then needed to create an additional step to restructure the exported XML into the structure they could actually use. New in Crystal Reports 2008 is the ability to define what the XML export structure should be. To define the XML output structure for your report, go to the File menu, Export, Manage Exporting XML Formats… From here the report author can define the output XML by clicking the Add button, then the button Import XML Transform and browsing for his *.xsl or *.xslt documents.

NOTE

> Resist the temptation to use this XML export as a substitute for a proper ETL (Extract Transform & Load) product. While the XML export delivers some light capability in this area, it is not an ETL product and attempting to use this feature as a substitute for a proper ETL process will probably result in disappointment at some point down the road. Business Objects, an SAP company, offers a rich ETL product named Data Services.

One export format that all Crystal Reports authors should be familiar with is the Report Definition. This export will create your documentation for you. Once the report is complete, exporting the Report Definition will create a document that will describe all groups, formulae, report fields, and more. This one-time-saving feature can save hours of painstaking documentation creation with the assurance that nothing is overlooked. The report is professionally documented in a detailed consistent format that reflects well on the report author's professionalism.

CRYSTAL REPORTS IN THE REAL WORLD—STANDARDIZED TEMPLATES

Arguably the most powerful use of report templates is simply adding consistent headers and footers. As described previously, the job of placing header and footer information in exactly the right place time after time is time-consuming and boring. A very simple template can give you a head start on basic formatting.

To create your template, an image of the company logo will be used. For this example, the Business Objects, an SAP company logo (saved in JPG format) from the corporate website is used.

1. Begin by creating a new report without a data source, as described earlier in the chapter. Your starting point should look like Figure 14.12.

14

Figure 14.12
A blank canvas for
the report template.

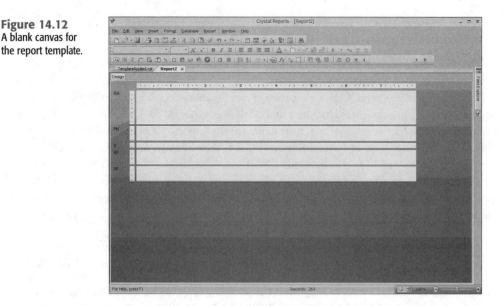

2. From the Insert menu, choose Insert, Picture. Browse for the logo (.jpg or .bmp) file and add it to the upper left of the report header. In the top right, add a text object and label it **Data as of:** and right justify the text. Add the special field Data Date to the right of the text.

3. Add the special field Report Title to the page header, center justify the text, widen the field so that it reaches to both edges of the report, change the font to 14, and add some vertical height so the text fits properly.

4. In the page footer, add the special field Page N of M, centered with the field stretched to both left and right edges of the canvas. The template is now ready to be applied to all reports, effectively standardizing fundamental elements of report look and feel.

NOTE

> To maximize flexibility, ensure that objects (such as the logo) used in the template make full use of the Repository. Not only is it important to standardize the look and feel, it should also be easy to update.

5. Save the template as StandardTemplate.rpt.

Figure 14.13
A sample standardized template.

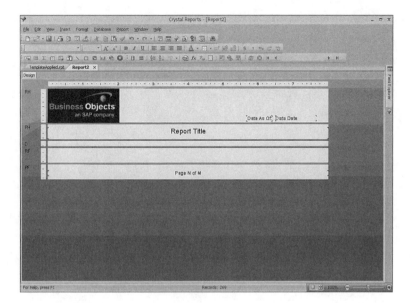

TROUBLESHOOTING

TEMPLATES

The template has a chart, but the chart fails to appear when applied to a report. Why is that?

Charts are typically built to show summary values. Make sure to group the data in the report and include one or more summaries. This is the most likely reason the chart failed to show.

Using the sample templates shipped with Crystal Reports works fine for everything except the Title and Report Description fields. These fields are blank and can't be edited. How can Title and Report Description fields be added to the report?

These are special fields accessible from the Field Explorer. To populate these fields, go to File, Summary Info. In the dialog box, the Title property assigns a value to the Title field and the Comments property assigns a value to the Report Description field.

ADDITIONAL DATA SOURCES IN CRYSTAL REPORTS

In this chapter

15

UNDERSTANDING THE ADDITIONAL CRYSTAL REPORTS DATA SOURCES

When thinking about data sources for Crystal Reports, most people tend to think about popular databases such as Microsoft SQL Server, Microsoft Access, Oracle, IBM DB2, and so on. However, the extent of Crystal Reports reaches far beyond these traditional relational databases. The data sources discussed in this chapter are as follows:

- .NET- and COM-based data sources
- Java-based data sources
- XML as a data source
- Integration kits

CONNECTING TO COM OR .NET DATA SOURCES

Crystal Reports provides *direct access* or *native* drivers for some databases. These drivers are written specifically for a particular database and are often the best choice. However, because hundreds of types of databases exist, BusinessObjects can't possibly write direct access drivers for all of them. So, often, users turn to using standard data access layers such as ODBC or OLEDB to connect to their databases. Often, the vendor of a database provides an ODBC driver or OLEDB provider so that other applications can access the vendor's database. Sometimes though, even this is not enough. Customers would like to report off of data that is not accessible by any Crystal Reports data source driver or via ODBC or OLEDB. To accomplish this, customers often turn to the COM Data Source driver, the ADO.NET Data Source driver, or the Java Data Source driver. This section describes the COM version of the driver, but much of the theory applies to the ADO.NET and Java Data Source drivers as well.

NOTE

The *ActiveX Data Object*, or *ADO*, is a Microsoft-based technology for software component development. ActiveX Data Objects are a language-neutral object model that expose data from an underlying OLE DB provider. The most commonly used OLE DB provider is the OLE DB Driver for ODBC. Business Objects provides sample applications to illustrate how to use Crystal Reports with these technologies. We'll examine one sample that you can download from here: `https://websmp130.sap-ag.de/sap(bD1lbiZjPTAwMQ==)` `/bc/bsp/spn/bobj_download/main.htm`. For Software Product, select Crystal Reports, Product Version select XI Release 2, and Software Type select Sample. Download the file labeled RDC ASP Samples for CR XI R2 (Developer Edition only). With the zip file downloaded and the contents extracted (be sure to put a check in the Use Folder Names setting), we'll review the code in the folder `ADORecordsetExample`.

Because ADO is a standard technology, Business Objects decided to leverage it to create an extensible data source driver mechanism. This ADO Data Source driver doesn't connect to a database—rather, it gets data from an ADO connection defined by you. This means that if you are somewhat savvy in the .NET world, you can write your own mini data source driver (called an *ADO data provider*) that enables access to data that would otherwise be unavailable.

To better understand the concept of writing your own ADO data provider, look at a few scenarios in which doing so can be beneficial.

LEVERAGING LEGACY MAINFRAME DATA

Although new technologies are surfacing at an alarming rate, many companies still have data held in legacy mainframe systems. Often, the nature of these systems doesn't allow for any kind of relational data access, and thus lowers the value of the system. However, these systems can often output text-based files, called *print files* or *spool files*, that contain the data held in the mainframe system. These text-based files are often more complicated than a set of simple comma-separated values and thus require a bridge between the files and a data access and reporting tool like Crystal Reports. Writing an ADO data provider can serve just this purpose. The data provider would read the text files, parse out the required data, and return it to Crystal Reports for use in numerous reports.

HANDLING COMPLEX QUERIES

Often, companies have a database that is accessible via standard Crystal Reports data access methods. However, the process of connecting to the database and performing a query can be quite complex. Sometimes this is because the database servers are constantly changing, queries are becoming more complex, and other business processes affect the complexity of the query. By writing an ADO data provider, a clever person can abstract the location and complexity of the database interaction away from the user designing a report. The user simply connects to the data provider, and the rest of the logic is done transparently in the background.

RUNTIME MANIPULATION OF DATA

Performing a simple query against a database that returns a set of records is often all that is needed. However, sometimes logic needs to be incorporated into the query that cannot be expressed in the database query language (using SQL). Other times, per-user manipulation of data needs to be performed, such as removing all salaries stored in a database for all users other than the currently logged-in user for confidentiality purposes (often called *data-level security*). This runtime manipulation can be performed by an ADO data provider.

These three scenarios outline just a few of the reasons why you might want to use the ADO data provider and create one of your own. The following sections describe the technical details of doing this. The example demonstrates creating a VB .NET ADO provider, but the same functionality can be provided from any .NET language. For the report author, both methods are equal and transparent.

REVIEW AN .ADO.NET DATA PROVIDER

ADO data providers can be written in any development language or platform with the capability of creating ADO objects. Most commonly, they are created in either VB .NET or C# (pronounced "see-sharp"). The following example uses VB .NET, but it can easily be translated to other development languages. To create a simple ADO provider, follow these steps:

1. Download one of the zip files of sample .NET applications from the Business Objects website at

   `https://websmp130.sap-ag.de/sap(bD1lbiZjPTAwMQ==)/bc/bsp/spn/bobj_download/main.htm`. For Software Product select Crystal Reports, for Product Version select XI Release 2, and for Software Type select Sample. Download the file labeled `RDC ASP Samples for CR XI R2` (Developer Edition only).

   The sample is named `aspxmps115.zip`. Extract the contents of the file to your machine—be sure to Use Folder Names so that the extract process creates a number of child folders. Open the folder `ADORecordsetExample`—it contains 10 files. See Table 15.1 for a summary of each file.

TABLE 15.1 SUMMARY OF THE SAMPLE APPLICATION FILES

Filename	Explanation of Purpose
`ADORecordSet.asp`	The main line of the application. Contains the custom code that defines which report to load and where to get the data from.
`ADORecordSetReport.rpt`	Sample report to connect to the data.
`ADOSample.ttx`	Data definition file that describes the data structure.
`AlwaysRequiredSteps.asp`	Steps common to all Crystal Reports ADO applications.
`Cleanup.asp`	Steps required to clean the memory used in the Crystal Report ADO application.
`JavaPluginViewer.asp`	File used to invoke the Java viewer for Crystal Reports.
`MoreRequiredSteps.asp`	Additional steps common to all Crystal Reports ADO applications.
`RDCrptserver115.asp`	File to set all the Crystal Report Engine properties.
`ReadMe.txt`	A help file that describes some of the application details.
`SmartViewerActiveX.asp`	File used to invoke the ActiveX viewer for Crystal Reports.

2. Using the steps from Chapter 9, "Custom Formatting Techniques," download the Xtreme 12 Sample Database. Create an ODBC DSN for this database and name it **Xtreme Sample Database 11.5** (note the ReadMe file DSN name is not correct). With the files downloaded, create a web share for the `ADORecordsetExample` folder.

3. Open a browser, navigate to your web share, and open the file `ADORecordSet.asp`. Your URL might look something like this: http://localhost/ado/ADORecordSet.asp if `ado` is the name of your web share. See Figure 15.1 for an example of the report.

Figure 15.1
Sample report in the browser with data from an ADO data provider.

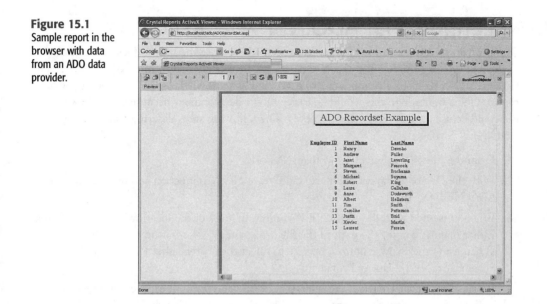

4. Despite all the .asp files, the only file that needs to be modified is ADORecordSet.asp. The other files in the sample could remain constant. Open the ADORecordSet.asp file to see what's happening. After all the comment lines are removed, running this application requires three essential steps: define the report, get the data, and display the report.

5. Define the report. The report name is defined by this line of code:

```
reportname = "ADORecordSetReport.rpt".
```

The include file AlwaysRequiredSteps.asp uses the value of reportname and creates the report object and opens the Crystal Report.

6. Get the data. The data is fetched using the following lines of code:

```
Set oADOConnection = Server.CreateObject("ADODB.Connection")
oADOConnection.Open ("Xtreme Sample Database 11.5")
Set oADORecordset = Server.CreateObject("ADODB.Recordset")
Set oADORecordset = oADOConnection.Execute _
("Select [Employee ID],[First Name], [Last Name] From Employee")
Set oRptTable = session("oRpt").Database.Tables.Item(1)
oRptTable.SetDataSource oADORecordset, 3
```

The preceding lines generally define the data connection, execute SQL against the data, and assign the results to the report defined in step 5. The include file MoreRequiredSteps.asp then merges the report from step 5 with the data from step 6.

7. Display the report. The last step is to open the report in a browser either using the Java viewer or the ActiveX viewer for the report. By embedding the include file SmartViewerActiveX.asp, the report will open in the ActiveX viewer. By embedding the include file JavaPluginViewer.asp, the report will open in the Java viewer.

CONNECTING TO AN ADO.NET XML RECORDSET

The preceding example can be difficult to work with because the report does not connect directly to the datasource but the data is passed to the report at run-time. An alternative is to have the ADO.NET application write to XML and use this XML as the data source for the report. One advantage to this would be easier report development because a sample XML file could be used for development purposes. The following steps describe connecting to ADO.NET XML data:

1. From the File menu, select New, Blank Report.

2. With the Database Expert open, expand Create New Connection and double-click on ADO.NET (XML).

3. When presented with the ADO.NET window, first select the location of the source file. Either manually enter the path to the file or use the Browse button to find the file. When using the Browse button, be sure to select the correct filter (XML File, XML Schema, or .NET Dataset Provider).

4. If you select a .NET dataset provider, the .NET dataset might expose multiple classes. To identify a specific class from the provider, check the box beside Use Classes from Project, and select the class from the list of available classes.

5. Multiple datasets might be exposed from a given class. To select a dataset from a class, check the box beside Use Dataset from Class and select the dataset from the list of available datasets.

CONNECTING TO JAVA-BASED DATA SOURCES

ADO.NET is targeted at .NET developers. Because Crystal Reports 2008 has a full Java SDK, an equivalent Java Data Source driver provides functionality equivalent to the ADO data provider for developers using the Java platform.

The process of creating a Java Data Source driver is conceptually similar to that of creating an ADO data provider. A Java class needs to be created that has a public function with a return type of ResultSet or CachedRowSet. A ResultSet is the standard object returned from a JDBC-based query, whereas the CachedRowSet is a disconnected recordset useful for parsing out things like XML. Listing 15.1 shows a simple Java data provider that returns a ResultSet.

LISTING 15.1 A JAVA DATA PROVIDER THAT RETURNS DATA FROM THE SAMPLE DATABASE

```
import java.lang.*;
import java.sql.*;

public class XtremeDataProvider
{
    public ResultSet Employee()throws java.sql.SQLException
    {
```

```
                        ResultSet rs = null;
                        Connection con = null;
                        String url = "jdbc:odbc:Xtreme Sample Database 11";
                        String JDBCBridge = "sun.jdbc.odbc.JdbcOdbcDriver";

                        try{
                                    // connect to the database
                                    Class.forName(JDBCBridge);
                                    con = DriverManager.getConnection _
                                    (url, "", "");

                                    // run a SQL query
                                    Statement stmt = con.createStatement _
                              (ResultSet.TYPE_SCROLL_SENSITIVE, _
                    ResultSet.CONCUR_READ_ONLY);
                                    String query = "SELECT * FROM Employee";
                                    rs = stmt.executeQuery(query);

             }catch (ClassNotFoundException e) {
                                    System.out.println("Check JDBC-ODBC bridge driver");
                                    e.printStackTrace();
                    } catch (SQLException e) {
                                    System.out.println("SQL Exception #" + e.getErrorCode()
➥ + " : " + e.getLocalizedMessage());
                                    e.printStackTrace();
                    }

                    // return the results of the query
                    return rs;
          }
}
```

To identify a Java class, simply compile the code into the .class file and place that compiled .class file into the JavaBeans classpath. To define the classpath, edit the following properties in the CRconfig.xml file in the default folder: C:\Program Files\Business Objects\ common\4.0\java\.

JAVADIR

This property must refer to a valid Java Runtime Environment (JRE) or J2SE Development Kit (JDK). If a JRE or JDK was detected during install, this property will already be set. If not, install JDK 1.4 and set the property manually. A valid setting is the complete path to the JDK: <JavaDir>c:\Program Files\Java\JRE\bin</JavaDir>.

JAVABEANSCLASSPATH

If the JavaBeans are unjarred, simply refer to the .class file's path:

```
<JavaBeans>
    <CacheRowSetSize>100</CacheRowSetSize>
    <JavaBeansClassPath>c:\myjavabean</JavaBeansClassPath>
</JavaBeans>
```

15

If the JavaBean class files are jarred, refer to the same location with the `.jar` extension:

```
<JavaBeans>
    <CacheRowSetSize>100</CacheRowSetSize>
    <JavaBeansClassPath>c:\myjavabean.jar</JavaBeansClassPath>
</JavaBeans>
```

During the process of creating a report, Crystal Reports searches through all classes contained in the classpath. It then provides a list of methods with return types of `java.sql.ResultSet`. The same rules about function arguments apply. Any arguments to the Java method are mapped to report parameter fields. Using Java code, you can control exactly what data comes back.

CONNECTING TO XML DATA SOURCES

Crystal Reports can connect to XML data in three ways. XML can be presented as source data as

- **Local data source**—This is a physical XML file that resides locally or on the network and is identified by passing in the fully qualified path and filename. If a schema (`.xsd`) file exists, it can also be specified.

- **HTTP(S) data source**—An HTTP(S) data source is XML-formatted data accessed from a servlet, an ASP page, or a JSP page. The URL to the source may be HTTP or HTTPS. When using HTTPS, the ID and password information passed into Crystal Reports is used for authentication.

- **Web service data source**—A web service data source can be a service on a local machine or network drive that is referenced either via a path and filename or via a servlet/dynamic web page (ASP/JSP). No schema is specified because it is derived through the web services framework. Web service data sources are accessed using Web Services Description Language (WSDL). After the WSDL is specified, the driver prompts for service, port, and method.

Regardless of the data source, from the File menu choose New, Blank Report. From the Data window, expand Create New Data Connection and double-click on XML and Web Services. From that point, follow one of the following paths.

CONNECT TO A LOCAL XML DATA SOURCE

1. Specify the fully qualified path and filename to the `.xml` file. If the `.xml` file does not have embedded schema information, a schema (`.xsd`) file must be identified. To identify the schema file, ensure that there is a check mark beside Specify Schema File.

2. Click on Next.

3. If the schema does not need to be specified, click on Finish; otherwise, you will be prompted for the location of the schema. The schema may be referenced using a fully qualified path or URL.

4. Click on Next and then on Finish.

CONNECT TO AN HTTP(S) DATA SOURCE

1. Select the radio button for Use HTTP(S) Data Source and enter the URL to the .xml file. If the .xml file does not have embedded schema information, a schema (.xsd) file must be identified. To identify the schema file, ensure that there is a check mark beside Specify Schema File.

2. Click on Next.

3. If authentication information is required, enter it here. Click on Next.

4. If the schema does not need to be specified, click on Next; otherwise, you will be prompted for the location of the schema. The schema may be referenced using a fully qualified path or URL. Click on Next.

5. As a final step, HTTP parameters may be added/modified/removed in order to modify the set of data returned. Then click on Finish.

CONNECT TO A WEB SERVICE DATA SOURCE

1. Select the Use Web Service Data Source radio button. No schema file is needed, so the option will be dimmed immediately on a selection of this data source type. Click on Next.

2. Specify the location of the web service. Either a local file or HTTP(S) location may be specified. Click on Next.

3. If prompted for it, enter authentication information and click on Next.

4. Select the service, port, and method from the lists. Click on Finish.

After the connection to the data source is complete, the report may be designed as any other. The XML data is presented as a table just as in any other Crystal Reports data source.

INTRODUCTION TO THE INTEGRATION KITS

The integration kits provide native access and integration to commonly used Enterprise Resource Planning (ERP) applications. They achieve this by providing unique access to the data via the ERP's application layer, via the application's published programming interfaces or APIs. New development for the Baan Integration Kit has been discontinued, and as a result no Baan Integration Kit will be released for Crystal Reports 2008. A Siebel Integration Kit for Crystal Reports 2008 has not been released. A complete list of supported ERP applications is defined in Table 15.2.

TABLE 15.2 FEATURES BY INTEGRATION KIT

	SAP		PeopleSoft	
Integration Kit	R3	BW	Enterprise	EPM
Software shipped with product			X	
Integrated security	X	X	X	X
Sample reports	X	X	X	X
Portal/UI integration	X	X		
Crystal Report access	X	X	X	
Web Intelligence access		X	X	
Voyager	X			

This unique approach to data access allows the integration kit to honor the security, access all the data, make sample reports, leverage the metadata of the ERP application, and provide real-time access to the data.

HONOR THE SECURITY

Organizations spend a lot of time and effort setting up security in their ERP applications. The integration kits are made so that users do not have to re-create this security. This results in organizations having to change security only once in their ERP application; this change is then reflected in the reports.

ACCESS TO ALL THE DATA

Many ERP applications, such as SAP, do not store all their data in the underlying database. Some of the data used in SAP can be found only in programmatic sources, such as cluster tables and other objects unique to SAP. Therefore, if your reporting tool could connect to only the underlying database, you would likely miss some critical pieces of data that might dramatically affect your business decisions. With the Business Objects integration kits, you do not have to worry about this problem because the kit connects to the application layer of SAP and can thus leverage SAP functionality and gain access to all forms of data storage that SAP provides.

SAMPLE REPORTS

Sample reports are provided for all the integration kits. These reports provide not only a basis on which to start but, more importantly, also provide examples on how to report off hierarchies and use variables—to name just a few.

LEVERAGE THE METADATA OF THE ERP APPLICATION

Changes made to the application might not necessarily be reflected in the database. The native drivers connect to the application's metadata and should see any of the changes. For example, SAP R3 has cluster tables that you will not find in the underlying database, but they are visible in the SAP R3 data dictionary.

> **NOTE**
>
> In determining whether your ERP application is supported by Business Objects integration kits, you should *not* be concerned with the specifics of the underlying database, but instead focus on the specific version or patch level of the application itself.

PROVIDE REAL-TIME ACCESS TO DATA

With this approach, data is not extracted from the ERP application in order to report against it. In some cases it might make sense to extract the data to a data mart or data warehouse, and the ERP provider or Business Objects might provide solutions for that. A lot of production reporting requires real-time data, however, and the ERP's own tools might prove inflexible and difficult to use.

SAP INTEGRATION KIT

The SAP integration kit includes drivers to allow connectivity to both R3 and Business Warehouse (BW). In addition, it includes a BW toolbar for Crystal Reports, a specific set of folders in InfoView with role-based links, sample iViews for Enterprise Portal, and an SDK in Java, COM, or .NET.

REPORTING OFF R3 DATA

The kit includes two drivers to allow Crystal Reports to connect to the ABAP data dictionary via a remote function call or *RFC*. The Open SQL driver allows the user to connect to SAP R3, displaying the field and the short text description of the tables and fields. The developer can join the tables accordingly, using the database expert, and then select the relevant fields from which to report. This driver displays not only transparent tables, but views, pool tables, cluster tables, ABAP (Advanced Business Application Programming) data clusters, and ABAP functions. This driver is geared toward a technical person with functional expertise in joining the tables and then creating the report.

> **NOTE**
>
> In Crystal Reports, you cannot check the SQL generated using the Show SQL Query option from the Database menu. You can check what Open SQL was generated by using SAP transactions.

The InfoSet driver allows the user to connect to an existing InfoSet, as defined by SAP transaction SQ02. Alternatively, you can use an existing ABAP query, as defined by SAP

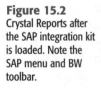

transaction SQ01. The benefit of this driver is that the user does not need to know where the data is stored or how to join the tables. Another advantage is that any prompts defined in the InfoSet become parameters in Crystal Reports.

NOTE

> To test the InfoSet query, run the InfoSet using your SAP GUI and ensure that it is pulling the required data before testing it in Crystal Reports.

REPORTING OFF BW DATA

When you're reporting off of BW data, the Business Objects integration kit consists of three drivers that are used to pull data.

The BW Query driver enables the user to connect to a BW query. To enable selection of a query with this driver, Crystal Reports has its own toolbar, as shown in Figure 15.2, and the user needs to select the New Report icon from this toolbar. The user then selects the required BW query and thus displays a listing of fields available in the query. The user can then create the report using any of those fields. Variables defined in the query automatically become Crystal Reports parameters. After the user has finished building the report, the user saves the report using the BW toolbar. This saves the report to BW, and if the user selects the option to do so, automatically publishes the report to BusinessObjects Enterprise. By using this workflow, BW creates an association between a given role in BW and the report allowing Crystal Reports to leverage BW security, saving SAP implementations significant costs.

Figure 15.2
Crystal Reports after the SAP integration kit is loaded. Note the SAP menu and BW toolbar.

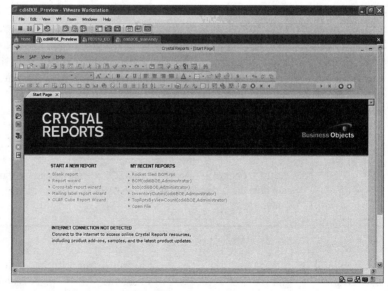

The MDX query driver supports using Crystal Reports to report off either a SAP BW query or a BW cube. Furthermore, it adds additional functionality by providing support for

- A structure in both the row and column of the BW query
- Hierarchy node and hierarchy node variables
- Free characteristics in a BW query

The Operational Data Store or ODS driver exposes the ODS tables, so that they look much like the tables of any relational database. However, because of the structure of the objects, it considers them to be like a database stored procedure.

Connecting to the ODS objects is not performed with the SAP toolbar described here, but rather by selecting the driver from the Data Explorer as shown in Chapter 1, "Creating and Designing Basic Reports." After the user has finished building the report, the report can be saved back to BW and published to BusinessObjects Enterprise by selecting the Automatically Publish to Enterprise check box, as shown in Figure 15.3.

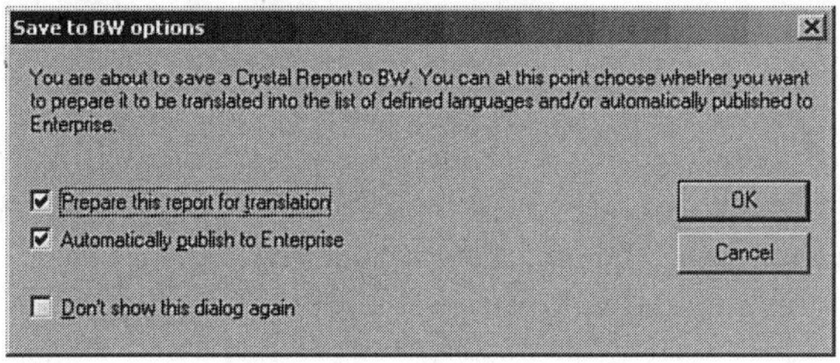

Figure 15.3
The additional options after saving a Crystal Report to SAP BW.

NOTE

> This publishing method requires some setup. Please refer to the Installation documentation for further details.
>
> Both the ODS and MDX drivers require SAP transports to be loaded on the SAP BW system. Please refer to the Installation CD in the `Transports` folder for further details.

USING VOYAGER OR WEB INTELLIGENCE TO REPORT OFF BW DATA

Included in the SAP integration kit are specific drivers to allow Voyager and Web Intelligence to report off of SAP BW.

To connect to a BW cube or query using Voyager, open the connection browser and select Add. Select SAP Business Information Warehouse and then proceed to fill in the relevant data, as shown in Figure 15.4.

15

Figure 15.4
The information
required to connect to
a BW cube or query
from Voyager.

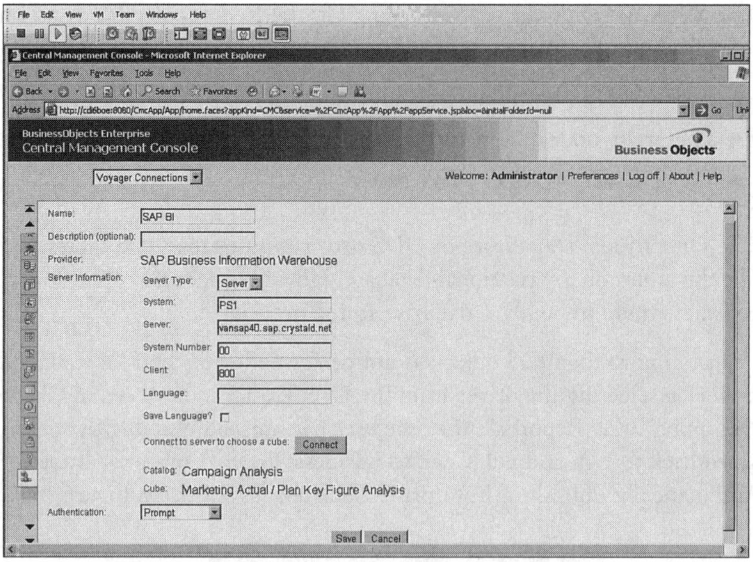

After you are connected, select the query or cube and process to build the report.

Web Intelligence requires that a universe be built on a BW cube or query. However, to aid in this process, Designer builds the universe for you. To do this, select SAP from the list of connects and fill out the required information, as displayed in Figure 15.5.

Figure 15.5
The information
required to connect to
a BW cube or query
from Web
Intelligence.

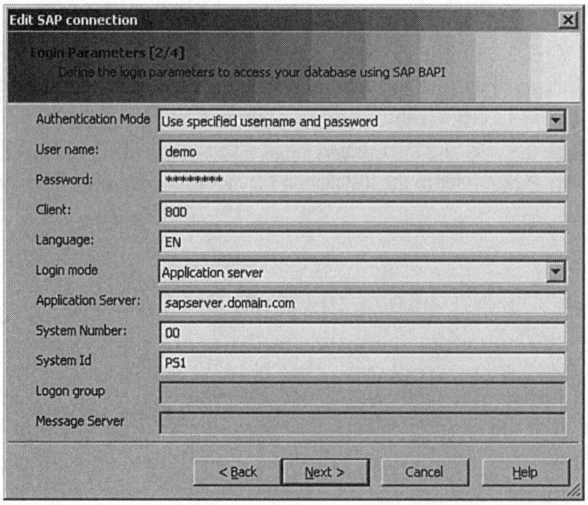

15

Finish the remainder of the wizard and when you click on OK, Designer generates the Universe for you. It might be necessary to move some of the objects around to suit your needs, but when you are finished, export to BusinessObjects Enterprise.

NOTE

> Only the BW query driver does not require the query be released for external access. The Web Intelligence, OLAP Intelligence, and MDX drivers require the user to release the BW query. To release a query, select the query properties in the BW Query Designer, select the Extended tab, and then check Allow External Access to This Query.

VIEWING THE REPORTS

Your SAP reports can be viewed either via InfoView or via SAP Enterprise Portal 6. The integration kit provides a number of sample iViews that can be imported by a portal administrator. These include

- **Folder iView**—The folders a user has access to are displayed, and from here a user can run her reports.
- **Alert iView**—Shows all the alerts that have been triggered by Crystal Reports. The user can then click on the report to view the report. The creation of alerts is defined in Chapter 11, "Using Record Selections, Sort Controls, and Alerts for Interactive Reporting."
- **Thumbnail iView**—This iView displays the Crystal Report as a thumbnail of the report. The user can then click on the thumbnail to run the report.

NOTE

> These are sample iViews. The organization can create its own iViews via the provided SDK.

BusinessObjects InfoView for SAP is a unique version of InfoView designed for integration with SAP BW systems. This integration includes features such as the ability to log on to InfoView using your SAP username and password. Related to authentication is the ability to access your roles and the Crystal Reports saved to these roles. The roles are defined in Enterprise as folders. The user can also schedule reports in the different languages loaded into SAP BW. This creates an instance for each language.

PEOPLESOFT INTEGRATION KIT

Crystal Reports has been embedded in PeopleSoft for many versions. The BusinessObjects integration kit for PeopleSoft extends the usefulness of the embedded reporting functionality by providing all the features of Business Objects XI to the report consumer.

REPORTING OFF PEOPLESOFT DATA

The native PeopleSoft driver connects to the PeopleSoft query as defined within the PeopleSoft system. Furthermore, because you are required to pass a username to the PeopleSoft system, the driver will honor the parameters and security (both query-level security and row-level security) defined by the PeopleSoft query. To access the PeopleSoft query, select the PeopleSoft driver from the list of drivers available to Crystal Reports. After authenticating, a list of accessible queries becomes available. Select a query, and Crystal Reports treats the query's resulting recordset the same way it treats a table. The developer is presented with a listing of fields that make up the query. These fields can then be dragged onto the report and the report can be developed as described in the first half of this book.

Business Objects also offers two more significant integration points with PeopleSoft: user security integration and an EPM Security Bridge. With the PeopleSoft security plug-in in place, users can log into Business Objects InfoView and Central Management Console using their PeopleSoft credentials. This means reduced administration and cost savings. The EPM Security Bridge maps EPM security rules to the Business Objects universe to allow Web Intelligence analysis of PeopleSoft EPM data.

VIEWING THE REPORTS

After the report is complete, the user can publish the report, and this report can then be viewed via InfoView. The integration kit allows for PeopleSoft authentication so that PeopleSoft users can log on to InfoView using their PeopleSoft credentials. The security integration creates a group in Business Objects XI for each mapped PeopleSoft role. A single install of Business Objects XI can be mapped to multiple PeopleSoft domains.

SIEBEL INTEGRATION KIT

The Siebel integration kit for Crystal Reports 2008 has not been released as of this writing.

TROUBLESHOOTING

PUBLISHING WITH A COM OR JAVA PROVIDER

I've published a report using a COM (or Java) data provider to BusinessObjects Enterprise, but I am getting errors when the report is run.

Whenever one of these types of reports is published to BusinessObjects Enterprise, you need to make sure that you copy the COM or Java component to the machines running the Page and Job servers. This component needs to be installed and registered properly before the report can invoke it.

I am receiving errors when I try to connect to the Java data provider.

Make sure that you have installed a Java Virtual Machine (*JVM*, also called the *Java Runtime Environment*). The JVM is required to connect to Java data providers.

SAP MENU AND TOOLBAR DO NOT APPEAR

After installing the SAP integration kit for BW, I was expecting the SAP menu and toolbar to appear in Crystal Reports, but they are not there.

Before installing the integration kit, ensure that you have the SAP GUI installed, including the BW add-ons, and that the GUI is patched to the correct level.

NO TABLES APPEAR WHEN I SELECT THE SAP TABLE, CLUSTER, OR FUNCTION DRIVER

When I'm searching for a table using the Open SQL driver, the expected table names do not appear in the list of tables.

Possible causes could be that you do not have SAP access in your profile either to the table or to the required Business Objects transports. Also, you could be filtering the tables using the Data Explorer option in Crystal Reports.

"NO ANALYTIC SERVERS AVAILABLE TO PROCESS THE QUERY" ERROR RECEIVED INTERMITTENTLY WHEN VIEWING CRYSTAL REPORT BASED ON PEOPLESOFT QUERY DATASOURCE.

Crystal Reports utilizes the PeopleSoft analytic server(s) when running reports based on queries. Large, complex reports with multiple subreports may consume more analytic servers within PeopleSoft than have been configured for the environment. Additional servers must be configured within PeopleSoft to remedy this issue.

"DATABASE CONNECTOR ERROR – RESULT IS INVALID OR QUERY IS NO LONGER RUNNING IN PEOPLESOFT ENTERPRISE" ERROR RECEIVED WHEN TRYING TO REFRESH CRYSTAL REPORT BASED ON PEOPLESOFT QUERY.

This error is commonly caused by incorrect configuration of the source PeopleSoft environment, specifically within the Query Access Services. This error is generally not a result of invalid permissions for the user running the report, because if a user does not have rights to view a query within PeopleSoft, the query will simply not appear as available in Crystal Reports.

CRYSTAL REPORTS IN THE REAL WORLD—LEVERAGING XML AS A DATA SOURCE

With the emergence of XML as a data interchange format, many customers wanted to create reports on XML documents. So, in Crystal Reports 8.5, a new driver was released that allowed just this scenario. This ODBC driver reads certain types of XML documents. Version XI of Crystal Reports provides the capability to read multiple XML files, most com-

15

monly a folder of XML files that have the same schema. When using this driver, you specify either a folder name or a file path to an XML file, as described in detail earlier in this chapter. Once connected, XML elements at the first level are represented as fields that you can place on a report. In Crystal Reports 2008, the sample reports ship with XML files for the datasources.

If you require more flexibility around reading XML files, a good approach to take is to write a COM or Java data provider to read the XML. That data provider can use one of the many readily available XML parsers to read in the XML and choose exactly what fields to return to Crystal Reports. Listing 15.2 is a sample Visual Basic COM data provider that reads in a simple XML file. This method is still used by developers who want to exert very strict control over the XML data provided to the report.

LISTING 15.2   A COM DATA PROVIDER THAT READS XML DATA

```
' Loads an XML document with the following structure:
'    <employees>
'      <employee>
'        <name>X</name>
'        <dept>X</dept>
'        <salary>X</salary>
'      </employee>
'    </employees>
    Public Function SimpleXML(ByVal fileName As String) As ADODB.Recordset
        Dim rs As New ADODB.Recordset>

        Dim xmlDoc As New MSXML2.DOMDocument
        xmlDoc.Load(fileName)

        rs.Fields.Append("Name", ADODB.DataTypeEnum.adBSTR)
        rs.Fields.Append("Dept", ADODB.DataTypeEnum.adBSTR)
        rs.Fields.Append("Salary", ADODB.DataTypeEnum.adCurrency)
        rs.Open()

        ' Loop through each employee element
        Dim employeeNode As MSXML2.IXMLDOMElement
        Dim childNode As MSXML2.IXMLDOMElement

        For Each employeeNode In xmlDoc.documentElement.childNodes
            rs.AddNew()
            For Each childNode In employeeNode.childNodes
                rs(childNode.nodeName).Value = childNode.Text
            Next
            rs.Update()
        Next

        SimpleXML = rs
    End Function
```

CHAPTER 16

FORMATTING MULTIDIMENSIONAL REPORTING AGAINST OLAP DATA

In this chapter

16

INTRODUCTION TO OLAP

The first 15 chapters exposed you to a wide variety of the reporting capabilities found in Crystal Reports. Up to this point, however, all the reports you created were based on relational data sources, often known as *Online Transactional Processing (OLTP)* databases, where most organizations generally keep their operational data.

In many organizations and for many people today, data reporting ends with Crystal Reports pointing at existing relational data sources such as Microsoft SQL Server, Oracle, DB2, Sybase, or even Microsoft Access. All those relational databases are designed for the efficient storage of information. These databases are not designed optimally, however, for the efficient extraction of data for aggregated analysis across multiple dimensions—that is where OLAP databases excel.

OLAP stands for *Online Analytical Processing*, which enables business users to quickly identify patterns and trends in their data while reporting against multiple dimensions at once. Examples of dimensions for analysis include time, geographic region, product line, financial measure, customer, supplier, salesperson, and so on. Crystal Reports provides powerful OLAP-based formatted reporting capabilities, and this chapter introduces them.

This chapter covers the following topics:

- Introduction to OLAP concepts and OLAP reporting
- Recently added OLAP features in Crystal Reports
- Creation of OLAP-based Crystal Reports

OLAP CONCEPTS AND OLAP REPORTING

OLAP is an analysis-oriented technology that enables rapid analysis of large sets of aggregated data. Instead of representing information in the common two-dimensional row and column format of traditional relational databases, OLAP databases store their aggregated data in logical structures called *cubes*. Designers create OLAP cubes around specific business areas or problems. Cubes contain an appropriate number of dimensions to satisfy analysis in that particular area of interest or for a specific business issue. OLAP is a technology that facilitates data viewing, analysis, and navigation. More than a particular storage technology, OLAP is a conceptual model for viewing and analyzing data. Table 16.1 highlights some common business areas and typical sets of related dimensions.

TABLE 16.1 BUSINESS AREAS AND COMMONLY ASSOCIATED OLAP DIMENSIONS	
Business Area	**Associated Business and Common OLAP Dimensions**
Sales	Sales Employees, Products, Regions, Sales Channels, Time, Customers, Measures
Finance	Company Divisions, Regions, Products, Time, Measures
Manufacturing	Suppliers, Product Parts, Plants, Products, Time, Measures

OLAP cubes pre-aggregate data at the intersection points of their associated dimension's members. A *member* is a valid field value for a dimension. For example, members of a time dimension could be 2006, 2007, Q1, or Q2; members of a product dimension could be Gadget1, Gizmo2, DooDah1, and so on. This pre-aggregation facilitates the speed-of-thought analysis associated with OLAP.

Precalculating the numbers at the intersection points of an OLAP cube's associated dimension members enables rapid high-level analysis of large volumes of underlying data that would not be practical with traditional relational databases. Consider the example of analysis on several years of sales data by year, quarter, and month and by region, sales manager, and product. The pre-aggregated nature of OLAP facilitates speed-of-thought analysis that otherwise would not be practical when working with the phenomenal amount of data and involved calculations required to provide answers on a traditional relational (OLTP) database system—it would simply take too long.

When a Crystal Report uses an OLAP cube as a data source, it presents the multidimensional data in a two-dimensional OLAP grid that resembles a spreadsheet or cross-tab. The focus of Crystal Reports when reporting against OLAP cubes is to present professionally formatted two-dimensional (or flat) views of the multidimensional data of particular business use for report-consuming end users and not necessarily analysts requiring interactivity—the more traditional OLAP end users.

The concepts of OLAP usually become more understandable after you explore them. To that end, later sections in this chapter step you through a Crystal Reports report creation example against an OLAP cube.

RECENTLY ADDED OR CHANGED OLAP FEATURES IN CRYSTAL REPORTS

This section is specifically targeted for users of older versions of Crystal Reports. Table 16.2 lists the newly added OLAP-oriented features of recent versions and their practical use or benefit. If you are a new user to Crystal Reports or you have not previously used the OLAP reporting features in the product, you might want to skip directly to the next section.

TABLE 16.2   LATEST OLAP FEATURES IN CRYSTAL REPORTS

OLAP Feature	Feature Benefit and Value
Row/Column Dimension Parameter links	Enables the direct linking of report parameters to member selection and filtering in the column and row dimensions of the selected cube. You access this feature through either the OLAP Report Creation Wizard or the OLAP Report Settings option under the Report menu.

continues

16

TABLE 16.2   CONTINUED

OLAP Feature	Feature Benefit and Value
Slice/Page Dimension Parameter links	This productivity feature enables the direct linking of report parameters to pages and slices in the OLAP grid. This enables the end user to dynamically specify the values of slices and pages in the OLAP grid. You access this feature in either the OLAP Report Creation Wizard or the OLAP Report Settings option under the Report menu.
Interactive OLAP Worksheet (Analyzer) in new Cube tab	The New OLAP Analyzer feature (a Cube tab in Crystal Reports Designer) is accessed by right-clicking on an existing OLAP grid object and selecting the Launch Analyzer option. The Cube tab provides a fully functioning drag-and-drop OLAP worksheet that enables rapid selection of the most appropriate OLAP viewpoint for the Crystal Report. The associated Crystal Reports OLAP grid, where you can apply advanced formatting, reflects all changes made in the Analyzer worksheet.
Interactive drill-down of OLAP grids in Preview tab	The OLAP grid presented in the Crystal Reports Preview tab is more fully functional. In addition to having access to advanced OLAP grid functionality including calculations, exception highlighting, sorting, filtering, and member reordering from the right-click button, the OLAP grid now enables the report designer to expand (drill-down) and contract members directly from within the Preview tab.
New and improved data sources	At the time of writing, Crystal Reports 2008 provides OLAP access to multiple versions of Hyperion Essbase, DB2 OLAP, SQL Server Analysis Services, and SAP BW.

The following sections explore the creation of an OLAP report through the OLAP Report Creation Wizard, the added value of the OLAP Expert, and the advanced interactivity features of Crystal Reports.

USING THE OLAP REPORT CREATION WIZARD AND OLAP EXPERT

Crystal Reports provides two easy ways to create reports against OLAP data sources. As introduced in Chapter 1, "Creating and Designing Basic Reports," Crystal provides several report wizards to step you through the creation of some popular types of reports—one of those is OLAP. The OLAP Report Creation Wizard involves five steps and walks you through the process of creating an OLAP grid and an optional supporting graphic based on an existing data source. You can access the OLAP Report Creation Wizard when you are creating a new report.

The second method of creating an OLAP-based report is through the OLAP Expert that you access from the Insert OLAP Grid on the Insert menu. This expert provides six tabs that step through the creation of an OLAP grid to be placed anywhere on a report.

The two methods of creation offer very similar degrees of functionality, and their respective dialog screens and tabs are almost identical. The OLAP Report Creation Wizard provides a built-in Charting screen not found in the OLAP Expert, whereas the OLAP Expert provides Style Customization and Label tabs not found in the OLAP Report Creation Wizard.

NOTE

> Although Crystal Reports has been designed to report off of numerous multidimensional/OLAP databases including Hyperion Essbase, Microsoft SQL Server Analysis Services, and SAP BW, for the purposes of demonstration in this chapter, examples will be based on the SQL Server 2005 sample Sales and Employee cube—FoodMart. If a different OLAP database is available, the general principles should be followed against that native OLAP cube.

SPECIFYING AN OLAP DATA SOURCE

The OLAP Data tab (or screen in the OLAP Report Creation Wizard) requests the OLAP data source on which the report is to be based. This wizard and its associated dialog screens are to multidimensional data sources what the data explorer, introduced in Chapter 1, is to relational data. Figure 16.1 shows the OLAP Data screen from the OLAP Report Creation Wizard.

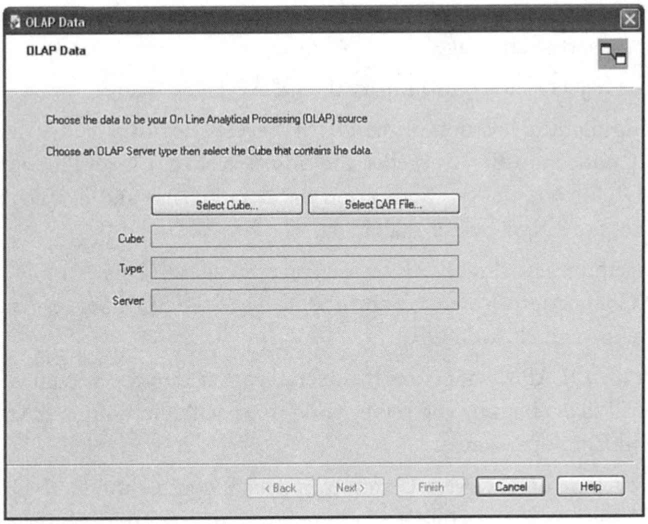

Figure 16.1
The OLAP Data dialog from the OLAP Report Creation Wizard.

When this screen first displays, you must use the Select Cube button to select a cube. Clicking on this button opens the OLAP Connection Browser, displayed in Figure 16.2. From the tree control presented in this dialog, select the desired cube.

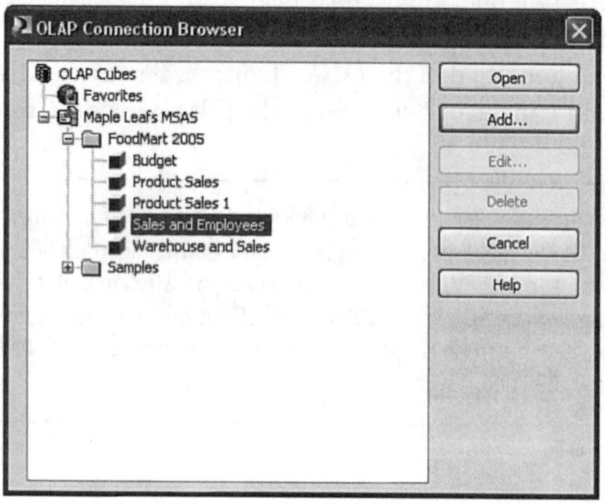

Figure 16.2
The OLAP Connection Browser enables the specification of an OLAP data source for the involved Crystal Report.

To help you learn about the creation of an OLAP-based Crystal Report, here are the introductory steps to doing exactly that against SQL Server 2005's sample FoodMart Sales and Employee cube (provided at usingcrystal.com). Other exercise steps will appear throughout the chapter after the presentation of related text and figures. For now, start the OLAP Report Creation process with the following steps:

1. Create a New Crystal Report by selecting the OLAP Cube Report Wizard from the Crystal Reports Start Page.

2. Click the Select Cube button from the OLAP Data dialog.

3. Assuming that the location of the OLAP Server has not already been identified to the OLAP Connection Browser, click the Add Server button and identify the location of your SQL Server Analysis Server and the sample Sales and Employees cube. Figure 16.3 shows the New Server dialog.

4. Enter a caption for the OLAP server you are adding. This caption appears in the OLAP Connection Browser. Enter the name of the SQL Server Analysis Server for the server name and click on OK.

5. Back in the OLAP Connection Browser, navigate into the presented list of servers (there will likely be only the server you just added) and double-click on the sample Sales and Employees cube.

6. Before clicking on the Next button to proceed, you see the Page Dimension Selector dialog. New to version 2008, from here you can select the specific dimensions from the cube that you would like to report on. For this exercise, select the highest level dimension from each group and click on OK to move forward. In the future you can use this functionality to restrict retrieved data/dimensions from larger cubes.

Figure 16.3
The Connection
Properties dialog for a
new OLAP server cre-
ates new connections
to OLAP data sources.

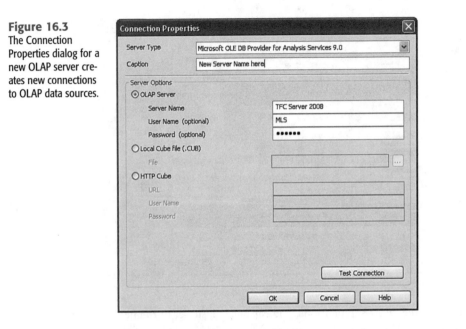

NOTE

A Select CAR File button exists on the Data screen of the OLAP Report Creation Wizard,
in addition to the Select Cube button. The name CAR comes from the legacy name
Crystal Analysis Reports (CAR). CAR files are created with the sister online OLAP product
to Crystal Reports used within BusinessObjects Enterprise. (This tool was formerly called
Crystal Analysis.) CAR files can be treated as multidimensional data sources because they
contain connectivity information to an underlying OLAP data source.

SPECIFYING OLAP ROWS AND COLUMNS

The Rows/Columns dialog screen enables you to select both the dimensions and fields to be
presented along the columns and rows of the OLAP grid. The Dimensions list box depicted
in Figure 16.4 lists all the available dimensions in the selected cube/data source.

To select a dimension for placement in the rows section or the columns section of the OLAP
grid, highlight the desired dimension and click either the column or row arrow (>) button. It
is possible to select multiple dimensions for display and to have them nested in the OLAP
grid by successively selecting multiple dimensions for either the rows or the columns section. It is also possible to remove dimensions from the existing row or column list boxes;
however, you cannot leave the column and row dimension list boxes empty.

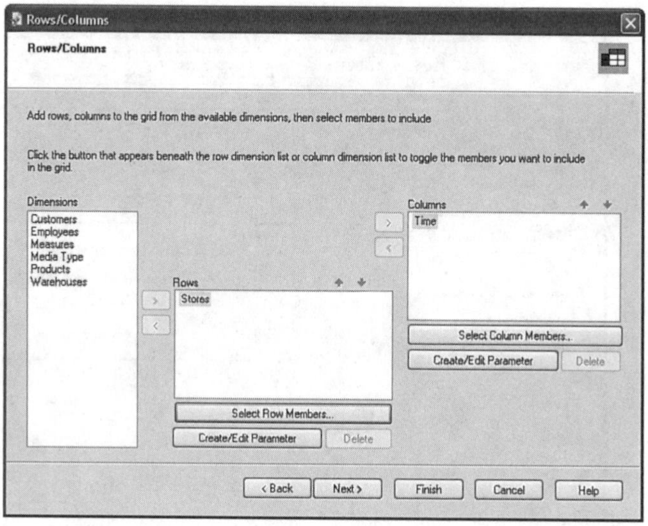

Figure 16.4
The Rows/Columns dialog of the OLAP Report Creation Wizard.

After selecting the desired dimensions, you can select a subset of the fields (also known as *members*) for those dimensions by using the Select Row Members or Select Column Members button. Examples of this include selecting only a certain subset of provinces or states in a region dimension or, alternatively, selecting only a certain year's worth of data in a time dimension. By highlighting a dimension in either the Rows or the Columns list box and then selecting the appropriate selection button, you can use the Member Selector dialog to select a subset of the members for the involved dimension, as shown in Figure 16.5.

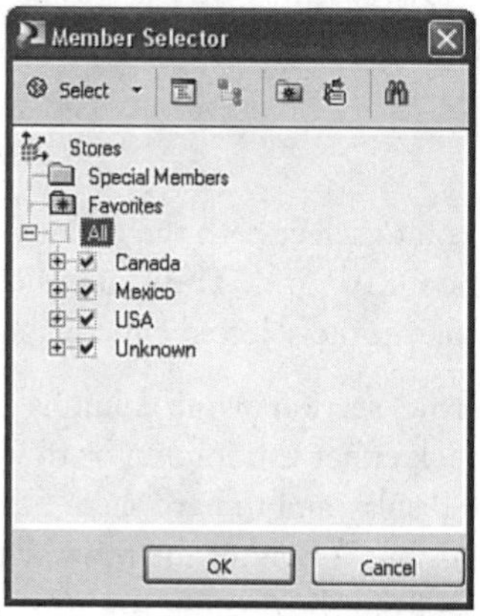

Figure 16.5
Use the Member Selector dialog to select default column and row dimension members.

The last and newest feature of the Rows/Column screen is the Create/Edit Parameter functionality provided for each of the row and column dimensions. This capability provides the business user or report consumer with the capability to interact with the report and control its content by entering parameters that directly affect the dimension members displayed in the OLAP grid(s) on the report.

Because Chapter 5, "Implementing Parameters for Dynamic Reporting," covered parameters in detail, you are familiar with this topic. Of significance for this wizard screen is that the parameter creation process is directly accessible here, and this facilitates the rapid development of formatted and interactive OLAP reports. If necessary, review Chapter 5 for a refresher on creating and editing parameters.

TIP

> The Member Selector dialog provides some powerful shortcuts for the selection of certain logical groups of members. These selection shortcuts are accessible through either the Select drop-down box or by right-clicking on any part of the Member Selection list box. Sample selection shortcuts include the ability to select all base level members or all members at a highlighted level.

Continuing with the creation of the sample report started in the last section, the following steps walk through the Rows/Columns screen part of this report creation example and allow for the refinement of the data to be viewed in the OLAP grid. Follow these steps to add rows and columns to your OLAP-based report:

1. Select the Stores dimension from the available dimensions list as the Row dimension using the row dimension arrow button. (Note: It will likely be necessary to remove a default dimension to ensure that this is the only dimension in the row dimensions list view.)

2. Using the Select Row Members button, select all the store country locations (for example, Canada, USA, and Mexico) from the Member Selector dialog, but deselect the aggregated top-level All field. This enables the OLAP grid to present all the different store types down the side of the grid as rows.

3. Select the Time dimension from the available dimensions list as the Column dimension using the column dimension arrow (>) button. (Note: It will likely be necessary to remove a default dimension to ensure that this is the only dimension in the column dimensions list view.)

4. Using the Select Column Members button, select the quarters Q1, Q2, Q3, and Q4 from the year 1998 from the Member Selector dialog, but be sure not to select any children members. This enables the OLAP grid to present a comparison of the four quarters of data in four side-by-side columns.

5. Click the Next button to proceed.

At this point, you will review the concept of OLAP dimension filters and pages in your OLAP report.

SPECIFYING OLAP DIMENSION SLICES (FILTERS) AND PAGES

The Slice/Page dialog of the OLAP Report Creation Wizard, shown in Figure 16.6, enables you to select values or members for the dimensions not selected to be row or column dimensions. In the OLAP world, these dimensions are *paged* or *sliced dimensions*.

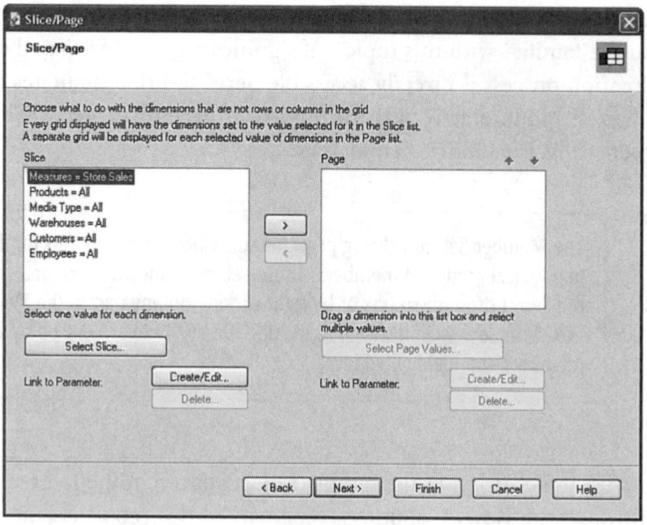

Figure 16.6
The Slice/Page screen of the OLAP Report Creation Wizard allows manipulation of the dimensions not selected for use on either the rows or columns.

The Slice list box lists all the paged dimensions and their current member settings. The default setting is usually all members for any given dimension. An example is that for the Media Type Dimension, the default slice setting is All. To change the member selection (slice) for a particular dimension, that dimension must be selected in the Slice list box, and the Select Slice button must be used to open the familiar Member Selection dialog (refer to Figure 16.5). This dialog is identical to the Member Selector dialog used previously except that you can choose only one member from the selected dimension. If multiple members from a slice dimension are required in a report, use the Page list box and create separate pages/grids for each selected value.

The Page list box is initially empty but can contain any dimensions outside the row and column dimensions that require multiple member selection. An example could involve selecting the three countries of North America as store regions. The selection of multiple values for a paged dimension creates completely separate grids (based on the same preselected rows and columns) for each selected member value. To select multiple members for a dimension, select the involved dimension in the Slice list box and move it to the Page list box using the transfer arrow buttons between the list boxes. After you move the dimension to the Page list box, the Select Page Values button enables multiple member selection through the Member Selector dialog.

The last, but perhaps most powerful, feature of the Slice/Page screen is the Link to Parameter functionality provided for each of the filtered and paged dimensions. This capability provides the business user or report consumer with the capability to interact with the report and control its content by entering parameters that directly affect the information displayed in the OLAP grid(s) on the report.

Of significance for this wizard screen is that the parameter creation process is directly accessible here, which facilitates the rapid development of formatted and interactive OLAP reports.

→ For more information on creating and editing parameters, **see** "Creating and Implementing Parameters Fields," **p. 134**

Continuing with the creation of the sample report, the following steps walk through the Slice/Page dialog part of this report creation example and enable you to select the measure to display in the OLAP grid. Follow these steps to select measures on the page/slice dimensions:

1. Select the Measures dimension from the Slice list box.

2. Instead of selecting a specific filter using the Select Slice button, click the Link to Parameter Create/Edit button to enable the business user to dynamically select this slice every time the report runs. The Create Parameter Field dialog appears, as shown in Figure 16.7.

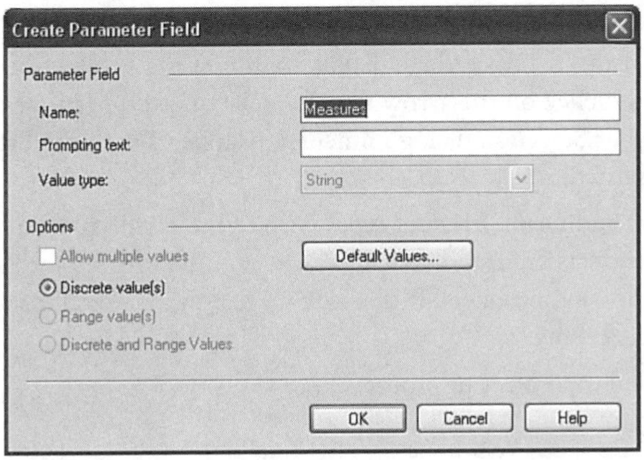

Figure 16.7
The Create Parameter Field dialog called from the Slice/Page screen.

3. In the Prompting Text text box, enter the text that you want your user to be prompted with when this report runs. In this case, it could be something similar to **Please select the measure to be used in your report**. Also, ensure that the Discrete Value(s) radio button is active because a range of entries is not required or allowed here.

4. To avoid requiring users to type in any text, defaults can be set so that selection from a drop-down box is possible. To do this, click the Default Values button. The dialog in Figure 16.8 appears.

5. The Measures table is preselected because the report respects the association with the previously highlighted dimension. Move all the available member values for the Measures dimension to the Description list box by clicking on the Select Default Values button and selecting all the members through the familiar Member Selector dialog.

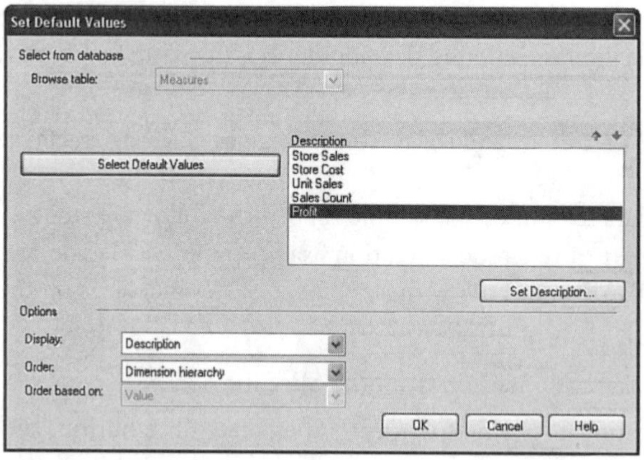

Figure 16.8
The Set Default Values dialog for the OLAP slice parameter.

6. Ensure that the Display drop-down box has Description selected and that the Order drop-down box has no sort selected. Click on OK twice to get back to the Slice/Page dialog of the OLAP Report Creation Wizard.

7. When you return to the Slice/Page dialog, highlight the Products dimension in the Slice list box, and click on the arrow transfer/select button to move it to the Page list box. The Member Selection dialog immediately appears with the Products Dimension Hierarchy presented.

8. Select the Food and Drink Product types (two of the children of All Products), and deselect the All Products field. Individual OLAP grids are created for each of the drink products and the food products. If this isn't clear now, it should make more sense when you visualize the report.

9. Click on OK and then Next to proceed.

CAUTION

> After parameters or multivalue paged dimensions have been set in the OLAP Report Creation Wizard, you can access them for editing only through the OLAP Design Wizard under the main Report menu. These settings are not configurable in the OLAP Expert.

ADDING REPORT STYLES IN THE OLAP REPORT CREATION WIZARD

The Style dialog in the OLAP Report Creation Wizard enables you to select any one of a predetermined number of styles for OLAP grids available in Crystal Reports. Figure 16.9 displays the Style dialog. The styles are a good starting point for formatting the OLAP grids on your reports. You can enhance them through the Customize Style tab of the OLAP Expert (described later in the chapter) and by using many of the advanced formatting features you have already learned about.

Figure 16.9
The Style dialog of
the OLAP Report
Creation Wizard.

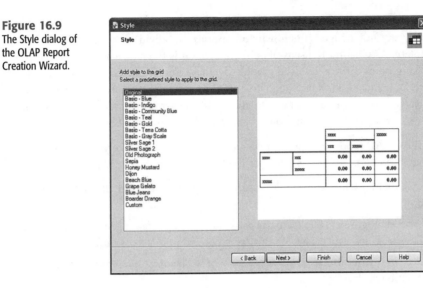

16

ADDING CHARTS VIA THE OLAP REPORT CREATION WIZARD

The Chart dialog provided in the OLAP Report Creation Wizard enables you to quickly add graphics to the OLAP report being created. The graphics available in the wizard, shown in Figure 16.10, are only a subset of the graphics available in Crystal Reports (see Chapter 8, "Visualizing Your Data with Charts and Maps," for a refresher), but they enable a rapid visualization of your OLAP data without using the Chart Expert.

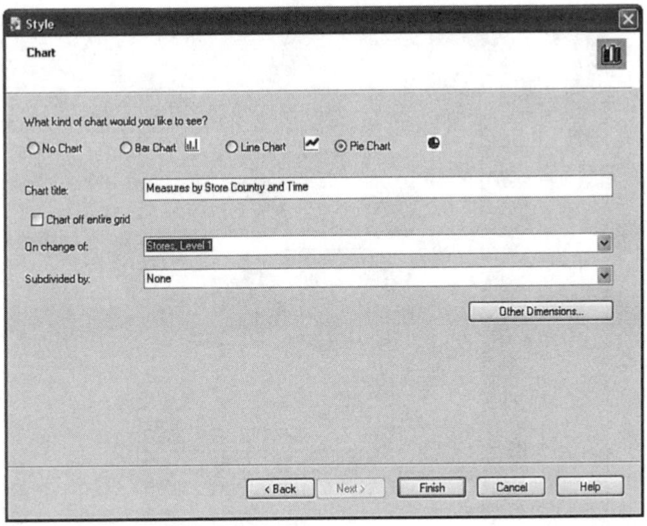

Figure 16.10
The Chart dialog of
the OLAP Report
Creation Wizard
enables you to select
between different
basic chart types.

Aside from selecting the type of chart (bar, line, or pie) and specifying a title on this screen, you must specify an On Change Of field with an optional Subdivided By field before this screen is complete. As Chapter 8 discussed, On Change Of is the data source field that provides the breaking point for the involved graphic. Examples could include country, region, year, store, product, and so on. The Subdivided By field can provide a second variable to base your charts on. An example of a two-variable OLAP chart using the FoodMart sample cube is a chart showing salary information by year and then subdivided by store type.

To complete the OLAP report creation process, the following steps take you through the addition of a style, a chart, and the creation of the finished report:

1. On the Style dialog, select any style that suits your preference, and click on the Next button.

2. On the Chart dialog, select Pie Chart as the chart type by selecting the associated radio button. This provides a nice way of visualizing comparables across different store types.

3. Give your chart a title similar to `Measures by Store Country and Time` by entering it in the Chart Title text box.

4. Select all grid column fields as the On Change Of field. This facilitates the comparison of the three store locales. Select all the grid row fields as the Subdivided By drop-down selection.

5. Click on the Finish button on the OLAP Report Creation Wizard. The wizard prompts you to select a parameter for the Measure dimension. After you select Store Sales (or another field if you prefer), the wizard generates a report that looks similar to Figure 16.11.

Figure 16.11
The sample OLAP report created using the OLAP Report Creation Wizard.

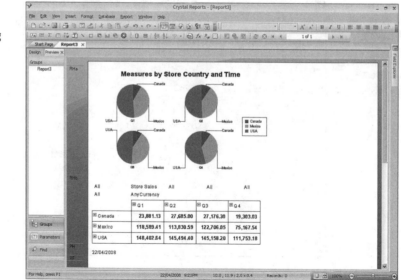

The OLAP Report Creation Wizard provides an efficient and effective method to getting value out of OLAP data in a short time. After placing an OLAP grid or OLAP chart on your report through the wizard, you can perform further formatting and analysis through a variety of built-in Crystal Reports formatting tools. The next two sections explore further customization options, and the three subsequent sections discuss the powerful interactivity available in Crystal Reports OLAP objects.

CUSTOMIZING STYLES IN THE OLAP EXPERT

After an OLAP grid has been added to a report, with or without a selected style, Crystal Reports provides the capability to enhance and customize the formatting of that grid through the Customize Style tab of the OLAP Expert. Figure 16.12 shows the OLAP Expert dialog, which you access by right-clicking on an existing OLAP grid object and selecting OLAP Grid Expert or by selecting the Insert OLAP Grid option from the Insert menu.

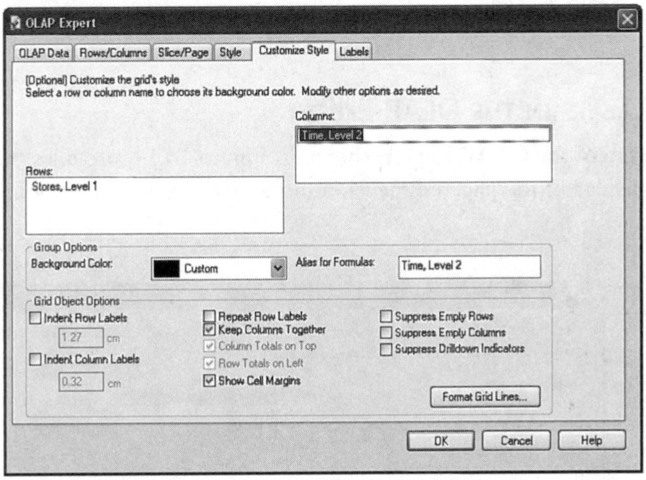

Figure 16.12
The OLAP Expert dialog provides the capability to edit many OLAP grid display properties including the customization of styles.

Four of the tabs in the OLAP Expert have identical functionality to that presented in the previous OLAP Report Creation Wizard sections. The Customize Style tab shown in Figure 16.12 is unique to the OLAP Expert and provides the capability to fine-tune the formatting of the row and column dimensions selected for the involved OLAP grid. By selecting any of the column or row dimensions from the presented list boxes, you can select custom colors for the backgrounds of the OLAP grid row and column headings. The Customize Style tab offers a number of formatting options for the presentation of the grid, including indentation, blank column/row suppression, margins, and labels. Also provided is an option to format grid lines, as shown in Figure 16.13. This dialog enables granular level formatting and selection of grid lines for display on the OLAP grid's layout.

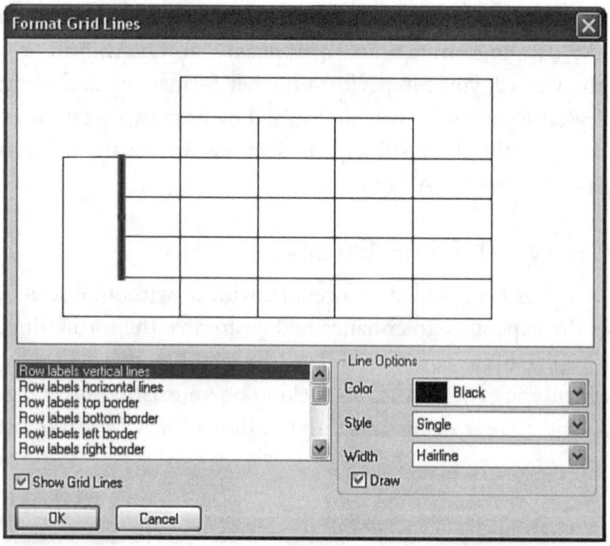

Figure 16.13
The Format Grid Lines dialog is accessed from the Customize Style tab of the OLAP Expert dialog and enables granular-level control of the grid lines in the OLAP grid.

CUSTOMIZING LABELS IN THE OLAP EXPERT

The Labels tab of the OLAP Expert, shown in Figure 16.14, provides the capability to customize the display of the paged dimension (non-row/column dimensions) labels on the OLAP grid.

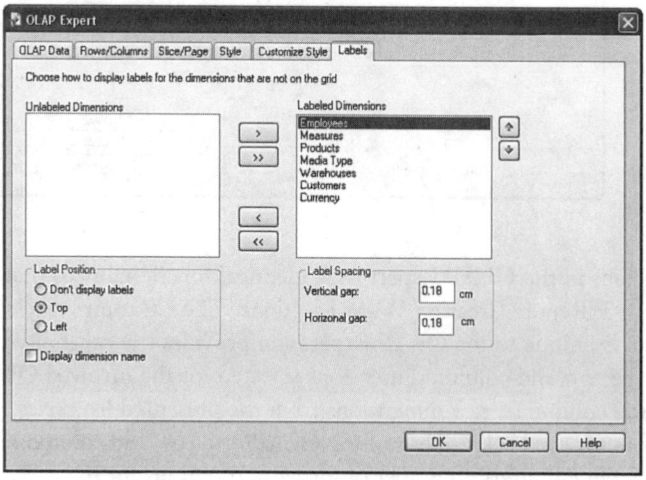

Figure 16.14
The Labels tab of the OLAP Expert enables you to specify display properties around the OLAP grid's dimensions.

Paged/sliced dimension member values for the display grid can be displayed or hidden by simply moving the selected dimension between the unlabeled dimension and labeled dimension list boxes using the transfer arrow (>, >>, <, <<) buttons. You can select additional labeling options such as label location, label spacing, and dimension names in this tab.

ADVANCED OLAP REPORTING

Up to this point, the OLAP Expert and OLAP Report Creation Wizard have demonstrated the capability of Crystal Reports to rapidly create OLAP-based reports. In addition to those capabilities, Business Objects provides advanced analytic capabilities against OLAP data sources through some advanced OLAP-oriented features in Crystal Reports and through a set of online OLAP functionality via BusinessObjects Enterprise's Voyager functionality (formerly called OLAP Intelligence and before that Crystal Analysis). The last four sections of this chapter introduce some of these advanced features for Crystal Reports.

INTERACTING WITH THE OLAP GRID

Crystal Reports provides some powerful interactive OLAP features from within the Crystal Reports Preview and Design tabs. Figure 16.15 displays the right-click menu that appears when you right-click on the year Q4 member in this chapter's sample report.

Figure 16.15
The right-click menu provides access to advanced OLAP features.

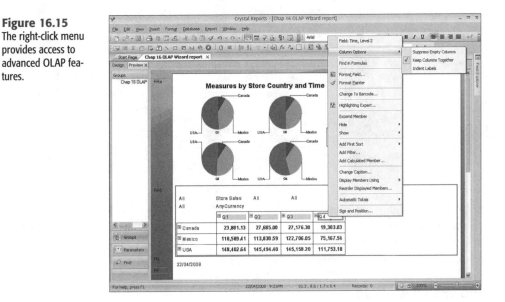

Advanced features made available here include conditional member highlighting, setting column display options, hiding and showing members for asymmetrical reporting, adding calculations, adding filters, reordering members, changing the member caption, expanding members (that is, drilling into the children members), adding sorts, and adding automatic totals to the OLAP grid. Although exploring these features in detail is beyond the scope of this chapter, it is important to note their availability for enhancing your OLAP grid presentations and reports. For detailed information on all these functions, you can review a legacy chapter on OLAP Intelligence that is available at www.usingcrystal.com.

One feature of note is the active nature of the column and row dimensions in the OLAP grid. By double-clicking on any member in either the row or column headings and assuming that the selected member has lower level members (children), the OLAP grid dynamically expands to include that member's children in the grid. In OLAP parlance, this is *drilling down*. Figure 16.16 shows the result of drilling down on the Q4 Header in this chapter's sample report. An alternative means to drilling down is to click on the + icon displayed beside any row or column dimension member.

Figure 16.16
Sample OLAP-based report with Q4 member's children expanded.

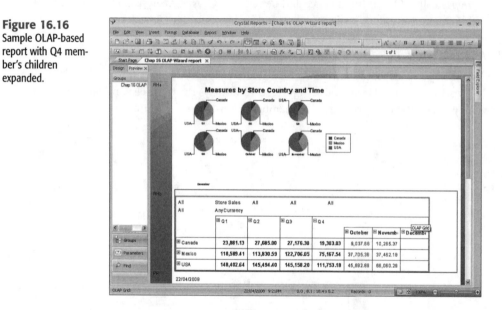

A dimension member can subsequently have its children contracted by double-clicking on the parent member or clicking on the – icon beside the involved parent member. This feature enables you to interactively determine the best static viewpoint to provide to the business user audience for the report.

PIVOTING THE OLAP GRID

After an OLAP grid has been added to a report, as in this chapter's sample, Crystal Reports provides the capability to easily swap the grid's columns and rows. OLAP parlance calls this *pivoting* the OLAP grid. Figure 16.17 highlights this chapter's sample report after pivoting with this function. To access this function, right-click on the OLAP grid and select the Pivot OLAP Grid option. Pivoting the OLAP grid does not affect any OLAP charts or maps already on the report.

This function is particularly useful when attempting to decide which viewpoint of the involved OLAP grid is most helpful to the business users of the report.

Figure 16.17
A preview of the sample report after pivoting the OLAP grid. Notice how the chart and the grid have changed.

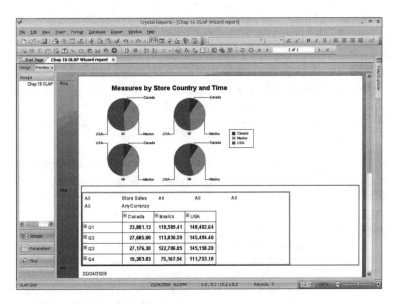

16

USING THE CUBE VIEW FUNCTIONALITY

The Cube View (previously called the OLAP Analyzer) is a powerful worksheet analysis tool introduced in version 9 of Crystal Reports. The Cube View is initiated through the View Cube option on the right-click menu of the OLAP grid (make sure that you don't have any specific grid objects selected) and is accessed through the Cube View tab in the Crystal Reports Designer (see Figure 16.18). Report designers and analysts familiar with other OLAP interface tools are instantly comfortable with the Analyzer because it provides access to the OLAP cube through a traditional OLAP worksheet.

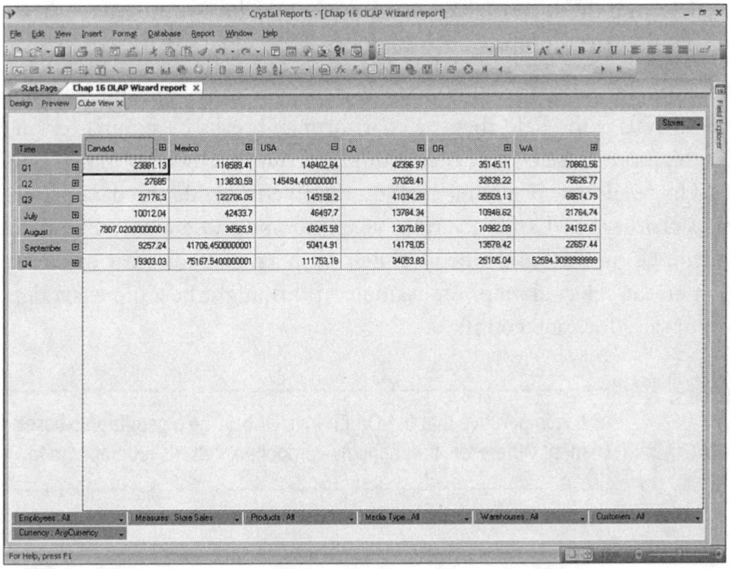

Figure 16.18
The Cube View tab launched by the OLAP Analyzer provides a powerful analytic tool for report designers and power users.

The Cube View tab's worksheet is designed for rapid analysis of the underlying OLAP data through a rich and interactive interface not available in the OLAP grid presented in the Crystal Reports Preview tab. Dimensions can be rapidly shifted, swapped, and nested by double-clicking on them and dragging them into any row, column, or paged dimension area. A dimension member can be quickly expanded and contracted by clicking on its associated + or – icon. A right-click menu in the OLAP Analyzer view of the cube offers access to additional calculations, sorts, filters, automatic totaling, exception highlighting, data analysis, and custom captions.

The Cube View is a powerful report design tool because it lets Crystal Reports developers create impressive flat views of the underlying multidimensional/OLAP data in a short time-frame and subsequently format the created OLAP grid in the Preview tab.

CAUTION

> Although both the Cube View tab and the in-place OLAP grids within the Crystal Reports Designer offer much of the same functionality, not all the work handled in the Cube View necessarily translates back to the related OLAP grid on Crystal Reports. Exception Highlighting and Field Formatting are two examples of functionality that does not cross over. It is generally recommended that the majority of formatting work be done in-place within the Crystal Report's Design or Preview tabs and that cube and dimension orientation be the primary focus of the Cube View tab.

USING CHARTS AND MAPS BASED ON OLAP GRIDS

As described in Chapter 8 and discussed briefly in the "Adding Charts via the OLAP Report Creation Wizard" section earlier in this chapter, OLAP grid data can be presented through visually appealing charts and maps. To create a chart or a map based on OLAP data, an OLAP grid must pre-exist on your report as a data source to form the basis of the chart or map. Selecting the Insert Chart or Map command from the Insert menu (or the respective icons on the Insert toolbar) enables the creation of an OLAP-based visualization.

The creation process for both charts and maps requires the specification of an On Change Of field. This is the field that the chart or map breaks its summaries on (for example, country, state, product, sales rep, and so on). You can specify an optional Subdivided On field as well. The results of specifying an extra variable to divide the data on has different results for various chart types. Explore various charts to find those most suitable for your business problem. Using the Subdivided On field with a map adds a bar or pie chart to every main region on the selected map. An example of this might be a pie chart depicting the break-down of sales for each country.

CAUTION

> It is imperative that the On Change Of field be a geographic-based field when creating a map. Otherwise, the mapping component returns an empty map.

TROUBLESHOOTING

ADDING AN OLAP GRID TO AN EXISTING REPORT

I want to add an aggregated OLAP grid view to an existing drill-down report.

You can quickly accomplish this by accessing the Insert OLAP Grid functionality from the main Insert menu. An alternative approach that might make sense in certain situations is to insert a subreport that points to the involved OLAP data source. Using a subreport to host the OLAP grid enables you to dynamically pass in parameters from the main report to the subreport and its associated OLAP grid. These parameters can dynamically filter the columns, rows, and slices of the involved OLAP grid(s).

CRYSTAL REPORTS IN THE REAL WORLD—OLAP SUMMARY REPORT WITH DRILL-DOWN

The scenario discussed here describes the flexibility behind accessing multidimensional and relational data sources in one report. The benefit of this type of functionality is to enable the user to see aggregated information coming from a cube while allowing drill-down on the relational data to provide greater detail. By using parameters in this report, you let the user decide which information elements to display.

1. Start by creating a simple sales report against the sample Xtreme data source. For the data, select the First Name, Last Name, and Last Year's Sales fields from the Customer table. Group the report by region, city, and then customer. Hide the Details section and the City and Customer groups and enable drill-down on these sections. The report at design time should look like Figure 16.19. Before moving on, add Summary fields for Last Year's Sales into each of the Group Header fields (Country, Region, and City). You can quickly accomplish this by using the new (in version 2008) Add to All Group Levels check box in the Insert Summary dialog.

2. Now add to this report an OLAP grid against the sample cube used earlier in this chapter—Sales and Employees from Foodmart. Using the steps described earlier in this chapter, point the grid at the sample Sales and Employee OLAP cube selecting only the Measures, Time, and Stores dimensions. Select the Stores dimension for the rows and the Time dimension for the columns. Change the Stores rows to include only USA, Canada, and Mexico to limit the number of rows displaying in the report. Also change the Time dimension members selected to Q1, Q2, Q3, and Q4 of 1998.

3. Drop the OLAP grid in the Report Header area. Now insert a bar chart based on the relational source that displays Last Year's Sales on change of values in the City field and place the chart in the Group Header for Country to enable the user to visually under-stand the contribution of sales from each of the selected cities. In design view, the report should look similar to Figure 16.20. Perform the same filtering task in the report Select Expert so that the relational data source is limited to the same three countries (USA, Canada, and Mexico).

Figure 16.19
Framework for drill-down integrating both relational and OLAP data.

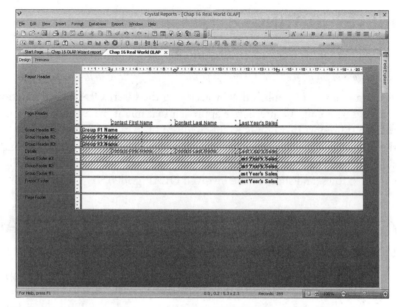

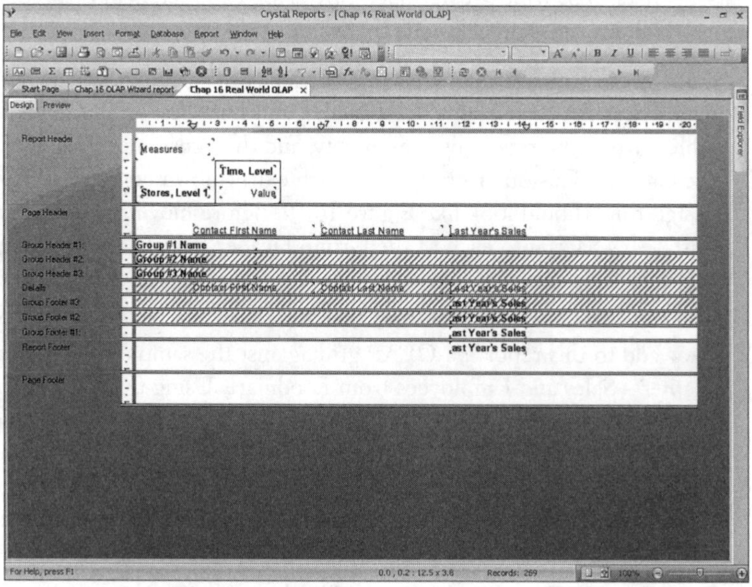

Figure 16.20
A report using both OLAP and relational data sources. The pie chart based on the relational data enables drill-down into the relational data details.

4. If the user viewed this report, he would currently see both the chart and the OLAP grid at the top of the report summarizing the same information but sourced from two different data sources: a pre-aggregated SQL Server data cube and a relational database. (This example assumes that similar data is the basis for both data sources.) To enable end users to turn off the grid display, create a parameter field that specifies whether to

display the grid. This enables users to decide whether they want to look at the summary information in both a grid and chart format or only in a chart.

5. Create a parameter of Boolean type called Display Grid.

6. Conditionally suppress the Report Header section containing the grid based on the values supplied to the parameters by right-clicking on the Report Header and selecting Section Expert from the Report Explorer. Click on the X+2 formula button next to the suppress option. Inside the formula editor, type

   `{?Display Grid}=false`

   and close the editor. Now when a user runs the report, he is prompted to select whether he wants to see the summary OLAP grid. Save the report. On display, it should look similar to Figure 16.21.

Figure 16.21
Report showing both the OLAP grid and charts and enabling drill-down from the high-level summary information displayed from the OLAP grid into the relational details.

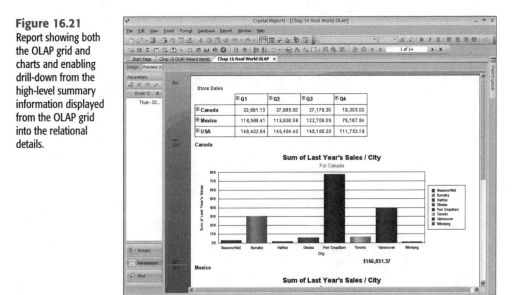

This example illustrates how to combine relational and multidimensional data in one report to allow for different views based on the same underlying data. This allows drill-down on relational elements and provides aggregate header information for views on summary OLAP data.

PART IV

REPORT DISTRIBUTION AND ADVANCED REPORT DESIGN WITH CRYSTAL XCELCIUS

INTRODUCTION TO CRYSTAL REPORTS SERVER, CRYSTALREPORTS.COM, AND THE CRYSTAL REPORTS VIEWER

In this chapter

WHAT IS CRYSTAL REPORTS SERVER?

Crystal Reports Server is a relatively new addition to the Crystal Reports product suite. It allows companies to create, manage, and deliver Crystal Reports over the web or embedded in Enterprise applications. It includes a complete set of reporting services to address all steps in the reporting process, from data access and report design to report delivery and management to portal and application integration to report maintenance. Designed for use on a single server, Crystal Reports Server is ideal for departmental reporting and sharing requirements.

On the surface, Crystal Reports Server looks like BusinessObjects Enterprise (or related mid-sized business product BusinessObjects Edge). Indeed, Crystal Reports Server provides a rich set of Enterprise-level reporting functions including

- Accessing any data source
- Designing any Crystal report
- Delivering and managing Crystal reports over the web
- Integrating reporting with applications and portals
- Maintaining Crystal reports with minimal IT overhead

In fact, the same object model is the basis for both Crystal Reports Server and the BusinessObjects Enterprise and Edge products. The following core components are included in the product:

- Crystal Report Designer (all drivers and access methods)
- Business views
- Report publisher
- InfoView web portal interface
- Portal integration kits
- Viewers
- Scheduler
- Security (BOE, Active Directory, LDAP [Lightweight Directory Access Protocol], and NT authentication)
- Software development kits (SDKs)
- Import Wizard
- Management console

The main differences between Crystal Reports Server and the BusinessObjects Enterprise and Edge products lie in the enterprise-level functionality. BusinessObjects Enterprise (and Edge) is a multiserver Business Intelligence (BI) platform designed to address large-scale reporting and BI requirements. The multiserver capability of the environment provides fault tolerance, load balancing, scalability, and reliability. BusinessObjects Enterprise also provides enterprise-level features such as auditing, Crystal Reports Explorer, dashboarding, and the Encyclopedia and Process Tracker.

Crystal Reports Server is a single-server enterprise reporting solution that delivers Crystal Reports over the web. It does not support Web Intelligence, Crystal Xcelsius, Performance Manager Dashboards, and Scorecards or other BI content.

Compared to BusinessObjects Enterprise, Crystal Reports Server focuses more on addressing the reporting infrastructure needs of small- to middle-sized companies. It has the following limitations over BusinessObjects Enterprise:

- **Concurrent access license (CAL) limitation**—Crystal Reports Server is limited to a maximum of 20 concurrent users. An error message displays when an administrator attempts to enter key codes for more than 20 CALs.
- **Scalability limitations**—Crystal Reports Server can run on only a single server and there is a license limiting the installation to a maximum four-processor server.
- **Platform limitation**—Crystal Reports Server runs only on Windows, Red Hat 3.0 Advanced / Enterprise Server, SuSe, and Linux 9.0, whereas BusinessObjects Enterprise runs on other operating systems, such as AIX and Solaris.
- **Content limitation**—Crystal Reports Server runs only Crystal Reports; it does not run Web Intelligence or Desktop Intelligence reports.

CRYSTAL REPORTS SERVER ARCHITECTURE

Crystal Reports Server is a multitier system. Although responsible for different tasks, components can form logical groups based on the type of work they perform.

Crystal Reports Server has five tiers: the client tier, the application tier, the intelligence tier, the processing tier, and the data tier. Figure 17.1 illustrates how each component fits within the multitier system.

The servers run as services on Windows machines. On UNIX, the servers run as daemons. These services can run in multiple instances on a single machine.

CLIENT TIER

The client tier is the part of the Crystal Reports Server system that administrators and end users interact with directly. This tier comprises the applications that enable people to administer, publish, and view web content such as Crystal Reports.

The client tier includes the Central Configuration Manager (CCM), Central Management Console (CMC), Publishing Wizard, Import Wizard, and InfoView.

Figure 17.1
The relationships between the BusinessObjects Enterprise tiers.

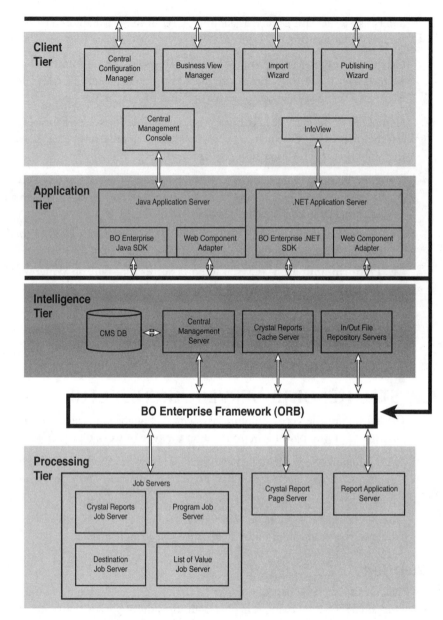

Application Tier

The application tier hosts the server-side components that process requests from the client tier as well as the components that communicate the requests to the appropriate server in the intelligence tier. The application tier includes support for report viewing and logic to understand and direct web requests to the appropriate Crystal Report server in the intelligence tier. The application tier includes application tier components, web development platforms, and web application environments.

For the Java and .NET platforms, the application tier includes the Application Server, Crystal Reports Server SDK, and Web Component Adapter (WCA). In Crystal Reports Server XI, the web server communicates directly with the Application Server.

Crystal Reports Server systems that use the Java SDK or the .NET SDK will run on a third-party application server.

The Application Server acts as the gateway between the web server and the rest of the components in Crystal Reports Server. The Application Server is responsible for processing requests from the user's browser and hosts InfoView and other Business Objects applications. The SDK is a software development kit that exposes the functionality of Crystal Reports Server to developers.

The WCA runs within the Application Server and provides all services not directly supported by the SDK. The web server passes requests directly to the Application Server, which then forwards the requests to the WCA. The Web Component Adapter provides support for the legacy Crystal Web Architecture CSP and CWR. These include the CMC, Active X, and Java Viewer.

INTELLIGENCE TIER

The intelligence tier manages the Crystal Reports Server system. It maintains all the security information, sends requests to the appropriate servers, manages audit information, and stores report instances. The intelligence tier includes the Central Management Server, Cache Server, File Repository Server, and Event Server.

The Central Management Server (CMS) is responsible for maintaining a database of information about the system. The data stored by the CMS includes information about users and groups, security, folders and report objects, and servers. The CMS also maintains the repository and a separate audit database of information about user actions.

The Cache Server is responsible for handling all report-viewing requests. The Cache Server checks whether it can fulfill the request with a cached report page. If the Cache Server finds a cached page that displays exactly the required data (with data that has been refreshed from the database), it returns that cached report page to the user. If the Cache Server cannot fulfill the request with a cached report page, it passes the request to the Page Server. The Page Server runs the report and returns the results to the Cache Server. The Cache Server then caches the report page for future use and serves the page to the viewer. By storing report pages in a cache, Crystal Reports Server avoids accessing the database every time a user requests a report. If multiple Page Servers are running for a single Cache Server, the Cache Server automatically balances the processing load across Page Servers.

There is an Input and an Output File Repository Server in every Crystal Reports Server implementation. The Input File Repository Server manages all the report objects and program objects published to the system by administrators or end users (using the Publishing Wizard, the Central Management Console, the Import Wizard, or a Business Objects designer component, such as Crystal Reports or the Web Intelligence Java or HTML

Report Panels). The Output File Repository Server manages all the report instances generated by the Report Job Server. The File Repository Servers are responsible for listing files on the server, querying for the size of a file, querying for the size of the entire file repository, adding files to the repository, and removing files from the repository.

The Event Server manages file events. When the appropriate file appears in the monitored directory, the Event Server triggers the file event and notifies the CMS that the file event occurred. The CMS then starts any jobs that are dependent on the file event. After notifying the CMS of the event, the Event Server resets itself and again monitors the directory for the appropriate file.

PROCESSING TIER

The processing tier accesses the data and generates the reports. It is the only tier that interacts directly with the databases that contain the report data. The processing tier includes the Report Job Server, Program Job Server, Report Application Server (RAS), Destination Job Server, List of Values Job Server, and Page Server.

A Job Server processes scheduled actions on objects at the request of the CMS. A Job Server can be configured to process either report objects or program objects. If configured to process report objects, a Job Server becomes a Report Job Server. The Report Job Server processes scheduled reports, as requested by the CMS, and generates report instances. (*Instances* are versions of a report object that contain saved data.) To generate a report instance, the Report Job Server obtains the report object from the Input File Repository, opens the report, executes the SQL for the report, and saves both the report object and the data to the Output File Repository when all the data has been returned to the report.

The RAS processes reports that users view with the Advanced DHTML viewer. The RAS service also provides the ad hoc reporting capabilities that allow users to create and modify Crystal Reports over the web. The RAS service is very similar to the Page Server: It, too, is primarily responsible for responding to page requests by processing reports and generating cache pages. However, the RAS service uses an internal caching mechanism that involves no interaction with the Cache Server. As with the Page Server, the RAS service supports COM, ASP.NET, and Java viewer SDKs. The Report Application Server also includes an SDK for report creation and modification, providing you with tools for building custom report interaction interfaces.

The Page Server is primarily responsible for responding to page requests by processing reports and generating Encapsulated Page Format (EPF) pages. Each EPF page contains formatting information that defines the layout of a single report page. The Page Server retrieves data for the report from an instance or directly from the database. When retrieving data from the database, the Page Server automatically disconnects from the database after it fulfills its initial request and reconnects to retrieve additional data if necessary. The Cache Server and Page Server work closely together. Specifically, the Page Server responds to page requests made by the Cache Server. The Page Server and Cache Server also interact to ensure the reuse of cached EPF pages as frequently as possible and to ensure that new pages generate as soon as they are required. Crystal Reports Server takes advantage of this behavior by ensuring that the majority of report-viewing requests go to the Cache Server and Page Server. (However, if a user's default viewer is the Advanced DHTML viewer, the RAS processes the report.)

DATA TIER

The data tier is made up of the databases that contain the data used in the reports. BusinessObjects Enterprise supports a wide range of corporate databases.

CRYSTAL REPORTS SERVER APPLICATIONS

Crystal Reports Server provides several client tier applications that enable people to administer the system as well as to publish, view, and manage web content.

CENTRAL CONFIGURATION MANAGER

The CCM is a server-management tool that allows you to configure the Apache Tomcat server and the Server Intelligence Agent (SIA). New for version 2008, other Crystal Report Server services are now only configurable through the Central Management Console and are no longer available here. This tool allows an administrator to start, stop, enable, and disable the Apache or SIA service and to view and configure advanced server settings on these two services. The CCM also allows an administrator to add or remove SIA servers from the Crystal Reports Server system.

To launch the CCM, go to the Start button and click on Programs, Crystal Reports Server 2008, Crystal Reports Server 2008, Central Configuration Manager. Figure 17.2 shows the CCM.

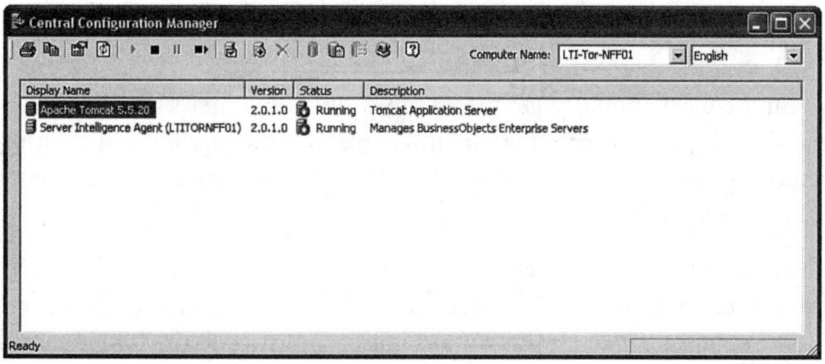

Figure 17.2
The Central Configuration Manager for the Crystal Reports Server. The pull-down menu by the computer name on the top-right corner of the CCM displays the Central Management Server to which the CCM is connected.

The CCM displays the Apache and SIA servers for the involved Crystal Reports Server implementation. To start, stop, enable, and disable servers, click on the corresponding buttons on the toolbar. To view and change the configurations of a certain server, right-click on the display name of the server and left-click on the Properties menu item on the pop-up

menu (see Figure 17.3). To add and remove servers, click on the Add Server and Delete
Server buttons on the toolbar.

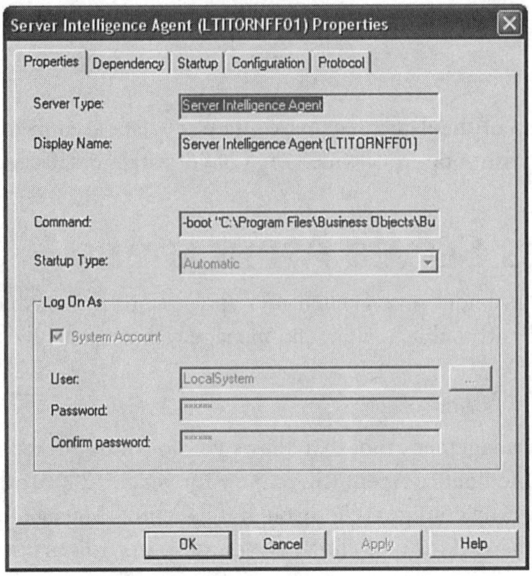

Figure 17.3
View server proper-
ties by using the
CCM.

USE THE CENTRAL MANAGEMENT CONSOLE (CMC)

You can launch the CMC via different menu paths, depending on which application tier is
used. For .NET, go to Microsoft Start, Programs, BusinessObjects 11 or XI, Crystal
Reports Server, .NET Administration Launchpad. For Java, go to Microsoft Start,
Programs, Crystal Reports Server 2008, Crystal Reports Server, Central Management
Console. After logging on, the administrator sees the CMC home page shown in Figure
17.4.

From the CMC home page, the administrator can enter various areas to conduct administrative tasks, such as creating, organizing, and removing folders; creating, organizing, and
removing users and user groups; and publishing reports and other content into the Crystal
Reports Server.

To create a new folder, click on the Folders link in the Organize area. Select the New
Folder action from the Manage drop down-box in the subsequent page. After selecting the
New Folder menu action shown in Figure 17.5, specify the folder name and other proper-
ties of the folders and click on OK.

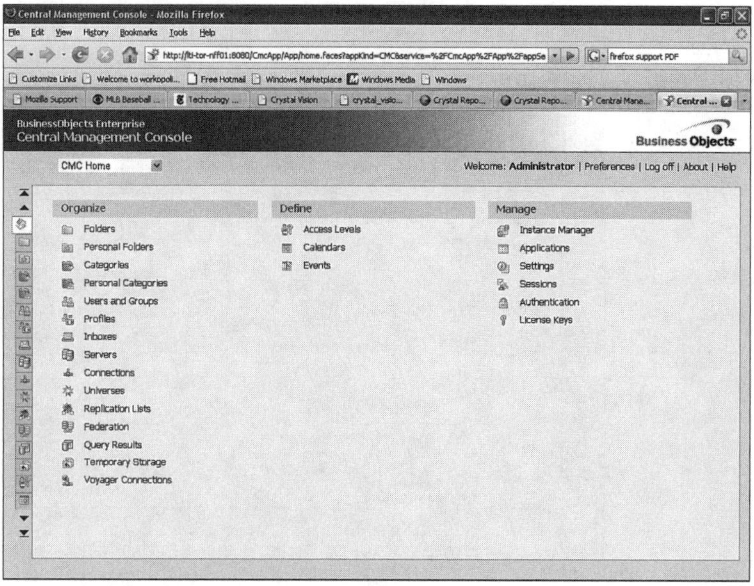

Figure 17.4
The Crystal Reports
Server Central
Management Console
home page.

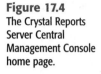

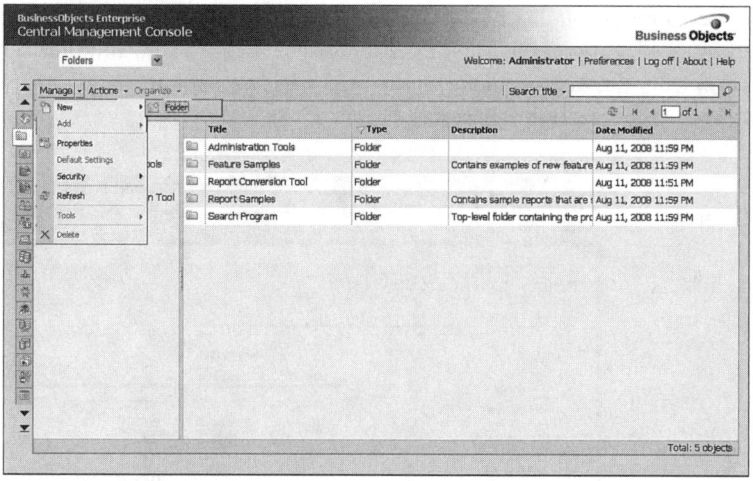

Figure 17.5
Create a new folder
in Crystal Reports
Server.

To publish a report to a specified folder in Crystal Reports Server, navigate to that folder in CMC and click the Manage drop-down menu. In the Manage drop-down menu, select the Add and Crystal Report options, and the New Object page displays as shown in Figure 17.6.

Specify the Crystal Report file to publish using the file browser, and click on OK.

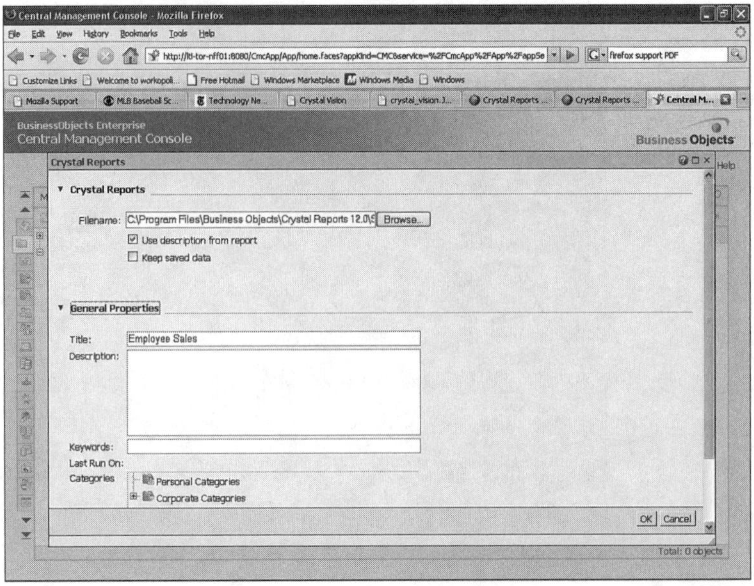

Figure 17.6
Publish a Crystal Report to the Crystal Reports Server.

To view a report on demand, navigate to the folder where the report is located, highlight the report by clicking on the title of the report you want to run, and then select the View menu option from the Actions menu. If the report has no parameters, the report viewer launches to display the resulting report (see Figure 17.7).

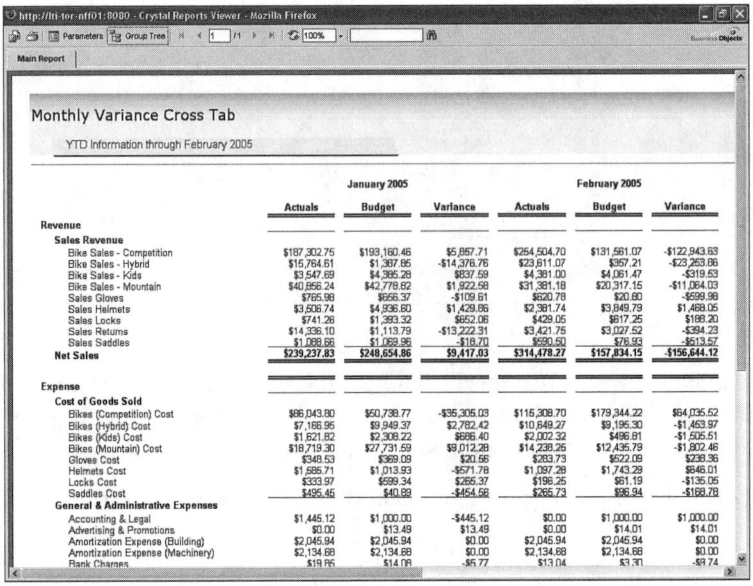

Figure 17.7
The Crystal Reports viewer.

If the report has report parameters, the report viewer launches to display the report parameter page for the user to fill in (see Figure 17.8). After the user specifies the input parameters and clicks on OK, the report viewer displays the resulting report.

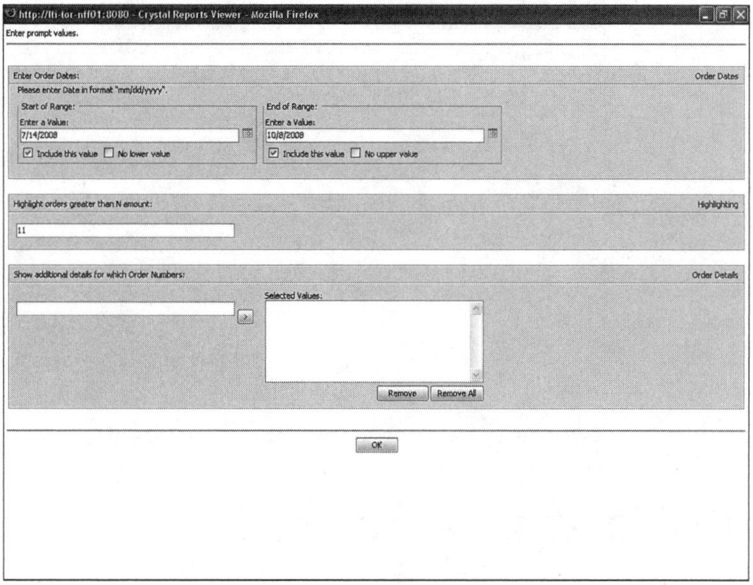

Figure 17.8
The report parameter page.

LAUNCH INFOVIEW

InfoView is a web-based portal interface for end users to view and schedule reports and to manage their content. To launch InfoView, go to Microsoft Start, Programs, Crystal Reports Server 2008, Crystal Reports Server, Java InfoView (or .NET InfoView, depending on whether the .NET or Java environment has been configured). Figure 17.9 shows the InfoView portal.

Recent versions of the InfoView and the providing BusinessObjects Enterprise infrastructure that supports both Crystal Reports Server and BusinessObjects Enterprise are covered in detail in chapters provided at www.usingcrystal.com.

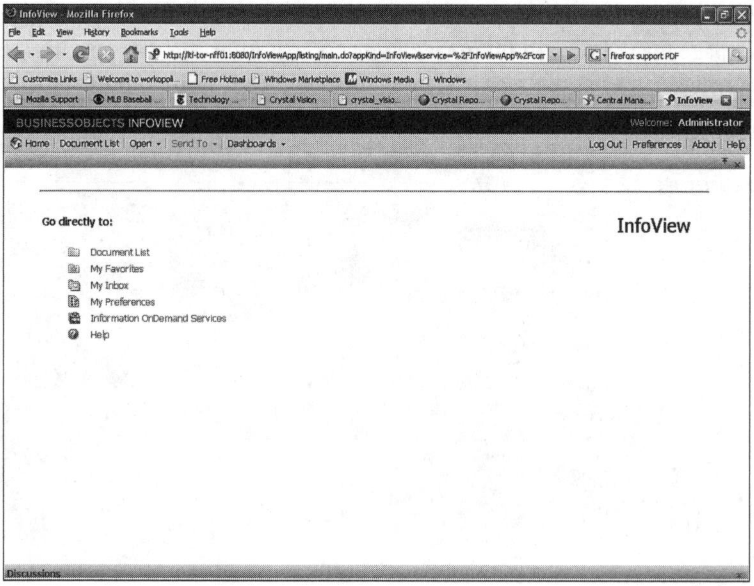

Figure 17.9
InfoView for Crystal
Reports Server.

WHAT IS CRYSTALREPORTS.COM?

Crystalreports.com is a new web-based report-sharing service that enables you to instantly share your Crystal Reports with other people in a straightforward manner over the web. Unlike Crystal Reports Server, described previously in this chapter, crystalreports.com does not require the installation of any software or the management of any servers. It is a hosted service provided over the Internet for distribution of Crystal Reports, Crystal Xcelsius reports, and related Crystal documents. Figure 17.10 displays a report viewed through crystalreports.com and highlights that nothing beyond a web browser is required to view previously published reports through this service.

For many firms and people unable to divert resources to support enterprise-level reporting solutions, the traditional alternative has been to export Crystal reports into static formats such as Excel or Adobe PDF and then deliver them via email or printed paper. Although a low-cost solution, it lacked security, scalability, and interactivity, and it clogged internal networks and email inboxes with hundreds of often overlooked files. Crystalreports.com provides a cost effective (free to start), secure, and scalable alternative.

GETTING STARTED WITH CRYSTALREPORTS.COM

The good news is that you can get started immediately with the Standard version of crystalreports.com by visiting the website and registering. This free version of the service enables you to publish up to 10 reports holding up to 50MB of data and share them with up to three users. Business Objects provides an upgrade path (with increased cost) to increased numbers of reports, size of data, and number of users if you decide to scale your use of the service. Figure 17.11 displays the home page for crystalreports.com.

Figure 17.10
A Sales Dashboard report displayed in a web browser at crystalreports.com.

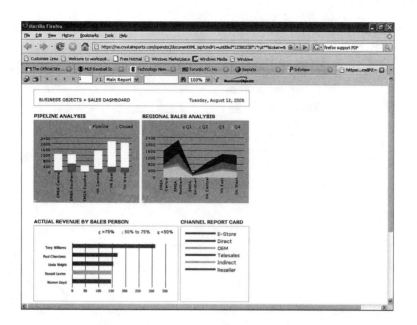

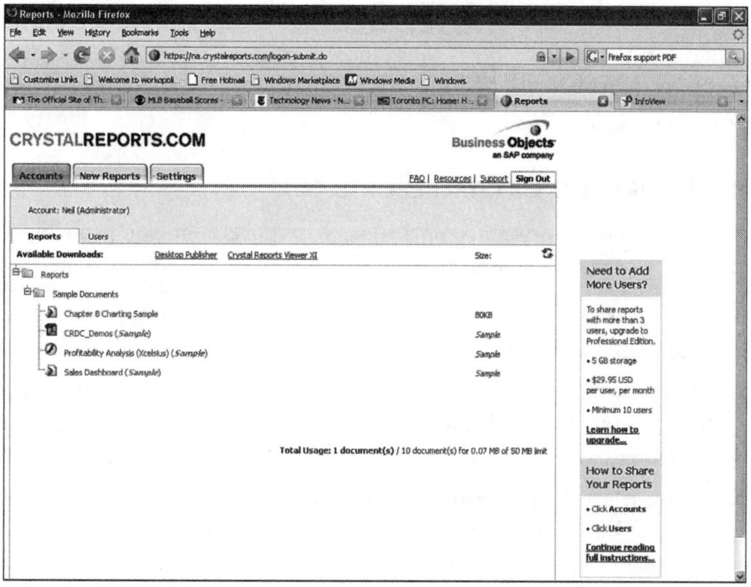

Figure 17.11
The crystalreports.com home page where you can register for each provided service level.

ADDING REPORTS TO CRYSTALREPORTS.COM

After you register with the crystalreports.com service, adding reports is very easy. From the Accounts tab of the user interface, click on the drop-down box indicator beside the folder that you want to add the report to. As Figure 17.12 highlights, select the Add Document menu option and select the relevant report to add from your desktop.

Figure 17.12
Adding a report to crystalreports.com is simple and easy.

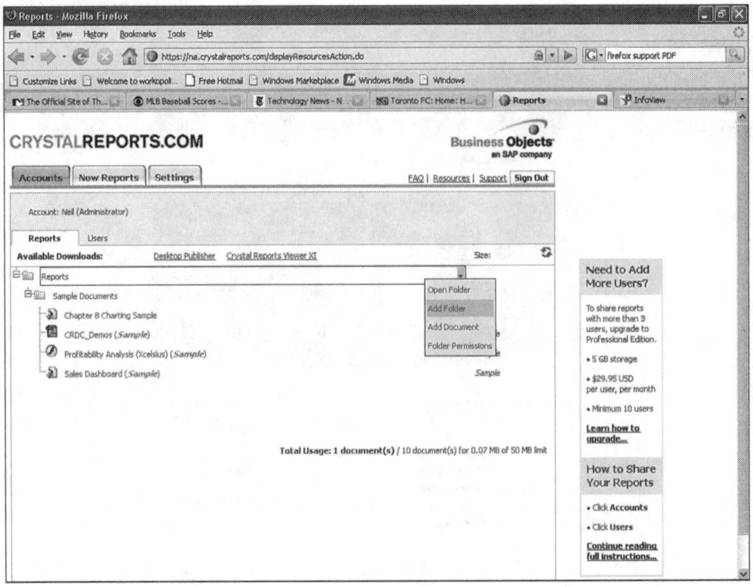

In addition to this simple method, crystalreports.com provides a report publisher that enables you to publish reports to crystalreports.com and update the saved data within them directly from your desktop. You can download this desktop report publisher from crystalreports.com.

SHARING REPORTS ON CRYSTALREPORTS.COM

After you add one or more reports to crystalreports.com, you probably want to share them with your report consumers. To accomplish this, follow a few simple steps:

1. Add a new user group to the system under the Accounts tab and the Users menu item as highlighted in Figure 17.13.

2. Select the newly added user group's drop-down indicator and grant group permissions to this group as you deem appropriate. These permissions map to the available folders, and you can allow certain users to see only particular folders.

3. Again, select the new group's drop-down indicator and select the Add User menu option. You receive a prompt for a user's email address and name. After you enter this information, the added user receives an email that provides a temporary password and a link to your reports.

You can view some of the book and website samples by logging on to crystalreports.com with the email ID sample@usingcrystal.com and the password BlueJays.

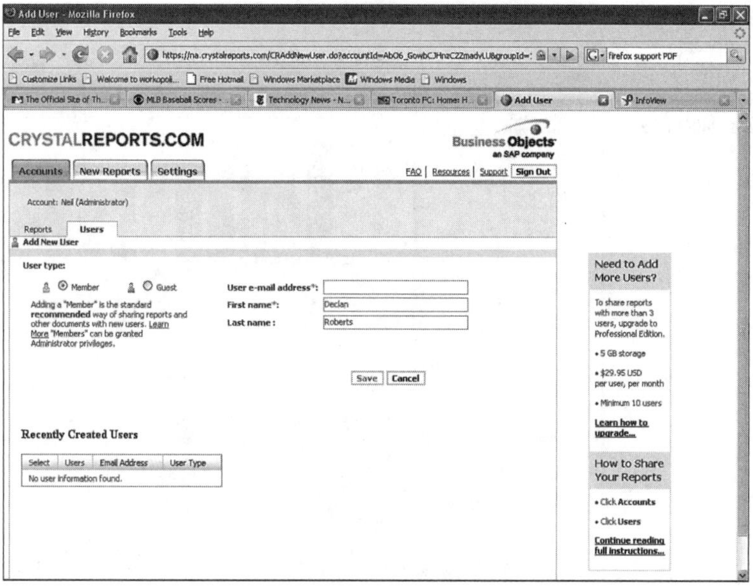

Figure 17.13
Adding a user group to crystalreports.com is the first step in securing access for your report users.

OFFLINE VIEWING WITH THE CRYSTAL REPORTS VIEWER

As you create Crystal Reports and begin to share them with your user community, it is expected that many of them will not have copies of Crystal Reports nor will they be licensed on any of the enterprise (or web) Crystal Reports distribution systems. If your current budget doesn't allow for securing any of those licenses and you want to avoid the need to export to Excel, PDF, or other formats, there is still a viable method to share your Crystal Reports: the free offline Crystal Reports Viewer. Crystal Reports Viewer is a free standalone RPT file viewer that allows users to open, explore, and view reports straight from their desktop when working both off and online. They can generate customized views of the data without the need for a report designer or report engine. Report sharing is also possible via email or with crystalreports.com, as discussed earlier.

The offline viewer is available as a free download to registered users of crystalreports.com and directly from the Business Objects website at http://businessobjects.com/products/reporting/crystalreports/viewer/en/register.asp. By distributing this viewer to your users, they can view reports that you have created, interact with them, print them, email them, and export them into different formats. Figure 17.14 highlights the Crystal Reports Viewer with one of the Chapter 8 sample reports.

Figure 17.14
Viewing a Crystal Report with the Crystal Reports Viewer is a viable preliminary step into report sharing.

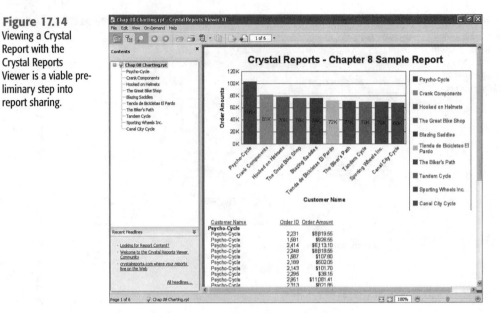

TROUBLESHOOTING

When trying to publish an Xcelsius model to InfoView, I get an error: `"The InfoObject plugin 'CrystalEnterprise.Flash' is not installed properly."`

The Web Services Wizard needs to be installed on the Business Objects Server. The install can be found on the CD in the folder `\Collaterals\Add-Ons\Web Services\`.

CHAPTER 18

CRYSTAL REPORTS JAVA COMPONENTS

In this chapter

OVERVIEW OF THE CRYSTAL REPORTS JAVA REPORTING COMPONENT

Business Objects has had a commitment to Java developers for quite some time. Crystal Reports version 9 included a Java edition of the Report Application Server Software Development Kit (SDK), and Crystal Enterprise version 8.5 had a Java edition of the Crystal Enterprise SDK. Both of these solutions consisted of a processing tier of non–Java-based services and then an application tier of Java-based objects that acted as the entry point to those services. The theme here was around multitier, large-scale, enterprise applications. This might sound quite natural to some Java developers, who would argue that's what Java is for.

In the version 11 suite of products, the Report Application Server and corresponding Java SDK have been moved out of the Crystal Reports product line and into the BusinessObjects Enterprise product line. This makes it clear that all servers are part of the BusinessObjects Enterprise offering. However, without any other changes, this would leave the Crystal Reports product without any Java-based developer components. Because developers have always been important to Business Objects—especially Java developers—the Business Objects folks have spent a significant amount of time building a new offering in version 2008 for Java developers: the Crystal Reports Java Reporting Component.

The key word in the name of the Java Reporting Component is *component*. There is a clear distinction between the Crystal Reports–based developer solutions and the Crystal Enterprise–based developer solutions. This is based around the distinction between components and servers. Crystal Reports provides reporting components, and BusinessObjects Enterprise provides reporting servers. The following sections describe some of the key differences between components and servers.

There have been a number of improvements made to the Crystal Reports 2008 Java components. This is especially true around the viewing components, where you will first notice the new look and feel of the user interface. But you'll also notice the additional functionality that has been added—such as the new parameter panel that allows you to see and change the parameter values within the viewer, and on report sort controls that allow you to sort the report by clicking on the up/down arrows next to the column header. Furthermore, you can now export the report to XML format right from within the viewer because this additional export format has been added to the list of export format options. Finally, worth noting here is the ability to embed Flash objects into the report. When viewing the report through the viewer, you can share the data between the report and the Flash object by using Flash variable support added to the report engine.

COMPONENTS RUN ON THE WEB APPLICATION SERVER

Components are self-contained and reside on the web application tier. They are single tier in that there is no separation between the programmatic interface and the report processing.

Although they can be run on multiple machines in a web application server farm, they themselves are individual components and have no built-in mechanism to load balance or share state.

Although this kind of deployment architecture is initially attractive to many Java developers, many eventually find that the report processing degrades the performance of the web application server to an unsatisfactory level. Keep in mind the size of your user audience before deciding to do all report processing on the web tier.

COMPONENTS ARE GENERALLY LESS SCALABLE

Although the actual report processing of a single report is generally done just as fast with a component as it is done with a server, the capability to scale the components differs. Although a farm can be created, components running on different machines are not aware of each other and thus don't have the smarts to figure out which component is least busy or has some information that is needed by another server. In general, the servers provide a more scalable, extensible solution for high-volume reporting. Obviously, cost can be a factor because the server solutions have higher licensing costs, so do your research about the product capabilities before you start development.

COMPONENTS ARE 100% PURE JAVA

Besides product line differentiation, the other reason Business Objects created the Java Reporting Component was so it would have a 100% pure Java reporting engine. Although the server solutions have a pure Java SDK, the Java Reporting Component consists entirely of native Java code. This is attractive to both Java purists and also partners who embed Crystal Reports technology inside Java-based applications, and finally for customers wanting to deploy a reporting component on a UNIX platform. Providing a 100% pure Java reporting engine means that Business Objects rewrote a portion of the Crystal Reports engine into Java. Because this was not a total port of the functionality, some reporting features are not available. However, in practical terms, most reports off standard relational data will run just fine.

UNDERSTANDING THE JAVA REPORTING COMPONENTS ARCHITECTURE

Now that you know why Business Objects created the Java Reporting Component and how it differs from some of the server solutions, you will move on to learning more about the components. The Java Reporting Component has three main pieces to it, as shown here:

- A report engine
- Report viewer controls
- Helper tag libraries

The report engine is the component that processes the reports. Its job is to load the report template (.rpt file), run the query to the data source, process the report's pages, and communicate with the report viewer controls to provide the information they need to render the reports. The main report viewer is an HTML viewer control that is used to display the report's output in JSP pages or servlets. The other viewer control is used to view the reports in other formats such as Rich Text Format (RTF) or PDF. Finally, there are helper tag libraries that make the process of using the report viewers easier by wrapping up their logic into a simple tag that can be inserted into JSP pages. Also of note is that the Java Reporting Component has integration with both Borland JBuilder and BEA WebLogic; more will be discussed on what this integration provides later in this chapter.

From an architecture point of view, all these components reside on the Java application server. The officially supported application servers are

- BEA WebLogic 7 (SP1)
- BEA WebLogic 8.1
- IBM WebSphere 5.0 (Fix-pack 2)
- Tomcat 4.1.27

NOTE

If the exact application server or version of application server you are targeting is not listed here, it does not necessarily mean that the Java Reporting Component will not work there. It just means that it was not one of the configurations explicitly tested by Business Objects, and although not "officially supported," chances are you will be able to use it. If you are unsure, contact Business Objects to see whether it is aware of any issues with that particular application server. There are customers using other application servers such as JBoss in production today.

Although the Java Reporting Component comes with some JSP and servlet samples, the actual API is simply raw Java classes. These classes can be used inside of JSPs (JavaServer Pages), servlets, EJBs (Enterprise JavaBeans), or other web-based technologies. The advantage here is that there is no dependency on any particular version of the J2EE specifications such as servlets or struts. You might have noticed that desktop applications have not been mentioned thus far. This is because there is not currently a desktop viewer control (that is, based on the AWT [Abstract Window Toolkit] or Swing frameworks). Because the viewer controls that exist are dependent on a web framework being in place—they require servlet-based objects in order to work—there is currently no way to view reports in desktop applications. At the time of this writing, Business Objects has expressed interest in producing a desktop report viewer for the Java world at some point in the future. Check back with the company if you're interested. In the meantime, a good solution for delivering reports inside desktop applications is to host a web browser applet inside of a Java form.

DIFFERENCES WITH THE JAVA REPORTING ENGINE

Although there are clear advantages to having a 100% pure Java reporting engine, the developers at Business Objects had to rewrite it from scratch. Anytime a large software component such as the Crystal Reports engine is rewritten, there are bound to be some differences, at least in the first version. Some of those differences are conscious decisions made by Business Objects to limit the scope of the development to meet the target release date. Other differences surface because of development platform differences: Java versus native Windows. The result is that some features are not currently supported by the report processing engine included with the Java Reporting Component. The following sections address some of these issues.

SUPPORTED FILE FORMATS

The first and most important limitation is that only versions 9, 10, and XI report files are supported. This doesn't mean that reports designed in version 8.5 or earlier are useless, but it does mean they have to be converted to version 9. To make this process easier, you can download a Report Conversion Utility from the Business Objects website. It can open up reports in batch, make any necessary changes, and save them into a version 9/10/XI file format. New reports can be created using the standard Crystal Reports 2008 designer.

TIP

> The file format has not had major changes between version 9, 10, XI, and 2008 of Crystal Reports. If you have report files created in version 11, you can generally use them in version 2008 applications.

18

SUPPORT FOR USER FUNCTION LIBRARIES IN VERSION XI OF THE JAVA REPORTING COMPONENTS

Historically, the ability to define your own functions that extend the power of the Crystal Report's formula language has been available through the ability to write your own COM libraries that can be utilized within the report's formula designer. Such functionality could be implemented by writing your own DLL in any COM development environment, such as C++ and Visual Basic.

As of version XI of the report designer component, this functionality can now be built and leveraged inside the Java report engine API. This is accomplished by implementing a class that exposes methods consumed by the Crystal Report.

NOTE

> Keep in mind that inside one report there can only be one flavor of the UFL (user function library) implementation, meaning you cannot utilize both COM and Java UFLs.

Example creating a user-defined function:

```
public class UserFunction1 implements FormulaFunction
import com.crystaldecisions.reports.formulas.*;
import com.crystaldecisions.reports.common.value.*;
public FormulaValue evaluate (FormulaValueReference[] arguments)
throws FormulaFunctionCallException
{
    String strArg0 = ((StringValue)arguments[0].getFormulaValue()).getString();
    String string1 = "Input entered: " + strArg0;
    FormulaValue formulaVal = StringValue.fromString(string1);
    return formulaVal;
}
}
```

In the preceding example, the function simply returns a string value supplied as an argument to the calling function inside the formula workshop. All user-defined functions appear under additional function tree items inside the formula editor.

THE JAVA REPORTING ENGINE USES JDBC

Another difference related to the Java platform is the way queries are run against the database. Although the Windows world has many different data access technologies, Java has just one: Java Database Connectivity (JDBC). Prior to version XI, Crystal Reports did not support JDBC, but a new JDBC driver is available since version XI is a website download, and version 2008 is the JDBC driver is available as part of the main installation.

For any new reports that you develop, choosing JDBC is generally the best approach. You will save yourself time and effort this way. The Crystal Reports JDBC driver shows up as "JDBC (JNDI)" in the Crystal Reports data explorer when creating a new report. It has two ways to connect to a data source: through a JDBC URL or a JNDI (Java Naming and Directory Interface) reference. This can be problematic at times because there are several steps involved in setting up your environment for JDBC access. Make sure you take your time going through the steps, and double-check the changes you are making.

When connecting via a JDBC URL, you need to specify two items:

- **Connection URL**—A standard JDBC URL that specifies a data source
- **Database classname**—The fully qualified classname of the JDBC driver

The best way to figure out what these two values should be is to consult the documentation for the JDBC driver you'd like to use. The following bullets provide sample connection information for connecting to SQL Server using the SQL Server JDBC driver. Figure 18.1 shows this information being used from the Crystal Reports designer.

- **Connection URL**—`jdbc:microsoft:sqlserver://abc:1433` (where `abc` is the name of the server running on port 1433)
- **Database classname**—`com.microsoft.jdbc.sqlserver.SQLServerDriver`

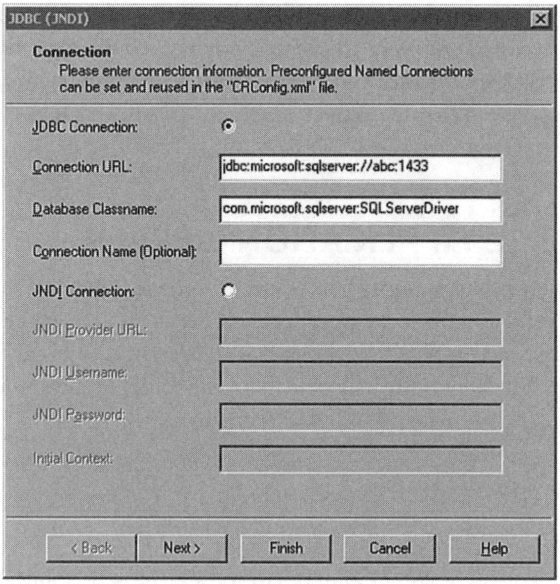

Figure 18.1
Connect to a JDBC
data source through
the Crystal Reports
designer.

Before you try to connect, you need to modify a configuration file. This file,
CRDB_JavaServer.ini, can be found at \Program Files\Common Files\Crystal
Decisions\2.5\bin\.

You should make the following changes:

- Set PATH to where your Java Runtime Environment (JRE) is; for example,
  C:\jdk1.4\bin.

- Set CLASSPATH to the location of the JDBC driver you want to use, and include
  C:\Program Files\Common Files\Crystal Decisions\2.5\bin\CRDBJavaServer.jar.

- Set IORFileLocation to a location where the driver can write temporary files; make sure
  this location exists.

The other method of connecting to JDBC is through a JNDI reference. JNDI is a Java standard around resolving names and locations to resources in complex environments. In the
case of the Crystal Reports JDBC driver, it is used to store JDBC connection strings.
Connecting via JNDI has a few key benefits. First, the person creating the reports doesn't
need to know the exact server name; he only needs to know an alias given to it in JNDI,
such as FinanceData. Second, if that connection information were to change, no report
change would be needed, only a change in the JNDI directory. Last, JNDI supports connection pooling, which the Crystal Reports JDBC driver can take advantage of. As a recommen-
dation, if you have an available JNDI server, use it to define all your database connections;
this will save you time and effort later on.

Any existing reports you deliver through the Java Reporting Component will be converted
on-the-fly to JDBC. This conversion is configurable using JNDI. To set up a configuration

mapping, register a JDBC connection in a JNDI directory under the same name as the existing report's data source. For example, an existing report is connecting via ODBC to Oracle. With the same name as the ODBC DSN name, create a JNDI entry for a JDBC connection to the same Oracle server. When the report is run, it looks to JNDI and resolves the connection to the Oracle server.

CONFIGURING THE APPLICATION SERVER

Although building web applications in Java is meant to be independent of application servers, the J2EE standard tends to be interpreted differently for each vendor's application server. Because of this, each application server has a different way of performing web application configuration. The general rule is that there is a folder structure like this:

```
\webApplicationFolder
    \WEB-INF
        web.xml
        \lib
        \classes
```

When setting up the Java Reporting Component for a given web application, the following steps are required:

- Copy all the Java Reporting Component `.jar` files from `C:\Program Files\Business Objects\Common\4.0\\java\lib` into the `lib` folder.
- Copy all the third-party `.jar` files from `C:\Program Files\Business Objects\Common \\ \3.4.0\java\lib\external` into the `lib` folder.
- Copy `CrystalReportEngine-config.xml` from `C:\Program Files\Business Objects\Common\4.0\\java` to the `classes` folder.
- Copy the `crystalreportviewer12` folder from `C:\Program Files\Business Objects\Common\4.0\` to the web application folder (`webApplicationFolder` in the previous example).
- Add the following entry to the `web.xml` file:
    ```
    <context-param>
        <param-name>crystal_image_uri</param-name>
        <param-value>crystalreportviewers12</param-value>
    </context-param>
    ```

There are two additional steps required if you intend to use the Crystal tag libraries:

- Copy `crystal-tags-reportviewer.tld` from `C:\Program Files\Common Files\Crystal Decisions\2.5\java\lib\taglib` to the `WEB-INF` folder.
- Add the following entry to the `web.xml` file:
    ```
    <taglib>
        <taglib-uri>
            /crystal-tags-reportviewer.tld
    </taglib-uri>
        <taglib-location>
            /WEB-INF/crystal-tags-reportviewer.tld
        </taglib-location>
    </taglib>
    ```

DELIVERING REPORTS IN WEB APPLICATIONS

Report viewing is done primarily through the HTML report viewer included with the Crystal Reports Java Reporting Component. This report viewer is a control that runs inside a JSP or servlet. Its job is to get the information the report engine produces for a given page of a report and render that data to HTML format into the page's response stream.

The programmatic entry point to the report viewer is a class called `CrystalReportViewer`. This class is found in the `com.crystaldecisions.report.web.viewer` package. It can be instantiated as follows:

```
CrystalReportViewer viewer = new CrystalReportsViewer();
```

Make sure you add the class's package name in the `import` attribute of the page clause like this:

```
<%@ page import="com.crystaldecisions.report.web.viewer.*" %>
```

This is the main class you use to render reports to HTML. Its two main methods used to view reports are `setReportSource` and `processHttpRequest`. These methods are outlined in the following sections.

THE setReportSource METHOD

This `CrystalReportViewer` object's `setReportSource` method is used to indicate to the viewer which report it should display. Specifically, it accepts an object that implements the `IReportSource` interface. The Java Reporting Component's engine supplies this object. There are generally three steps involved in setting the report source.

The first step is to create a `JPEReportSourceFactory` object found in the `com.crystaldecisions.reports.reportengineinterface` package. As the name implies, this object's job is to create report source objects. This object has one relevant method: `createReportSource`. Its definition is as follows:

```
IReportSource createReportSource(object reportPath, Locale userLocale)
```

The `reportPath` argument should be a string consisting of the filename of the report file (`.rpt`). With the Java Reporting Component, the path from where the report file should be loaded is configured in the `CrystalReportEngine-config.xml` file. This XML configuration file has a `<reportlocation>` element that indicates the location of the report files relative to the location of the config file. The default value for the reportlocation is `..\..`, which (if the config file is in the `classes` folder as outlined in the previous section) would point to the `webApplicationFolder` folder. It's a good idea to create a `reports` folder inside the `web application`'s folder and store all your reports there. Then change the report location setting to `..\..\reports`. Then when reports are referenced in the call to `createReportSource`, you need only pass the name of the report, not the folder location.

The second argument to `createReportSource` is a `Locale` object. Generally, you should pass in `request.getLocale()`. This means that whatever the user's locale is, it is passed down to the report engine so that any locale-specific formatting can be applied.

18

THE processHttpRequest METHOD

After the viewer is told which report it needs to view, the only other method left to call is the processHttpRequest method. This method kicks off the actual report processing and renders the report to HTML. Its definition is as follows:

```
void processHttpRequest(HttpServletRequest request,
                        HttpServletResponse response,
                        ServletContext context,
                        Writer out)
```

The first argument passed in is the current servlet's request object. The report viewer uses this to access the HTTP request's form data where the viewer holds its state information, such as what page it was showing, what level of drill-down, and so on. Also stored in the form data is the piece of data that indicates what action is to be performed. For example, the user might have clicked on the Next Page button or might have also drilled down. You simply pass in the servlet's request object.

The second argument is the response object. The report viewer uses this object to access the page's response stream so that it can write the HTML output of the report. Here, you simply pass the servlet's response object.

The third argument is the servletContext, which is used to access the servlets container. Generally, you pass getServletConfig().getServletContext() for this argument. The final argument is a Writer. You generally pass null here unless you want to provide your own Writer. Listing 18.1 shows all these concepts brought together in a JSP page that displays a report.

LISTING 18.1   VIEWING A REPORT IN HTML

```
<%@ page contentType="text/html;charset=UTF-8"
    import="com.crystaldecisions.reports.reportengineinterface.*,
            com.crystaldecisions.report.web.viewer.*"  %>

<%
// name of report file
String reportFile = "Income_Statement.rpt";

// create the JPEReportSourceFactory
JPEReportSourceFactory rptSrcFactory = new JPEReportSourceFactory();

// call the createReportSource method
Object reportSource = rptSrcFactory.createReportSource(reportFile,
                                                       request.getLocale());

// create the report viewer
CrystalReportViewer viewer = new CrystalReportViewer();

// set the report source
viewer.setReportSource(reportSource);

// tell the viewer to display the report
```

```
viewer.processHttpRequest(request,
                          response,
                          getServletConfig().getServletContext(),
                          null);

%>
```

The output of this page is shown in Figure 18.2. All content for the report consists of HTML elements, keeping all formatting and layout preserved. Every once in a while you will find a discrepancy in the report output between the designer and the HTML viewer, but the advantages of the HTML viewer generally outweigh the disadvantages. Besides drilling down or hyperlinking from the report's main content, a toolbar along the top provides a way for the end user to interact with the report. Buttons for page navigation as well as printing and exporting are present. When the user performs a command such as navigating to the next page or drilling down, the report viewer using a JavaScript function causes a form post to occur back to the same page. Both the current state and the new command are sent as part of the form's post data. The JSP or servlet reruns, and the new state of the report is again rendered back to HTML.

Figure 18.2
This is the HTML report viewer in action.

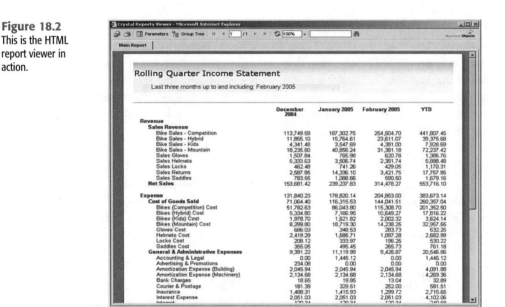

There is a collection of methods that the `CrystalReportViewer` object exposes that can be used to customize how the viewer looks and behaves. For the full list of methods, consult the API documentation; however, the following sections cover some of the more useful types of customizations.

CUSTOMIZING THE TOOLBAR

Each button or set of buttons on the report viewer toolbar can be individually turned off and on. This is done by a set of simple methods that accept a Boolean argument. They are listed here:

- `setHasToggleGroupTreeButton(boolean)`

- `setHasExportButton(boolean)`

- `setHasPrintButton(boolean)`

- `setHasViewList(boolean)`

- `setHasRefreshButton(boolean)`

- `setHasPageNavigationButtons(boolean)`

- `setHasGotoPageButton(boolean)`

- `setHasSearchButton(boolean)`

- `setHasZoomFactorList(boolean)`

- `setHasLogo(boolean)`

Finally, the entire toolbar can be turned off by calling `setDisplayToolbar(boolean)`. If the toolbar is turned off, the user does not have a way to interact with the report, such as navigating pages. To facilitate this, there are other methods on the `CrystalReportViewer` object that can be called to drive the page navigation, including `showFirstPage`, `showPreviousPage`, `showNextPage`, `showLastPage`, and `showNthPage`. Similar methods exist to re-create the functionality of most of the other buttons as well. In general, the methods related to toolbar customization are almost self-explanatory.

CUSTOMIZING THE GROUP TREE

The group tree's width can be set via the `setGroupTreeWidth` method. To change the formatting of the group tree's text, change the CSS styles defined in the `default.css` file found in `crystalreportviewers12/css`. Alternatively, the entire group tree can be hidden by passing `false` to the `setDisplayGroupTree` function.

USING THE CRYSTAL TAG LIBRARIES

Now that you understand how the report viewer works, it's beneficial to understand some of the ways that it can be used in a more productive manner. Java tag libraries are a great way to accomplish this. A *tag library (taglib)* is an HTML-like tag that can be embedded inside a JSP page; it has some compiled code logic behind it that knows how to render itself to HTML. The beauty of a tag library is that you don't need to clog up your JSP page with a bunch of code; you simply need to insert the tag. When Business Objects created the HTML report viewer, it was wise enough to create some Java tag libraries alongside it. This is not to say you could not create your own tag libraries to suit your own needs, but the ones provided with the product will probably meet most requirements.

Refer to the application server configuration section in this chapter for steps to configure the Crystal tag libraries. After you've finished the setup, you can start adding the tags to your page. The first step in using the tag is to add the `taglib` directive to the top of your JSP page. This directive looks like this:

```
<%@ taglib uri="/crystal-tags-reportviewer.tld" prefix="crviewer" %>
```

This indicates to the JSP page that anytime it finds a tag prefixed with `crviewer`, it should look in the `crystal-tags-reportviewer.tlb` file to find out how to work with that tag.

There are two tags that must be added to the JSP page: `viewer` and `report`. Listing 18.2 shows a simple page using the `viewer` and `report` tags.

LISTING 18.2   USING THE TAG LIBRARIES

```
<%@ taglib uri="/crystal-tags-reportviewer.tld" prefix="crviewer" %>
<crviewer:viewer viewerName="" reportSourceType="reportingComponent">
  <crviewer:report reportName="Income_Statement.rpt"/>
</crviewer:viewer>
```

The `viewerName` and `reportSourceType` attributes of the `viewer` tag are required. The `viewerName` can be set to blank unless there are multiple viewer tags on the same page, in which case you'll need to name them uniquely. There is only one report source type supported in the Java Reporting Component, which is `"reportingComponent"`. Inside the `viewer` tag, you'll see a `report` tag. For the `reportName` attribute, pass in the name of the report you want to display. The output of this page would be the same as the output of the previous code example using inline Java code. The advantage of this page is that it is cleaner and simpler. To customize the viewer, rather than writing code, simply add attributes to the `viewer` tag. For example, adding the following attribute to the `viewer` tag hides the group tree:

```
displayGroupTree="false"
```

There are many other attributes supported. Consult the documentation for a full list, but the general rule is that most methods on the `CrystalReportViewer` object have a corresponding tag library attribute.

18

EXPORTING REPORTS TO OTHER FILE FORMATS

You've learned so far how the `CrystalReportViewer` object can be used either in code or as a tag library to view reports in HTML format. This is useful for having a quick look at a report online, but users often require the capability to save the report to their own machine either for their own reference or so that they can send the report elsewhere. Exporting is a perfect solution to this. The Java Reporting Component supports exporting reports to both Adobe PDF and RTF. There are two ways exporting can be done: via the Export button on the toolbar and via code.

EXPORTING VIA THE TOOLBAR BUTTON

By default, the Export button on the report viewer's toolbar is hidden. To enable it, either set the `displayToolbarExportButton` attribute to `true` if you are using the tag library or call the `setHasExportButton` method if you are using the viewer directly.

NOTE

> Even though you instruct the viewer to show the Export button, you might find that it is still now showing up. This is most likely because you have not told the viewer that it owns the whole page. This is done via the `setOwnPage` method or `isOwnPage` attribute for the viewer or tag library, respectively.

When the Export button is clicked on, a pop-up window asks the user which document format she would like to export the report to and which pages she would like to export to. This is shown in Figure 18.3.

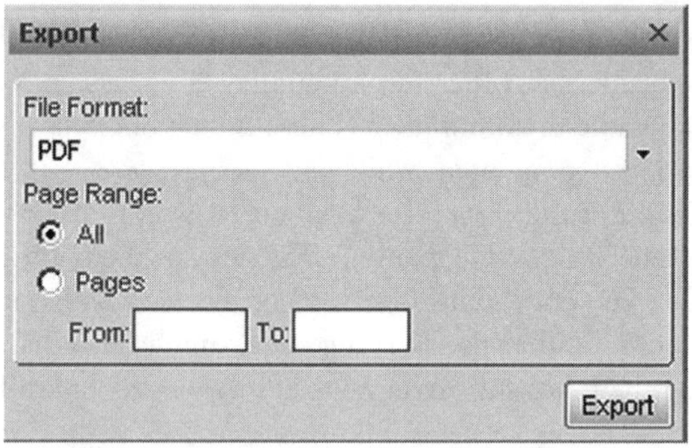

Figure 18.3
Export a report through the report viewer.

When the user clicks on OK, the browser sends back the report in the requested format. Figure 18.4 shows the Income Statement report from the previous examples, exported to PDF.

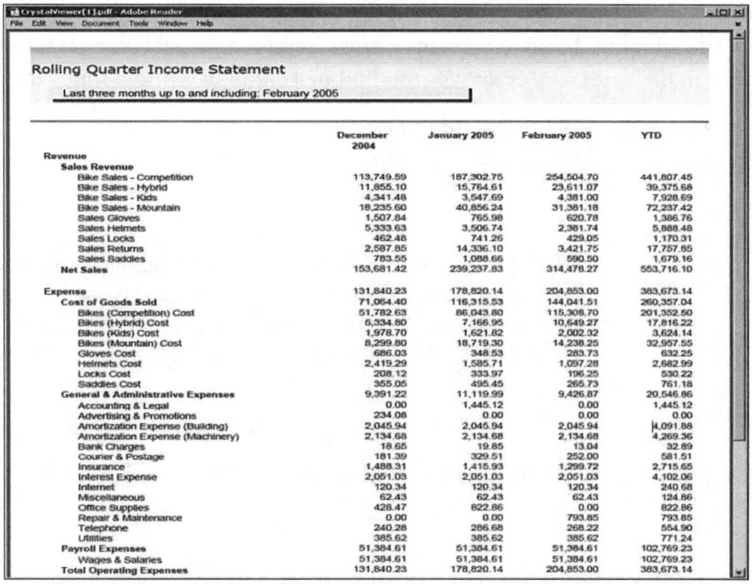

Rolling Quarter Income Statement

Last three months up to and including: February 2005

	December 2004	January 2005	February 2005	YTD
Revenue				
Sales Revenue				
Bike Sales - Competition	113,749.59	187,302.75	254,504.70	441,807.45
Bike Sales - Hybrid	11,855.10	15,764.61	23,611.07	39,375.68
Bike Sales - Kids	4,341.48	3,547.69	4,381.00	7,928.69
Bike Sales - Mountain	18,235.60	40,856.24	31,381.18	72,237.42
Sales Gloves	1,507.84	765.98	620.78	1,386.76
Sales Helmets	5,333.63	3,506.74	2,381.74	5,888.48
Sales Locks	462.48	741.26	429.05	1,170.31
Sales Returns	2,587.85	14,336.10	3,421.75	17,757.85
Sales Saddles	783.55	1,088.66	590.50	1,679.16
Net Sales	153,681.42	239,237.83	314,478.27	553,716.10
Expense	131,840.23	178,820.14	204,853.00	383,673.14
Cost of Goods Sold	71,064.40	116,315.53	144,041.51	260,357.04
Bikes (Competition) Cost	51,782.63	86,043.80	115,308.70	201,352.50
Bikes (Hybrid) Cost	6,334.80	7,166.95	10,649.27	17,816.22
Bikes (Kids) Cost	1,978.70	1,621.82	2,002.32	3,624.14
Bikes (Mountain) Cost	8,299.80	18,719.30	14,238.25	32,957.55
Gloves Cost	686.03	348.53	283.73	632.25
Helmets Cost	2,419.29	1,585.71	1,097.28	2,682.99
Locks Cost	208.12	333.97	196.25	530.22
Saddles Cost	355.05	495.45	265.73	761.18
General & Administrative Expenses	9,391.22	11,119.99	9,426.87	20,546.86
Accounting & Legal	0.00	1,445.12	0.00	1,445.12
Advertising & Promotions	234.08	0.00	0.00	0.00
Amortization Expense (Building)	2,045.94	2,045.94	2,045.94	4,091.88
Amortization Expense (Machinery)	2,134.68	2,134.68	2,134.68	4,269.36
Bank Charges	18.65	19.85	13.04	32.89
Courier & Postage	181.39	329.51	252.00	581.51
Insurance	1,488.31	1,415.93	1,299.72	2,715.65
Interest Expense	2,051.03	2,051.03	2,051.03	4,102.06
Internet	120.34	120.34	120.34	240.68
Miscellaneous	62.43	62.43	62.43	124.86
Office Supplies	428.47	822.86	0.00	822.86
Repair & Maintenance	0.00	0.00	793.85	793.85
Telephone	240.28	286.68	268.22	554.90
Utilities	385.62	385.62	385.62	771.24
Payroll Expenses	51,384.61	51,384.61	51,384.61	102,769.23
Wages & Salaries	51,384.61	51,384.61	51,384.61	102,769.23
Total Operating Expenses	131,840.23	178,820.14	204,853.00	383,673.14

Figure 18.4
Here is a report exported to the PDF format.

EXPORTING VIA CODE

There are a few reasons why you might want to export via code. Perhaps you always want to deliver reports in PDF or RTF format instead of using the report viewer. Or perhaps you want to control the user interface for exporting. In any case, this section describes how to export using the `ReportExportControl`.

NOTE

> Although some developers find it attractive to bypass the Crystal Report HTML viewer, and instead use either PDF or RTF as the primary way to deliver reports, this is not often the best way to go. Exporting is one of most processor-intensive operations and thus should be used sparingly if possible. In addition, when you export reports, you lose all the interactive functionality such as drill-down and group tree navigation. Use exporting where appropriate.

The `ReportExportControl` is the Java object used to render reports to both PDF and RTF. Because it is derived from the same class as the `CrystalReportViewer` object, it has many of the same properties and methods. The two main methods used in the report viewer—`setReportSource` and `processHttpRequest`—are used in the same way in the `ReportExportControl`. Also, when exporting there is an additional method that is required: `setExportOptions`. This method is used to tell the `ReportExportControl` which export format should be used, and optionally, which pages should be exported.

The argument passed into the setExportOptions method is an object of type ExportOptions. This is found in the com.crystaldecisions.sdk.occa.report.exportoptions package. With it, you call the setExportFormatType method passing in one of the following values:

- ReportExportFormat.PDF (for PDF)
- ReportExportFormat.RTF (for RTF)

NOTE

> Although the ReportExportFormat object has additional export formats not mentioned here, such as MSExcel and Text, these are not currently available with the Java Reporting Component. These show up because the ExportOptions object is a shared object between other Crystal products that do support those export format types.

Listing 18.3 pulls all this together and shows a JSP page that exports a report to PDF format.

LISTING 18.3 EXPORTING VIA THE ReportExportControl

```
<%@ page contentType="text/html;charset=UTF-8"
import="com.crystaldecisions.reports.reportengineinterface.*,
        com.crystaldecisions.report.web.viewer.*,
om.crystaldecisions.sdk.occa.report.exportoptions.*"  %>
<%

// name of report file
String reportFile = "Income_Statement.rpt";

// create the JPEReportSourceFactory
JPEReportSourceFactory rptSrcFactory = new JPEReportSourceFactory();

// call the createReportSource method
Object reportSource = rptSrcFactory.createReportSource(reportFile,
                                            request.getLocale());

// create the report viewer
ReportExportControl exporter = new ReportExportControl();

// set the report source
exporter.setReportSource(reportSource);

ExportOptions exportOptions = new ExportOptions();
exportOptions.setExportFormatType(ReportExportFormat.PDF);
exporter.setExportOptions(exportOptions);

// tell the viewer to display the report
exporter.processHttpRequest(request,
                            response,
                            getServletConfig().getServletContext(),
                            null);

%>
```

There are a few additional options that you might find useful. The first is the capability to specify which page numbers should be exported. This enables you to export just a small number of pages from a very large report. This is accomplished by creating either the RTFWordExportFormatOptions or PDFExportFormatOptions objects and calling their setStartPageNumber and setEndPageNumber methods. The resulting object is passed into the setFormatOptions method of the ExportOptions object. The code snippet shown in Listing 18.4 illustrates this.

LISTING 18.4   SPECIFYING PAGE NUMBERS WHEN EXPORTING

```
ExportOptions exportOptions = new ExportOptions();
exportOptions.setExportFormatType(ReportExportFormat.PDF) ;

RTFWordExportFormatOptions rtfOptions = new PDFExportFormatOptions();
rtfOptions.setStartPageNumber(1);
rtfOptions.setEndPageNumber(3);
exportOptions.setFormatOptions(rtfOptions);

exporter.setExportOptions(exportOptions);
```

The other option related to exporting is whether the resulting exported report should be sent back to the browser as an attachment or inline. When they report is sent as an attachment, the browser pops up a dialog asking the user whether he would like to save or open the file. This is useful if you think most of your users will want to save the file to their machines. The default behavior is for the report to open inside the browser window in either the Adobe or Microsoft Word embedded viewer. This is controlled via the setExportAsAttachment method of the CrystalReportViewer. This method simply takes a Boolean value, which determines whether the file should be an attachment.

PRINTING REPORTS FROM THE BROWSER

Viewing reports in electronic form is very valuable, but as much as the "paperless office" is talked about, people still need to print reports to printers. The Java Reporting Component has the capability to print reports via the Print button on the viewer's toolbar. Like the Export button, for the Print button to show, the viewer must be set to own the page via the isOwnPage attribute or setOwnPage method of the CrystalReportViewer object. When this button is clicked on, a window opens asking the user which pages he wants to print. This dialog is shown in Figure 18.5.

When the user clicks on the Print button, the report opens in the Adobe PDF viewer, from which the user can then click on Adobe's Print button. This prints the report to the user's printer.

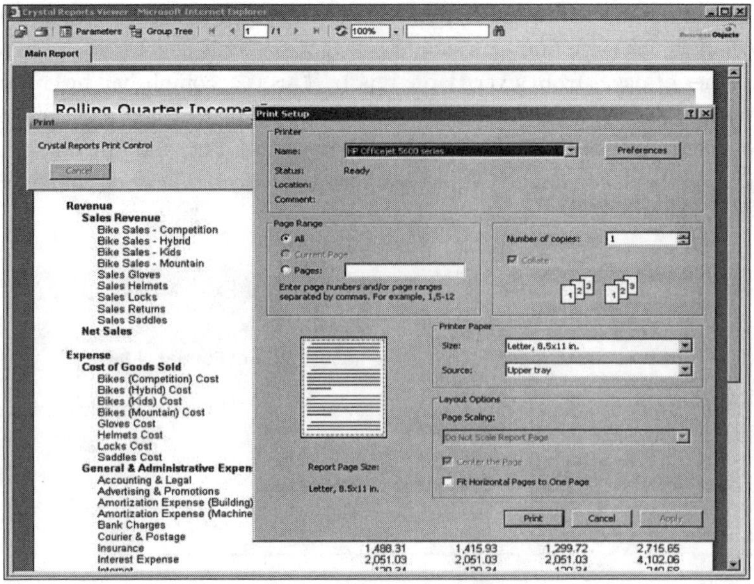

Figure 18.5
Print a report using
the report viewer.

COMMON PROGRAMMING TASKS

The different delivery mechanisms for the report viewer have been discussed. Now let's look at some of the common programming tasks that go along with delivering reports. This includes passing parameters to the report viewer and setting or changing the data source. The following sections will discuss these topics.

PASSING PARAMETERS

One of the most common programming tasks with any Crystal Reports product is to pass parameters to the report viewer. This really isn't a hard task, but developers often find this difficult because of a lack of proper examples in the product documentation. This chapter will attempt to provide concrete examples. Typically, reports are designed to be dynamic and so have multiple parameters that drive how the report functions. There are two ways to handle parameters: either have the report viewer prompt the user for the parameters automatically or pass the parameter values via code. Which method you choose is determined largely by whether you want the users to pick their own parameter values.

Using the automatic parameter prompting requires no extra code or configuration. Simply view a report using either the viewer class or tag library, and a default parameter prompting screen is displayed. Alternatively, you can pass the parameter values by code. This involves creating a series of objects as outlined later in this chapter.

The first step in passing parameter values is to create an instance of the `Fields` class. This is a container class for parameter fields. This and the other objects are found in the `com.crystaldecisions.sdk.occa.report.data` package. Next, create an instance of the

`ParameterField` object. To determine which parameter you are setting values for, call the `setName` method passing in the name of the parameter. To set the parameter values, create an instance of the `Values` class, which is a container for parameter value objects. Finally, create a `ParameterFieldDiscreteValue` object and call the `setValue` method to pass in the actual parameter value. This collection of objects is then passed to the report viewer via the `setParameterFields` method. Listing 18.5 shows a parameter being passed.

LISTING 18.5   PASSING A SIMPLE PARAMETER

```
Fields fields = new Fields();
ParameterField param = new ParameterField();
param.setName("Country");
Values vals = new Values();
ParameterFieldDiscreteValue val = new ParameterFieldDiscreteValue();
val.setValue("Canada");
vals.add(val);
param.setCurrentValues(vals);
fields.add(param);
viewer.setParameterFields(fields);
```

Because there tends to be a bunch of objects you need to create, a nice way to handle this is to wrap up the parameter logic into a function. Listing 18.6 provides a sample function like this.

18

LISTING 18.6   A SAMPLE PARAMETER-HANDLING FUNCTION

```
public ParameterField createParam(string name, object value) {
   ParameterField param = new ParameterField();
   param.setName(name);
   Values vals = new Values();
   ParameterFieldDiscreteValue val = new ParameterFieldDiscreteValue();
   val.setValue(value);
   vals.add(val);
   param.setCurrentValues(vals);
   return param;
}
```

After you have a function like this in place, passing parameters looks as simple as in Listing 18.7.

LISTING 18.7   CALLING THE SAMPLE PARAMETER-HANDLING FUNCTION

```
Fields fields = new Fields();

field.add( createParam("Country", "Canada") );
field.add( createParam("Product Line", "Widgets") );

viewer.setParameterFields(fields) ;
```

SETTING DATA SOURCE INFORMATION

Setting data source information is similar to the way setting parameters works. There is a collection of objects that you create, which then gets passed to the report viewer. In this case, the method used is `setDatabaseLogonInfos`. This method takes a `ConnectionInfos` object, which is found in the `com.crystaldecisions.sdk.occa.report.data` package. The `ConnectionInfos` class is a container class for any data source information for a given report. Each connection's information is held in an object called `ConnectionInfo`. This object has `setUserName` and `setPassword` methods for passing credentials. Also, each `ConnectionInfo` has a collection of properties associated with it called a *property bag*. The property bag contains information such as server name, database name, connection type, and so on. The property bag stores information in a name/value pair structure. There are variations as to what items are held in the `ConnectionInfo`, but the best way to figure it out is to look in the Set DataSource Location dialog from the Crystal Reports designer. There you can see which items are associated with a connection. Listing 18.8 shows how to pass logon information for a report.

LISTING 18.8   PASSING DATA SOURCE CREDENTIALS

```
ConnectionInfos connections = new ConnectionInfos();

ConnectionInfo connection as new ConnectionInfo();
connection.setUserName("Ryan");
connection.setPassword("123BAC");

connections.add(connection);
viewer.setDatabaseLogonInfos(connections) ;
```

DEVELOPING WITH A VISUAL DEVELOPMENT ENVIRONMENT

Not only has Business Objects delivered a full Java reporting offering with the Crystal Reports Java Reporting Component, but it also provides integration with some of the major Integrated Development Environments (IDEs) in the market to drive developers to build applications with the Java Reporting Component more quickly. The vendors Business Objects is currently working with on IDE integration are BEA and Borland. The integration consists of the following:

- **An integrated project item for reports**—This enables developers to add a report to their projects easily. It launches the Crystal Reports designer to edit the report automatically.

- **A report viewer wizard**—This is a visual wizard that walks users through the process of adding the report viewer tag to their JSP page.

Figure 18.6 shows the integration info BEA WebLogic Workshop, and Figure 18.7 shows the integration into Borland JBuilder X. There are various other plug-ins to the IDEs as well that can be explored, such as automatically importing the Crystal libraries and configuring the web.xml.

Figure 18.6
The Java Reporting Component integrated into BEA WebLogic Workshop.

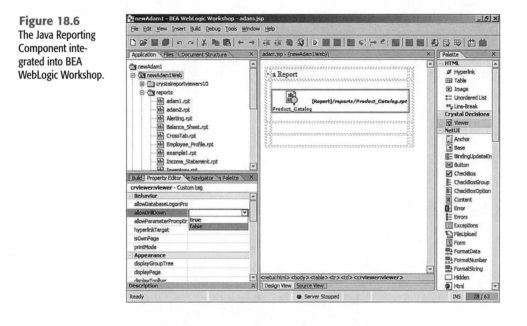

Figure 18.7
The Java Reporting Component integrated into Borland JBuilder X.

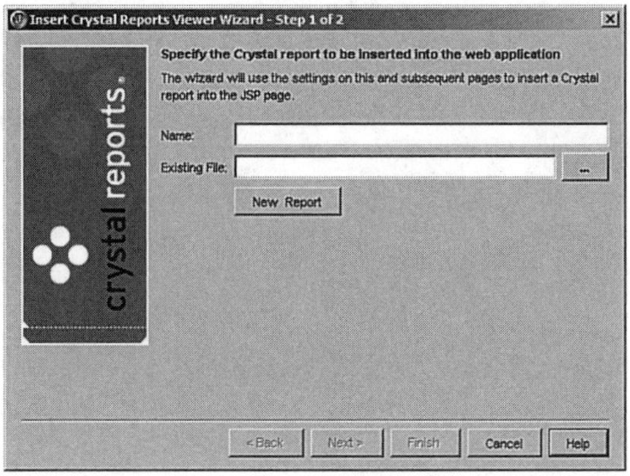

For more information on IDE integration into these and other developer tools, visit the Business Objects website.

CHAPTER **19**

CRYSTAL REPORTS MICROSOFT .NET COMPONENTS

In this chapter

UNDERSTANDING MICROSOFT'S .NET PLATFORM

Business Objects has a long partnership history with Microsoft. This has continued with Microsoft's .NET platform. This chapter provides an overview of the various .NET reporting technologies available both within Visual Studio .NET and with Crystal Reports 2008.

Microsoft .NET is a next-generation platform that enables developers to create programs that transcend device boundaries and harness the connectivity of the Internet. .NET and the tools and languages that compose it are the foundation for building Windows-based components and applications, creating scripts, developing websites and applications, and managing source code.

Many of the terms used in this chapter are specific to the Microsoft .NET solution or the Visual Studio .NET development environment. Before you learn the Crystal components, review some of the key .NET technologies that are relevant to Crystal Reports developers:

- **XML web services**—A *web service* is a unit of application logic providing data and services to other applications. Applications access web services via ubiquitous web protocols and data formats such as HTTP and XML, with no need to worry about how each web service is implemented. Web services combine the best aspects of component-based development and the web and are a cornerstone of the Microsoft .NET programming model.

- **ASP.NET**—*ASP.NET* is a set of technologies in the Microsoft .NET Framework for building web applications and XML web services. ASP.NET pages execute on the server and generate markup such as HTML, WML, or XML that is sent to a desktop or mobile browser. ASP.NET pages and ASP.NET XML web services files contain server-side logic (as opposed to client-side logic) written in Visual Basic .NET, C# .NET, or any .NET-compatible language.

- **ADO.NET**—*ADO.NET* is an evolutionary improvement to Microsoft *ActiveX Data Objects (ADO)* that provides platform interoperability and scalable data access. Using *Extensible Markup Language (XML)*, ADO.NET can ensure the efficient transfer of data to any application on any platform.

- **SOAP**—*SOAP (Simple Object Access Protocol)* is a lightweight and simple XML-based protocol designed to exchange structured and typed information on the web. The purpose of SOAP is to enable rich and automated web services based on a shared and open web infrastructure.

For more detailed information on the Microsoft .NET solution, refer to Microsoft's website at http://msdn.microsoft.com/library/default.asp.

19

UNDERSTANDING THE DIFFERENT CRYSTAL .NET COMPONENTS

There have been multiple releases of both Visual Studio .NET and the Crystal Reports .NET components. This has created some confusion in the marketplace. In an attempt to clear this up, the following section describes the history of the various Crystal .NET products. Way back in 1993—a long time ago in the computing industry—Business Objects (then called Crystal Decisions) signed an agreement with Microsoft to include Crystal Reports version 2 with Visual Basic 3.0. This relationship continued over the years as the Microsoft developer community embraced Crystal Reports technology. Late in the year of 2000, when Microsoft began to create the next generation of its development platform, it again looked to Business Objects to provide the reporting solution. The Crystal folks ran full speed ahead with this project and embraced all the new technologies composing the .NET development platform.

In March of 2002, Visual Studio .NET shipped with a new product as part of the install: Crystal Reports for Visual Studio .NET. This was a special edition of Crystal Reports targeted at the .NET developer. It was seamlessly integrated with both the Visual Studio .NET integrated development environment (IDE) and the .NET Framework. It provided report viewer controls for both the Windows Forms and Web Forms application frameworks, a managed report engine object model, and a report designer integrated into the Visual Studio .NET IDE.

Another variant of the Crystal Reports .NET product came about when Microsoft released Visual Studio .NET 2003 (code-named Everest). This was a point release of Visual Studio .NET and again included an updated edition of Crystal Reports for Visual Studio .NET. There were no new features per se, but the latest patches and updates were included. Many developers today have one of these Crystal Reports editions and believe that they have the most recent and complete Crystal Reports release. This is not true.

Subsequent to that release, Business Objects updated its .NET offering by adding new features such as additional report viewer controls, more functionality through its API, and support for more data sources. This functionality was bundled with the Crystal Reports 9 release. Therefore, Crystal Reports 9 Advanced Edition served as an upgrade to Crystal Reports for Visual Studio .NET. Finally, version 10 and XI again include upgrades to the .NET components that shipped with version 9. The rest of this chapter covers the functionality of the .NET components included with Crystal Reports 2008.

There have been a number of improvements made to the Crystal Reports 2008 .NET components. This is especially true around the viewing components, where you will first notice the new look and feel of the user interface. But you'll also notice the additional functionality that has been added—such as the new parameter panel that allows you to see and change the parameter values right within the viewer, and on report sort controls that allow you to sort the report by clicking on the up/down arrows next to the column header. Furthermore, you can now export the report to XML format from within the viewer because this additional export format has been added to the list of export format options. Finally, worth noting here is the ability to embed Flash objects into the report. When viewing the report through the viewer, you can share the data between the report and the Flash object by using Flash variable support added to the report engine.

AN OVERVIEW OF THE CRYSTAL REPORTS 2008 .NET COMPONENTS

Crystal Reports XI provides developers working within Visual Studio .NET with a fast, productive way to create and integrate presentation quality, interactive reports to meet the demands of their application's end users. Crystal Reports 2008 enhances the .NET platform by allowing you to

- Create reports from virtually any data source
- Save time and write less code by leveraging existing Crystal Reports and report creation knowledge within .NET projects

To accomplish this, Crystal Reports 2008 provides a broad offering of .NET technologies for delivering reports inside .NET applications. The following sections cover each component at a high level. They are

- The report designer
- The Report Engine Object Model
- The Windows Forms viewer
- The Web forms viewers

THE REPORT DESIGNER

Like the original Crystal Reports for Visual Studio .NET product, Crystal Reports 2008 provides an integrated report designer inside the Visual Studio .NET development environment. This edition of the report designer enables you to create and edit reports from within the comfort of Visual Studio .NET. Figure 19.1 shows the report designer in action.

To add a new report to a project, select Add New Item from the Project menu. Select Crystal Reports from the Add New Item dialog. The filename you use here maps to the name of the report file as well as the name of the class created behind the scenes for the report (called the *code-behind class*).

NOTE

Many of you might be familiar with the Visual Basic report designer that was part of the Report Designer Component package made for Visual Basic 6.0. This new Visual Studio .NET report designer is the evolution of that component and works in a similar manner.

Figure 19.1
This is a report being designed in the Visual Studio .NET report designer.

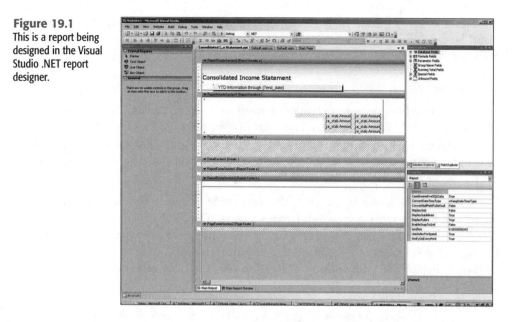

After you select Crystal Reports from the Add New Item dialog, the Report Wizard displays. Select Using the Report Wizard or As a Blank Report to create a new report from scratch. The From an Existing Report option provides the capability to import any existing Crystal Report file (.rpt) and use the Visual Studio .NET report designer to make further modifications. This is a great way to leverage any existing work an organization has put into Crystal Reports. A report that is added or imported into a Visual Studio .NET project is just a standard RPT file. This means you can use the standalone report designer to edit the report. The Visual Studio .NET report designer supports almost all the features of the standalone report designer and can be used to create everything from simple tabular reports to highly formatted professional reports. Although the feature sets of these two editions of the designer are almost the same, there are a few things for which the standalone designer is good, namely being able to preview the report without having to run the application.

TIP

A quick way to launch the standalone designer from within Visual Studio .NET is to right-click on a report in the Solution Explorer and select Open With. In the dialog that opens, select crw32.exe. This is the executable for the standalone report designer. This usually proves to be a better method to build reports anyway because you have a built-in and active preview screen available for dynamic viewing, editing, and testing.

Even though the capabilities of the two editions of the designers are similar, there are some differences in the way the designer works. This is not meant to be inconsistent, but rather to adapt some of the standalone report designer tasks to tasks that Visual Studio .NET

19

developers would be familiar with. Ideally, the experience of designing a report with the Visual Studio .NET report designer should be like designing a Windows Form. The following sections cover these differences.

UNDERSTANDING THE REPORT DESIGNER'S USER INTERFACE CONVENTIONS

Several user interface components work differently in the Visual Studio .NET report designer. One of the first things you'll notice is that the section names are shown above each section on a section band as opposed to being on the left side of the window. However, the same options are available when right-clicking on the section band. This actually takes up less real estate and tends to be preferred by developers.

The Field Explorer resides to the left of the report page by default but can be docked anywhere, as can most Visual Studio .NET tool windows. The Field Explorer can be easily shown or hidden by clicking the Toggle Field View button on the designer toolbar. Other Explorer windows found in the standalone designer, such as the Report Explorer and Repository Explorer, are not available in the Visual Studio .NET report designer.

> **NOTE**
>
> Reports that contain objects linked to the Crystal Repository are fully supported; however, no new repository objects can be added to the report without using the standalone designer.

The menus that you would normally find in the standalone report designer can be found by right-clicking on an empty spot on the designer surface. The pop-up menu provides the same functionality.

THE PROPERTY BROWSER

To change the formatting and settings for report objects in the standalone designer, right-click on a report object and select Format Field from the pop-up menu. Doing so opens the Format Editor, which gives you access to changing font, color, styles, and other formatting options. In the Visual Studio .NET report designer, this scenario is still available; however, there is an additional way to apply most of these formatting options—via the Property Browser.

The Property Browser is a window that lives inside the Visual Studio .NET development environment. It should be very familiar to developers as a way to change the appearance and behavior of a selected object on a form or design surface. In the context of the report designer, the property browser is another way to change the settings (properties) for report objects. In general, any setting that is available in the Format Editor dialog is available from the property browser when that object is selected. This generally proves to be a faster and better way to set properties than using the Format Editor. To see which properties are available for a given object, click to highlight the object, and then check out the Property Browser window shown in Figure 19.2.

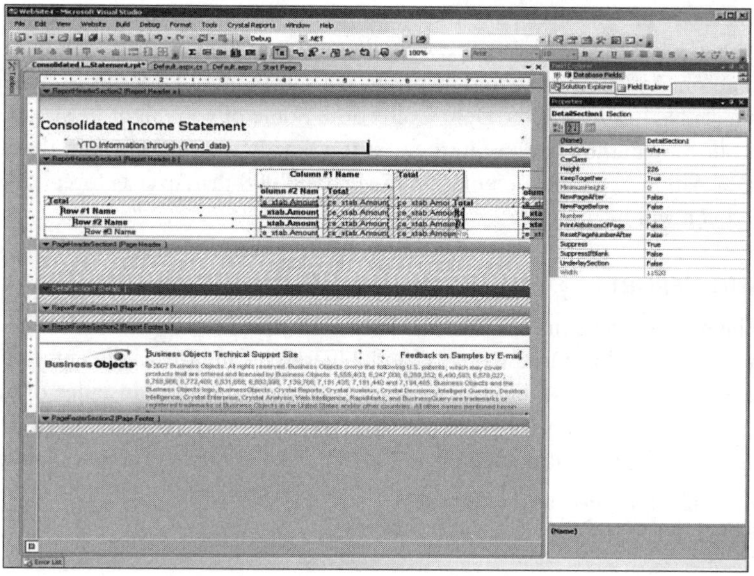

Figure 19.2
Using the Property
Browser window to
modify a report
object's settings.

The property names are listed on the left, and the current values are listed on the right. To click a value, simply click on the current value and either type or select from the drop-down list.

One property to pay attention to is the Name property. This becomes relevant in the next section when you learn how to use the Report Engine Object Model to manipulate the report on the fly at runtime. This is the way to reference that object in code.

THE REPORT ENGINE OBJECT MODEL

The Report Engine Object Model is the .NET programmatic entry point to the Crystal Reports engine. It provides a collection of objects, methods, and properties that enable you to process, save, export, and print reports. While doing that, you are able to manipulate the report by modifying parameter values, database credentials, sorting, and grouping. The Report Engine Object Model (hereafter referred to as the *object model*) consists of a standard .NET assembly called CrystalDecisions.CrystalReports.Engine.dll. As the name of the DLL implies, the namespace for all the objects contained in this DLL is CrystalDecisions.CrystalReports.Engine. Because this is a standard .NET assembly, the object model contained within it can be used from any .NET programming language or tool. All sample code within this chapter uses the Visual Basic .NET language, but any .NET-compliant language could, of course, be used. Keep in mind that although the object model is pure managed code, the underlying report engine is not. This means you can't perform a pure xcopy deployment that Microsoft likes to advertise that all .NET applications can do.

There are many objects, and thus capabilities, in the object model. This chapter does not explain all of them but rather covers the most common scenarios. For a complete reference of all objects, properties, and methods, consult the Crystal Reports 2008 documentation that is installed in the MSDN Help Collection. Some of you might be skeptical about the product documentation because in the past it was very sparse. However, there is much more information in the documentation in version 2008 than ever before; have a look through it, and you will be impressed.

OPENING REPORTS

The main object you use when working with the object model is the `ReportDocument` object. It is the root object in the object model hierarchy and forms the entry point to opening reports. The first step in opening reports is to create a new instance of the `ReportDocument` class. To open a report file, call the `Load` method. This method takes a single parameter, which is a string that points to the RPT file. An example of this is as follows:

```
Dim Report As New ReportDocument
Report.Load("C:\My Reports\Sales.rpt")
```

NOTE

> One common way to handle file paths is to use `Application.StartupPath` to determine the current location of the Windows Forms executable and reference report files relative to there.

The other way to load a report is to use a strongly typed report object. A *strongly typed report object* is an object automatically generated when a report is added to the Visual Studio .NET project. This object (sometimes called *code-behind*) is specific to the report file both in its class name and properties. For example, a report added to the project called `InvoiceReport.rpt` would in turn have a class called `InvoiceReport`. Instead of calling the `Load` method, a developer needs only to create an instance of the `InvoiceReport` class. This class knows how to locate the report. In the case of strongly typed reports, instead of having an external RPT file, the report file is compiled into the application executable. The report is loaded out of the application's resources from there. Whether you use a `ReportDocument` (untyped report) or a strongly typed report, the rest of the object model is the same.

EXPORTING REPORTS

One of the most common uses of the object model is to run a report and export it to another file format. In past versions, exporting required a good-sized chunk of code. Fortunately, exporting in version XI is very easy with the updated object model. First, a `ReportDocument` object needs to be created and a report loaded into it. After that is done, several exporting methods are available to you:

- **ExportToDisk**—This is the simplest way to export a report; it accepts an argument to indicate the export format type to use and a filename to export to. This method is useful when you just need to export a file to the disk.

- **ExportToStream**—This method accepts only a single argument—the export format type. The return value of this method is a `System.IO.Stream` object. This is actually a `MemoryStream` object, so you can cast it to a `MemoryStream` if need be. This method is useful when you intend to send the exported report elsewhere as a stream without having to write to an intermediate disk file. It's best to call the steam's `Close` method when finished with the stream to release memory.

- **ExportToHttpResponse**—This method is similar to the `ExportToStream` method in that it is intended to be used when the resulting report is streamed back to the user. However, this method accepts as an argument the ASP.NET `HttpResponse` object and automatically streams the exported report back to the web browser handling the MIME type and response stream for you.

- **Export**—This is the master export method. It accepts an object called `ExportOptions` as an argument that describes the export format type and destination type. You can think of this as the longhand way of exporting, but it does allow for a few additional options such as email, Exchange destinations, and page range options.

A common argument to all these exporting methods is the export format type. This is specified using the `ExportFormatType` enumeration found in the `CrystalDecisions.Shared` namespace. It's generally a good idea to add a reference to `CrystalDecisions.Shared.dll` because you will find many common objects used in the object model located in this assembly. The following list describes the members of the `ExportFormatType` enumeration:

- **Excel**—Microsoft Excel format
- **ExcelRecord**—A variation of the Microsoft Excel format that just exports the data, not the formatting
- **HTML32**—HTML for Netscape Navigator or other uncommon browsers
- **HTML40**—HTML for Microsoft Internet Explorer
- **PortableDocFormat**— Adobe PDF
- **RichText**—Microsoft's Rich Text Format (RTF)
- **WordForWindows**— Microsoft Word format
- **Text**—Plain text format
- **CrystalReport**—Standard Crystal Reports (RPT) format
- **XML**—XML format

19

TIP

> When exporting to Crystal Reports format, a standard RPT file is created; however, the report has saved data. This is quite useful because you can run a report once, export to Crystal Reports format, and then have many people view that report using the saved data. In this scenario, only one hit is made to the database even though many people are viewing the report. This is similar to creating a report instance in the BusinessObjects Enterprise environment. This feature can be used to affect a greater scalability by introducing a report instance delivery model.

A common scenario for exporting would be processing many reports in a batch job. This is a great use of the object model. Here are a few tips to help you do this effectively. First, clean up to make sure that memory is released, and second, use multiple threads to maximize the time available for processing reports. The report engine object model is thread safe. Listing 19.1 illustrates a multithreaded report processing class. Listing 19.2 shows how this class could be called.

LISTING 19.1 MULTITHREADED BATCH PROCESSING CLASS

```
Imports System.Threading
Imports CrystalDecisions.Shared
Imports CrystalDecisions.CrystalReports.Engine

Public Class BatchProcessor
    Private ReportList As New ArrayList
    Private OutputFolder As String
    Private BatchCounter As Integer

    ' Call this method to add a report to the list of reports
    ' to be processed by the batch processor
    Public Sub AddReportJob(ByVal ReportPath As String)
        ReportList.Add(ReportPath)
    End Sub

    ' This runs an individual report job
    Private Sub ProcessNextReportJob(ByVal Index As Object)
        Dim report As New ReportDocument
        Dim outputFileName As String

    ' Load the report based on index
        report.Load(ReportList(Index))
    ' Construct an output filename
        outputFileName = "Report" & Index & ".pdf"
    ' Call the ExportToDisk method
        report.ExportToDisk(ExportFormatType.PortableDocFormat, _
                            OutputFolder & "\" & outputFileName)
    ' Make sure to clean up the report object
        report.Close()

    ' Decrement a counter of remaining jobs
        BatchCounter = BatchCounter - 1
    End Sub
    Public Sub ExecuteBatch(ByVal OutputFolder As String)
        Me.OutputFolder = OutputFolder

        BatchCounter = ReportList.Count

        ' Grab the current time
        Dim startTime As DateTime = DateTime.Now

        ' Start the batch job
        Dim i As Integer
        For i = 1 To ReportList.Count
```

```
    ' Use the .NET ThreadPool class to handle the multiple requests
        Dim wc As New WaitCallback(AddressOf ProcessNextReportJob)
        ThreadPool.QueueUserWorkItem(wc, i - 1)
    Next

    While BatchCounter > 0
        Thread.Sleep(250)
    End While

    Dim elapsedTime As TimeSpan = DateTime.Now.Subtract(startTime)
    MessageBox.Show("Batch completed in " + _
                    elapsedTime.Seconds.ToString() & " seconds")
    End Sub

End Class
```

LISTING 19.2   CALLING THE BATCH PROCESSOR

```
Dim bp As New BatchProcessor

bp.AddReportJob("C:\Temp\Reports\Report1.rpt")
bp.AddReportJob("C:\Temp\Reports\Report2.rpt")
bp.AddReportJob("C:\Temp\Reports\Report3.rpt")
bp.AddReportJob("C:\Temp\Reports\Report4.rpt")
bp.AddReportJob("C:\Temp\Reports\Report5.rpt")
bp.AddReportJob("C:\Temp\Reports\Report6.rpt")
bp.AddReportJob("C:\Temp\Reports\Report7.rpt")
bp.AddReportJob("C:\Temp\Reports\Report8.rpt")
bp.AddReportJob("C:\Temp\Reports\Report9.rpt")
bp.AddReportJob("C:\Temp\Reports\ReportXI.rpt")

bp.ExecuteBatch("C:\Temp\Output
```

PRINTING REPORTS

Although the fantasy of a paperless office floats around our heads, the reality today is that no matter how much technology for viewing reports is produced, people will always want to print them. Along these lines, the object model supports printing reports to printers. This is accomplished by calling the ReportDocument's PrintToPrinter method. It takes the following arguments, which determine basic print settings:

- **nCopies**—An integer representing the number of copies to print
- **collated**—A Boolean value indicating whether the printed pages should be collated
- **startPageN**—An integer representing the page number on which to start printing
- **endPageN**—An integer representing the page number on which to end printing

19

In addition to these printing options, there is another set of more advanced options. These options are in the form of properties and are contained in the ReportDocument's PrintOptions object:

- **PaperSize**—An enumeration of standard paper sizes, such as Letter or A4
- **PaperOrientation**—An enumeration to indicate the orientation of the paper, such as portrait or landscape
- **PageMargins**—A PageMargins object containing integer-based margin widths
- **PageContentHeight/PageContentWidth**—Integer-based width and height for the main page area
- **PaperSource**—An enumeration containing standard paper tray sources such as upper and lower
- **PrinterDuplex**—An enumeration containing duplexing options for the printer
- **PrinterName**—A string representing the name of the printer device or print queue

NOTE

> Keep in mind that whatever account the Report Engine Object Model is running under needs access to the printer when the PrintToPrinter method is invoked. Sometimes when the object model is used in ASP.NET, it is running under a Guest-level account, which does not have access to the machine's printers. If this is the case, you need to install and grant access to the printers for that account.

DELIVERING REPORTS WITH THE WINDOWS FORMS VIEWER

After reports are imported into or referenced from a Visual Studio .NET project, the next obvious step is to have a way to view those reports. This section covers report viewing in Windows Forms applications.

Windows Forms is the new .NET technology for building rich-client applications. It is the evolution of the COM and ActiveX platform that Crystal Reports was so popular in. When it came to .NET, Business Objects decided to write a native .NET control based on the Windows Forms technology. This control is simply called the Windows Forms Viewer. Its corresponding class name is CrystalDecisions.Windows.Forms.CrystalReportViewer.

Like other Windows Forms controls, this control ultimately inherits from the System.Windows.Forms.Control class. It has many public methods and properties that enable you to drive the appearance and behavior. In addition to these runtime capabilities, the Windows Forms Viewer has design-time support to increase the efficiency and ease of using the control. The control can be found in the toolbox on the Windows Forms tab. You can see what the control looks like after being dropped onto a form in Figure 19.3.

Figure 19.3
A Crystal Report displayed in the Windows Forms Viewer control.

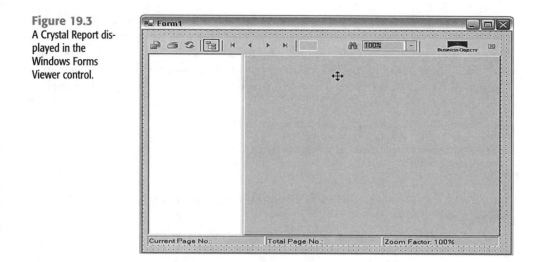

THE ReportSource PROPERTY

Although there are many properties and methods, the ReportSource property is key. This property indicates to the viewer which report it should display. Because the ReportSource property's data type is object, it can accept multiple types of values, the most common of which are listed here:

- **Filename**—The full path to an RPT file as a String object.
- **Report object**—An instance of a CrystalDecisions.CrystalReports.Engine.ReportDocument class. This report should already have been loaded by calling the ReportDocument's Load method.
- **Strongly typed report object**—An instance of a strongly typed report object derived from ReportClass.

The following code shows VB .NET examples of setting the types of report source objects:

```
' #1 - A filename as a string
Viewer.ReportSource = "C:\Program Files\My Application\Reports\Sales.rpt"

' #2 - a ReportDocument object
Dim Report = As New ReportDocument()
Report.Load("C:\Program Files\My Application\Reports\Sales.rpt")
Viewer.ReportSource = Report

' #3 - A strongly typed report object
Dim Report As New SalesReport()
Viewer.ReportSource = Report
```

If the viewer is visible when the ReportSource property is set, it displays the report immediately. If the viewer is not visible yet (that is, the form has not been shown yet), the viewer waits until it is shown onscreen to display the report. After a report source is provided to the viewer, it maintains that report until the viewer is destroyed or another report source is passed into it.

19

Because the viewer can generically accept report filenames and report objects, a single viewer can be reused for viewing multiple reports. One of the ways you could handle this is to create a form dedicated to report viewing. This form would contain the Windows Forms viewer. To easily invoke this form and pass in a report source, make the viewer a public variable and then create a shared method to accept a report source as an argument. An example of this function is shown here:

```
Public Shared Sub Display(ByVal ReportSource As Object)
    Dim newForm As New ReportViewerForm()
    newForm.Viewer.ReportSource = ReportSource
    newForm.ShowDialog()
End Sub
```

After this is in place, to invoke the report viewer from anywhere in the application, use the following code:

```
strReportPath = ...
ReportViewerForm.Display(strReportPath)
```

CUSTOMIZING THE WINDOWS FORMS VIEWER

There are many properties and methods of the report viewer that can be used to customize its appearance. The first level of customization is to show or hide the individual components of the viewer. The group tree on the left side can be shown or hidden via the `DisplayGroupTree` Boolean property. The toolbar works the same way via the `DisplayToolbar` property.

In addition to hiding the entire toolbar, each button or button group on the toolbar has corresponding properties that allow them to be individually hidden or shown. These properties can be found in the property browser or accessed via code. They all start with `Show`, such as `ShowExportButton`, `ShowPrintButton`, and so on. The names should be self-explanatory.

TIP

> There is a status bar at the bottom of the viewer that does not have a corresponding show/hide property. It tends not to add a lot of value and ends up more of an annoyance than anything. A trick to hide this status bar is to drop a panel control onto the form and drop the viewer onto the panel. Set the viewer's `Dock` property to `Fill` so that the viewer always sizes itself to the size of the surrounding panel. Then set the `DockPadding.Bottom` property of the viewer to -20. This sizes the height of the viewer to 20 pixels more than the panel, effectively hiding the status bar below the extents of the panel. Keep in mind that any methods and properties that need to be accessed from the report viewer after you've done this have to be accessed via the panel object's controls collection. Figure 19.4 shows the report viewer with no group tree, no toolbar, and the status bar hidden.

Figure 19.4
The report viewer is shown here with its status bar hidden.

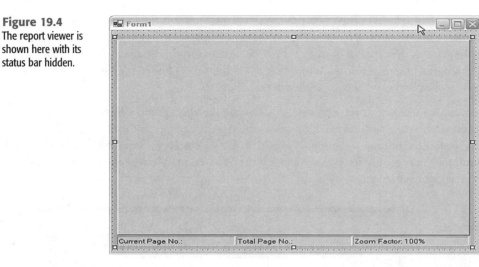

Another property that can be used to change the behavior of the report viewer is the `EnableDrillDown` property. Setting this Boolean property to `false` disables the user from performing any drill-down operations. Finally, the `SelectionFormula` and `ViewTimeSelectionFormula` properties can be used to create and append filters to the report. Keep in mind that the filtering is actually done by the report engine, but the report viewer simply exposes the property and then sends the information down to the report engine. The `SelectionFormula` property should be used when creating or overwriting a selection formula. To append to an existing formula, use the `ViewTimeSelectionFormula` property, which automatically appends using an `AND` operator.

DELIVERING REPORTS WITH THE WEB FORMS VIEWER

An equivalent viewer to the Windows Forms Viewer exists for ASP.NET-based applications; it's called the *Web Forms Viewer*. This is an ASP.NET control derived from the `WebControl` class. This means that it is a server-side control that renders only HTML to the client browser. No special controls, applets, or files are required on the client to view reports with the Web Forms Viewer.

Like the Windows Forms Viewer, the Web Forms Viewer can be found in the Visual Studio .NET toolbox and is called CrystalReportViewer. It is found in the `CrystalDecisions.Web` namespace and the `CrystalDecisions.Web.dll` assembly. Many objects used in the Web Forms Viewer are contained in the `CrystalDecisions.Shared` namespace. The Web Forms Viewer has many properties and methods that control how it displays reports. This section covers these.

The first step to using the viewer is to drop it onto a Web Form from the toolbox. From there, properties can be set via the property browser or via the code-behind for the ASPX page. The first relevant property for the Web Forms Viewer is the `ReportSource` property. The nice thing is that the types of objects that can be passed into the `ReportSource` property are the same as the types of objects that can be passed into the Windows Forms Viewer's `ReportSource` property. For more information on the `ReportSource` property, refer to "The `ReportSource` Property" section earlier in this chapter.

After the `ReportSource` property is set, you can run the application. When the page is processed, the viewer is created; it processes the report specified in the report source and then renders the output of the report page to HTML, which gets written to the response stream for the page. Figure 19.5 shows what the Web Forms Viewer looks like in action when rendering a report.

Figure 19.5
A Crystal Report is shown being displayed through the Web Forms Viewer control.

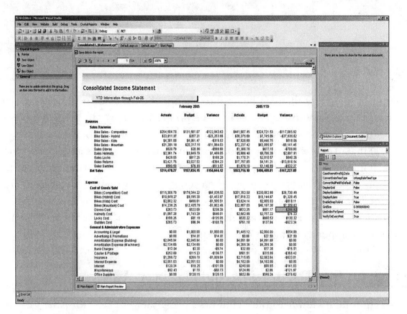

The next section describes some of the common properties used to customize the appearance and behavior of the report viewer.

CUSTOMIZING THE WEB FORMS VIEWER

The first level of customization is to show or hide the main components of the report viewer. The `DisplayGroupTree` and `DisplayToolbar` properties show and hide the group tree and toolbar, respectively. `PageToTreeRatio` is a handy property that enables you to set the width of the group tree as a ratio to the width of the rest of the page. The default value is 6. To show or hide individual toolbar buttons, there is a collection of properties beginning with `Has`, such as `HasExportButton` and `HasRefreshButton`. Using these properties, you can control each button or button group on the toolbar to meet your needs. In addition, the toolbar buttons are standard GIF files contained in the `C:\Program Files\Common Files\Business Objects\3.0\crystalreportviewers11\images\toolbar` directory.

These GIF files can be changed using any graphics-editing program or even replaced by entirely new images assuming that the filenames are kept the same. Finally, there is a style sheet associated with the Web Forms Viewer that can be overridden to change the viewer's colors, fonts, alignment, borders, and more. By default, the viewer looks for the CSS file in the location /crystalreportviewers11/css/default.css. This location translates to the following physical path: C:\Program Files\Common Files\Business Objects\3.0\crystalreportviewers11\css\default.css.

You can either modify this default.css file or create multiple copies of the CSS files, effectively having several skins for the viewer, and dynamically point the viewer to one of the CSS files based on a user preference. The CSS file location is set via the CssFilename property of the Web Forms Viewer.

By default, the viewer renders one page of the report at a time, just as the report designer would do. However, sometimes users find that it would be easier to have all the report's content contained on a single web page. You can do this by setting the SeparatePages property to false instead of its default value of true. When this is done, the viewer renders each page under one another, effectively producing a single web page with the entire report's data.

DATABASE CREDENTIALS

One of the nice things about the version 2008 Crystal Report Viewers as opposed to previous versions is that if the report needs database credentials, it prompts the user for this information. Figures 19.6 and 19.7 show the Windows Forms and Web Forms Viewers database credential prompting.

Figure 19.6
The Windows Forms Viewer prompts for database credentials.

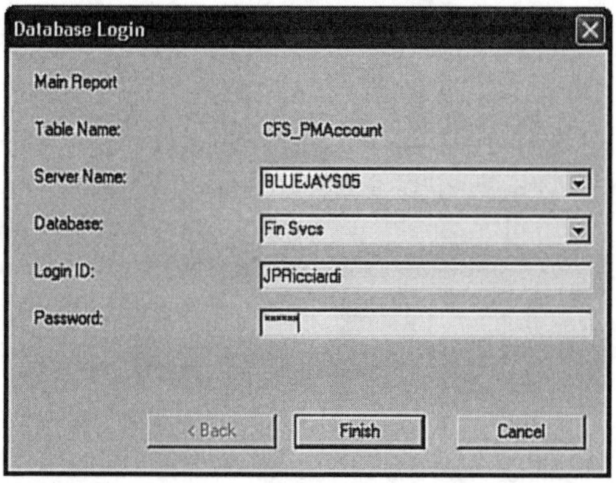

19

Although this is a nice feature, you will often want to suppress this and handle the database credentials. The first reason to do this is to change the appearance or behavior of the database credential process. This could be as simple as customizing the look and feel of the user interface or perhaps changing the behavior in some way. For example, you could have the user prompted the first time but offer to save the credentials for later. This could be accomplished by writing the credentials to a cookie or database. The second reason for suppressing the viewer's prompting would be to set the credentials transparently behind the scenes so that the user won't need to enter them at all. The logic of the viewers is to determine whether credentials have been supplied through the viewer directly, and if not, to see whether the corresponding report has them defined and finally, if not, to prompt the user. Therefore, the solution to customizing or eliminating the database credential prompts is to simply set them before the report is viewed.

Figure 19.7
The Web Forms
Viewer prompts for
database credentials.

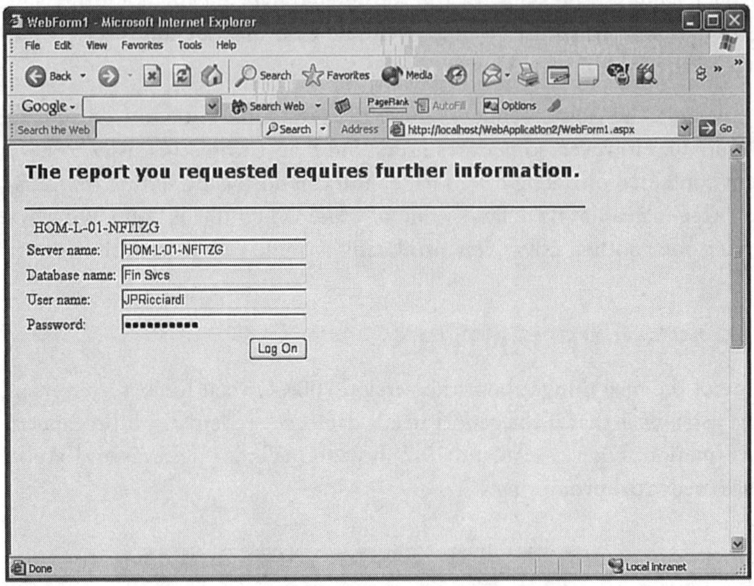

The easiest way to do this is to use the ReportDocument's SetDatabaseLogon method. This function is overloaded for several different argument types. There are really only two of them that you will use. The simplest version of SetDatabaseLogon accepts two strings: a username and password. Keep in mind that Crystal Reports stores the information required to connect to the database inside the RPT file, so unless you want to change the database, you only need to set the username and password. The following code shows an example of this:

```
Dim Report As New ReportDocument()
Report.Load("C:\Reports\Finance.rpt")
Report.SetDatabaseLogon("username", "password")
Viewer.ReportSource = Report
```

In this case, the Viewer object could be either a Windows Forms Viewer or a Web Forms Viewer, because they both have the ReportSource property.

The other version of the SetDatabaseLogon method takes four string arguments: username, password, server name, and database name. This is useful for taking reports based off a test database and pointing them to a production database. Simply pass in the server name and database name you want the report to use, like this:

```
Report.SetDatabaseLogon("username", "password", "SERVER01", "SalesDB")
```

SETTING PARAMETERS

Parameter fields work almost exactly the same as database credentials. Both viewers prompt for parameters if they are required by the report but not supplied by the developer. These parameter prompting screens are shown in Figures 19.8 and 19.9.

Figure 19.8
The Windows Forms Viewer prompting for parameter values.

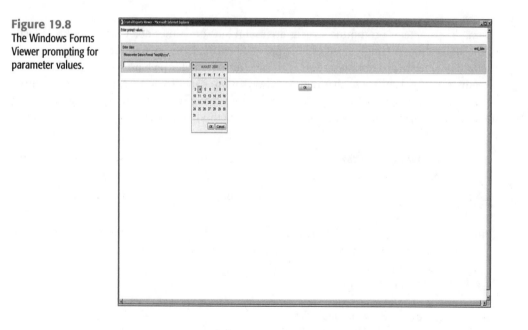

19

Figure 19.9
The Web Forms
Viewer prompting for
parameter values.

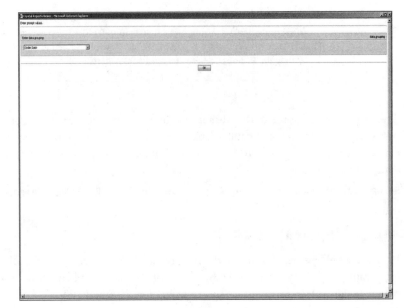

Again, the parameter prompting screens are useful but sometimes don't fit the look and feel of the application or simply need to be suppressed entirely. Another common usage of customized parameter prompting screens is to have the parameter pick list's values come directly from the database so that they are always up to date. To do that, you would use the ReportDocument object to set the parameters before passing it to the viewer to display. This is done via the ReportDocument's SetParameterValue method. There are three versions of this method:

- SetParameterValue(index As Integer, val As Object) is used to set a parameter value by index.

- SetParameterValue(name As String, val As Object) is used to set a parameter value by name.

- SetParameterValue(name As String, val As Object, subreport As String) is used to set a parameter for a subreport by parameter name and subreport name.

An example of this is

```
Dim Report As New ReportDocument()
Report.Load("C:\Reports\Orders.rpt")
Report.SetParameterValue("Geography", "North America")
Report.SetParameterValue("Start Date", DateTime.Now)
Viewer.ReportSource = Report
```

For parameters that accept multiple values, pass in an array of those values.

UNDERSTANDING THE REPORT APPLICATION SERVER BRIDGE

An important change has occurred to the report engine object model in version XI of Crystal Reports. In fact, you might not even have realized this change had taken place after using Crystal Reports 2008 for quite some time; however, it's important to understand. The object model that was previously supplied with the various .NET offerings that Business Objects has produced has talked directly to the Crystal Reports print engine. In version XI, the object model talks to the Report Application Server (a component of BusinessObjects Enterprise and Crystal Reports Server), and then in turn to the Crystal Reports engine. Although there is no immediate noticeable change to the way the engine operates, this is an important change for two key reasons:

- The Report Application Server exposes more functionality than the report engine object model discussed thus far, and this additional functionality can now be leveraged from the report engine object model.

- Because the Report Application Server is a part of the BusinessObjects Enterprise framework, any application using the Crystal Reports 2008 report engine object model and viewers can now be easily upgraded onto the BusinessObjects Enterprise framework.

As for the first point, the Report Application Server's API is available through the standard report engine object model. To access it, use the `ReportClientDocument` property of the `ReportDocument` object. The `ReportClientDocument` is the equivalent to the `ReportDocument` for the Report Application Server. It includes the capability to not only open and change reports, but also to create reports from scratch, add new report objects, add new data sources, and so on.

CREATING A CRYSTAL REPORTS WEB SERVICE

Another notable facet of working in the .NET environment is the capability to create a Crystal Report that is available as a web service and that can be consumed by other applications. To highlight how simply this can be accomplished, Figure 19.10 shows Visual Studio after having added an existing sample Crystal Report (World Sales Report) to a new web service project. Enacting the Publish as Web Service function from the right-click menu creates an `.asmx` file with the name of the report prefixing the text *service*.

You can test out this Crystal Reports web service by setting the corresponding `WorldSalesReportService.asmx` file as the starting page for this web service. This option is accessed through the right-click menu of the `.asmx` object and can be viewed in the browser by accessing http://localhost/WebServiceName/WorldSalesReportService.asmx (see Figure 19.11). You will be presented with a list of the different operations that the report web service supports. You can view sample SOAP request-and-response information using placeholders by clicking on any of the available operations.

Figure 19.10
Visual Studio .NET enables the quick and easy publishing of the World Sales Report as a web service.

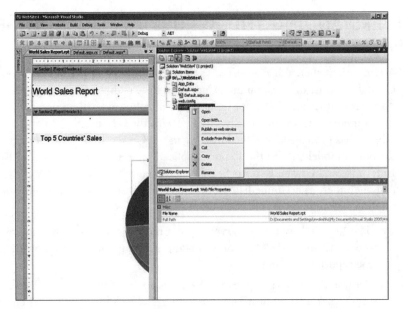

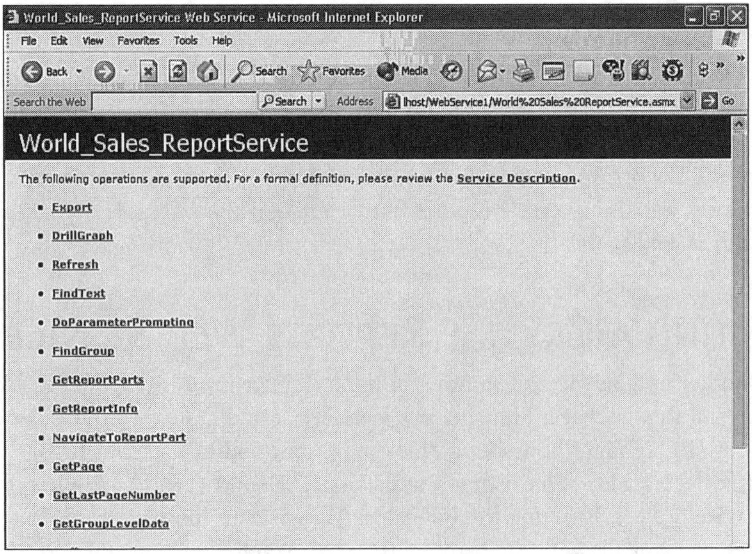

Figure 19.11
Viewing the Crystal Reports web service and its associated operations.

To use this web service from another application, you can quickly create a new ASP.NET application called ShowSalesReport (or anything you prefer) and, after adding a CrystalReportViewer from the new form's toolbox, bind the ReportSource to either the web service or the involved web service's URL as follows:

```
CrystalReportViewer1.ReportSource = http://localhost/WebService1/
➥World Sales ReportService.asmx
OR
CrystalReportViewer1.ReportSource = New localhost.WorldSalesReportService
```

TIP

> When adding a Crystal Reports web service, it is recommended that you eliminate any spaces from the created .asmx web service file. You might experience problems in attempting to click through on the report operations provided by the Crystal Reports web service when spaces have not been eliminated. Also, remember to build your solutions/projects before testing them in your browser.

TROUBLESHOOTING

APPLICATION DEPLOYMENT WITH XCOPY

I am having problems using Xcopy to deploy applications.

Although the object model is pure managed code, the underlying report engine is not. This means you can't perform a pure Xcopy deployment that Microsoft likes to advertise that all .NET applications can do.

PRINTING REPORTS

I can't seem to print a report.

Sometimes when the object model is used in ASP.NET, it is running under a Guest-level account, which does not have access to the machine's printers. If this is the case, you need to install and grant access to the printers for that account.

CHAPTER 20

BASIC XCELSIUS DEVELOPMENT

In this chapter

BusinessObjects Xcelsius 2008 is an intuitive, flexible, and highly customizable data visualization tool, designed to create stunning interactive analytics and dashboards with the ability to securely connect to live data through BusinessObjects Enterprise. Next-generation graphics and easy-to-use prebuilt components allow Xcelsius dashboards to provide maximum impact without months of effort. This chapter will introduce you to basic Xcelsius practices for developing simple interactive dashboards.

INTRODUCTION TO DASHBOARDS WITH XCELSIUS

Xcelsius is a powerful development environment for designing interactive data visualization applications. Xcelsius is capable of producing robust dashboards and calculators that connect directly to Crystal Reports or any other web service connection. Xcelsius dashboards often lead to high user adoption rates because of their stunning aesthetics and ease of use for navigating and visualizing data. Xcelsius dashboards are often deployed to information consumer user groups that need only summarized views of key metrics. An Xcelsius dashboard can then serve as a launch pad into detailed information facilitated by Crystal Reports. Xcelsius technology is deeply integrated with Crystal Reports and BusinessObjects Enterprise to create a seamless transition between technologies, creating a productive and pleasurable end user experience.

Creating Xcelsius dashboards is accomplished by mixing technical and design best practices to ensure that business information is easy to consume. There are a few basic rules of design that will help you to provide the best possible experience for effectively assimilating information.

- Present summarized information that can be easily consumed and understood
- Refrain from adding content or graphics that impede the assimilation process
- Provide sufficient information to drive action or a mechanism to drill into more information to drive action
- Create an intuitive and easy-to-use interface for navigating information without severing the visual association between analytics

XCELSIUS DEVELOPMENT PARADIGM

Xcelsius provides a unique development paradigm that empowers you to create dashboards using Excel or web service connections as a data source. The Xcelsius integrated development environment (IDE) is where you assemble the dashboard project.

When publishing a dashboard from the Xcelsius development environment, the output is an Adobe SWF (Shockwave File). Adobe Flash Player 9 or higher is required to open and run the SWF, which most Internet browser computers already have. This technology enables the highest flexibility to deploy and integrate Xcelsius dashboards within your organization. Adobe SWF technology also enhances the graphic aesthetics and interactivity that Xcelsius is recognized for.

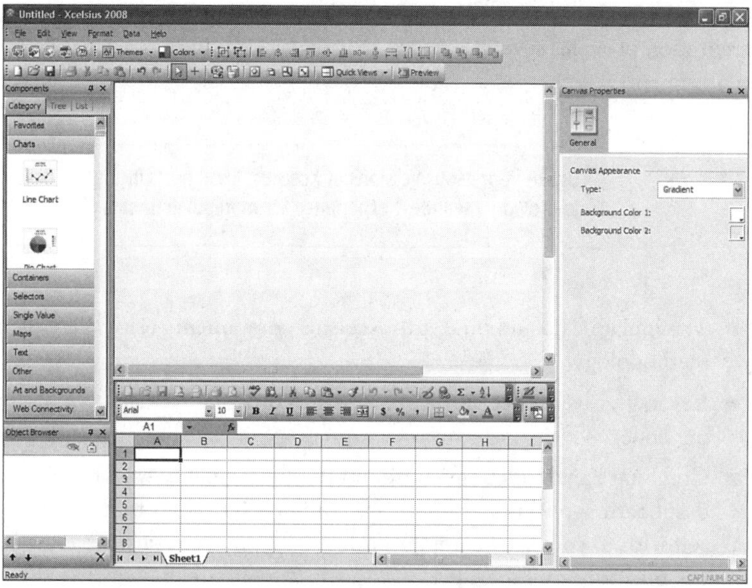

Figure 20.1
The Xcelsius IDE enables dashboard development with no coding required.

Figure 20.2
SWF files generated from Xcelsius provide high-quality vector graphics and an interactive interface.

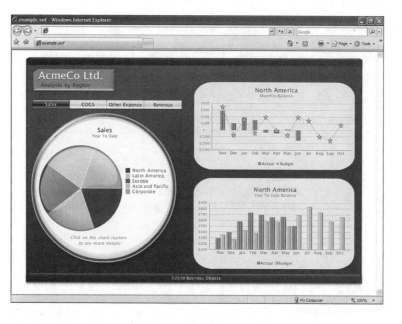

NOTE

Xcelsius-generated SWFs can exist within the most commonly used business applications, including Internet browser, PDF (Portable Document Format), PPT (PowerPoint), and Word.

A critical proponent of the Xcelsius development paradigm is use of Microsoft Excel. This integration provides several benefits that make Xcelsius a powerful dashboard development environment.

> **NOTE**
>
> Unlike in previous versions of Xcelsius, Excel nests inside the development environment to provide a seamless experience for manipulating data and configuring components.

- Manipulate data and bind it to Xcelsius components using a simple point-and-click methodology.
- Leverage Live Office and XML maps to provide live data to a dashboard without writing code.
- Combine Excel functions to extend the functionality with more complex calculators and dashboard applications. There are common functions that you should familiarize yourself with to construct complex dashboards with Xcelsius. Chapter 21 further explains the functions in Table 20.1.

TABLE 20.1 COMMON EXCEL FUNCTIONS FOR BUILDING XCELSIUS DASHBOARDS

Functionality	Formula Examples
Runtime analysis	SUM(), AVERAGE()
Conditional logic	IF(), IF(AND)
Dynamic lookups	VLOOKUP(), INDEX()

> **NOTE**
>
> Xcelsius uses Microsoft Excel only during the dashboard development process. When Xcelsius compiles a SWF, it encodes all the data, metadata, formatting, and logic into the output SWF during the publishing process. That means the SWF can exist without the original Excel sheet.

XCELSIUS INTEGRATED DEVELOPMENT ENVIRONMENT

Xcelsius is capable of producing many unique applications ranging from visual calculators to personalized connected dashboards. The large collection of components and connectivity options provides a broad palette of tools for development. Before you build any applications with Xcelsius, you will familiarize yourself with the development environment.

COMPONENTS

The Components window is an organized collection of preassembled user interface controls and data visualization elements. You can arrange any combination of components on the canvas to achieve a desired interface and layout. Each component has a unique set of properties that can be configured and connected to data and are categorized based on their function within a dashboard. If the Components window is not visible, click on the View menu and then click on Components. Learning to work with the components is critical to understanding how to tap into the visualization power of Crystal Xcelsius. Let's get started with the following steps:

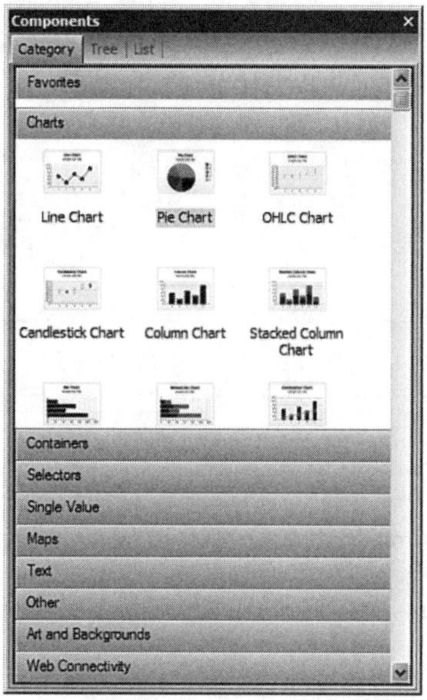

Figure 20.3
The Components window is a sliding accordion menu.

1. Add any chart component to the canvas by clicking on and dragging or clicking once on the component, and then clicking on the canvas.

PROPERTIES

2. Double-click on the component located on the canvas to access the Properties window. All component instances added to a canvas have a properties window that enables you to

   • Bind data from the spreadsheet in the General tab
   • Define how the component behaves in the Behavior tab
   • Modify visual aesthetics in the Appearance tab
   • Set alerts for specific single value, chart, and selector components in the Alerts tab

20

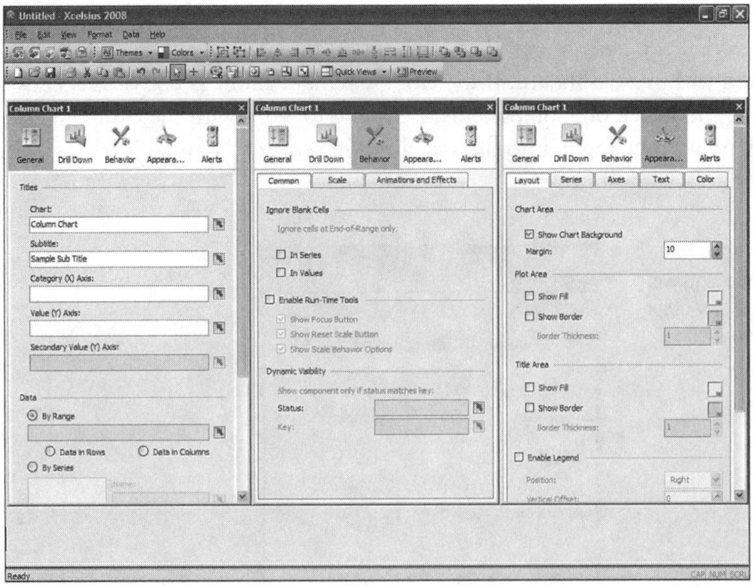

Figure 20.4
Access the properties window by double-clicking or right-clicking on any component located on your canvas.

TIP

Select multiple components on the canvas by holding the Ctrl button while clicking. You can also group multiple selected components. If they are the same type of component, you can change a single properties sheet to affect all involved components at the same time.

NOTE

The quickest way to learn how to use Xcelsius components is to choose a single component from each category and explore the properties sheet. Components from each component category employ similar properties fields, making this learning process efficient.

OBJECT BROWSER

3. Click on the View menu and ensure that the Object Browser is selected. Notice that the component selected on the canvas is also highlighted in the Object Browser.

The Object Browser is a convenient tool for managing multiple components on the canvas and serves as a critical time-saver for complex dashboard projects. The Object Browser displays components in ascending order, which indicates the layer where a component resides in relation to other components. Items at the bottom of the Object Browser list appear as the top layer on the canvas. Changing the layering order of components, and adding and removing components from a group, is possible by clicking on and dragging the related components within the Object Browser window.

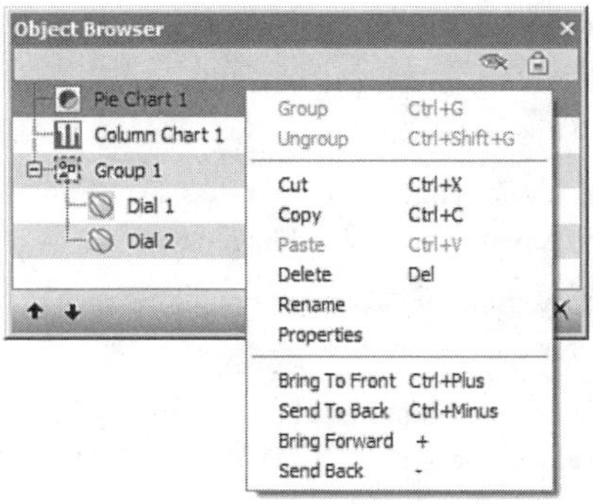

Figure 20.5
The Object Browser has significant built-in functionality to streamline the dashboard design process.

4. Add a second and third component to the canvas, and explore the following Object Browser options:

- Rename objects
- Group and ungroup objects
- Drag objects in and out of groups
- Lock and hide components
- Change the order of multiple objects

TIP

Right-clicking on a component in the Object Browser or canvas provides a menu to copy/paste, group, change the z-order (layer level), and rename a component. You can also use the Ctrl and Shift keys to select multiple components in the Object Browser to facilitate your selected operations.

DATA MANAGER

Xcelsius 2008 features a Data Manager window—the single location for configuring all connections to live data that originates outside a dashboard. Each connection, covered in Chapter 21, has a unique set of properties for connecting to live data. All connection options have a Definition tab where connectivity properties are set. Xcelsius 2008 provides 10 methods for connecting to data through the Data Manager as shown in Table 20.2.

TABLE 20.2   XCELSIUS CONNECTION METHODS

Connection Method	Description
Query as a Web Service	Web service connection that connects only to Query as a Web Service universe queries.
Web Service Connection	Web service connection to most web services that use SOAP standards.
XML Data	Web Service connection that uses a specific <ROW><COLUMN> XML schema to send and load data.
Flash Variables	Push method for loading variables originating in a browser or application.
Portal Data	Method for passing data between two SWFs using Windows SharePoint Services or IBM WebSphere portal integration kits.
Crystal Report Data Consumer	Integration that enables an SWF to nest and consume data from Crystal Reports 2008.
FS Command	A traditional method for passing parameters between an multiple SWFs.
LCDS Connection	Integration allowing for real-time communication and data broadcasting using Adobe Life Cycle Data Services (LCDS).
Excel XML Maps	Web service connection using Excel XML maps as the mechanism for defining the method binding the XML structure.
Live Office Connections	Web service connection to Business Objects web service configured using Live Office.

Although it is premature to dive into the exploration of these data connections at this point, follow the next steps to establish some familiarity with the process that you will explore in the next chapter:

1. Launch the Data Manager and add a Web Service connection. Access the Data Manager through the toolbar icon, within the Data menu, or the Ctrl+M shortcut.

2. Click on the Usage tab to explore the Refresh Options and Load Status. You will learn more about these options in Chapter 21, "Using Crystal Xcelsius for Dashboarding—Advanced."

Figure 20.6
Add and configure
multiple connections
using the Data
Manager.

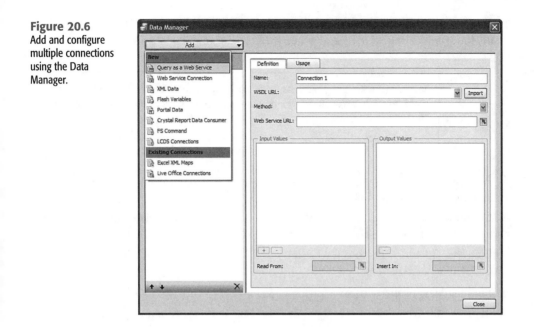

BASIC COMPONENT CATEGORIES

Xcelsius provides a large collection of robust components that, when combined, provide rich functionality to end users. Fortunately, Xcelsius employs a consistent methodology for using components that facilitates a short learning curve for mastering the basic component sets. The initial challenge for new users is in deciding on what components to use in various scenarios to maximize screen real estate and to provide the most productive experience for end users.

SINGLE VALUE COMPONENTS

Single value components have the least complex properties compared to other Xcelsius components. Combining single value components with Excel formulas can enable what-if analysis within a dashboard. All single value components have identical properties sheets, so after you learn how to use one, you have the entire set under your belt.

1. Insert the data in Table 20.3 inside a new Xcelsius project. You might have to highlight and delete the objects that you previously added to the reporting canvas, or you can simply start a New Xcelsius report from the File menu by selecting the New with Spreadsheet option.

TABLE 20.3   EXCEL SPREADSHEET DATA

	A	B
1	Revenue	Adjustment
2	2000	500

2. Change the Excel tab's name to Single Value by double-clicking on the tab located in the lower-left corner of the Excel window. By default, the tab's name is Sheet1.

> **TIP**
>
> To make your Xcelsius project easy to manage and share with other designers, always name Excel tabs according to their purpose. Xcelsius supports multiple tabs within a single dashboard project.

3. Navigate within the Components window to the Single Value Components category, and then insert a Gauge component.

4. Open the Gauge properties window by double-clicking or right-clicking on the component after you add it to the canvas area.

5. Bind the Title property to cell A1 using the source data button, located to the right of the Title input box.

6. Bind the Data property to cell A2.

7. Type **0** in the Minimum Limit input box and **5000** in the Maximum Limit input box.

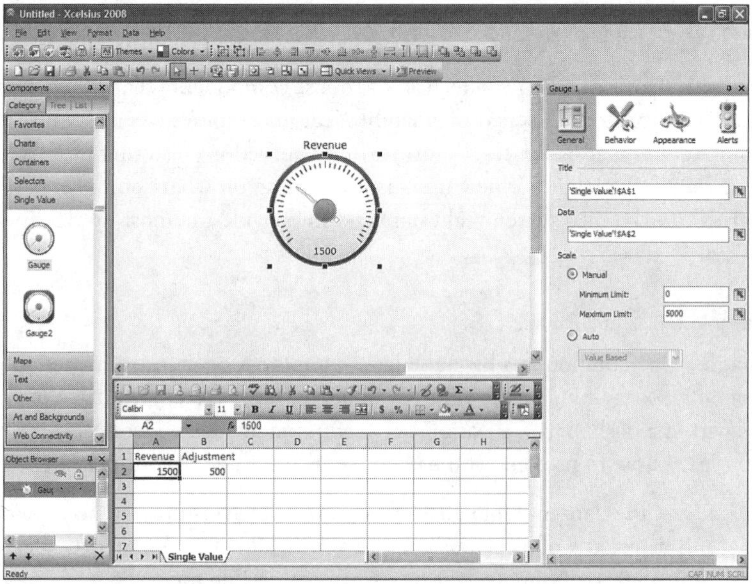

Figure 20.7
Configure the properties sheet by entering data or binding values from the spreadsheet.

> **TIP**
>
> When you start developing your own dashboards from a blank Excel sheets , it is a best practice to leave the first column and top 10 rows empty to make room for titles, labels, selector destination values, and Excel formulas. Grouping meta data and commonly used functions together at the top of your spreadsheet will save you time as you scale and manage your dashboard project.

8. Preview the dashboard by clicking on the toolbar button labeled Preview or pressing Ctrl+Enter. Preview mode generates the SWF inside Xcelsius, providing an exact representation of the dashboard as end users will experience it.

9. Return to design mode by clicking on the Preview button again in the toolbar.

Figure 20.8
Preview mode provides instant validation for designers to ensure that they have configured their dashboard correctly.

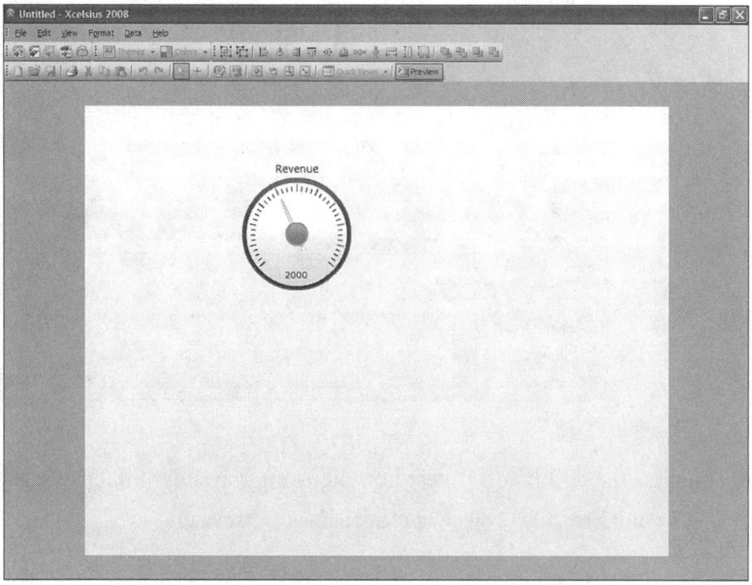

10. Navigate to the Gauge Behavior tab to explore the various properties, including Needle Movement, Limits, Interaction Options, and Dynamic Visibility. As you explore these properties, make sure to preview the dashboard and view how the property changes affect the SWF.

NOTE

Although an end user can technically interact with any single value component, some of these components are for displaying values. Traditionally, the Gauge, Value, and Progress Bar components are *output* visual controls, meaning that an end user does not intuitively expect to click on or interact with the control.

20

11. Insert a Horizontal Slider component from the Single Value components section, and bind the Data property to cell B2.

12. Type **1000** into the Slider Maximum Limit field.

13. Modify cell A2 in the embedded Excel worksheet to reflect the following formula that creates interactivity between the Gauge and Slider components:

```
=1500+B2
```

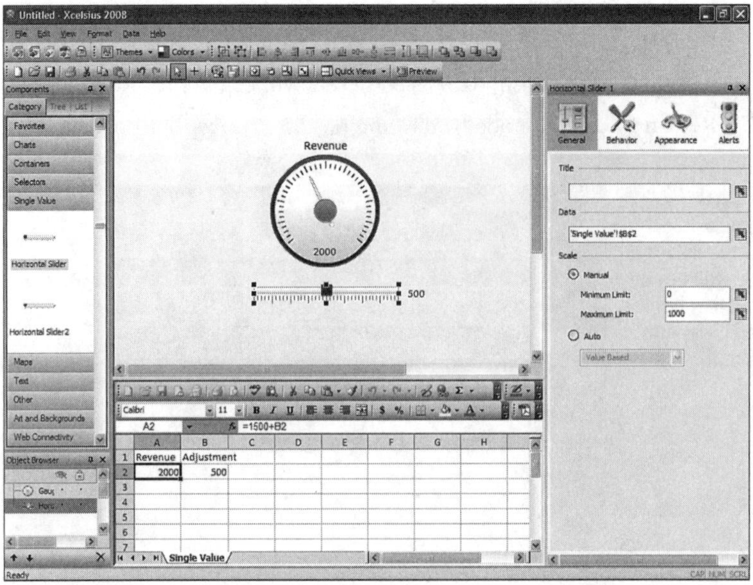

Figure 20.9
Insert a slider and
bind the formula to
create basic interac-
tive analysis.

14. Preview the dashboard to test how adjusting the slider affects the gauge's output value.

15. Save your Xcelsius project as Chapter20_SingleValue.xlf.

NOTE

Using gauges consumes valuable screen real estate, so carefully consider the incremental value that each element adds to the user experience. Also, although the flashy nature of a gauge or progress bar is attractive aesthetically, you could inadvertently misrepresent values if you have no target values to measure against.

CHARTS

Xcelsius includes many of the most common and compelling charts available for visualizing quantitative information. Xcelsius employs similar chart-naming conventions and configuration processes to Excel. In the following exercise, you create a chart and manipulate common properties.

1. Add a new Excel Sheet tab to the Xcelsius project by right-clicking on the existing tab, clicking Insert, and then clicking on OK.

2. Rename the tab to Chart.

3. Insert the data in Table 20.4 inside the Chart Excel tab.

TABLE 20.4   EXCEL SPREADSHEET DATA

	A	B
1	Sales	
2	Q1	2000
3	Q2	2500
4	Q3	3500
5	Q4	4000

4. Navigate to the Charts component category within the Components window, and insert a Column Chart.

5. If not already displayed, open the properties window for the Column Chart through the View, Properties menu option. You might notice that there are many similarities between the General tab on the properties window and the Excel interface for creating charts.

Figure 20.10
All chart components have a similar General tab to make the chart configuration process consistent.

6. Bind the chart Title to cell A1 and delete the chart Subtitle.

7. Bind the Data Range to A2:B5. Xcelsius has logic built into the Chart component to recognize and auto-fill the series values and the axis labels. To bind these values individually or modify them, change the radio button from By Series to By Range.

NOTE

After you select By Series, Xcelsius provides a toggle to enable second Y-axis to create a dual axis chart. Defining a second Y-axis exposes additional appearance and behavior options that enable powerful comparative visualizations.

8. Click on the Behavior tab and check both Ignore Blank Cells check boxes. Ignore Blank Cells is an important feature to scale a dashboard when the number of data points in a range varies. The value of Ignore Blank Cells is the ability to configure a chart to consume a large range of data but only plot the available data points. This feature becomes mandatory when introducing connectivity.

Figure 20.11
Ignore Blank Cells is available for both values and series.

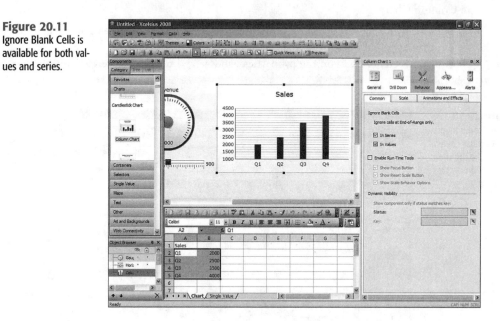

9. Navigate back to the General tab and select the By Series radio button.

10. Rename the Series Name from Series 1 to Revenue. Xcelsius displays the series name in a legend and when end users roll over a data point.

11. Expand Values(y) to B2:B8. Although the data range expands, nothing changes on the chart because there are blank values. The Ignore Blank Cells feature prohibits the chart from plotting these blank cells until data is present.

12. Type **1000** into cell B6. As new values are inserted into the chart data range, the chart dynamically displays them.

13. Save your Xcelsius project as Chapter20_Chart.xlf.

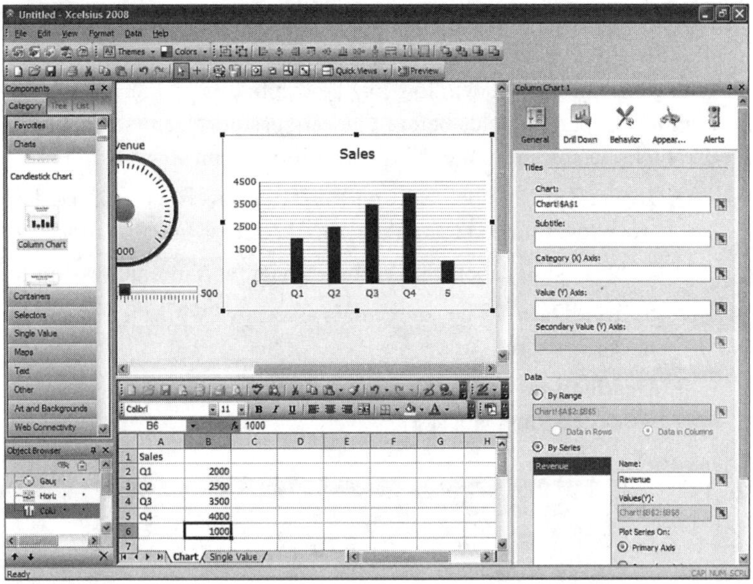

Figure 20.12
Ignore End Blanks allows charts to scale with the introduction of new data.

SELECTORS

Selectors provide a navigation layer to Xcelsius dashboards using common controls, including list boxes and label menus. There are two common uses for selectors.

■ Selectors combined with dynamic visibility toggle components to display and hide based on an end user's selection. You learn more about dynamic visibility in Chapter 21.

■ Selectors that isolate a small range of data from a larger data set using an insertion type. The following exercise leverages a selector to navigate data.

In the following exercise, you transform the bar chart created in the previous exercise to a dynamic visualization tool using a selector to filter data.

1. Insert a new Excel tab within the same Xcelsius project file and label it Selectors.

2. Insert the data in Table 20.5 inside the new Selectors tab.

TABLE 20.5   EXCEL SPREADSHEET DATA

	A	B	C
1		East	West
2	Q1	2000	350
3	Q2	2500	320
4	Q3	3000	360
5	Q4	4000	400

20

3. Navigate to the Selector component category within the Components window, and insert a combo box.

4. Launch the properties window for the combo box. You need to understand the following four properties fields before you can master selectors. Xcelsius uses these fields to drive all selector components' functionality within Xcelsius.

   - **Insert Type**—The insert type dictates how labels, source data, and destination work together to create the desired selector functionality.

   - **Labels**—The labels that end users view and interact within the selector interface.

   - **Source Data**—The source data associated with each label. The insertion type dictates the source data.

   - **Destination**—The destination is where source data values are placed when an end user clicks on a label.

Figure 20.13
All selectors feature the same four fields within the General tab.

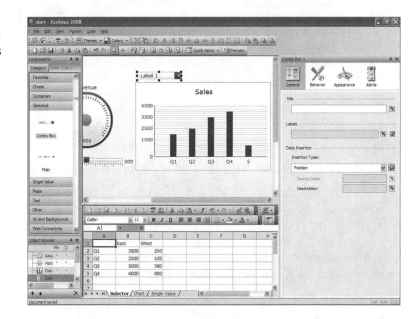

TIP

> Before proceeding, spend some time investigating all seven available insert types using inline help movies provided within the Xcelsius Properties window. Located on the right side of the Insert Type drop-down menu is a help icon that launches a pop-up movie to quickly illustrate the current selected insert type.

5. Bind the labels to B1:C1. The selector automatically populates the labels.

6. Click on the Insertion Type combo box and select Column to define the function that will take place when an end user makes a selection. In this simple scenario, the goal is to isolate each region's column of data when an end user clicks on a selector label.

7. Bind the source data to B1:C5 to assign one column per label.

8. Navigate to the Chart Excel tab from the previous exercise, and bind the destination range to Chart!B1:B5. The destination is bound as a column because the column insertion type was selected. Binding the selector destination column to the same range as the Chart soure data will cause the chart to plot the selector source data. The Destination column should always have the same number of rows as the source data.

Figure 20.14
Configure the combo box to insert rows associated with labels.

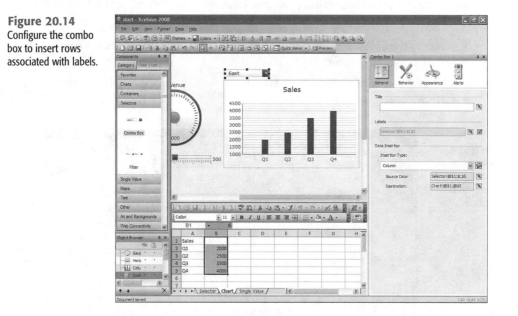

> **TIP**
>
> Setting up a new selector requires additional space within the spreadsheet as a dashboard's data range grows. To save time from having to restructure the Excel sheet, always put the destination range above the source data, or even at the top of the spreadsheet with all other destination cells, rows, and columns. This can be a huge time-saver when troubleshooting or linking components.

9. Preview the dashboard to see the combo box dynamically change the chart.

10. Save your Xcelsius project as Chapter20_Selector.xlf.

> **TIP**
>
> A selector destination cell(s) should not contain data and will never contain formulas. To ensure that you can quickly identify where the selector insert rows are, implement color-coding standards that identify Excel ranges and make Xcelsius development more efficient.

CONTAINERS

Container components streamline the process for navigating groups of components. Both the Panel Container and Tab Set components visually group objects as you add them from the Components window into the container canvases. The Tab Set component provides additional utility with multiple canvases and a tab navigation paradigm to navigate to each view. Their simplicity of use and ability to streamline dynamic visibility (see Chapter 21) for multiple components make containers valuable time-savers in the dashboard development process. The next set of steps introduces this powerful functionality:

1. Navigate to the Container component category within the Components window, and insert a Tab Set component.

2. Double-click on Tab 1 to launch the properties window and expose the buttons to add and remove tabs.

Figure 20.15
Access the Tab Set properties window by double-clicking or right-clicking on the Tab Set buttons.

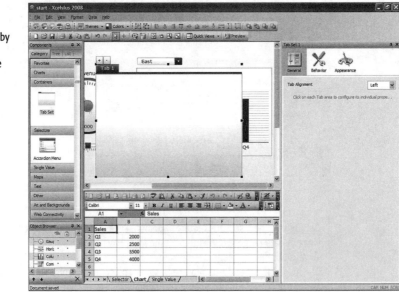

3. Click on the + button, located next to Tab 1 on the canvas, add a second tab, and then name it Revenue.

4. With the second Revenue tab selected, drag the revenue gauge and slider from the first exercise into the container. When inside the container, the components are designated to the corresponding canvas.

5. Click on the Tab 1 button on the Tab Set component to show its unique canvas view, which should be blank.

6. Double-click anywhere within the Tab Set canvas to open the Tab 1 canvas properties window. Each canvas has its own unique properties sheet where you can modify the canvas name, scroll behavior, and appearance.

Figure 20.16
Each tab within the Tab Set component represents an independent canvas view.

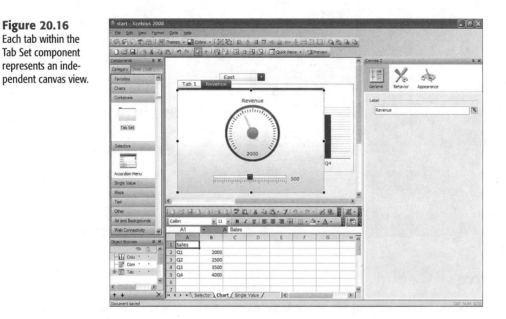

TIP

To drag or scale a Tab Set component, click on a tab and not the canvas area.

7. Rename Tab 1 to Sales through the canvas properties window. To access the canvas properties window, click anywhere inside the container component.

8. Drag and drop the sales chart and combo box selector from the previous exercise into the Sales tab.

9. Spend some time altering the appearance of the Revenue tab to become familiar with the various options.

10. Save your Xcelsius project as Chapter20_Container.xlf.

20

Figure 20.17
Components retain their same behavior, even inside a container.

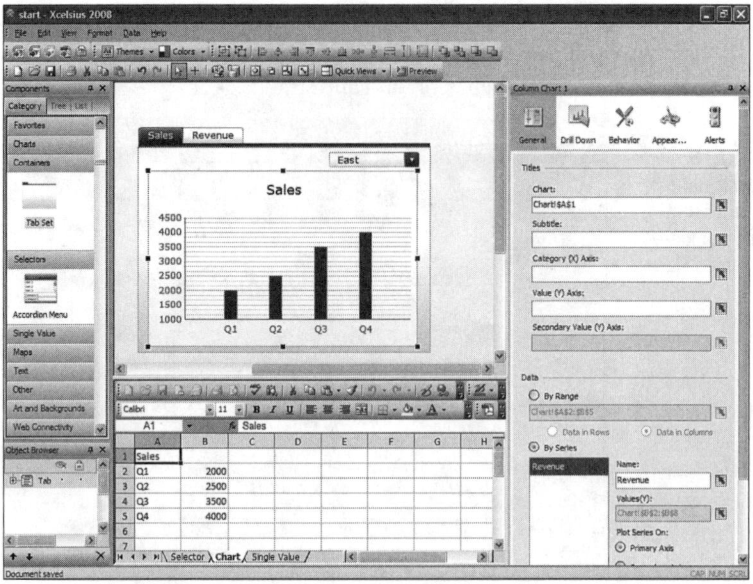

ALERTS

Alerts are critical elements for any dashboard project to ensure that end users can quickly identify areas that require specific attention or action. Alerts within Xcelsius serve as a visual indicator when actual values fall within tolerance of a target value. Single value components, charts, and selectors come equipped with alert properties for designating target values and displaying color-coded thresholds.

In this exercise, you learn how to configure Xcelsius alerts using a single value component that allows you to use the Alerts tab and view the utility of the alerting functionality. And, in doing so, you learn to understand the same concepts in their applicability to chart and selector alerts.

1. Insert a new Excel tab within the same Xcelsius project file and label it Alerts.
2. Insert the data in Table 20.6 inside of the Alerts tab.

TABLE 20.6 EXCEL SPREADSHEET DATA

	A	B
1	Market Share	Target
2	70%	50%

3. Navigate to the Revenue tab within the existing Xcelsius project.
4. Insert a new Gauge component from the properties window into the container.
5. Bind the title to A1 and the data to A2.
6. Type 1 for the gauge maximum limit.

NOTE

> When you enter values into a properties sheet, Xcelsius evaluates whole numbers. In this scenario the gauge represents a percentage, so the maximum value must represent a percentage (1.00 = 100%).

7. Select the Alerts tab within the Gauge properties window, and check Enable Alerts.

Figure 20.18
You can customize the Alerts tab to fit most alert scenarios.

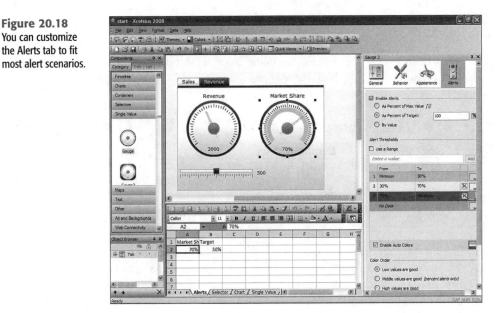

Xcelsius features three alert methods that dictate how alert thresholds are set:

- As Percent of Max Value measures the actual value for a single value component against the component max value. This alert method is available only for single value components.
- As Percent of Target measures how the actual value matches against a single declared target.
- By Value measures how the actual value matches against multiple incremental target values.

NOTE

> The most common alert scenario is Percent of Target because alert thresholds are usually relative to a target number rather than targets themselves. In a less common scenario where there are multiple targets, the By Value alert scenario is the best choice.

20

8. Select the Percent of Target alert method, and bind the value to B2.

9. Enter the following alert thresholds in Table 20.7 for the gauge alerts. Alert threshold colors values can be hard-coded or bound to the spreadsheet.

TABLE 20.7 ALERT THRESHOLDS

1	Minimum	65
2	65%	75%
3	75%	Maximum

10. Select High Values Are Good as the color order. This modifies the gauge alert colors appropriately, where the high color is green and not red. Table 20.8 provides common examples for the three Color Order options.

TABLE 20.8 COLOR ORDER OPTIONS

Alert Color Order	Common Uses
Low Values Are Good	Costs, violations
Middle Values Are Good	Supply
High Values Are Good	Revenue, profit

The effective use of color-coded alert indicators is extremely important to avoid confusion among dashboard end users. Because a small percentage of users are color blind, they cannot naturally interpret red, yellow, and green alert colors. A proper solution is to use the same color hue and change the color intensity or lightness to differentiate alert levels. Xcelsius provides this functionality with auto alerts.

11. Click on the Auto Alerts icon, located on the right side of the Enable Auto Colors. A pop-up window displays multiple alert color options to satisfy color-blind users. Review these color options before moving back to your report to preview the results of your alert-activated gauge.

12. Save your Xcelsius project as Chapter20_Alerts.xlf.

Figure 20.19
Auto Alerts provides multiple options to address all end user populations or alerting standards.

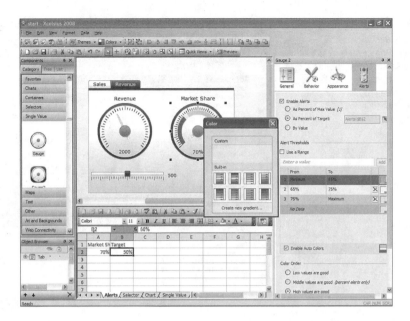

DASHBOARD DESIGN ENHANCEMENTS

The freeform approach of Xcelsius to designing dashboards provides maximum flexibility in layout and content options. The control that Xcelsius provides over color selection and stylized graphics is streamlined to easily create aesthetics that match or complement any design standards.

COLOR SCHEMES

Color schemes introduce a global color palette to all components inserted on the canvas, as well as new components imported from the Components window. The benefit of using color schemes is the ability to establish uniformity across multiple components or dashboard projects.

1. Click on the Color Scheme drop-down from the Format toolbar (or select the Color Scheme menu option from the Format menu) to quickly toggle between standard or custom color schemes.

2. Click on the Create New Color Scheme label, or click on View, Color Schemes to launch the Custom Color Scheme window.

3. Click on Advanced Settings to configure detailed color settings for each component type.

20

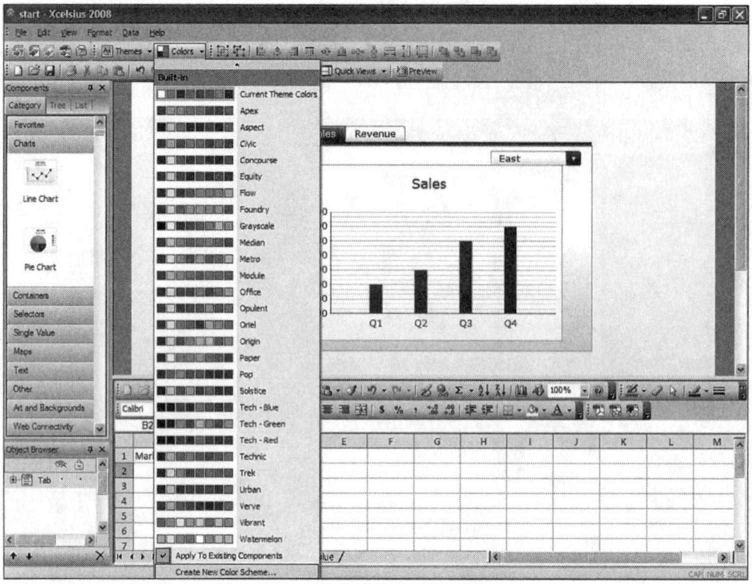

Figure 20.20
Selecting the Color Scheme drop-down is a time-saver compared to changing Appearance properties for individual components.

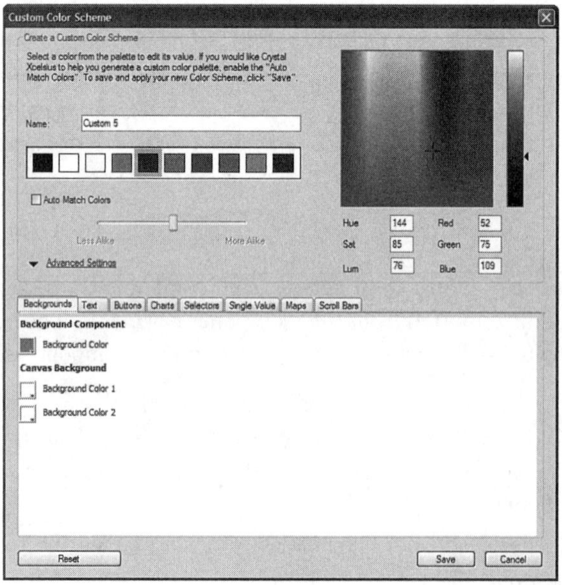

Figure 20.21
The Custom Color Scheme window is a powerful tool because of its granular control over individual component colors.

TIP

You can customize any existing color scheme by right-clicking while the color scheme drop-down is exposed.

THEMES

A *theme* is a stylized graphical composition that affects all components within a single dashboard project. A theme consists of a highly stylized skin and color scheme that you can change at any point in the development cycle. Xcelsius comes bundled with nine themes, each of which has its own unique style—ranging from the basic Halo theme to the over-the-top Admiral.

TIP

> If you select a new theme while developing a dashboard, you overwrite any changes made within the appearance properties of individual components. To avoid overwriting and losing previous work, make sure to save regular versions of your dashboard projects.

Figure 20.22
You can apply all nine themes at any point in the development cycle.

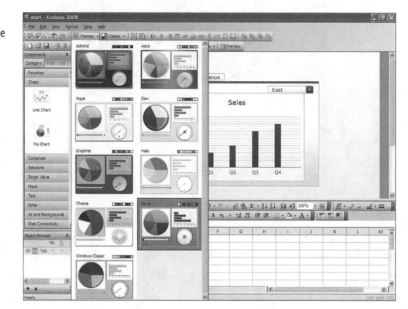

4. Insert any new component onto the canvas. The new component inherits the currently selected theme.

BACKGROUNDS

The Art and Backgrounds component category provides design elements that help transform a collection of components on the canvas to a complete dashboard application. Xcelsius provides a unique background for each theme. When layered on top of each other, they create visual separation between components on the screen. By design, the backgrounds are ordered so that they complement each other in style and color contrast.

1. Open a new Xcelsius project and navigate to the Art and Backgrounds component category.

2. Insert the Background4 and stretch it on the canvas so that it is slightly larger than the Tab Set container.

3. Right-click on the Background component and click Send to Back.

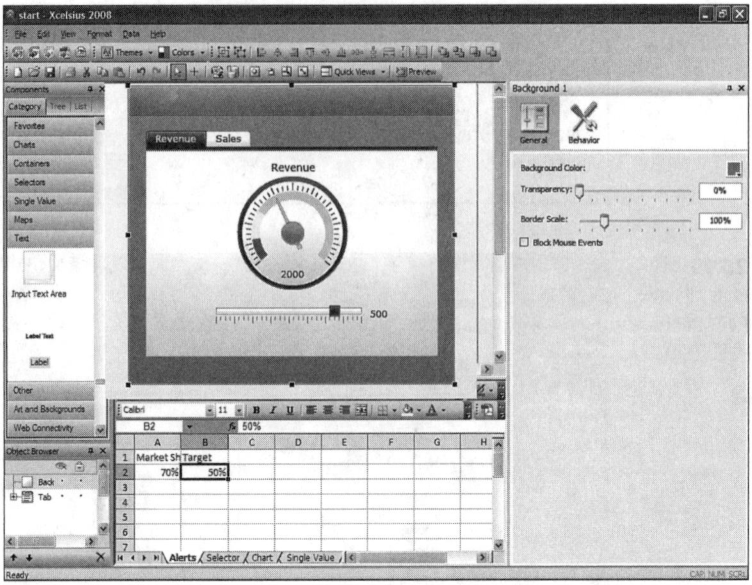

Figure 20.23
Background components create the look and feel of an application with minimal effort.

LABEL TEXT

Most dashboards require additional text, labels, or titles to identify qualitative information. The Label component is capable of displaying formatted text strings or scrollable text blocks.

1. Insert a Label component, from the Text component category, into the upper-left corner of the Background component.

2. Type **Executive Dashboard** into the Enter Text field.

3. Stretch the Label component so that the title displays on the same line.

4. Navigate to the Appearance tab and then the Text tab.

5. Test the various text-formatting options to achieve your preferred style.

6. Save your completed Xcelsius project as Chapter20_Dashboard.xlf.

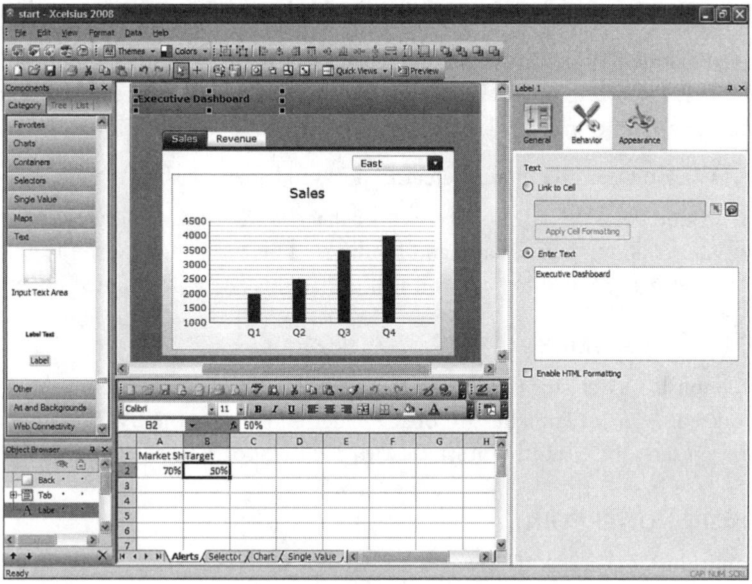

Figure 20.24
Label components are perfect for supplying additional qualitative data within a dashboard.

IMAGE COMPONENT

Another important component within the Art and Backgrounds category is the Image component. The Image component is a container for importing JPG, PNG, GIF, and BMP images or other SWF files into Xcelsius. The imported images embed inside the SWF upon compilation. This component is widely used when the provided Xcelsius backgrounds and artwork are not sufficient for a specific design requirement. A common example is the introduction of company logos or brand-specific graphics.

NOTE

The Image component is recommended for JPGs and SWFs generated by Flash or Flex using ActionScript 3. Although you can nest a published Xcelsius dashboard inside a parent Xcelsius project, I recommend using the Slideshow component for multilayer dashboards. Chapter 21 covers this topic in detail. Though the image component is not capable of embedding an SWF generated from Xcelsius, it will successfully display the content. The parent SWF containing the image component and the loaded child SWF will be copied into the same directory when publishing the dashboard.

PUBLISHING AND DEPLOYMENT

The last step before deploying a dashboard to end users is to publish the SWF output. Xcelsius is capable of exporting a wide variety of file formats that serve as a container or framework for the SWF. Regardless of the deployment type, an SWF retains its interactivity and connectivity. Clicking on File, Export displays a list of export options.

ADOBE SWF

A standalone SWF file is executable using a desktop version of the Flash player or a web browser. Exporting to SWF is necessary in any scenario where a dashboard loads into another application, portal, or framework that supports SWF file formats.

1. Click on the File menu, select Export, and then Flash (SWF).

2. Name the SWF file Chapter 20_Dashboard. Xcelsius generates an SWF file containing all the components, data, and bindings. This file is now portable and does not require Xcelsius or Excel to run. You will utilize this SWF in the next chapter.

ADOBE PDF DOCUMENT

To publish an Xcelsius dashboard to a PDF document, only the Adobe Acrobat Reader is required. Xcelsius launches Acrobat Reader and inserts the SWF as an embedded object where users can instantly interface with the dashboard as they open the PDF document.

MICROSOFT POWERPOINT

Publishing to Microsoft PowerPoint embeds the SWF as an object on a slide. While in the PowerPoint Design mode, the SWF is resizable like any other object but is not interactive. PowerPoint must be in Presentation mode to interact with the SWF.

> **TIP**
>
> Do not stretch an SWF object to fill the entire PowerPoint slide. Because the SWF file is an object, the presenter must click outside of the SWF object to proceed to the next slide. If the SWF provides no space to click outside the object, it leaves the presenter stuck on the current slide.

MICROSOFT WORD

A dashboard published to Microsoft Word, by default, stretches to fit the document width while maintaining the SWF's original aspect ratio.

> **NOTE**
>
> Before publishing your dashboard, make sure the canvas is not significantly larger than the area you consume with components. The canvas-sizing options are located in the View menu and ensure that there is no excessive whitespace. To define the canvas size in pixels, access the Document Properties located in the File menu.

BUSINESS OBJECTS ENTERPRISE

Xcelsius provides a secure publishing option directly to the BusinessObjects Enterprise platform, where you can load a dashboard inside InfoView or add it to a Dashboard Manager screen as a new analytic. For more information on Xcelsius' integration points into BusinessObjects Enterprise, read the next chapter.

HTML

Exporting to HTML generates an SWF and an HTML file that contains the correct markup syntax to load the SWF. The SWF must reside in the same directory as the HTML file unless the HTML code is modified.

CRYSTAL REPORTS

Crystal Reports 2008 supports embedded SWF files, which is a powerful delivery mechanism for delivering interactive analytics or what-if analysis to support standard reporting functionality. Although Xcelsius does not provide a built-in feature for exporting to Crystal Reports, the following process provides Crystal Reports as an additional deployment method for Xcelsius. Chapter 21 covers additional connectivity integration between Xcelsius and Crystal Reports.

1. Click on the Xcelsius File menu, and export to an SWF file format.

2. Click on Crystal Reports 2008 Insert menu, and then click on Flash.

3. Browse the local folder structure to find an Xcelsius-generated SWF and click on OK. The SWF file behaves like any other object in a Crystal Report but retains the Xcelsius interactivity and connectivity. Chapter 21 provides additional connectivity instructions for connecting Crystal Report data to an embedded SWF.

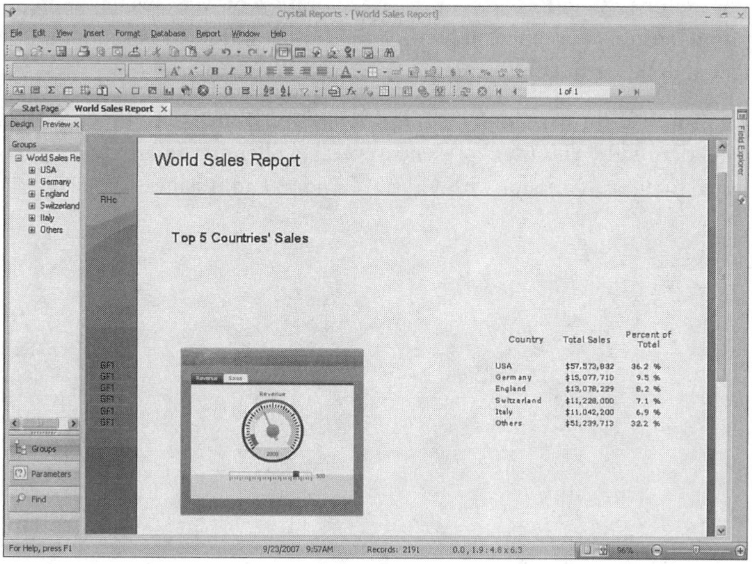

Figure 20.25
An Xcelsius dashboard embedded inside a Crystal Report.

TROUBLESHOOTING

An Xcelsius dashboard can potentially become a complicated compilation of components, logic, and queries that utilize Excel for binding input and output. This process can lead to user error, making it difficult to troubleshoot because an SWF does not expose the underlying spreadsheet during runtime. There are two methods for gaining visibility to the underlying bindings and logic:

- The spreadsheet table is the quickest method available for visualizing the underlying table structure while in preview mode. Using this component as a troubleshooting aid provides instant feedback over questionable cells when data does not appear or when the dashboard does not behave as anticipated.

- The snapshot feature is accessible only in Preview mode and generates a copy of the original spreadsheet based on the current state. This feature is extremely powerful for troubleshooting Excel logic or complicated combinations of selectors. To create a snapshot, select File, Snapshot, Current Excel Data.

After completing this chapter's exercises, you should have a solid foundation for constructing basic dashboards using Xcelsius components. Xcelsius utilizes a consistent methodology for configuring dashboards, which makes exploration of additional features much easier. The speed and flexibility for deploying dashboards makes Xcelsius the perfect complementary solution for Crystal Reports. Further exploration of Xcelsius, including Crystal reports integration, ensures that you can provide a robust solution by combining best-of-breed reporting and dashboard technologies.

The processes for matching technical Xcelsius features with functional dashboard requirements desired by end users presents several challenges. In Chapter 21, you will also learn how to integrate Xcelsius with Crystal Reports and Business Objects.

ADVANCED XCELSIUS VISUALIZATION AND CONNECTIVITY

In this chapter

With an understanding of core Xcelsius development techniques and components, you are prepared to take dashboard development to the next level using the advanced features and connectivity of Xcelsius. This chapter's sections will introduce you to Xcelsius concepts for transforming simple models for visualizing information through to the creation of robust connected dashboards.

ADVANCED GLOBAL FEATURES AND TECHNIQUES

All the basic component categories introduced in the previous chapter have advanced features that you can harness to enhance a dashboard. Using existing components, you will learn how to apply advanced features and techniques to provide granular control over the user experience and to provide increasingly powerful data display and navigation.

DYNAMIC VISIBILITY

Dynamic Visibility is a global property located in the Behavior tab for every Xcelsius component that is intended to manipulate the visibility behavior. Dynamic Visibility consists of two fields, Status and Key, which dictate when a component is visible to end users as they interact with a dashboard. The first of the two fields is Status, which serves as a listener when bound to a cell. The second field, Key, is a value that the Status field listens for. Whenever a Status cell contains the defined Key, a component displays on the screen. When the Status contains any value other than the Key, a component hides on the screen. Developers primarily use Dynamic Visibility to create multiple views based on a user's interaction. Because screen real estate is limited, many scenarios call for multiple levels of analysis based on the relevance and importance of provided information. In the following exercise, you will use a selector to toggle the visibility of two chart components.

1. Open a new Xcelsius project with a blank Excel sheet.

2. Rename the Excel tab to Dynamic Visibility by double-clicking on the tab located in the lower-left corner of the Excel window. By default the tab will be Sheet1.

   Navigate within the Components window to the Charts components category and insert both a pie chart and a column chart.

3. Navigate to the Selectors components category and insert a radio button selector.

4. Open the Radio Button Properties window by double-clicking or right-clicking on the component.

5. Click on the Labels icon, located at the extreme right of the Labels area beside the Source Data icon, to manually define two labels: Column and Pie. You can also delete the third Label option created by default in this dialog.

6. Change the insertion type to Labels, and bind the destination to cell A1.

7. Navigate to the column chart's Properties window, and select the Behavior tab.

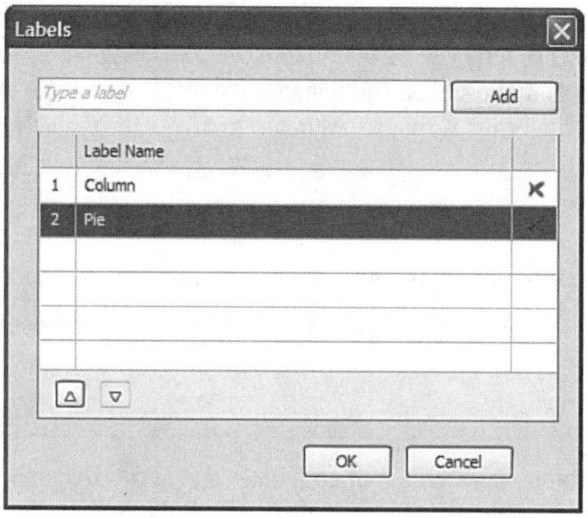

Figure 21.1
The Labels icon is located to the right of the Source Data icon.

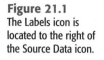

8. Bind the Dynamic Visibility Status field to cell A1. This instructs the column chart to listen to cell A1 for a specific key.

9. Type **Column** as the dynamic visibility key. When the value Column is present in A1, the column chart appears on the screen. If any value other than Column is present in cell A1, the chart will be invisible. Because the radio button inserts into cell A1, this selector causes the chart to appear or disappear during runtime.

Figure 21.2
Column chart with Dynamic Visibility configured.

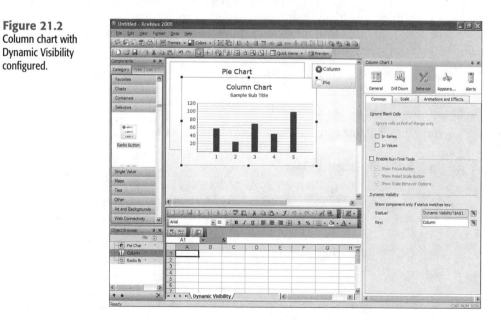

10. Bind the Pie chart's Dynamic Visibility status field to A1, and define Pie as the key.

21

NOTE

A Status or Key property can be bound to a cell containing logic that provides more flexibility over events that dictate a component's visibility. An example of this scenario is a combination of selectors within a dashboard to trigger the visibility of a component.

11. Align the bar and line charts vertically, and then preview the dashboard. This provides a visual effect to end users as they toggle between the two charts using the radio button selector.

TIP

As you layer components on top of each other and assign Dynamic Visibility, the canvas area becomes a conglomeration of controls. This is the perfect scenario to leverage the Object Browser for hiding or locking components while in Design mode.

CHART DRILL DOWN

Most Xcelsius charts contain a Drill Down Properties sheet tab that enhances a chart from static visualization component to selectable control. A chart with Drill Down enabled allows end users to click directly on a data point to trigger a selector insertion type. This option is an efficient way to provide intuitive drill-down, eliminate redundancy, and save screen real estate. The configuration process for chart drill-down employs the same configuration methodology as selector components within Xcelsius.

1. Add a new Excel sheet tab to the Xcelsius project by right-clicking on the existing tab, clicking on Insert, and then clicking on OK.
2. Change the tab's name to Chart Drill Down.
3. Insert the data in Table 21.1 inside the Chart Drill Down tab.

TABLE 21.1   EXCEL SPREADSHEET DATA

	A	B
1		
2	Q1	20
3	Q2	40
4	Q3	60
5	Q4	80

4. Open the existing column chart's Properties sheet from the Dynamic Visibility exercise.
5. Bind the source data to A2:B5.

6. Select the Drill Down tab and check Enable Drill Down. Drill Down employs the same configuration properties as a selector with an option to set up unique Data Source and Destination properties per series. Because each data point in a chart serves as a label that an end user can click on, the Labels property is absent from the Drill Down tab.

7. Select Row as the insertion type.

8. Select Series 1 inside the Series list box.

9. Bind the source data to A2:B5. Each data point represents one row of data, so selecting the entire range allows the chart to insert the corresponding row into the Destination row.

10. Bind the destination to A1:B1.

11. To finish off the chart, type **Quarterly Sales** for the chart title and delete the subtitle.

Figure 21.3
A chart configured with drill-down capability functions like a selector.

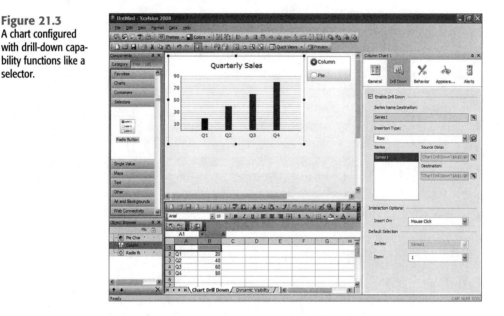

12. Insert a Horizontal Progress Bar component (from the Single Value component category) onto the canvas, and navigate to its Properties sheet.

13. Bind the title to A1 and the data to B1.

14. Preview the dashboard and click on the various chart columns. Notice the dynamic effect of the progress bar values based on your drill-down behavior.

TIP

Although chart capabilities might seem intuitive as an Xcelsius developer, end users might not recognize that it is possible to click on a chart. Depending on the sophistication of your end user community, it is good practice to label components with instructions to click when the drill-down option is available on a chart.

21

INSERT FILTERED ROWS

Insert Filtered Rows is an advanced selector insertion type often used in conjunction with connected dashboards. A connected dashboard consumes data from live data sources including Crystal Reports or web services and returns data in a flat vertical table, as shown in Table 21.2. The challenge as a dashboard designer is to allow end users to choose between dimensions using a selector and then display the associated values in a chart. Insert Filtered Rows is the perfect solution to automatically parse and display unique labels and then insert the associated rows into a destination range. Although Insert Filtered Rows utilizes the same property fields as all other insertion types, the method for binding labels, source data, and destination is slightly different. In the following exercise, you will configure Insert Filtered Rows to enable an end user to choose a region and view the associated products in a chart.

1. Add a new Excel sheet tab to the Xcelsius project by right-clicking on the existing tab, clicking on Insert, and then clicking on OK.

2. Change the tab's name to Filtered Rows.

3. Insert the data in Table 21.2 inside the Insert Filtered Rows tab.

TABLE 21.2   EXCEL SPREADSHEET DATA

	A	B	C
1			
2			
3			
4	West	Cars	500
5	West	Boats	510
6	East	Cars	800
7	East	Boats	810
8	East	Trains	820

4. Navigate to the Selectors components category and insert a Combo Box selector.

5. Open the Combo Box Properties window and select Filtered Rows from the Insertion Type drop-down.

6. Bind the labels to A4:A8. Unlike other insertion types, Insert Filtered Rows automatically parses the selected labels range and displays unique values within the selector.

TIP

If the range of data includes end blanks, enable the selector Ignore End Blanks feature located in the Properties sheet Behavior tab. That feature prevents blank label values from displaying in the selector.

7. Bind the source data to A4:C8. Although the Filtered Rows insertion type does not require you to include the labels in column A, this data can be leveraged for titles within the dashboard.

8. Bind the destination to A1:C3. The destination range should always match or exceed the maximum number of possible filtered rows from the source data. In this exercise there are three labels with the value East. Selecting three rows as the destination range ensures that all data is accommodated.

Figure 21.4
A combo box with
Insert Filtered Rows
configured properly.

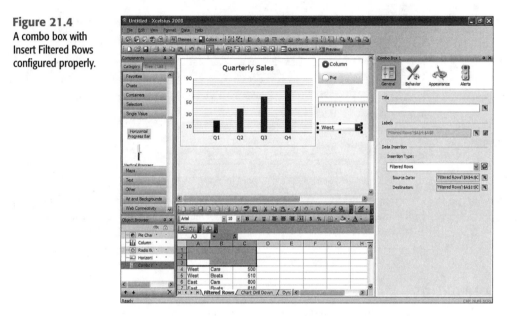

9. Use the existing pie chart from the Dynamic Visibility exercise, or insert a new pie chart.

10. Bind the data values to C1:C3 and the labels to B1:B3.

11. Bind the pie chart title to A1, and delete the subtitle.

12. On the Behavior tab of the Pie chart, check the In Values check box under Ignore End Blank Cells. At this point the pie chart is empty because it is bound to ranges that are currently empty. When you preview the SWF file, the Combo Box selector dynamically inserts the filtered ranges based on the region selection.

13. Check the In Values box under Ignore Blank Cells on the Behavior tab of the Pie chart to ignore the blank cells at the end of the range.

14. Preview the chart to see the selector insert filtered rows and display them inside of the chart. Depending on where you placed the Combo Box and Bar Chart components, you might need to move them around to ensure that you can view all the values of the Combo Box when it is selected. Alternatively, you can bring it forward by using the right-click functionality in the designer while that object is selected.

21

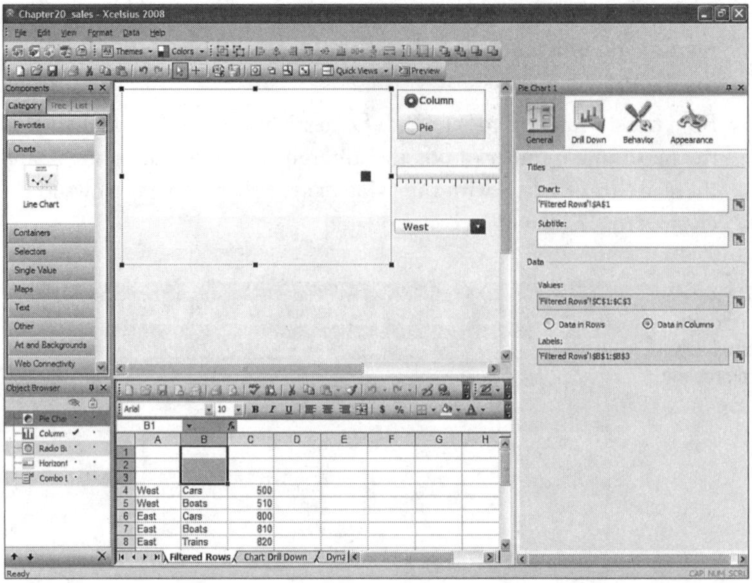

Figure 21.5
Pie chart configured to consume data provided by the Combo Box selector.

NOTE

The Insert Filtered Rows insertion type does not require contiguous matching labels values to correctly filter and insert rows into the destination range.

MAP COMPONENTS

The Map Components category in Xcelsius features an extensive collection of maps that you can use as navigation controls and as visual alert indicators. Xcelsius maps are configured to work similar to selectors, but with a few variances due to the Region Labels property already defined. In the next exercise, a world map enables the user to display values and drill into detailed information.

1. Add a new Excel sheet tab to the Xcelsius project by right-clicking on the existing tab, clicking on Insert, and then clicking on OK.

2. Change the tab's name to Map.

3. Insert the data in Table 21.3 inside the Map tab.

TABLE 21.3 EXCEL SPREADSHEET DATA

	A	B
1		
2	Africa	500
3	Asia	600
4	Australia	700

	A	B
5	Europe	800
6	North America	900
7	South America	1000

4. Navigate to the Map Components category and insert a World by Continent map.

5. Open the map Properties window and click on the view Region Keys icon located to the right of the source data button. A pop-up window will display a list of map keys.

6. Delete the region keys for Antarctica and Oceania by double-clicking on the item located in the Region Key column. This prevents both regions from displaying within the map.

Figure 21.6
Delete the region keys that do not have data present. In this case Antarctica and Oceana have been deleted.

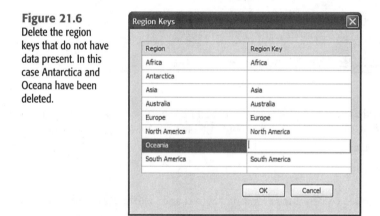

7. Bind the map display data to A2:B7. The data in column B displays as a ToolTip when an end user hovers over a continent.

8. Bind the source data to A2:B7 and set the insertion type to Row.

> **NOTE**
> Unlike other selectors, map components require the region keys within the left column for display data, source data, and alert target. The region names must reside in contiguous cells so that the data links to the correct region.

9. Bind the destination to A1:B1.

10. Insert a Value component from the Single Value Components category.

11. Bind the value component title to A1 and the data to B1.

12. Preview the dashboard to test the map as a selector.

Figure 21.7
Map component
properly configured
to include the keys
with source data.

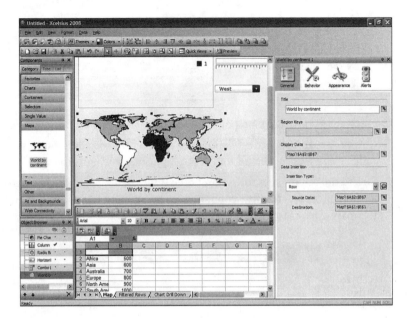

13. Publish your dashboard as an SWF by clicking on the File menu, selecting Export, and then selecting Flash (SWF). Save the dashboard to your local machine, and name the SWF file Chapter21_sales.swf.

14. Save your Xcelsius project file (XLF) as Chapter21_sales.xlf.

Maps are an ideal user interface control for navigating regions and visualizing color-coded alert indicators. Xcelsius map components make great alternatives to using selector components when countries or states dictate how an end user will navigate information. If you are building a dashboard that uses a country or state as a dimension, remember to browse the maps component category to see whether there is a map to suit your application requirements.

MULTILAYER DASHBOARDS

Multilayer dashboard is a term used to describe a single parent dashboard that loads multiple child SWFs into a nested container. Multilayer dashboards are intended to create a single interface for seamlessly toggling between multiple dashboard views. A common use for implementing a multilayer dashboard is a large-scale project with multiple SWFs that need to be coupled in one application.

In the following exercise, you will use two SWF files generated from previous Xcelsius exercises, Chapter20_dashboard.swf and Chapter21_sales.swf. You will create a single multilayer dashboard that dynamically loads each SWF into a single container.

1. Navigate to the directories on your computer containing two Xcelsius-generated SWFs for this exercise, Chapter20_dashboard.swf and Chapter21_sales.swf, and copy them to the same directory where you will save your multilayer dashboard exercise.

2. Insert the data in Table 21.4 inside a new Xcelsius project.

TABLE 21.4 EXCEL SPREADSHEET DATA

	A	B
1		
2	Executive View	`Chapter19_dashboard.swf`
3	Sales View	`Chapter20_sales.swf`

3. Insert a new component from the Selectors category called Label Based Menu.

4. Bind the labels to A2:A3.

5. Select the Row insertion type and bind the source data to A2:B3.

6. Bind the destination to A1:B1. Cell B1 will drive the dynamic toggle between both child SWFs.

7. Navigate to the Web Connectivity category within the Components window and insert the Slide Show component below the Label Based Menu selector.

8. Stretch the Slide Show to fit the entire canvas area below the Label Based Menu. The size of the canvas component dictates how a child SWF scales, so it is important that the canvas is the same size or larger than the child SWF to prevent unnecessary scaling.

9. Open the Slide Show Properties window and bind the URL to cell B1. As the value in B1 changes, the slideshow refreshes with the new child SWF based on the URL. A relative path is used in this scenario and dictates that the child SWFs reside in the same directory as this parent dashboard.

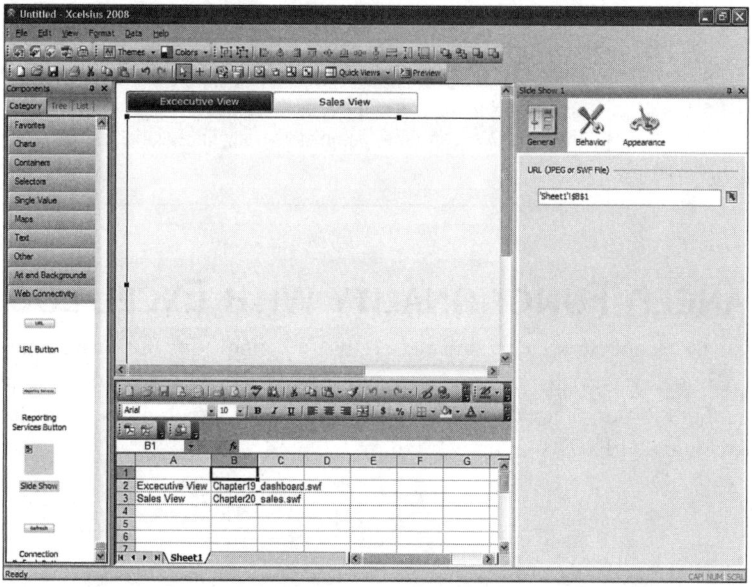

Figure 21.8
Stretch the slideshow to fit the entire canvas below the Label Based Menu.

NOTE

To ensure that a multilayer will maintain a consistent scale, ensure that all child SWF files are the same canvas size. To set canvas sizing, navigate to Document Properties, located in the File menu.

10. Navigate to the File menu and export an SWF as `Chapter21_multi-layer.swf` to the same directory as the two child SWFs.

11. Save the Xcelsius project file as `Chapter21_multi-layer.xlf`.

12. Open the parent dashboard with a web browser to view both `Chapter20_dashboard.swf` and `Chapter21_sales.swf` load in the Slide Show container.

NOTE

A multilayer dashboard loads child SWFs from their respective URLs instead of embedding the SWF inside of the parent. You can use both relative and absolute paths within the parent dashboard as long as the dashboard end user has access to a folder or server where the child SWFs resides.

Multilayer dashboards are extremely powerful for scaling a dashboard that might contain a high volume of charts and analytics. This feature also provides a nice way to "componentize" a large dashboard project as multiple files, making it much easier to manage and edit. Although Dynamic Visibility and container components provide a similar end user experience, a multilayer dashboard is the only way to combine multiple disconnected Xcelsius dashboards into a single seamless interface.

TIP

Multilayer dashboards can send parameters from the parent to the child by appending parameters to the end of the child SWF path (example: `dashboard1.swf?param=xyz`). The child SWF consumes parameters using Flash variables, which is covered later in this chapter.

ADVANCED FUNCTIONALITY WITH EXCEL LOGIC

Excel logic facilitates sophisticated events and conditions not provided as native Xcelsius functionality. Xcelsius components combined with Excel functions present an unlimited number of options for delivering most desired user experiences. Xcelsius supports a high percentage of Excel functions listed in Table 21.5.

21

TABLE 21.5   SUPPORTED EXCEL FUNCTIONS IN XCELSIUS

ABS	DEGREES	HLOOKUP	NETWORKDAYS	SLN
ACOS	DEVSQ	HOUR	NORMDIST	SMALL
ACOSH	DGET	IF	NORMINV	SQRT
AND	DIVIDE	INDEX	NORMSINV	STANDARDIZE
ASIN	DMAX	INT	NOT	STDEV
ASINH	DMIN	INTERCEPT	NOW	SUM
ASSIGN	DOLLAR	IPMT	NPER	SUMIF
ATAN	DPRODUCT	IRR	NPV	SUMPRODUCT
ATAN2	DSTDEV	ISBLANK	OFFSET	SUMSQ
ATANH	DSTDEVP	KURT	OR	SUMX2MY2
AVEDEV	DSUM	LARGE	PI	SUMX2PY2
AVERAGE	DVAR	LE	PMT	SUMXMY2
AVERAGEA	DVARP	LEFT	POWER	SYD
BETADIST	EDATE	LEN	PPMT	TAN
CEILING	EOMONTH	LN	PRODUCT	TANH
CHOOSE	EVEN	LOG	PV	TEXT
COMBIN	EXACT	LOG10	QUOTIENT	TIME
CONCATENATE	EXP	LOOKUP	RADIANS	TIMEVALUE
COS	EXPONDIST	LOWER	RAND	TODAY
COSH	FACT	MATCH	RANGE_COLON	TRUE
COUNT	FALSE	MAX	RANK	TRUNC
COUNTA	FIND	MEDIAN	RATE	UPPER
COUNTIF	FISHER	MID	REPLACE	VALUE
DATE	FISHERINV	MIN	REPT	VAR
DATEVALUE	FIXED	MINUS	RIGHT	VDB
DAVERAGE	FLOOR	MINUTE	ROUND	VLOOKUP
DAY	FORECAST	MIRR	ROUNDDOWN	WEEKDAY
DAYS360	FV	MOD	ROUNDUP	WEEKNUM
DB	GE	MODE	SECOND	WORKDAY
DCOUNT	GEOMEAN	MONTH	SIGN	YEAR
DCOUNTA	GT	N	SIN	YEARFRAC
DDB	HARMEAN	NE	SINH	

> **NOTE**
>
> Because of the conversion process that takes place when Xcelsius generates an SWF, not all Excel functions and features are supported. Xcelsius transforms Excel functions into proprietary code that the Flash player can interpret, which alleviates a reliance on Excel.

CONDITIONAL FORMULAS

Conditional formulas provide significant flexibility in controlling dashboard events based on user interaction. An IF() statement can facilitate complex logic used to toggle visibility or calculations. Conditional formulas are commonly used to control data displayed within a chart or table. Although this logic is most valuable in more complex examples, the following exercise illustrate a simple use of the IF conditional formula. The logic evaluates a logical statement and then enters designated value when the condition is TRUE or FALSE.

> **TIP**
>
> To prevent performance lag within a dashboard, replace complex nested IF statements with IF(OR) or IF(AND) formulas.

1. Open a new Xcelsius project with a blank Excel sheet.
2. Change the Excel tab's name to IF.
3. Insert the data in Table 21.6 inside of the IF tab.

TABLE 21.6   EXCEL SPREADSHEET DATA

	A	B	C	D
1				
2		Actual	Target	Logic
3	Q1	5000	4500	
4	Q2	2400	2200	
5	Q3	3400	3500	
6	Q4	2200	2000	

4. Navigate to the Selectors components category and insert a Checkbox selector.
5. Open the Checkbox properties window, and enter **Show Target** as the component title.
6. Bind the destination to cell B1.

> **NOTE**
>
> By default, all toggle selectors, including the check box, icon, and toggle button, have default source values of 0 (off) and 1 (on).

7. Enter the following formula into cell D3, where B1 represents the destination for the check box and C3 is the target value. The goal is to show the target value in column C only when the check box is checked. If the check box is unchecked (B1=0), the formula leaves D3 blank.

    `=IF($B$1=1,C3,"")`

8. Repeat the formula in range D4:D6 using the same formula pattern. For example, D4 should look like the following:

    `=IF($B$1=1,C4,"")`

9. Insert a combination chart, and change the title to Quarterly Sales.

10. Select the By Series radio button to manually define two ranges.

11. Click on the + symbol twice at the bottom of the Series list to add two new series items. You will configure each one of these series individually.

12. Bind the first range name to B2 and the values to B3:B6.

13. Bind the second range name to C2 and the values to D3:D6. The values in column D are dictated by the IF function, which is driven by the Checkbox selector.

14. Bind the Category Labels(x) located at the bottom of the Chart properties sheet to A3:A6.

15. Navigate to the chart's Behavior tab, and then check the In Series and In Values check boxes under Ignore Blank Cells. This property will cause the chart to ignore blank cells at the end of range.

Figure 21.9
The target series is bound to a range containing an IF() statement that hides the series when the check box is unchecked.

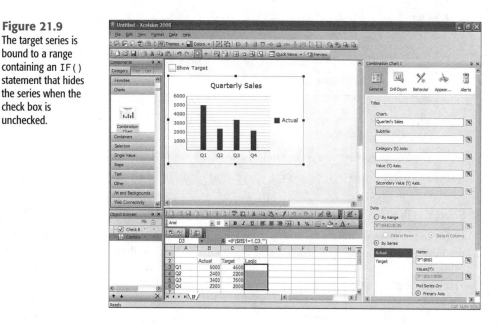

16. Preview the dashboard to test how the check box toggles the data visibility.

The IF() formula expands your potential for constructing complex navigation and user experience options that cannot be achieved with basic Xcelsius component properties. The IF statement can be extended with additional functions (AND, OR) to provide a simple solution for complex conditional logic.

LOOKUP FUNCTIONS

Lookup functions, including MATCH, INDEX, VLOOKUP, and HLOOKUP, are lightweight alternatives to using selector insertion types that might not fill your functional requirements for specific dashboard functionality. Lookup functions are commonly used to look up values in a cross-tab or when selector insertion types are not sufficient. The following exercise will use the INDEX function to look up values in a cross-tab using two selectors.

1. Add a new Excel sheet tab to the Xcelsius project by right-clicking on the existing tab, clicking on Insert, and then clicking on OK.

2. Change the tab's name to INDEX.

3. Insert the data in Table 21.7 inside the INDEX tab.

TABLE 21.7   EXCEL SPREADSHEET DATA

	A	B	C
1	Region		
2	Product		
3	Lookup		
4		West	East
5	Cars	60%	65%
6	Planes	56%	45%

4. Insert a Combo Box selector onto the canvas and bind the labels to B4:C4. This selector defines the region.

5. Select the Position insertion type; bind the destination to B1.

6. Insert a Combo Box selector onto the canvas and bind the labels to A5:A6. This selector defines the product.

7. Select the Position insertion type; bind the destination to B2.

8. Insert the following INDEX function into cell B3. This formula evaluates B5:C6 and uses the positions defined by the product and region drop-downs to look up a single index value.

```
=INDEX(B5:C6,B1,B2)
```

NOTE

After creating the INDEX logic, cell B3 might show an error because the region and product values are not defined. To test the INDEX function within Excel, enter numeric values in cells B1 and B2.

9. Insert a Gauge component. Bind the Data property to B3 and assign a maximum limit of 1.

10. Navigate to the Appearance tab and select the Text tab. Choose Value, and then change the number format to Percent.

11. Change the Decimal Places to 0.

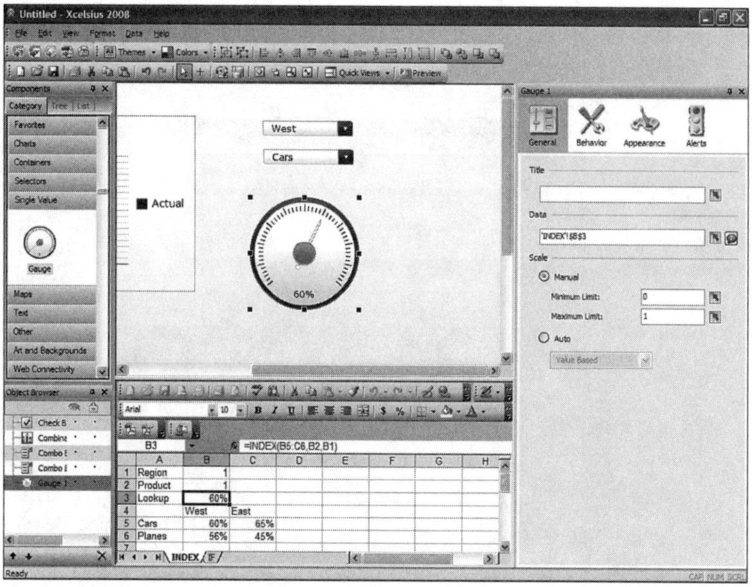

Figure 21.10
The INDEX function is used to look up a value in a cross-tab based on the combination of selections.

12. Preview the dashboard to view how both selectors combined with INDEX logic will look up and display the appropriate value in the gauge.

    INDEX formulas can also be used to look up values within a single row or column. This exercise uses row insertion methods for both combo boxes, which provides the row and column numbers for the INDEX function. To look up the current selected region and product, you can leverage the INDEX formula again.

13. Insert the following INDEX function into cell C1:
    =INDEX(B4:C4,1,B1)

14. Insert the following INDEX function into cell C2:
    =INDEX(A5:A6,B2,1)

The INDEX and VLOOKUP functions provide maximum flexibility to dynamically structure data within a dashboard. The benefit to using a lookup formula is the ability to dynamically look up values and extend basic Xcelsius selector capabilities.

CONCATENATING VALUES

Concatenation of multiple cells and text strings delivers functionality not possible with component properties. The Concatenation function is valuable for creating dynamic titles when multiple inputs or dimensions dictate information displayed in a chart. The following steps concatenate two combo box selections to provide a meaningful title for end users:

1. Enter the following formula into cell E1 on the INDEX tab. The & symbol is used to concatenate cells and text within quotation marks.

   `=C1&": "&C2`

2. Bind the Gauge component's title to cell E1.

3. Publish the dashboard as `Chapter21_logic.swf`, and save the Xcelsius project as `Chapter21_logic.xlf`.

Figure 21.11
The chart title is a concatenation of the destination cells for region (A2) and product (A3) selectors.

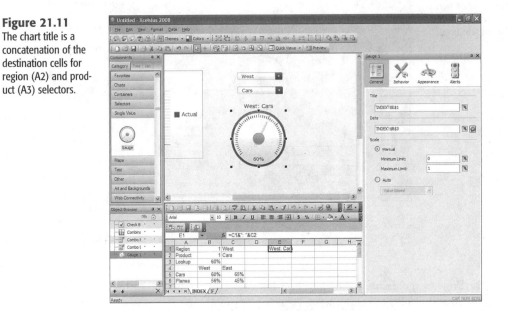

TIP

> Although Excel does provide a concatenate function, it is best to use an & (ampersand) to concatenate multiple values together because this method provides better performance.

NOTE

> Another common use for the concatenation formula is generating dynamic URL strings. This method is used for passing parameters to web services or launching reports using selectors to dictate parameters. This is covered in more detail later in this chapter in the section "Launching Parameterized Reports from Xcelsius."

WORKING WITH DATES

When connecting dashboards to live data, the challenge of matching data formats will occur. Dashboards that pass a date or time parameter often require a specific date format. Coupling DAY(), MONTH(), and YEAR() functions with Concatenate provides flexibility to generate any date format.

TIP

> The NOW() function provides the current date and time within a dashboard and can be used to calculate the difference between the current date and past dates.

ADVANCED CONNECTIVITY AND INTEGRATION

Xcelsius dashboards are capable of loading data originating from sources including web services, XML, Crystal Reports, and Query as a Web Service (QaaWS). Within the Xcelsius development environment, all data connections are managed within the Data Manager introduced in Chapter 20. Each connection has its own unique properties for loading or sending data. All connection types have the commonality of using the same Excel binding paradigm that Xcelsius components rely on.

Choosing the appropriate connectivity option ensures a smooth development process, leading to a dashboard that scales and performs appropriately. Developing a dashboard that uses one or multiple Data Manager connections typically requires more planning than a self-contained Excel-based dashboard. To ensure that the development process goes smoothly, make sure that you have resources who can obtain the required data, and then build reports, queries, or web services for Xcelsius to consume. The quickest and easiest method for producing dynamic and secure dashboards with Xcelsius is through Crystal Reports, Web Intelligence, and QaaWS, which are covered in detail in this chapter.

A few general guidelines will lead to a successful connected dashboard deployment:

- Use parameterized queries to restrict the volume of data when larger record sets are required for data visualization and navigation.
- Utilize the query-triggering options to chain or delay queries based on when end users need access to the data.
- Develop queries with query response times of 3 seconds or less. The longer end users have to wait for data, the more difficult it is to gain user adoption.
- Leave adequate space within the spreadsheet for data results to grow, and enable the Ignore End Blanks option within all selectors and charts.
- Keep all commonly used functions and titles on a single tab or at the top of each tab.

21

DATA MANAGER USAGE TAB

Most connection types within the Data Manager have a Usage tab. The Usage tab provides properties that dictate when a connection will trigger and connection status feedback options.

The connection refresh options provide granular control over events that trigger a single query to refresh. Xcelsius can trigger a query to refresh when a dashboard is loaded, on a time-based interval, or using a Trigger Cell event. A Trigger Cell is a single cell that serves as a listener for a specific event. When one of the following events occur, the query will refresh.

- **When Cell Updates**—Triggers the connection whenever a value is inserted into a cell, even if it is the same value.

- **When Value Changes**—Triggers the connection only when the value within a trigger cell changes.

- **When Value Equals**—Triggers the connection only when a value within the trigger cell matches a specified key—similar to Dynamic Visibility. This key can be bound to a cell, which provides unlimited flexibility in triggering options if conditional formulas are used to dictate the trigger key.

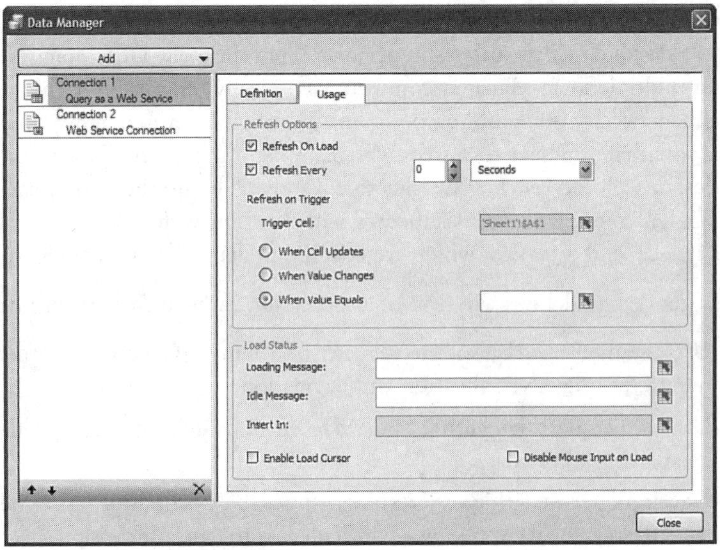

Figure 21.12
The Data Manager's Usage tab provides control over refresh events and load status options.

The Usage tab also features multiple load status properties that provide real-time feedback while an SWF connects to live data.

- The load status' `Loading` and `Idle` messages can be bound to a cell and then bound to a Label component to provide a visual indication of which analytic or chart is being refreshed.

■ The Enable Load Cursor property changes the mouse pointer into an hourglass during the length of a connection refresh period.

> **TIP**
>
> The Enable Load Cursor property is highly recommended to provide visual indication to end users that data is loading.

■ The Disable Mouse Input on Load property prohibits a dashboard end user from clicking on any controls while a query is loading. This feature is important to avoid triggering multiple queries by accident while waiting for data to load.

> **TIP**
>
> If a selector drives a query through a trigger cell, check the Disable Mouse Input on Load option to prevent inadvertently triggering multiple queries.

CONNECTION REFRESH BUTTON

The Connection Refresh button is accessible from the Web Connectivity components category and works in conjunction with the Data Manager. This component is available as a user interface control to provide a clickable method to execute a query. After a connection is added to the Data Manager, it is an accessible option within the Connection Refresh Button Properties window.

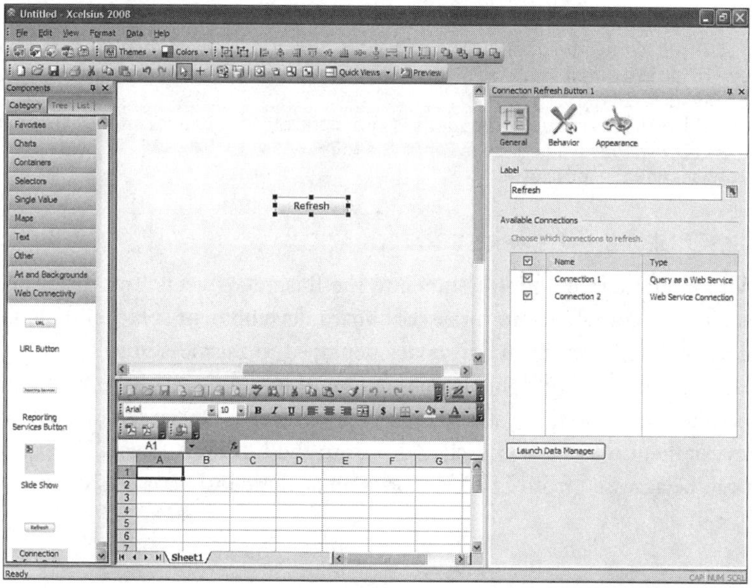

Figure 21.13
The Connection Refresh button can trigger any combination of connections from the Data Manager.

LIFE CYCLE MANAGEMENT CONSIDERATIONS

Most enterprise dashboards built with Xcelsius reside in a secure environment and connect to live data. Assuming that the dashboard design process transpires in a development environment before migration to production, there are a few considerations to ensure seamless life cycle management. All common connectivity methods used for enterprise dashboards utilize a variation of a web service URL. In a scenario where the SWF resides on the same application server as the data source, the web service URL can be streamlined as a relative URL path. This modification alleviates changing web service URLs for every environment the SWF is deployed to. With the exception of a Live Office connection, all web service connectors have a bindable web service URL. That URL can be controlled through Flash variables to provide a seamless transition from production to development. Flash variables are covered later in this chapter.

NOTE

> Using a relative path works with most server configurations, but rarely when a reverse proxy is used.

CROSS-DOMAIN POLICY

When an SWF is deployed to a server different from the data source, a cross-domain policy file will need to reside in the root directory where the web services reside. This cross-domain policy file is part of the enhanced security options in the latest version of the Adobe Flash player. A cross-domain policy file is always named `crossdomain.xml` and should contain the following XML code:

```
<?xml version="1.0"?>
<!DOCTYPE cross-domain-policy SYSTEM "http://www.macromedia.com/xml/dtds/cross-
domain-policy.dtd">
<cross-domain-policy>
    <allow-http-request-headers-from domain="*" headers="*" secure="false" />
    <allow-access-from domain="*" secure="false" />
</cross-domain-policy>
```

BUSINESSOBJECTS ENTERPRISE INTEGRATION

With multiple integration points into the BusinessObjects Enterprise platform, Xcelsius facilitates a complete enterprise dashboard development solution including security, connectivity, and deployment. A dashboard deployed to BusinessObjects Enterprise automatically inherits data security rights from one of multiple connectivity options, including Web Intelligence reports, Crystal Reports, and Universe Queries. The Xcelsius development environment offers a single-click export to the BusinessObjects Enterprise repository, where it can be accessed from InfoView or as an analytic inside of Dashboard Manager.

Figure 21.14
Xcelsius dashboards can be loaded as a new Dashboard Manager analytic or within BusinessObjects Enterprise InfoView.

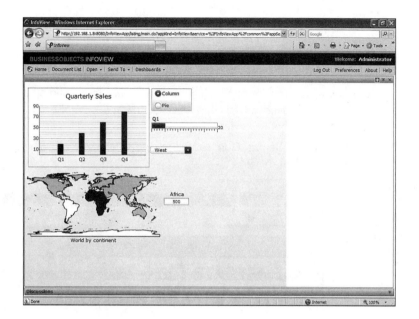

LIVE OFFICE CONNECTIVITY

An Xcelsius dashboard is capable of connecting directly to Crystal Reports or Web Intelligence reports through web services. Connectivity to either reporting solution is configured using Live Office for Microsoft Excel. This add-in facilitates the process for connecting report parts to Xcelsius. BusinessObjects Live Office is a BOE Premium product or can be added on to BOE Professional. Architecturally, there is no difference between how Crystal Reports or Web Intelligence provides data to an SWF because both use the same web service layer, which is part of BusinessObjects Enterprise. The choice of which reporting solution to use should be dictated by the reporting standards that are in place within your organization.

An Xcelsius dashboard will automatically consume all the metadata that the Live Office Excel add-in generates when you bind a Crystal Report or Web Intelligence report to an Excel range. Inside of Xcelsius, you will define connectivity properties using the Live Office connection inside the Data Manager.

NOTE

Xcelsius' integration with Live Office is only utilized during design time to define the fields and properties required to transact data from the Crystal and Web Intelligence reports to the dashboard. During runtime, an SWF uses the inherited metadata from Live Office to connect directly to the reports via BusinessObjects web services.

21

1. In Microsoft Excel, select the Live Office menu item and then click on Insert Crystal Report content. If you are using Excel 2007, the Live Office options are located in the Add-Ins menu.

2. Enter your username and password within the Live Office login screen to BusinessObjects Enterprise XI 3.0. Your Live Office install should be configured to connect to a web service URL that looks like the following: http:// servername: portnumber/dswsbobje/services/session.

3. Select the Crystal Report, Comparative Income Statement.rpt to be used as a data source, and click on Next.

Figure 21.15
Select a Crystal Report containing data to use within the dashboard.

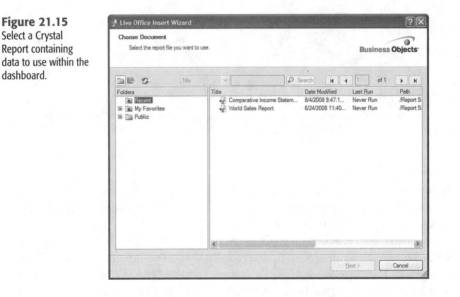

4. Click and drag to select the report part containing data that will be bound to an Excel range.

5. Click on Next, and then click on Finish within the Live Office Insert Wizard window to insert the selected report part data into the Excel range. Right-clicking on any cell within the range displays a Live Office menu for refresh or additional configuration options.

6. Save the Excel file to your local PC as Chapter21_LiveOffice.xls.

7. Open a new Xcelsius project. You will enable a feature required for working with Live Office inside of Xcelsius.

NOTE

Close all instances of Excel when working with Live Office connections inside of Xcelsius to ensure that Xcelsius will properly communicate with the Live Office add-in for Excel.

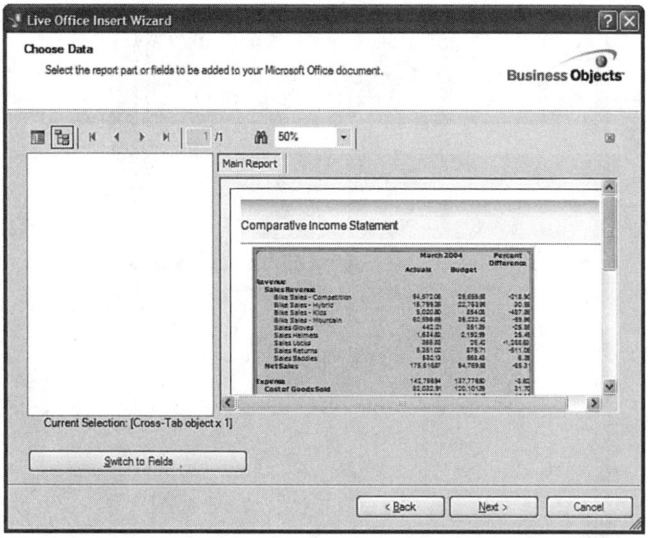

Figure 21.16
Click and drag within the report window to select the report part(s).

8. Click on the File menu, Preferences, and then navigate to the Excel Options menu.

9. Click on the Enable Live Office Compatibility option, and then click on OK to close the Preferences window. This option allows Xcelsius to communicate with Live Office.

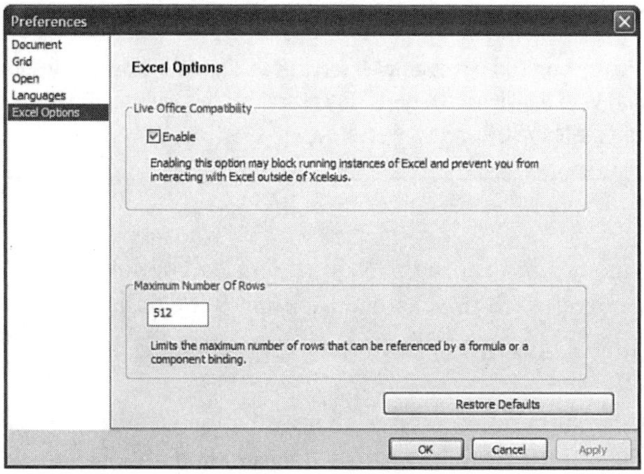

Figure 21.17
Enable Live Office compatibility mode within Xcelsius.

10. Click on the Data menu, and then click on Import.

11. Navigate to Chapter21_LiveOffice.xls, and then click on Open.

12. Launch the Data Manager window and add the Live Office Connections. Xcelsius automatically displays all Live Office reports within the Data Manager.

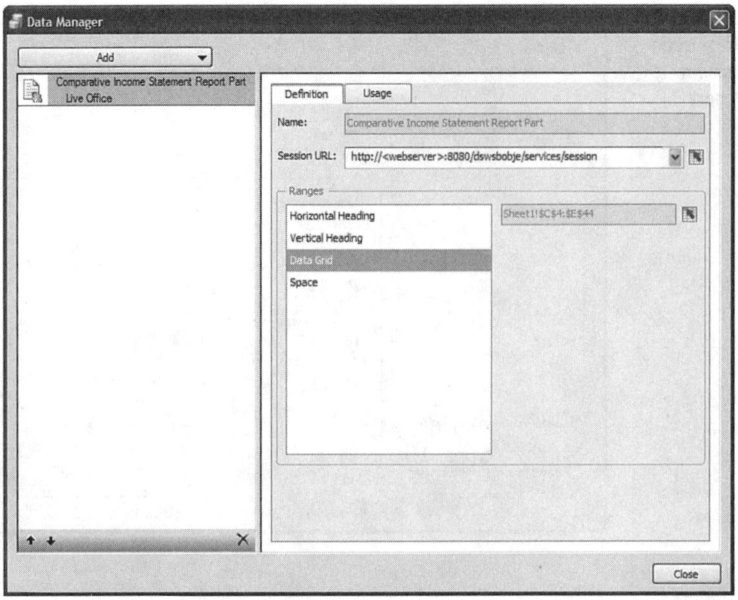

Figure 21.18
Add Live Office connections within the Xcelsius data manager.

13. Replace the `<webserver>:8080` portion of the session URL with your BusinessObjects Enterprise server and port number.

> **NOTE**
>
> The session URL accesses web services that an SWF uses to consume data from Crystal and Web Intelligence reports. To ensure that this web service is functioning properly, you can paste the URL into a web browser.

14. Select the Usage tab and check the Refresh on Load option. The Live Office connection will now refresh each time an end user opens the dashboard.

15. Save the Xcelsius dashboard as `Chapter21_LiveOffice.xlf`.

To make certain that your end users have all information required to make decisions, you can import multiple reports or report parts into a single dashboard to ensure a holistic view of metrics and trends. The benefit of using Crystal and/or Web Intelligence reports is the ability to consolidate and summarize large volumes of data that can easily be integrated into a dashboard. The goal is not to load thousands of rows of data into a single dashboard, but rather smaller digestible bits that the end user will visualize and make decisions with. Another benefit of using either reporting solution is the ease for mashing up summarized data from multiple data sources. For example, a single Xcelsius dashboard is capable of displaying report data originating from finance, CRM (customer relationship management), and marketing systems to provide rich analysis that drives business decisions.

SCHEDULED INSTANCES VERSUS LIVE REFRESH

Scheduling Crystal Reports and Web Intelligence reports maximizes query response time for reports that normally take long periods to refresh. Xcelsius can consume cached data from scheduled report instances to provide instant access to data with minimal latency for end users. In contrast, both reporting solutions allow for runtime refresh in scenarios when the database is frequently updated or when parameters are used to filter query results. By default, a Live Office connection will refresh the latest instance of a report, meaning the data will not be refreshed from the database. The settings for refreshing Live Office connections with live data are toggled using Live Office.

> **NOTE**
>
> Although Web Intelligence will not enable parameterized scheduled reports, Crystal Reports' interactive parameters offer the best of both worlds with parameterized queries within a scheduled instance. For more information about interactive parameters, see Chapter 5, "Implementing Parameters for Dynamic Reporting."

1. In the Excel file with configured Live Office connectivity (`Chapter21_LiveOffice.xls`), right-click on the range containing the Live Office connection, and then click on Refresh Option.

2. Select the On Demand: From the Database option. Doing so refreshes the Crystal Report each time the Live Office connection is triggered rather than consuming data from the last report refresh.

While the On Demand option retrieves data directly from the database, the latency in your dashboard will be a direct result of how long the report takes to refresh. A good way to benchmark how the dashboard connectivity performance will affect your end users is to run the report standalone. If you are not using parameterized reports, the Use Report Saved Data option might be the best choice for providing data to your dashboard. In this scenario, you will need to schedule your report on a daily or weekly basis.

PARAMETERIZED REPORTS

Both Crystal and Web Intelligence reports offer powerful features for summarizing, filtering, and structuring data. Both reporting solutions have prompting features for transacting parameterized data to a dashboard through Live Office web services. Once the report prompts are bound to Excel ranges, Xcelsius components and logic can dictate the prompt values. The end result is a dashboard that can execute parameterized queries based on an end user's interaction. The benefit of this configuration is a dashboard that scales when large volumes of data need to be visualized during a single dashboard session. The following exercise explains the process for binding prompts after the report has been inserted into Excel using Live Office.

21

TIP

> If a report prompt is bound to a cell, the existing formula is overwritten. It is recommended to replicate the same logic in an adjacent cell to avoid rewriting logic each time a Live Office prompt is reconfigured.

1. In the Excel file with configured Live Office connectivity (Chapter21_LiveOffice.xls), click on the Live Office menu, and then click on Prompt Setting.

2. Click on the Choose Excel data range radio button to bind a parameter to an Excel cell.

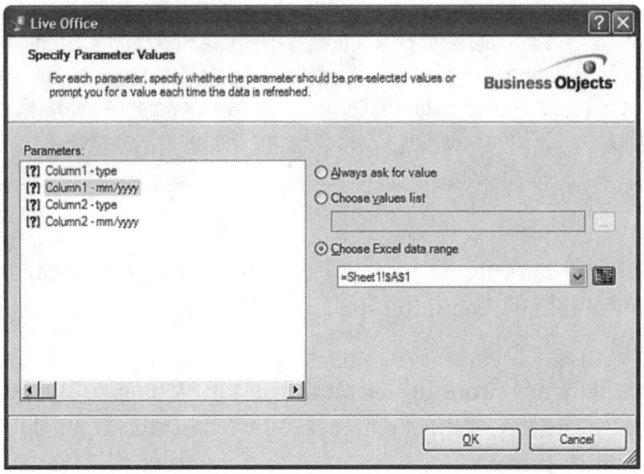

Figure 21.19
Bind a prompt to a cell within the Excel range.

Once a report parameter is bound to an Excel cell, you can leverage Xcelsius selectors or logic to dynamically control the value. Each time the Live Office connection is refreshed, the report will return filtered or calculated data to the dashboard. Using parameterized reports to supply data to an Xcelsius dashboard is the most efficient method for scaling a dashboard where large volumes of data are required.

UNIVERSE QUERY WITH QUERY AS A WEB SERVICE

QaaWS comes packaged with BusinessObjects Enterprise Professional and employs a client tool that resembles the Web Intelligence query panel to generate web services. Xcelsius can leverage these web services using a native QaaWS connector in the Xcelsius Data Manager. The primary benefit of using QaaWS is the alleviation of writing reports or a reliance on Live Office for configuring connectivity. The following exercise explains the process for binding an existing Universe query into the Data Manager.

TIP

> Data received from QaaWS loads into Xcelsius as a vertical table. If the intent is to load a cross-tab or horizontal table, Live Office integration is a better choice for connectivity.

WEB SERVICE CONNECTION

Xcelsius' Web Service connection can interpret web services that use Simple Open Access Protocol (SOAP) standards. Xcelsius imports the Web Service Definition Language (WSDL) to define a web service method, input values, and output values. Configuring a SOAP-based web service is achieved using the same process as QaaWS, which also uses WSDL for configuring web services.

NOTE

> Xcelsius supports only WSDL with a single schema block containing single value strings and arrays. Complex data types will not import properly when defining WSDL, which prohibits the web service from being configured.

1. Paste the WSDL URL and click on the Import button. Xcelsius will display the web service URL, input values, and output values.

2. Select a method from the combo box, if multiple methods are available.

3. Bind the input values.

4. Bind the output values to a cell or range.

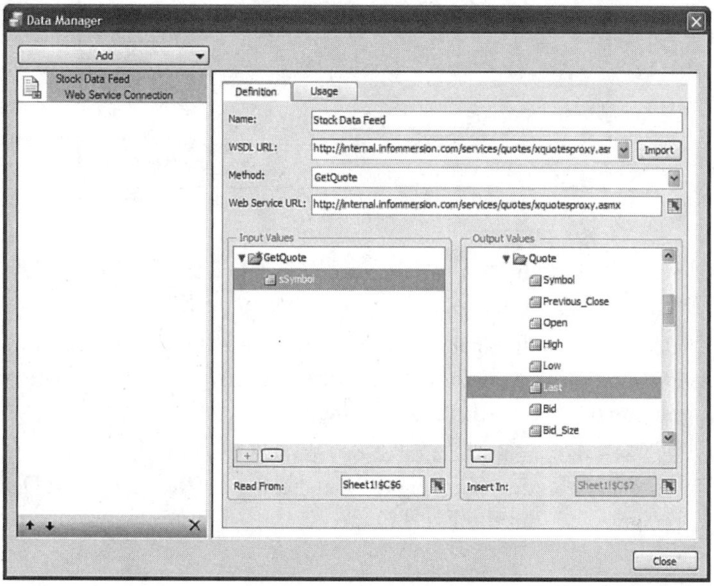

Figure 21.20
A web service connector configured to a real-time stock data feed.

EXCEL XML MAPS

Similar to Live Office, Xcelsius can interpret an Excel-based feature, XML Maps, to interpret most XML structures. XML Maps establishes a generic schema for most XML structures before they map to an Excel range. The result is an SWF that can connect directly to

XML files or web services that stream XML. The following exercise will illustrate how to load a simple XML file into the Xcelsius project and how to configure connectivity using the Data Manager.

1. Launch the XML Source window from the Data menu within the Excel window. Because Excel 2003 does not display the menu bar, initial XML maps connectivity might need to be established in Excel and then imported into Xcelsius.

NOTE

For Excel 2007 users, if the Developer tab is disabled, right-click (while in Excel 2007 only, not Xcelsius) on the Quick Access toolbar and select Customize Quick Access Toolbar. Change the Choose Commands From drop-down selection to All Commands. Scroll down and select XML, click on Add then OK. The next time you use Xcelsius, the XML Quick Access Shortcut will be available.

2. Scroll to the bottom of the XML Source window and click on the XML Maps button.

Figure 21.21
Excel XML Maps can load an XML file or XML schema file.

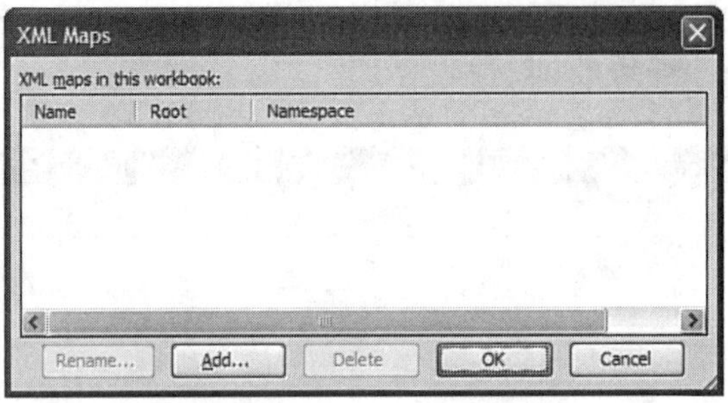

3. Click on the Add button to select an XML file from the local file system or enter a URL for a web service that will return streaming XML.

4. Click and drag individual elements or an entire element group from the XML Source window into an Excel range. Excel automatically inserts the element headings and highlights the live XML range in blue.

5. Load XML data from the source by right-clicking on the mapped range within the Excel sheet, selecting XML, and then clicking on Refresh XML Data. The XML data will populate within the Excel range.

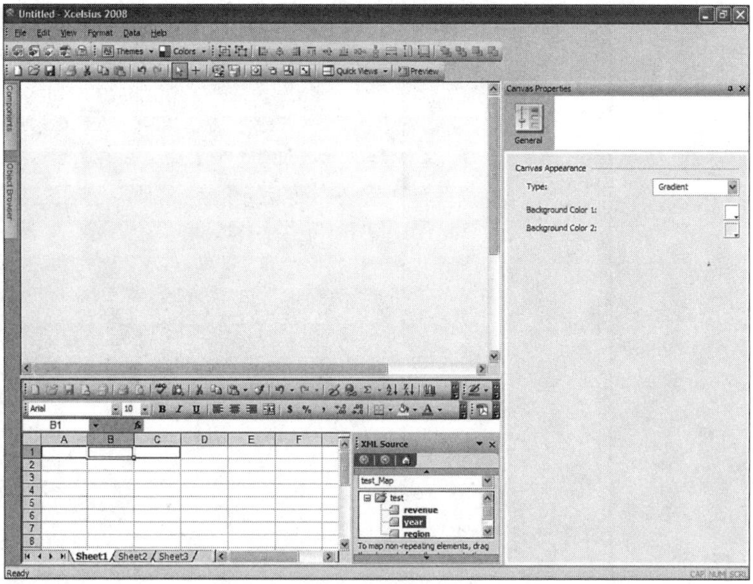

Figure 21.22
XML Elements can be inserted in any order within the spreadsheet.

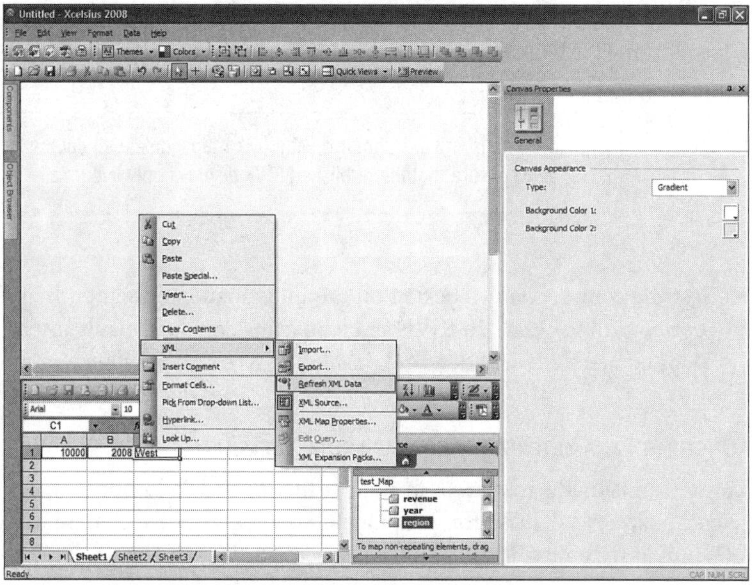

Figure 21.23
The XML Map range expands as it populates the data into Excel.

6. Launch the Xcelsius Data Manager and add the Excel XML Map connection. The XML Data URL will dictate where the dashboard will retrieve XML data from during runtime. This URL can be modified or bound to a cell.

21

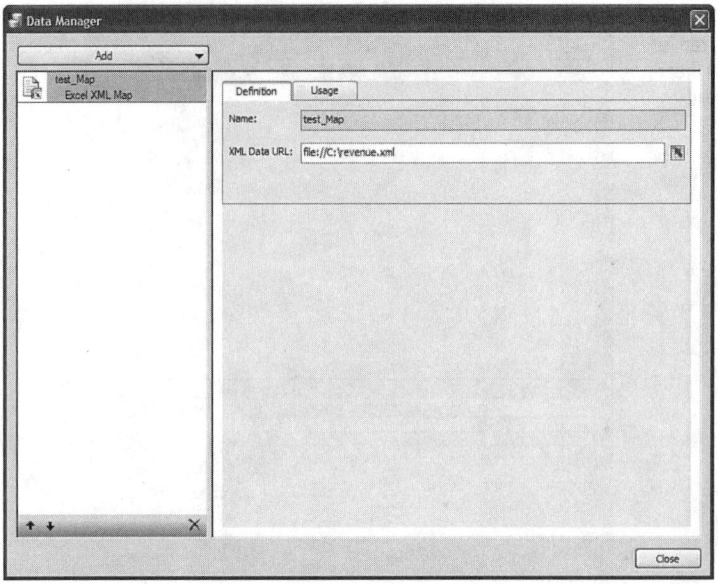

Figure 21.24
The XML Map URL can be modified or bound to a cell.

7. Insert a Spreadsheet Table selector from the Components window, and bind the display data to the XML Map range.

> **TIP**
>
> Before publishing a dashboard with XML maps, delete all data within the XML Maps range to ensure that the published SWF displays only live data.

8. Test the connection by clicking on the File menu and then on Export Preview. Export preview will generate an SWF and load it inside your default Internet browser. XML Maps connectivity will not work inside the Xcelsius designer.

LAUNCHING PARAMETERIZED REPORTS FROM XCELSIUS

Xcelsius can launch parameterized reports that provide additional analysis to supplement the dashboard. A URL Button component coupled with Excel logic will transform a static URL into a dynamic URL driven by a selector to launch Crystal and Web Intelligence reports.

1. Copy a URL into cell A1 within a new Xcelsius project. The following URL launches a parameterized Crystal Report using a `Region` parameter:

   `http://servername:port/.../openDocument.jsp?sDocName=Widget&sType=rpt&sRegion=`

2. Type the value `"West"` into cell A2. This value is the dynamic `Region` parameter that will be appended to the initial URL. Though this example uses a static value, normal implementations of this technique use selectors or logic to manipulate the parameter in A2.

3. Type the following formula into cell A3 to concatenate the URL:
   =A1&A2.

4. Insert the URL Button component from the Web Connectivity category, and bind the URL to cell A3.

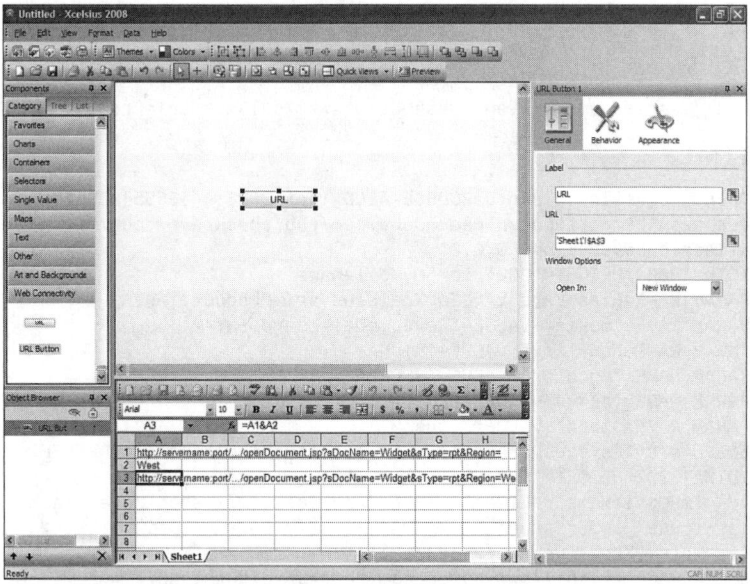

Figure 21.25
Bind the URL component to the concatenated dynamic URL.

5. Insert any selector and bind the destination to cell A2. This action illustrates how a selector can dynamically change the Region parameter. A production implementation of this procedure would use the Label insertion type.

> **TIP**
>
> Launching parameterized reports that reside in the BusinessObjects repository uses a specific syntax for defining parameters using openDocument.jsp.

USING FLASH VARIABLES

Xcelsius dashboards are capable of consuming variables from HTML using the Flash variables connection. Flash variables provide a data push method to Xcelsius, using comma-separated values or XML. Flash variables can originate as nested variables inside HTML or as appended parameters to the end of a URL string. Flash variables are the first events that trigger when an SWF initializes before any other connector or event. In both examples shown later, the variable name is XcelsiusVar1, which is defined as a Flash variable inside the Data Manager.

21

NOTE

> An SWF published to BusinessObjects Enterprise is stored as an object within the repository. Inside the Central Management console, the SWF object has a tab called FlashVars where you can modify Flash variables. This capability provides additional control for modifying parameters or URLs instead of republishing an SWF.

URL String

```
http://servername/ RevenueDashboard.swf?XcelsiusVar1=Product
```

HTML

```
<OBJECT classid="clsid:D27CDB6E-AE6D-11cf-96B8-444553540000"
codebase="http://fpdownload.adobe.com/pub/shockwave/cabs/flash/
swflash.cab#version=9,0,0,0"
WIDTH="800" HEIGHT="600" id="myMovieName">
<PARAM NAME=FlashVars VALUE="XcelsiusVar1=Product1">
<PARAM NAME="movie" VALUE="RevenueDashboard.swf">
<PARAM NAME="quality" VALUE="high">
<PARAM NAME="bgcolor" VALUE="#FFFFFF">
<PARAM NAME="play" VALUE="true">
<PARAM NAME="loop" VALUE="true">
<EMBED src="RevenueDashboard.swf" quality=high bgcolor=#FFFFFF
WIDTH="800" HEIGHT="600"
NAME="myMovieName" ALIGN="" TYPE="application/x-shockwave-flash"
play="true" loop="true"
FlashVars="XcelsiusVar1=Product1"
PLUGINSPAGE="http://www.adobe.com/shockwave/download/
index.cgi?P1_Prod_Version=ShockwaveFlash">
</EMBED>
</OBJECT>
```

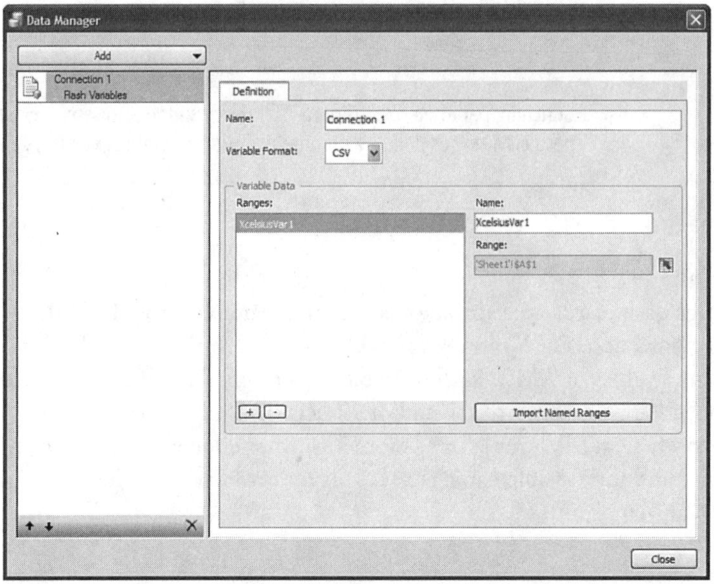

Figure 21.26
XcelsiusVar1 is
an example of a Flash
variable. The screen
shows it is configured
in the Data Manager.

PORTAL INTEGRATION

Xcelsius 2008 includes proprietary portal integration kits for Microsoft SharePoint Services and IBM WebSphere. Both server-side installs permit the Data Manager's Portal Data connection to work within both portal environments. The Portal Data connection includes a Provider and Consumer method for passing data between two independent SWF files. An additional Parameters option within the Portal Data connection will allow portal users to modify the parameters within the portal environment.

NOTE

Two SWF files that communicate via provider and consumer connections provide only one-way communication. That means a single SWF cannot have both a provider and a consumer.

INDEX

Page Header, 17
Report Header, 17
Section Expert, 18
Standard toolbar, 18
ToolTips, 19
View menu, 20
Window menu, 21
Workbench, 23

**destination cells in selectors,
473**

**Destination property field
(Xcelsius), 472**

**Detail Size option (Section
Expert, Layout tab), 191**

Details section, 17, 186
lines, adding between, 236
template, created by, 336

direct access drivers, 23

**Disable Mouse Input on
Load property (Xcelsius,
Data Manager Usage tab),
507**

**Display String option
(Format Editor, Common
tab), 167**

**display strings, cross-tabs
with, 264-266**

distinct records option, 306

**divide-by-zero errors, cus-
tom functions, 126-129**

Do/While structures, 119

docking design explorers, 22

Dot Density maps, 219

**dragging/dropping objects,
171**

**Drill Down feature
(Xcelsius), 490-491**

drill-down functionality
commands for, 386, 389-391
OLAP, 372, 386, 389-391
report sections, 186-187,
201-202

drill-down reports
group paths for, 71
hiding details, 72-73
icon for, 71

navigating for, 72
purpose of, 71
Suppress (No Drill-Down)
option, 73

drivers
direct access database, 23
indirect access database, 24

**Drop Shadow option
(Format Editor, Border
tab), 168**

**DSNs (Data Source Names),
24**

DTSToDate function, 278

**dynamic cascading prompts,
289-292**

**Dynamic List of Values
properties, 135, 147**

**dynamic parameters,
147-149**

**Dynamic Visibility
(Xcelsius), 488-498**

E

email addresses
columns, 165-166
Email address option
(Format Editor, Hyperlink
tab), 169

**Edit Mask property (parame-
ter fields), 136-137**

Edit menu (Designer), 19

editing
alerts, 284-285
charts, 221
column titles, 163-164
cross-tab summaries, 270

**Editing area (Formula
Editor), 101**

**Enable Load Cursor prop-
erty (Xcelsius, Data
Manager Usage tab), 507**

Enter Values dialog, 29

**equals to (=) operators,
parameter fields, 152**

**ERP (Enterprise Resource
Planning) integration kits**
application support,
359-360
full data access, 360
metadata in, 360
real-time data access, 361
sample reports, 360
security, 360

errors
looping errors, 119
runtime, variable data,
324-326

**ETL (Extract Transform &
Load) products, XML for-
mat as, 347**

**EvaluateAfter() function,
120, 126**

**Event Server, Crystal
Reports Server, 400**

Excel (MS)
dashboard development,
460, 466
reports, exporting to, 346
Xcelsius
Chart Drill Down fea-
ture, 490-491
concatenating values,
503-504
conditional formulas,
500-501
dashboard development,
460
date functions, 505
Excel Sheet tab, 468
Excel tabs, 466
IF() statements, 500-502
INDEX function,
502-503
Insert Filtered Rows fea-
ture, 492-493
lookup functions,
502-503
Map Components fea-
ture, 494-496
multilayer dashboards,
496-498

K - L

U - V

ETL products, 347
reports
    exporting to, 347
    Web services, 434, 453-454

XML Maps (Excel), Xcelsius, 515-516, 518

Y - Z

zero, dividing by (custom functions), 126-129

Zoom In/Out options (Map Expert), 228

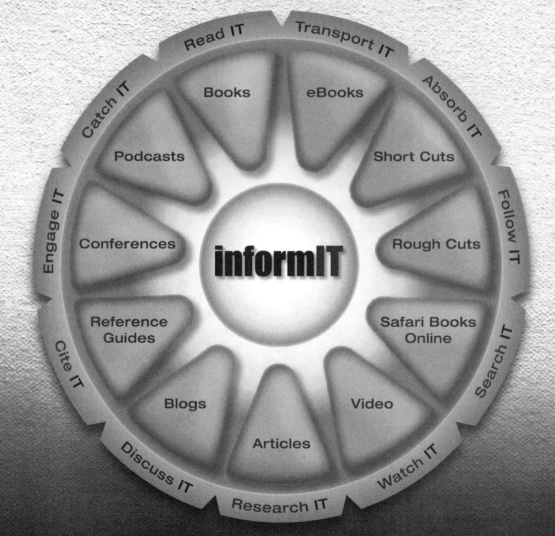

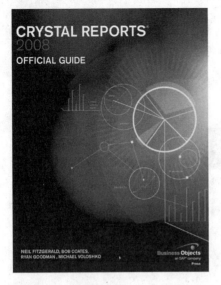

FREE Online Edition

Your purchase of **Crystal Reports® 2008 Official Guide** includes access to a free online edition for 45 days through the Safari Books Online subscription service. Nearly every Sams book is available online through Safari Books Online, along with more than 5,000 other technical books and videos from publishers such as Addison-Wesley Professional, Cisco Press, Exam Cram, IBM Press, O'Reilly, Prentice Hall, and Que .

SAFARI BOOKS ONLINE allows you to search for a specific answer, cut and paste code, download chapters, and stay current with emerging technologies.

Activate your FREE Online Edition at www.informit.com/safarifree

> **STEP 1:** Enter the coupon code: B3EE-PBEC-LLT7-KPCF-3K7A.

> **STEP 2:** New Safari users, complete the brief registration form.
> Safari subscribers, just log in.

If you have difficulty registering on Safari or accessing the online edition, please e-mail customer-service@safaribooksonline.com

Addison Wesley AdobePress ALPHA Cisco Press FT Press IBM Press. lynda.com Microsoft Press New Riders

O'REILLY Peachpit Press PRENTICE HALL Que Redbooks SAMS SAS Publishing Sun microsystems WILEY